PUBLIC PAPERS OF THE PRESIDENTS

OF THE UNITED STATES

PUBLIC PAPERS OF THE PRESIDENTS

OF THE UNITED STATES

Lyndon B. Johnson

Containing the Public Messages, Speeches, and

Statements of the President

U. S. President

1965

(IN TWO BOOKS)

BOOK II—JUNE 1 TO DECEMBER 31, 1965

UNITED STATES GOVERNMENT PRINTING OFFICE

WASHINGTON : 1966

PUBLISHED BY THE
OFFICE OF THE FEDERAL REGISTER
NATIONAL ARCHIVES AND RECORDS SERVICE
GENERAL SERVICES ADMINISTRATION

For sale by the Superintendent of Documents, U.S. Government Printing Office
Washington, D.C. 20402 - Price $6.25

CONTENTS

Book I

Book II

LIST OF ITEMS, Book I

[List of Items, Book II, starts on page XXXI]

List of Items, Book I

Page

List of Items, Book I

List of Items, Book I

List of Items, Book I

List of Items, Book I

LIST OF ITEMS, Book II

List of Items, Book II

List of Items, Book II

Page

Lyndon B. Johnson

June 1 – December 31, 1965

BOOK II

June 1 – December 31, 1965

288 Statement by the President on the Department of Defense Actions in Support of the War on Poverty. *June 1, 1965*

BY MAKING available its vast resources and the diverse skills of its men and women, the Department of Defense has greatly assisted our national mobilization for the war on poverty. Without in any way reducing their combat effectiveness or interfering with their basic military mission, our Armed Forces have contributed to a speedier implementation of many antipoverty programs than would otherwise have been possible. And through their experience and efficiency, they have also achieved substantial economies in putting those programs into operation.

These accomplishments provide further proof that the American people, and their Government, are firmly determined to prosecute the war against poverty to a successful conclusion.

NOTE: The President's statement (made public at Austin, Tex.) is part of a White House release which also included the text of a memorandum from Secretary of Defense Robert S. McNamara.

The memorandum reported on assistance provided by the Department of Defense through May 1, 1965, for which, as provided by law, the Office of Economic Opportunity had reimbursed the Department. As of March 30, 1965, Secretary McNamara told the President, the reimbursement totaled $3,731,289.

The memorandum summarized the assistance furnished as follows:

"*Excess Installations and Personal Property.* Department of Defense installations and related personal property no longer needed for military purposes have been made available for Job Corps Urban and Rural Training Centers. Installations which have been turned over to the Job Corps for Urban Centers, each with a capacity for one thousand men or more, are: Camp Parks, Calif., Camp Atterbury, Ind., Fort Rodman, Mass., Fort Custer, Mich., Camp Kilmer, N.J., Camp Gary, Tex.

"Former Department of Defense installations at Fort Breckinridge, Ky., and Tongue Point, Oreg., have also become Job Corps Urban Centers. The Navajo Army Depot in Arizona, the Cottonwood Radar Station in Idaho, and the Dickinson Radar Station in North Dakota have been made available for Job Corps Rural Centers.

"The Office of Economic Opportunity has a number of other Defense installations under consideration for future use, including Fort Slocum, N.Y., and Indiantown Gap, Pa. The Department of Defense's Office of Economic Adjustment is working closely with the Office of Economic Opportunity on plans for possible use of other excess military installations, and the Army Engineers are assisting in rehabilitation and construction work. Special arrangements have been made by the military departments and the Defense Supply Agency to expedite transfer of excess personal property to the General Services Administration for use by the Job Corps.

"*Clothing and Subsistence.* The Defense Supply Agency has been providing clothing for Job Corps enrollees and, as of April 30, 1965, had filled clothing requisitions valued at $1,042,233. The Defense Supply Agency and the Army are working with the Office of Economic Opportunity to develop a distinctive Job Corps uniform. The Defense Supply Agency also provides both perishable and nonperishable foods to the Urban Training Centers at Camps Atterbury, Park and Gary. Subsistence to other Centers is provided by local military installations. MacDill Air Force Base, Fla., and the Defense Supply Agency provide subsistence to the Women's Training Center at St. Petersburg, Fla. Such subsistence is furnished only where there is a saving to the Government.

"*Financial Services.* The Army Finance Center is now administering a complete program of payroll services for both the Job Corps and Volunteers in Service to America (VISTA).

"*Medical Services.* The Army Surgeon General is assisting the Office of Economic Opportunity in developing a comprehensive medical program for members of both the Job Corps and VISTA.

"When particular non-military medical facilities are unavailable, and their regular workload permits, the military departments conduct medical examina-

tions and immunizations for the Job Corps and VISTA. Approximately 3,000 such examinations had been performed by May 1, 1965.

"*Assistance by Defense Personnel.* Nearly 50 Department of Defense specialists in such fields as civil engineering, management analysis, civilian personnel management, training techniques, recreational program planning, and vocational curriculum development, have been temporarily assigned to the Office of Economic Opportunity. One of these specialists, Mr. Raymond Stellar of the Army Corps of Engineers, recently was commended for saving the Job Corps more than $2,000,000 in rehabilitation costs at Camp Kilmer."

289 Remarks at the Commencement Exercises of the National Cathedral School. *June 1, 1965*

Presiding Bishop Hines, Bishop Creighton, Dean Sayre, members of the faculty, members of the 1965 graduating class and their parents, families, ladies and gentlemen:

The office of President presents many challenges, but I am sure that every father that is here this morning will understand sympathetically that few challenges could compare with the exacting demands of speaking before the graduating class of your own daughter.

I have been reminded repeatedly—before this morning—that in talking here I really have a family reputation to uphold. I only hope that it is not principally a reputation for talking.

For members of the class of '65, I know this is a very proud and happy and rewarding day for you. Speaking for myself, as a parent, I find this moment both sad and glad. I shall miss the small comfort of knowing that no matter how much homework I might bring to the White House every night, Luci still would have brought more from NCS. But at the same time I am glad and I am

eternally grateful that by the time that she reached her junior year here at NCS Luci had learned to spell her name correctly, with an "i" instead of a "y."

Most of you here this morning will go on from here to serve your country in many ways. So this morning I want to ask your assistance in a very special way. This particular occasion will be broadcast and reported to millions of people—some in other lands. Now, this is not a tribute to me or to you, but it is a tribute to the importance of our beloved country. So this morning I would like to discuss with you and the Nation a matter which concerns me and about which I have given much thought.

FREEDOM OF DEBATE IN TIME OF DANGER

As is true for most national issues, we have had much discussion here of late about the various aspects of American foreign policy. I have disagreed with some of the views that have been expressed. I know that the large majority of Americans support our country's

598

efforts everywhere to stop aggression.

But I also know that such discussion is one of the great strengths of American democracy. How rare is the land and extraordinary the people who freely allow and really encourage, as I have on many occasions, the citizens of our Nation to discuss and to debate their Nation's policies in time of danger. So, let no citizen that is secure in his own liberty ever forget how precious it is and how brave we must be if we are to keep it, how many generations of men have perished in order to guard its light, and how many scattered throughout the world are dying still to protect it.

Our soldiers are falling in Viet-Nam. Twenty have died and more than a hundred have been wounded on guard in the Dominican Republic so that men may always rise with perfect safety to criticize and to try to influence the leadership of their government.

Nor should we forget that the purpose of liberty is not merely to allow error, but to discover truth; not only to restrict the powers of the Government, but to enrich the judgment of the Nation. So, by testing ideas in the forum of the Nation we discover their strength as well as their wisdom. As the Bible says: "Where no counsel is, the people fall: But in the multitude of counselors there is safety."

Therefore we welcome and we ask for new ideas from serious and concerned men and women, from universities and journals and public platforms all across this land. We are constantly searching for views and proposals which might strengthen and unite and help your Government. Of course, there can be no decision with which we all agree. But all will be heard.

Let no one ever think for a moment that national debate means national division. For even among those who do not support our Government policies, the very process of discussion rests on a broad and deeply set foundation of shared belief, principle, faith and experience.

There are, first of all, the assumptions of American democracy. Thus, most of those who disagree are really trying to influence the democratic process and not rip it and tear it apart. They are really seeking to exercise their own freedom and not deny it to others. They try to affect the decisions of the Nation, not flaunt or ignore them.

Secondly, even among those who quarrel with particular acts, most believe, as I believe, in the principles which have shaped American world policy now for more than a generation:

We seek neither conquest nor domination.

We seek to work toward a goal where every country can run its own affairs, can shape its own progress, can build its own institutions according to that country's own desires and needs.

We do all that can be done to find enduring peace—at the same time resisting aggression by any who wish to subdue others and gobble them up and really try to destroy us.

We seek to reserve our special friendship for those governments that are dedicated to social justice and progress for all of the people—all the people, not just a privileged few.

It is these principles which I am trying so hard, as best I can, for your Government to support in every continent of the world today. Because I think these are also the beliefs of the American people. Therefore, we need never shrink from debate because debate can only strengthen our determination and our ability to follow this course.

In a democracy, the people have to want to do what must be done—and that particularly includes students like you.

THE COMMITTED GENERATION

I have visited many campuses and I have talked to many students, and I can tell you that this generation of young Americans is a generation of which I am deeply proud. And I think you are very lucky to be joining them.

This is not the lost generation or the silent generation or the indifferent generation. This is the concerned and the committed generation. And I, for one, believe that adult America should be proud and should be thankful that young America—youthful America—is so concerned for their country, so committed and dedicated to a genuine understanding of all of America's problems and they are uncowed in their determination to be a part of the answers that we are seeking and that we need.

A RESTLESS WORLD

This world that we live in is a restless world. It is a world filled with revolution and even violence, and we must never make the sad mistake of thinking that this is only the work of our enemies. Of course, our enemies are at work like ants, constantly united and dedicated and determined. But they thrive on the desperate struggle by the poor of the world to try to create a more hopeful life.

Our life in America is good. Our land is rich. Our comforts are many. But more than 2 billion of the 3 billion people in the world have an income of less than $20 per month. Half of the world's children today have no school to go to at all and have

never darkened a schoolroom. Two hundred million people in the world today have no safe water to drink any day of their lives. More than half the population of Asia and Africa and Latin America, by our standards, have no home at all in which to live.

Now this is the world that you live in and, whether you know it or not, it is a world of slums and shacks; it is a world without lights or water in the homes; it is a world without food on the shelves or health in the bodies; a world with too few teachers and too few doctors. In Viet-Nam, they have 200 doctors. And if they had the same ratio of doctors that we have in this country they would not have 200, they'd have 5,000.

So, this is a world where hope is too rare and help is too scarce. Wherever and whenever men struggle to escape this misery no nation ought to be neutral—whatever be the continent or the creed or the color of those who reach upward striving and yearning for a better life.

Were there no cold war—and no communism at all—this planet would still be wracked and seething with man's heroic battle to secure justice for himself and his loved ones.

OUR MORAL COMMITMENT

For myself, I do not propose that this powerful Nation which I lead shall stand alone or shall stand apart from this most decisive struggle of our times. Concerned as I am with the future of freedom for America, concerned as I am with the world that my daughters shall know, I would commit the American Nation to face up to its obligation to be with the world's people on their march toward the life that all God's children should know on this earth.

This is not a political commitment nor even an economic commitment that we alone must make. This is a moral commitment that we have made and that we must keep in all that we do.

Look around this great cathedral. Every day men and women come here to fulfill their spiritual and their moral needs. Every day they come here to seek the blessings and the strength and the guidance of God. But as people we shall never satisfy the command of God, or the responsibilities of country, simply by coming to the houses of worship.

When the time of judgment comes, it will be no excuse to say that they were far away, or their language was strange, or their color was different, or I did not know their names.

It will be asked of you, and it will be asked of me: What did you do—you, the children of abundance—what did you do to help those who were hungry, and those who were sick, and those who were fatherless, and those who were homeless?

What did you do? You were conceived in hope, and you have been raised in opportunity, and your parents have made great sacrifices so that you could be in this place of honor today. But what did you do to brighten the promise of those who, from the moment of their birth, the moment they discovered the world, could see only the darkness of fear and insecurity and poverty.

I propose that when the day of answering comes, the American Nation and the American people shall be able to answer that we kept the trust of our abundance, that we kept the faith of our moral beliefs, because we were good and faithful servants of the ideals which we promulgated and for which we said that we stood.

You must give the hours of your life, and the fruits of your learning, and the courage of your spirit, and the substance of your home to those in need in every continent of the earth. You must, in the words of the Bible, "Let your light so shine before men that they may seek your good works."

Then only will you have earned what you have so abundantly received, as is in evidence here this morning.

Then only will you have really met your duty to your God and your country and your family, but most of all to yourself.

EDUCATION'S GREATEST GIFT

To do all of these things you must prepare yourself.

You have been doing that in this school. Whether you go on to college or not you will continue your education for the rest of your life. For to stop learning, at any age, is to relapse into ignorance.

And one of the greatest satisfactions that come to me in my hours of sunshine and sorrow, and my nights of trouble, is the knowledge that my daughter, who is a part of you, has decided to spend her life healing the sick and ministering to the needs of the needy.

Yes, you are going to learn many things in the years to come, but I hope that you will remember that education's greatest gift is not just particular knowledge. Education's greatest gift is a spacious and a skeptical mind—a curious mind. It is the willingness to accept fresh ideas, even if they challenge the most cherished assumptions.

And here, I think, I can pay a very special tribute to Miss Lee and to the faculty of this great institution. Whatever else may be said about them, they do develop and instill, at least from my personal observation, a reasonable amount of independence and independent thinking among their graduates.

So, it is this ability to seek the right, to

seek the right while never forgetting that you could be wrong, and that you may be wrong.

THE PRICE OF LEADERSHIP

But if you are to be among those who lead and who act then even this is not enough. It is not hard to act when you know that you are right. I find it far more difficult to act when I just believe that I am right, but sometimes knowing that I could be wrong. Yet that is the burden that responsibility imposes on thought. And that is the price that leadership exacts of free men and free thinkers.

A great statesman once said that he would rather be right than President. Well, I must try to be both. I must try as best I can, with whatever the good Lord gave me and with whatever help God chooses to give me now, to seek the right course not just for myself but for you to whom I have a special responsibility, and to the Nation who relies on me.

And as President of your country I must act, in this 20th century—often swiftly, always decisively—according to judgment.

So, we will proceed with the course that we are on, glad of the overwhelming support of the American people, always open to criticism and the flow of ideas, but proceeding as we believe that we must, following the path that we believe is right, however the transient winds of opinion may blow.

This is what I believe the American people expect of their President.

And this is what they shall receive from me.

But, I guess, this is enough of such grave and weighty matters.

Recently I gave a speech, and when I came back to the White House that night my wife and my two daughters were sitting on the bed talking and reading, and I asked Lady Bird what she thought about what I had said that evening—as I will ask her when we go home this morning. She said, "Darling, you were wonderful, except you did miss several good opportunities to sit down."

Well, I will take that opportunity now. This is a shining spring day. You are all so young and beautiful, and this is a wonderful moment for me. And I think it is very nice of you sparkling, scintillating, fresh, intelligent young ladies to let a much older and a rather solemn man come here and talk to you about his problems. I hope that you know how it lifts my heart to just look at you, and to understand and to believe and to know that a little of what I will do today, and tomorrow, and the years ahead, may possibly enrich your lives and ensure peace for you and your families.

Thank you so much.

NOTE: The President spoke at 11:13 a.m. in Washington Cathedral on the occasion of the graduation of his daughter, Luci Baines Johnson, from the National Cathedral School. In his opening words he referred to the Right Reverend John E. Hines, Presiding Bishop of the Episcopal Church, the Right Reverend William F. Creighton, Bishop of Washington, and the Very Reverend Francis B. Sayre, Jr., Dean of the Washington Cathedral. Later the President referred to Katharine Lee, Headmistress of the National Cathedral School.

290   Remarks at a Swearing-In Ceremony for Several Government Officials. *June 1, 1965*

Ladies and gentlemen:

I think that we might dedicate this ceremony this morning to Kermit Gordon.

Over the past months, Kermit, as Director of the Budget, has been preaching to me the virtues of consolidation. Today, as he finally takes leave of public service, it seems to me that we are putting into practice what Kermit has been preaching, in consolidating this swearing in.

This is an occasion to make any President very proud and very glad—proud to have men and women of this quality and this caliber willing to serve in positions of highest trust and glad that we are able to make all of these gains with relatively few losses.

Considering the numbers present this morning, I expected to have a long list of farewells but actually other than in two instances, there is no incumbent departing from Government service.

We shall miss both of those who are, or who think they are, or who say they are returning to private life—Budget Director Kermit Gordon and Under Secretary of Commerce for Transportation, Clarence Martin. These men have told their wives that this is the end of their public service, and I never dispute publicly what a man tells his wife, but in these instances I suspect that their information to their wives is only temporarily correct.

Clarence Martin has written for himself and for his country a most outstanding record in a most challenging position. His leadership has afforded us a strong and solid start for the monumental task of meeting this Nation's transportation needs. We are sorry to see him depart Washington. But few of his friends, other than perhaps his wife, believe that this is really the end of his public service.

As for Kermit Gordon, I would not—I just could not express in any words of mine just how much this most able and dedicated public servant has meant to me as President, or has meant to this Nation which I try so hard to lead.

There have been many distinguished men in the office of the Director of the Budget which Mr. Gordon now holds, but I genuinely and sincerely believe his record must be ranked as one of the most, if not the most outstanding ever made.

The office of the Director of the Budget is not the best base from which to win friends here in Washington, but Kermit Gordon has won both friendship and respect throughout the Government for his fair, his objective, his always just, his always reasonable and intelligent handling of this job—a job in many ways the most single vital position in the executive branch of the Government.

I hope that I will have other opportunities to express myself on the subject of Kermit Gordon. I would like though to say to him and to his wife today that I am very glad they won't be leaving Washington. It will save them moving expenses when we find some way to lure him back to public duty where he really belongs.

The departure of these men is offset by the qualities of those who are taking up their duties and other duties throughout the executive branch. Time does not permit me to speak as I might like about all of those who are taking up new challenges and opportunities this afternoon—Alan Boyd, Franklin D. Roosevelt, Jr., Charles Murphy, Dr. John Schnittker—all have my deep personal gratitude for their willingness to assume new positions, for their willingness to continue their fine public service to this country.

The fields that they enter are among the most dynamic and decisive in our contemporary society—transportation, agriculture; most vital of all, the field of human rights. By experience, by instinct, by conscience, by conviction, each man we believe, and we have made a good many investigations with the help of Mr. Hoover across the street, is peculiarly suited for the office that he is now assuming. Much is asked of each of them in these posts. And they wouldn't be there if I didn't believe that each has much to give and if I thought that I could find a better in the Nation.

Mr. Charles Schultze returns to public life after only the very briefest interlude outside. I suppose I might as well admit that before allowing him to leave in the first place, I felt that he just had to return at a very early date.

Now if I may put it frankly, I would say no one that I have appointed has a harder act to follow than Kermit Gordon. But Kermit, as well as I, think Charlie is the right and the best choice for this undertaking.

The management and the direction of an organization as large as our executive branch necessarily cause us to focus on fiscal matters, but the heart and the soul of this Government has never been and must never be just money and management. It is, and it always will be, assuring the rights and the dignity and the opportunities of all Americans.

I am very proud today to welcome the members as well as the Chairman, Franklin D. Roosevelt, Jr., my longtime friend, of the Equal Employment Opportunity Commission—Mrs. Hernandez, Mr. Graham, Mr. Jackson, and Dr. Holcomb. These men and women under the leadership of Chairman Roosevelt will represent a broad cross section of America. They reflect, I believe, a strong and sure cross section support of the Nation's dedication to the simple justice of equal

opportunity. The task they undertake, the work they shall do, ranks at the top of our national priorities.

So this is a very proud occasion, a very happy occasion, and a somewhat crowded occasion. In all these fields there is much work to do, so we shall now proceed to clear the way for this vital work to be carried forward.

I am quite honored that my old and beloved friend, Justice Black, has consented to come here and distinguish this occasion. Justice Black.

NOTE: The President spoke at 12:47 p.m. in the Rose Garden at the White House. Justice Hugo L. Black, Associate Justice of the Supreme Court, administered the oaths of office to the following officials: Alan S. Boyd as Under Secretary of Commerce, Charles S. Murphy as Chairman of the Civil Aeronautics Board, John A. Schnittker as Under Secretary of Agriculture, Charles L. Schultze as Director of the Bureau of the Budget, and Franklin D. Roosevelt, Jr. (Chairman), Mrs. Aileen Hernandez, Richard Graham, Samuel C. Jackson, and Rev. Luther J. Holcomb as members of the Equal Employment Opportunity Commission.

During the course of his remarks the President referred to J. Edgar Hoover, Director of the Federal Bureau of Investigation.

Kermit Gordon served as Director of the Bureau of the Budget from December 28, 1962, through June 1, 1965. The text of his letter of resignation, dated May 26, 1965, and the President's reply was released on June 2, 1965.

Clarence Martin served as Under Secretary of Commerce for Transportation from February 9, 1961, through June 1, 1965.

The President's letter accepting the resignation of Charles L. Schultze as Assistant Director of the Bureau of the Budget was released by the White House on February 9, 1965.

291   Statement by the President Announcing the Calling of a White House Conference on Education. *June 1, 1965*

THE NATION has begun to make great progress in meeting its educational needs, but much more remains to be done.

Education is the key to opportunity in our society, and equality of educational opportunity must be the birthright of every citizen.

No other challenge concerns me more than this one. None is of greater importance to the American people. For this reason, I am asking leaders of American education, business, labor, and other public groups to meet with me in Washington on July 20 and 21 at a White House Conference on Education.

I have asked John W. Gardner, president of the Carnegie Corporation of New York, to serve as conference chairman. A list of Governors and educators who will serve on the conference committee will be made available to you at the close of this press conference.

All of us can benefit from a lively exchange of views on the major problems confronting our schools and colleges. We need to pool our best ideas about how to stimulate and to enrich the Nation's adventure in learning.

NOTE: On the same day the White House released the names of 10 educational leaders who had been invited to serve as vice chairmen and to preside over conference panels. The release stated that Governor Edmund G. Brown of California, Governor John B. Connally of Texas, Governor Richard J. Hughes of New Jersey, and Governor John H. Reed of Maine were appointed vice chairmen-at-large for the conference.

The release also stated that approximately 500 leaders from Government, education, business, labor, and other groups were expected to attend and that special attention would be given promising young academic leaders, teachers, and students. The release noted that the last White House Conference on Education had been held in 1955.

See also Item 374.

292   Statement by the President and Letter on the Agreement on the Importation of Educational, Scientific, and Cultural Materials. *June 1, 1965*

I AM releasing the text of a letter to the Vice President and Speaker of the House of Representatives urging passage of legislation to implement the Florence Agreement. This legislation would eliminate duties on imports of educational, scientific, and cultural materials.

Forty-seven countries have already carried out the Florence Agreement. Enactment of such legislation would benefit our schools and universities, science laboratories, libraries, museums, and other institutions.

Freedom of access to the knowledge and culture of other nations is the hallmark of open society. I urge prompt congressional consideration of this measure during International Cooperation Year.

A copy of my letter is being made available.

Dear Mr. Vice President: (Dear Mr. Speaker:)

The Agreement on the Importation of Educational, Scientific and Cultural Materials, commonly known as the Florence Agreement, was opened for signature at Lake Success, New York, on November 27, 1950. This Agreement is now in force in forty-seven countries.

The United States participated in the negotiation of the Florence Agreement. It was signed on behalf of the United States on June 24, 1959, and the Senate gave its advice and consent to its ratification on February 23, 1960. It now remains for the Congress to approve the legislation to permit the United States to implement this important Agreement.

The purpose of the Florence Agreement

is to promote the growth of international understanding by reducing trade barriers to the flow of knowledge in all directions across all frontiers.

Enactment of the legislation would be of very material benefit to our schools and universities, science laboratories and research foundations, libraries, art galleries, museums, and institutions and organizations devoted to the welfare of the blind.

The fullest freedom of access to the knowledge and culture of other nations is the hallmark of the open society.

Passage of this legislation would be particularly timely in 1965, which has been designated as International Cooperation Year.

Accordingly, I ask the Congress to approve promptly the legislation implementing the Florence Agreement.

LYNDON B. JOHNSON

[Honorable Hubert H. Humphrey, President of the Senate; Honorable John W. McCormack, Speaker of the House of Representatives]

NOTE: The text of the Agreement on the Importation of Educational, Scientific, and Cultural Materials is printed in the Department of State Bulletin (vol. 41, p. 425).

293 Statement by the President on the Distribution of Food and Medical Supplies in the Dominican Republic. *June 1, 1965*

I WANT to call your attention to the very effective and selfless emergency relief work done by representatives of our Government, in cooperation with the OAS.

From the very earliest days, we have been distributing food and medical supplies to ward off starvation and epidemic. This work has been under the very able direction of Mr. Anthony Solomon, who is being sworn in this afternoon as Assistant Secretary of State for Economic Affairs.

Under his direction we have now distributed more than 9 million pounds of food, and distribution continues at a rate of half a million pounds a day. We have given out rice, cornmeal, powdered milk, beans, and flour.

In the same way, we have provided medical supplies from U.S. Army sources in repeated shipments. They have included antibiotics and other medicines, oxygen tanks, serums for immunization, power generators for the hospitals, and surgical supplies.

Both food and medical supplies have been distributed all over the country by nine food teams of Spanish-speaking Americans working to relieve need on a straight humanitarian basis. These teams have cooperated fully with private charitable agencies like Catholic Relief, CARE, and the Church World Service. They have been subjected to harassment in about equal measure by suspicious members of both contending groups.

We have also reopened lines of fuel supply for the civilian economy—while at the same time we have resisted pressure to provide fuel for either of the contending military forces.

It is entirely natural that while the shooting continued, public attention focused heavily on the fighting. But it is time now for us all to pay tribute to the work of these peaceful representatives of our country. They have saved uncounted lives and they have taken the lead in the first steps toward the peaceful reconstruction of the Dominican Republic.

294 Special Message to the Congress on the Need for Additional Foreign Aid Funds for Southeast Asia. *June 1, 1965*

To the Congress of the United States:

The American people want their government to be not only strong but compassionate. They know that a society is secure only where social justice is secure for all its citizens. When there is turmoil anywhere in our own country, our instinct is to inquire if there is injustice. That instinct is sound. And these principles of compassion and justice do not stop at the water's edge. We do not have one policy for our own people and another for our friends abroad.

A vast revolution is sweeping the southern half of this globe. We do not intend that the Communists shall become the beneficiaries of this revolt against injustice and privation. We intend to lead vigorously in that struggle. We will continue to back that intention with practical and concrete help.

In Southeast Asia today, we are offering our hand and our abundance to those who seek to build a brighter future. The effort to create more progressive societies cannot wait for an ideal moment. It cannot wait until peace has been finally secured. We must move ahead now.

I know of no more urgent task ahead. It requires more of us, more of other prosperous nations, and more of the people of Southeast Asia.

For our part, I propose that we expand our own economic assistance to the people of South Viet-Nam, Thailand and Laos.

I propose we start *now* to make available our share of the money needed to harness the resources of the *entire* Southeast Asia region for the benefit of all its people. This must be an international venture. That is

why I have asked Mr. Eugene Black to consult with the United Nations Secretary General and the leaders of the poor and advanced nations. Our role will be vital, but we hope that all other industrialized nations, including the Soviet Union, will participate.

To support our own effort, *I ask the Congress to authorize and appropriate for FY 1966 an additional $89 million for the Agency for International Development for expanded programs of economic and social development in Southeast Asia.*

This money will serve many purposes:

1. *Approximately $19 million* will provide the first installment of our contribution to the accelerated development of the Mekong River Basin. This is an important part of the general program of regional development which I outlined at Johns Hopkins University on April 7. This money will enable us to meet a request for half the cost of building the Nam Ngum Dam, which the international Mekong Committee has marked "top priority" if the Mekong River is to be put to work for the people of the region. This will be the first Mekong power project to serve two countries, promising power to small industry and lights for thousands of homes in Northeast Thailand and Laos. The funds will provide also for

—power lines across the Mekong linking Laos and Thailand;

—extensive studies of further hydroelectric, irrigation and flood control projects on the Mekong main stream and its tributaries;

—expansion of distribution lines in Laos.

2. *Five million dollars* will be used to support electrification cooperatives near three provincial towns—Long Xuyen, Dalat and

Nha Thang—in South Vietnam. Co-ops, which have been so important to the lives of our rural people, will bring the benefits of low priced electricity to more than 200,000 Vietnamese. We hope this pattern can be duplicated in towns and villages throughout the region. I will ask that we provide further support if the pattern meets the success we believe possible.

3. *Seven million dollars* will help provide improved medical and surgical services, especially in the more remote areas of Vietnam, Laos and Thailand. South Vietnam is tragically short of doctors; some 200 civilian physicians must care for a population of 15,000,000. In Laos the system of AID-supported village clinics and rural hospitals now reaches more than a million people. But that is not enough. We propose to extend the program in Laos, assist the Thailand Government to expand its public health services to thousands of rural villages, and to organize additional medical and surgical teams for sick and injured civilians in South Vietnam.

Better health is the first fruit of modern science. For the people of these countries it has far too long been an empty promise. I hope that when peace comes our medical assistance can be expanded and made available to the sick and wounded of the area without regard to political commitment.

4. *Approximately $6 million* will be used to train people for the construction of roads, dams and other small-scale village projects in Thailand and Laos. In many parts of Asia the chance of the villager for markets, education and access to public services depends on his getting a road. A nearby water well dramatically lightens the burdens of the farmer's wife. With these tools and skills local people can build their own schools

and clinics—blessings only dreamed of before.

5. *Approximately $45 million* will be used to finance increasing imports of iron and steel, cement, chemicals and pesticides, drugs, trucks and other essential goods necessary for a growing civilian economy. This money will allow factories not only to continue but, through investment, to expand production of both capital and consumer goods. It will provide materials for urgently needed low-cost housing. And it will maintain production incentives and avoid inflation. It is not easy for a small country, with a low income, to fight a war on its own soil and at the same time persist in the business of nation-building. The additional import support which I propose will help Vietnam to persevere in this difficult task.

6. *An additional $7 million* will supplement the present program of agricultural development and support additional government services in all three countries, and will help in the planning of further industrial expansion in the secure areas of Vietnam.

Much of the additional assistance I request is for Vietnam. This is not a poor and unfavored land. There is water and rich soil and ample natural resources. The people are patient, hard-working, the custodians of a proud and ancient civilization. They have been oppressed not by nature but by man. The failures of man can be redeemed. That is the purpose of the aid for which I now ask additional authorization.

We are defending the right of the people of South Vietnam to decide their own destiny. Where this right is attacked by force, we have no alternative but to reply with strength. But military action is not a final solution in this area; it is only a partial means to a much larger goal. Freedom and progress will be possible in Vietnam only as the people are assured that history is on their side—that it will give them a chance to make a living in peace, to educate their children, to escape the ravages of disease and, above all, to be free of the oppressors who for so long have fed on their labors.

Our effort on behalf of the people of Southeast Asia should unite, not divide, the people of that region. Our policy is not to spread conflict but to heal conflict.

I ask the Congress, as part of our continuing affirmation of America's faith in the cause of man, to respond promptly and fully to this request.

LYNDON B. JOHNSON

The White House
June 1, 1965

NOTE: The Foreign Assistance Act of 1965, which appropriated an additional $89 million for use in Southeast Asia, was approved by the President on September 6, 1965 (see Item 495).

In his message the President referred to Eugene R. Black, adviser to the President on Southeast Asian social and economic development and former President of the World Bank, and to U Thant, Secretary General of the United Nations.

295 The President's News Conference of June 1, 1965

THE PRESIDENT. Good afternoon, ladies and gentlemen.

WITHDRAWAL OF MARINES FROM THE DOMINICAN REPUBLIC

[1.] The situation in the Dominican Republic continues to be serious. That is why we welcome the additional efforts which are being made in the OAS today to enlarge and to strengthen the efforts to find a peaceful settlement there. We continue to give our full support to Secretary General Mora [1] in his outstanding service under existing OAS resolutions, but we share his judgment that a very strong and sustained effort is going to continue to be needed.

Meanwhile, I have been advised today by General Alvim, the Commander in Chief of the Inter-American Force, and by Lieutenant General Palmer, the Deputy Commander of the Inter-American Force, that conditions in the Dominican Republic will now permit the further withdrawal of the United States military personnel from the Inter-American Force. This recommendation has the concurrence of Secretary General Mora and Ambassador Bennett.[2]

I am, therefore, accordingly, ordering the immediate withdrawal of one battalion landing team of United States Marines, plus headquarters and supporting personnel. This will total approximately 2,000 people.

Now to another subject.

ANNIVERSARY OF THE UNITED NATIONS

[2.] This month of June marks a very historic anniversary in the affairs of man. Twenty years ago, while war still raged in the world, the nations of Europe assembled at San Francisco to sign the charter of hope that brought into being the United Nations. Men were mindful that in these times humankind must choose between cooperation or catastrophe.

[1] José A. Mora, Secretary General of the Organization of American States.

[2] W. Tapley Bennett, Jr., U.S. Ambassador to the Dominican Republic.

At San Francisco there was brought into being a great instrumentality for international cooperation, and we can believe today that the cooperation engendered by the United Nations has helped to avert catastrophe in this century. So today we have to work not on the things that divide us, but instead on the things that unite nations in the bonds of common interest.

On June 24th, 25th, and 26th of this year, the General Assembly of the United Nations will meet for commemorative sessions in San Francisco. It is my hope and plan at this time to be in San Francisco and to address the delegates at that time during the meetings of the sessions there.

FOREIGN AID FUNDS FOR SOUTHEAST ASIA

[3.] This afternoon I am sending to the Congress a very special message requesting an additional appropriation to help in the peaceful economic and social development of southeast Asia.[3] This is another forward step toward carrying out my April proposal for a massive effort to improve the life of man in that conflict-torn corner of the world.

The American people, I think, want their own Government to be not only strong but compassionate. They know that a society is secure only when there is full social justice for all of its people, and these principles of compassion and justice never stop at the water's edge.

So we do not intend that the enemies of freedom shall become the inheritors of man's worldwide revolt against injustice and misery. Therefore, we expect to lead in that struggle, not to conquer or to subdue, but to give each people the chance to build its own nation in its own way.

My personal representative, Mr. Eugene

Black,[4] has already begun extensive and hopeful discussions with interested parties around the world. Thus, the groundwork has already been laid for a long-range development plan for all of southeast Asia, led by Asians, to improve the life of Asians.

In South Viet-Nam today, brave and enduring people are carrying on a determined resistance against those who would destroy their independence. They will win this fight, and the United States of America is going to help them win it.

But there is another and a much more profound struggle going on in that country, and that is the struggle to create the conditions of hope and progress which are really the only lasting guarantees of peace and stability.

The 16 million people of South Viet-Nam survive on an average income of $100 per year. More than 60 percent of the people have never learned to read or write. When disease strikes, medical care is often impossible to find.

As I remarked the other day here, there is only one doctor for every 29,000 people, compared with one for every 740 in the United States. They have 200 doctors; whereas, they need 5,000. This poverty and this neglect take their inevitable toll in human life. The life expectancy there is only 35 years. That is just about half what it is in our country.

Now, we think that these are the common enemies of man in South Viet-Nam. They were there before the aggressor struck. They, of course, will be there when aggression is completely gone. These enemies, too, we are committed to help defeat.

Today's request will be used to help de-

---

[3] See Item 294.

[4] Eugene R. Black, adviser to the President on Southeast Asian social and economic development and former President of the World Bank.

velop the vast water and power resources of the Mekong basin. They will be used to bring electricity to small towns in the provinces. We have had REA teams, as you know, there working for several weeks making these surveys and planning to build several REA systems.

We will build clinics and provide doctors for disease-ridden rural areas. We will help South Viet-Nam import materials for their homes and their factories, and in addition, the members of the American Medical Association have already agreed with us to try to recruit surgeons and specialists, approximately 50 of them. We are particularly very much in need of plastic surgeons to go to Viet-Nam to help heal the wounds of war and to help them, as well, to deal with the ravages of unchecked disease.

Now, this is just a part of the beginning. This appropriation today calls for only $89 million, but in the future I will call upon our people to make further sacrifices because this is a good program, and the starts that we are making today are good starts. This is the only way that I know in which we can really win not only the military battle against aggression, but the wider war for the freedom and for progress of all men.

Now I will be glad to take any questions you may have.

QUESTIONS

THE OAS PEACE FORCE

[4.] Q. Mr. President, in your speech at Baylor on Friday,[5] you spoke of new international machinery being needed to counteract any future aggression or subversion in this hemisphere. Could you spell out in any further detail just what your concept of this is, militarily or diplomatically?

---
[5] See Item 286.

THE PRESIDENT. Yes. I think that we are very delighted that for the first time in history, we have presently on the military side an Inter-American Force that is functioning—and functioning effectively—under the leadership of General Alvim in the Dominican Republic. A good many of the nations in this hemisphere are supplying forces to that Inter-American Force, and others will be making contributions, we hope, in the next few days.

On the political side, we are now considering the Organization of American States' certain solutions for the Dominican Republic which could very well serve as an indication of what might come in similar situations down the road. We have had very enlightened and very positive leadership under Mr. Mora, the Secretary General of the OAS, in the Dominican Republic, and we hope not only can they supply forces to help provide the military answer to the necessities in that field, but that they can evolve a formula that will provide judicious determinations in connection with political judgments that we need to make in the near future.

U.S. EFFORTS IN THE DOMINICAN REPUBLIC

Q. Mr. President, could you spell out for us, sir, the efforts and role that the United States has been playing in seeking a compromise government in the Dominican Republic and what you think the chances for success are?

THE PRESIDENT. Yes, I will be very glad to. We found it necessary, in order to preserve our own citizens' lives, and in order to stop the wholesale killing of hundreds and even thousands of Dominicans, to intervene in the Dominican Republic. Since that time, we have counseled at great length and sought the assistance of the OAS in connection with contributing the military forces that would bring about a cease-fire and preserve the peace.

At the same time, we have urged the OAS to establish machinery to help find a political solution, and awaiting the establishment of that machinery, which we are really considering in the OAS today, we have sent some of the best people in this Government to maintain contacts with the broad base of leadership in the Dominican Republic in the hope that there would, in due time, evolve a broadly based government that would meet with the approval of the Dominican people.

I have had Mr. Vance, Mr. Bundy, Mr. Mann, Mr. Vaughn,[6] and others maintain liaison with various leaders of various groups there. Those conferences have been taking place from day to day and we have been keeping the OAS and their representatives fully informed. We are hopeful that in due time they will reach conclusions as to how they think it can be best handled and that we will be able to contribute our part and cooperate with them. As you know, they were discussing the matter over the weekend and today, and we hope that a decision will be in the offing in the immediate future.

We have no desire to insist upon our particular brand of military solution or political solution. We think it is an inter-American matter, and we want to cooperate fully with them. Prior to our intervention, we consulted and discussed the gravity of the situation there with 14 Latin American nations, beginning on Saturday when the revolution took place, up through Wednesday when we sent the Marines in.

During that same period, we met with the Peace Committee of the OAS on Tuesday, and we met with the OAS Council on Wednesday. It has been our desire all along to contribute all we could to a cease-fire, to the eventual evolution of a stable government that would be broadly based, and to make our appropriate contribution to the necessary reconstruction of that country.

We feel that when the OAS reaches its decision, that that decision will be communicated to the people of the Dominican Republic. We hope that they will be able to find agreement between the inter-American body and the folks there that will ultimately lead to an expression of opinion by the people of the Dominican Republic and ultimately lead to a broadly based government that will include none of the extremes.

MAYOR WAGNER'S CANDIDACY

[5.] Q. Mr. P r e s i d e n t, do you feel Mayor Wagner[7] should run again?

THE PRESIDENT. I think that is a matter not for the President to determine.

THE OAS SECRETARY GENERAL

[6.] Q. Mr. President, do you think that the attacks which have been made on OAS Secretary General Mora in the Dominican Republic may have undermined his usefulness as a peace negotiator?

THE PRESIDENT. No, I don't think so. I think it may have had that objective in mind. That may have been its purpose. But you know the old story—when a man gets in the role of a mediator, both sides usually hit at him. But we think, as I said in my opening statement, that the Secretary General has performed a very useful role, a very intelligent one, and a very objective one, and

---

[6] Cyrus R. Vance, Deputy Secretary of Defense, McGeorge Bundy, Special Assistant to the President, Thomas C. Mann, Under Secretary of State for Economic Affairs, and Jack H. Vaughn, Assistant Secretary of State for Inter-American Affairs and United States Coordinator, Alliance for Progress.

[7] Robert F. Wagner, Mayor of New York City.

we have every confidence in his efforts. We have regretted to see the attacks come upon him as we have regretted to see the attacks come upon us. But we much prefer the attacks to what could have happened except for our action and except for his action.

FREEDOM OF SPEECH

[7.] Q. Mr. President, this morning, sir, you said "We welcome and ask for new ideas in foreign policy from universities and journals and public platforms across the land." Two questions, sir: Does this mean you approve of the university teach-in techniques, and what is your view of dissenting comment on Viet-Nam and other foreign problems?

THE PRESIDENT. I will answer the latter question first. I think that this administration profits from the suggestions and recommendations of leaders in other branches of government, from men who occupy public platforms, from general discussions. I think that is the strength of the American system, instead of a weakness. I am hopeful that every person will always exercise the free speech that the Constitution guarantees him, and I would prefer, of course, that it be constructive and it be responsible, and I think generally that has been true.

I am glad that I live in a nation where, in the midst of conflict, when men are dying to preserve our freedom, that our citizens still do not fear to exercise it, and I can assure you that they do exercise it.

INCREASED ACTION IN VIET-NAM

[8.] Q. Mr. President, there has been a flareup of the fighting in Viet-Nam. Could you give us an estimate of the situation there, the military situation?

THE PRESIDENT. We had anticipated that

we would have some actions of this type at this season of the year. We have had a rather serious engagement in the last few hours, in the most immediate past. The South Vietnamese have lost, according to the reports we have, dozens, even hundreds, of people.

We do not know exactly the extent of the Viet Cong losses, although we believe them to be substantial. We do not announce those, perhaps unfortunately, along with the announcement of our own losses. We know how many we lose, but we don't know how many they lose until we get out there and count them, so their losses never really catch up with the original story of our losses.

Suffice it to say I think it has been serious. We are concerned about it. It is occupying our attention. As you know, General Taylor[8] plans to be here in the next few days and he will probably have more definite information at that time, just about the details of this particular engagement.

COMMUNIST THREAT IN THE DOMINICAN REPUBLIC

[9.] Q. Mr. President, sir, last month when you spoke to the Nation on the Dominican Republic, you indicated that the threat of Communist control of the rebel movement was very serious. More recently we have included the rebel leaders in these talks for coalition. Do you feel that the Communist threat in the Dominican Republic is now over?

THE PRESIDENT. Oh, no. If you want me to elaborate on that a little bit, I will say that the threat was greater before 21,000 Americans arrived there. It always is. The Communists did not, in our judgment, originate this revolution, but they joined it and

---

[8] Gen. Maxwell D. Taylor, U.S. Ambassador to South Viet-Nam.

they participated in it. They were active in it, and in a good many places they were in charge of it.

We think that following the action that this Nation took—it served a very good purpose and some of the men who had originally participated in the revolution, and had to take asylum, returned, and more moderate forces took leadership—the Communist elements have not been so active, although their presence is still noted hour by hour. Their effectiveness is still observed. From day to day we see their handiwork in the Dominican Republic and elsewhere throughout the world, particularly in the propaganda field.

REGIONAL PEACE FORCES

[10.] Q. Mr. President, do you foresee that an inter-American peace force which may be set up permanently would be used only to suppress Communist-directed revolutionary movements in Latin America, or would it also be used to thwart revolutions by military juntas which were attempting to destroy elected governments?

I would also like to ask, in view of the precedent which may be created by such a force, would you look with favor upon the creation of similar regional forces in such areas as Africa and the Arab world?

THE PRESIDENT. I would not want to anticipate what action the OAS is going to take.

REAPPORTIONMENT

[11.] Q. Mr. President, today the Supreme Court handed down several decisions in reapportionment cases in line with its doctrine of "One man, one vote." However, as you know, there are several proposals already introduced in Congress for constitutional amendments which would nullify this doctrine in part. Could you tell

us what your administration's position is on this legislation?

THE PRESIDENT. The President does not take action in connection with constitutional amendments. I have reviewed some of the proposals that have been made. I am generally sympathetic with the reapportionments taking place throughout the country in compliance with the Supreme Court's decision. I would not want to get into detailed discussion of the individual programs about which the President will not act one way or the other, because a constitutional amendment does not require White House action. It is a matter for the representatives of the people to decide.

In submitting it, the Congress takes that action. The people themselves have an opportunity to judge it. When the Congress does get down to debating the question and considering it, I will, of course, spend some time on it and become thoroughly conversant with it, but I wouldn't want to predict at this time just what measure would emerge in the form of an amendment or what action Congress or the people might take on it.

FORTHCOMING GEMINI FLIGHT

[12.] Q. Mr. President, the astronaut flight on Thursday is going to have more maneuvering than was originally announced. Was this increase done at your suggestion or urging, sir?

THE PRESIDENT. No.

VIET-NAM

[13.] Q. Mr. President, if the situation in Viet-Nam—in which you have promised the United States to help that country achieve victory—becomes such that American combat troops are used in the combat there, would you give that order, sir, in the event that there was an invasion from the north?

THE PRESIDENT. I don't see that I can do you any good, the country any good, or myself any good by discussing future operational plans. I know of no real reason why we ought to photograph them or decide them until we are confronted with that possibility.

REGIONAL PEACE FORCES

[14.] Q. Mr. President, in connection with your statement on the United Nations, the Secretary General of the U.N. has expressed the apprehension that the OAS action in the Dominican Republic might have established, I think, what he called an embarrassing precedent, that the Arab League might act in its region and the African states might act in theirs. I was wondering whether you shared those apprehensions about the U.N.?

THE PRESIDENT. I do not.

THE "JOHNSON DOCTRINE"

[15.] Q. Mr. President, some persons claim that you have enunciated a new Johnson doctrine under which American troops would be used to prevent the establishment of a Communist government anywhere in the Western Hemisphere. In sending American troops to Santo Domingo and explaining your actions afterwards, did you have any such purpose in mind?

THE PRESIDENT. No. I am afraid that the people that have branded the Johnson doctrine were unfamiliar with the fact that the nations of this hemisphere have repeatedly made it clear that the principles of communism are incompatible with the principles of the inter-American system, just as Presi-

dent Kennedy made it abundantly clear. That is the basis of our own attitude on the matter, as I explained in my television appearance.

That does not mean, of course, that this Government is opposed to change. The greatest purpose of the Alliance for Progress, which we are working on so hard and making such substantial contributions to, is to encourage economic and social change. We believe that will benefit all the people of this hemisphere. We are doing our best to provide encouragement for those changes. But I think it is a well-known and well-advertised doctrine of the hemisphere that the principles of communism are incompatible with the principles of our inter-American system. President Kennedy enunciated that on several occasions. The OAS itself has enunciated that. I merely repeated it. I am sorry I got some folks excited by it.

THE DECISION TO INTERVENE IN THE
DOMINICAN REPUBLIC

[16.] Q. Mr. President, I would like to ask you two questions about the Dominican rebellion, one dealing with its origin and one dealing with the possible future. Do you think that it would have been helpful if Juan Bosch [9] had returned; and do you think he might have exercised a restraining influence on some of the left-wing extremists, or Communists, who are in there? And secondly——

THE PRESIDENT. I will answer your first one. I don't want to get into personalities. Go ahead.

Q. On the second one regarding the future, do you think it would be useful if the Dominicans were to follow the example of the Founding Fathers in this country and

[9] Former President of the Dominican Republic.

hold a constitutional convention themselves to talk out some of their differences before they try to set up a new government?

THE PRESIDENT. We have taken several steps in the order of priority that we felt was required. Many months ago we became aware of the increasing tensions there, and the difficulties that would likely confront us. On the Sunday before we went in there on Wednesday, we asked the Ambassador, who had already come to Washington at our calling, to leave his family's home and come here to meet with us.

Ambassador Bennett met with us on Monday. We rushed him back to the Dominican Republic and set in motion certain steps.

First, was to attempt to obtain a cease-fire. Second, was to take the precautionary steps necessary to protect approximately 5,000 Americans, as well as thousands of other nationals, if that should be required. We moved our ships up there on Sunday.

The Ambassador arrived there on Monday. He talked to various leaders. We did all we could to bring about a cease-fire in cooperation with the Papal Nuncio and others who were active on the scene. On Wednesday at noon it became apparent that danger was lurking around the corner and the Ambassador gave us a warning in a cable about 1 o'clock.

We had met on Monday and we had met on Tuesday. We had met on Wednesday and we had had many conversations on Sunday that we did not issue any handouts on. During that period, I think from the time we were notified on Saturday, until we intervened on Wednesday, we spent a good part of both day and night giving our attention to this matter, from moving the ships up to making the final decision.

I had 237 individual conversations during that period and about 35 meetings with various people. Finally, on Wednesday afternoon at 4–something, we got another warning that we should have a contingent plan ready immediately, and a little before 6 o'clock we got a plea, a unanimous plea from the entire country team, made up of the Ambassador, the AID Director, CIA and the USIA, and the Army, Navy, and the Air Force, to land troops immediately to save American lives.

Now, of course, we knew of the forces at work in the Dominican Republic. We were not unaware that there were Communists that were active in this effort, but 99 percent of our reason for going in there was to try to provide protection for these American lives and for the lives of other nationals. We asked our Ambassador to summon all our people immediately to the Ambassador Hotel, to put them in one central group. In the presence of Secretary Rusk, Secretary McNamara, Secretary Ball,[10] Mr. Bundy, and Mr. Moyers [11] of my staff, we consulted with the Latin American desk, Mr. Vaughn and his experts, and Mr. Vance and the Joint Chiefs of Staff.

In the neighborhood of 6 o'clock Wednesday evening we made the decision, it was a unanimous decision, about which there was no difference of opinion either at the Dominican Republic level, or the country team, or the Cabinet level here, to send in the troops. We did not want to announce that they were on their way until they had landed, for obvious security reasons. But when I made the decision, I pointed out to the Secretary of State that we had been consulting since the weekend with some 14 Latin American nations, that we had had a meeting of the Peace Committee of the OAS, and we had had a meeting of the Council of the OAS.

---

[10] George W. Ball, Under Secretary of State.
[11] Bill D. Moyers, Special Assistant to the President.

I thought it was very important that we notify all the Latin American Ambassadors forthwith.

So the decision was to notify the Congress and ask them to come down so we could review with them developments, notify the Ambassadors, and ask for an immediate session of the OAS, and to notify the troops, because the lives of our citizens were in danger.

Men were running up and down the corridors of the Ambassador Hotel with tommyguns, shooting out windows, and through the roof and through the closets. Our citizens were under the beds and in the closets and trying to dodge this gunfire. Our Ambassador, as he was talking to us, was under the desk. We didn't think we had much time to consult in any great detail more than we had talked about up to that time, but we did make the announcement about 8 o'clock and immediately asked the OAS for an urgent meeting the next morning.

Since that time we have had two purposes in mind: One was for them to take action that would give us a military presence and provide a military solution so that we could quit killing people. I think that the Armed Forces are entitled to one of the greatest tributes ever paid that group in war or peace for the marvelous operation they conducted. They moved in there and landed within an hour from the time the Commander in Chief made the decision. They surrounded the hotel and protected the lives of a thousand American citizens and many hundreds of other nationals. They did not lose one civilian. They opened the route of 7 miles to the port and they evacuated 5,600 people.

Those people came from 46 different countries.

The next step that we thought should be followed was to provide food and clothing and sustenance for those people, so we sent an economic team of 32 people, headed by Mr. Solomon,[12] who was sworn in today as Assistant Under Secretary of State in charge of economic matters. And we started feeding the 3½ million people of the Dominican Republic. We have provided food and other necessities, medicine, since that time, to those people without regard to which side they were on.

In addition, we have treated more than 15,000 with our medical facilities.

So having gone in and secured the place, having evacuated 5,600 people, and now the commercial planes are running and they can come out on their own stint, having obtained a cease-fire, having provided the economic aid, having sent our best people there to talk to all groups and all factions and leadership, to try to find a government that would appeal to all the Dominican people, we now think that there are two essential things that are left to be done: One is to find a broadly based government under the leadership of the OAS that will be acceptable and approved by the Dominican people; and second, to engage in the comprehensive task of reconstruction of that nation, in trying to make it possible for 3½ million to have an economic comeback.

ALVIN SPIVAK (United Press International): Thank you, Mr. President.

NOTE: President Johnson's forty-third news conference was held in the East Room at the White House at 4 p.m. on Tuesday, June 1, 1965.

---

[12] Anthony M. Solomon, Assistant Secretary of State for Economic Affairs.

296   Remarks at the Presentation of the President's Award for Distinguished Federal Civilian Service.   *June 2, 1965*

Good morning, ladies and gentlemen:

It is a very exceptional pleasure to welcome all of you this morning.

Mr. Ball, Mr. Secretary of State, Members of the Congress, ladies and gentlemen:

Public service being what it is, I am sure that the wives and children will welcome the opportunity to see their husbands and their fathers again this morning in daylight.

Considering the current situation to natural beauty, I regret that the most colorful sight in the Rose Garden this morning is my sunburn.

Several people have written to Mrs. Johnson suggesting that if she is serious about beautifying America she ought to start working on me. After she pondered that task for a while she left just a moment ago for the Virgin Islands.

We have come here this morning to bestow our high civilian honor upon these five men who have distinguished themselves and honored their country by their very good and faithful service in high positions of public trust.

Over the years, in both public and private organizations, it has been traditional to honor employees for records of attendance, and punctuality, and seniority, and other kindred virtues. Such qualities, of course, are commendable, but in these times much more is asked and far more is given, as the record of these men so amply attest.

Today, in public service especially, we ask and we expect and we receive the highest order of originality, and initiative, and even of independent thought and inquiry.

In this largest organization of its kind, the executive branch of the Government of the United States, the emphasis is no longer on the faceless mass, but the emphasis is on individual excellence. In fields as diverse as the collection of statistics and the exploration of space, these five men have quested after excellence and, in so doing, they have enriched and expanded the sum of human knowledge and human capability. The service each has rendered is far more than mere service to the state.

No command, or no order, or no edict of a party, no directive from dictatorial authorities could have ever evoked from any of them the genius and the greatness and the constructiveness and the compassion that has come from their own voluntary desire to serve freedom responsibly and to serve it well.

In this century of contest, it is well for us all to remember that the harder the contest is, it remains always whether the men shall serve the state or whether the state shall serve men.

Our Government, and indeed all of our institutions, will be stronger as we trust independence rather than relying upon suppression of the individual.

In a free society, skepticism toward Government is both healthy and imperative and we should welcome it, but private citizens should always guard against allowing such healthy skepticism to corrode or to destroy their respect for their fellow citizens who serve them. For it really is the loyalty, and the efficiency, and the effectiveness of our public servants which stand as the first line of defense for the stability and the ultimate success of our organized society.

Half a world away, in the land of South Viet-Nam, we are reminded of this anew each day. There, for years, the enemies of freedom have been on the attack in a very cruel and a very vicious war. All through this period, the point of that attack has been the public servants, who were leading the organizations, and the development of a free society. In the villages and the hamlets and the countryside, the guerrillas in the night have stricken down by knives and guns and hand grenades Government officials. The losses there have been equivalent to the loss in the United States of more than 30,000 of our public officials—our mayors, our city councilmen, and our Government servants.

So, the men we honor this morning, and many tens and hundreds of thousands more like them that serve our Government throughout the United States, are devoting their lives and their minds to making our freedom more secure, and our success more certain.

We honor them for their contributions, not to the greater power of Government, but to the greater glory of man. The trust they are keeping is really the most noble trust on earth.

And now the citations will be read and the awards will be presented. But prior to that time, I want, on behalf of the Vice President and myself, to express to them the entire gratitude of a grateful Nation.

Thank you very much.

NOTE: The President spoke at 11:50 a.m. in the Rose Garden at the White House. In his opening words he referred to George W. Ball, Under Secretary of State and Chairman of the Distinguished Civilian Service Awards Board, and Dean Rusk, Secretary of State.

A White House release of the same date, listing the recipients of the awards, contained the following quotation from the President's memorandum informing the heads of executive departments and agencies of his selections for the award:

"Each of these men has demonstrated in his field that extra measure of professional excellence needed to effectively carry out our many action programs in the people's service. The work of each has been distinguished by courage, vision and ingenuity—qualities that make for greatness in men who serve the people. Collectively, they have made immense contributions to the Nation's well being and advancement.

"I know you share my great pride and satisfaction in the exemplary accomplishments of these public servants, which underscore for our fellow citizens how much excellence there is in the career ranks of the Federal service.

"Government programs are advanced as much through people and their efforts as through the language of laws and Federal regulations. We must make certain that we express our appreciation to the outstanding individuals in positions at all levels of Government who supply the special creative ability, the extra productive effort, or the unusually superlative skill that is vitally needed to carry out Federal programs to the topmost heights of excellence."

The recipients of the awards and the highlights of their citations as released by the White House are as follows:

Howard C. Grieves, Assistant Director of the Bureau of the Census, who "has contributed impressively to the effective functioning of the National economy by vastly improving the timeliness and reliability of the statistical products of our census system."

Homer E. Newell, Associate Administrator for Space Science and Applications, National Aeronautics and Space Administration, who "has been significantly responsible for this Nation's success in the unmanned satellite and space probe projects."

Frank B. Rowlett, Special Assistant to the Director, National Security Agency, Department of Defense, who "by his inventive genius and managerial skill has contributed profoundly to the security of the Nation."

Clyde A. Tolson, Associate Director of the Federal Bureau of Investigation, Department of Justice, who "has been a vital force in raising the proficiency of law enforcement at all levels and in guiding the Federal Bureau of Investigation to new heights of accomplishment through periods of great National challenge."

Philip H. Trezise, Deputy Assistant Secretary for Economic Affairs, Department of State, who "has developed imaginative solutions to vital and complex economic problems arising in United States relations with foreign countries."

297   Special Message to the Congress Proposing Changes in the Coinage System.   *June 3, 1965*

To the Congress of the United States:

From the early days of our independence the United States has used a system of coinage fully equal in quantity and in quality to all the tasks imposed upon it by the Nation's commerce.

We are today using one of the few existing silver coinages in the world. Our coins, in fact, are little changed from those first established by the Mint Act of 1792. For 173 years, we have maintained a system of abundant coins that with the exception of pennies and nickels is nearly pure silver.

The long tradition of our silver coinage is one of the many marks of the extraordinary stability of our political and economic system.

Continuity, however, is not the only characteristic of a great nation's coinage. *We should not hesitate to change our coinage to meet new and growing needs. I am, therefore, proposing certain changes in our coinage system—changes dictated by need— which will help Americans to carry out their daily transactions in the most efficient way possible.*

There has been for some years a worldwide shortage of silver. The United States is not exempt from that shortage—and we will not be exempt as it worsens. *Silver is becoming too scarce for continued large-scale use in coins. To maintain unchanged our high silver coinage in the face of this stark reality would only invite a chronic and growing scarcity of coins.*

We expect to use more than 300 million troy ounces—over 10 thousand tons—of silver for our coinage this year. *That is far more than total new production of silver expected in the entire Free World this year.* Although we have a large stock of silver on hand we cannot continue indefinitely to make coins of a high silver content—in the required quantity—in the face of such an imbalance in the production of silver and the demand for it.

We must take steps to maintain an adequate supply of coins, or face chaos in the myriad transactions of our daily life—from using pay telephones to parking in a metered zone to providing our children with money for lunch at school.

The legislation I am sending to the Congress with this Message will ensure a stable and dignified coinage, fully adequate in quantity and in its specially designed technical characteristics to the needs of our Twentieth Century life. It can be maintained indefinitely, however much the demand for coin may grow.

Much as we all would prefer to retain the silver coins now in use, there is no practical alternative to a new coinage based on materials in adequate supply.

THE NEW COINAGE

I propose no change in either the penny or the nickel.

The new dime and the quarter—while remaining the same size and design as the present dime and quarter—will be composite coins. They will have faces of the same copper-nickel alloy used in our present five cent piece, bonded to a core of pure copper. The new dime and quarter will, therefore, outwardly resemble the nickel, except in size and design, but with the further distinction that their copper core will give them a copper edge.

This type of coin was selected because, alone among practical alternatives, it can be used together with our existing silver coins in the millions of coin-operated devices that Americans now depend upon heavily for many kinds of food and other goods.

THE HALF DOLLAR

Our new half dollar will be nearly indistinguishable in appearance from the present half dollar.

It will continue to be made of silver and copper, but the silver content will be reduced from 90 percent to 40 percent. It will be faced with an alloy of 80 percent silver and 20 percent copper, bonded to a core of 21 percent silver and 79 percent copper. The new half dollar will continue to be minted with the image of President Kennedy. Its size will be unchanged.

THE SILVER DOLLAR

No change in this famous old coin, or plans for additional production, are proposed at this time. It is possible that implementation of the new coinage legislation that I am proposing, greatly reducing the requirement for silver in our subsidiary coinage, will actually make feasible the minting of additional silver dollars in the future. Certainly, without this change in the silver content of the subsidiary coinage, further minting of the Silver Dollar would be forever foreclosed.

It is our intention that the new coinage circulate side-by-side with our existing coinage. We plan to continue the minting of our current silver coins while the new coinage is brought into quantity production.

The new coins will be placed in circulation some time in 1966.

In terms of the present pattern of coin usage, adoption of the new coinage will

permit a saving of some 90 percent of the silver we are now putting into coins annually.

I want to make it absolutely clear that these changes in our coinage will have no effect on the purchasing power of our coins. The new ones will be exchanged at full face value for the paper currency of the United States. They will be accepted by the Treasury and by the Federal Reserve Banks for any of the financial obligations of the United States. The legislation I am proposing expressly recognizes the new coins as legal tender.

It is of primary importance, of course, that our new coins be specifically designed to serve our modern, technological society. In the early days of the Republic, silver coins served well because the value of a coin could only be measured by the value of the precious metal contained in it. For many decades now the value of a particular coin has depended not on the value of the metal in it, but on the face value of the coin. Today's coinage must primarily be utilitarian. The new coinage will meet this requirement fully, while dispensing with the idea that it contain precious metal.

It is, above all, practical. It has been specifically designed to function, without causing delays or disruptions of service, in coin-operated merchandising machines.

Furthermore, it is composed of materials low enough in value and readily enough available to insure that we can have as many coins as we need.

The legislation I am proposing also contains these additional recommendations:

OTHER AUTHORITY REQUESTED

First—As a useful precautionary measure, I request stand-by authority to institute controls over the melting and export of coins to assist the protection of our existing and our new silver coinage.

Second—I request authority to purchase domestically mined silver at not less than $1.25 per ounce.

Third—I am asking for authority to reactivate minting operations temporarily at the San Francisco Assay Office.

Fourth—As a safeguard for assured availability of the new coinage, I am asking for new contracting authority for the procurement of materials and facilities related to it.

Fifth—I propose the establishment of a Joint Commission on the Coinage, composed of certain members of the Congress, the Public and the Executive Branch of the Government, to report to me later the progress made in the installation of the new coinage and to review any new technological developments and to suggest any further modifications which may be needed.

WHY THE SILVER CONTENT OF THE COINAGE
MUST BE REDUCED AT THIS SESSION

These recommendations for revision of our silver coinage rest upon extensive study of the silver situation, and of alternatives to our present coinage, by both governmental and private specialists. The Treasury Department's comprehensive report, known as the Treasury Staff Silver and Coinage Study, is being released today as background to my recommendations. Its principal finding *was that the supply of silver in the Free World has become progressively incompatible with the maintenance of silver in all our subsidiary coins.*

On the average, in the five years from 1949 through 1953, new silver production in the Free World amounted to about 175 million troy ounces per year, while consumption amounted to more than 235 million ounces.

There was an average deficit in those five post-war years of more than 60 million ounces of silver per year.

In the latest complete five years, 1960 through 1964, Free World consumption of silver has averaged 410 million ounces annually, but new production has averaged a little less than 210 million ounces a year. The result has been an average annual deficit of about 200 million ounces. That is three times the average annual deficit in the five years from 1949 through 1953.

If no silver at all had been used for coinage there would have been a deficit in new production in Free World silver during the last five years averaging over 40 million troy ounces, or some 1,370 tons, a year.

The gap between the production of silver and silver consumption is continuing to increase. In 1964 the silver production deficit swelled to over 300 million ounces— half again the 1963 figure. And in 1964, the use of silver in coinage, and the use of silver for the arts and industry of the Free World were each—taken separately—greater than new production.

There is no dependable or likely prospect that new, economically workable sources of silver may be found that could appreciably narrow the gap between silver supply and demand. The optimistic outlook is for an increase in production of about 20 percent over the next four years. This would be of little help. Further, because silver is produced chiefly as a by-product of the mining of copper, lead and zinc, even a very large increase in the price of silver would not stimulate silver production sufficiently to change the outlook.

Short of controls that are undesirable in a peacetime free society, there is no way to diminish the bounding growth of private demand for silver for use in jewelry, silverware, photographic film and industrial processes. The one part of the demand for silver that can be reduced is governmental demand for use in coinage.

Most Free World countries no longer use silver in their coins. A few—as we now propose—continue to make limited use of it. It is true that United States coinage does not currently depend upon new silver production, because for many years we have supplied silver for our coinage out of large Treasury stocks, which still amount to 1 billion troy ounces.

But—and this is the crux of the matter— at the present pace, this stock cannot last even as much as three years. We would then be shorn of our ability to maintain the coinage, and, if there were no alternative to our present silver coinage, the nation would be faced with a chronic coin shortage. That is why definitive action is necessary at this session of the Congress.

PROTECTION OF THE COINAGE

It is necessary for the United States government to have large stocks of silver in addition to the quantity needed for coinage.

We need these stocks because our silver coins in circulation must be protected from hoarding or destruction. Protection of the silver coinage will continue to be a necessity since we plan for it to continue to circulate alongside the new coins. Our silver coins are protected by the fact that the government stands ready to sell silver bullion from its stocks at $1.29 a troy ounce. This keeps the price of silver, as a commodity, from rising above the face value of our coins. This, in turn, makes hoarding or melting of the silver coinage unprofitable.

It is as additional protection for the existing coinage that I am requesting stand-by authority to institute controls over the melting, treating or export of United States coins.

It may be asked why we seek stand-by control authority since we retain a large stock of silver with which to protect our silver coins through operations in the silver market.

The answer is clear. Given the magnitudes by which demand for silver is outrunning new production, we must consider the possibility, however unlikely, that the silver stock we possess could itself require the support and protection that would be afforded by authority to forbid melting and export of our coins.

We believe our present stocks of silver to be adequate, once the large present drains from coinage are greatly reduced, to meet any foreseeable requirements for an indefinite period. *However, prompt action on a new coinage will help us protect the silver coinage by freeing our silver reserves for redemption of silver certificates at $1.29 per ounce. Thus, we can assure that no incentive will be created for hoarding our present coins in anticipation of a higher price for their silver content.*

There is the opposite, although in all likelihood short-run, possibility that a fall in the price of silver might result from the enactment of this legislation largely removing silver from our subsidiary coin. *It is for the purpose of protecting silver producers from a precipitate drop in the price of silver resulting from the action of the government that I am requesting authority for the Secretary of the Treasury to purchase any newly mined domestic silver offered to him, at the price of $1.25 per troy ounce.*

THE SAN FRANCISCO ASSAY OFFICE

Coinage operations at the San Francisco Mint were ended in 1955. Legislation converting the Mint to the San Francisco Assay Office was passed in 1962. As part of our efforts to overcome the coin shortage of the past year, coin blanks have been cut and annealed at the San Francisco Assay Office. Present law forbids full minting there. However, we will temporarily need the facilities of this plant to move into large quantity production of the new coinage and to continue production of existing coins until enough new small money is made to make certain we have adequate supplies. *Consequently, I am asking for authority to reactivate minting operations at San Francisco on a temporary basis.*

A new, fully modern mint is to be built in Philadelphia. However, it cannot be completed and in operation before late 1967. It is our expectation that when the new Philadelphia Mint's capacity is added to that of the Denver Mint, our coinage requirements can be met efficiently and economically. Consequently, no more than temporary authority to mint coins in San Francisco is recommended in the draft legislation I am sending to you.

WHY COMPOSITE COINS ARE RECOMMENDED

We have no choice but to eliminate silver, for the most part, from our subsidiary coinage. The question was: What would be the best alternative? After very thorough consideration of all aspects of this highly complex problem, we have settled upon the two types of composite, or clad, coins I have already described. These are 10-cent and 25-cent pieces with cupronickel alloy faces bonded to a solid copper core, and a new half dollar with outer and inner layers of differing silver-copper alloys.

This type of coin was found to be necessary if the new coinage is to be compatible with the existing silver coinage in all the 12 million coin operated devices in use in the United States.

The convenience of using coins in automatic merchandising and service devices is a fact that, like the coins in our pockets and in our store tills, we take for granted. But if our coinage were suddenly to be such that it would not work in coin-operated devices, the public would be subjected to very great inconvenience and serious losses would occur to business with harmful effects upon employment.

The automatic merchandising industry is a large and growing part of our national economy. Last year, $3½ billion worth of consumer items were sold through 3½ million of these machines. On more than 30 *billion* separate occasions a consumer made a purchase by putting a coin in a machine. In growing numbers, factories, hospitals and other places now depend upon automatic vending for the service of goods. A million and a half people now rely upon coin controlled vending for at least one meal a day. The use of coin operated devices is expanding rapidly, not only in merchandise vending, but also in a number of other services.

Six million of our coin-operated devices, including nearly all vending machines, have selectors set to reject coins or imitations of coins that do not have the electrical properties of our existing silver money. Highly selective rejectors are a necessity in these machines if they are to be a low-cost source of food and other goods and services. Otherwise, fraudulent use would soon make them costly.

The sensors in these machines are set to accept or reject coins on the basis of the electrical properties of our traditional coins, which have a high proportion of silver. To be compatible in operation with our existing coinage, therefore, our new coins must duplicate the electrical properties of a coin that is 90 percent silver. No single acceptable metal or alloy does so. The composite coins, made of layers of differing metals and alloys, that I am asking the Congress to approve, are coins made to order to duplicate the electrical properties of coins with a high silver content. They are the only practical alternatives we have discovered to our present coinage.

Selectors exist that can handle coins with the widely varying electrical properties of, say, nearly pure silver and nearly pure nickel. But that is not enough. When the selectors are set to accept coins with greatly differing electrical properties, the selectivity of the mechanism declines and they will accept wrong coins and imitations. Unless the coins in use have very similar electrical properties, the coin-operated machines become subject to a high degree of fraudulent use. This would be costly to all concerned.

The future may bring selectors of a different kind able to accept coins of widely varying electrical properties while at the same time rejecting imitations and wrong coins. They are not available now. When and if they become available, our new coinage will work in them. On the other hand, if we now chose an incompatible coinage, there would be delays and interruptions lasting a year to three years in the services of these machines. This would impose heavy inconveniences upon the public and would cause business and employment losses in a large and growing industry.

In view of these considerations of public interest, we have concluded that our new coinage must without fail be able to carry out the technical merchandising functions of a modern coinage, working alongside our existing silver coinage. *The new coins that I am recommending to you do this, and do it well, because they were specifically designed for the task.*

The new half dollar was designed with the strong desire in mind of many Americans to retain some silver in our every-day coinage. We believe that by eliminating silver from use in the dime and the quarter, we will have enough silver to carry out market operations in protection of our existing silver coinage—and to make a half dollar of 40 percent silver content. It is clear and unmistakable that we would not have enough silver to extend this to the dime and quarter: they are heavily used, indispensable coins that we must have at all times in large quantity. We are convinced that we can include a 40 percent silver half dollar in the new coinage, but we cannot safely go beyond that. As a precaution, we intend to concentrate at first on getting out large quantities of the new quarter and dime before we embark upon quantity production of the new half dollar.

THE JOINT COMMISSION ON THE COINAGE

We believe the recommendations being made for a new coinage are sound and durable and in the best public interest. However, the installation of a new coinage is a matter so intimately affecting the life of every citizen, and so delicately related to the nation's commerce, that it is impossible to be certain in advance that all problems have been foreseen, even by such a long and arduous process of research as has gone into the selection of the proposed new coins.

Consequently, I am including among my recommendations the proposal for a Joint Commission on the Coinage. It will be composed of the four officers of the Executive Branch most directly concerned with matters affected by the coinage—the Secretary of the Treasury, the Secretary of Commerce, the Director of the Budget Bureau and the Director of the Mint; of four members representing the public interest, to be appointed by the President; of the Chairmen and ranking members of the Banking and Currency committees of the House and the Senate; of one member each from the two houses of the Congress, to be appointed by the Vice President and the Speaker of the House. The Commission will be appointed soon after the new coinage is issued. It will study such matters as new technological developments, the supply of various metals, and the future of the silver dollar. It will report as to the time and circumstances in which the government should cease to maintain the price of silver. It will be directed to advise the President, the Congress and the Secretary of the Treasury on the results of its studies.

THE COINAGE—CURRENT AND PROSPECTIVE

I am pleased to report to the Congress substantial progress toward overcoming the coin shortage the Nation has been experiencing. Greatly increased minting has eliminated the shortage of pennies and of nickels. We are still somewhat on the short side of the demand for dimes and quarters, but this deficit is rapidly being overtaken. A severe shortage of the half dollar continues, due to the popularity of the new 50 cent pieces bearing the image of President Kennedy.

I want to emphasize that we will continue to make the existing coins while the new ones come into full production, and that we contemplate side-by-side circulation of the old and new coins for the indefinite future. *There is no reason for hoarding the silver coinage we now use, because there is no reason for it to disappear.*

We are gearing up for maximum production of the new coins as soon as they are authorized by the Congress. Supply of the materials for them is assured. Both copper and nickel are economical and available in North America. Their usage in coins will not add enough to overall employment of these metals to create supply or price problems.

In the first year after new coins are authorized, we expect to make 3½ billion pieces of the new subsidiary coins. That is a billion and a half more pieces than will be made of the corresponding silver coins in the current fiscal year.

In the second year after authorization of the new coinage, we expect to be able to double the first year's output of the new coins, reaching a production total of 7 billion pieces.

We expect in this way to avoid any new coin shortage in the transition to production of the new coins, and within a period of less than three years to reach a point at which we could if necessary meet total coinage needs out of production of the new coins.

I am satisfied that, taking into account all of the various factors involved in this complex problem, the recommendations that I am making to you are sound and right. Your early and favorable action upon the proposed legislation will make it possible to produce and issue to the public a coinage that will be acceptable, provide the maximum convenience, and serve all the purposes—financial and technical—of modern commerce. In considering this problem the needs of the economy and the convenience of the public have been placed ahead of all other considerations. They are the factors that have resulted in my recommendations to the Congress. I urge their approval at the earliest possible date.

LYNDON B. JOHNSON

The White House
June 3, 1965

NOTE: The Coinage Act of 1965 was approved by the President on July 23, 1965 (see Item 380).

298   Remarks on the Youth Opportunity Campaign.
June 3, 1965

VICE PRESIDENT HUMPHREY. *Mr. President, Secretary Connor, Secretary Wirtz, members of the Youth Opportunity Campaign Task Force and, Mr. President, we have some trainees with us and distinguished guests:*

Ten days ago the President announced a nationwide youth opportunity campaign to provide job opportunities for the out-of-work young people between the ages of 16 and 21. The President asked me to head a task force to implement this campaign. I am pleased to report that the response to the President's appeal among Federal, State, and local government agencies, private businesses, our unions, and nonprofit organizations has been most encouraging. And we meet here this afternoon to honor those firms and organizations who responded most promptly to the youth opportunity campaign.

We should, however, recognize the excellent cooperation that we have received from Federal officials, State governments, and countless mayors throughout our country.

I am very pleased now to present to you the President of the United States.

THE PRESIDENT. *Mr. Vice President, members of the Cabinet, distinguished businessmen, young Americans, ladies and gentlemen:*

This has been a very exciting morning for all of us. Our prayers have been answered, our young men in the space program have been safely launched. Our prayers will be with them until they return. We are very grateful and very pleased that things have gone well thus far.

I picked up the morning paper and reviewed it carefully, always knowing in the back of my mind that the clock was ticking and that very shortly this great event in our national history would take place. I saw in one column of the paper about the Johnson administration's foreign policy, and I did not recognize it. I thought they were talking about this administration but from the description it could have been another administration somewhere. I looked over to another column and I saw the Johnson administration economic problems and the fears that were being expressed. I did not recognize that, either.

I guess when you have 4 or 5 million people working in the administration, you are not always sure what one of them is going to say under the name of the Johnson administration. But this program that we are meeting about this morning is a Johnson program. And if any of my people get tired of worrying about foreign policy and have time to stop giving interviews, I'd like for them to start worrying about getting young people jobs. And if any of our people get concerned about the economy going too fast or going too slow, I wish they would just quit worrying and go to worrying about getting kids jobs. That is the real important assignment that faces us on the domestic front.

I was looking at some of Bill Wirtz's figures last night and unemployment is down in this country now to 4.6—which is an encouraging thing for me—from 4.9. I observed that the unemployment among our young people is still 15 percent, and among our married adults is just a little over 2 percent.

So, we ought to really face up to this problem where it is. And I would hope that every businessman in this country that just insists on worrying would start worrying about how to get young people jobs; that every Government man that wants to give out an interview about something that he doesn't know much about would start worrying about how to get young people jobs, because we are going to add 25,000 in the Federal Government; that every labor official that has concern for his country will try to figure out how we can give these people training and how we can employ these young people, because unless we meet that challenge we'll have been a failure.

Some of you may remember the story of President Coolidge when a reporter asked him, "Do you wish to say anything about the strike?" And the President said, "No." And the reporter—as some of them are occasionally—was rather aggressive. He said, "Do you have any comment on the farm bloc?" And again the President said, "No." And the reporter kept insisting a little bit, and he said, "Do you have any comment about the World Court?" The President said, "No." Well, the reporter turned to go away and kind of showed his independence, and President Coolidge said, "Wait just a minute, don't quote me."

So, I asked the reporters here today because I want you to quote me. I want every businessman, not just those of you who have come here this morning because you are trailblazers and you are among the first, because you are aggressive leaders in your group, I want all of them to know that America faces the crisis of the first order this summer, and we ought to get ready for it.

That crisis is the unemployment among its young people. One out of eight of the total labor force is a youngster between 16 and 21. But one out of every three unemployed Americans is in that group. And the irony is that as teenage unemployment worsens

the overall employment situation continues to improve.

We can all take great pride in the figures for May which are being released today by the Bureau of Labor Statistics. They show major improvement on almost every front. Unemployment fell by 220,000 between April and May, down to a total of 3,300,000. This was triple the decline which usually takes place at this time of the year. As a result, the seasonally adjusted unemployment rate fell, as I stated a moment ago, from 4.9 percent in April to 4.6 percent in May—the lowest figure in 91 months.

Now, when we lose 10 or 12 or 15 lives in Viet-Nam we have headlines that say this is the highest number that we have lost any day, and when we send 200 planes out we say this is the largest number of planes. But these are facts and figures that I think are encouraging to every American of whatever party he belongs to—that unemployment fell from 4.9 to 4.6, and that is the lowest figure in 91 months. That's almost 8 years.

So, these returns represent the first available figures on employment for the 51st and recordbreaking month of peacetime expansion. Between February of 1961 and May of 1965:

—The number of workers went up by 3,900,000, but the number of jobs went up even more, by 5,300,000. As a result, the number of jobless declined by 1,400,000 during the 51-month period of expanding economic activity.

—The unemployment rate fell from 6.9 percent to 4.6 percent, and that is a drop of one-third.

—Every worker group showed a marked improvement during this time—except for the teenagers.

And that brings us to this occasion.

I have asked you here to thank you for the response to the youth opportunity campaign that we launched last month. Your actions—and those of businessmen throughout the country—mean new hope and a new chance for thousands of our young people. Two million young Americans will be without jobs this summer unless this administration's program is successful.

I expect the Vice President, and the Secretary of Commerce, and the Secretary of Labor, and the head of the Space Agency that has such a wonderful thing to be thankful for this morning, and other members who are leaders in the Government to stay after this young employment program until we get successful results.

In my initial announcement, this administration—the Johnson administration—asked every employer, public and private, to find work for at least one young man or woman for each 100 employees already at work. You employers that are here this morning, and you young people that are here, are an indication of the response to that request.

Already, I am told by the Vice President, more than 5,000 employers have come through with job openings for 75,000 young people. The response has come from some of the Nation's largest private employers, and some of the Nation's smallest local firms; it has come from labor unions, church and fraternal organizations. We have pledges from the State and the county and the municipal governments.

American Telephone and Telegraph has pledged to hire at least 1 summer trainee for each 100 employees.

Bill Roland, a general contractor in Lorain, Ohio, intends to hire 2 young people—1 who will go on to college, and 1 who will return to high school.

The International Brotherhood of Electrical Workers has promised to hire 6 young people between 16 and 21.

The pastor of the Holy Angels Church in Aurora, Ill., is going to put 10 high school boys to work on the task of the church.

At my request, as I stated a moment ago, the departments and agencies of the Federal Government will hire 1 trainee for each 100 workers now on the payroll. This will mean an additional 25,000 jobs, one of which will be an assignment with our astronauts. I have instructed the Neighborhood Youth Corps summer project to add another 50,000 openings for young people.

I read last night—in my night reading—a letter from Mr. John Knight, publisher of the Knight Newspapers. He had complete pages of young people want ads that he had furnished free in an attempt to really put a push behind finding jobs for young people.

I say to you that there is no more important project of this administration at this time than this project. Now this is only the beginning. We have a long way to go yet. But the fact that you employers have already made this start and you are present here today is all the proof that I need to realize that we are going to do the job.

I want to publicly commend and compliment the Vice President for the vision that he and his committee have demonstrated, at the industry they have shown, and the results they have obtained. But, I want to warn them and the employers of this Nation that the clock is ticking, that the time to find these jobs is now, that it is better to be making an investment to provide a job for a man than to be paying taxes to take care of a young person that has had to be incarcerated and found necessary for the Government to support him otherwise.

Here we are with profits of corporations

of 36.5 billion—the largest in our history, after taxes; with personal payrolls running 76 billion more than they have before taxes. If there ever was a time when we could share some of our prosperity and some of our accumulation with those who are to carry on afterwards, it is now.

It is not going to be long before some of you men in Government and before some of you employers are going to be up at St. Peter's door rapping on it, and asking for admission. And he is not just going to ask you if you tithed 10 percent, he is not just going to ask you if you went to church every Sunday, he is not just going to be content that you followed the Ten Commandments. He is going to ask you what you did with your affluence and what you did as a beneficiary of this great system of government to help others who wanted to help themselves.

I'll tell you one thing, I hope you can jot down, in the year of our Lord 1965, the month of June, I met at the White House with the President and I told him I was going to provide the leadership to get these young people off the streets and behind the bench, training them to do something and to let them work to help themselves.

I don't have any special dispensation to speak for St. Peter but my own judgment is that that will make a very favorable impression.

Thank you.

NOTE: The ceremony was held at 12:15 p.m. in the Cabinet Room at the White House. During his remarks the President referred to, among others, Vice President Hubert H. Humphrey, who introduced him, John T. Connor, Secretary of Commerce, W. Willard Wirtz, Secretary of Labor, and James E. Webb, Administrator, National Aeronautics and Space Administration.

Certificates were presented to the first 10 corporations which had responded to the President's youth opportunity campaign to provide summer jobs for young people.

299 Remarks in Chicago at the Cook County Democratic Party Dinner. *June 3, 1965*

Mr. Chairman; my old friend, the brave and valiant Governor of Illinois, Otto Kerner; my longtime devoted friend and as great a political leader and city administrator as there is in this world, your great mayor, Dick Daley; one of my great counselors, my former colleague, the conscience of the United States Senate, who speaks not just for Illinois but speaks for the entire United States, your fighting Marine, Senator Paul Douglas; Members of one of the Congress' most valued and effective delegations, the men who served Cook County in the House of Representatives, Congressman Bill Dawson, Congressman Bill Murphy, Congressman John Kluczynski, Congressman Frank Annunzio, Congressman Danny Rostenkow-

ski, Congressman Sid Yates, Congressman Roman Pucinski:

I am very proud that all of you are here tonight. I am prouder still that you stayed in Washington to pass our reorganization bill before you came.

My fellow countrymen:

I am constantly reminded that Chicago is the center of our country. When Dick Daley isn't reenforcing that thought, Otto Kerner and Paul Douglas are.

What a magnificently beautiful setting this is here tonight and how lovely, how truly lovely is this great city of Chicago which belongs to you! This is a great party. Actually I really like small parties. As a matter of fact, I told Senator Everett Dirksen the other day how partial I was to small parties and I pointed out to him that his party was just about the size I like to see it.

But on this occasion, honoring the founders of our party—Thomas Jefferson and Andrew Jackson—no words of ours could be so eloquent as their own expressions about each other. When Thomas Jefferson was asked what he thought of Jackson as a prospect for President, Jefferson replied without hestitation, "He is one of the most unfit men I know of for such a place." What "Old Hickory" said of Jefferson cannot be repeated in Cook County.

Needless to say I am glad to be here in Cook County where I am sure the Democrats never talk that way about each other.

Well, there is always a time and a place for party talk. I do not believe that this is an appropriate place tonight for partisanship. I say to you in Illinois what Woodrow Wilson said 50 years ago in Indiana: I love the Democratic Party but I love America a great deal more. And what difference does party make when mankind is involved?

Well, mankind is involved in every decision that will be waiting on my desk when I return to the White House tonight. America does not need, and I am confident Democrats do not want, a President who would ever allow those decisions to be influenced by considerations of party.

That is why I want to speak, not about partisanship or party tonight, but about what matters most to us all—the peace of mankind.

On this subject I believe there is a need now for plain speaking.

In this city of Chicago, 28 years ago, a President of these United States then described the condition of the world in these words:

"Without a declaration of war and without warning or justification of any kind, civilians, including vast numbers of women and children, are being ruthlessly murdered . . . ships are being attacked . . . without cause or without notice. Nations are fomenting and taking sides in civil warfare in nations that have never done them any harm. . . . Innocent peoples, innocent nations, are being cruelly sacrificed to a greed for power and supremacy which is devoid of all sense of justice and human considerations."

The world did not heed the vision or the wisdom of Franklin D. Roosevelt when he called upon all peace-loving nations to join together to quarantine the aggressors. And those who loved peace above all else, lost their peace and all else.

That history need not—and that history must not—be allowed to repeat its full course again in our time.

The peace of mankind must not, and will not, be lost again.

If similarities are many between the worlds of 1937 and 1965, the differences are far more numerous. The peace-loving nations are not weak now as they were then—not lacking in will now as they were then.

Educated in the adversity of a great war, tested in the trial of continuing danger, united in the face of ever-present peril, the peace-loving peoples have built strength in the 1960's that they never had in the 1930's.

That strength has one unmistakable meaning. For aggression there is no prize. At the end of the road of conquest, the only sure reward is sure ruin.

For 20 years we have applied what Abraham Lincoln said would be the great lesson of peace——

"Teaching men that what they cannot take by an election, neither can they take by war; teaching all the folly of being the beginners of a war."

But there are other differences, too, between 1937 and tonight in 1965. The people of Communist countries are somewhat wiser, too. While their leaders have chosen to close a curtain about them to keep out knowledge of the free world's peaceful intention, the people of the Soviet Union and Eastern Europe really know, above all other peoples on this earth, what the cost and the catastrophe is to their homeland of 20th century warfare.

The men and women of Russia, the men and women of all the nations of Eastern Europe, I believe want peace and want the taste of its sweet fruits. And none want them to have peace more than do we, the people of the United States of America.

Between the great powers of East and West, there is no history of conflict on the battlefields of the past. Between the people of the Soviet Union and the people of the United States, there has been friendship and there can be greater understanding.

The common interests of the peoples of Russia and the peoples of the United States are many—and this I would say to the people of the Soviet Union tonight: There is no American interest in conflict with the Soviet people anywhere. And no true Soviet interest is going to be served by the support of aggression or subversion anywhere in the world. We of the United States of America stand ready tonight, as always, to go with you onto the fields of peace—to plow new furrows, to plant new seed, to tend new growth—so that we and so that all mankind may some day share together a new and a bountiful harvest of happiness and hope on this earth.

Jefferson said of Americans: "Peace is our passion."

And I say to you here in Chicago tonight—peace is our passion still.

In this Union, in this hemisphere, in every region of this world, in every forum of nations, the United States is working for peace—and that work will never cease.

But as I have spoken to Communist countries, let me also tonight speak to the free world.

I carry in my pocket—and I often read to those who visit the White House—some wise words that were written by a man of peace, the late Secretary General of the United Nations, Dag Hammarskjold. The words are these:

"The qualities that peace requires are those which I believe we all need today—perseverance and patience, a firm grip on realities, careful but imaginative planning, a clear awareness of the dangers—but also of the fact that fate is what we make it."

In the 1930's, we made our fate not by what we did but what we Americans failed to do. We propelled ourselves—and all mankind—toward tragedy, not by decisiveness but by vacillation, not by determination and resolution but by hesitancy and irresolution, not by action but by inaction.

The failure of free men in the 1930's was not of the sword but of the soul—and there just must be no such failure in the 1960's.

So, let us not delude ourselves again by the belief that peace can be secured by submissiveness or peace can be extended by expediency.

Let us not adopt again the arrogance that peace is less important to the peoples of less important countries because they are distant or different from our own.

Let us not return again to the impulsiveness which accepts as safe every promise of peace from the enemies of peace and rejects as dangerous every proposal for strength from its friends.

Persevering and patient, firmly gripping realities, proceeding in clear awareness of the dangers, let us proceed with the careful but the imaginative planning that is necessary to assure peace and justice and progress for all the peoples of the earth.

This is the course that we of the United States have chosen—and this is the course that we shall faithfully hold—for we believe that this course leads to peace in the world.

Let me make it clear to all here and all listening in other parts of the world, that the United States seeks dominion over no people. Everywhere in the world we, the United States, seek decency for all.

Out among the earth's peoples, Americans are working tonight—as few peoples have ever worked before—to bring learning and light and health and housing and hope to the family of man. Food from our fields is feeding 100 million people—including 70 million children. Medicine from our laboratories is saving the lives of many millions more. And I dare say there is not one citizen present here tonight who would have his country conduct its course otherwise.

George Washington once told us that we would have one option:

"Whether (to) be respectable and prosperous or contemptible and miserable as a nation."

Today, we are prosperous, as the able Senator Douglas told you, more prosperous than any other nation in all the history of man. We have enjoyed 51 consecutive months of economic expansion—the longest ever known in any peacetime and the end is not yet in sight.

Our people are happy. They are prospering. They are moving on and on, and upward. Just last year the number of families living on less than $3,000 income decreased by 18 percent, and the number of families with more than $10,000 income per year increased by 22 percent.

But I must remind you that money is no

measure of the moral force at work among Americans today.

For we are committed—by a broad and a broadening consensus—to bringing brightness into lives where darkness dwells. We are committed to opening beauty to lives that are closed over by ugliness and guaranteeing the rights that God gave them to those man had forgotten.

The consensus within America tonight is a consensus of courage—and let none abroad believe that this consensus stops at the water's edge. For there is in our beloved America a consensus—a strong and a deep and an abiding majority consensus—that the world shall not walk again the road to darkness that led mankind into the valley of war 30 years ago.

The united will of the American people is itself the ultimate and the most profound difference between 1937 and 1965, and let neither friends of peace—or foes—underestimate the meaning of that unity.

The American people want to be a part of no war. But the American people want no part of appeasement or of any aggression.

Over the years of our history our forces have gone forth into many lands, but always they returned when they are no longer needed. For the purpose of America is never to suppress liberty but always to save it. The purpose of America is never to take freedom but always to return it, never to breach peace but to bolster it, and never to seize land but always to save lives.

One month ago it became my duty to send our Marines into the Dominican Republic and I sent them for these same ends.

I have been informed tonight by the Commander in Chief of the Inter-American Forces, General Alvim, and the Deputy Commander, Lieutenant General Palmer, that conditions in the Dominican Republic now permit further reductions of our military personnel. I am therefore ordering the withdrawal of all remaining units of the United States Marine Corps totaling approximately 2,100 men.

America's purpose is—and always will be—to serve the peace of mankind.

Let me say this to you: A man does what he must—in spite of personal consequences, in spite of obstacles and dangers and pressures—and that is the basis of all human morality.

Those words are not mine. They were written by the man whose great steps I follow—John Fitzgerald Kennedy. But I would want you to know that it is that spirit which guides me in all that I do.

For men, as for nations, the way of the peacemaker is never an easy way.

While all men hate war, they too often hate still more the discipline and the duty and the demands of acting to preserve the peace that they love. I am certain that this generation of Americans is willing to accept demands that are stern in order to enjoy a world that is safe.

For we know—as all men must know wherever they live—that after losing peace twice in this century, mankind just must not lose that peace again, and it is the united will of all the people of our beloved America that it shall not be lost.

NOTE: The President spoke at 9:30 p.m. at McCormick Place in Chicago. In his opening words he referred to Governor Otto Kerner of Illinois, Mayor Richard J. Daley of Chicago, Senator Paul Douglas of Illinois, and Representatives William L. Dawson, William T. Murphy, John C. Kluczynski, Frank Annunzio, Dan Rostenkowski, Sidney R. Yates, and Roman C. Pucinski, all of Illinois.

Later he referred to, among others, Senator Everett M. Dirksen of Illinois, General of the Army Hugo Panasco Alvim of Brazil, Commander of the OAS Inter-American Force in the Dominican Republic, and Lt. Gen. Bruce Palmer, Jr., of the United States, Deputy Commander.

300 Joint Statement Following Discussions With Chancellor Erhard. *June 4, 1965*

PRESIDENT Johnson and Chancellor Erhard met today at the White House with their senior advisers.

The President and the Chancellor expressed their satisfaction with the close and cooperative relations between their two countries and the political, economic, and military strength of the Atlantic Alliance. The President and the Chancellor also agreed on the continuing importance of maintaining an intimate and dynamic Alliance.

The Chancellor welcomed the President's assurance that the United States would maintain its forces in Europe, backed by nuclear power, so long as they were wanted and needed for the peace and security of Europe.

The Chancellor emphasized Germany's vital interest in the continued progress of European unity. And the President, in turn, agreed that European unity was an important factor in the strengthening of the Alliance. The President also expressed his appreciation for the Federal Government's effort to further European economic integration and to contribute to the development of increasingly closer economic ties between Europe and America and the rest of the world.

The Chancellor told the President of his appreciation for the President's strong support to efforts to resolve the German problem. The President and the Chancellor agreed that their governments, together with the other responsible powers, must continue to seek all available means to end the unjust division of Germany as soon as possible.

They agreed too that improvements in relations with the countries of Eastern Europe would help to contribute to peace and security and that a common allied policy would contribute to this end.

The President and the Chancellor also discussed the serious threats to peace and stability in a number of other areas of the world, and especially in southeast Asia. In this connection, the Chancellor emphasized the importance of mutual solidarity in dealing with communist aggression. He told the President his support for the American determination to turn back aggression in Viet-Nam and welcomed the United States Government's efforts to bring about a peaceful settlement of that conflict. The Chan-

cellor also told the President of his interest in the projected Asian Development Bank and the German Government's desire to participate in it and also provide economic assistance which would contribute to the establishment of political and economic stability in this area of the world.

The President and the Chancellor also expressed their hope for continuing progress in the Dominican Republic, leading to the restoration of peace and representative government there.

Finally the President and the Chancellor reaffirmed the strong and close friendship of their peoples and governments, working together for peace and freedom in the future as they have in the past. For this reason, they agreed to meet regularly and to discuss questions of common interest.

301 Commencement Address at Howard University: "To Fulfill These Rights." *June 4, 1965*

Dr. Nabrit, my fellow Americans:

I am delighted at the chance to speak at this important and this historic institution. Howard has long been an outstanding center for the education of Negro Americans. Its students are of every race and color and they come from many countries of the world. It is truly a working example of democratic excellence.

Our earth is the home of revolution. In every corner of every continent men charged with hope contend with ancient ways in the pursuit of justice. They reach for the newest of weapons to realize the oldest of dreams, that each may walk in freedom and pride, stretching his talents, enjoying the fruits of the earth.

Our enemies may occasionally seize the day of change, but it is the banner of our

revolution they take. And our own future is linked to this process of swift and turbulent change in many lands in the world. But nothing in any country touches us more profoundly, and nothing is more freighted with meaning for our own destiny than the revolution of the Negro American.

In far too many ways American Negroes have been another nation: deprived of freedom, crippled by hatred, the doors of opportunity closed to hope.

In our time change has come to this Nation, too. The American Negro, acting with impressive restraint, has peacefully protested and marched, entered the courtrooms and the seats of government, demanding a justice that has long been denied. The voice of the Negro was the call to action. But it is a tribute to America that, once aroused, the courts and the Congress, the President and most of the people, have been the allies of progress.

LEGAL PROTECTION FOR HUMAN RIGHTS

Thus we have seen the high court of the country declare that discrimination based on race was repugnant to the Constitution, and therefore void. We have seen in 1957, and 1960, and again in 1964, the first civil rights legislation in this Nation in almost an entire century.

As majority leader of the United States Senate, I helped to guide two of these bills through the Senate. And, as your President, I was proud to sign the third. And now very soon we will have the fourth—a new law guaranteeing every American the right to vote.

No act of my entire administration will give me greater satisfaction than the day when my signature makes this bill, too, the law of this land.

The voting rights bill will be the latest, and among the most important, in a long series of victories. But this victory—as Winston Churchill said of another triumph for freedom—"is not the end. It is not even the beginning of the end. But it is, perhaps, the end of the beginning."

That beginning is freedom; and the barriers to that freedom are tumbling down. Freedom is the right to share, share fully and equally, in American society—to vote, to hold a job, to enter a public place, to go to school. It is the right to be treated in every part of our national life as a person equal in dignity and promise to all others.

FREEDOM IS NOT ENOUGH

But freedom is not enough. You do not wipe away the scars of centuries by saying:

Now you are free to go where you want, and do as you desire, and choose the leaders you please.

You do not take a person who, for years, has been hobbled by chains and liberate him, bring him up to the starting line of a race and then say, "you are free to compete with all the others," and still justly believe that you have been completely fair.

Thus it is not enough just to open the gates of opportunity. All our citizens must have the ability to walk through those gates.

This is the next and the more profound stage of the battle for civil rights. We seek not just freedom but opportunity. We seek not just legal equity but human ability, not just equality as a right and a theory but equality as a fact and equality as a result.

For the task is to give 20 million Negroes the same chance as every other American to learn and grow, to work and share in society, to develop their abilities—physical, mental and spiritual, and to pursue their individual happiness.

To this end equal opportunity is essential, but not enough, not enough. Men and women of all races are born with the same range of abilities. But ability is not just the product of birth. Ability is stretched or stunted by the family that you live with, and the neighborhood you live in—by the school you go to and the poverty or the richness of your surroundings. It is the product of a hundred unseen forces playing upon the little infant, the child, and finally the man.

PROGRESS FOR SOME

This graduating class at Howard University is witness to the indomitable determination of the Negro American to win his way in American life.

The number of Negroes in schools of higher learning has almost doubled in 15 years. The number of nonwhite professional workers has more than doubled in 10 years. The median income of Negro college women tonight exceeds that of white college women. And there are also the enormous accomplishments of distinguished individual Negroes—many of them graduates of this institution, and one of them the first lady ambassador in the history of the United States.

These are proud and impressive achievements. But they tell only the story of a growing middle class minority, steadily narrowing the gap between them and their white counterparts.

A WIDENING GULF

But for the great majority of Negro Americans—the poor, the unemployed, the uprooted, and the dispossessed—there is a much grimmer story. They still, as we meet here tonight, are another nation. Despite the court orders and the laws, despite the legislative victories and the speeches, for them the walls are rising and the gulf is widening.

Here are some of the facts of this American failure.

Thirty-five years ago the rate of unemployment for Negroes and whites was about the same. Tonight the Negro rate is twice as high.

In 1948 the 8 percent unemployment rate for Negro teenage boys was actually less than that of whites. By last year that rate had grown to 23 percent, as against 13 percent for whites unemployed.

Between 1949 and 1959, the income of Negro men relative to white men declined in every section of this country. From 1952 to 1963 the median income of Negro families compared to white actually dropped from 57 percent to 53 percent.

In the years 1955 through 1957, 22 percent of experienced Negro workers were out of work at some time during the year. In 1961 through 1963 that proportion had soared to 29 percent.

Since 1947 the number of white families living in poverty has decreased 27 percent while the number of poorer nonwhite families decreased only 3 percent.

The infant mortality of nonwhites in 1940 was 70 percent greater than whites. Twenty-two years later it was 90 percent greater.

Moreover, the isolation of Negro from white communities is increasing, rather than decreasing as Negroes crowd into the central cities and become a city within a city.

Of course Negro Americans as well as white Americans have shared in our rising national abundance. But the harsh fact of the matter is that in the battle for true equality too many—far too many—are losing ground every day.

THE CAUSES OF INEQUALITY

We are not completely sure why this is. We know the causes are complex and subtle. But we do know the two broad basic reasons. And we do know that we have to act.

First, Negroes are trapped—as many whites are trapped—in inherited, gateless poverty. They lack training and skills. They are shut in, in slums, without decent medical care. Private and public poverty combine to cripple their capacities.

We are trying to attack these evils through our poverty program, through our education program, through our medical care and our other health programs, and a dozen more of the Great Society programs that are aimed at the root causes of this poverty.

We will increase, and we will accelerate,

and we will broaden this attack in years to come until this most enduring of foes finally yields to our unyielding will.

But there is a second cause—much more difficult to explain, more deeply grounded, more desperate in its force. It is the devastating heritage of long years of slavery; and a century of oppression, hatred, and injustice.

SPECIAL NATURE OF NEGRO POVERTY

For Negro poverty is not white poverty. Many of its causes and many of its cures are the same. But there are differences—deep, corrosive, obstinate differences—radiating painful roots into the community, and into the family, and the nature of the individual.

These differences are not racial differences. They are solely and simply the consequence of ancient brutality, past injustice, and present prejudice. They are anguishing to observe. For the Negro they are a constant reminder of oppression. For the white they are a constant reminder of guilt. But they must be faced and they must be dealt with and they must be overcome, if we are ever to reach the time when the only difference between Negroes and whites is the color of their skin.

Nor can we find a complete answer in the experience of other American minorities. They made a valiant and a largely successful effort to emerge from poverty and prejudice.

The Negro, like these others, will have to rely mostly upon his own efforts. But he just can not do it alone. For they did not have the heritage of centuries to overcome, and they did not have a cultural tradition which had been twisted and battered by endless years of hatred and hopelessness, nor were they excluded—these others—because of race or color—a feeling whose dark intensity is matched by no other prejudice in our society.

Nor can these differences be understood as isolated infirmities. They are a seamless web. They cause each other. They result from each other. They reinforce each other.

Much of the Negro community is buried under a blanket of history and circumstance. It is not a lasting solution to lift just one corner of that blanket. We must stand on all sides and we must raise the entire cover if we are to liberate our fellow citizens.

THE ROOTS OF INJUSTICE

One of the differences is the increased concentration of Negroes in our cities. More than 73 percent of all Negroes live in urban areas compared with less than 70 percent of the whites. Most of these Negroes live in slums. Most of these Negroes live together—a separated people.

Men are shaped by their world. When it is a world of decay, ringed by an invisible wall, when escape is arduous and uncertain, and the saving pressures of a more hopeful society are unknown, it can cripple the youth and it can desolate the men.

There is also the burden that a dark skin can add to the search for a productive place in our society. Unemployment strikes most swiftly and broadly at the Negro, and this burden erodes hope. Blighted hope breeds despair. Despair brings indifferences to the learning which offers a way out. And despair, coupled with indifferences, is often the source of destructive rebellion against the fabric of society.

There is also the lacerating hurt of early collision with white hatred or prejudice, distaste or condescension. Other groups have felt similar intolerance. But success and achievement could wipe it away. They do not change the color of a man's skin. I have seen this uncomprehending pain in the eyes of the little, young Mexican-American schoolchildren that I taught many years ago. But it can be overcome. But, for many, the wounds are always open.

FAMILY BREAKDOWN

Perhaps most important—its influence radiating to every part of life—is the breakdown of the Negro family structure. For this, most of all, white America must accept responsibility. It flows from centuries of oppression and persecution of the Negro man. It flows from the long years of degradation and discrimination, which have attacked his dignity and assaulted his ability to produce for his family.

This, too, is not pleasant to look upon. But it must be faced by those whose serious intent is to improve the life of all Americans.

Only a minority—less than half—of all Negro children reach the age of 18 having lived all their lives with both of their parents. At this moment, tonight, little less than two-thirds are at home with both of their parents. Probably a majority of all Negro children receive federally-aided public assistance sometime during their childhood.

The family is the cornerstone of our society. More than any other force it shapes the attitude, the hopes, the ambitions, and the values of the child. And when the family collapses it is the children that are usually damaged. When it happens on a massive scale the community itself is crippled.

So, unless we work to strengthen the family, to create conditions under which most parents will stay together—all the rest: schools, and playgrounds, and public assistance, and private concern, will never be enough to cut completely the circle of despair and deprivation.

TO FULFILL THESE RIGHTS

There is no single easy answer to all of these problems.

Jobs are part of the answer. They bring the income which permits a man to provide for his family.

Decent homes in decent surroundings and a chance to learn—an equal chance to learn—are part of the answer.

Welfare and social programs better designed to hold families together are part of the answer.

Care for the sick is part of the answer.

An understanding heart by all Americans is another big part of the answer.

And to all of these fronts—and a dozen more—I will dedicate the expanding efforts of the Johnson administration.

But there are other answers that are still to be found. Nor do we fully understand even all of the problems. Therefore, I want to announce tonight that this fall I intend to call a White House conference of scholars, and experts, and outstanding Negro leaders—men of both races—and officials of Government at every level.

This White House conference's theme and title will be "To Fulfill These Rights."

Its object will be to help the American Negro fulfill the rights which, after the long time of injustice, he is finally about to secure.

To move beyond opportunity to achievement.

To shatter forever not only the barriers of law and public practice, but the walls which bound the condition of many by the color of his skin.

To dissolve, as best we can, the antique enmities of the heart which diminish the holder, divide the great democracy, and do wrong—great wrong—to the children of God.

And I pledge you tonight that this will be a chief goal of my administration, and of my program next year, and in the years to come. And I hope, and I pray, and I believe, it will be a part of the program of all America.

WHAT IS JUSTICE

For what is justice?

It is to fulfill the fair expectations of man.

Thus, American justice is a very special thing. For, from the first, this has been a land of towering expectations. It was to be a nation where each man could be ruled by the common consent of all—enshrined in law, given life by institutions, guided by men themselves subject to its rule. And all—all of every station and origin—would be touched equally in obligation and in liberty.

Beyond the law lay the land. It was a rich land, glowing with more abundant promise than man had ever seen. Here, unlike any place yet known, all were to share the harvest.

And beyond this was the dignity of man. Each could become whatever his qualities of mind and spirit would permit—to strive, to seek, and, if he could, to find his happiness.

This is American justice. We have pur-sued it faithfully to the edge of our imperfections, and we have failed to find it for the American Negro.

So, it is the glorious opportunity of this generation to end the one huge wrong of the American Nation and, in so doing, to find America for ourselves, with the same immense thrill of discovery which gripped those who first began to realize that here, at last, was a home for freedom.

All it will take is for all of us to understand what this country is and what this country must become.

The Scripture promises: "I shall light a candle of understanding in thine heart, which shall not be put out."

Together, and with millions more, we can light that candle of understanding in the heart of all America.

And, once lit, it will never again go out.

NOTE: The President spoke at 6:35 p.m. on the Main Quadrangle in front of the library at Howard University in Washington, after being awarded an honorary degree of doctor of laws. His opening words referred to Dr. James M. Nabrit, Jr., President of the University. During his remarks he referred to Mrs. Patricia Harris, U.S. Ambassador to Luxembourg and former associate professor of law at Howard University.

The Voting Rights Act of 1965 was approved by the President on August 6, 1965 (see Item 409). See also Items 548, 613.

---

302   Commencement Address at Catholic University. *June 6, 1965*

Bishop McDonald, Bishop Swanstrom, Speaker McCormack, Mrs. McCormack, Mr. Norris, my fellow countrymen:

On this campus dedicated to the glory of God, it is fitting that we meet on this first day of the week. For this is the day kept by Christendom as a day of remembrance, a day of renewal, a day of rededication to the moral values by which we guide our lives.

In our temporal affairs—no less than in the affairs of the spirit—this is a season for remembrance, for renewal, for rededication to the moral values by which men guide the course of their governments on this earth.

On this occasion, then, I come to speak, at this time and at this place, about the morality of nations. For while I believe devotedly in the separation of church and state, I do not believe it is pleasing in the sight of God for men to separate morality from their might.

Your Nation is a mighty nation—the mightiest in all the milleniums of man. But let none who would measure that might—or test it—be deceived and let us never deceive ourselves.

The strength of our society does not rest in the silos of our missiles nor lie in the vaults of our wealth—for neither arms nor silver are gods before which we kneel.

The might of America lies in the morality of our purposes and their support by the will of the people of the United States.

It was Mr. Jefferson who said that: "Our interests . . . will ever be found inseparable from our moral duties."

That standard guides us still.

For America's only interests in the world today are those we regard as inseparable from our moral duties to mankind.

This is the truth—the abiding truth—about your land, America. Yet all through this century, men in other lands have—for reasons of their own—elected to discount moral duty as the motivation that moves America.

In its place, they have erected and embraced myths of their own creation—the myths of American isolationism and imperialism, the myths of American materialism and militarism.

I would recall the words that were once spoken by a man who deeply understood these times, this land, and the truth about them—our late, beloved President John Fitzgerald Kennedy. For he once said:

"The great enemy of the truth is very often not the lie—deliberate, contrived, and dishonest—but the myth—persistent, persuasive, and unrealistic."

If we cannot persuade other men to disbelieve their own persistent, persuasive, and unrealistic myths about America's motivations, we at least can urge them to seek after the truth—for the truth about America has been chronicled on every continent in this century.

Twenty-one years ago today, on the 6th day of June 1944, it was neither isolationism nor imperialism that sent our sons ashore in Normandy to intervene in the destiny of the continent of Europe where our culture was cradled.

Nor was it materialism that moved this Nation to the works of the postwar world—committing her crops to the care of the hungry, dedicating her dollars and determination to reconstruct the ruined lands of friend and foe, sharing her skills and resources to strengthen the foundations for emerging nations all around the globe.

Neither was it militarism that motivated this Nation to dismantle her arms in good faith when victory was won and offer up the atom in good faith for control by all nations. Nor is it militarism now that motivates America to stand her sons by the sons of Europe and Asia and Latin America in keeping a vigil of peace and freedom for all mankind.

What America has done—and what America is doing around the world—draws from deep and flowing springs of moral duty, and let none underestimate the depth of flow of those wellsprings of American purpose.

On this, let me speak forthrightly—to you and to the entire world.

All through history the doubt of men for the morality of their own generation has been exceeded only by their doubt for the morality of the next generation. As long ago as ancient Chaldea, when history was just beginning, there was a popular verse, saying:

"We are fallen upon evil times,

And the world has waxed very old and
wicked,
Politics are very corrupt,
The sons of men are not so righteous
As their parents were."

Whatever some may say, you of this class
of '65 know that words such as these do not
describe your America in these times. This
is a new time in our land—a time that is
young in spirit, a time of renewal, a time of
resurgence for those forces which fashion a
finer and a fairer society.

The people in their politics are keeping
faith with American ideals as never before.
They are doing it in education, in health, in
the human environment. That great American commitment to equality for all men—
in the sight of the law as in the sight of
God—is, at last, being fulfilled. Sons of
men—and daughters, too—are giving of
themselves as volunteers for good and noble
works in a manner their parents never
thought of doing.

So, if men elsewhere say they have never
met such an America before, they are right—
and we are honored and proud.

For this is an America morally aware,
morally aroused—an America determined to
end at home the compromise of its own
moral duty which has, for much too long,
given credence to those who would doubt us
or misrepresent us elsewhere in the world.

Myths, misrepresentations, and misunder-
standings are enemies of truth—and enemies
of America—but they shall not be masters
of either.

The truth of America's purposes cannot
be veiled.

Sure of its moral purposes—surer of its
own moral performance—America shall not
be deterred from doing what must be done
to preserve this last peace man shall ever
have to win or lose.

We have—as our forefathers had—a de-

cent respect for the informed opinions of
mankind, but we of this generation also
have an abiding commitment to preserve
and perpetuate the enduring values of
mankind.

And we shall keep that commitment.

Our purpose, our policy—our constant and
continuing commitment—was set forth just
18 years ago this weekend by the then great
Secretary of State, George C. Marshall.

In a speech the world will never forget,
that great citizen of war and peace said this
for the United States:

"Our policy is directed not against any
country or doctrine but against hunger, and
poverty, and desperation and chaos. Its
purpose should be . . . to permit the emer-
gence of political and social conditions in
which free institutions can exist."

Well, that is America's purpose now—our
only purpose—in the hungry and poor and
desperate and chaotic lands to the farthest
corners of this earth. In the policies that
guide us abroad—as in the principles that
govern us at home—we of the United States
cherish the right of others to choose for
themselves what they shall believe and what
their own societies and institutions shall be.

On this right rests all morality among
nations, and we intend to guard and defend
this right for others as for ourselves.

But the shade of a shield is not enough
to cause stable societies to grow and free
institutions to flower in integrity.

Pope John XXIII reminded us that peace
would be only "an empty-sounding word"
unless it rested upon, as he put it, ". . . an
order founded on truth, built according to
justice, vivified and integrated by charity,
and put into practice in freedom."

That is the next imperative of morality
among nations—to integrate the system of
nations and peoples by charity, not the charity of callous and calculating dole, but the

compassionate charity of learning and love.

This, too, has been—and will continue to be—the purpose of the American people: to maintain in our policies toward all nations a spirit of compassion and caring. For we believe, as Pope John said, "there is an immense task incumbent on all men of good will, namely the task of restoring the relations of the human family in truth, in justice, in love, and in freedom."

And that, finally, is the highest morality of nations—the noblest purpose to which great powers can put their great persuasion: to restoring relations between the human family.

Our world has been scarred and sundered by war since the beginning of time and man. On every continent, men of every color—and every creed—live with memories of wars that are past and they dread of wars yet to come.

Peace is still a stranger, knocking at the door.

We of America—and we of all the free world—are ready, as we are always ready, to open that door and invite peace to enter, to dwell in the house of all nations forever.

So on this Sunday morning, as you are here to bear witness, then, I would say to the people, and to the leaders, of the Communist countries, to the Soviet Union, to nations of Eastern Europe and southeast Asia; we extend to you our invitation—come, now, let us reason together.

As peace knocks, our door is unlatched.

Our table is set.

We are ready, and we believe mankind is ready with us.

So, we wait only for those of the human family who have barred their doors and closed their windows to pull back your curtains and signify to mankind that you are ready, too, to welcome peace to the table of man.

A great American President—Franklin Delano Roosevelt—once said, "The most serious threat to our institutions comes from those who refuse to face the need for change."

Today, in both the open world of freedom and in the curtained world of communism, men and their families are enjoying the comfort and the contentment of a life none have ever known before.

There is still discontent, but there is less despair. There is still need, but the wants are not so mean. There is still futility today, but there is much more faith for tomorrow.

The most serious threat—the only threat—to this improving condition of all peoples lies with those who refuse to face the need for change, and who refuse to face the need for renouncing war in all of its ugly guises.

The will of the world—the great and growing moral force of mankind—presses for that renunciation. For men know today, as they have not been able to know before, that war serves no necessary end of any nation anywhere on earth.

Only a few days ago, an American son stepped out into the void of space and walked his way from the coast of the Pacific to the coast of the Atlantic over this continent. When his walk was complete, he did not want to return to the capsule from which he had emerged.

And, in many ways, this epitomizes our age.

The peoples of earth—in lands that are old and young—are today enjoying experiences that man has never known before, and they will not willingly return to the old world of war from which they have finally emerged.

On this campus, then—on this day of peace and promise—I would offer one message to men everywhere and to their leaders in every nation.

We of the United States welcome the gains

and the progress that all people have realized since the brutal and bitter years of war and devastation and exploitation.

We are grateful for the progress that we ourselves have achieved. We are blessed, and we are determined to press forward—not for our gain and our greatness alone, but rather for the gain and the good of all mankind everywhere.

But the need of man—the need of these times—is not for arms races or moon races, not for races into space or races to the bottom of the sea. If competition there must be, we are ready and we are willing always to take up the challenges and to commit our country to its tasks. But this is a moment when the opportunity is open and beckoning for men of all nations to come and to take a walk together toward peace.

The stranger knocks. Peace seeks admission at all our doors. Let us then open our doors and go forth together to walk at each other's side toward peace.

For let us never forget, the longest journey begins with a single step.

NOTE: The President spoke at 10:55 a.m. in the gymnasium on the campus at Catholic University in Washington, after being awarded an honorary degree of doctor of laws. In his opening words he referred to Bishop William J. McDonald, Rector of the University, Bishop Edward E. Swanstrom, General Secretary, Catholic Relief Services, National Catholic Welfare Conference, Representative John W. McCormack of Massachusetts, Speaker of the House of Representatives, and his wife, and James J. Norris, prominent Catholic layman and official of Catholic Relief Services.

Later he referred to Maj. Edward H. White 2d, the astronaut who left the spacecraft and walked in space during the Gemini 4 flight (see Item 304).

303   The President's Toast at a Luncheon in Honor of Sir Robert Menzies, Prime Minister of Australia. *June 7, 1965*

Mr. Prime Minister, distinguished guests:

Under any circumstance, this would be a very happy day for us in this country—and in this house.

After a momentous journey of more than 1 million miles, our two American astronauts have splashed down safely in the Atlantic Ocean. We are proud of them, and happy for the success of this peaceful adventure on mankind's newest frontier.

But in this house there is an added cause for happiness today.

After a journey of somewhat fewer miles—but not many less—the Prime Minister has "splashed down" here in the White House. And we are very proud to have him with us for this occasion of friendship and fellowship.

The affection and mutual admiration between Americans and Australians is well and widely known. Over the years of this century, that friendship has been a source of strength for the cause of freedom—and a source of despair and frustration for the purposes of those who have followed the path of aggression.

We of the United States are honored, Mr. Prime Minister, that your flag and our flag fly together, side by side, in the efforts these times require to preserve the peace of the world.

All through these times, men in other lands have questioned whether the democracies would stir themselves to stop aggression and save freedom. At the same time there have been those in the free countries who, so long as danger seemed far away, have asked whether such efforts should be made.

I remember that in 1940—before he became Prime Minister of Great Britain—Winston Churchill said that sometimes he was asked: "What is it that Britain and France are fighting for?" To that question, Churchill answered: "If we left off fighting, you would soon find out."

The appetite of aggression feeds on success. If the strong nations should fail or forfeit their trust, both the strong and the weak would today "soon find out" what it is and why it is that we make our efforts together today.

On this same day 21 years ago, sons of all our countries were united in the great effort to push ashore in Normandy and liberate the peoples of Europe, and bring relief from the ravages of war experienced so brutally by the peoples of the Soviet. There was a common purpose then—a full unity and a full accord on our objectives. Because of that unity, and that accord, peace was finally won.

I do not despair of an abiding personal belief that the peoples—and the leaders—of the free democracies can achieve the same unity and find the same great common purpose in peace that we had in war.

The events in space remind us that all mankind has entered a new age. The world of 1965 is greatly changed from the world of the 1940's. At no other time, in all history, have peoples of earth had so much to unite them, so many tangible opportunities to work together in peace, so little provocation to walk different roads toward war and ruin.

We want them to walk together towards peace.

We live by no illusion that the way toward peace is easy or that the distance is short. We know that the course is steep, the obstacles are many. The tests will come often and the trials will be demanding. But all of us—in lands both rich and poor—have gained too much to gamble on either aggression or appeasement.

All through this country's program of manned space flight, the paths of our spacecraft have crossed over the land from which our visitor comes. Most often the flight has passed Australia during the darkness of night. On such occasions, the citizens of cities of Australia have turned on their lights—testing to see whether those lights are visible to man up among the stars.

In many ways, this is symbolic.

All around the world, where there is darkness, men are willing, I believe, to turn on their lights. And America is looking for those lights—looking through the darkness and shadows to see the signals that will mean there is hope for peace.

We are searching the horizons now—looking for the glimmer of light that will tell us and will tell the world that others are ready to join with us in peace and understanding, for the gain and the good of all mankind.

This is the purpose that binds America and Australia together always.

To this purpose, then—to the purpose of peace and to the friendship between our peoples—I ask you now to join with me in raising your glass, as we express our gratitude for the privilege and pleasure of sharing this hour with our good friend, His Excellency, the Prime Minister.

NOTE: The President proposed the toast at a luncheon in the State Dining Room at the White House.

As printed above, this item follows the prepared text released by the White House.

304 Telephone Conversation Between the President and Astronauts James McDivitt and Edward White. *June 7, 1965*

THE PRESIDENT. Major McDivitt?

MAJOR McDIVITT. Yes, sir, Mr. President, this is Major McDivitt.

THE PRESIDENT. I just wanted to say to you and Major White, "Well done." We are all in this country very proud of you and, I think, the entire world is grateful for what you have done and, particularly, for your safe return. You have both written your names in history and in our hearts. God bless you both and your very fine families.

MAJOR McDIVITT. Mr. President, you certainly make me proud saying something like that. As you know, this is one of the happiest days of my life.

THE PRESIDENT. Major White, there are several million people in this country that have been wondering for 3 days what you were doing to Jim's windshield when he called you a dirty dog.

MAJOR WHITE. Mr. President, this is Major White.

THE PRESIDENT. Major, there are several million people in this country that have been wondering for 3 days what you were doing to Jim's windshield when he called you a dirty dog.

MAJOR WHITE. There wasn't too much I could do. We were pretty close, but there wasn't much I could do about it.

THE PRESIDENT. Well, we're mighty glad that you have had a safe return. We're all very proud of you, and we are looking forward to seeing you.

Major McDivitt, you had a little trouble talking Ed back in from his walk the other day, do you think you might be able to persuade him to come to see us this weekend down in Texas if I can get down there?

MAJOR WHITE. This is Major White on here still, sir. I'll get Major McDivitt on it. But I think that will be very fine. Just a moment.

MAJOR McDIVITT. Mr. President, this is Major McDivitt again.

THE PRESIDENT. I said you had a little trouble talking Ed back in from his walk the other day, do you think you might be able to persuade him to come up to see me this week if I can get down to Texas?

MAJOR McDIVITT. Well, I don't think there will be any trouble whatsoever.

THE PRESIDENT. Well, you talk to your families and we'll see if we can't get together down at the ranch about Friday or Saturday. I've been saving a little something for you.

MAJOR McDIVITT. Yes, sir. It would make me the happiest man in the world. I'm sure this will make Ed equally happy.

THE PRESIDENT. I heard Major White's wife say she wanted to go to Colorado, but you tell her to just hold off that trip until you get up to the ranch. I'll have my military aide get in touch with you in a day or two and I hope we can make it probably Saturday morning.

MAJOR McDIVITT. Yes, sir, we certainly would love that.

THE PRESIDENT. Now, I just want to say this finally to the two of you. What you have done will never be forgotten. We can hope and we do pray that the time will come when all men of all nations will join together to explore space together, and walk side by side toward peace. And you two outstanding men have taken a long stride forward in mankind's progress. And everyone in this Nation and, I think, in the free world feels in your debt.

MAJOR McDIVITT. Thank you very much, sir, we appreciate that.

THE PRESIDENT. I'll see you Friday or Saturday, and we'll be in touch with you through Mr. Webb.

MAJOR McDIVITT. Yes, Mr. President.

THE PRESIDENT. Goodby.

MAJOR McDIVITT. Goodby, Mr. President.

NOTE: The President spoke at 5:46 p.m. from the Fish Room at the White House to the astronauts, Maj. James A. McDivitt and Maj. Edward H. White 2d, who were resting on board the carrier *Wasp* following the successful completion of the Gemini 4 flight on June 6.

The 62-orbit, 1,609,684-mile voyage around the earth lasted 97 hours, 56 minutes, and 30 seconds, and set a new space endurance record.

At the end of the third orbit Major White left the spacecraft, took a 23-minute walk in space, and looked through the windshield at Major McDivitt who was inside the craft.

See also Items 310, 318, 320.

305 Remarks at the Signing of the Bill Providing for a National Technical Institute for the Deaf. *June 8, 1965*

Members of the Congress, Secretary Cele-brezze, ladies and gentlemen:

I want to welcome all of you to the White House and to the flower garden.

If these surroundings seem to be spruced up more than usual today, it is only partly because we were expecting you. It is mainly because the lady of the house returned home last night, and at the White House as in every other home in the land, everything runs better when the wife is at home.

Lady Bird made some news swimming around underwater down in the Virgin Islands. I told her I do that all the time up here without ever leaving dry land.

This is a very welcome and gratifying occasion and I am so happy that you could be here with us.

More than a hundred years ago Abraham Lincoln signed the charter of Gallaudet College here in Washington. From that time until this, Gallaudet stands as the only institution of higher learning in the world for those that are afflicted by deafness.

Americans ought to know more of that fine institution than they do because we can all be proud of it and the work which is done there.

Through a longtime friendship with the late Mary Thornberry, the mother of Congressman Thornberry, I first came to know Gallaudet College. I have been there on a number of occasions and visited with them and I have been inspired and stimulated by the great work that they are doing.

This institution will help to meet the needs of hundreds of deaf young people, both students and adults, who want to be and can be trained for various technical occupations and placed in very useful careers. Deafness is not and need not be regarded as the handicap that men thought it was in the past. Given the opportunity to learn and to prepare themselves, the deaf can fill a wide array of useful and important positions in our industries and our professions throughout our society.

Human talent is our most precious national resource. Strong and successful as America is, we cannot allow any of our human potential to be wasted or neglected. This conviction motivates us now in all that we do in the field of education.

This legislation is another example of the determination of the people of the United States and their Congress that education and all of its blessings must reach every American citizen.

I am personally very grateful to the leadership of Secretary Celebrezze, Commissioner Keppel, Commissioner Switzer for the commitment they have made to this effort. I appreciate especially the support that's been given by Senator Hill and other members of his committee, Senator Morse; by their colleagues in the House, Mr. Powell, Mr. Carey, and other members of the Labor committee; the membership of the committee of both parties in both houses have been helpful in this connection.

I am moved to make this further observation, that sometimes it seems deafness is not simply an affliction of individuals, but an affliction of nations as well. In this day of dramatic change and rapid progress, we have achieved capabilities of communication that were never dreamed of by any man before. We can now communicate sight and sound around the world in a single instant. Even at this moment, as we meet here, we are in communication with the Mariner rocket that speeds one hundred million miles away from earth toward the planet Mars. But here on earth we wait and we listen and we strain to hear with every antenna at our command for that word from other lands which will signify a willingness to talk of peace and a willingness to work for justice.

The will of free men for peace has been broadcast to all the world. We have done it again, and again, and again. The people of this peaceful Nation of which you are a member, the peaceful peoples of every na-

tion, wait and wonder what the answer will be. Will it be the tread of marching feet or will it be the saner sound of softly moving feet of millions and millions walking towards peace.

I say here today as I have said before, our guard is up but our hand is always out; our ears are open and our minds are not closed. If it comes in a whisper or if it comes in a shout, the world will hear and will welcome any word of peace.

This is a country of both courage and compassion. We have no purpose other than peace for mankind—peace that assures freedom to all who choose it, peace that assures honor to all who help keep it. So, then, in this spirit, I am proud today to sign this legislation which in my opinion embodies the compassion and understanding of the American people. And I am glad you could be here to join with us on this occasion.

NOTE: The President spoke at 12:45 p.m. in the Rose Garden at the White House. In his opening words he referred to Anthony J. Celebrezze, Secretary of Health, Education, and Welfare. Later he referred to Homer Thornberry, Representative from Texas 1949–1964, and his mother, Mrs. William M. Thornberry, Francis Keppel, Commissioner of Education, Mary E. Switzer, Commissioner of Vocational Rehabilitation, Senators Lister Hill of Alabama, Chairman of the Senate Committee on Labor and Public Welfare, and Wayne Morse of Oregon, member of the Committee, and Representatives Adam C. Powell of New York, Chairman of the House Committee on Education and Labor, and Hugh L. Carey of New York, member of the Committee.

As enacted, the bill (H.R. 7031) is Public Law 89–36 (79 Stat. 125).

306 Remarks to the Presidential Scholars. *June 8, 1965*

YESTERDAY Major McDivitt and Major White came down from their momentous maneuvers in space and they will be visiting with us later this week.

Today, though, we have the very great pleasure of greeting other outstanding young Americans—you who are the Presidential Scholars of 1965.

You and the astronauts have hardly been sharing the same experiences, but you have shown one fundamental quality in common—you have done your task, and you have done it superbly. You have achieved excellence and I congratulate each of you.

We are delighted to greet the parents of the scholars this afternoon. For having gone through the experience of graduating our second daughter last week, Mrs. Johnson and I feel it might be in order to give parents medals, too.

We do understand your feelings of pride and relief as parents. All of you have such a special reason for a glow of satisfaction in these young Americans that you have raised.

In the year 2000, most of you scholars will be no older than I am today. If you fulfill your promise you will be the leaders in all the various enterprises of American life, whether as a scientist, a businessman, a scholar, a doctor, or a mother or a housewife.

Intricate and subtle problems will daily confront you. And it is your responsibility to bring to the solution of these problems a set of values drawn from the long wisdom of the democratic process. Those values are many—honor and integrity, a love for justice, an unremitting enmity for oppression, an abiding faith in man himself, a decent respect for yourself and for your own potential.

All of these, and many more, are qualities essential for the fulfillment of the gifted talents that each of you possess. But there is still another value that I regard as very nearly supreme—that of believing that every man created in the image of God has something to say to his time, and has the right to be heard by his contemporaries without prejudice or without misconception.

All your lives, and in these times now, much has been heard about national power and its uses. Yours is a strong Nation, strong in its arms and more powerful in its heart and in its soul, and that is the only power which shall really prevail.

All through history, nations have built power to put down among their own peoples, and other peoples, the precious and the fragile things of the spirit and the soul—such as the love of liberty, the love of justice.

And it is for such a world that we work today. Not to conquer, not to subjugate, but rather to liberate the human spirit and allow it to grow and flourish in a climate of universal and in a climate of lasting understanding.

Emerson told us long ago that the true test of civilization is not the census, nor the size of the cities, nor the crops, but the kind of man that the country turns out.

So, here in America we are appreciating this more than ever before. We have bigness. We have strength. We have wealth. But we are concerned, and we must remain even more concerned, with the kind of man and the kind of woman that America turns out.

I am looking out there today upon this group of outstanding young Americans, and I am sure all Americans are grateful for the promise that each of you represent. The life of your land is in good hands as its destiny passes, as it will, into your hands.

I believe passionately that your future is light and not darkness; decency and not depravity. Every hour of every day that is mine is devoted to doing what we know to do to assure that kind of future for you.

You and your generation have much to say to mankind and much to say about mankind's future.

So, to each of you today, and to the parents who have played such a part in your life,

I want to say congratulations. We are glad you are here. We hope you have many happy and prosperous, comforting years ahead.

And God bless each of you.

NOTE: The President spoke at 6:05 p.m. in the East Room at the White House. In his opening words he referred to the astronauts, Maj. James A. McDivitt and Maj. Edward H. White 2d, who had completed the successful Gemini 4 flight on June 6 (see Item 304). Later he referred to his daughter, Luci Baines Johnson, who had graduated from the National Cathedral School on June 1 (see Item 289). Following the President's remarks he presented a bronze medallion to each of the Presidential Scholars.

The 121 Presidential Scholars of 1965, announced by the President on May 30, were chosen for their superior intellectual attainment and potential from among the Nation's outstanding secondary school graduates. The scholars were selected by an independent commission appointed by the President and chaired by Dr. Milton S. Eisenhower. The group included several students from each State, the District of Columbia, and Puerto Rico.

307 Remarks to the Members of the Iowa Trade Mission. *June 9, 1965*

I AM HAPPY to welcome you from out where the tall corn grows—to this little garden of ours where the sharp thorns grow.

I am glad Governor Hughes is with you.

I was afraid his dog might get loose again and you would have to leave my good friend behind, running through the streets of Des Moines.

It has been said that traveling makes men wiser, but less happy. I hope you return to Iowa, after your trade mission, both wiser and happier. Having bought a few Iowa hogs myself, I have full respect for your trading abilities.

As long as we have been a nation, peace, commerce, and honest friendship with all nations have been our aims—as Thomas Jefferson once said.

Those are still our aims—and will be always.

In this world, in these times, America seeks no domination over foes, no domination over friends. There is no war we want to fight—except to join with other nations to war on war itself.

When you are in Europe—visiting the cities and the peoples there—I hope you will each speak from your own hearts to convey to them how deeply runs the commitment of Americans to peace for all mankind.

America is a land of many interests around the world—for our cause is the cause of all mankind. But the peoples of the lands you will visit are ever close to our hearts, bound there by blood and beliefs forever. So, also, the heart of America's purposes and policies is concerned with the strength, the safety, the stability, and the greater success of the Atlantic lands and peoples.

In Europe—and in America, too—there are now, as there are always, those who would divide us and set us against one another. Such efforts have never succeeded—and they will not succeed now.

This Nation, this Government, this administration have no foes in the capitals of the free world. We have no feuds to follow, no vendettas to vindicate, no profound differences to pursue or prolong. We seek only—and always—to fashion with our friends in Europe and other free lands stronger supports for the security that keeps the peace and the progress that promises prosperity.

Central to our purposes with Europe—and

all the world—is our desire to foster increasingly free trade and peaceful commerce.

You residents of Iowa know the value of trade. You know what trade means to Iowa farmers, what it means to Iowa manufacturers, what it means to more than 100,000 jobholders in your State.

Last year our exports reached the record level of $25.2 billion—30 percent above the level in 1960. Agricultural exports of the United States rose 14 percent in the last calendar year—to $6.3 billion. Foreign markets took the output of 1 out of 4 acres of American farmland.

Free trade is both sensible economics and sane politics. And I believe we must move together in that direction.

Old obstacles are obvious. Old myths are many. But the time has come when all nations must think far beyond the thinking

they have done before. If the people of the world are to raise up their incomes, step up their growth, and lift up the standards by which men live, this is essential.

In our increasingly interdependent world, there is no room for the restrictiveness that leads to counter-restriction—and finally to the rivalries and conflict that undermine the foundations of free alliances and the pillars of peace.

On your journey abroad, I wish you good luck and Godspeed.

NOTE: The President spoke at 11:45 a.m. in the Diplomatic Reception Room at the White House. During his remarks he referred to Governor Harold E. Hughes of Iowa.

The group consisted of about 110 prominent businessmen, industrialists, bankers, and agricultural specialists, who were en route to Europe to broaden the State's economy through increase in the sales of Iowa products abroad.

As printed above, this item follows the prepared text released by the White House.

308   Remarks to Winners of a Contest Sponsored by the National Rural Electric Cooperative Association. *June 9, 1965*

Mr. Ellis, and my young friends:

I just had the pleasure of receiving a report from the distinguished Commander of the Veterans of Foreign Wars—Comdr. John Jenkins, who has just returned from Viet-Nam where he has visited with hundreds of our young men who are out there defending freedom in order that we may have liberty in the world. I want to present to you briefly, Commander Jenkins.

I am very proud to welcome to the White House today this wonderful group of allowance spending, chaperone managed, free, private young Americans.

Clyde Ellis gives me credit for originating the program that brings you here because back in 1957 I had a suggestion along that

line. I am very proud of the program and of you. But when I made that first suggestion back there 8 years ago, I had no idea whatever that Clyde would show up here some afternoon around dinnertime with 700 guests.

But having you come this afternoon has much meaning for me. Over the years of my public career, no other domestic activity has been closer to my heart than the program which has lighted the homes and the lives of rural America—and that is our program of rural electric cooperatives.

The contribution that rural electrification has made to our Nation's strength and success can never be measured adequately and, now, we see its finest result in the talent, and the intelligence, and the enthusiasm of you young men and women who have so much to offer our country.

In a very real sense, the REA program of the last 30 years is symbolic of the purpose that is always first in the hearts of Americans. Wherever men live in darkness, wherever there is an unbroken night of despair, and fear, and oppression, we of this great country want only to put our hands with theirs to turn on the lights and let brightness shine in a peaceful world. And you of this group are here in Washington today to study the operations of this great system.

It is valuable and it is important for Americans, young and old, to understand their system better in order that many people can benefit from it. And I hope that all of you will keep in mind all of your lives that what America is, rests really and finally not upon its system but on its soul.

As Macaulay once said: "It is the spirit that we are of and not the machinery we employ which binds us together." And I am greatly heartened by the spirit that binds us together in America.

When I came into this office many of the issues on my desk as President were very nearly the same issues that had been on my desk when I arrived in Washington 34 years earlier as a Congressman—civil rights, education, medical care for the aged, improvement of our cities, housing, farm incentives. All these, and more, were issues that are twice your age, some were even older than your parents, and some of them had been around here as long as your grandparents.

A nation such as ours cannot be true to itself, and cannot be true to its youth, if it fails to face up to the demands of duty. But that is what we are doing today. That is what we are doing now. That is what we

are doing at home. And that is what we are doing out in the world.

Duty is a very demanding word. It is never easy. It is not always clear. But it is always inevitable. When duty makes its call upon us there is no escaping judgment, whether we act or whether we fail to act.

I believe the young people of America want to be a part of a society that meets its duty, and that never fails its duty.

Your generation is showing this spirit in all that you do. Out in the world, nearly 10,000 of your contemporaries are now serving in 46 countries as members of the Peace Corps. Here at home, you are responding to the call and opportunity of your Nation's efforts to help the poor, to give the less fortunate young people a better chance, to assure the children of poor families a headstart in school. In the Neighborhood Youth Corps there are 90,000 youths at work already in 350 communities. Thousands more have stepped forward as Volunteers in Service to America—as part of the VISTA program—to help the needy, to help the poor. Still more are participating in helping 530,000 preschool children from impoverished homes, helping them to prepare themselves for school this fall.

We started the Job Corps with only 10,000 places to be filled, and 250,000 young Americans have already applied for those places.

So, you are a part of what I like to call "The Volunteer Generation." You have talents and abilities that are far beyond your parents at the same age, and you want to put them into service of your fellow man. And I am proud of you and I am grateful to the country that we have such a generation as you.

This country has no war that we want to fight, but the war on war itself. And in other times other generations have been called to fight for what we believe on the battlefields of war. But it is our hope, and it is our prayer, and it is our determination, that your generation shall have a chance to fight the wars of peace, the wars of poverty, the wars of disease, the wars of ignorance and injustice, and on bias and on prejudice and on bigotry.

I have the highest confidence that you will, by your hands and your hearts, turn on many lights at home and in the world, to make this a brighter world for your fellow man.

And to Congressman Ellis, and others who have contributed so much to so many in

bringing you here, I say, thank you, and well done.

NOTE: The President spoke at 5:40 p.m. on the South Lawn at the White House. In his opening words he referred to Clyde T. Ellis, Executive Manager, National Rural Electric Cooperative Association, and United States Representative from Arkansas 1939–1943. Later he referred to John Jenkins, Commander of the Veterans of Foreign Wars of the United States.

The group was composed of more than 600 rural high school students who won the trip on the basis of essays written on the topic "Rural Electrification—Good for All Americans." The essay contest was sponsored by the National Rural Electric Cooperatives of 19 States.

See also Item 357.

309   Message to the Congress Transmitting Annual Report of the Office of Alien Property. *June 10, 1965*

To the Congress of the United States:

I am proud to transmit the Annual Report of the Office of Alien Property for the fiscal year ended June 30, 1964.

This is the twenty-second report, as required by law, of proceedings under the Trading with the Enemy Act, as amended. There is special significance in this report because it signals the completion of the functions of the Office of Alien Property in the near future. I feel it is appropriate, therefore, to review the record of this Office which has led to the successful conclusion of the purpose for which it was established by the Congress.

Upon our entry into World War II, Congress broadened the terms of the Trading with the Enemy Act of 1917 to permit effective use of enemy-owned or controlled property in our own war effort, and also to deny its use to the enemy.

The Office of Alien Property Custodian was reconstituted as an independent agency in 1942 and by February 1943, personnel

of the Office had reached its peak of almost 1,300 persons. Offices were opened in Washington, New York, Chicago, San Francisco, Manila, and Honolulu—and after the war in Munich, Germany and Tokyo, Japan. In 1947, the Office of Alien Property Custodian was terminated and its functions transferred to the Office of Alien Property within the Department of Justice.

Thus far, a total of $861,000,000 has been realized from all World War II vestings. Seizures affected assets of every description from the huge General Aniline & Film Corporation stock holdings to scrip certificates valued at only a few cents. Assets administered and liquidated have included personal property, trusts, estates, patents, copyrights, trademarks, stocks, bonds, industrial equipment, mineral rights, farms, urban real estate, mortgages, entire businesses, and objects of art.

In 1946, following the cessation of hostilities, Congress authorized return of vested property to individuals who were within countries which had been occupied by the enemy and to individuals who had been substantially deprived of their rights of citizenship on racial and religious grounds. Additionally, Congress authorized the payment of claims of American creditors from the vested property of their German debtors. More than 67,000 claims were filed under this authority—and, at this writing, only 134 claims involving about $25,000,000 remain for processing and decision.

Under the Act, the net proceeds of vested property which are not returnable must be placed in the War Claims Fund where it will be used to compensate American citizens who have suffered war damage. To date, about $314,000,000 has been transferred by the Office of Alien Property to the War Claims Fund. An additional amount of $165,000,000 recently obtained from the sale of the stock of General Aniline & Film Corporation will also be available for deposit to the War Claims Fund in the future.

During the years since 1942, the Office has participated in more than 7,000 litigated cases involving its assets. I am pleased to report that this caseload has now been cut drastically so that only 60 cases remain in litigation currently.

I am able to report to you now that the Department of Justice expects to complete the administration of World War II property, and to terminate the Office of Alien Property as an organizational entity, by June 30, 1966. This achievement is the result of a planned and purposeful effort made since 1961 to close the Office within five years.

Throughout its entire existence, the Office of Alien Property has been self-supporting from the proceeds of its vested property. Since July 1, 1961, the annual budget authorization of $690,000 for each year has supported a staff of about 50 persons. The Office's budget request of $369,000 for fiscal year 1966 is designed to support a staff of 21 persons during its last year as an organization.

After June 30, 1966, certain minimal functions will remain, including the administration of the blocked assets of several satellite countries which cannot be terminated until adequate financial agreements are reached with those countries. This function which requires the full time services of only one employee may be assigned to another agency. At present, no other alien property matters are expected to require the full time services of any employee beyond June 30, 1966.

At an appropriate time, in connection with the budget for fiscal 1967, I will propose recommendations on how the burden of the few remaining alien property functions can continue to be discharged with non-appropriated funds even though the functions may be performed by persons on appropriated fund payrolls.

The termination of the Office of Alien Property as of June 30, 1966, will bring to a close a chapter of American history which began in World War I. The first provision for an Alien Property Custodian in United States legislation is found in The Trading with the Enemy Act of October 6, 1917.

The termination of the last remaining World War I functions—impeded by the outbreak of World War II—was not accomplished until 1956, some thirty-eight years after the conclusion of hostilities. Fortunately, we shall be able to conclude the affairs related to World War II in only twenty-one years, and I welcome this occasion to report that this objective is now finally in sight.

I would take this opportunity to observe that we of the United States enjoy the unique and blessed distinction of having, as a nation, no traditional or historic, and certainly no "natural" enemies, among other nations and other peoples on this earth. We greatly prize this good fortune and I know it is the will of the people, of the Congress, and certainly of the Chief Executive that such amity and friendship may be preserved forever, through growing understanding and un-wavering pursuit of our objective of peace with honor among all men and nations.

LYNDON B. JOHNSON

NOTE: The report, together with a letter of transmittal from Attorney General Nicholas deB. Katzenbach, is contained in "Annual Report, Office of Alien Property, Department of Justice, Fiscal Year Ended June 30, 1964" (23 pp., processed).

310 Remarks in Houston at the NASA Manned Spacecraft Center. *June 11, 1965*

Mr. Webb, Dr. Dryden, Dr. Seamans, my fellow Americans:

Monday was a very happy day for you and for the Nation, but this opportunity to visit with all the members of America's space team is no anticlimax for me.

So, to each of you who contributed to the success of America's most historic peacetime adventure, I am proud and I am privileged to say to each and to all of you: Well done.

The television commentators and the newspaper writers have all had a good bit to say about the sterling qualities and virtues of Major McDivitt and Major White. Of course, I have detected a certain greater objectivity in the remarks made publicly by both of their lovely wives.

Be that as it may, what impresses and gratifies me most about these two heroes—and all of the other astronauts—is the quality of personal modesty and humility.

I haven't yet met a man who has not come down from space wanting to give more credit to all the men and women on the ground than he would accept for himself up there.

Ed and Jim are no exceptions.

I invited them to bring their families to the ranch tomorrow, or the next day, because I wanted to present both of them with a token of their country's great esteem and respect. But I learned last night from the Administrator, Mr. Webb, that both men felt a ceremony at the ranch would focus too much credit on them and exclude all of you who supported their flight here so impressively at this new NASA Spacecenter in Houston.

So, we have arranged our plans gladly to come here—with one proviso. A little later, next week or the early part of the following week, we expect to see the McDivitts and their three children, and the Whites and their two children, and the manager of the Gemini program, Mr. Mathews and his family, in Washington at the White House.

At that time we're going to pay them the honor all of you know they deserve, no matter what they say about it.

But today, as I said to you when we were talking a few hours ago, I promised to bring these two heroes a little token. Well, I am going to keep my promise. I am nominating Major McDivitt and Major White for promotion to the rank of lieutenant colonel for their spectacular achievements on behalf of all the people of their country and the free world. And I am saying, also, that that is something you can eat as well as wear.

Incidentally, I might announce today that Maj. Gordon Cooper will be promoted on July 15th to the rank of lieutenant colonel.

And I am not going to forget the fourth Air Force astronaut to make an orbital flight, so I complete my announcement today by nominating Maj. Gus Grissom for promotion to lieutenant colonel, also.

When our manned space program began, many said about space what men probably said 500 years before about America itself—that the environment was hostile, that the climate was no good, that there was nothing there worth the trip anyway. These two young Americans have changed that conception forever.

All people have a new sense of thrill, and excitement, and anticipation about space exploration because of the flight of Gemini 4.

The joy and the thrill and the exhilaration that Ed White experienced on his walk from the Pacific Ocean to the Atlantic ran through the veins of us all. Our attitudes about space will never entirely be the same again.

And let me make one other observation. I read with mixed emotions yesterday that Major White had decided to claim this State of his birth as his home State. Well, as President, I am supposed to be neutral on matters of State pride, but the glimmer of pride I allow myself to feel is subdued just a bit. I know some will say that as soon as Americans got themselves up into space a Texan had to go and put his foot in it.

Seriously, I hope that the clear and obvious meaning and promise of this great adventure, which all of you have really shared, will not be lost upon mankind.

Only a few years ago, this great Nation was unmistakably behind in space. Abroad—and at home—some prophesied that America would remain behind, that our system had failed, that the brightness of our future had dimmed and would grow darker. But no such prophecies are heard today.

Proceeding openly—openly admitting our failures, openly sharing and offering to share our successes—the United States of America has proceeded with the determination and the zeal that burns in the hearts of men who love liberty. And, today, we know that America's success is very great indeed.

All that we have accomplished in space—all that we may accomplish in days and years to come—we stand ready to share for the benefit of all mankind. Whether we stand first in these endeavors matters to our momentary pride but not to our continuing and permanent purpose. The race in which we of this generation are determined to be first is the race for peace in the world.

In the labors of peace—as in the explorations of space—let no man in any land doubt for a moment that we have the will, and the determination, and the talent, and the resources required to stay the course and see those labors through.

So, I would end this week as I began it last Sunday morning, saying to all nations and all peoples, East and West, that we of America—a strong, a confident, a proud, and a peaceful America—invite you to open your curtains, come through the doorways and the walls that you have built, and join with us to walk together toward peace for all people on this earth.

Thank you.

[*At this point Major McDivitt and Major White presented to the President pictures of their orbital flight; the President then resumed speaking.*]

Thank you, Colonel McDivitt, and thank you, Colonel White.

I just want to say this, before I look at your Center, that I conducted the first investigations in the space field as a Member of the Senate. And as I looked out over this group today and this great installation that just did not exist those few years ago, I thought of what Jim Webb and Dr. Dryden had said 4 years ago, or more, when they left my office the first day they were to undertake this assignment. I saw Dr. Seamans and Dr. Gilruth here today and all of the thousands of people who have participated in this great adventure.

You don't know the gratitude I feel to each of you and how proud I am of all of you.

Thank you.

NOTE: The President spoke at 3:38 p.m. at the NASA Manned Spacecraft Center in Houston, Tex. In his opening words he referred to James E. Webb, Administrator, National Aeronautics and Space Administration, Dr. Hugh L. Dryden, Deputy Administrator, and Dr. Robert C. Seamans, Jr., Associate Administrator.

Later he referred to Maj. James A. McDivitt and Maj. Edward H. White 2d, the astronauts who completed the successful Gemini 4 flight on June 6, Charles W. Mathews, manager of the Gemini space flight program, Maj. L. Gordon Cooper, Jr., and Maj. Virgil I. Grissom, astronauts, and Dr. Robert E. Gilruth, Director of the Manned Spacecraft Center.

See also Items 304, 318, 320.

---

311   Statement by the President Following a Review of Agency Compliance With His Memorandum on "June Buying." *June* 12, 1965

I AM gratified by the thoroughness of the measures instituted throughout the executive branch to make certain that our cost reduction efforts are not circumvented or compromised by indulgence in the obsolete practice of "June Buying."

Following my memorandum of May 18, the head of each department and agency has assumed personal responsibility for making certain that orders, purchases, and contract commitments made during the last month of the present fiscal year will not exceed planned and necessary expenditures. In some instances, the agency heads have required that procurement requests for materials or services costing in excess of $500 must have the personal approval of appropriate office heads and be supported by written justifications. In other instances, agencies operating on other than appropriated funds have installed regulations complying fully with the spirit of my memorandum, even though their operations are exempt from the letter of that directive.

I want to express my appreciation to all who are participating in making this program successful—not only to the heads of the departments and agencies, but to the personnel at the requirements and purchasing level. The effective and imaginative cooperation they are offering is a vital factor in the success of our entire cost reduction program.

The old practice of "June Buying" is a relic from the past. In our governmental programs today, we recognize that sloth and indifference toward the management of fiscal affairs impairs the progressiveness of the Government in responding to the needs of our changing society. In the last fiscal year, responsible self-discipline every month of the 12 months enabled us to return more than $800 million to the Treasury at the close of the year. During the present fiscal year, departments and agencies have operated under even more exacting budgetary standards, but I am hopeful that the amount of unexpended funds on June 30 will again be substantial. On the basis of the reports I have reviewed, I am certain that there will be less unnecessary and unjustifiable spending during the month of June than in any comparable period during recent fiscal years.

NOTE: See also Item 267.

312   Statement by the President on Extending the Automated
        Merchant Vessel Report System to the Pacific Coast.
        June 12, 1965

IN 1958, the United States Coast Guard inaugurated a program of mutual maritime assistance called Automated Merchant Vessel Report, or AMVER.

Under this program, any vessel of any nation making an offshore voyage in the Atlantic may, if it wishes, periodically report its position to the AMVER nerve center in New York City. This information, along with available data on the search and rescue capabilities of the ship, is fed into an electronic computer. The computer keeps constant track of the ship's precise location. Should any emergency occur, any recognized search and rescue agency of any nation may request—and promptly receive—from AMVER accurate and pertinent data on the predicted whereabouts of any ship that has taken advantage of AMVER.

Since the start of the program 7 years ago, more than 8,000 vessels of all maritime nations have chosen to participate voluntarily in the AMVER program. While unheralded, this program represents a significant and valuable contribution to cooperation among nations and reflects the purpose of our Nation impatiently pursuing the tangible works of peace.

Because of the success achieved by the AMVER program in the Atlantic, I am privileged today to announce that it will be expanded to include the Pacific coast as well as the Atlantic coast.

The headquarters for the Pacific coast operation will be operated at San Francisco.

We are thus achieving another significant step in this country's efforts to advance the works of peace and to extend the hand of friendship in peril or in need anywhere in the world.

313   Statement by the President on Rate Reductions by the Rural
        Electric Cooperatives.   *June 12, 1965*

THE REDUCTION in rates for electricity used by farmers and other rural residents is as significant as a gain in rural income. The objective of the REA program throughout its existence has been to achieve parity of electric service and costs between city and country. I am gratified that the cooperatives are applying their resources and growing skills to keep faith with this important objective and purpose of our rural electrification program.

NOTE: The President's statement was part of a White House release which announced that a new record would be set in fiscal year 1966 by rural electric cooperatives on reductions of rates to their consumers. The release stated, in part, "With the end of the current fiscal year approaching 112 rural electric systems financed by the Rural Electrification Administration have made rate reductions this year which will amount to a savings of more than $3.8 million annually to consumers. . . .

"Eighty-six other rural electric systems presently are considering rate reductions, which, if adopted, will amount to another $3 million in annual savings to consumers. . . ."

314   Remarks at the White House Festival of the Arts.
June 14, 1965

Ladies and gentlemen:

Thomas Jefferson often spoke of America's good fortune in being distant from the Europe of his day. But in a letter in 1785, he spoke of his great pleasure in the architecture, painting, sculpture, music, and other arts of Europe. "It is in these arts they shine," he said. And he wrote: "It is the only thing which from my heart I envy them."

Well, I wish Thomas Jefferson could be here today. He would find that the last cause for envy had disappeared.

For most of our history we have bowed to that observation of Jefferson. We have had great artists. But the central flame of American art has been fed by the model of other invention, and fanned by the standard of other judgment. Almost unaware in recent decades, we have realized this is no longer so. In every field we have produced artist after artist, equipped to stand in the front rank of creative talent. Our painting and music, architecture and writing have profoundly shaped the course of modern art. From jazz and folk song to the most complex abstractions of word and image, few parts of the world are free from the spreading influence of American culture.

I do not pretend to judge the lasting values of these works. But if art is important to man, then American art is deeply important to mankind.

So today the Nation honors its artists.

No people can afford to neglect the creative minds among it. They enrich the life of the Nation. They reveal the farthest horizons of man's possibility. And Government—as representative of all the people—should always play a role in stimulating our people.

First, and most important, it can leave the artist alone. Art is not a tender or fragile thing. It has kept alive in the habitations of cruelty and oppressions. It has struggled toward light from the manifold darkness of war and conflict and persecution. Yet it flourishes most abundantly when it is fully free—when the artist can speak as he wishes and describe the world as he sees it without any official direction. In no country in all the world—East or West—is the artist freer than here in America. There are pressures. But they come from inner desire and not external coercion.

Secondly, the Government can offer direct encouragement. Most of this help will come, as it always has, from private and local sources. But the Nation has its obligation. And that is why we have proposed a bill to establish a National Foundation for the Arts and Humanities. That historic bill has already been passed in the United States Senate. I would hope that it could soon become law.

Third, we can work to create an atmosphere for the arts to thrive. Fundamentally this flows from the values and the thoughts and the hopes of the Nation itself. It is shaped by our schools and by our surroundings and by the nature of our society.

So by honoring artists and their work, by recognizing the importance of their contribution, we not only reflect, but we help to mold the values of this country.

Every President has known that our people look to this city, and to this house—not to follow but to lead, not to listen but to teach, not only to obey their will but to help design their purpose. The Presidency is not just a center of action and administration. It is, perhaps most importantly, a wellspring of leadership. We are, for example, using this great power to help move toward justice for all of our people, not simply because I believe it, but because American freedom depends on it. And we are trying to stimulate creation, not because of our personal tastes or desires, but because American greatness will rest on it.

So, this is the true meaning of this occasion. Those of you who are participating in this day are not simply sharing an isolated event. You are sharing in an effort to enrich the life of this country and all of its people. You have been asked to come not because you are the greatest artists of the land, because in the judgment of those who made up this guest list you may be and you do distinguish yourselves in the world of American art, but by your presence you help in the struggle to liberate all the talent and energy which this Nation has in such abundance. And you help us awake, in all of our people, the knowledge and the appreciation which can add so much to their lives.

Your art is not a political weapon. Yet much of what you do is profoundly political. For you seek out the common pleasures and visions, the terrors and the cruelties of man's day on this planet. And I would hope that you would help dissolve the barriers of hatred and ignorance which are the source of so much of our pain and danger. In this way you work toward peace—not only the peace which is simply the absence of war—but the peace which liberates man to reach for the finest fulfillment of his spirit.

Stephen Vincent Benet called upon the "American muse, whose strong and diverse heart—so many men have tried to understand." You are still reaching for the understanding beyond capture. But in that effort you not only explain a nation. The search itself enlarges America in heart, in spirit, in purpose, and in grandeur.

We have created an American culture. It is a great achievement. But with it come great responsibilities that can no longer be cast off on others: to lift and to strengthen—in partnership or rebellion—a nation; in itself and for the dreams it shares with all mankind.

Thank you.

NOTE: The President spoke at 8 p.m. on the South Lawn at the White House.

The Festival of the Arts lasted over 12 hours and was attended by more than 300 artists, art patrons, and critics. The program ranged from pop art and jazz to poetry readings and ballet. Mrs. Johnson spoke briefly at the close of the program.

The National Foundation on the Arts and the Humanities Act of 1965 was approved by the President on September 29, 1965 (see Item 534).

315   Remarks to a Delegation From the American Institute of Architects and the Pan American Congress of Architects. *June 15, 1965*

Mr. Chairman, ladies and gentlemen:

I am grateful to you for this certificate honoring our efforts to foster a greater attention to natural beauty in this spacious and beautiful country of ours.

Your profession is one which I personally greatly admire. I believe that in the fullest sense no society can fulfill its greatness until its ideals and aspirations are expressed eloquently and effectively in its architecture.

Here in this country, moving as we are into an age of much greater urbanization, it is more important than ever that attention be given to the quality and character of our architecture.

I am delighted to see that you had our

neighbors in this hemisphere join with you here this morning. I am glad not only to welcome them but I know that from them we have learned much and will learn more.

Our cities in America can be great centers of inspiration for the finest qualities of the human soul if, but only if, that aspiration is captured and reflected through the architecture of these cities.

So it is my hope and my intention that the efforts of the Federal Government of the United States be devoted to encouraging and contributing to these high standards. Cities are for people—for all of our people. We know they can be formless and oppressing and degrading to the human spirit, or they can be beautiful as well as livable, pleasant as well as practicable.

We do not want and we do not accept the idea of a standard governmental architecture. This must never be. But we do look to the individual creativity of the members of your profession to provide the leadership that will express the aspirations of our society and exalt the full dimensions of the human spirit.

While you are here, I thought that it might be interesting to you and certainly to some of our friends from the hemisphere, to show to you and for the first time announce publicly the acceptance of the design for a major new building that the Federal Government is doing here in the District of Columbia. We are going to begin a significant development of necessary Federal buildings in the 10th Street and Independence Avenue section of the District of Columbia.

The central building in this undertaking is this structure shown here. This building will house a number of units of our defense establishment and bring them together. They are not now located in the Pentagon; they are scattered around the area—approximately 6,000 Army and Air Force personnel will be employed here.

This structure will be one of our very finest buildings in the Federal complex and I want it to have one of the finest names that I know. I am therefore, in the presence of all of you here this morning, designating this building to be known as the Forrestal Building, honoring this Nation's first Secretary of Defense, a man in whose office I worked as a young man, my good friend, the Honorable James Forrestal.

I have conferred with Mr. Knott, the General Services Administrator I know most of you men are acquainted with, and we are going to try to do our very best to get the best designs, to have outstanding committees from the architectural profession help us in connection with the selection of architects, in connection with the design of public buildings in the hope that we can add much economy, convenience and beauty to the construction of all Federal buildings throughout this land.

Thank you very much.

NOTE: The President spoke at 12:58 p.m. in the Cabinet Room at the White House. His opening words "Mr. Chairman" referred to Arthur Gould Odell, Jr., President of the American Institute of Architects. Later he referred to Lawson B. Knott, Jr., Administrator of General Services.

The joint assembly of the American Institute of Architects and the Pan American Congress of Architects, which met in Washington June 14-18, 1965, presented the President with a citation for his "leadership in inspiring the people of this nation to act on their obligations and opportunities for conserving their God-given environment and improving their man-made surroundings."

316   Remarks at the Graduation Ceremony of the School for Capitol Page Boys.   *June 15, 1965*

Ladies and gentlemen:

Woodrow Wilson once said that "the Office of President requires the constitution of an athlete, the patience of a mother, and the endurance of an early Christian." Personally, I think he may have overstated the requirements of the Presidency. But from very long and close observation of 34 years, it seems to me that President Wilson may have been describing the requirements for congressional page.

So, whether your experience on the Hill has been long or brief, each of you in this page class this morning has been through a very rigorous and a very demanding test. And I want you to know—each of you to know—that I am extremely proud of you.

From this point on you will turn upward along many different paths. All of you are exceptional young men with exceptional training. I am sure that in your choices of professions or other pursuits many of you will achieve exceptional success. Whatever your pursuit, however, I hope that the experience you have had at the heart of our representative democratic system will always be a part of your life.

Even if you do not choose a career of public service, I hope as private citizens you will live your lives with a high and an active sense of public duty and responsibility.

This is a time of change in America. All of us are awakening to the fact that America today is far different from the land into which my generation or your generation was born. The answers, the attitudes, and the approaches of 30 years ago, or 20 years ago, or even 5 years ago, are not now adequate to meet the new obligations or the new opportunities of the 1960's.

As one who shares with you a very abiding respect and affection for the Congress, I am especially gratified and pleased by the response that Congress itself has made last year and this year toward meeting the change of our changing times. Congress has done much to silence the critics and the cynics who have belabored it and who have attempted to downgrade it.

You can all be proud that you served during a season when the Congress of the United States was strengthened and revitalized as a functioning, responsive, and conscientiously responsible branch of our system of government. And I am pleased that at their own direction they are now engaging in a considerable amount of introspection and study on how they can make the Congress stronger and better and more effective.

As this is a changing land, so America stands as a part of the changing world. There are some who would have mankind believe that the only choices of these times are choices between political philosophies. Actually, I do not believe that this is the case. In a real sense, the choice facing men in every nation today, old or young, large and small, is a choice between moving into the modern world with all of its unlimited potential or turning back toward the restrictive world that is dominated by the dogma and the doctrine of the 19th century.

So, in your lifetimes, and in the lifetimes of a majority of the nations on earth, the total of human knowledge has doubled twice. The growth of human knowledge has made obsolete many of the causes of friction and contention and division among nations. Certainly the advance of human knowledge has made war itself obsolete and impossible as a means of resolving differences between large or small nations. Above all, the growth of human knowledge has rendered obsolete and archaic the doctrine on which the dogma of communism was constructed.

Man today has in his capacity the potential of ending human misery or ending human life. We can really, for the first time, see the promise and the prospect of eliminating hunger and poverty, illness, bias, and prejudice in our own land and, we would hope, all around the world.

So, this is the work that we want to do. And this is the work which your generation will do. And that is why I have said over, and over, and over again that we of the United States invite all peoples—East and West—to pull back their curtains, and to tear down their walls, and to come out of the darkness of dogma and walk all together in the bright light of human knowledge and human freedom toward the peace that mankind must make together, and must keep together, on this earth.

I have seen many classes of Capitol pages graduate throughout the years. I would say that the class of which you are members faces the brightest and the most thrilling and the most hopeful prospects of any. For never before have young men like yourselves had so sure and so strong a prospect of being a part of the constructive building of a sane and a sensible and a rational world.

Whatever profession you choose as your own, I hope you will never forget that the ultimate success of our system rests upon the contributions that every citizen makes to public service.

And I would hope that as the days and weeks go by that you would, too, engage in a little introspection and ask yourselves, upon occasions at least: What did I do today to make my country better, to make it stronger, to make my Government more efficient and more useful? And whether as the elected or the elector you will have a great opportunity to be leaders of your times in fostering the responsible and the responsive politics that is needed at every level—local and State, as well as national and international?

You have been privileged to know some of the great leaders of these times in the legislative halls. And I hope that when your time comes you will keep faith by being leaders then in the cause of peace and freedom for the world, and for progress for all of humankind.

I went to sleep last night after reading a letter from a mother who was the mother of only one child, and that boy was now 20 years of age. And she had just gotten a letter from him and he said in 20 days he would be on his way to Viet-Nam. And she said, "Mr. President, I hesitate to take your time to write this letter, but I did not want to see my boy go away unless and until I could have your assurance that our Government and our country needs that boy and needs him where he is going."

He had lost his father. He was an only child. It was a difficult letter to dictate an answer to, but I had to write it this morning. And I told her that our liberty and our freedom was so precious, and liberty and freedom was in danger. And we had to call upon those who were capable and equipped to help us protect it. And all of us in our own way were doing the very best we could to preserve freedom, and that I did think it was necessary.

The mother had said in her letter that if I felt that, that she wouldn't, under any circumstances, object, although she did have to admit that while she did not want him out of the service, and she did not want him not to face up to his duty, she had to admit that she did not look with any favor to his going to that place at this time.

So, those of you who in a short time will be in the service of your country in one capacity or another, know how blessed you are to live in a system that was inherited by you as the result of the sacrifice of many thousands of young men like yourselves.

I believe that as you leave your present work that you will have gained from the halls of the Congress a sense of duty and a sense of responsibility that will always make the job of serving your country a pleasant one for you.

Thank you very much.

NOTE: The President spoke at 12 noon in the Rose Garden at the White House at the graduation ceremony of the Capitol Page School.

317 Remarks at the Signing of the Pacific Northwest Disaster Relief Act. *June 17, 1965*

Members of the Congress, ladies and gentlemen:

This is a very happy and gratifying occasion for all of us—for the legislative branch and for the executive branch alike.

It is also a gratifying occasion, I think, for the people of this country and those who love our system of government.

The legislation before me now very clearly represents and, I think, symbolizes the spirit of constructive cooperation, and more than that, responsible understanding that prevails today between the great branches of our great Federal system.

The legislation which I will shortly sign has the highest of humanitarian purposes. It will provide additional and essential funds to further the reconstruction of areas of our great Pacific Northwest, a section that has the finest potential in our country. This area was severely devastated by the unprecedented floods last winter.

On the objectives involved, there has never been the slightest disagreement between any of us in either party. However, when the legislation came to me a few days ago, there were provisions in it which made it necessary for a self-respecting executive to withhold approval at that time. For me, I can

tell you such a decision was not reached lightly. I was troubled. I believe devotedly in our system of division of power in checks and balances.

On November 27, 1963, when I first spoke after assuming the burdens of this Office, I told the Congress in person that for 32 long years Capitol Hill had been my home. Then I went on to add, as one who has long served in both Houses of the Congress—12 in the House and 12 in the Senate—I see some of you out there that were responsible for my going there even though you may not want to admit it—I firmly believe in the independence and the integrity of the legislative branch of the Government, and I promise you that I shall always respect this. It is deep in the marrow of my bones. For this philosophy guides me still, and will always.

Let none think I worship the veto. I exercise it rarely and only when required. I never welcome either the opportunity or the necessity to make use of that power in this Office. But I do believe that it is imperative to the order and to the success and to the strength of this great constitutional system—and some of the great constitutional lawyers in our country are standing behind me this morning—that the division of responsibilities as well as the division of powers be faithfully and religiously maintained. And that is why I took the decision to withhold my approval of this legislation originally and to set forth my views very respectfully and very carefully in an attempt to be as inoffensive as possible to the Congress.

The result has been a very slight delay of about a week in securing this legislation which does uphold, I think, the vital principles on which our whole system was built and upon which it stands.

I am very grateful and I am most appreciative and, if I could, I would ask their constitutents to take judicial notice of the sponsors of this legislation, particularly the chairmen of the Senate and House committees, Senator McNamara and Congressman Fallon, Senator Morse and others, for their willing cooperation in achieving this prompt and this constructive action.

As I have said, this cooperation should be reassuring to all the American people—reassuring that this is not, that there is not, and there will not be a stalemate in our democracy.

As we of the executive branch ask respect for the division of executive responsibilities, I want all within the executive branch to hear me now say loud and clear, that we extend to the legislative branch that same respect.

I want every employee and every bureaucrat in this Government to know that I am going to exercise the responsibilities of the executive department but I recognize the equal and sometimes more compelling responsibilities of the legislative department. And I want them to recognize them, too, and to honor them and to respect them and to cooperate with them, and not infringe upon them. So when laws have been enacted and

when they have been signed, I want them faithfully and fully upheld in the spirit of the law. Although we in the executive branch might not have agreed with every curlicue or every comma or every paragraph, they do express the will of the Congress, and the only will that governs our land under law is the will of the people. And the will of the people is expressed through their elected representatives, not as well expressed as I would always have it, but it is expressed, and once it is expressed, that is it.

This will and this way must be respected and honored to the fullest in both spirit and letter of the constitutional intent. Our system stands on mutual respect and trust. It will never grow, it will never flourish, it will never persist, it will never endure on division, or on contention, or on quarrels, or on name calling, or on labels.

It is that spirit which must govern and must guide us as we face our challenges at home and when we meet our tests abroad.

So I am very proud and I am very pleased, and I am very honored in the presence of those of you here this morning to be able now to give my approval to this valuable legislation for the benefit of a strong and a growing region of our great land, and to be able to give it consistent with the spirit of our Constitution, consistent with our division of powers, consistent with the kind of relationship I want to exist between the branches of Government.

I think I can truthfully say that I doubt there has ever been a period in American history when the Court and the Congress and the Executive were working more harmoniously, and were discharging their duties more effectively.

We don't spend our time on name calling and talking about somebody else. We just spend our time on passing bills for the benefit of the people and hoping the Court will uphold it.

Thank you very much.

NOTE: The President spoke at 11:17 a.m. in the Rose Garden at the White House. During his remarks he referred to Senator Pat McNamara of Michigan, Chairman of the Senate Public Works Committee, Representative George H. Fallon of Maryland, Chairman of the House Public Works Committee, and Senator Wayne Morse of Oregon.

As enacted, the Pacific Northwest Disaster Relief Act of 1965 (S. 2089) is Public Law 89-41 (79 Stat. 131).

318 Remarks at the Presentation of NASA Exceptional Service Awards Following the Flight of Gemini 4. *June 17, 1965*

Mr. Vice President, Administrator Webb, and all of the McDivitts, and the Whites, and the Mathews, large and small:

I hope it is not too much of a disappointment for you younger members of the families to settle for the White House instead of the ranch house.

I had planned this morning to salute the astronauts as colonels, but your alma mater— Michigan—seems to have topped that. So, I suppose I should just greet you here in the Rose Garden as Dr. McDivitt and Dr. White.

One week ago, at the spacecenter in Houston, I extended you my own very personal greetings. Today, I am very proud to offer to you—and to Mr. Mathews—the appreciation, and gratitude, and the very special congratulations of an admiring Nation.

All your countrymen are very proud of you, and are proud of all who contributed to the success of your historic mission—and they are legion.

While he never likes to be included, and he rarely is included in our public remarks, this morning I am going to take a moment to express my deep, personal gratitude and my admiration to the man whose ability and whose great brain, whose energy and whose diligence, whose imagination and initiative and abiding faith represent one of America's major assets—the Administrator of NASA, Jim Webb.

I asked him to come to the Senate Office Building in the Capitol before he took this job and asked him to take it. He turned me down. I asked him to come back again. The second time he did not turn me down. I asked Dr. Dryden to come up there. And that morning we presented them to each other, and they have made a fine team and developed a team that is unequaled in this country. And every American ought to be grateful to those two men, and all of the people who work under them, because their achievements have been unbelievable and have been phenomenal, and we are deeply in their debt.

I said to one of the members of the Cabinet the other day what I thought about Jim Webb. And he said, "Why don't you have him in your Cabinet?" I said, "I would have if his job weren't more important." And that is how we feel about the space effort in this country. There is just no job that is more important.

Also, there is another whose role is growing every day in the space field as in many other vital fields. The imagination and the application and the inspiration that he has given this program, and the executive branch, and the legislative branch, should be acknowledged this morning. He is a man whose judgment I value highly, whose friendship I cherish deeply, and in whom I have complete and absolute confidence—the

666

Chairman of the National Space Council, the Vice President of the United States, Hubert Humphrey.

Now, if everything had not gone right, the men responsible for it having gone wrong are also here. They are the chairmen of the Senate committees, and the members of the House and Senate Space Committees. And I hope that their constituents and the people of a grateful Nation will take due notice of the great successful enterprise that they have contributed to, which we have just completed and for which we will continue to work in the future.

Back in 1958, when we were making the great effort to launch this Nation's serious space effort, there were those in the Senate, and some elsewhere, who scoffed at our interest in space, who laughed at it, who ridiculed it—to borrow a memorable phrase—but not Senator Humphrey.

Ten years ago, in July 1955, President Eisenhower first announced this country's plan to orbit several small, unmanned satellites during the International Geophysical Year. And the leaders of both parties worked and planned to bring the Space Administration into existence. President Eisenhower was the leader of our country at that time, and he made valuable contributions, and I want to thank him for his leadership.

Our purpose then was to cooperate with other nations in the peaceful exploration of the domain of space. And that has been our unchanging purpose every minute, every step of the way since then.

It is our purpose still.

In 1961, under our beloved President John F. Kennedy, we committed ourselves as a Nation to achieving leadership in space. For wherever there is an opportunity to advance the hopes for peace, America intends to be second to none.

And there is a hope—a strong and a genuine and living hope—that cooperation in exploring the avenues of space could lead men and nations to cooperate in exploring the avenues to peace on earth.

In terms of our national goals of leadership in space, it can be said—and it should be said—that the brilliant performance of both spacecraft and crew on the flight of the Gemini 4, together with the progress on our Apollo program, clearly indicates that the United States of America has closed the gap in manned space flight.

But I believe that the Gemini 4 has done more than that.

Your successful mission has raised hopes—at home and abroad—that the day may now be much nearer when all the world can enjoy the benefits of close cooperation among all nations in exploring and using space for the common good and for the peaceful interests of mankind.

Americans noted with great satisfaction the message that you received, shortly after you landed in the Atlantic, from Major Gagarin. He expressed the hope that all space flights may serve the world and benefit all mankind. And we very much welcome that expression.

While the Gemini 4 was still in orbit, I spoke here in Washington, and I would like to repeat what I said then:

"The need of man—the need of these times in which we live—is not for arms races, and it is not for moon races. . . . If competition there must be, we are ready and we are willing to take up the challenges and commit our country to its tasks. But this is a moment when the opportunity is open and beckoning for men of all nations to take together a walk toward peace in space."

That is no new impetuous thought on my part. That is the view I expressed in 1958—7 years ago—when I was privileged to present, at the request of the President of our

667

country, President Eisenhower, America's proposals on space to the United Nations in New York. That is the view Americans will always have in their hearts, and that spirit is not new.

In 1958, while I was serving as leader of my party in the Senate, President Eisenhower asked me to present this Nation's proposals to the United Nations for cooperation among all nations in the peaceful exploration of space.

On November 17th of that year, I said to the United Nations in New York, and I quote:

"Men who have worked together to reach the stars are not likely to descend together into the depths of war and desolation. . . . Barriers between us will fall as our sights rise to space."

The sights of mankind are rising. And I hope and I am confident that barriers between us must and will begin to fall.

We know that you men of Gemini have opened the doors to space a great deal wider. And how much more we would prefer to see you all riding together in a spaceship to a new adventure, to conquering a new world, than to shoot down each other's planes, as we had to last night.

So, we can hope and we can trust that others will recognize—and I want to emphasize again, and again, and again—that the doors to cooperation and peace are opened wider, too. And here, in America, we welcome those who want to join us with open arms.

If men and nations will reason together, if they will cooperate together, if they will make the improvement of the condition of man their common goal, then I am confident that we can safely predict—and I do predict here this morning—that during the next decade of the 1970's many more nations will

be joined together in the adventure of space—developing its potential for bettering life on this earth. And my, what a glorious moment that will be when those nations do join with us!

For 8 years I have believed—as I believe now—that space is the great breakthrough for humankind. Human progress has never come on a slow and steady curve. But progress comes by great advances which move us forward, which cause many other obstacles to fall aside.

So here, to this little group this morning at this very special occasion, I am confident that the breakthrough in space will permit all mankind—in developed nations and emerging nations—to overcome and leave behind many obstacles that today retard human progress in health, that retard human progress in education, in agriculture, in the control of weather and man's environment, in industry and economic growth, and, above all, in understanding among nations.

So, you are the Christopher Columbuses of the 20th century. You are the peacemakers. Peace is your mission. And notwithstanding the great advance that your performance will bring us in science, in agriculture, in controlling the weather, in all the things that we knew not of, your greatest contribution will be "peace is your mission." And ultimately you will be the men, and those associated with you, who brought us all together.

So, this is a very happy moment for you, and for your families, and for your Nation.

You are symbols of a new world. You are symbols of a new horizon. You are symbols of a new potential—not just for yourself or your country, but for 3 billion human beings everywhere. All our thoughts leap forward to the kind of world we want to pass on to these youngsters in your fine

668

families. And not just your kids; we want to do it for all the children on the earth, wherever they live.

So, let us then here—in this peaceful garden of the White House, whose occupants all have and all still do work for peace throughout the world—let us stress again our readiness to join hands and minds and technologies with all men who seek the betterment of mankind on the way to the stars.

And that is what you do seek. Not just scientific knowledge. Not just weather information. Not just to dominate space as we dominated the air since World War II, and as the British dominated the seas for generations. But so that you may lay the stone that ultimately builds the walk to understanding between men.

Now, I have not been successful, but I did try to participate. I tried to persuade my Secretary of State and my Administrator of NASA to not only have you come to Washington to appear as a symbol of the 20th century, our progress in bettering mankind, but I also expressed the hope that it might be possible for you to inspire the peoples of the world, as you are inspiring those here in the Capital of the United States today. And I am sorry that you are not going abroad tomorrow. It is not my fault, but I am going to keep working at it.

Now I know that you don't want to listen to speeches all day. You came here to the White House. But the person that is providing great leadership and inspiration, not only in this field but in many other fields of this Government, is Chairman of the National Space Council, and we honor and we respect and I particularly applaud the way he has come into this new undertaking and picked it up and provided it with leadership and stimulation and inspiration. And I am just going to insist that I be permitted to listen to a very brief speech, the kind of speech he used to make in the Senate—and, with amendment, I want to strike that word brevity. Vice President Humphrey.

NOTE: The President spoke at 11:45 a.m. in the Rose Garden at the White House before the presentation of NASA Exceptional Service Medals to Lt. Col. James A. McDivitt and Lt. Col. Edward H. White 2d, Gemini 4 astronauts, and to Charles W. Mathews, manager of the Gemini space flight program.

In his opening words he referred to Vice President Hubert H. Humphrey and James E. Webb, Administrator, National Aeronautics and Space Administration. Later he referred to Dr. Hugh L. Dryden, Deputy Administrator of NASA, and to Maj. Yuri Gagarin, Soviet astronaut.

Following the President's remarks the Vice President spoke briefly. The text of his remarks was also made public by the White House.

See also Items 304, 310, 320.

319   The President's News Conference of June 17, 1965

THE PRESIDENT. [1.] I had some announcements that I thought would be of interest to you, and some of them are going to take some time. We normally take from 12 to 15 minutes on our announcements, so what I thought we'd do would be to just go ahead and make all the announcements and we'll send them to the mimeograph and have them made available to you as soon as possible.

And then we'll reserve 20 minutes for questioning afterwards, and we'll depend on AP or UP here to tell us when that 20 minutes is up, if that is agreeable to all of you. If none of you have any suggestions, what I plan to do is read these announcements, and as I read them, send them to the mimeograph. And if you prefer any other way I'd be glad to do it.

The Vice President has been talking to me about the developments on the Hill, the legislative program he's working on, some agriculture legislation—now in the Fish Room with a number of people. The Chairman of the Atomic Energy Commission has been here discussing a variety of matters with me. I'll refer to those a little bit later.

Q. Sir, we don't hear a word.

THE PRESIDENT. The Vice President has been here—now can you hear me?—discussing some legislative matters with me. He has been in the Fish Room working on an agricultural message with various interested parties—and various would include Members of Congress, and departmental members, and agriculture people, and others— some items on the cotton bill. He has also reported to me on certain legislative developments and targets. We'll have a meeting of the leadership, if it is convenient with them, in the early part of the week, at which time we will review our remaining legislation and look at the dates that they have it targeted for.

DEPARTMENT OF URBAN AFFAIRS

[2.] We have some very good news from Capitol Hill in the last few days—in a variety of fields.

I was especially gratified by the action of the House yesterday in giving approval to the legislation establishing departmental status for urban affairs. I hope, and I believe, that the Senate will act favorably. The vote in the House was impressive and decisive, and exceeded our expectations. I believe it reflects the realization throughout the land that our cities constitute the decisive challenge of these last decades of the 20th century.

By the year 2000 we estimate that approximately 80 percent of our people will be living in urban areas, so we must meet the needs of the cities because the cities are really the homes for most of our people. What our country is to mean for most Americans, therefore, depends upon the quality of life in our cities.

This is a long and a historic step forward. I congratulate the House on this forward-looking action in support of building a better America for all of our people, and I communicated my thanks and appreciation to the leadership of the House and asked them to express that view to the Members that supported the legislation.

EXCISE TAX REDUCTION

[3.] Another subject. I am pleased that the Congress has now completed action on the reduction of excise taxes. The bill remains to be enrolled, and there are certain steps that you take before a bill is sent to the President. But we expect to get it later in the week. After we get it, we will have it reviewed by the experts and the Budget and the Treasury, and any other agencies that could be concerned with it, and collect their recommendations. After we get those recommendations and read them we'll take action.[1] I think it is safe to predict it will not be a veto, in light of what I said this morning.

This bill will realize about $1¾ billion extra purchasing power in the economy for the rest of 1965, and another $1¾ billion on top of that beginning next January. The bill itself is a little over $4 billion and adds to the $14 billion tax reduction last year, totaling something over $18 billion.

Under the bill, consumers will no longer be paying this $4 billion into the Federal

---

[1] The Excise Tax Reduction Act of 1965 was approved by the President on June 21, 1965 (see Item 326).

Treasury, and will have it to spend instead on the products of our farms and factories.

It will help maintain the steady growth of jobs and production that are the mark of a healthy economy.

It will extend the string of production gains that the Federal Reserve Board announced yesterday—gains that have brought our total industrial production rate more than 7½ percent above a year ago.

It will support the continuing growth of our economy that has already served us so well for the recordbreaking 52 months. It will maintain stability of prices.

Yesterday, the Chairman of the Council of Economic Advisers announced that the Council, and the Treasury, and the Bureau of Labor Statistics initiated some time ago a study of the impact of excise tax reduction on prices. I am sure the study will show that businesses throughout the Nation have passed along to consumers in lower prices the tax reductions that the Congress enacted.

CEASE-FIRE VIOLATIONS IN THE DOMINICAN REPUBLIC

[4.] In the Dominican Republic in the last 2 days there has been renewed, and repeated, and totally unjustified firing on the Inter-American Force. This is in flagrant violation of a cease-fire.

This firing has been accepted without reply by the Inter-American Force for periods up to one-half hour before the necessary replies were given under the orders of General Alvim of Brazil and General Palmer of the United States.[2] In these actions 3 of our fellow Americans have lost their lives, and

[2] General of the Army Hugo Panasco Alvim of Brazil, Commander of the OAS Inter-American Force in the Dominican Republic, and Lt. Gen. Bruce Palmer, Jr., of the United States, Deputy Commander.

37 more Americans and 5 Brazilians have been wounded.

These unprovoked attacks on the Inter-American Force appear to have been premeditated by elements which seek to prevent the establishment of peace in Santo Domingo. Our forces there have no other mission, and they will continue to observe the same soldierly restraint that they have shown now for more than 7 weeks, in the face of more than 900 cease-fire violations, and they have already suffered almost 200 casualties.

ATOMIC ENERGY PROGRAMS

[5.] Dr. Seaborg[3] and I talked about the International Atomic Energy Agency's safeguards system and nonproliferation. At present, facilities in 15 countries are being inspected by the International Atomic Energy Agency. I believe we should do everything we can to point out the important contributions to nonproliferation and the world's peace that the International Atomic Energy Agency is making. And I plan to make further reference to that in a speech that I now have in the works.

We discussed the progress report on nuclear power and the nuclear powerplants that are being selected by American utilities because of economic considerations alone. About 20 utilities are considering such large plants and several are on the verge of announcing their orders. The Commissioner estimates that 5,000 megawatts of nuclear generating capacity by 1970, and 70,000 megawatts by 1980 seems reasonable.

The AEC and Department of Interior program on desalting also seems very promising. I have directed him, today, to undertake a

[3] Dr. Glenn T. Seaborg, Chairman of the Atomic Energy Commission.

new study in connection with the associated Government agencies, particularly Interior, in connection with certain cooperative efforts—that I expect to announce at a later date with other nations—in the field of desalting in an attempt to make the deserts bloom.

We discussed the United States and U.S.S.R. exchanges in atomic energy in some detail. This program is making a very effective and very positive contribution to the U.S.-U.S.S.R. relations. Dr. Seaborg reports that Ambassador Kohler has emphasized to us the great value of this program. As you know, he is our Ambassador in Russia. Dr. Seaborg stated that during his visit to the Soviet Union in May 1963 his counterpart, Chairman Petrosyants,[4] and Dr. Seaborg signed a memorandum of understanding in the peaceful uses of atomic energy, which has since provided us numerous scientific exchanges.

We are hopeful and we are going to labor to the end that the scientists become a bridge between nations of differing philosophies in the hope that we can bring about, through their efforts, much better understanding.

In the last 2 years, four U.S. teams have visited the U.S.S.R. Those teams are made up of 7 to 10 men each. And four Soviet teams visited the U.S. on a reciprocal basis. Three American scientists have been sent to the U.S.S.R. on an extended basis, and reciprocally three Soviet scientists have come here to the U.S. The success of this program has furthered our hope that science can serve as a common ground between East and West even in these troubled times.

You now have a mission there, don't you?

DR. SEABORG. Yes.

THE PRESIDENT. How many men?

DR. SEABORG. We have a couple of scientists working there on a long-term basis in one of the labs. The last team was a Soviet team that came to this country just last week. That is a team of 10 scientists in the field of radioactive waste disposal.

REDUCTION IN BUDGET DEFICIT

[6.] THE PRESIDENT. This one I'll go a little slow on. Earlier this year I announced to you that our expanding economy would produce more revenues than we had anticipated in our prediction to Congress in the January budget.

I also announced that the drive to keep Federal expenditures under tight rein would reduce expenditures below the estimates we made in January. We do not have any final figures for June, but I do have a final, rather strong, memorandum to all the agencies about this June spending. And on the basis of the reductions we were able to make in June spending last year, and the best estimates that the career men and Budget can make today, we want to report that our progress on both fronts is much better than we had previously expected, according to Mr. Schultze,[5] of the Budget Bureau, and the Secretary of the Treasury.

Instead of revenues increasing by $1.4 billion above our budget estimate, as it appeared earlier, we now anticipate a $1.6 billion revenue improvement. Our latest reports also indicate that expenditures will be in the neighborhood of $900 million lower than our January estimate. So, we expect to have a very unique thing happen to us—at present, taking in $1.6 billion more than we said we would, and spending in the neighborhood of $900 million less than we said we would spend. That will make a difference of $2.5 billion.

---

[4] Andronik M. Petrosyants, Chairman, State Committee for Use of Atomic Energy in Soviet Union.

[5] Charles L. Schultze, Director of the Bureau of the Budget.

Now, as a result, we expect revenues to be $92.8 billion and expenditures $96.6 billion. This could be off a hundred or so million either way, but this is the estimate they make, and they have been very good on it and this is the middle of June. The budget deficit, therefore, will be only $3.8 billion, which is $2.5 billion less than the $6.3 billion estimated in our January budget.

REDUCTION IN UNEMPLOYMENT

[7.] Continuing improvement in the Nation's economy has now, today, reduced to 22 the number of major manpower centers classified by the Federal Government as having substantial unemployment. The figure is the lowest since May of 1957. There were 39 such areas at this time last year, and 101 such areas in March and April of 1961.

Last month's data on employment and unemployment collected in the Nation's 150 largest manpower centers has resulted in our reclassification of 16 areas to categories denoting lower unemployment. Fifteen of these were removed from categories of substantial unemployment and were redesignated as areas of relatively low or moderate unemployment.

The Governor of Georgia told me that before they were acting on requests for new facilities they were making very careful studies because their unemployment rate is down in a good many areas 2 percent or less. Now before people come in and make surveys they try to bring them up to date. I just add that parenthetically. This is what he told me arriving at the airport yesterday.

The improved conditions can be credited to the effects of Federal programs of tax reduction, manpower training, area development, cooperation and trust and confidence between employees and business and labor

and Government, in addition to the general improvement in the economic climate and the strong confidence existing in the business community, so far as new plant investments are concerned.

BALANCE OF PAYMENTS DEFICIT

[8.] Another item is in connection with our voluntary cooperation program to control and reduce the balance of payments deficit. Many cooperating bankers and businessmen have asked what the Federal Government is doing for its part in the program. I have reviewed with the Secretary of the Treasury, and night before last with the Secretary of Commerce, and I will meet with Mr. Robertson of the Federal Reserve Board, and Mr. Maisel, a Federal Reserve Board member,[6] tomorrow. We don't want to be overoptimistic, and we want to caution everyone to be prudent in their predictions. We are pleased with the balance of payments and it is exceeding our expectations. But these bankers and businessmen that I was speaking about—their concern is quite proper.

I have just received a report from the Budget Director today on the matter and here is what it shows. The net balance of payments costs of the Federal program— that is just Federal; what I said a moment ago has to do with banks alone, capital investments by business—this has to do with Federal programs. The net balance of payments costs of Federal programs through regular transactions abroad—keeping our troops there, Korea, Germany, our headquarters in France, and our foreign aid to all the countries—through regular transactions abroad declined 23 percent, or $635 million from fiscal 1963 to 1965.

----

[6] J. L. Robertson and Sherman J. Maisel, members, Board of Governors, Federal Reserve System.

According to present plans, these costs will decline another 13 percent, or $290 additional million, by 1967.

We have certain actions and decisions that have already been made but have to be tapered out. This major improvement has been possible because of efforts throughout the Government to reduce overseas dollar payments and to increase our receipts from abroad. The most substantial contribution to date has resulted from a reduction in overseas payments of $720 million from 1963 through 1965. In the next 2 years our receipts from abroad—loan repayments, receipts from the sale of Government-owned agricultural commodities, and even advance repayments on loans made since World War II, and we hope some of these days some from World War I—will increase sharply.

These we welcome gladly, and some of them are coming back, and some are coming back in advance, and that is what reduced this 23 percent and 13 percent. So, these contributions of Federal agencies toward sharing the burden of reducing the balance of payments deficit were also reflected in the reduction in Federal employment in foreign countries. As I reported several weeks ago, there were 8,614 fewer civilian Federal employees overseas in December 1964 than a year earlier—approximately 9,000 reduced.

These improvements have been obtained without sacrificing essential U.S. commitments abroad, and in the face of rising price and wage levels in most overseas countries where we spend our dollars.

REDUCTION IN NUMBER OF GOVERNMENT EMPLOYEES

[9.] Employment last month, I believe, is down something like over 4,000 employees

in the Federal Government. I'll get those exact figures if Bill Moyers,[7] or someone else, will get them for me. That is contrasted with 2.1 million more people working this May than worked last May.

RESIGNATIONS AND APPOINTMENTS

[10.] I have today accepted the resignation of Secretary of the Army, Stephen Ailes, effective July 1st. I plan to nominate Stanley R. Resor, currently Under Secretary of the Army, to replace Mr. Ailes as Secretary of the Army. Mr. David E. McGiffert, currently Assistant Secretary of Defense, will replace Mr. Resor as Under Secretary of the Army. Secretary Ailes served as Under Secretary of the Army from February 9, 1961, until January 28, 1964, when he succeeded Cyrus Vance as Secretary of the Army. He has served in that post continuously since that time. Secretary Ailes is returning to his Washington law practice.

I have spent a good portion of my time in the last few days going back and forth—yesterday to Georgia, and other places, reading reports and evaluating employees. I expect to have some today when it is convenient to give you a number of other appointees. We are having changes from time to time. There will be more in the Defense Department. There will be a good many in the Justice Department. Some on commissions. We are in good shape with our appointees but we have a dozen or so now under active consideration.

[11.] I have today accepted the resignation of Under Secretary of the Navy, Kenneth E. BeLieu, effective July 1st. I will nominate Robert H. B. Baldwin of New Jersey, currently a partner in the investment firm of Morgan Stanley, and a con-

---

[7] Bill D. Moyers, Special Assistant to the President.

sultant to the Secretary of the Navy, to take Mr. BeLieu's place.

Q. What does he do?

THE PRESIDENT. He is consultant to the Secretary of the Navy and a partner in private life—he comes from the firm of Morgan Stanley.

CABINET TO REVIEW INTERNATIONAL SITUATION

[12.] I called a meeting of the Cabinet for 11 a.m., Friday. We will have a thorough review and discussion of the international situation, and U.S. policies. I will ask the Secretary of State to review the dozen or more diplomatic proposals and initiatives that we have considered and received and proposed, so that all the members of the Cabinet may evaluate and discuss them and be informed about them in greater detail than has been permitted before.

In addition, we will explore with members of the Cabinet certain other hopes for peace that we are evaluating and considering. The Secretary of Defense will report on the status of the men in uniform, who protect us and who defend us, and the quality of their performance, the dangers that they have undertaken, the commitments that we have made to certain areas of the world. That will be thoroughly and carefully reviewed, and members of the Cabinet will make—those not on the National Security Council—the Secretary of the Treasury is, and the Attorney General comes frequently, and, of course, the Vice President is always there—but others will make any suggestions that they come to, and very likely will make some suggestions to new initiatives which we have already tried, and some unsuccessfully.

I think that is all I have at this time.

QUESTIONS
RESIGNATIONS AND APPOINTMENTS

[13.] Q. Mr. President, will Mr. BeLieu have any office in Government?

THE PRESIDENT. He has resigned from his office and he has not informed me what he expects to do.

When Mr. McNamara came over the other day to talk about personnel matters he presented these resignations and made these suggestions, and while studies have been made of the men—investigations that we normally make, we brought them up to date, and since that meeting—whenever it was, 3 or 4 days ago, it was on the record—I have decided to name Mr. Resor and Mr. Baldwin.

CONGRESSIONAL COMMENTS AND THE NEGOTIATIONS IN VIET-NAM

[14.] Q. Mr. President, since you made a recent speech, you expressed a willingness and acceptance of the fact that your foreign policy was very subject to public discussion and such open remarks as this——

THE PRESIDENT. I have always believed that.

Q. Yes, sir, but in the last day or two, this criticism or discussion on Capitol Hill has become a little more pointed——

THE PRESIDENT. In recent days it has become a little more what?

Q. Pointed. Senator Clark of Pennsylvania says we must negotiate with the Viet Cong or we will never get a peace without it. What do you think of a statement like that by a member of the Foreign Relations Committee?

THE PRESIDENT. First, I think Senator Clark is a very able member of the Foreign Relations Committee. He has been interested, I recall, through the years when I was leader—he wanted to go on Foreign Relations and has been added to Foreign Relations recently. I think he has a perfect right to express himself—and a duty. His suggestion is one that I think has been carefully considered by Secretary Rusk and Secretary Ball,[8] and for that matter the entire Security Council and the President.

I think that you must observe—as accurate and perceptive as you are a good many times—and I think we all wish we could settle these differences by discussion and by reasoning them out instead of the way we are attempting to settle it.

I have no doubt—I am sure other Senators who are real familiar with this matter, including Senator Clark, have no doubt that if the Viet Cong had a viewpoint to present and were anxious to negotiate they would have no difficulty finding the government to negotiate.

I don't think that you would have a group that feels very strongly—maybe like the group at the Pentagon yesterday, or maybe State—I don't believe we'd ever agree to someone negotiating that is not a government. I am not aware of any government the Viet Cong has. What would you think about the State of Mississippi negotiating for us in this matter? Although it is a State it is not a sovereign government.

Now, if there is any indication, or anyone has information—I remember one time Senator Borah[9] said he had better information than the President. At that time, Smitty,[10] it was a matter of much more point than it is now, and much more equal, I am glad to say. But our information is when we asked them to come into the United Nations last August, after we said you bring these people in and let's try to work through the U.N., they weren't the slightest interested—the North Vietnamese were not.

In February, we started the program of trying to curtail their ammunition supply and trying to eliminate their bridges and make it more difficult for them to come in, and attempting to convince them we were there to keep our commitment and we were going to keep it although they believed from some things said in word and writing, we might not. We attempted to convince them.

They told our representatives, our spokesmen, people who were negotiating for us (not members of this Government), and this is an example that I have used in talking to a good many people in the Congress and elsewhere, "this inflexibility characterizes the position of this entire regime, and illustrates its great measure of confidence in itself. It considers it holds all the trump cards; that world opinion is becoming more sympathetic; that the United States retaliation is limited; that South Viet-Nam is having its difficulties and they are not the slightest interested."

On February 15th, the same man reported to us and just a few days ago, I believe it was June 7. And the message on June 7 was just about the same as the message on February 15. It is a confidential message but I will unclassify a paragraph or two of it for you.

He is completely persuaded, from his conversations with the officials, they are not now interested in any negotiation of any kind. He said he was able to see—he names a high official—and he followed the standard line that the United States offer of unconditional discussion was deceitful. He asked them to elaborate on any proposal they would consider. He remained deliberately vague and gave no clear answer. We pressed him

---

[8] Secretary of State Dean Rusk and Under Secretary of State George W. Ball.

[9] William E. Borah, Senator from Idaho 1907–1940.

[10] Merriman Smith of United Press International.

specifically about this matter but only received a vague and very indefinite reply.

He just talks about being impressed by an American in a foreign country, and he concludes the paragraph that his impressions from all of his meetings and discussions was there has been no change whatever in their position or at least they did not seem about to let such change be known.

Now, if any of these people want to negotiate they would have no difficulty finding a way. I told them in Baltimore we would like to go and would hope to do, and have repeated it since, and we have indicated many, many times we would be glad to negotiate with any government. Now they are going into groups of people.

Well, that is the current line. You remember first we had no policy. Second, we wouldn't explain it. Third, we ought to negotiate. Fourth, we ought to have a halt. These things originate and in about a month they come to us. You will find a good deal of it in the next few weeks—negotiate directly with the Viet Cong. And I would say the Viet Cong would have no difficulty, since they are controlled, directed, and masterminded from North Viet-Nam, in getting any view to us they wanted.

Q. Mr. President, this man who is reporting in, is this an American national?

THE PRESIDENT. You don't need to give him a blood test.

Q. This man was talking to Hanoi?

THE PRESIDENT. Yes. The negotiations, or who is carrying it on and how, I don't see how that could be of any value. The substance is what you want; not how much he weighs, how tall he is, or what country he represents. What we are trying to do is get them to talk to us.

Q. Mr. President, the Commonwealth meeting in London agreed to contact countries principally involved. Would you care to comment on that, sir?

THE PRESIDENT. Yes, I think the Prime Minister of Great Britain and the Prime Ministers of other Commonwealth countries are deeply interested in this matter and we are happy they are. We have reviewed their ideas and we are keeping close touch with them. We are very happy they have made this suggestion. We have talked to them, communicated with them about it, and they will have our full cooperation and we are delighted.

As I indicated the day after I took over as President, I'd be glad to go anywhere, do anything, see anybody, anytime that offered any hope of peace, and this is hope. We hope they can select a good committee that will be fair to all sides and we will be glad to meet with them, and we hope that every other country involved will be glad to meet.

We welcome any attempt, as we told them about the Cambodian conference [11] and we replied to the 17 nations,[12] as we said in 44 States and as we tried to repeat in some length in Pat Furgurson's [13] town of Baltimore some time ago.

THE FUTURE OF THE UNITED NATIONS

[15.] Q. Mr. President, what is to be done about the bad financial condition of the U.N.?

THE PRESIDENT. Well, that is a matter that

---

[11] On April 25, 1965, Secretary of State Dean Rusk stated that the U.S. would gladly participate in any conference on Cambodia. The text of his remarks is printed in the Department of State Bulletin (vol. 52, p. 711).

[12] On March 15, 1965, at Belgrade, Yugoslavia, a conference of 17 nonaligned nations adopted a declaration on the war in Viet-Nam. The 17-nation declaration and the U.S. reply are printed in the Department of State Bulletin (vol. 52, p. 610).

[13] Ernest B. (Pat) Furgurson of the Baltimore Sun.

deeply concerns us. We don't want to see the U.N. wrecked on account of a dollar. At the same time, we recognize the responsibilities of the member nations and there are differences of opinion there and we are trying to carefully consider the merits of the positions of various governments and find an area of agreement.

I am sorry to say we are not in a position to go any further at this time but we are very concerned about it, very anxious to find an answer to it, and we have great hopes for the U.N. and we think it would be tragic if because of a relatively minor amount of money, compared to the total budgets of the various nations, the U.N. should become less effective because of that.

I plan to—I want to put it this way, I hope that I may be able to go to San Francisco next Friday, and I wouldn't take that as a commitment that I am going to be there, but I hope to go and if I do, I may have something to say about the future of the U.N. at that time.

THE SITUATION IN VIET-NAM AND THE
DOMINICAN REPUBLIC

[16.] Q. Mr. President, with the situation in Viet-Nam and the Dominican Republic, what is your personal assessment of the chances of improving international relations right now?

THE PRESIDENT. What is the first part of your question?

Q. With the situation in Viet-Nam and the Dominican Republic, what is your assessment?

THE PRESIDENT. I would say it is very difficult. They are strained. We are going to do everything we can to avoid provoking any controversies or straining any relations, and there has been no statement of ours to-

ward any of the leaders of other governments, no propaganda of ours toward other peoples; and in our judgment, no act of ours that would justify irritating anyone who really loved peace and hated war.

We recognize that other nations keep their commitments and are true to their alliances and we assume that they would allow us the same privilege they reserve for themselves. We agreed to help the signatories of the Southeast Treaty Organization and the protocol states, and pursuant to that commitment we are trying to help them save their freedom from aggression. And we intend to save it.

In the Dominican Republic, forces moved in and overthrew the government. And while I am not passing on the merits of the actions that take place many times in many places, where they change governments— and we believe in change of conditions, and we are trying to obtain them through the Alliance for Progress—but in this particular instance, a fact that has been emphasized all too little, I think, some 1,500 innocent people were murdered and shot, and their heads cut off, and six Latin American embassies were violated and fired upon over a period of 4 days before we went in.

As we talked to our Ambassador to confirm the horror and tragedy and the unbelievable fact that they were firing on Americans and the American Embassy, he was talking to us from under a desk while bullets were going through his windows and he had a thousand American men, women, and children assembled in the hotel who were pleading with their President for help to preserve their lives.

We didn't start that. We didn't intervene. We didn't kill anyone. We didn't violate any embassies. We were not the perpetrators. But after we saw what had happened we took the necessary precautions as I have said so often and as I repeat again: We do not want to bury anyone and we don't intend to, but we are not going to be buried ourselves. And as we had to go into the Congo to preserve the lives of American citizens and haul them out when they were being shot at, we went into the Dominican Republic to preserve the lives of American citizens and citizens of a good many other nations—46 to be exact, 46 nationals.

While some of the nations were denouncing us for going in there their people were begging us to protect them. And the American Marines protected them. Twenty died. We removed 5,600 people from 46 nations and we didn't sprain an ankle doing it. But we had 20 of our boys killed by the rebels who fired first and who tried to keep us from evacuating these people. We established a peace zone.

We had only two purposes there. One, to get an Inter-American Force in there to bring about a cease-fire and preserve peace, that is all. We are not after their money or after their philosophy or trying to dominate them. We said that. And we tried our best to get them there as quick as we could and we finally got them—and General Alvim is doing an excellent job under great difficulties.

Yesterday I saw one of his cables, and it was 23 minutes after they started shooting before he replied. I don't know how many of you are anxious to stand up and be shot at by tommyguns, and you ask a lot of these boys to do that. That is the first thing.

The second was to have a government broadly based to be acceptable to the people of the Dominican Republic. We are not pointing, we are not matching a computer and saying, here is what the government will be. We asked Mr. Bundy, Mr. Vance, Mr.

Mann, Mr. Vaughn [14] and everyone we knew to talk to the extreme elements—some to talk to the other side, some to the loyalists, the rebels—hoping we could have a cease-fire until we could have a broadly based government, and until the OAS could give help, counsel, and mediation.

They have appointed a very fine committee. They appointed the best men they could find and they are there talking to every group, going all over the land. They are making progress, and we hope that the OAS will have a recommendation on the political matter like they did on the military matter. We don't want it to be unilateral. We much prefer that the forces of all nations go in to save people of 46 nations. But it is taking us 7 weeks to get the two things we have done up to now and haven't got the final answer yet.

We first had a committee appointed, then a man, then another committee appointed from the OAS, and we are proud of what the OAS is doing but it is not a matter that can save lives. As a matter of fact, we landed our people in less than 1 hour from the time the decision was made. It was a decision we considered from Saturday until Wednesday evening. But once we made it, in the neighborhood of 6 or 6:30 that evening, they landed within 1 hour. But they didn't save 1,500 lives.

CONGRESSIONAL RESOLUTION OF SUPPORT

[17.] Q. Mr. President, because of the growing commitment of American combat troops in Viet-Nam, there have been some

[14] McGeorge Bundy, Special Assistant to the President, Cyrus R. Vance, Deputy Secretary of Defense, Thomas C. Mann, Under Secretary of State for Economic Affairs, and Jack H. Vaughn, Assistant Secretary of State for Inter-American Affairs and United States Coordinator, Alliance for Progress.

discussions in Congress that you should go back to Congress for another resolution of support?

THE PRESIDENT. The evidence there is very clear for anybody that has read the resolution.[15]

First, the authority of the President is very clear and unquestioned without a resolution. The Commander in Chief has all the authority that I am exercising. But because of my desire to have the support of the Congress and to have them a part of any decision we make after consulting their leadership, exchanging viewpoints, and carefully drawing a resolution, we submitted to the Congress language that we thought would make it clear for all time, to one and all.

That language, just as a reminder to you, said the Congress approves and supports the determination of the President as Commander in Chief "to take all—all—all necessary measures to repel any—any—any armed attack against the forces of the United States" and, "to prevent further aggression."

Furthermore, the United States is prepared, as the President determines, to take all necessary steps, including the use of armed forces to assist any member or protocol state of the Southeast Asia Collective Defense Treaty requesting assistance in the defense of freedom.

Now, the resolution—and we carefully put this in, and this, I think, will give a full response to your question—this resolution shall expire when the President shall determine that the peace and security of the area is reasonably assured by international conditions created by the action of the U.N. or otherwise; it may be terminated earlier by

concurrent resolution of the Congress. I couldn't veto that resolution. We purposely put it in.

Anytime they want to take the authority the resolution gives me, they can take it away. It is just an expression and they just approved the position that we were taking. So we think that if there is anyone—and there will be some in a body of a hundred when from time to time we ask them to make appropriations, and there are such things as the military bills reported out today, and military assistance which has a lot of testimony in this connection and the economic bill just last week.

Anyone that wants to cannot only speak against us but can vote against us. We don't encourage it, and we think we are very fortunate that we are as unified as we are. The first vote was 502–2 and my study of history would indicate that that is rather unusual even for most extreme times.

I remember Jeannette Rankin of Montana[16] voting against a declaration of war. And on the last vote, I believe it was 10 out of 35. So we are very happy at the support we are receiving and the people are supporting us not only in this country but other places.

I told Senator Long[17] yesterday morning: Do not be dissuaded and do not become discouraged because I remember your father telling about the Louisiana farmer that stayed awake night after night because of the frogs barking in the pond. Finally he got irritated and angry and the way you all describe me—those of you that never come around here—and he went out and drained the pond and killed both frogs.

We aren't going to kill anybody but we recognize the frogs and the ponds and they

---

[15] The joint resolution (H.J. Res. 1145) to promote the maintenance of international peace and security in southeast Asia was approved on August 10, 1964 (Public Law 88–408, 78 Stat. 384).

[16] Jeannette Rankin, Representative from Montana 1917–1919 and 1941–1943.

[17] Senator Russell B. Long of Louisiana.

keep us awake sometimes. That is the freedom we love.

President Eisenhower told me about a prominent Soviet general who came into his office during the war and criticized one of the newspaper reporters. He was talking about some bad articles that had been written about him, and he thought they were unjust. And President Eisenhower told him he would consider it. The next day the Soviet general came back to the headquarters and said he wanted Merriman Smith, or whoever it was, court-martialed.

President Eisenhower said, "Here is a big book compiled on what they said about me." He said, "Before I left here I went home to see my mother and there were five Eisenhower boys there, and Milton is a liberal, progressive head of a university; one is a banker, the other is a constitutional lawyer; one is a professor; and one is an engineer." He said, "My father was a railroad man who married my mother when she was 19 years old and gave birth to five children. She had five boys—there had been six but there were five there that day, I believe it was, but two of those boys are ultra-conservatives and two of those boys are progressive liberals and one of them is General of the Army. I am over here fighting for that right and to preserve that right where a railroad man can marry a 19-year-old girl and produce five children and two of them can develop into conservatives and two liberals and one General of the Army."

So, I have been around Congress too long—35 years—not to understand that there are going to be different viewpoints but I applaud and appreciate the assistance that General Eisenhower, who is the only President of the other party that is living, has given me.

I read last night a very lengthy report of a briefing that he had received and his reac-

tions and I have asked him to come back to the White House from time to time, and don't you think there is an emergency when he walks in. He is going to be here the latter part of this month, speaking to Howard.[18] I am going to talk to him then.

I consult with President Truman from time to time, but the strength the opposition party has given me is very much appreciated and the support of my own people. I don't know of any similar period in history with the great difficulties we are facing now that the Congress has performed more magnificently.

I may question some individual member some time close to election, but I am not going to quarrel with any this early.

FRANKLIN D. ROOSEVELT, JR.

[18.] Q. Mr. President, Franklin Roosevelt[19] said he would like to talk to you as to whether he should run for mayor or not. Are you going to see him?

THE PRESIDENT. I have not seen him. I have not talked to him. I will be happy to talk to him. I like him. He performed a very valuable service to this administration but I am not in the business of selecting mayors for any cities. I would, of course, be happy to talk to any prominent citizen, and I include Mr. Roosevelt in that group, who desire to talk to me about his future or any others. As a matter of fact, I talked to Franklin Roosevelt, Sr., about my future a good many times and I would feel very bad if I refused.

---

[18] On June 17, 1965, former President Dwight D. Eisenhower addressed an audience at Howard University in Washington, D.C., at a ceremony honoring 320 college students who were to spend the summer in Europe as "people-to-people" ambassadors.

[19] Franklin D. Roosevelt, Jr., Chairman, Equal Employment Opportunity Commission.

THE SUPERSONIC TRANSPORT

[19.] Q. Mr. President, is there anything you can tell us on the supersonic transport?

THE PRESIDENT. Yes. The Russians have made considerable advances in that field. We watched them with interest and we are glad they have been successful.

The French and the British have made rapid strides in that field and as you know it won't be long before they have their plane ready. We have carefully studied it and tested the sonic boom and other things necessary. I told the committee of the Vice President, the Secretary of the Treasury, Mr. Webb, Mr. McNamara, Mr. Halaby,[20] and others—we are going to build it if the Congress gives us some money. We want the best plane and we want one the airlines will buy, so, therefore, it must be a sizeable undertaking involving hundreds of millions— over a billion dollars for the first plane—and it has got to be at a price they will buy and can use to haul people 2,000 miles an hour, or however fast it goes—2,200 some of them. The Russian, I think, is 1,600.

To do that we have got to get the best brains in this country who know how to build a plane, and that is not a civil service worker or ex-governor or even manager of an airport.

So, Mr. McNamara and the Secretary of the Treasury—because of the balance of payments we want these people to buy our planes instead of buying abroad—Mr. McCone[21] worked with us because of his experience in business before he left; Mr. Webb because of the NASA interest. And we looked to try to get the best man in the United States without regard to politics, without regard to anything, and we think we got the best man in the United States. His name is "Bozo" McKee.

He was the head of Wright Field, he was a procurement expert, and Mr. McNamara said he has been on a good many different sides with him and against him, but he considered him the best man. Mr. Webb grabbed him up for the space program—he is 50 and some odd years and he has an $8,000 retirement—and so he got him and sent him to some of his NASA centers to give expert advice on procurement and building and construction, because that is his business. He built a lot of airplanes. He was in charge of Wright Field.

I called him one morning at 7:30—they agreed he was best—and I said, "What are you doing?" And he said he didn't have his britches on. And I said, "Get them on and come on up." I asked him to take this job and he said he didn't like the idea of being tied down and looked forward to a vacation. I said he could have it after he gave us air supremacy, and if he could do it after 2 or 3 years he could go back to Palm Springs or Nassau. And like most men trained by West Point and Annapolis, or whatever, he said, "If that is what the Commander in Chief wants me to do I will do it." ("I have been separated from my wife in three wars . . ."—that was Maxwell Taylor[22] who was separated from his wife.) I asked Mr. McKee to do the job. But they had gotten into an argument with General Quesada[23] and they had put a provision in the act that the head must be a civilian.

---

[20] James E. Webb, Administrator, National Aeronautics and Space Administration, Robert S. McNamara, Secretary of Defense, and N. E. Halaby, Administrator, Federal Aviation Agency.

[21] John A. McCone, former Director of the Central Intelligence Agency.

[22] Gen. Maxwell D. Taylor, U.S. Ambassador to South Viet-Nam.

[23] E. R. Quesada, former Administrator, Federal Aviation Agency.

The head or deputy is a general but he is not going to build a transport. We want the man to head it and be responsible for it, and we asked the Congress—as you do in extreme cases—to permit this man to move over from NASA, where he didn't have to be confirmed, to FAA at the same salary.

He kept his $8,000 retirement and got the job, whatever it pays—28 or 30. So, we sent the bill up there and Congressman Harris had been against the General because of the problem with General Quesada. But he thought it was merited, and I called him down in Arkansas and he said we ought to get the best man.

But he is the most experienced and he is the best now. The bill has passed the House overwhelmingly. Only one Democrat voted against it. It is in the Senate. It is up today and I hope, as I speak, the roll is called on it and I hope McKee will take that job.[24] And I told him we want him to go full steam ahead, around the clock, until we obtain the best plane at the best price that was achievable.

THE DENVER FLOOD DISASTER

[20.] Q. Mr. President, have you been apprised of the Denver flood disaster and have you taken any action?

THE PRESIDENT. Mr. Ellington[25] has that matter before him. It is a matter for the Governor. The Governor called me. I haven't been able to talk to him. Governor Ellington will talk to him and we will make all resources available to him.

Reporter: Thank you, Mr. President.

---

[24] A bill (H.R. 7777) authorizing the President to appoint Gen. William F. McKee to the office of Administrator, Federal Aviation Agency was approved on June 22, 1965 (Public Law 89–46, 79 Stat. 171).

[25] Buford Ellington, Director, Office of Emergency Planning, and former Governor of Tennessee.

FURTHER ANNOUNCEMENTS BY THE PRESIDENT
THE WHITE HOUSE STAFF

[21.] I have a couple of additional announcements to make. Doug Cater[26] has been working with Health, Education, and Welfare on the education bill and health bill, and he's been doing so well that I want to get him back where his time is not so divided. I hope that he can get back with the work of the Security Council, and I am going to ask him to. And as soon as I can I am going to move him over from the Executive Office Building. And I will probably move Horace Busby,[27] too. Both of them will be devotees of Mr. Bundy.

Are the wire services here?

Q. We'll tell them, Mr. President.

THE PRESIDENT. This is that pool that you're always seeking there. Busby will undertake a variety of duties. As you know, he now prepares statements for me, and does research, and analyzes, and gives me advice on a good many matters. But he will concentrate some on space, on defense, on various regions of the world, and various messages and correspondence that we will be sending to other countries. We have an exchange of things that go back and forth, and I'll have him attend to and specialize in that field, and there will be others, including this but not limited to this.

Mr. Cater will be working in foreign policy, generally. He'll be doing what he can to give us advice on cooperative efforts that we can make in matters like saline water, or against the ancient enemies of mankind, or in food, health, education, with other nations. That is a big problem. If

---

[26] S. Douglass Cater, Jr., Special Assistant to the President.

[27] Horace Busby, Jr., Special Assistant to the President.

we can get those people some food and clothing and housing and some education and
health, we would not be having all this
bombing. It would not be necessary to
make them.

They'll be working with USIA, keeping
in close touch with them. Both of them
will be working with certain international
organizations: SEATO, CENTO, NATO,
U.N.

They'll have increasingly important roles
in the preparation of all of my statements
and my press conferences. For that reason, they'll be kept informed of all major
national security matters, and they'll be present on all security matters. They may not
go to lunch with me on Tuesday. But they
don't mind. I'd be glad to have them there,
but they'll be in on official meetings and on
a good many of the unofficial ones. They
have both worked very closely with me for
a good many years on a series of subjects,
and they have been very helpful to me in
Viet-Nam, and the Dominican Republic,
and in other areas.

Now, Mr. Bundy will continue to head
the staff. He has several people specializing
in various areas, Bob Komer, Cooper,[28] and
different ones, and they'll still have their
regions. But these men will be working
within the fields I've told you about.

JUDICIAL APPOINTMENTS

[22.] I anticipate that I will name very
shortly Judge Homer Thornberry to the Circuit Court of Appeals of the 5th District of
Texas, and former Governor J. P. Coleman
of Mississippi.[29] Mr. Coleman is a former

---

[28] Robert W. Komer, Deputy Special Assistant to
the President for National Security Affairs, and
Chester L. Cooper, senior member of the National
Security Council staff.

[29] Also appointed to the United States Court of
Appeals for the Fifth Circuit.

attorney general of that State, a former judge
of that State, and a former Governor of that
State. Thornberry is a former district attorney, a former member of the city council, a former member of the legislature, a
former Member of the Congress. He's now
a district judge and he'll be promoted to
the circuit court.

Q. What was Governor Coleman to be?

Q. How about replacements?

THE PRESIDENT. That's a matter we'll
have to look into. I want to get the recommendation from the Bar Association. I
want to consult with Senator Yarborough.

Under the Constitution, the President ap-
points judges and the Senate confirms
judges. It doesn't mean necessarily that
when a bar association checks them because
of a practice they're in that we give the Bar
Association the appointment power of the
President. It doesn't mean that we give the
Senate the appointment power. If they're
not qualified they can always reject them.
The Bar Association does a good many times
in their judgment, and the President goes
ahead and acts anyway. I don't have the
record but a good many have been rejected.

A good many times men not qualified may
be personally obnoxious, but I would try to
select one that is qualified to meet the Bar
Association's requirements, one that is not
obnoxious. And I prefer someone who is
actually supported by Senator Yarborough
and is not offensive to any Member of the
Senate and has the qualifications of the job
beyond the peradventure of a doubt. I have
not gone in and considered anyone.

Judge Adrian Spears will move to Austin
and will reside in Austin and will succeed
Congressman Thornberry there.

Q. Mr. President, of course——

THE PRESIDENT. This is not another press
conference.

Q. Mr. Busby and Mr. Cater, of course,

will retain their present titles?

THE PRESIDENT. Yes, their same present titles. This is just an expansion of their duties.

Reporter: Thank you, Mr. President.

NOTE: President Johnson's forty-fourth news conference was held in his office at the White House at 4:15 p.m. on Thursday, June 17, 1965.

320   Remarks at a Ceremony in the State Department Auditorium in Honor of the Gemini 4 Astronauts. *June 17, 1965*

Mr. Secretary, Your Excellencies, astronauts, Mr. Mathews, Mr. Webb:

I am happy to be able to join with the Vice President here this evening to participate in this ceremony, to enjoy the film that we have just seen, to pay our respects to the astronauts, and to meet all of our visitors.

I am seldom accused of being at a loss for words. But I am sure all of you agree that there are no words that are really adequate to describe what we have just seen on that screen.

I should like to say to you gentlemen, that if I had seen your films before I saw you last week in Houston I might have made you full colonels.

It is so unusually fitting that we could view these films tonight here in the company of our diplomats and their families, including their young children, from every corner of the globe.

In 1958, when I presented this country's space proposals to the United Nations, I said then that we of America are determined that our quarrels and divisions here on this earth shall not be carried into this new and this very peaceful domain of space.

And sitting here watching this film, it struck me again how imperative it is. Colonel McDivitt and Colonel White were soaring 100 miles from this planet. And from that perspective, when the sun shines in all of its purity, how small, how meaningless seem the differences among men and among nations down below.

Surely, we on this earth, the heads of state, the diplomats, and the private citizens, can some way find it within ourselves to search for, and to reach for, those new perspectives which will enable us to understand one another a little better, and assure peace among the peoples of the world forever.

We of the United States are quite proud of this accomplishment by these fine young men, and by all who are part of our space exploration team.

But I would say to you tonight, from all the nations of earth, that pride is not what motivates us, and pride is not the end that we seek. We of America are motivated in these efforts to extend the human frontiers by the desires in our hearts for peace—and peace is the end that we seek in everything that we do.

I have said it before. I want to say it again. The world has no need for arms races or for moon races. What we ask and what we want is for all peoples in all lands— East and West—to pull back the curtains, to come through the walls, to join hands in common cause, and to take a great walk together towards peace on this earth.

And may I say to you, Colonel McDivitt, and to you, Colonel White, and you, Mr. Mathews, and you, Mr. Webb, that this may not make me too popular with your families. But I am going to ask you tonight— in the very next few hours—to take the Presidential plane and travel outside this country again.

685

Many peoples in many lands are thrilled, as we are thrilled, by what you have done. And as the details can be worked out, I want you to join our delegation in Paris at the Paris Air Show, and go out among the friendly peoples of earth to share with them the excitement and the thrills of your experience.

Always, we have meant for America's successes to be shared by all mankind, and we welcome the opportunity for all mankind to know you, and to see you, and to understand from you that our mission—and our only mission—is peace.

And the highest ranking official of this Government other than the man speaking to you, the distinguished Vice President is an apostle of peace. He has preached it in the Congress and in the world wherever he has gone. And I am going to ask him to have Mrs. Humphrey join you as an escort, and as a leader, and as a symbol of the Government of the United States, in the next few hours if you are ready. You won't travel quite as fast or nearly so far, but I hope you will enjoy your mission.

NOTE: The President spoke at 9:10 p.m. in the Department of State Auditorium. In his opening words he referred to Dean Rusk, Secretary of State, the Ambassadors and heads of missions from foreign countries, Lt. Col. James A. McDivitt and Lt. Col. Edwin H. White 2d, Gemini 4 astronauts, Charles W. Mathews, manager of the Gemini space flight program, and James E. Webb, Administrator, National Aeronautics and Space Administration.

On June 18 the astronauts and their wives left for Paris, accompanied by Vice President Hubert H. Humphrey and Mr. Webb.

See also Items 304, 310, 318.

321 The President's Statement to the Cabinet Following Passage of the Excise Tax Reductions. *June 18, 1965*

THE CONGRESS has acted with unparalleled promptness and cooperation in approving the reduction of excise taxes.

Chairman Mills, Chairman Byrd, Senator Long, the committees that handled the bill, and the entire Congress deserve a hearty vote of thanks for their fast action.

I am pleased with the strong bipartisan support which has brought about this long overdue relief for both consumers and producers.

The bill will reach the White House today.

I will immediately ask the Treasury Department, the Bureau of the Budget, the Council of Economic Advisers, and my own legal staff to begin the necessary technical review of the measure. I expect them to complete this review over the weekend. While they are working, our merchants will have time to take the necessary inventories to establish floor stock refunds.

The benefits of this measure will begin flowing to consumers, producers, and retailers on Tuesday.

This is the second major tax reduction I will have signed into law in the last year and one-half since I became President. These two measures will reduce the taxes of our citizens by about $18 billion each year.

Despite these reductions, Federal revenues during the period 1961–66 will grow about $18 billion. This compares with the $17.5 billion increase in the preceding 6-year period when there were no tax cuts.

We have also been able to reduce taxes while reducing our deficit almost in half. The deficit in 1964 was $8.2 billion. The budget deficit for the current year was estimated in my January 1965 Budget to be $6.3 billion, and now estimated at $3.8 billion.

These are solid and significant gains. They have come because Government, business, and labor have learned to work together.

This cooperation has been a decisive factor in the recordbreaking expansion of the American economy. We are now in the 52d month of that expansion. This is unequaled in peacetime. The reduction in excise taxes will help us to continue to grow.

I believe producers and retailers will match the responsible conduct of the Congress with equal responsibility by passing these reductions along to consumers. This will bring us lower prices, more purchasing power, and new jobs. Two million, two hundred thousand more Americans were working this May than last May. That is a great gain, but we can and must do better. Our tax cuts will help us to do better.

The Treasury has prepared a table showing the distribution of excise tax reduction next year by States.

First, it shows only the amount of tax reduction for calendar 1966—the July and January cuts. The additional reduction will be staged over several years following 1966.

Second, as this tax reduction, which represents increasing purchasing power, is spent and respent throughout the economy, the eventual benefit will be several times the total amount of the tax reduction itself, both for separate States and for the economy as a whole.

NOTE: The President delivered the statement at 11 a.m. to a meeting of the Cabinet in the Cabinet Room at the White House. In the statement he referred to Representative Wilbur D. Mills of Arkansas, Chairman of the House Ways and Means Committee, Senator Harry F. Byrd of Virginia, Chairman of the Senate Finance Committee, and Senator Russell B. Long of Louisiana, member of the Senate Finance Committee.

After the Cabinet meeting, the President addressed a gathering of White House correspondents as follows:

"The Press Office will have a statement from the President to the Cabinet on the passage of the excise tax reductions. We expect to receive that bill later in the day. The statement is self-explanatory, and I won't elaborate on it.

"We received detailed reports this morning on the international situation from Secretary of State Rusk, and Secretary of Defense, Mr. McNamara, in connection with the military figures.

"Mr. McNamara had an extended press conference yesterday, or the day before, and he has met with groups, and I think I will just ask Secretary Rusk today to review with you what he said to the Cabinet, and to be available for any questions that you may care to ask.

"I will have to excuse myself, and certain other Cabinet members have planes to catch, and luncheon appointments and so forth, and so if they want to, they can retire through the exit. Mr. Secretary, I submit you to their mercies."

Following the President's remarks, Secretary Rusk spoke to the group on U.S. efforts to reach a peaceful settlement in southeast Asia. The text of his remarks, released by the White House on June 18, is printed in the Department of State Bulletin (vol. 53, p. 6).

The Excise Tax Reduction Act of 1965 was approved by the President on June 21, 1965 (see Item 326).

322   Remarks at a Ceremony Marking the Progress of the Neighborhood Youth Corps. *June 18, 1965*

Secretary Wirtz, Mr. Shriver, Members of the Congress, honorees, ladies and gentlemen:

The Presidency has its cares and has its burdens, but it also has its great joys. And I am keeping no secret when I tell you that this is one of them.

It is a great pleasure for me this morning to welcome to the White House you three young people whose personal stories, I believe, help to explain what the war on poverty is all about—in a small way, really, what this Nation is all about.

I am happy to introduce to you Miss Bernice Del Rosso of Newark, New Jersey, the first volunteer who enrolled in the Youth Corps; Miss Shirley Rolland of Rienzi, Mississippi, Youth Corps enrollee number 10,000; and Mr. Robert Martinez of Wilmington, California, who just this very week became Youth Corps member number 100,000.

Last January the Youth Corps got its start by Secretary Wirtz and his associates taking the leadership after months of patient preparation. Bernice became the first enrollee. Since then, 532 Youth Corps programs in 50 States, the District of Columbia, and Puerto Rico have gone into operation.

The Federal Government is providing funds to States and to local governments, and to other nonprofit employers, so that they may enable young people to be contributors to society instead of society's burdens.

All Youth Corps programs have a common purpose—that is, to provide employment to young people while they finish their high school education, to provide full-time work and training to those who have dropped out of school and who lack the training and the skills to find jobs.

It is true that we live in a time of general economic expansion and national prosperity, for which we are very grateful. Total employment in May stood at 72,400,000—a gain of more than 900,000 since December. Factory employment today is at its highest peacetime level. Average weekly earnings are at an alltime high. But these averages do not cloud the fact that not all Americans share our prosperity.

Young people are the only group in our economy whose employment situation has not improved significantly in 1965. Gains in youth employment have not been enough to offset the enormous number of postwar babies that are now approaching adulthood.

Teenage unemployment stands at 14½ percent—more than three times the average for the population as a whole—and six times as many Negro youths as white youths are unemployed. Such conditions would be a tragedy in any nation. They are intolerable in America, because we are the wealthiest and the most powerful in all the world.

So, what are we doing? Well, we are determined to use our wealth, and to use our power, and to use our ingenuity to change these conditions.

I just received from our very able and popular Vice President a report on the youth opportunity campaign, which we recently launched. It is a new offensive on poverty and on unemployment. The Vice President reports that so far more than 300,000 summer jobs for young people have already been provided by Federal, and by State, and by local governments, and by private industry. This is a magnificent response and the reports of the progress are still coming in, which indicate that we will soon reach our goal and go over the top with a 500,000 figure that we originally set.

These young people whom we greet today are living symbols of the success of the Youth Corps, and I am very happy to take these few moments this afternoon to meet with them, to reaffirm our deep conviction that the work of this Nation is not constructing bombs but building opportunities for greater liberty and security and happiness for all of our citizens.

I have talked to a number of the Governors in the States of this Union, and I have asked them to take the leadership that we are trying to take in the Nation—to call together not only their State officials who have employer contacts and who do a lot of employing themselves, but to call together the leaders of industry in their areas to see what can be done now to correct this 14½ percent teenage unemployment.

Thank you for coming here. We look forward, in the days ahead, to getting the results which we have talked about.

NOTE: The President spoke at 1:30 p.m. in the Rose Garden at the White House. In his opening words he referred to W. Willard Wirtz, Secretary of Labor, and R. Sargent Shriver, Jr., Director of the Office of Economic Opportunity.

The ceremony honored Bernice Del Rosso of Newark, N.J., the 1st volunteer to enroll in the Youth Corps, Shirley Rolland of Rienzi, Miss., the 10,000th volunteer, and Robert Martinez of Wilmington, Calif., the 100,000th volunteer. Beverly Jackson of Cleveland, Ohio, the 1,000th volunteer, was congratulated earlier by the Secretary of Labor at his office. She was not present at this ceremony.

323   The President's Statement to the Cabinet on Project Head Start. *June 19, 1965*

THIS SUMMER more than 500,000 children from low-income families will be enrolled in Project Head Start Child Development Centers throughout the United States. More than 2,000 communities will join in giving these children a better chance to succeed when they start to school next fall. Tens of thousands of Americans are giving unselfishly of their time and skills to this nationwide war on poverty. Their dedication is the best proof we have that this war will be won.

Mrs. Johnson is Honorary Chairman of Project Head Start. On June 30, Sargent Shriver, Director of the Office of Economic Opportunity, will present her with the insignia of Head Start. On that day, in all the communities with a Head Start project, the local officials will raise a similar flag. It will serve as a symbol of hope to the thousands of families whose children will take part in Head Start.

Mrs. Johnson and I are proud of the Nation's response to Head Start. I want to call on all Americans to join with us in declaring Wednesday, June 30, Head Start Day, and to give wholehearted support to this vital undertaking.

NOTE: On June 30, 1965, in a ceremony held in the East Room at the White House, Mr. Shriver presented the first Head Start flag to Mrs. Lyndon B. Johnson. The red, white, and blue banner, with a design of building blocks, had an arrow pointing upward to represent the uplifting of spirits.

324   The President's Statement to the Cabinet on Approving New Guidelines for Employee Health Service Programs. *June 20, 1965*

THE EFFICIENCY and productivity of Government employees is one of our primary concerns. We have made excellent progress in reducing costs and improving operations and will continue to press vigorously for savings and increased efficiency.

Employee productivity depends on a number of factors—motivation, training, challenging work, fair pay, and recognition of superior performance. But there is another factor that we must not overlook—good health. In some ways it is the key factor.

Good health and good work go together. Within the Government itself, we must do all we can to avoid the waste that results from sickness and disease. The Federal health benefits program provides prepaid health and medical protection to our employees. But it is just as important to provide for a strong preventive health service program.

—Each year about 20 million days of sick leave are taken by Federal civilian employees.

—If we can reduce the amount of sick leave taken by the average employee by just one-half day, it means the equivalent of over 1 million man-days per year. We will improve the motivation and productivity of our employees and at the same time reduce costs through better placement and utilization.

In the final analysis, it is up to each employee—and each top official—to take care of his own health. Health is a personal responsibility. I want to emphasize that.

But we can be a good employer. We can help our workers to maintain their health and thereby prevent the kind of illness and disablement that brings discouragement, hardship, and loss of productivity.

Private industry in the United States discovered long ago that a good employee health maintenance program is a paying proposition. The Federal Government has not kept up with the example set by private employers. I want that situation to change.

I want the Federal Government to start to catch up with the practices of our efficient private enterprise—and in time become a model.

We must be prepared—to the best of our ability—to assure our employees of

—prompt attention to on-the-job illness and injury,

—correction of working conditions that may be detrimental to employees' health,

—education in health maintenance,

—health examinations, including in-service examinations as needed, and

—disease screening examinations and immunizations.

I repeat that the individual employee must bear the primary responsibility to obtain frequent health checkups, and otherwise to take proper care of himself.

In 1950, President Truman issued health service guidelines to the Federal agencies but there has been no updating since that time. I have approved new guidelines for employee health service programs to be issued by the Director of the Budget. The Chairman of the Civil Service Commission will take the leadership in developing and improving this program in cooperation with the Secretary of Health, Education, and Welfare and the Secretary of Labor.

NOTE: On June 18, 1965, the Director of the Bureau of the Budget issued a memorandum to the heads of executive departments and establishments on Federal employees' occupational health service programs (Circular No. A–72, 5 pp., mimeographed).

325 Statement by the President on Announcing the First International Symposium on Water Desalination. *June 20, 1965*

A SHORTAGE of fresh water is one of the most critical problems facing the nations of the world. Developing nations which face rapid population growth must establish adequate fresh water supplies if they are to achieve their potential. The world's seas and oceans offer an inexhaustible supply of fresh water—if economically feasible methods of desalting can be developed.

The United States has been deeply involved in recent years in desalination research, sharing the results of this research with other nations:

—A study is underway, supported jointly by the United States and Israel, to determine the feasibility of a large dual-purpose power-water plant for construction on the Mediterranean coast south of Tel Aviv.

—American experts have visited the United Arab Republic and Tunisia to review water needs there and to study possible ways of solving water-supply problems through desalting.

—The United States has offered the services of the Office of Saline Water, an agency of the Department of the Interior, to the Government of Saudi Arabia as it works to bring water to the arid Jidda area.

—Teams of visitors from Greece, Italy, Spain, Mexico, and other nations have visited U.S. desalting facilities and shared information with this Nation's experts in the field. And the United States recently agreed with the Soviet Union to exchange information and visits by specialists in the water-desalting field.

Much of the information about desalting provided to other nations has been based on Government and industrial work in desalting to solve domestic water supply problems:

The largest water desalting plant operating in the United States produces over a million gallons of fresh water a day, and even more efficient forms of desalting are under study. The Interior Department's Office of Saline Water has awarded 15 contracts for design studies aimed at achieving a desalting plant which would produce up to 50 million gallons of water per day.

The State of California, the city of San Diego, and the Interior Department cooperated in the construction of the Point Loma Desalting Plant, which was moved to Guantanamo Bay, Cuba, in 1964 to meet U.S. Navy water needs there.

Discussions have begun between the Interior Department and the State of California for a joint Federal-State research station in California to test components of multi-million gallon per day desalting plants. Studies by the Atomic Energy Commission and the Interior Department are inquiring into the possibility of building a nuclear desalting installation in southern California.

The knowledge developed through these programs will be available at the October symposium to all nations which need it and can benefit from work in the area of salt-water conversion.

NOTE: The First International Symposium on Water Desalination, held in Washington October 3–9, 1965, was attended by delegates from 54 countries. It was one of the major events of the International Cooperation Year.

See also Items 494, 547, 558.

---

326   Remarks at the Signing of the Excise Tax Reduction Bill.
June 21, 1965

Distinguished Members of the Congress, ladies and gentlemen:

This is a bright day for all Americans.

Very shortly I will sign into law a bill that at midnight will lift $1¾ billion of onerous taxes from the American economy; that next January will ease the tax burden by a further $1¾ billion; that will pay big dividends in lower prices, in more jobs, in more sales, and in more production, not just in this year of

1965, but in 1966 and in many years to come thereafter.

So, this afternoon I want to personally congratulate the entire Congress for its very prompt and its very efficient and effective action on this matter. I asked the Congress on May 17 to reduce excise taxes. They have now completed action on that bill in exactly 32 days.

This is another shining chapter in the legislative record that a great Congress is writing—a new chapter of progress in American life.

The enactment of this bill reflects the confidence of the administration and the Congress that the benefits of excise tax reductions will be passed along to the American consumer. We can expect no less from our competitive business system.

This bill is now our third major tax action in 3 years.

The Revenue Act of 1962 introduced a bold new concept without precedent in American fiscal history—a 7-percent tax credit for business investment in new equipment. It laid the foundation for a sustained advance in business investment.

That uninterrupted advance has brought investment in equipment in the first quarter of 1965 to $38 billion, an increase of 52 percent in 4 years. And it is continuing. It is bringing rich rewards in the modernization of our entire industrial plant, in better products, in more efficient production, in lower costs, and, finally, in hundreds of thousands of new jobs for the working people of America.

Early last year, the Congress, in its wisdom, passed the Revenue Act of 1964. This second major tax reform simplified our income taxes, and made them fairer, and it reduced by $14 billion the taxes that American consumers and businesses owe on their 1965 incomes.

And this bill, which I am signing today, will eliminate an additional $4.7 billion of excise taxes.

The tax actions of 1962, and 1964, and 1965, taken together, are the mark of a vigorous new philosophy in our fiscal affairs.

Through the rigorous and never-ending pruning of waste, we have found the means for new programs already in education, in health, in urban and regional development, in the war on poverty, in large-scale strengthening of social efforts toward a better America, and in many new health programs.

Through a careful concern for private incentives, our tax system now better promotes growth, and efficiency, and opportunity.

And through a prudent control over total expenditures and total revenues, we have supplied consumers and businesses an expanding volume of purchasing power. The use of that growing purchasing power:

—has carried national output to a rate that is currently running in excess of $650 billion—compared with $500 billion in the first quarter of 1961;

—has raised wages and salaries by $76 billion in 4 years;

—has raised corporate profits after taxes by $17 billion;

—has reduced the unemployment rate from 7.1 percent in May 1961 to 4.6 percent in May 1965;

—has created more than 5½ million new jobs in these 4 years.

When we cut taxes last year, there were some who felt that lower taxes could renew an expansion already old by all past standards. They were wrong.

Today that old expansion has surpassed all peacetime records for duration. In its 52d month, it displays today the youthful vigor, the healthy balance, which promises to keep it going as far into the future, as the

Secretary of the Treasury said only yesterday, that we can really see.

Others feared that we were squandering the Federal revenues that were needed to reduce our deficit. And they, too, were mistaken.

Our budget has really fared better than most of us had expected.

In January 1964, we estimated a deficit for fiscal year 1964 of $10 billion. It turned out to be $8.2 billion. In January 1965, we expected a deficit of $6.3 billion for fiscal year 1965. It now appears that it will be close to $3.8 billion.

In the 5-year period 1961 to 1966 we expect that Federal revenues will have increased more than in the preceding 6 years—when there were no tax cuts at all.

We have proved that a healthy budget depends on a healthy economy. And all of us—Government officials, managers, employees, and consumers—are determined to keep our economy healthy.

A healthy economy is free of inflation. Over the past 5 years our price stability has been unmatched in the industrial world. The average level of our wholesale prices in May was only 1.7 percent higher than its average in 1958.

So, this price stability has reflected both prudent monetary and fiscal policies and the responsible actions of both labor and management.

In May, the average manufacturing worker earned $4.56 more a week than he did in May of last year. And he was also earning better pensions, and better vacations, and better insurance. Yet because the gains in his union contracts stayed, on the average, within the rise in productivity, average unit labor costs in manufacturing last month were really lower than a year earlier—or lower then they were 4 years earlier.

So, we are counting on management and on labor to continue to act responsibly in setting prices and wages. The Nation both expects and deserves it to act in the national interest.

And this excise tax bill will make its maximum contribution to our economic health only if businesses pass along to the consumers the full amount of the reduction in the tax. And today I urge every manufacturer, and every retailer in this country, to do just that.

I am pleased that the Congress saw fit to leave substantially unchanged my recommendations for excise tax reduction in 1965 and 1966.

The only major change the Congress made was the additional reduction in the automobile tax in later years.

I had recommended a five-point reduction in that tax, and the Congress decided to increase this to nine points.

But by postponing the additional four-point reduction, the Congress allowed time for possible modification if future developments should indicate that that would be desirable.

We in the executive branch will be carefully considering the possible constructive uses that might be made of the 1 percent automobile excise which the Congress decided to retain. This revenue could help to solve such related national problems as automobile safety, air pollution, highway beauty, and the disposal of discarded and abandoned automobiles.

If we should find that the need for these purposes—or the fiscal situation generally—should require retention of more than the 1 percent tax on automobiles, there will be ample time for the Congress then to consider our recommendations.

When there is again opportunity for tax revision, we hope, in particular, to provide further tax relief to those in our Nation who need it most—those taxpayers who now live in the shadow of poverty.

Tax revision is a job—as all of you congressional leaders know—that is really never finished. Our tax system must be continually geared to the needs of a healthy and a growing economy.

Such an economy provides both the foundation for our national security and for a better life for all of our citizens.

So, to the members of the Senate Finance Committee, and to the members of the House Ways and Means Committee, and to the membership of the two Houses respectively, I say to you, on behalf of a grateful people, you have done your job well.

Thank you.

NOTE: The President spoke at 4 p.m. in the East Room at the White House.

As enacted, the Excise Tax Reduction Act of 1965 is Public Law 89–44 (79 Stat. 136). For the President's message to Congress of May 17, 1965, requesting the legislation, see Item 255.

Reports to the President on the effect of the excise tax reduction on consumer prices by Gardner Ackley, Chairman of the Council of Economic Advisers, were released by the White House on July 24, August 18, September 22, and November 29 (1 Weekly Comp. Pres. Docs., pp. 4, 108, 299, 542).

327   Statement by the President on the Death of Bernard Baruch. *June 21, 1965*

BERNARD BARUCH was in the robust tradition of the philosopher-politician: one who thought and cared mightily about the course of his country but who did not shrink from actively doing what needed to be done to keep his country on course.

He loved his Nation and he lived for his Nation and that was enough to enroll him in an aristocracy of humanity.

328   Letter to the Secretary, Smithsonian Institution, on the Transfer to the Institution of the Original Corcoran Gallery of Art. *June 23, 1965*

Dear Dr. Ripley:

I am enthusiastic about your suggestion that the Smithsonian Institution take over the old U.S. Court of Claims Building and establish it as a gallery of arts, crafts and design.

No more appropriate purpose for the building could be proposed than to exhibit, in the restored gallery, examples of the ingenuity of our people and to present exhibits from other nations, whose citizens are so proud of their arts.

I would hope that tours of this Gallery might play a memorable part in the official Washington visits of foreign heads of State, offering them not only a glimpse of our art but an opportunity to enjoy the friendliness and hospitality of our people.

I have therefore approved your recommendation, and am instructing Mr. Lawson Knott, Administrator of the General Services Administration, to transfer the building to the Smithsonian Institution under existing authority. This is contingent, of course, upon your obtaining authorization for the funds necessary to renovate the building for use as a gallery.

With kindest regards,

Sincerely,

LYNDON B. JOHNSON

[Dr. S. Dillon Ripley, Secretary, Smithsonian Institution, Washington, D.C.]

NOTE: Excerpts of the letter were made public as part of a White House release which stated that the President's letter was in reply to a suggestion by Dr. Ripley that the building, which was occupied by the Corcoran Gallery from 1869 until 1897, be restored to use as an art gallery. The building was designed by James Renwick, architect of the original Smithsonian Institution building, and was acquired by the United States in 1901.

The release noted that the project would be undertaken as part of the renovation of the Lafayette Square area.

329   Remarks at the Democratic Congressional Dinner in the Washington Hilton Hotel. *June 24, 1965*

Senator Long, Senator Mansfield, Senator Hayden, Senator Magnuson, Congressman Albert, Congressman Kirwan, Chairman Bailey, Neil Curry, and distinguished and beloved committee c h a i r m e n of the Congress:

I came here tonight not to bury the Congress, but to praise it. I came not to purge its selection, but to urge its reelection. I come not to talk about the mistakes of the past, but to rejoice in the adventures of the future.

I am a child of the Congress. For more than 30 years the Hill was my home, and I am here tonight among those that I know, and that I respect and that I love.

And as if to give towering substance to my words tonight, this Congress that I speak about, in one day—today—moved on many, many fronts toward even higher achievements.

Today the Education-Labor Committee of the House reported the higher education bill to the House, a bill which will be one of the enduring monuments of this Congress.

Today this Committee under the chairmanship of Chairman Powell, reported the arts and humanities bill, and the mine safety bill, and the disaster relief bill.

Today the Senate Finance Committee, under the leadership of Senator Long and Senator Anderson and other Senators here present this evening, voted out the medical care for the aged bill that Chairman Mills passed a few days ago. Next Wednesday, this bill, second in importance only to the social security bill and of the highest value to every citizen of our land, will be on the floor of the Senate for debate according to Senator Mansfield's plans.

Today the Senate Banking and Currency Committee voted out the housing bill of 1965.

Today the Senate Labor and Public Welfare Committee reported out the heart and the cancer and the stroke measure, the community mental health center bill, the health research facilities amendment, and all three of these bills the majority leader, Senator Mansfield, tells me will be on the floor of the Senate tomorrow for action.

Today the Government Operations Subcommittee voted out the Department of Urban Affairs bill in the Senate. It has already passed the House.

Today the Senate passed, by a vote of 74 to 9, the silver coinage bill.

Today the House passed the juvenile delinquency bill and the extension of the area redevelopment bill.

Today the conferees agreed on the Presidential disability and succession bill; and the conferees reported the Post Office, Treasury, and Executive Office appropriation bill.

All of this happened in one day, in time for us to come to dinner tonight.

I used to think when I had some little position up in the Congress that I had had a good week, but when I look over these 17 measures that have been handled in the House committee and the House floor, and the Senate committee and the Senate floor, I just wonder if I wasn't in the kindergarten class.

So no wonder this 89th Congress will leap into history as the most effective and the most rewarding Congress in the history of our Nation.

And I want to say to each person at this head table and to every person in this audience, that you can be proud that you are doing your part to help reelect a Democratic Congress come next year.

We know of the sacrifices you have made, we know of the tickets you have bought, we have got the greatest and the biggest and the finest dinner in the history of the party, and we thank each one of you and love you for it.

Over the years, the opponents of our party and our purposes have followed one consistent strategy over and over again. On every issue they have tried to divide Democrats—but without success, until tonight.

I have always had the fear that if anything ever split the Democratic Party in two, it would be one of our two dinners.

So I suppose it might be said that a good Democrat needs a good head and a good heart all the time, and good legs and feet at election time, and certainly a good stomach in between times.

You don't know how proud I am to be here with you tonight.

Our system in this land is the most successful that any nation has ever known. And, at this moment in our national life, that system is functioning more successfully than we have ever known.

We are strong.

We are sure of our purposes.

We enjoy peace.

We have plenty—and we mean to see that all of our people share more fully in our abundance.

All that we have in these good times has not come to us in the last 20 months—or the last 40 months—or even the last 40 years. It is the harvest of the hard labors and the patient toils of all the generations of Americans who have helped to guide and who have helped shape our destiny through the full course of this Republic's 189 years.

But when men seek the secret of America's success it seems to me that the answer lies along two long and bright and unbroken threads woven in the fabric of our national life.

The first of these is that great body of the representatives of the people—which stands at the very center of our system—the Congress of the United States of America.

In peace and in war, and in prosperity and in depression, the men and women chosen by the people themselves have never failed the purposes or the principles or the responsibilities of just and decent, and unselfish and unfearing people. There have been strong Congresses and there have been weak ones. There have been good Congresses and there have been poor ones. But I am prepared to argue—with more than usual persuasion, and twist an arm if it is absolutely necessary—that the Congress that is meeting now will be remembered in our history as the greatest of them all.

What this Congress has done to meet the responsibility of educating America's youth would of itself assure its rank high in history—and when it is concluded, this Congress will be remembered for having—

—guaranteed to every American the right to vote whatever his color and wherever he lives.

—guaranteed to every American past the age of 65 protection against the cost of hospital care and other incidental benefits.

This Congress will be remembered by these measures—and by many more—which add to the health and the happiness and the vitality of our people as well as the prosperity of our system. But this Congress will also be remembered in history for the strong and the resolute and the uncompromising support that it has given—and is giving now—to support and to defend freedom against aggression and subversion in the world.

And so I want to say to you, my friends, here tonight, that your country has only one purpose—the purpose that I believe is in each of your hearts: that purpose is peace for all peoples. We covet no territory. We seek no dominion. We want nothing for ourselves except that our neighbors and our friends and our fellow free men shall be able to live their lives and work their destinies unmolested by their neighbors in any part of the world.

And this Congress—like the great Congresses before it—is taking the hard choices and making the brave decisions that have and will continue to keep this world free and safe for all of the works of lasting peace.

The responsibility of the Congress is one of the golden threads that brighten the fabric of our national life.

Along with the vital role that Congress has played in all of our history, there is the responsible role of which we are all heirs and of which we are all trustees: that is the role of the great Democratic Party of which we are all members.

For 165 years—since it was founded in 1800 by that great Democrat, Thomas Jefferson—our party has received the people's trust because it has been and it is tonight the party that is striving to fill the people's needs

and the people's aspirations—and we will not fail.

You and I are present in Washington at a time I believe to be one of the most exciting and one of the most creative and one of the most significant in the history of our national life. Seldom before have any people anywhere ever undertaken—as the American people are undertaking now—to shape consciously the quality and the worth and the value of our society for many generations yet to come.

Along their streets and in their gardens, and through the rural countryside, Americans are now volunteering to add beauty to their lands and to their lives. But, far more importantly, they are going into the dark corners and the shadows of our society to extend their helping hand to the children of the poor who have never seen a picture book, or heard a story read, or looked at a television, or had a tablet in their homes on which they could draw and make their marks and their letters.

Yes, Americans are volunteering their time and their talent and their spirit—in unparalleled numbers—to help their fellow man, the young and the old, the forgotten and the neglected.

This spirit that runs in our land knows no partisanship—it knows no party. But we as Democrats are trustees of that spirit—and we must ever be faithful to that trust.

We must give, ourselves, all the energy and talent of our party to those specific things that unite America—not to those things that divide America.

I hope I haven't said a thing disrespectful of anyone or a thing that would divide any American because we must have the courage to fulfill not only the ideals of our party but the aspirations of our society and the promises of our Constitution.

Our house is large—and it is open. It is

open to all, those who agree and those who dissent. And we mean to keep it open—for if our society is to be great, it must first of all be free.

I shall never forget when I came here in 1931. I went over with a young Congressman who had just been elected, and I was his secretary, and carrying along the briefcase, and he met the great leader from the great State of Arizona—Carl Hayden.

He asked that beloved character for advice. He had come to the Congress when his State came in the Union, and he had enough experience to give it. He said then what I have thought of so often these 20 months that I have been President. He said, "Congressman, I learned after I had been here only a few days that there are two kinds of horses in the Congress—the showhorses and the workhorses." He said, "There will be a time when it comes for you to speak, and speak your heart and your head. But wait for that time and always remember that you don't ever have to explain something you didn't say."

Well, I recounted for you just a moment ago what, under the leadership of Mike Mansfield, my beloved friend, my cherished neighbor, Carl Albert, what the House and Senate did today—17 bills moved on up the Hill toward serving the needs of a growing, a developing, a vital America.

It gives me so much pleasure and so much pride to be able to say to my great Chairman, John Bailey, that the work that you did for

us in 1964—that you said so little about—is now showing up on the statute books of our country. And when I go from here to the other dinner this evening—the dinner that divided us—and I have checked out my desk before I left and I am sure that it is locked and nobody is going to break into it, but while these people talk about ethics, we are going to talk about the future. And after I shall have concluded over there I am going on out to see one of the great men of our times and one of the greatest fighting leaders our party ever had—Harry Truman.

And I think I will be able to tell him tomorrow morning at 7 o'clock at breakfast, not about that awful, terrible, do-nothing 80th Congress of showhorses, but I will be telling him about that wonderful Congress of workhorses.

NOTE: The President spoke at 9:20 p.m. at the Washington Hilton Hotel.

In his opening words he referred to Senator Russell B. Long of Louisiana, majority whip of the Senate, Senator Mike Mansfield of Montana, majority leader of the Senate, Senator Carl Hayden of Arizona, President of the Senate Pro Tempore, Senator Warren G. Magnuson of Washington, Representative Carl Albert of Oklahoma, majority leader of the House of Representatives, Representative Michael J. Kirwan of Ohio, John M. Bailey, Chairman of the Democratic National Committee, and Neil J. Curry of Los Angeles, honorary chairman of the Democratic congressional dinners.

Later he referred to Representative Adam C. Powell of New York, Senator Clinton P. Anderson of New Mexico, and Representative Wilbur D. Mills of Arkansas.

Following his remarks the President left for the District of Columbia Armory where another congressional dinner was in progress (see Item 330).

330 Remarks at the Democratic Congressional Dinner in the D.C. Armory. *June 24, 1965*

Mr. Kirwan, Mr. Speaker, Senator Magnuson, Chairman Bailey, distinguished committee chairmen, my fellow Democrats, ladies and gentlemen:

I am enjoying this night much more than you really know. With not one but two dinners to attend, I have an excuse to eat two desserts tonight and Lady Bird can't say a thing about it—at least until we get back to the White House.

I am very proud to join in this salute to the 89th Congress and to all the Democratic Members in both the House of Representatives and the Senate. I came out here tonight not to bury the Congress but to praise it. I came not to purge its selection but to urge its reelection. I came not to talk about the mistakes of the past but to rejoice in the adventures of the future.

I am a child of the Congress. For more than 30 years the Hill was my home. I am here tonight among those that I know, and those that I respect, and those that I love.

And as if to give towering substance to my words tonight, the Congress in one day—today—moved on many fronts toward even higher achievements.

Today the Education and Labor Committee of the House of Representatives reported the higher education bill to the House, and that is a bill which will be one of the enduring monuments of this Congress.

Today this same Committee, under the chairmanship of Chairman Powell, reported the arts and humanities bill, and the mine safety bill, and the disaster relief bill.

Today the Senate Finance Committee voted out our medical care bill for the aged. We liberals have talked about that bill for many years, but this year we Democrats are going to pass it. Next Wednesday this measure, that is second in importance only to the Social Security Act and of the very highest value to every citizen of our land, will be on the floor of the Senate for debate.

Today the Senate Banking and Currency Committee voted out the housing bill.

And today the Senate Labor and Public Welfare Committee reported out the heart and cancer and stroke health measure, and the community mental health center bill, and

the health research facilities amendments, and all three of these bills will be on the Senate floor tomorrow, and I hope before the sun goes down they will have passed that body.

Today the Government Operations Subcommittee voted out the Department of Urban Affairs bill in the Senate—and the House has already passed that bill, I need not tell you.

Today the Senate passed, by a vote of 74 to 9, the silver coinage bill.

Today the House passed the juvenile delinquency bill; and the House passed an extension to the Area Redevelopment Administration bill.

And today the conferees of the House and the Senate agreed on the Presidential inability and succession bill; and the conferees reported the Post Office, Treasury, and Executive Office appropriation bill—and that is a real important bill.

And Mrs. McCormack, all this happened in just one day—17 bills.

Now I know you are proud of your husband, the beloved Speaker, but we are proud of all the Congress, and no wonder—this 89th Congress will leap into history as the most effective and the most rewarding Congress for all the people in all the history of America.

And no one knows better than I do that the record of any Congress—and the record, for that matter, of any President—depends finally upon the quality of the leadership in both Houses of the legislative branch.

I am very proud to say that this 89th Congress has leadership—good, strong, wise, experienced, progressive Democratic leadership of the very highest quality.

When some day the world lives in peace, and when the peoples of this hemisphere live together in justice and prosperity, men will honor the name of the good and gentle man who leads the Democratic Party in the Senate of the United States, Mike Mansfield, the majority leader.

And, likewise, when Americans see the ideals of their system fulfilled, and when they live in a society that is made great by the people's will, they will give their credit to the man who led the historic legislative breakthrough—the majority leader of the House of Representatives, Carl Albert of Oklahoma.

But history has already reserved a very large and a very important place of respect and affection for the great and good American who puts his country ahead of his party, and always his party ahead of himself—the wise and the diligent, the conscientious warmhearted friend of all the people of the United States, Speaker John McCormack of Massachusetts.

I paid my respects to that young progressive from the South, Russell Long, at the other dinner, but all these measures that we have talked about had to have votes to pass them and to report them and send them to the White House. And we couldn't have gotten those votes except for the enduring patience, and perseverance, and hard work, and intelligent grasp of matters as exhibited in the House of Representatives by our beloved friend, Hale Boggs from New Orleans—and George Smathers from Florida.

George and Hale are not only two of the best looking men in the Senate and the House—and the country—but they are two of the most effective.

Now, at this point I think I should announce that I have only 357 more Democrats to go—before I begin the speech of the evening!

Well, I came out here tonight because I wanted to say to you that as Americans—and as Democrats—we are an honored generation. We are living in a very rare and

a very special moment in history.

No other Americans—certainly no other Democrats—have had entrusted to their hands the substance of history such as this moment has placed in ours now.

The more than 50 major bills enacted last year—because they were presented to the Congress by that fearless, outstanding, beloved late President of ours, John Fitzgerald Kennedy, we kept his faith and the Congress was true to his trust; and those bills were enacted and became law because of his vision and his foresight—the 19 major measures that we have already passed this year, and the some 70 more that are still to come, do not represent victories of party but they do represent victories of and for and by the people.

So, in these times of our abundance and our comfort and our safety, it is an enduring victory—for all the people—when their Congress is moved and motivated, as the people themselves are, by conscience and by courage and by abiding conviction.

It is a victory for the people when conscience moves their Congress—

—to declare war on human poverty in this land and to do something about it;

—to open the abundance of our harvest to the hungry people all around the world and to do something about it;

—to offer fresh hope to the worn region of Appalachia and to do something about it;

—to promise the dignity of medical care to our aged and then to do something about it, as we are going to do next week.

Yes, this is a very great victory for the people of America when conscience and courage and conviction moves their Congress—

—to guarantee, as this Congress very soon will, every American in this land the right to vote,

—to assure, as Congress did last year, that

every American shall be treated equally in places of public accommodation without fear of indignity because of his color or his creed,

—to assure, as Congress will this year, that families may be reunited from other lands—I hope I am prophesying correctly, Mr. Speaker—and that valuable new citizens can come to America from places across the seas to see their families without humiliation or inhumanity,

—or to make certain, as Congress has, in the most important measure that I think I shall ever sign, that every boy and girl born in America, regardless of his race or religion or his creed, shall have the opportunity for the best education that he or she can absorb from the first grade onward to the highest grades.

Yes, I think it is a victory—a victory for the people—when Congress is moved by the courage—

—to lift off the burden of wartime tax rates on incomes and place its confidence in our economy to produce the growth that produces jobs to keep America's promise to our growing population,

—to reduce taxes by more than $18 billion in less than 18 months to sustain the longest peacetime economic expansion that this Nation, or any other nation, has ever known,

—to face up squarely to the challenges of America's cities, where 80 percent of our people will live in 35 years, and

—to meet boldly the opportunities of conservation and b e a u t y in America's countryside.

Yes, it is, finally, a victory for the people when Congress is moved by abiding convictions, deep within the heart and soul of this Nation, to stand up before the world to declare the will of the United States of America to resist aggression, to defend freedom, to honor our treaties, and, above all,

to work without ceasing anywhere, anytime for the peace of mankind everywhere in the world.

In a very short while I shall be leaving this hall to fly across the continent—first to meet with a man whose name is written forever among the heroes of freedom, Harry S. Truman—and then to fly on to San Francisco to renew there the pledge of support that President Truman gave 20 years ago this week to the United Nations.

For 20 years now—20 years of trial and testing—the purpose of this Nation has never wavered for a moment, and I want to tell you that it is strong, and it is steady, and it is sure tonight. And in this week we seek nothing of others. All we want is peace and justice for all—and that is America's purpose.

For 20 years we have journeyed a road of danger—and neither the journey nor the danger is near an end. In our land—and around the world—we would far rather use our hands than our arms. For we want to walk and to work at the side of mankind to help him overcome poverty and disease and ignorance and bias and fear. But we cannot do the works that we want to do—mankind cannot make the gains that all peoples yearn to make—so long as there are those who are unwilling to leave their neighbors alone and in peace.

And I take with me the assurance of the Congress—and my own determination that:

—So long as peril remains we shall remain prepared.

—So long as peace is weak we shall remain strong.

—So long as Communist aggression challenges freedom we shall meet it.

I remember that a great Democrat, Woodrow Wilson, once told us that there is "something better . . . that a man can give than his life." That is, Woodrow Wilson

701

said, "his living spirit—given to a service that is not easy, to resist counsels that are hard to resist, to stand against purposes that are difficult to stand against."

Well, you are giving such a living spirit—and in so doing you honor your party by honoring first your country. For it is not as Democrats, and it is not as partisans, and it is not as members of factions that we shall prove ourselves worthy of the public's trust, but it is only as free men and only as Americans first.

My heart bursts with pride tonight when I look at this head table and come back to the scenes of my childhood, so to speak. I see the distinguished chairman—I can't see all the way down there—Mike Monroney, and Alan Bible, and Everett Jordan, and Bill Dawson, and that wonderful Tom Morgan, Joe Evins, and the rest of them at the other end of the table. And I am proud to say to you that although the Republicans have been trying to divide our party, ever since we got a 15 million mandate and carried every State in the Union except 5, it is only tonight that they finally succeeded—and I am glad they did, because they divided us into two groups of about 4,000 each. We could not get them all in one hall.

And so as we return to our homes this evening I hope that each of you that have made this sacrifice to buy a ticket and come out here to help elect or reelect Democratic Congressmen and Democratic Senators—that will come here and follow the leadership of John McCormack, and Carl Albert, and Hale Boggs, and Mike Mansfield, and Russell Long, and George Smathers, and all of these great committee chairmen—I hope that you know that we are grateful to each of you for taking away from your families some of the things that you could give them and giving it to your party and, I hope, to the benefit of your country.

We notice it. We like it. We appreciate it. And it is absolutely necessary.

And I have been assured by those great Democrats—Warren Magnuson, Mike Kirwan, Neil Curry, who put on this dinner, and my friend that came a long way, like my beloved friend Jim Sewell that sits out there in the front row who came here from Texas, and he's one of the greatest Democrats of them all—that we can assure him and every other Democrat in this room that there are going to be no locks on the desks, there are going to be no drawers pulled open, there are going to be no tape recorders around. And we are going to take what you have put here, and put on this table, and we are going out to the hustings and we are going to break the record. Instead of suffering losses in the off year we are going to bring you back gains for your sacrifices here tonight—gains that you and your children will be proud of.

Thank you.

NOTE: The President spoke at 10:12 p.m. at the District of Columbia Armory.

In his opening words he referred to Representative Michael J. Kirwan of Ohio, Representative John W. McCormack of Massachusetts, Speaker of the House of Representatives, Senator Warren G. Magnuson of Washington, and John M. Bailey, Chairman of the Democratic National Committee.

Later he referred to Representative Adam C. Powell of New York, Chairman of the House Education and Labor Committee, Senator Mike Mansfield of Montana, majority leader of the Senate, Representative Carl Albert of Oklahoma, majority leader of the House of Representatives, Senator Russell B. Long of Louisiana, majority whip of the Senate, Representative Hale Boggs of Louisiana, Senator George A. Smathers of Florida, Senator A. S. Mike Monroney of Oklahoma, Senator Alan Bible of Nevada, Senator B. Everett Jordan of North Carolina, Representative William L. Dawson of Illinois, Representative Thomas E. Morgan of Pennsylvania, Representative Joe L. Evins of Tennessee, Neil J. Curry of Los Angeles, honorary chairman of the Democratic congressional dinners, and James L. Sewell of Dallas, Tex., President of the Delhi-Taylor Oil Corp.

Earlier in the evening the President spoke at the

Washington Hilton Hotel where another congressional dinner was in progress (see Item 329).

Following his remarks at the Armory the President left for San Francisco to address a meeting of the United Nations. On the way he stopped at Kansas City, Mo., for breakfast with President Truman.

331   Address in San Francisco at the 20th Anniversary Commemorative Session of the United Nations. *June 25, 1965*

Mr. President, Mr. Secretary General, Your Excellencies, distinguished representatives, Governor Brown, ladies and gentlemen:

On my journey across the continent, I stopped in the State of Missouri, and there I met with the man who made the first such pilgrimage here 20 years ago as the 33d President of the United States—Harry S. Truman.

Mr. Truman sent to this Assembly his greetings and good wishes on this anniversary commemoration. He asked that I express to you for him—as for myself and for my countrymen—the faith which we of the United States hold firmly in the United Nations and in the ultimate success of its mission among men.

On this historic and happy occasion we have met to celebrate 20 years of achievement and to look together at the work that we face in future meetings. I come to this anniversary not to speak of futility or failure nor of doubt and despair—I come to raise a voice of confidence in both the future of these United Nations and the fate of the human race.

The movement of history is glacial. On two decades of experience, none can presume to speak with certainty of the direction or the destiny of man's affairs. But this we do know and this we do believe.

Futility and failure are not the truth of this organization brought into being here 20 years ago.

Where, historically, man has moved fitfully from war toward war, in these last two decades man has moved steadily away from war as either an instrument of national policy or a means of international decision.

Many factors have contributed to this change. But no one single factor has contributed more than the existence and the enterprise of the United Nations itself.

For there can be no doubt that the United Nations has taken root in human need and has established a shape, and a purpose, and a meaning of its own.

By providing a forum for the opinions of the world, the United Nations has given them a force and an influence that they have never had before. By shining the light of inquiry and discussion upon very dark and isolated conflicts, it has pressed the nations of the world to conform their courses to the requirements of the United Nations Charter.

And let all remember—and none forget—that now more than 50 times in these 20 years the United Nations has acted to keep the peace.

By persuading nations to justify their own conduct before all countries, it has helped, at many times and in many places, to soften the harshness of man to his fellow man.

By confronting the rich with the misery of the poor and the privileged with the despair of the oppressed, it has removed the excuse of ignorance—unmasked the evil of indifference, and has placed an insistent, even though still unfulfilled, responsibility upon the more fortunate of the earth.

703

By insisting upon the political dignity of man, it has welcomed 63 nations to take their places alongside the 51 original members—a historical development of dramatic import, achieved mainly through peaceful means.

And by binding countries together in the great declarations of the charter, it has given those principles a strengthened vitality in the conduct of the affairs of man.

Today then—at this time of anniversary—let us not occupy ourselves with parochial doubts or with passing despair. The United Nations—after 20 years—does not draw its life from the assembly halls or the committee rooms. It lives in the conscience and the reason of mankind.

The most urgent problem we face is the keeping of the peace.

Today, as I speak, clear and present dangers in southeast Asia cast their shadow across the path of all mankind.

The United Nations must be concerned.

The most elementary principle of the United Nations is that neighbors must not attack their neighbors—and that principle today is under challenge.

The processes of peaceful settlement today are blocked by willful aggressors contemptuous of the opinion and the will of mankind.

Bilateral diplomacy has yielded no result.

The machinery of the Geneva conference has been paralyzed.

Resort to the Security Council has been rejected.

The efforts of the distinguished Secretary General have been rebuffed.

An appeal for unconditional discussion was met with contempt.

A pause in bombing operations was called an insult.

The concern for peace of the Commonwealth Prime Ministers has received little and very disappointing results.

Therefore, today I put to this world assembly the facts of aggression, the right of a people to be free from attack, the interest of every member in safety against molestation, the duty of this organization to reduce the dangers to peace, and the unhesitating readiness of the United States of America to find a peaceful solution.

I now call upon this gathering of the nations of the world to use all their influence, individually and collectively, to bring to the tables those who seem determined to make war. We will support your efforts, as we will support effective action by any agent or agency of these United Nations.

But the agenda of peace is not a single item.

Around the world there are many disputes that are filled with dangers—

—many tensions that are taut with peril,

—many arms races that are fraught with folly among small nations as well as large.

And the first purpose of the United Nations is peace-keeping. The first work of all members now, then, just must be peace-making. For this organization exists to resolve quarrels outside the confines of its headquarters—and not to prolong quarrels within.

Where there are disputes, let us try to find the means to resolve them—through whatever machinery is available or is possible.

Where the United Nations requires readily available peace forces in hours and days—and not in weeks or months—let all pledge to provide those forces. And my country is ready.

On another front of our common endeavors, I think nothing is more urgent than the effort to diminish danger by bringing the armaments of the world under increasing control. Nations rich and poor are burdened down by excessive and competitive and frightening arms. So let us all urgently commit ourselves to the rational reduction of those arms burdens. We of the United States would hope that others will join with us in coming to our next negotiations with proposals for effective attack upon these deadly dangers to mankind.

And after peace, high on the agenda of man is devotion to the dignity and to the worth of the human person—and the promotions of better standards of life in larger freedom for all of the human race.

We in this country are committing ourselves to great tasks in our own Great Society. We are committed to narrow the gap between promise and performance, between equality in law and equality in fact, between opportunity for the numerous well-to-do and the still too numerous poor, between education for the successful and education for all of the people.

It is no longer a community or a nation or a continent but a whole generation of mankind for whom our promises must be kept—and kept within the next two decades.

If those promises are not kept, it will be less and less possible to keep them for any.

And that is why—on this anniversary—I would call upon all member nations to rededicate themselves to wage together an international war on poverty.

So let us then together:

—raise the goal for technical aid and investment through the United Nations.

—increase our food, and health, and education programs to make a serious and a successful attack upon hunger, and disease, and ignorance—the ancient enemies of all mankind.

Let us in all our lands—including this land—face forthrightly the multiplying problems of our multiplying populations and seek the answers to this most profound challenge to the future of all the world. Let us act on the fact that less than $5 invested in population control is worth $100 invested in economic growth.

For our wars together on the poverty and privation, the hunger and sickness, the despair and the futility of mankind, let us mark this International Cooperation Year by joining together in an alliance for man.

The promise of the future lies in what science, the ever more productive industrial machine, the ever more productive fertile and usable land, the computer, the miracle drug, and the man in space all spread before us. The promise of the future lies in what the religions and the philosophies, the cultures, and the wisdoms of 5,000 years of civilization have finally distilled and confided to us—the promise of the abundant life and the brotherhood of man.

The heritage that we share together is a fragile heritage.

A world war would certainly destroy it. Pride and arrogance could destroy it. Neglect and indifference could destroy it. It could be destroyed by narrow nationalism or ideological intolerance—or rabid extremism of either the left or the right.

So we must find the way as a community of nations, as a United Nations, to keep the peace among and between all of us. We must restrain by joint and effective action any who place their ambitions or their dogmas or their prestige above the peace of all the world. And we just must find a way to do that. It is the most profound and the most urgent imperative of the time in which we live.

So I say to you as my personal belief, and the belief I think of the great American majority, that the world must finish once and for all the myth of inequality of races and peoples, with the scandal of discrimination, with the shocking violation of human rights and the cynical violation of political rights.

We must stop preaching hatred, we must stop bringing up entire new generations to preserve and to carry out the lethal fantasies of the old generation, stop believing that the gun or the bomb can solve all problems or that a revolution is of any value if it closes doors and limits choices instead of opening both as wide as possible.

As far back as we can look—until the light of history fades into the dusk of legend—such aspirations of man have been submerged and swallowed by the violence and the weakness of man at his worst.

Generations have come and gone, and generations have tried and failed.

Will we succeed?

I do not know.

But I dare to be hopeful and confident.

And I do know this: whether we look for the judgment to God, or to history or to mankind, this is the age, and we are the men, and this is the place to give reality to our commitments under the United Nations Charter. For what was for other generations just a hope is for this generation a simple necessity.

Thank you very much.

NOTE: The President spoke at 11:30 a.m. at the San Francisco Opera House. In his opening words he referred to Alex Quaison-Sackey of Ghana, President of the 19th session of the United Nations General Assembly, U Thant, United Nations Secretary General, Chakravarthi V. Narasimhan, Under Secretary for General Assembly Affairs, Pierre DeMeuleneester, United Nations Chief of Protocol, and Edmund G. (Pat) Brown, Governor of California.

332 Memorandum Directing Full Use by Federal Agencies of the ZIP Code System. *June 27, 1965*

[Released June 27, 1965. Dated June 18, 1965]

THE 5-digit ZIP Code system developed by the Post Office Department will

—contribute to the development of commerce and trade by speeding the delivery of business mail.

—increase the efficiency and economy of postal operations, with resultant benefits to the taxpayers.

—permit faster communications between individuals in both their business and personal affairs.

—keep our postal system abreast of improvements in other methods of communication.

—improve the accuracy of mail deliveries.

A complete transition to the ZIP Code system will not be accomplished without substantial effort by both the Post Office Department and the general public. The full use of ZIP coding by the Government it-

self is essential to the proper development of the system.

I expect, therefore, that the agencies of the Government will take the lead in adopting the ZIP Code system, including the presorting of quantity mailings. The operations of Federal agencies should provide an example to private mailers who are expected to conform to the new system.

I have instructed the Postmaster General to issue regulations governing the use of the ZIP Code by all Federal agencies. These regulations will be designed to

—improve governmental services to the public.

—contribute to efficiency and economy in Government by improving the operations of all agencies, particularly those of the Post Office Department.

—provide an example to private mailers

in the effective use of the ZIP Code system.

I shall expect each one of you to insure that his agency is ready to comply fully with the Postmaster General's regulations on the dates which he will specify in the regulations.

The Director of the Bureau of the Budget will take appropriate action to see that forms in use throughout the Federal Government are changed as may be necessary to provide the information required for ZIP coding of addresses on Government mailings.

LYNDON B. JOHNSON

NOTE: The memorandum was released at Austin, Tex.

333 Remarks at a Ceremony Marking the First Commercial Communication Satellite Service. *June 28, 1965*

THIS MOMENT marks a milestone in the history of communications between peoples and nations.

For the first time a manmade satellite of earth is being put into commercial service as a means of communication between continents.

The occasion is as happy as it is historic, and that is for many reasons.

This is, first of all, a very tangible and valuable realization of the promise and potential of man's exploration of space. On ahead, we shall take many more and, I think, many longer strides forward. But we can know, from this step today, that mankind's growing knowledge of space will bring growing improvement for life on this earth.

So, it is especially fitting that this historic step comes not as the achievement of any single nation—but as the work of many nations. This represents a joint venture of 44 countries, with still more participants in prospect. For us in the United States, that is especially gratifying. Since the earliest days of the age of space we have urged—as we still do—that all nations join together to explore space together and to develop together its peaceful uses.

Finally, for us—and, I am sure, for our friends in Europe as well—it is a particularly happy circumstance that this service is another bond in the many ties that join us together across the North Atlantic.

Other satellites, in days to come, will open new communications pathways for all the world. But we are especially pleased that this first service brings closer together lands and people who share not only a common heritage but a common destiny—and a common determination to preserve peace, to uphold freedom, to achieve together a just and a decent society for all mankind.

In these times the choice of mankind is a very clear choice between cooperation or catastrophe. Cooperation begins in the better understanding that better communications bring.

On this occasion, then, I am pleased to extend my congratulations to all the international participants in this system and to the Communications Satellite Corporation.

And I would express the hope that all nations may become willing to join in such great enterprises for the good of mankind, and that all of our labors may be blessed by a rich and a bountiful harvest of peace on this earth.

NOTE: The President spoke at 11:43 a.m. from the Cabinet Room at the White House. His remarks were addressed, via Early Bird satellite, to officials in six European nations. The ceremony marked the beginning of commercial operations by the Communications Satellite Corporation.

Immediately following his remarks, the President heard messages from Louis Jacquinot, French Minister of State, Ludwig Erhard, West German Chancellor, Hans-Peter Tschudi, Swiss President, Harold Wilson, British Prime Minister, and Ramon Gaspari, Italian Undersecretary of Posts and Telecommunications.

334 Remarks at the White House Fellows Ceremony. *June 28, 1965*

Mr. Rockefeller, distinguished guests:

The first occupant of this house, John Adams, once said that if he could have his wish, ". . . There should never be a show or a feast made for the President while I hold the office."

Well, I like people too much to subscribe entirely to that Adams doctrine for myself. But I will say—and Mrs. Johnson joins me in this—nothing makes us happier than to be hosts, rather than honorees, at such functions as the one arranged here this afternoon.

We are glad you're here. It is our privilege to welcome you to your house—this house of all the people.

This has been an unusually significant day for me in the White House. This morning I sat in the Cabinet Room—over in the West Wing. And there—by means of communications satellite—I talked with and I listened to the heads of governments of friendly nations across the Atlantic.

As I sat there, several thoughts passed through my mind which, I think, seem appropriate for this occasion now.

First of all, there was the thought that all nations—not just a few nations—could have been, and should have been, joined together in that conversation and many others like it. It is true that modern technology has brought peril to human existence. But that peril need not dominate us—and it need not paralyze us—if politics and politicians will put our technological progress to work serving the purposes of peace

and the betterment of all mankind.

But another thought was present in my mind this morning. In times such as these, a society which cherishes freedom—a society which has a yen and a zest for higher values of man—cannot be a spectator society.

In its deepest sense, freedom requires a sense of participation—a full, zestful sense of participation. A spectator society is doomed to be a listless society.

And this is true whether we speak of our American society, or the great Atlantic society, or the broad, global society of all men who aspire for justice and decency and freedom in human affairs.

For whatever our continent, or our culture, or our creed, or our color, all of us on this earth are all involved today in really determining the destiny of man—both by what we do and perhaps more by what we neglect to do.

Our collective involvement, then, is real.

Our individual commitment, then, must be real, too.

So, I am quite pleased and very proud that in America so many of our people are showing today a new and a growing spirit of commitment to the values of this society of which we are so proud. Just as one measure, I think I could mention that in the Peace Corps and in the programs of the war on poverty there are now more than 500,000 Americans, of all ages, serving as volunteers—more than a half million volunteering to make their individual commitment and their individual contribution to our society through these efforts.

So, more than any other generation of this century, today's Americans are involved, and they are committed, and they are willing, and they are ready to give themselves and to give their talents in order to enrich the lives of others, both here at home and in the lands around the world.

And in the final analysis, a democratic society achieves excellence not just by its arts alone, nor by its commerce or enterprise, nor by the magnitude of its abundance, but always and only by the standards of citizenship which each citizen demands of himself.

Last spring I established this new program of White House Fellows to recognize and to provide an outlet for the very high demands that some of our younger citizens are so worthily making of themselves. We invited those who wanted to share first-hand, high-level experience in their Government to apply—and do you know that more than 3,000 did from all the various professions.

A distinguished commission, headed by a most distinguished man and a patriot, Mr. David Rockefeller, made the final selections. And one Fellow now will be assigned to the Vice President, one to each member of our Cabinet, and four members will join the White House staff. I expect their prestige and their presence to add to the quality of our labors.

We are very grateful to Mr. John Gardner and the Carnegie Foundation for helping to make this program possible.

And to each of you who have been selected, I am very proud to offer my heartiest congratulations. In the year that you spend here, I am confident that you will contribute much to us. And I am confident also that you will take away from this association a new and a deeper conviction that your land—and its leadership today—have but one purpose. That purpose, above all else, is to preserve peace with honor, with freedom, with justice, progress with equal opportunity for all men and all time.

Now, it is my great pleasure to ask Mr. Rockefeller to come forward and read the list of the winners of the White House Fellows for the year 1965, and to thank each of you for coming here and honoring us with your presence.

NOTE: The President spoke at 5:50 p.m. in the East Room at the White House. In his opening words he referred to David Rockefeller, President of the Chase Manhattan Bank in New York City, and Chairman of the Commission on White House Fellows. Later he referred to John W. Gardner, President of the Carnegie Corporation which sponsored the program, and a member of the Commission.

The program, designed to give outstanding young Americans top-level experience with the workings of the Federal Government, was established by the President on October 3, 1964 (see 1963–64 volume, this series, book II, Item 622).

On October 1, 1965, the President announced the names of the first 15 persons chosen for the White House Fellows Program as follows: William R. Cotter of New York City, John A. DeLuca of Los Angeles, Calif., Richard L. deNeufville of Boston, Mass., Edwin B. Firmage of Columbia, Mo., Wyatt T. Johnson, Jr., of Macon, Ga., Robert R. Lee of Palo Alto, Calif., Maj. Ronald B. Lee of Wheaton, Md., Charles M. Maguire of New York City, David C. Mulford of Rockford, Ill., Howard N. Nemerovski of San Francisco, Calif., Robert E. Patricelli of West Hartford, Conn., Harold A. Richman of Chicago, Ill., Thomas C. Veblen of Minneapolis, Minn., Michael H. Walsh of Portland, Oreg., and Kimon S. Zachos of Manchester, N.H.

335 Remarks to the YMCA Youth Governors' Conference. June 29, 1965

I KNOW who you're really applauding for and I am so proud that you gave him such a warm welcome.

This is the Chancellor of the Exchequer, Mr. Callaghan, of Great Britain. And the distinguished Secretary of the Treasury I think you know. And this is the distinguished British Ambassador, Mr. Patrick Dean.

I am sorry that I have been delayed, but I have been delayed in a good cause. We have been talking about the problems that affect you and that will affect governors in many places in the world.

Bernard Shaw once said that "youth is too precious to be wasted on the young." And if he could be here today to greet you governors, I think he might retract his statement.

For the young people of today are a generation that is excitingly different from any which has come before. I have said upon many occasions, as the young men and women come here to visit the White House, that you are the committed generation. You have inherited a world which seethes with crises and danger, yet you face these problems and you don't shirk them.

You have courage and you have imagination. And that is demonstrated in our Peace Corps throughout the world, in our job opportunities program, where we now have more than 500,000 young people working, and it is demonstrated in the rice paddies of Viet-Nam as we meet here this afternoon.

So, it is a great pleasure for me to welcome you to the White House and to say to you—of this committed generation—that you are much better prepared to face the problems that come to you than were any of us who face the ones that we are dealing with today.

We hope that your studies here and your visit here will improve your general knowledge of the conditions we face and will better equip you to provide leadership in dealing with those problems.

We are at the moment living in a relatively peaceful and prosperous world, and the goal of your Nation and our allies, who are associated with us here today, is, first of all, peace for ourselves and all the peoples of the world. And second, for prosperous people to do something about the ancient enemies of mankind—disease, and ignorance, and illiteracy that stalks so many parts of the world.

I thank you for coming here. I am sorry my visit will be limited. You give us all inspiration by your interest and your leadership, and I hope you can come back again soon.

Thank you.

NOTE: The President spoke at 6:35 p.m. in the Fish Room at the White House.

The third annual YMCA Youth Governors' Conference was attended by 42 young people from throughout the United States, chosen in Statewide elections by the members of YMCA's Hi-Y programs. The conference, which was sponsored by the Reader's Digest Foundation of Pleasantville, N.Y., was held in Washington June 25-30, 1965.

336   Remarks at the Presentation of the Young American Medals. *June 30, 1965*

Mr. Attorney General, Mr. Hoover, ladies and gentlemen:

It is always a very proud occasion here when we have the opportunity to honor young Americans.

America's greatest asset will always be our young people. If our society has achieved a measure of distinction and greatness, it is because we have held a very high regard and a sincere respect for our young people.

Many years ago, before our Government came into being, Thomas Jefferson wrote a letter to a friend, and in that letter he said, and I quote: "The fortune of our lives depends on employing well the short period of youth."

Today, contrary to much that is said—and some that is written and believed by at least a few—young Americans of this generation are employing well the period of their youth.

So, this is a responsible generation, a reasoning generation, a reliable generation—constructive, committed, and concerned in both its principles and its purposes. All the libels and slanders which the conduct of a few may bring upon the many cannot alter this truth about the overwhelming majority of the youth in America today.

So, on this occasion today here in the Cabinet Room, we are marking the 15th year of the award of the Young American Medals. This very fine program was conceived by Congressman Frank Chelf, the popular Congressman from Kentucky, and under his leadership it was enacted in 1950.

Since that time, Young American Medals have been presented to some 35 American boys and girls—24 for acts of exceptional courage and swift decision, and 10 for extraordinary character and public service in their home communities.

These medals honor more than the acts of individuals. They honor a spirit of our youth—a spirit of courage and conscience that is part of the fiber of our Nation's character.

Those qualities of character have been tested for other generations on fields of battle throughout the world. And for whatever tests the times ahead may bring, I have complete and absolute faith that young Americans of the present will be equal to the demands that destiny might make of them.

But I wish to say to all our young people—and to all the youth of the entire world—that it is the consistent, determined, and daily purpose of this Nation's leadership that the young people of our nations may live out their lives in a peaceful world. For we believe the only heroic battles of these times are the humane battles, the battles to improve the life and the lot of mankind—by warring on poverty, illness, illiteracy, prejudice, and despair.

And I think that in the few months that I have been in this office I have concentrated, both from the pulpit, from the Rose Garden, the legislative halls of the Congress, and all the States of the Union, for a program that declares war on the ancient enemies of mankind—poverty, ignorance, illiteracy, prejudice, and bigotry.

And so, it is today a very high privilege to be here in the company of these distinguished individuals—the Attorney General, and Mr. Hoover, and my colleagues from the Senate and the House of past bygone days—to present these medals to these young Americans.

The Governors of 18 States forwarded to the Attorney General the names of 46 young people whose deeds were all quite noteworthy. And out of this number only 4 have been selected.

And for each of these young Americans I am very proud, and I am very privileged, to offer the congratulations, the admiration, and the gratitude of all the American people.

Thank you very much.

NOTE: The ceremony was held at 12:10 p.m. in the Cabinet Room at the White House. In his opening words the President referred to Attorney General Nicholas deB. Katzenbach and J. Edgar Hoover, Director, Federal Bureau of Investigation.

The President presented the gold Young American Medals for Bravery to the following:

Kenneth Pilago Magallanes, aged 13, of Pearl City, Hawaii, who descended twice into a noxious, abandoned cesspool to rescue a 2-year-old child who had fallen into the pool; Barbara Ann Lynch, aged 16, of Atco, N.J., who ran back into the family's burning home to rescue her invalid grandmother; and Mr. and Mrs. Carlos Espin, parents of Rosa Linda Espin, aged 7, of Charlotte, N.C., who was honored posthumously for having given her life to rescue her tiny brother from their burning house.

Dennis J. Power, aged 18, received a service medal for organizing his friends into a volunteer remedial reading school for Puerto Rican and Negro children in the Spanish quarter of Harlem in New York City.

Winners were selected by the Young American Medals Committee, composed of Mr. Hoover, Solicitor General Archibald Cox, and Jacob Rosenthal, Director of Public Information, Department of Justice.

337   Statement by the President Following Passage of the Housing Bill by the House of Representatives.   *June 30, 1965*

THE House of Representatives today took a historic step toward assuring every American a decent place to live.

The passage of the housing bill—with its pathbreaking provision for rent supplements—gives us new and expanded weapons for meeting the housing needs of all our people.

The rent supplements will provide new homes for hundreds of thousands of our people now condemned to slums and substandard homes.

It will give private industry an opportunity and an incentive to build for our future needs and to overcome our present failures.

It will help toward eliminating the arbitrary and unhealthy division of families and communities by income and age—an inevitable consequence of many present programs.

With the new tools of this bill, and with others yet to come, we can move toward the construction of communities and neighborhoods rather than housing units and isolated projects. For the city we aspire to is not just a collection of homes, but a community in which men and their families can live the good life.

NOTE: The Housing and Urban Development Act of 1965 was approved by the President on August 10, 1965 (see Item 415).

338   Statement by the President Upon Signing Bill Limiting Duty-Free Imports by Tourists.   *June 30, 1965*

ON FEBRUARY 10th of this year I proposed a 10-point program to help deal with the deficit in our balance of payments that measured $3.1 billion in 1964. Congress has differed with my recommendations only in an area involving 1.3 percent of that deficit which we are attempting to close. The administration proposed limiting to $50 retail value the amount tourists could bring back duty-free. Congress felt this amount should be $100 retail value instead of the present $100 wholesale value. This change represents a fair and reasonable adjustment on a relatively minor part of the overall program and still gives a $60 million assist to the balance of payments problem.

This legislation is important because it assures that we will continue to benefit from the continuation of previous reductions in the duty-free exemption.

In addition, it will provide new savings in our balance of payments of about $60 million a year—more than half of the amount we originally sought.

Had Congress failed to pass this measure, we would have had losses, not gains.

This may seem like a small step forward.

I believe it is significant because it reflects a strong determination by our Government and this Nation to eliminate our balance of payments deficit.

With the help of this measure, and all the other measures large and small that we have taken, and that we will take, I am sure we will achieve our goal.

Thanks in good part to that program, and thanks also to the voluntary cooperation of the business and financial community of this Nation, we have made substantial progress toward that goal since February 10th.

I am confident that this voluntary cooperation will continue to be given, and will continue to be effective.

I am equally confident that both management and labor will continue the responsible conduct which they have shown in recent years in protecting our Nation from inflationary wage and price increases, thus insuring not only our domestic economic gains, but also helping to keep our export trade strong and healthy.

We have made substantial economic progress both at home and abroad.

I have every confidence that we will continue to make economic progress—both at home and abroad.

In this way we will continue to keep the dollar strong throughout the world and to provide a better life and greater opportunity for all Americans.

NOTE: As enacted, the bill (H.R. 8147) is Public Law 89–62 (79 Stat. 208).

For the President's message to Congress on international balance of payments, see Item 60.

---

339 Remarks at the Swearing In of General McKee as Administrator, Federal Aviation Agency. *July 1, 1965*

Secretary McNamara, General McKee, Mr. Halaby, Mr. Thomas, General Grant, my friends in the Congress, ladies and gentlemen:

If it won't cause the press to think a news conference is beginning, I will start out this morning by saying that I have a few announcements to make—short and to the point, as always.

Right now, I am very happy to be able to welcome all of you here—with the advice and the consent of the Senate—Senator Magnuson.

This is a ceremony of more than usual significance. It is one of the relatively rare occasions when a native of the State of Texas is leaving the Government voluntarily. I hope that none will regard that as an ominous link in an ominous chain.

Jeeb Halaby gave up the quiet, everyday pleasures of being a test pilot to face the perils and the dangers of bureaucratic life in

Washington. But every passenger who flies across this country in a plane owes him a deep debt of personal gratitude. In 4 years of dedicated, tireless service he has done much to assure public confidence in the safety of air travel.

By the inspiration of his vigorous leadership, he has greatly advanced the performance of the fine agency that he has headed. And certainly Mr. Halaby has won a place in history as the first regulator—in my memory—to fine himself for violating one of his own regulations. I am grateful to him for his willingness to serve his country by remaining in his post at great personal sacrifice for many months, and I wish him every success ahead.

Now the man who takes the direction of the FAA today leaves the perils and the dangers of retirement to resume the quiet, everyday pleasures of an 18-hour workload.

I don't know whether it is more politic to call him "General," or "Mister," or "Bill," but whatever the title of the man, I know that every knowledgeable person in this Government and out of it calls "Bozo" McKee the best man for the important job that I am assigning him this morning.

You know without my repeating it what that assignment is. It is to develop a supersonic transport which is, first, safe for the passenger, second, superior to any other commercial aircraft, and third, economically profitable to build and operate.

All about the man and about his record, I think, is conclusive evidence that he is the man to direct this effort. I am very proud to have him aboard. And in that connection, I have this announcement to make.

I have received the second interim report of the President's Advisory Committee on Supersonic Transport.

This Committee has conducted an intensive appraisal of the status of our supersonic transport program. Based on this review, the Committee members have recommended a plan of action to move the program forward at the fastest possible rate consistent with the attainment of those goals that I have outlined—that is, to develop a supersonic transport, safe for the passenger, superior to any commercial aircraft, and economically profitable to build and to operate.

The Committee advises me that substantial program progress has been made within the last several months. The Committee believes there is a high degree of probability that with future work on the basic technological problems, a commercially profitable supersonic transport can be developed. It has also stated, however, that much work must be done before construction of a prototype aircraft is initiated—if the large financial and developmental risks underlying the program are to be minimized.

On this basis, the Committee has recommended a substantial increase in the tempo of the program.

I have approved the Committee's five recommendations. I have directed their implementation as soon as possible. Those five recommendations might well be mentioned here and they are that:

1. The next phase of design cover an 18-month period beginning about August 1, 1965.

2. The four manufacturers—Boeing Company, Lockheed Aircraft Company, General Electric Company, Pratt & Whitney Division of United Aircraft Corporation—be invited to continue in this phase of the program.

3. The FAA Administrator be authorized to enter into contracts with the airframe manufacturers to undertake detailed airframe design work and tests over the next

18 months.

4. The FAA Administrator be authorized to enter into contracts with the engine manufacturers to construct and to test over the next 18 months demonstrator engines to prove the basic features of the engines.

5. And finally—and very importantly, Mr. Magnuson—that the Congress be requested to appropriate—Mr. Mahon—the necessary funds to initiate the next phase of the program. And for this purpose I shall request an appropriation of $140 million.

The objectives of this 18-month design phase are as follows:

First, to provide a sound foundation upon which realistic estimates of operating performance and development and production costs can be based.

Second, to take advantage of the flight experience of the SR-71, the XB-70, and the variable sweptwing F-111—all of which will be extensively flown at supersonic speeds over the next 18 months.

Third, to reduce developmental risks and developmental costs while retaining the capability to accelerate the program in its later phases, depending upon the technological progress of the manufacturers.

And, fourth, to provide a basis for judgment as to the manner in which the program should proceed after the 18-month period, and to determine with much greater precision and knowledge the work that should be done in the succeeding phases of the program.

I might add here that all of the talent in the Federal Government is going to be available to the FAA Administrator in cooperating and in coordinating with him in this great job. The distinguished Secretary of Defense is going to offer counsel and assistance and facilities and resources of his Department. The distinguished Secretary of Commerce, the Secretary of the Treasury, the Space Administrator, and others, are all involved in this effort, and it is going to succeed.

The program that I have just approved represents a very significant increase in the level of our effort—and a threefold increase in the amount of funds that we are spending. We believe that the increase is clearly justified by the progress that has been made over the last 4 years and particularly by that made over the last several months under the plan of action approved last May.

The program demands much hard work and much hard thinking. As I have been since President Kennedy first asked me to chair this Committee, I am confident that this country can achieve the level of technological advance that is required to develop and produce a supersonic transport.

So, given the ability of industry and the Government and the people all working together, I have not the slightest doubt that under the predicate laid and the preliminary work done through the years by men like Jeeb Halaby, and carried through under the direction of Bozo McKee, America will proudly reach her goal in due time and on time.

Thank you very much.

NOTE: The swearing-in ceremony was held at 11:27 a.m. in the Cabinet Room at the White House. In his opening words the President referred to Robert S. McNamara, Secretary of Defense, Gen. William F. McKee, incoming Administrator of the Federal Aviation Agency, N. E. Halaby, outgoing Administrator, David D. Thomas, Associate Administrator for Programs, and Lt. Gen. H. W. Grant, Deputy Administrator.

During his remarks he referred to Senator Warren G. Magnuson of Washington and to Representative George H. Mahon of Texas, Chairman of the Appropriations Committee of the House of Representatives.

The six-page report on supersonic transport, entitled "Memorandum for the President—Second

Interim Report of the President's Advisory Committee on Supersonic Transport," is dated May 8, 1965.

The Supplemental Appropriation Act, 1966, which appropriated $140 million for development of civil supersonic aircraft, was approved by the President on October 31, 1965 (Public Law 89–309, 79 Stat. 1133).

340 Remarks in New York City Before the Convention of the National Education Association. *July 2, 1965*

Secretary Celebrezze, Senator Morse, majority leader of the House of Representatives, Congressman Carl Albert, Dr. Edinger and Dr. Carr—who have labored in education's cause and helped us so much—and all of my fellow educators:

I have brought with me today Secretary Tony Celebrezze, the great administrator of the HEW and the best lobbyist the teachers of this country has; Senator Wayne Morse, the valiant fighter for education and the chairman of all the Senate committees that report these bills constantly—Senator Morse; the distinguished majority leader, Carl Albert, a Rhodes Scholar and education leader, majority leader in the House of Representatives, and my neighbor from Oklahoma; and I, too, want you to meet one of the great fellows that works on my staff, and who has been assigned the special subject of education and has made it his day and night work all year—Douglass Cater.

I greet you as the shapers of American society.

Emerson said: "The true test of a civilization is not the census, nor the size of cities, nor the crops, but the kind of man that the country turns out."

Education, more than any single force, will mold the citizen of the future. That citizen, in turn, will really determine the greatness of our society. And it is up to you to make that education equal to our towering expectations of the America that we love and the America that is to come.

And I came here today to reaffirm to you your Government's intention to continue to help in that task.

In the last 19 months your Congress and your President have worked shoulder-to-shoulder together in the most fruitful partnership for American education in all the history of the American Nation.

We passed the Higher Education Facilities Act.

We passed the Library Services Act to improve our libraries as storehouses of learning.

We passed the Vocational and Technical Education Act.

We passed the Nurses Training Act.

We passed the poverty measure—the Economic Opportunity Act, appropriating hundreds of millions of dollars, requested a billion-two this year, offering millions of young people the necessary training to help them escape from poverty.

We passed the $1,200 million Elementary and Secondary Education Act of 1965—the broadest, the most meaningful, and the most sweeping Federal commitment to education that this Nation has ever made.

And this is the first week of the first fiscal year in which funds, under this act, will begin to flow to States and communities in every part of this land, in every State in this country.

We are going to pass the higher education bill to provide help to colleges and students this year.

We are going to pass the Federal arts and humanities foundation bill to help those engaged in the study of the humanities and in the practice of the arts, and we are going to pass it this year.

And next year—in my next State of the Union Message—I intend to offer more new proposals to improve the education of all Americans. And I am here to tell you today that we are not going to stop until every child in this great and beautiful land of ours can have all of the education, of the highest quality, which his or her ambition demands and his or her mind can absorb.

So, I come here this afternoon to speak to you not of our triumphs, but of our tasks; not of the success that we have had, but the sacrifices that are to be made; not of the achievements of yesterday, but the aspirations of tomorrow. For this is not an occasion for self-congratulations. It is rather a time to reflect on our mounting needs and on our present deficiencies.

More than 1 million students—who are not here to speak for themselves this afternoon—drop out of school, their talents wasted, their intelligence lost to the Nation, their futures shattered by their failure and by our failure.

In the next 5 years attendance in elementary and secondary schools—at 48.1 million now, in the fall of 1964—will increase by more than 4 million—almost 1 million students per year. We will need 400,000 new classrooms to meet this growth—while a half million of our present classrooms are already more than 30 years old.

And beyond 1970 the demand for education—at every level—will continue to increase.

We will need more classrooms, we will need more books, we will need more teachers, we will need more schools on a scale that we have never dreamed of even a decade ago.

Nor is it enough to give a student a place

to sit and a teacher to learn from. We must make sure that the quality of that education is equal to his capacity to learn. We must make sure that it stimulates creativity rather than stifling it. We must make sure that it enlarges the mind rather than narrowing it—that he receives not merely a diploma but learning, in its real, broadest, and most meaningful and most humane sense.

In pursuit of these goals, I have asked the White House to send out invitations to the White House Conference on Education. That Conference—I hope it is the largest and best of its kind ever held in this Nation—will take place on July the 20th and 21st of this year at the White House in Washington. It will bring together educators and informed citizens from every State in this Nation. It will seek the answer to the immense question: How can a growing nation in an increasingly complex world provide education of the highest quality for all of its people?

The search for this answer radiates into every corner of American life. It must deal with educational opportunity and techniques from pre-school age to the most advanced of studies. It must look beyond the classroom to the family, and to the surroundings and the environment of the student.

For the process of learning is not a carefully defined and isolated segment of a person's life. It is part of an organic whole, embracing all the forces which shape the man.

And if we ignore these forces we do so at the peril of learning itself. Nothing is more dangerous than the easy assumption that simply by putting more money into more schools we will emerge with an educated, a trained, and an enlightened Nation.

And it is this kind of assumption that I came here to challenge today. I want you to bring all the tools of modern knowledge—from physics to psychology—to bear on the increase of learning. And if these tools are still inadequate then it is our job to fashion new ones and better ones.

To guide discussion in this Conference we are formulating a series of questions. And I hope you will give these questions your most careful thought and your boldest imagination in the weeks between now and the Conference.

They include:

How can we bring first-class education to the city slums and to the impoverished rural areas? Today the children of 5 million families are denied it.

How can we stimulate every child to catch the love of learning so he wants to stay in school? One million children now drop out of school each year.

How do we guarantee that new funds will bring new ideas and new techniques to our school system—not just simply expand the old and the outmoded?

How can local, and State, and Federal Government best cooperate to make education the first—the first among all of this Nation's goals?

These are a few of the important questions which I hope the White House Conference examines. And I would like to mention one other: Our country today is among the leaders in the community of nations of the world. How well is our education system preparing our citizens of this one Nation for their responsibility to some 120 other nations in the world?

But even as we prepare for this Conference, your Government is acting. We are now completing a thorough overhaul and reorganization of the Office of Education. We are equipping it to deal with its new and its future responsibilities of the 20th century.

We have also established a National Center for Educational Statistics, an office of programs for educating the disadvantaged, an Office of Equal Educational Opportunity so people of all races, of all creeds, of all sections, are given equal treatment. And we are, at this moment, in the process of preparing more and exciting new programs that our task force is working on this week to present next year when the Congress comes back.

In the next few days I will propose a National Teachers Corps to enlist thousands of dedicated teachers to work alongside local teachers in city slums and in areas of rural poverty where they can really serve their Nation. They will be young people, preparing for teaching careers. They will be experienced teachers willing to give a year to the places in their country that need them the most. They can bring the best in our Nation to the help of the poorest of our children.

And I announce today that your President will submit to the Congress and will support a program of fellowships for elementary and secondary schoolteachers so that they can replenish their knowledge and improve their abilities. And this program will assist teachers—displaced by the process of school integration—to acquire the skills that are necessary to permit them to perform new and challenging jobs in a new environment, in a new century.

For you and I are both concerned about the problem of the dismissal of Negro teachers as we move forward—as we move forward with the desegregation of the schools of America. I applaud the action that you have already taken.

For my part, I have directed the Commissioner of Education to pay very special attention, in reviewing the desegregation plans, to guard against any pattern of teacher dismissal based on race or national origin.

When the upgrading of the teaching staff is required in newly integrated districts, I have instructed educational officials to provide funds for teacher institutes and to assist the school districts through title IV of the Civil Rights Act.

And where an integrated school system requires fewer teachers than those required to operate two segregated school systems, I have directed Federal officials to provide special reemployment services through a national program carried out by the U.S. Employment Service.

And when unemployed teachers need and when they desire refresher training, I have ordered Federal officials to provide this training, with full allowances, under the Manpower Development and Training Act that we have already passed. And such a training program, I think you know, has already proven its great value in this city. It is being sponsored by the Urban League at Yeshiva University.

Now, in these and in many other ways we continue to pursue this—the central goal of this administration.

But the basic thought, and the programs of future action, must come from you teachers. And the deeds which give meaning to the law must also come from you teachers. For a Federal law is not an education. A national program is not a developing child. A Presidential speech is not a trained Nation.

But as a teacher—I'm still on leave of absence from Houston public school—who has labored with you through the years in the elementary, high schools, and a short while in the colleges, I remind you that we have talked together, and dreamed together, and philosophized together about the need, the great need, for all of these things for 30 years or more since I finished college. We have even urged, since then, that they

be put in the annual party platforms of both the Republican and Democratic Party for your consideration on election day.

Well, I'm here to tell you this afternoon that this is a different day, a different hour, and a different month. The time for talking and dreaming and philosophizing and writing platforms is gone, and the time for doing things instead of talking about them is here.

All these things are empty and they are sterile without the will and without the effort at every level of our national life that is needed to transform intention into reality—the mandate of the law into the fulfillment of life. And in this, too, the hopes of our Nation are resting on you.

I do not need to talk to this audience about the importance of education. It's been your life work. No strain in our national life is more deeply rooted or more enduring than this faith in learning. It is the pathway to opportunity and the good life. It is the key to wise and satisfying use of our leisure time. It is the door to each man's highest use of his highest powers—which is happiness. It can bring fulfillment to the many, and to the happy few those transcendent achievements which really enrich the human race.

And if these things are true for every society, how much more important they are to our free society.

In every corner of this world in which we live, not only *our* democracy but the *idea* of democracy itself is today being challenged. As the world grows in danger and as it grows in complexity, and as humanity seems dwarfed by the forces it has loosed, man's ability to govern himself is again being questioned.

We will not prove democracy's strength by faith or even by the experience of our past. We will prove it by the works of the future.

I am not concerned with all the promises

that have been made to you all through the years. I am not concerned with the times you have been taken up on the mountain and asked to look out at the future beyond.

I am not concerned with your hopes, or your plans, or your dreams of the past when you went out as the pioneers did with their gun on their shoulder in search of food for their families. What I am concerned with, and what I want you to be concerned with, is results—the coonskins that they bring back and put on the wall.

And, as I said earlier, together we are not just going to talk and dream. We are going to do. The day of the talkers is gone. The day of the doers is here.

And with that kind of a comment I better come to a speedy conclusion and go on and get on with the job.

That future—hopeful but still unknown— is today struggling to be born in millions of young and waiting minds in thousands of classrooms in this restless continent.

So, when you go back from this great convention, in this first city of our land, I hope that you will remember the words of a great leader of Government and a great educator who, in the early days of our Republic, warned us that "an educated mind is the guardian genius of democracy. It is the only dictator that free men recognize, and the only ruler that free men desire."

Today we are faced with many trying and complex and difficult decisions and problems. But I can tell you here this afternoon that I have never been prouder of my country than I am now. And the pride that I have in my country is largely due to the years of toil and dedication and satisfaction of the teachers who made it so.

Thank you.

NOTE: The President spoke at 5:17 p.m. at Madison Square Garden in New York City before a crowd of 7,000 persons who attended the final session of the National Education Association convention.

In his opening words he referred to Anthony J. Celebrezze, Secretary of Health, Education, and Welfare; Senator Wayne Morse of Oregon; Representative Carl Albert of Oklahoma, majority leader of the House of Representatives; Dr. Lois V. Edinger, retiring President of the NEA; and Dr. William G. Carr, Executive Secretary of the NEA. During his remarks the President referred to S. Douglass Cater, Jr., Special Assistant to the President. In the next to the last paragraph he referred to Mirabeau Buonaparte Lamar, second President of the Republic of Texas.

The National Education Association held its convention in New York City June 27-July 2, 1965.

For the President's remarks to the delegates to the White House Conference on Education, see Item 374.

341   Remarks at the Swearing In of Homer Thornberry as Judge, U.S. Court of Appeals, Fifth Circuit.   *July 3, 1965*

My friends:

This is a very happy occasion for Lady Bird and me and all the members of our family.

We are so pleased that we could be honored with the presence of Judge Brown this morning, Judge Spears, and Judge Jones, who is a longtime personal friend of Judge Thornberry and a former partner of his.

Homer and Eloise have been with us the last few days while they went through the necessary constitutional requirements getting confirmed, and we have enjoyed their presence so much.

I don't know of anyone that is missed more from Washington than this wonderful Thornberry family. But I know, too, that the people that they serve in this area of the United States are very happy that they could be here.

We hated to see him leave the legislative halls, but we are glad to see him preside in the temples of justice. Because we know that there is no more courageous person, no better and finer human being, and no man with a greater sense of justice and fairness and feeling of equality for all human beings, wherever they live, whatever their color, or whatever their religion, than Homer Thornberry.

So, it is a peculiar delight for us to come back here to the porch of our little home and ask the Thornberry family, and the Engles, and Thornberry children, to come here to see Homer administered the oath as Circuit Judge of the Fifth Judicial District, in the Fifth Circuit Court, in the presence of his neighbors here, and some of the best friends he has in the world.

I now want to present one of those best friends—Judge Herman Jones.

NOTE: The swearing-in ceremony was held at 11:01 a.m. on the front lawn of the LBJ Ranch at Johnson City, Tex. During his remarks the President referred to Judge John R. Brown of the Fifth Circuit Court of Appeals, Judge Adrian Spears, Judge Herman Jones, and Mrs. Homer (Eloise Engle) Thornberry.

342   Statement by the President on Ordering Further Withdrawal of U.S. Forces From the Dominican Republic.   *July 3, 1965*

I HAVE been advised today by General Alvim, the Commander of the Inter-American Force, and Lieutenant General Palmer, the Deputy Commander of the Inter-American Force, that conditions in the Dominican Republic now permit further withdrawal of United States military personnel from the Inter-American Force. This recommendation has the concurrence of the special committee of the Organization of American States and Ambassador Bennett.

I am therefore ordering the withdrawal of two battalions of the 82d Airborne Division, totaling approximately 1,400 personnel.

NOTE: In his statement the President referred to General of the Army Hugo Panasco Alvim of Brazil, Commander of the OAS Inter-American Force in the Dominican Republic, Lt. Gen. Bruce Palmer, Jr., of the United States, Deputy Commander, and W. Tapley Bennett, U.S. Ambassador to the Dominican Republic.

The statement was released at Austin, Tex.

343   Statement by the President on Announcing U.S. Participation in the International Agency for Research on Cancer.   *July 4, 1965*

THIS ACTION taken jointly by five governments constitutes a most welcome and significant contribution toward the solution of one of the world's oldest and most serious health problems. I am especially pleased that we are doing this during International Cooperation Year. The battle against cancer was one of my foremost thoughts when I proclaimed 1965 International Cooperation Year in the United States last fall. I said then that I hoped my cancer committee could come up with some good results. This is a valuable step in the right direction.

NOTE: The statement was made public as part of a White House release announcing that the U.S. Government had that day notified the World Health Organization of its acceptance of the statutes establishing an International Agency for Research on Cancer.

The release stated that action to establish the agency was taken at the initiative of France and was the result of 18 months of negotiations by delegates of France, West Germany, Italy, Great Britain, the United States, and the Director General of the World Health Organization.

The release further stated that the agency would concentrate on epidemiological research, the training of research workers, and support of research in national laboratories. The research facilities would be made available to all nations which could make effective use of them, the release concluded, and the results of the research would be for the benefit of all.

Proclamation 3620 "International Cooperation Year" is dated October 2, 1964 (3 CFR, 1964 Supp., p. 76). For the President's remarks upon signing the proclamation, see 1963–64 volume, this series, book II, Item 616.

On March 7, 1964, the President announced the establishment and membership of the President's Commission on Heart Disease, Cancer, and Stroke (see 1963–64 volume, this series, book I, Item 211 [6]).

The statement was released at Austin, Tex.

344   Statement by the President on Announcing a Mission To Consider U.S. Cooperation in Establishing a Korean Institute for Industrial Technology and Applied Science.   *July 4, 1965*

THE TALENTS of trained Korean scientists and engineers are a rich resource for the country's development and progress. I believe it is important that efforts on their part to advance the level of technological achievement in Korea should receive encouragement and support. If the Institute contributes toward channeling Korea's talents effectively into accelerating the pace of Korean economic growth, it will serve as an inspiring example of what can be accomplished through international cooperation in science.

NOTE: The statement was made public as part of a White House release announcing that Dr. Donald F. Hornig, the President's science adviser, would

leave for Korea on July 7 to explore possibilities for U.S. cooperation in establishing an Institute for Industrial Technology and Applied Science.

The release stated that Dr. Hornig would be accompanied by his wife, Dr. Lilli Hornig of Trinity College in Washington, D.C., and by three advisers: Dr. Albert I. Moseman, Director of Agricultural Sciences, the Rockefeller Foundation of New York City, Dr. James B. Fisk, President of Bell Laboratories, Murray Hill, N.J., and Dr. B. D. Thomas, President of the Battelle Memorial Institute, Columbus, Ohio.

The Presidential mission planned to spend one week in Korea meeting with government officials, businessmen, industrialists, scientists, and educators.

The Institute was first proposed in the joint statement issued at the end of President Park's visit to Washington (see Item 257).

See also Item 407.

The statement was released at Austin, Tex.

345   Remarks at the Swearing In of LeRoy Collins as Under Secretary of Commerce.   *July 7, 1965*

Secretary Connor, Governor Collins, Senator Smathers, distinguished guests:

It is a pleasure to welcome you to the White House for this happy occasion this morning.

Judging by the holiday suntans I see, it would appear to me, Secretary Connor, your message is getting through about seeing the U.S.A. first.

In years gone by, the Fourth of July traditionally marked the beginning of a 3-months' doldrums in our Capital City, when very little went on. But that is not the case this year.

This is a new season in Washington and I am confident that we are beginning a new sort of summertime—a constructive and creative time of major accomplishment.

These are challenging times in which we live, as we all realize.

These are demanding times, as we all expect.

But above the challenges and above the demands, we see more clearly the opportunities of an age and a time that man has never known before.

I think it is symbolic that in only a few more days the rocket Mariner will fly by the planet Mars and man's reach will have been extended to the farthest reaches of our universe.

So our knowledge is growing each day. Our mastery of the mysteries of the ages is growing each day. Our capabilities for greatness are growing—not just American capabilities alone, but the capabilities of all the human race.

So in such times as these, I do not believe that mankind will turn—or be turned—down the forlorn and fading road of trial and tragedy which lies behind us. The opportunities which are ours now must be and shall be fulfilled in order to make life better on this earth for people who cherish freedom and who love peace in the world.

So in a real sense, Governor Collins, this ceremony today epitomizes this strong and and this new spirit in the United States of America. For too many years the Department of Commerce has been regarded narrowly by some as a dry and a dull and a lifeless organization. Now we recognize that in its work—as in the work of all of our organizations, both public and private— there is a most creative and constructive role for the Department to fill.

Secretary Connor is carrying forward the fine start made by Secretary Hodges before him. We have a new vigor, a new vitality, a new sense of purpose. A new pride, I think, is permeating the Department. And it is contagious.

When I returned the other day I said to my staff that I doubt if the Government anywhere has a better management team than has been assembled in the Department here of late. I think this forward thrust is being given momentum by the new men that Secretary Connor has brought into the Department.

So we have come here today to welcome one of those new men to that team, one of its most distinguished members—LeRoy Collins, a great public servant in the State of Florida. Governor Collins is one of our most respected citizens. On the basis of the record that he has already written at the State level and the Federal level, both public and private life, he ranks very high.

Last year—at considerable personal sacrifice—he came to the White House and agreed to pick up the unpleasant challenge of directing the Community Relations Service under the Civil Rights Act of 1964. He is peculiarly equipped by training and experience and personality and soul to do that job. And his leadership there has been of the greatest value to this Nation.

I doubt that any of us, even in our greatest moments of optimism, would have ever been prone to predict that the compliance and the mediation that has been brought about as a result of his leadership would have ever reached such proportions.

So today his talents turn to the Office of the Under Secretary of the Department of Commerce. This is an appropriate reminder, I think, that in our society, social progress must rest on a basis of solid well-being for our economy—and the well-being of our enterprise rests finally on a broad base of a decent, and just, and fair society.

As I was last year, I am again this morning very grateful to Governor Collins and to all the members of his family for this unselfish demonstration and willingness to serve where he is most needed, and I think where he is most able. I predict that he will be a bright star in the new Commerce team, and I am very proud to welcome him, and to congratulate him, and to thank him for this new role of service.

NOTE: The President spoke at 11:15 a.m. in the Cabinet Room at the White House.

In his opening words he referred to John T. Connor, Secretary of Commerce, LeRoy Collins, incoming Under Secretary of Commerce and former Governor of Florida, and George A. Smathers, Senator from Florida. Later he referred to Luther H. Hodges, former Secretary of Commerce.

346 Remarks Upon Signing World Law Day Proclamation. July 8, 1965

Ladies and gentlemen, Justice Goldberg, Attorney General Katzenbach, Dean Storey, and other most distinguished guests and friends:

I welcome you this morning to the Rose Garden. By tradition and custom, and by direction of the Congress, and on petition of the public, the Presidents sign many proclamations each year on many subjects. Some are of great significance and great impact. Others are, as I am sure the press will agree, of somewhat lesser significance and import. But today we are meeting in this manner to observe the signing of a proclamation which, in its way, expresses something of the greatest importance about the purposes of the American people and the purposes of the American Nation. And that is our commitment to, and our quest toward, a world where all men may live in peace with the hope of justice under the rule of law.

That goal cannot be made real by any proclamation that I issue or sign. It cannot be attained by the observance of any single day of the year. But I do believe that by observing together one day designated as World Law Day, we may remind ourselves, and we hope call to the attention of others, that a decent world ruled by just law is not a vain dream.

It can be real. It will be true—if the peace-loving peoples uphold the beginnings of world law with the same resolve as they defend the end of individual liberty.

In this 20th century, millions of men and women have fought and have died and have struggled and sacrificed to win or to redeem their liberty or freedom. The fighting and the dying and the struggle and sacrifice go on as even we meet here today.

But this century has really seen the beginning of a will and an effort to establish respect for the rule of law over the conduct of the nations of the world. Those beginnings must not perish under the heel or by the hand of those who refuse to honor their own agreements, or refuse to keep their own treaties, or refuse to respect the borders or the rights of their own neighbors. And this is central to the purposes of the American people and the policies of the governments around the world.

And by faithfully honoring our agreements, by faithfully keeping our treaties to which we are party, we seek to assure substance for the dream of a world that is ruled by law.

This year, in September, the leaders of the law for many nations will assemble here in Washington. In observance of this International Cooperation Year, they will confer on this most vital and on this most basic subject of strengthening the hope for world peace by strengthening the rule of law among world nations.

And so to honor this significant occasion, I am today proclaiming September 13, 1965, as World Law Day. In so doing, I would call upon citizens throughout the land to join in appropriate observances on that date to reaffirm our abiding American goal of a world where all men live in obedience to the rule of laws that they have chosen, rather than in subjugation to the rule of men that they have not chosen.

It is a great pleasure to have the leadership that we have present with us here this morning.

I will now sign the proclamation.

NOTE: The President spoke at 12:23 p.m. in the Rose Garden at the White House just prior to signing Proclamation 3662 "World Law Day" (30 F.R. 8773; 3 CFR, 1965 Supp.). In his opening words he referred to Associate Justice Arthur J. Goldberg of the Supreme Court of the United States, Attorney General Nicholas deB. Katzenbach, and M. Robert Storey, former President of the American Bar Association and Dean of the Southern Methodist University Law School in Dallas, Tex.

For the President's remarks on September 16, 1965, to the delegates to the Conference on World Peace Through Law, see Item 516.

347 The President's News Conference of July 9, 1965

THE PRESIDENT. After you have had a chance to write your stories, we will be going to Texas and will be there over the weekend. I thought you might have some questions you wanted to ask me, and if you do, I have a few minutes to answer them.

REPORT ON VIET-NAM

[1.] Q. Mr. President, in the light of recent news developments concerning Viet-Nam, I wonder, sir, if you could give us an up-to-date assessment of how the war is going out there, what is happening, and what sort of news you think the country can expect in the next month or two?

THE PRESIDENT. Well, we will have a somewhat better picture of that after Secretary McNamara and Ambassador Lodge[1] return a week from next Wednesday. I spent an hour or so with the Secretary this morning reviewing the reports that have come in from there, and evaluating them and discussing with him the work that he is going to do with Ambassador Lodge when he is out there.

The incidents are going up: that is, the Viet Cong attacks. The casualties are going up. From June 15th through July 3d there were 4,556 Viet Cong dead counted, and some 1,900 South Vietnamese forces, and some 40 Americans. We have lost in the neighborhood of some 300 men in the period since I have been President. We expect that it will get worse before it gets better. They have had substantial increases in the aggression forces. They are swinging wildly. They are suffering substantial losses in their sneak attacks.

Our manpower needs there are increasing, and will continue to do so. We have some 60,000-odd people there now, and they are landing each day. There are some 75,000 that will be there very shortly. There will be others that will be required.

Whatever is required I am sure will be supplied. We have met and taken action to meet the requests made by General West-

---

[1] Henry Cabot Lodge, newly appointed U.S. Ambassador to South Viet-Nam, who had previously served in that position from July 1963 to June 1964.

moreland,[2] and as other needs appear, we will promptly meet them.

We committed our power and our national honor, and that has been reaffirmed by three Presidents. I have neither a rosy nor a gloomy report to make. It will require understanding and endurance and patriotism.

We have suffered 160,000 casualties since World War II, but we did not allow Greece or Turkey or Iran or Formosa or Lebanon or others to fall to aggressors, and we don't plan to let up until the aggression ceases.

I will ask Secretary McNamara to talk to you before he leaves, or talk to the press before he leaves. I reviewed with him in some detail this morning his plans, and I am sure he will tell you all about them that he can.

MEETINGS WITH FOREIGN POLICY ADVISERS
AND WITH TASK FORCE GROUPS

[2.] Q. Mr. President, I understand that you met until well after midnight last night with a group of foreign policy advisers. Could you tell us about that meeting?

THE PRESIDENT. Well, that is not a correct statement. I met until about 8 o'clock with them, maybe 8:30. I don't recall exactly. After I left that meeting, I met with a number of members of my task forces and chairmen of the task groups that are studying our program for next year and making our plans that will be submitted in the State of the Union Message, so they probably got those two meetings mixed up.

We discussed the balance of payments situation, and we had a brief report from Secretary Fowler. We discussed the European situation, NATO, and our relations with European countries and had a brief re-

port in that connection from Secretary Ball,[3] who left today for a meeting of the Deputy Prime Ministers in Europe.

We discussed the Latin American situation, including the Dominican Republic and other sensitive areas, and we had a brief report from Secretary Mann.[4]

We discussed the Asian situation, and the problems in India, and Pakistan, and their economic plans. Reports were received from Mr. George Woods[5] of the International Bank. Secretary Rusk reviewed them in some detail. We discussed our plans and ideas in the field of disarmament and proliferation. Mr. Bundy[6] went into some detail on that. We spent a substantial amount of time on Viet-Nam—I expect more time on that than on all of the other subjects. I will get Bill[7] to supply you with the time we went in and went out.

I went from that meeting to a meeting with the task force in the mess. I had my dinner with them and stayed until after midnight.

I will give you the subjects that we discussed. (I asked Bill to get them for me, and he did, but I misplaced the list.) I can give you pretty generally the basic ones—resources, education, health, fiscal policy, economic foreign policy, beautification, and the basic things.

THE DOMINICAN REPUBLIC

[3.] Q. Can you give us an evaluation of the Dominican situation now?

---

[2] Gen. William C. Westmoreland, Commander of United States Forces in South Viet-Nam.

[3] George W. Ball, Under Secretary of State.
[4] Thomas C. Mann, Under Secretary of State for Economic Affairs.
[5] George D. Woods, President, International Bank for Reconstruction and Development.
[6] McGeorge Bundy, Special Assistant to the President.
[7] Bill D. Moyers, Special Assistant to the President.

THE PRESIDENT. Yes, we are having very thorough reports from there. Ambassador Bunker [8] will be back to spend the weekend. We have been conferring with every interested group of citizens from all factions, and the OAS committee feels quite encouraged. There is a minimum of disorder. There is some economic dislocation and some strikes that have given some difficulties, but under all the circumstances we have made remarkable progress.

The OAS is entitled to our thanks for the diligence of their representatives there, and their effectiveness. I would hope that we will have some specific plans that will be acceptable, and that the OAS will make specific recommendations that will be acceptable to all concerned at an early date.

BALANCE OF PAYMENTS

[4.] Q. Are the reports, sir, that the balance of payments deficit is wiped out in the last 3 months true, and if so, what about some worry among economists that this could hurt the economy of Europe, that they will not have the dollars that they had before?

THE PRESIDENT. The reports that I have read are highly inaccurate. They cannot be confirmed. We do not have the exact information. I asked the Secretary of the Treasury to give me even his speculation, and he refused to do that yesterday. After I read the wire service stories, and stories in other periodicals, I asked the Chairman of the Economic Advisers, the Secretary of Commerce, and the Secretary of the Treasury. All of them were unfamiliar with it. They said that the only thing they could say was that it was premature, it was inaccurate,

and was undependable so far as the President is concerned.

Now, in the days ahead they may be exactly on the nose, but they are unwilling to say that in their position today, even to me, or to the task forces.

RESIGNATION OF AMBASSADOR TAYLOR; APPOINTMENT OF HENRY CABOT LODGE

[5.] Q. Mr. President, it seems inevitable that Ambassador Taylor's resignation is going to encourage or promote stories which allege that the real reason that he resigned was because of policy and/or strategic differences with the administration on how to conduct the war in Viet-Nam. Would you care to comment on these reports even before they become current?

THE PRESIDENT. I would not think that they were inevitable. I would think any such comment would be irresponsible and inaccurate and untrue. There have been no such facts to justify any conclusion of that kind. The letters reveal that, I think, clearly. [9]

To assume that, you would have to assume that neither the President nor General Taylor would tell the truth. General Taylor, at my request, was drafted to take this job. He told me when I asked him to take it that he would do whatever his Commander in Chief said, but that he hoped I would assure him that at the end of 12 months, 1 year, he would be relieved; that he had been taken from his family three times in 45 years, during three wars, and he looked forward to retiring from Government service.

Very shortly after he had retired he had

---

[8] Ellsworth Bunker, United States Representative to the Organization of American States.

[9] Gen. Maxwell D. Taylor served as U.S. Ambassador to South Viet-Nam from June 1964 to July 1965. His letter of resignation, dated July 7, and the President's reply, dated July 8, were not made public by the White House.

been called back to serve his country. He had done that in connection with the Bay of Pigs study. When he concluded that, they asked him to be Chairman of the Joint Chiefs, and that now he still looks forward to it, but if we needed him there, he would go for 12 months.

So we assured him that we would relieve him at the end of the 12-month period. That period was due to be about June 1st when he returned to Columbia University for a degree that they were to give him.

As usually happens, before General Taylor planned to come back, we had a serious problem there. We had a change of government about that time. It was necessary for him to delay his return for a few days until he had maintained contact with that situation. So he was delayed in departing.

When he came back, in the light of the developments out there, at his suggestion he returned, feeling that he did not want to leave that situation without going back and having an orderly transition that would not have been necessary if it had the same government. But we had a new government.

On March the 23d I had received from Ambassador Lodge an indication that he would be available for service to the Government. I had asked him to take another assignment. He told me that he would be glad to do it if I felt that that is where he could be best used, but if I had any thought of asking him to go back to Viet-Nam after General Taylor's year was up, that he would be available to do that.

I said, "Well, you think it over and talk to Mrs. Lodge, and call me back the next morning. And let us wrap this one up."

On the morning of March 24th he called me back and said he would be available. Since that time we have had him go to SEATO, and to NATO countries. We have had him appear before the Congress,

and at the debate at Oxford. We have kept him in complete touch with the situation. When General Taylor was ready to be relieved, it was agreed that this was the most effective and desirable way for us to do it.

Does that answer your question?

[6.] Q. Mr. President, in connection with Mr. Lodge's appointment, as you know, there has been a good deal of criticism about his appointment, especially because of his role during the overthrow of President Diem.[10] I would like to ask whether you anticipated those criticisms and how deeply concerned you are about them?

THE PRESIDENT. I know that some people can find fault with almost anything you do. I always anticipate that there will be some difference of opinion. I believe that in the Government there is none. The Secretary of State, the Secretary of Defense, the Assistant to the President in charge of matters of this kind, Mr. Bundy, and the President, all felt that Mr. Lodge had a grasp of the situation, a knowledge of the situation, that no other American had; that he was the best equipped, the best qualified, and the most experienced to do this work.

He had a combination of military experience, actual service in World War II, and diplomatic experience. He had gone to the SEATO nations and the NATO nations. He had been Ambassador there for some time and his service was highly respected by the governments of that area that he worked with, and by the people in this Government that he worked with.

It was with great regret that we accepted his resignation when he decided he should come home prior to the Republican Convention. It was with great pleasure that we

---

[10] Ngo Dinh Diem, former President of South Viet-Nam, who was executed after his government was overthrown by a military coup on November 2, 1963.

learned he would respond to the President's request to go back.

I think that we have the best man that is available to the United States in one of the most difficult jobs. I think the representatives of the people and the people will think so, too. He asked for 2 days' notice to notify his employers and to discuss the matter with General Eisenhower. I had discussed it with him some time before. I discussed Mr. Lodge with him and his Government service at a meeting 2 or 3 weeks ago and we gave him that 2 days' notice. That is why we made the announcement yesterday.

THE COMMON MARKET

[7.] Q. Mr. President, do you have any comment on the Common Market situation? Did you discuss that yesterday with Mr. Heller? [11] Did you reach any conclusions?

THE PRESIDENT. Yes, Mr. Heller made a brief report on his meetings that involved the Common Market situation. It involved the monetary situation; it involved the views that the Europeans have about our country, our leadership, and the soundness of the dollar, and so forth. It was an encouraging report generally, although there were some disappointments in it. I asked him to review the matters that he thought he could review with you.

TASK FORCE PERSONNEL

[8.] The task forces I talked to were the intergovernmental fiscal cooperation, transportation, metropolitan and urban problems, income maintenance task force, cost reduction task force, sustaining prosperity task force, foreign economic policy task force,

natural resources task force, preservation of natural beauty, Government reorganization, and education.

I will ask the Press Office to get you those.

Q. Mr. President, are these the same personnel as those who worked on the task force reports?

THE PRESIDENT. There are some adjustments. We have some substitutes, some additions. We think we have the best people available in these respective fields in the country. We have some new Government personnel working with them. For instance, Mr. Schultze [12] of the Budget is new; Mr. McPherson [13] is new. There will be other new ones that I hope to announce over the weekend.

I am going to have a rather busy weekend on appointments. I will try to make available to Bill information on them, and I will try to have a televised press conference, for those of you who are interested in that type of information, sometime next week.

CALL UP OF RESERVES

[9.] Q. Mr. President, in the light of the increased troop commitment to Viet-Nam, is it conceivable that you might call up some specific reserve units and also, perhaps, extend the draft to cover the other services?

THE PRESIDENT. When we have any plans or announcements to make of that nature, I will get in touch with you.

MISSION TO HANOI

[10.] Q. Mr. President, would you say, sir, to what extent you are being kept informed of the mission of Mr. Harold Davies

---

[11] Walter W. Heller, former Chairman of the Council of Economic Advisers.

[12] Charles L. Schultze, Director, Bureau of the Budget.

[13] Harry C. McPherson, Jr., Special Assistant to the President.

that Prime Minister Wilson is sending to Hanoi,[14] and what opportunity there may be for a peace talk?

THE PRESIDENT. We are informed about it.

INCOME TAX CUT

[11.] Q. Mr. President, in the light of the previous performance of the Government's receipts, have you moved any further along in your thinking about a possible further income tax cut next year?

THE PRESIDENT. We have a task force working on it, and the Secretary and the tax experts are working on it. I spent some time discussing fiscal matters with the Secretary of the Treasury yesterday.

We have a rather thorough report that I am sending to the Cabinet this week that will be released,[15] I think, about the middle

of the week by Secretary McNamara that shows $4.6 billion were actually realized during fiscal 1965 in savings, and that was $2.1 billion more than we estimated we could realize.

Savings of $6.1 billion a year by fiscal 1969 and each year thereafter has been set as our new long-range goal. We have the chart, the details of how it is done, the explanations and the challenges of change. We will make those available to the Cabinet and to some 30,000 other individuals that are involved. Secretary McNamara will discuss them in some detail with you a little later.

We cannot foresee at this moment the exact effect of defense expenditures at this time, but we have task forces in each department working on abolishing old programs and cutting down on present expenditures so that we may have some funds available for the subjects I discussed.

Merriman Smith, United Press International: Thank you, Mr. President.

NOTE: President Johnson's forty-fifth news conference was held in his office at the White House at 1:25 p.m. on Friday, July 9, 1965.

---

[14] In early July Prime Minister Harold Wilson of the United Kingdom sent Harold Davies, parliamentary secretary at the Ministry of Pensions, to Hanoi in an attempt to persuade President Ho Chi Minh to meet with a Commonwealth peace mission. The discussions in Hanoi were not successful.

[15] See Item 360.

---

348 Statement by the President Following Passage of the Medicare Bill by the Senate. *July 9, 1965*

THE 22-YEAR fight to protect the health of older Americans is now certain of swift and historic victory.

For these long decades bill after bill has been introduced to help older citizens meet the often crushing and always rising costs of disease and crippling illness. Each time, until today, the battle has been lost. Each time the forces of compassion and justice have returned from defeat to begin the battle anew. And each time the force of increased public understanding has added to our strength.

This bill is a great achievement for this Congress. But it flows from the long-enduring, and often thankless, efforts of earlier Presidents and earlier Congressmen. This is their victory too. It is the victory of Harry Truman and of great Congressmen like Aime Forand and James Murray and Robert Wagner and John Dingell. And it is also the victory of another who does not share this day.

I stood beside John Kennedy in the Senate in 1960 as he battled for the cause of justice, and watched in later years as his courage and his refusal to accept defeat gradually helped shape the forces which led us to this day. This bill is another stone in the enduring monument of his greatness.

When the conference has completed its work, a great burden will be lifted from the shoulders of all Americans. Older citizens will no longer have to fear that illness will wipe out their savings, eat up their income, and destroy lifelong hope of dignity and independence. For every family with older members it will mean relief from the often crushing responsibilities of care. For the Nation it will bring the necessary satisfaction of having fulfilled the obligations of justice to those who have given a lifetime of service and labor to their country.

This bill is sweeping in its intent and impact. It will help pay for care in hospitals. If hospitalization is unnecessary, it will help pay for care in nursing homes or in the home. And wherever illness is treated—in home or hospital—it will also help meet the fees of doctors and the costs of drugs. Its benefits are as varied as the techniques of modern treatment themselves.

This is a great day for older Americans. And it is a great day for America. For we have proved, once again, that the vitality of our democracy can shape the oldest of our values to the needs and obligations of today.

NOTE: The Medicare bill was approved by the President on July 30, 1965 (see Item 394).

In the statement the President referred to Aime Forand, Representative from Rhode Island 1937–1939 and 1941–1961, James E. Murray, Senator from Montana 1934–1961, Robert F. Wagner, Senator from New York 1927–1949, and Representative John D. Dingell of Michigan.

The statement was released at Austin, Tex.

349 Statement by the President Following Passage of the Voting Rights Bill by the House of Representatives. *July 10, 1965*

I CONGRATULATE the House of Representatives on its passage of the voting rights bill. That bill is not only a monument to this Congress, it is a shining moment in the entire history of the United States Congress.

I also congratulate the House on its decisive defeat, by a vote of 215–166, of the substitute amendment—supported by the Republicans' leadership—which would have seriously damaged and diluted the guarantee of the right to vote for all Americans.

These votes are not only a victory for the American Negro and the Democratic Party. They are a victory for every American who believes the strength of our democracy rests on the right of every citizen to share in its direction.

I hope the Senate and House conferees— in the same spirit of wisdom and urgency which has marked their earlier action—will resolve their differences and speed the bill to the White House for signature. For then every citizen can prepare to make himself eligible to choose his Government.

Thus we near the completion of a process almost as old as America itself. Our Revolution established the principle of democratic self-government—a reality for ourselves, a guiding hope for a world then drowned in monarchy and despotism. From that day to this we have labored and fought to extend the suffrage—the central mark of democratic dignity—to more of our people. Barrier after barrier—from property to sex— has fallen before the resistless progress of this most consistent political movement in American history. One major barrier alone remains, that of race and color. Now this too is tumbling.

Once this barrier is down, and if the right is fully exercised, we will enter a new and more hopeful stage in the progress of the Negro American. Possessing this most fundamental instrument of political redress, he can make his needs and his just demands heard and heeded in the politics and, ultimately, in the life of this land. We have been awakened to justice by the sound of songs and sermons, speeches and peaceful demonstrations. But the noiseless, secret vote will thunder forth a hundred times more loudly—inspiring the faithful, summoning the reluctant, and strengthening a Nation in its search for the promise of equality.

But a law is not a ballot. The right to vote is not a vote. The law must be enforced. It is my pledge to every American that as long as I am President I will enforce it. Every concerned citizen must help his fellows understand their rights, register, and use their vote wisely. Above all, American Negroes must strive to transform the promise of this law into strength at the polling places. They must teach and work—State by State,

district by district, street by street, house by house. It takes brave and dedicated men to win a battle. But our history tells us it takes equal, and often greater, dedication and endurance to reap the fruit of victory.

If this is done, Negro voting will double and redouble in years to come. A new force will have entered American political life. And the presence of that force will speed the day of equal opportunity for all.

Of course the vote alone will not fulfill the aspiration of the Negro Americans. It will require the guarantee of a wide spectrum of legal rights. And it will take a national effort to cope with the manifold ills which flow from the history of oppression.

But it is a vital step. It is an important addition to the sum of rights and obligations we call freedom. And, perhaps more importantly, it enriches the life of every one of us—white and black. For men are fully free only in the company of the free. And thus, today, we can all be a little prouder to be Americans.

NOTE: The Voting Rights Act of 1965 (S. 1564) was approved by the President on August 6, 1965 (see Item 409).

The statement was released at Austin, Tex.

350   Letter to the President of the Senate and to the Speaker of the House Transmitting a Report on the Development of the Passamaquoddy-St. John River Basin. *July 12, 1965*

Dear Mr. President: (Dear Mr. Speaker:)

I am transmitting herewith a report on the Passamaquoddy-St. John River Basin power development, together with a recommendation for the immediate authorization of the Dickey-Lincoln School project on the St. John River. Construction of this project would be contingent upon the completion of necessary arrangements with the Government of Canada.

This report, which has my approval, was prepared under the general direction of the Secretary of the Interior, and in cooperation with Federal, State, and local agencies concerned.

The report in draft form has been circulated to the Federal agencies concerned and to the Governors of the New England States for their review and comments. These comments accompany the report.

Authorization of the Dickey-Lincoln School project and the carrying forward of the other recommendations contained in the report is a highly important step in the future economic growth of the New England area.

New England is an area of exceptionally high power costs. The Federal Power Commission's 1964 National Power Survey revealed that the cost of producing, transmitting, and distributing power in New England is 28 percent above the national average.

To some extent, this reflects a lack of native resources of coal, oil and natural gas and the consequent high cost of these fuels when used for electric generation. To an equal extent, however, it reflects the relative lack of large-scale generation and transmission facilities.

The Dickey-Lincoln School project is among the best of the unexploited resources of New England and fits admirably into plans for broad scale and long-term improvement for energy costs in New England.

Much of the 794,000 kilowatts of power which would be installed ultimately at the Dickey-Lincoln School project can be made available to meet peakloads on systems elsewhere in New England at estimated costs to these systems in the range of $15.50 per kilowatt-year and 3 mills per kilowatt-hour. These costs compare favorably with the more economic sources of peaking power which have been developed in many other parts of the Nation.

The Dickey-Lincoln School project would save New England power consumers more than $7 million annually by comparison with costs of currently planned alternative new sources of power supply in the area. In comparison with present average costs for equivalent power in New England, the sav-

ing would be more than $9 million annually.

The location of the Dickey-Lincoln School project in northern Maine and in relatively close relation to load centers and transmission networks in neighboring Canadian Provinces, could provide the basis for important mutual gains by Canada and the United States. The further strengthening of the interconnections between our two countries, permitting the appropriate exchange of available capacity and energy and mutual support under emergency conditions, could be a significant extension in the program of international cooperation which has aided so much in the mutual improvement of our electric energy resources.

While power developments will make significant contributions to the economic well-being of the New England region, comprehensive planning for the multiple use of the natural resources of the region should also be pursued to provide for a balanced program of regional economic development.

I am requesting that the Federal agencies, working in full cooperation with State and regional planning groups, continue and accelerate the preparation of an overall plan for the development of the region's resources. Particular attention will be given to the historic sites and values in New England which form such an important part of our national heritage, including any recommendations the Roosevelt Park Commission may make to the United States and Canadian Governments for a more extensive program of development of President Franklin Roosevelt's summer home on Campobello Island.

I am confident that this program for the development of the resources of the New England areas will make a major contribution to the region, the Nation, and indeed—looking ahead to the future—to the well-being of the people of Canada as well. I commend this report to the Congress for its consideration.

Sincerely,

LYNDON B. JOHNSON

NOTE: This is the text of identical letters addressed to the Honorable Hubert H. Humphrey, President of the Senate, and to the Honorable John W. McCormack, Speaker of the House of Representatives. A portion of the letter was made public as a White House release.

The report is printed in House Document 236 (89th Cong., 1st sess.).

351 Memorandum Following Release of the Labor Department's Employment Figures for June. *July 12, 1965*

Memorandum from the President for Cabinet Officers and Agency Heads:

A new job can mean

—The launching of a young person's career;

—Another lease on economic life for someone dropped by a shrinking industry or an outmoded occupation;

—A bright horizon for a housewife who has brought up her children; and

—A ticket to join the steady movement from farm to city.

Jobs are our economy's most important product, and I want you to know where our job record stands at mid-year.

The news is good. Although it is not good enough and although unemployment remains too high for many groups and many areas, we are moving forward toward our ultimate aim of job opportunities for everyone willing and able to work.

New figures for June released by the Labor Department this afternoon show that, in the first half of 1965, we added 1.1 million jobs to non-farm payrolls. This is even a substantially better gain than we made in the first half of 1964.

Employment in manufacturing, wholesale and retail trade, service industries, and state and local governments all increased substantially, while the Federal government was not adding to the number of its employees.

And these most recent figures show that the pace is being maintained, with a 210,000 increase in payroll jobs during June.

For the second quarter of this year, the unemployment rate was 4.7 percent of the civilian labor force, the lowest since the third quarter of 1957. Nearly all groups in our labor force have shared the improvement since unemployment began a steady decline from the 5.6 percent rate of the last quarter of 1963. But the unemployment rate for teenagers remains near 15 percent because of the rapid growth of teenagers in the labor force. And though it has shown encouraging improvement in the past year, the rate for Negro workers remains far too high at 8 percent.

These are problems we must face and solve. I know I can count on all of you to work to improve our record. I know that we will be working to promote and extend the prosperity of 53 months that has added 5½ million jobs for Americans. I know that we must and we can develop and carry out programs to make more efficient and more humane use of our precious manpower resources.

And I know that we will work in full cooperation with business and labor, because full employment opportunity is a task and a goal for the whole nation.

LYNDON B. JOHNSON

NOTE: The memorandum was released at Austin, Tex.

352 White House Statement on the Report on U.S.-Canadian Relations Prepared Jointly by Ambassadors Livingston Merchant and A. D. P. Heeney. *July* 12, 1965

THE PRESIDENT and the Prime Minister of Canada are making public today a report prepared at their request by Ambassador Livingston Merchant of the United States and Ambassador A. D. P. Heeney of Canada.

In their first working meeting in Washington in January 1964, the President and the Prime Minister agreed on the need for a study of the basic principles of relations between the United States and Canada. Later, they commissioned Ambassador Merchant and Ambassador Heeney to make this study together. The two Ambassadors made their report on Friday, July 9, and the President and the Prime Minister have agreed that it deserves prompt publication.

The President emphasizes again the ex-traordinary importance of close and friendly relations between the United States and Canada, which have lived together as the best of neighbors in two centuries. The President believes that this report is a serious and constructive contribution to still better relations between Canada and the United States. He has asked Secretary of State Rusk to take the lead for the United States in a prompt review of the report and its recommendations. The Secretary's review will be the basis for further United States action on this report.

NOTE: The report of the two Ambassadors, dated June 28, 1965, and entitled "Canada and the United States—Principles for Partnership," is printed in the Department of State Bulletin (vol. 53, p. 193).

The White House statement was released at Austin, Tex.

353 The President's News Conference of *July* 13, 1965

THE PRESIDENT. Good afternoon, ladies and gentlemen.

VIET-NAM

[1.] Secretary McNamara and Ambassador Lodge [1] will be leaving tomorrow evening for Saigon. When they return next week, we will give careful consideration to their recommendations, as well as those of Ambassador Taylor [2] and General West-moreland.[3] And we will do what is necessary.

The present center of the struggle is in South Viet-Nam, but its root cause is a determined effort of conquest that is directed from Hanoi. Heavy infiltration of North Vietnamese forces has created new dangers and difficulties in South Viet-Nam. Increased aggression from the North may require an increased American response on the ground in South Viet-Nam. Increased aggression from the North continues to re-

[1] Henry Cabot Lodge, U.S. Ambassador to South Viet-Nam.

[2] Gen. Maxwell D. Taylor, former U.S. Ambassador to South Viet-Nam, who resigned on July 7, 1965.

[3] Gen. William C. Westmoreland, Commander of United States Forces in South Viet-Nam.

quire very careful replies against selected military targets in North Viet-Nam.

Meanwhile, General Westmoreland has the authority to use the American forces that are now in Viet-Nam in the ways which he considers most effective to resist the Communist aggression and the terror that is taking place there. These forces will defend their own bases. They will assist in providing security in neighboring areas, and they will be available for more active combat missions when the Vietnamese Government and General Westmoreland agree that such active missions are needed.

So it is quite possible that new and serious decisions will be necessary in the near future. Any substantial increase in the present level of our efforts to turn back the aggressors in South Viet-Nam will require steps to insure that our reserves of men and equipment of the United States remain entirely adequate for any and all emergencies.

Secretary McNamara and Ambassador Lodge will concern themselves also with the political and economic situation. We have had Mr. Eugene Black visiting southeast Asia and he has given me an oral report on his encouraging visit to that area.[4] We mean to make it plain that our military effort is only a necessary preliminary to the larger purpose of peace and progress.

---

[4] On July 10, 1965, the White House announced that Eugene R. Black, adviser to the President on southeast Asian social and economic development, had telephoned the President and given him an encouraging report on his visit to the Far East. During his trip Mr. Black had participated in meetings of the Consultative Committee of the United Nations Economic Commission for Asia and the Far East on the establishment of an Asian Development Bank. He reported to the President that all had gone well, and the Bank would begin operating early in 1966.

DOMINICAN REPUBLIC

[2.] In the Dominican Republic, Ambassador Bunker[5] and his colleagues are continuing their skillful and determined effort to find a peaceful solution. We believe, as they do, that it is urgent that a solution be found, and found promptly.

We are encouraged by indications that leaders on both sides are prepared to stand aside in favor of a new government which will enjoy the confidence of the Dominican people as a whole. Those on both sides who show good will and those who join a new government in the work of restoring peace will deserve the thanks of all of their countrymen. Right now, here, we are both cautious and hopeful.

NOMINATION OF THURGOOD MARSHALL AS SOLICITOR GENERAL

[3.] I am very pleased to announce today that I am nominating Judge Thurgood Marshall to be Solicitor General of the United States. He will succeed the Honorable Archibald Cox, who is retiring after more than 4 years of distinguished service to return to Massachusetts.

The Solicitor General directs all Government litigation before the Supreme Court of the United States and the other appellate courts. Judge Marshall brings to that significant job an outstanding record of legal and judicial experience. He has served on the United States Court of Appeals for the Second Circuit since 1962, and at very considerable financial sacrifice is resigning in order to meet the needs of his Government.

---

[5] Ellsworth Bunker, U.S. Representative to the Organization of American States.

For a quarter of a century before his appointment to the bench, Judge Marshall was the leading legal champion of equal rights under the law, appearing before the Supreme Court more than 30 times. His vast experience in the Federal courts, and especially in the Supreme Court, has gained Judge Marshall a reputation as one of the most distinguished advocates in the Nation. I know him to be a lawyer and a judge of very high ability, a patriot of deep convictions, and a gentleman of undisputed integrity.

So it is an honor to appoint him as the 33d Solicitor General of the United States. He is here this afternoon and I would like to ask him to stand.

Judge Marshall.

OTHER NOMINATIONS

[4.] I intend to nominate Mr. Leonard Marks of Washington, D.C., to be the Director of the United States Information Service, succeeding the Honorable Carl Rowan.

Mr. Marks has an excellent record as a teacher, as a lawyer, and as a Government servant. President Kennedy appointed him to be an original member of the board of directors of the Communications Satellite Corporation in 1962. Since that time he has been reappointed. Mr. Marks, who has had a long interest in international communications, has represented the United States at broadcasting conferences and activities in Italy, India, Pakistan, Switzerland, Afghanistan, Turkey, and Iran.

Phillips Talbot, the Assistant Secretary of State for Near Eastern and South Asian Affairs, will be nominated as United States Ambassador to Greece. He will succeed Mr. Henry R. Labouisse, who is Executive Director of the United Nations Children's Fund.

A most experienced Foreign Service Officer, the Honorable Raymond A. Hare, who is presently Ambassador to Turkey, will succeed him in his post as Assistant Secretary of State. Ambassador Hare has been in the Foreign Service since 1927. He has served in France, Egypt, Saudi Arabia, Lebanon, the United Arab Republic, and Yemen.

I have asked Mrs. Penelope Hartland Thunberg of Maryland to become a member of the United States Tariff Commission. She will serve in the position last held by Commissioner Walter Schreiber for a term expiring June 16, 1970.

Mrs. Thunberg is an international economist presently serving as Deputy Chief of the International Division, Economic and Research Area, Central Intelligence Agency. She was a Phi Beta Kappa graduate from Pembroke College and holds the M.A. and Ph. D. degrees from Radcliffe College. She is here this afternoon and I would like for you to meet her. Please stand up.

RECONVENING OF THE DISARMAMENT COMMITTEE

[5.] Yesterday the Soviet Government notified the United States Government that it is agreeable to the resumption of negotiations of the 18-nation Disarmament Committee at Geneva. The United States has suggested a date no later than July 27th for this resumption. Mr. William C. Foster now is in the process of inquiring whether this date is agreeable to the other 16 members of the Disarmament Committee.

At the conclusion of the Geneva conference last September, it was agreed that the two cochairmen, the Soviet Union and the United States, would consult and would agree on a date for resumption, after which the other members of the Committee would be con-

737

sulted in order to obtain their agreement as well.

Mr. Foster met with the Soviet spokesman in New York on June 15th on instructions to urge reconvening of the Disarmament Committee as soon as possible. Yesterday's Soviet response is an encouraging development. As we have stated before, peace is the leading item on the agenda of mankind, and every effort should be made to lead us toward that goal. As I stated in San Francisco, we will come to these next negotiations with proposals for effective attack on these deadly dangers to mankind, and we hope that others will do the same.

Now I am prepared to take your questions.

QUESTIONS

MANPOWER NEEDS FOR VIET-NAM

[6.] Q. Mr. President, in your statement about the situation in Viet-Nam, sir, you referred to the necessity for maintaining adequate reserves and adequate equipment. I wonder, sir, in view of the increased fighting and the increasing manpower commitment, are you giving any thought, is the Government giving any thought, first, to calling up additional Reserves, or second, to increasing draft calls?

THE PRESIDENT. The Government is always considering every possibility and every eventuality. No decisions have been made in connection with the Reserve or increasing draft calls. We will be in a better position to act upon matters of that kind after the Secretary returns from his trip.

AMBASSADOR HARRIMAN'S TRIP TO MOSCOW

[7.] Q. Mr. President, could you tell us whether Governor Harriman's [6] trip to Mos-

---

[6] W. Averell Harriman, Ambassador at Large and former Governor of New York.

cow has any connection with the Soviet position in Viet-Nam?

THE PRESIDENT. I think that the Governor has best explained that trip himself by saying it is a vacation. That is on the wires today. It is not an official Government trip. He was not sent there by the President, although the Governor is a man of a wide range of interests and experience. I approved heartily of his statement that he would be glad to visit with any people that cared to visit with him. It is a personal trip, and a vacation trip in nature.

POSSIBILITY OF AVOIDING MAJOR WAR IN ASIA

[8.] Q. Mr. President, what do you think, in your judgment, are the chances at this time of avoiding a major land war in Asia?

THE PRESIDENT. I don't think that anyone can prophesy what will happen from day to day, or week to week, or month to month. I think it is well for us to remember that three Presidents have made the pledge for this Nation, that the Senate has ratified the SEATO treaty by a vote of 82 to 1, pledging the United States to come to the aid of any nation, upon their request, who are parties to that treaty or protocol.

President Eisenhower made our first commitment there in 1954. That was reaffirmed by President Kennedy many times in different ways. The present President has reiterated the stand of the United States that we expect to keep that commitment.

Our national honor is at stake. Our word is at stake. And it must be obvious to all Americans that they would not want the President of their country to follow any course that was inconsistent with our commitments or with our national honor.

MERGER OF RESERVES AND NATIONAL GUARD

[9.] Q. Mr. President, sir, in view of the situation in North Viet-Nam and South Viet-Nam, are you thinking of continuing the plans for a merger of Reserves and the National Guard?

THE PRESIDENT. So far as I am aware, the situation there has no effect on the merger one way or the other.

Q. Would it not affect the efficiency of our forces?

THE PRESIDENT. It is contended that the merger would improve the efficiency, but I do not think that it is a matter that would be considered in connection with what happens out there, one way or the other.

MANNED ORBITING LABORATORY

[10.] Q. Mr. President, could you give us a status report on the Air Force's manned orbiting laboratory, and specifically whether you intend to give it a "go-ahead," and if so, when?

THE PRESIDENT. No, I am not in a position to make a statement on that at this time. The Space Council has had some briefings in connection with the matter. There is a study going on every day in that connection, but I would not want to go further than that now.

RELATIONS WITH SOVIET UNION

[11.] Q. Mr. President, in view of the Disarmament Conference and the Soviet response, and Ambassador Harriman's conversations with the Soviet Union, could you give us your assessment of the Soviet-American relations as they stand now? Could you give us a temperature reading?

THE PRESIDENT. We are very anxious to maintain close relations with the Soviet Union, and we had felt that considerable progress had been made in the last several years. Unfortunately, the situation that developed in North Viet-Nam has placed a strain on those relations. We regret it very deeply, but we have felt that, as I said earlier, our national honor required us to pursue the course of conduct that we have followed.

We will be looking for every opportunity that we can to work with the Soviet Union in the interest of peace. We think that the resumption of the Disarmament Conference is one step in that direction. We would like to improve the relations any way we can.

MANPOWER NEEDS FOR VIET-NAM

[12.] Q. Mr. President, you told us last week, sir, that things in Viet-Nam will probably get worse before they can get better. And today you indicate that we will probably send a lot more forces there than we have now. Can you give us any appraisal as to how many, or are we going to change our fighting, or is a new concept going to be introduced? Can you give us any indication of that?

THE PRESIDENT. As I said in my opening statement, the aggression has increased. The forces that are pursuing that aggression have greatly increased in number. It will be necessary to resist that aggression and, therefore, to have substantially larger increments of troops which we have been supplying from time to time.

I do not think that anyone can tell at this date any special figure that will be required, but I think that following Ambassador Lodge and Secretary McNamara's trip we will have a better estimate of what the rest of the year will hold for us.

GOVERNMENT IN SAIGON

[13.] Q. Mr. President, some people have questioned the ability of the South Vietnamese to govern themselves at this point—most recently, Senator Stennis of Mississippi. Can you give us some indication of what you see in the future for the re-establishment of democratic civilian rule in Saigon?

THE PRESIDENT. We would hope that if the North Vietnamese would cease their aggression we could immediately take steps to have the people of South Viet-Nam exercise their choice and establish a government of their choosing. We, of course, would hope that that would be a very efficient and effective and democratic system.

SEARCH FOR A PEACEFUL SETTLEMENT

[14.] Q. Mr. President, with the increasing number of American troops going to Viet-Nam, would you say if there will be a continuing or any increasing diplomatic probing for a peaceful settlement?

THE PRESIDENT. Yes, we will constantly be on the alert to probe, and to be ready and willing to negotiate with the appropriate people. I must say that candor compels me to tell you that there has not been the slightest indication that the other side is interested in negotiation or in unconditional discussions, although the United States has made some dozen separate attempts to bring that about.

RELATIONS WITH THE PRESS

[15.] Q. Mr. President, quite a bit has been written recently about your relations with the press. Some of these stories have been openly critical, to say the least, sir. We seem to have heard from everybody but you. I wonder if you could give us your views on the subject?

THE PRESIDENT. I think that the press and the Congress and the people of the United States have, generally speaking, with very minor exceptions, given me during the time I have been President very strong support and very excellent cooperation. I know that there are some in each segment that have been disappointed in some of my decisions and some of my actions. I like to think that those who talk about them the most see us the least, and so far as I am concerned, I have no criticism to make of any other people in helping me do my job.

We have a very fine Cabinet. Nearly every person I have asked to come and help the Government has done so. I think that there are very few Presidents in the history of this country that have had more support of more publishers and more magazines than the present President. I am grateful for that, although I recognize it is an essential part of their duty to point up weaknesses that they think exist.

I have seen that take place for some 35 years, and as long as they point them out, in the manner in which they are pointing them out, and the people continue to support us, and the Congress continues to support us, I am not going to find any fault with them. During the period that we have had the most hectic, distressing moments here in Washington, the poll has gone up 6 percent out in the country, so I sometimes think maybe it just may be July in the Nation's Capital.

REPEAL OF THE POLL TAX

[16.] Q. Mr. President, are you taking any position at this point on the poll tax repealer in the House version of the voting rights bill?

THE PRESIDENT. Yes, I have taken a position since making my recommendations to the Congress early in the year, that I would like to see the poll tax repealed. I am against the poll tax. I have tried to get it repealed every time that I have had a chance, when I thought we could do it legally.

I have asked the Attorney General to attempt to work with the conferees of both House and Senate to see if they cannot agree on satisfactory language that will give us the most effective repeal provision that is obtainable and that we think can be supported in the courts. I have no doubt but what a very satisfactory solution will be found. And I think that would be quite desirable.[7]

VACANCIES IN USIA

[17.] Q. Mr. President, have you discussed with Leonard Marks as yet the particular man or the type of men that you and he might like to fill the other two key vacancies in the USIA—the Deputy Director and the head of the Voice of America?

THE PRESIDENT. No. The Deputy Director is now being handled by a very able man with experience who will be there for a while yet. I am sure that after Mr. Marks reviews the organizations and talks to the present Deputy Director and the present Director, Mr. Rowan, he will come up with some suggestions and recommendations. I believe that they will be acceptable.

---

[7] The Voting Rights Act of 1965 was approved by the President on August 6, 1965 (see Item 409). The act did not abolish the poll tax as a precondition for voting in State elections, but it authorized the Attorney General to test the constitutionality of the poll tax in the courts.

HOUSE ACTION ON VOTING RIGHTS

[18.] Q. Mr. President, in view of your long history of seeking to keep civil rights a bipartisan matter, why did you single out the House Republican leadership for criticism in your statement on voting rights last week?[8]

THE PRESIDENT. I didn't single out anyone. We had had several days' debate about the relative merits of two proposals. It had been observed that the administration proposal was dripping in venom and was inadequate and went too far, and a good many things had been said about it. Finally, when it was put as a test to the judgment of the House and they made their decision, I commended that decision and said that I believed that they were wise in acting as they had. Because had they adopted the so-called Ford or McCulloch substitute for the committee bill, as advocated by Judge Howard Smith and Governor Tuck and others, I was of the opinion it would have diluted and taken strength from the bill that they had passed.[9]

I am very proud of the action of the House. I am very proud of the judgment they exercised in that connection. But people are allowed to comment on the relative merits of legislation either before or after a vote, and I found there have been a good many comments on my proposals. I thought it would be appropriate if I carefully limited

---

[8] See Item 349.

[9] Representative Gerald R. Ford of Michigan, minority leader of the House of Representatives, and Representative William M. McCulloch of Ohio, ranking Republican member of the House Judiciary Committee, sponsored a substitute for the administration's voting rights bill. The substitute bill was supported by Representatives Howard W. Smith and William M. Tuck, both of Virginia.

myself to an observation that the substitute would have diluted the right of every American to vote.

I think all of us are aware of the fact that in years gone by we could have done much more than we have in that field. I have become very conscious of that as I have traveled over this Nation and talked to our people. I think the House acted wisely, and I have every confidence in the action that will follow the conference report. I ask the cooperation of members of both parties. I do not think the substitute was as effective as the bill that was adopted. And I would not like to see us return to it.

THE PRESIDENT'S VIEWS ON CIVIL RIGHTS GENERALLY

[19.] Q. Mr. President, in connection with civil rights and the colloquy between you and the Republican leaders, they have suggested that over the years you have changed your position on civil rights. I wondered if you could give us your concept of your developing philosophy on civil rights legislation?

THE PRESIDENT. Yes, I think that all of us realize at this stage of the 20th century there is much that should have been done that has not been done. This bill is not going to solve the problem completely itself. There will be much to be done in the years ahead. I think the problem of the American Negro is one of the two or three most important problems that we must face up to with our legislation again next year.

I am particularly sensitive to the problems of the Negro and the problems of the city and the problems which the shift in population has caused, the problems of education. I have task forces working on those things. And perhaps it is because I realize, after traveling through 44 States and after reading

some 20,000 or 30,000 letters a week, digests from them, that it is a very acute problem and one that I want to do my best to solve in the limited time that I am allowed.

I did not have that responsibility in the years past, and I did not feel it to the extent that I do today. I hope that you may understand that I think it is an acute one and a dangerous one, and one that occupies high priority and one that should challenge every American of whatever party, whatever religion. I am going to try to provide all the leadership that I can, notwithstanding the fact that someone may point to a mistake or 100 mistakes that I made in my past.

THE SOVIET UNION'S AID TO HANOI

[20.] Q. Mr. President, the Soviet Union announced yesterday a new aid agreement to North Viet-Nam. I think they said it was over and beyond what they are now supplying. Do you see this as a serious, perhaps dangerous contribution to the increased aggression you spoke of earlier that is being directed from the North?

THE PRESIDENT. Peter,[10] I don't think that we can tell the extent of that agreement and how far it will reach. They gave no figures. They did not explain what materials they were going to supply. We have known for some time now that they are furnishing equipment and they are furnishing supplies and they are making contributions of aid in one form or the other to North Viet-Nam; this is no surprise to us at all.

I read the very general announcement that they had made. There is nothing that I could detect from it, or that our experts could detect, that would give me any more information than contained in the announcement.

---

[10] Peter Lisagor of the Chicago Daily News.

EFFECT OF TEACH-INS ON VIET-NAM

[21.] Q. Mr. President, do you think it possible that increased aggression and infiltration by North Viet-Nam springs from a misreading on the other side, a perhaps mistaken belief that the teach-ins and whatever criticism there has been here in the United States of your policy, that this represents the voice of the American people?

THE PRESIDENT. No, I don't think that the teach-ins and the differences of opinion have increased the strength of the North Vietnamese or the aggression that has taken place. I do think that at times our allies, particularly the South Vietnamese people, and particularly our own soldiers, do get concerned about how strong we are behind them and how united we are in this very serious undertaking.

But I am glad to say that I don't think it has had any serious or damaging effect there. I get several letters a day from soldiers in Viet-Nam, service people, the Navy, Marines, Army, and Air. I hear from their parents. And I have yet to receive a single complaining letter.

On occasions they wish that the folks back home, who are following this with such dedicated interest, understood the position as they feel they understand it. But I don't think it has damaged our effort out there and I don't think it will. I think we will be united in this effort.

There will be some differences of opinion about the wisdom of some courses that the President takes, the Executive takes, but whenever and wherever we can, we will try to explain those to the people involved and at least try to get their understanding.

THE SECRETARY OF STATE

[22.] Q. Mr. President, there have been reports published from time to time that you might contemplate a change in the office of the Secretary of State. In the months to come, do you foresee such a change?

THE PRESIDENT. None whatever. And I think you do a great damage and a great disservice to one of the most able and most competent and most dedicated men that I have ever known, Secretary Rusk. He sits to my right in the Cabinet room. He ranks first in the Cabinet and he ranks first with me.

SELECTION AS VICE PRESIDENTIAL CANDIDATE
IN 1960

[23.] Q. Mr. President, there are two recently published versions as to how President Kennedy selected you as his vice presidential running mate in 1960, Mr. Graham's [11] and Mr. Schlesinger's.[12] Which of these, in your judgment, is closest to the truth, or do you have your own version?

THE PRESIDENT. I would not want to get into a dispute with my friends who have written these memorandums. I don't see anything to be gained by that.

The President asked me, on his own motion, to go on the ticket with him, and I gave him my reasons for hesitating. He told

[11] The late Philip L. Graham, former President of the Washington Post. His account of the 1960 nomination for Vice President is in the form of a memorandum to himself. It is published in "The Making of the President" by Theodore H. White (New York: Atheneum Publishers, 1960).

[12] Arthur M. Schlesinger, Jr., "A Thousand Days— John F. Kennedy in the White House" (Boston: Houghton Mifflin Co., 1965).

me he would speak to Speaker Rayburn and others, and he did. Subsequently, he called me and said, "Here's a statement I am going to read on television, unless you have an objection." I listened to it. After I heard it, I felt that I should do what I did. I don't know just how much these men may know about what actually happened, but they are entitled to their opinions. Of course, I know why I did what I did.

Merriman Smith, United Press International: Thank you, Mr. President.

NOTE: President Johnson's forty-sixth news conference was held in the East Room at the White House at 1 p.m. on Tuesday, July 13, 1965.

354 Remarks at the Signing of the Older Americans Act. *July 14, 1965*

Members of the Congress, my old friend Aime Forand, distinguished guests, His Excellency the Ambassador from Malawi, Ambassador Gondwe:

I have just had a delightful visit with the Ambassador who comes from the African Continent, who was telling me that the average life expectancy in his country is little less than 40 years of age. I was reminded that in 1900, when this century began, the life expectancy in this country was 47 years of age, and what great improvements we have made here in our own land, and what great opportunity we had in the world to contribute to their improvements.

This year, the century has reached the age of 65, and nearly one out of ten Americans have lived that full span or longer.

Lengthening the lifespan is a major achievement of our time. It is also the source of one of the major challenges to the values and the vision of our Great Society.

This Older Americans Act that we meet here this morning to bring into being—the act of 1965, the act that is authored by the distinguished, socially-conscious gentlemen from Rhode Island and Michigan, my old friend, John Fogarty, and my colleague of many years, Pat McNamara—known as the Fogarty-McNamara bill—will help us to

meet that challenge for more than 18 million Americans who have already reached age 65, as well as the hundreds of thousands or more who are becoming 65 at the rate of 1 every 20 seconds. I know that doesn't apply to any of you out there, but that is what is happening in America.

Congressman Fogarty, Senator McNamara, and my distinguished Cabinet colleague here, Secretary Tony Celebrezze, and many more, deserve our gratitude for their leadership and their achievement in this legislation.

The Older Americans Act clearly affirms our Nation's sense of responsibility toward the well-being of all of our older citizens. But even more, the results of this act will help us to expand our opportunities for enriching the lives of all of our citizens in this country, now and in the years to come.

This legislation is really the seed-corn that provides an orderly, intelligent, and constructive program to help us meet the new dimensions of responsibilities which lie ahead in the remaining years of this century.

Under this program every State and every community can now move toward a coordinated program of services and opportunities for our older citizens. We revere them; we extend them our affection; we respect them. We have been talking about it all these years, now we are doing something about it. It is a *fait accompli*. The talk has gone ahead of us, the bills have been drafted, they are here for signature, and they become the law of the land.

Now many of our States and communities are already demonstrating imagination and initiative in this particular field, and it comes pretty late. It is too late to do a lot for a good many older Americans. They have already gone on. But a few communities have achieved the coordinated, community-wide programs which we think are needed, and we hope that this will just be a kickoff point for others to emulate their example.

The Older Americans Act will make it possible for us to move faster in these places where we have already started. It will permit us to travel new ways where old ways have not worked before. It will permit new beginnings where none have been made before.

The grants under this law will be modest in dollars, but will be far-reaching in results. Its results will come where they are needed—always at the hometown level. I am hopeful, as I know and believe that the Congress is hopeful, that this will permit us to find greater uses for the skills and the wisdom and the experience that is found in the maturity of our older citizens.

The importance of meeting this challenge just cannot be overstated. At present, 1.5 million Americans reach age 65 each year—1½ million. Since 1900 the proportion of persons in our population age 65 and over has already doubled. What a tribute that is to our medical profession. And you haven't seen anything yet.

When the conference committee reports in the Senate, and the House adopts their report, we have the Medicare act that this great man introduced many, many years ago—it was almost dangerous for him to walk down the corridor, after he introduced that bill, for several years. When it comes into being, there will be a real new day for older Americans in this country.

I understand that of all the persons that have reached age 65 since the dawn of civilization, 25 percent of them are alive today. These older generations need to participate in what we are doing and, as a Nation, we can profit from their participation.

This Congress has already done more for the youth of America in terms of education than any Congress of this century. And Senator Morse, who doesn't always endorse everything I do abroad, does endorse practically everything we do at home, and helps us to do it; and I want to salute him and all the other legislators for what they have done in making this the greatest education Congress in history. And before this session is concluded, I am confident we may be able to say the same of the record of this Congress as far as older people are concerned that we are able to say about education.

I am very proud to have the privilege of now signing into law this measure for the benefit of the men and women who have done so much in this century to build in America a just, a decent, a free, and a peaceful society. I hope that every person within the sound of my voice will be willing to continue to unite behind us in not only expanding the life expectancy in this country, but in trying to help our neighbors in the world to achieve the same remarkable results that all of you members of both parties, by working together, have achieved in this country.

This is really a bright spot in my public career, and the only thing I regret is that so many of the older Americans, including my college president, and including my mother who inspired me many years ago to take an interest in this field, are not here to see the results of the Fogarty-McNamara legislation and the legislators, each of whom made a major contribution in this field.

I asked Senator Douglas when he got out of the Senate someday if he wanted to be my Comptroller General, because he is always finding ways to save money that I can use on good things like education, health, and older Americans. And if we can find ways in these departments that just stop part of the waste, we will have much of our resources to use in fields of this kind.

Thank you very much.

NOTE: The President spoke at 11:55 a.m. in the Rose Garden at the White House. In his opening words he referred to Aime Forand, Representative from Rhode Island 1937–1939 and 1941–1961, and to Vincent Gondwe, Ambassador to the United States from Malawi.

During his remarks the President referred to Representative John E. Fogarty of Rhode Island, Senator Pat McNamara of Michigan, Secretary of Health, Education, and Welfare Anthony J. Celebrezze, Senator Wayne Morse of Oregon, and Senator Paul H. Douglas of Illinois.

As enacted, the Older Americans Act of 1965 is Public Law 89–73 (79 Stat. 218).

355   Remarks at a Luncheon for Members of the Joint U.S.-Japan Committee on Trade and Economic Affairs.   *July* 14, 1965

Distinguished guests, gentlemen:

We are deeply grateful for the time that the Ministers of the Cabinet of Japan have given to this visit to our country. We have found our discussions to be both pleasant and productive.

It seems that it is very difficult to avoid some tragedy in meetings of this kind, because I remember almost 20 months ago when members of the American Cabinet were enroute to Tokyo for discussions that we first learned of the death of our beloved President John Fitzgerald Kennedy.

A few moments before this luncheon began today, I received word that the great and good man, Adlai Stevenson, had died in London.

Of course, my immediate reaction was to cancel this luncheon meeting. But after talking to some of the members of my own Cabinet and some of his friends, we all realized that Adlai Stevenson would not have had us do any such thing. He would want us to continue, because he was first, and he was foremost, concerned that the works of peace and the works of progress and, most important, the works of understanding, which have prevailed and predominated throughout this meeting, must go on.

So this, then, is our legacy from Adlai Stevenson—a charge to continue the quest for a decent world, for a better world order, for a life for man that is free of war and destruction and the oppression of his spirit.

So, this is our pledge to the memory of this great man who is really, as all of you here know, a true citizen of the world—a pledge to devote our energies and our talents and our resources and our wills to the cause for which he died.

We realize that America lost its foremost advocate and its most eloquent spirit and one of its finest voices for peace in the world. The world of freedom has lost, I think, perhaps its most dedicated champion.

So, I would like to ask each of you to stand with me in a moment of silent tribute to this great lover of peace, this great statesman, Adlai E. Stevenson.

[*At this point there was a moment of silence.*]

NOTE: The President spoke at 2:10 p.m. in the State Dining Room at the White House. Foreign Minister Etsusaburo Shiina of Japan responded as follows: *"Mr. President, your Excellencies:*

"I am deeply grieved to hear of the passing of a truly great American, Ambassador Stevenson. It was last December that I had the privilege of meeting him for the first time at the United Nations when I attended the General Assembly meeting. His life, I believe, symbolizes the conscience of humanity upon which the United Nations is built.

"He will be deeply missed by all those who seek peace. Let me express my heartfelt sympathy and condolence to the remaining members of his family and to the people of the United States.

"We are greatly pleased to be honored in this way, to be accorded the privilege of meeting and talking with you at this luncheon, and I should like to thank you very much for the words that you have spoken. I am reminded that at the beginning of this year, I and Mr. Miki, who is here with us today as our Minister of International Trade and Industry, had the honor to be present on the occasion of Prime Minister Sato's visit to you.

"One of my favorite expressions in classical Chinese, if I may attempt to translate it, is: 'To the same pole, but by a different route.' It suggests the fact that it is entirely natural for two countries with such different historical and geographical backgrounds to pursue their respective national interests in a different manner, but it suggests also that we ultimately seek the common goal of world peace and prosperity.

"This is the most natural mode of cooperation between our two countries, and is the basis of a permanent and positive relationship. The results of the conversations between you, Mr. President, and Prime Minister Sato, have been welcomed in Japan with nationwide support, and have been regarded as a demonstration that the relations between our countries have entered an era of cooperation on a higher plane, in the way I have just tried to suggest. And to borrow Secretary Rusk's expression at the time of those talks, that we have entered into a 'new chapter' of our relationship.

"Since the beginning of this year, we have witnessed various developments in the international scene, mainly in Asia. In certain areas, the efforts we have directed towards achieving freedom, peace, and prosperity in Asia are producing fortunate results, and they appear to be opening the way for new developments conducive to future advance.

"However, the general situation in Asia seems to be one of persistent tension and strain, and is growing more serious with each day. In such a continually changing international scene, the close cooperation between our two countries serves a very significant role in sustaining a measure of international stability and prosperity.

"This joint United States-Japan Committee on Trade and Economic Affairs, attended by Cabinet members of both Governments, and allowing a frank exchange of views to take place, is a unique arrangement which symbolizes our close and cordial ties. Our present session has nearly been completed, and we believe that this fourth meeting has been as productive as the past three meetings. I am confident that this session has not only served to create a better and deeper understanding of the problems we face in our respective countries, but has contributed also to the promotion of peace and progress throughout the world.

"Thank you."

See also Items 356, 359, 373, 504.

REMARKS PREPARED FOR DELIVERY AT THE
LUNCHEON

The text of the remarks which the President had intended to deliver at the luncheon follow:

This is a great pleasure, and a welcome privilege, to welcome to this house in peace, friendship, and a common purpose, all of you who have come from across the great Pacific.

This is the fourth meeting of our two Cabinets, and the second such meeting here in Washington. For me, it is a meeting to which I have looked forward since the constructive and productive meeting earlier this year with your Prime Minister. I was most impressed with him at that time—and it confirms my estimate to know that he is able to conduct the affairs of your Government with so many members of his Cabinet so far from his side today.

Your presence here in Washington is a tribute to the importance which both you and we attach to the close friendship between Japan and the United States. These sessions between the Cabinet officers of our two countries are without precedent or parallel—and we can be very proud of them. Such meetings reflect to the world the importance our Governments and our peoples attach to our continuing ties as great nations of the free world.

Destiny has placed before us both great opportunities, responsibilities, and challenges. Together we shall meet them with enthusiasm, with courage, and—I am confident—with success.

On this day, when the genius of man has been able to probe the far-distant planet of Mars, I am privileged to pledge my country anew to explore

747

with vigor and imagination the pressing problems which confront us here on earth.

As Pacific countries, we have different assets and—in terms of narrow economics—some different interests. But we share the common purpose of contributing to the peace and prosperity of that part of the world.

Mankind as a whole faces a great challenge in finding ways to restore and maintain peace in southeast Asia. We know that merely yearning for peace will not bring it about.

An international effort enlisting commitments from peoples in the area—and all the nations interested in peace in the area—is needed to assure progress within that great region.

I am confident that if Japan and the United States can share their wisdom, and share their endeavors side by side, we can contribute greatly to the realization of this noble purpose.

We in the United States welcome your thoughts, your initiatives, and your cooperation in seeking objectives which are not only in our mutual interest, but in the interests of peoples everywhere.

In particular, I believe that our two great countries should together strive, first: to engage a broad range of developed countries in the task of promoting the economic development of southeast Asia, to strengthen the foundation for stability there and for world peace everywhere.

Secondly, I believe our two countries should together strive to help foster regional cooperation and a sense of common interest in the economic field.

Finally, I believe we should strive to persuade all countries in the area, especially those which are now committed to encouraging or supporting aggressive wars of national liberation, that their own patriotic self-interests would be better served by participating with others in peaceful economic development.

The basic conflict of our times is not over economic ideas or between economic systems. We do not believe any one peoples—or any one nation—stand as the sole possessors of all the truth. We do believe, however, that men and nations must have the right to develop their own systems and their own societies without fear of neighbors, and without a return to the dangers and perils of the past.

To end aggression as an instrument of national policy would bring great opportunities for progress and better welfare to unhappy millions throughout all of Asia. That is our goal in the United States—and our only goal.

Between us—in your country and in ours—we have mutual problems and mutual concerns. But much more important are our great mutual opportunities.

Let us hope that this meeting serves well the common purposes which we share together as we look to a broader, better, more peaceful horizon for ourselves and for all mankind.

Now may I ask you to join with me in a toast to the Sovereign whose distinguished Cabinet Ministers we proudly and warmly welcome today. Ladies and gentlemen, His Imperial Majesty, the Emperor of Japan.

356 Statement by the President on the Death of Adlai Stevenson. *July* 14, 1965

THE FLAME which illuminated the dreams and expectations of an entire world is now extinguished. Adlai Stevenson of Illinois is dead.

I am sending a delegation of distinguished Americans, headed by Vice President Humphrey, to London to bring back his body to America on the airplane of the President of the United States.

His great hero, Abraham Lincoln, said at the beginning of his political career, "I have no other ambition so great as that of being truly esteemed of my fellow men, by rendering myself worthy of their esteem."

And although his disappointments were many, in this, like Lincoln, he was vindicated.

Like Lincoln he was rooted in America's heartland, yet his voice reached across every boundary of nation and race and class.

Like Lincoln he was a great emancipator. It was his gift to help emancipate men from narrowness of mind and the shackles which selfishness and ignorance place upon the human adventure.

Like Lincoln he will be remembered more for what he stood for than for the offices he held, more for the ideals he embodied than the positions in which he served. For history honors men more for what they were than who they were. And by this standard, Adlai Stevenson holds a permanent place on that tiny roster of those who will be remembered as long as mankind is strong enough to honor greatness.

It seems such a short time ago, that out of Illinois came that thoughtful eloquence summoning an entire Nation back from its dangerous drift toward contentment and complacency. For an entire generation of Americans he imparted a nobility to public life and a grandeur to American purpose which has already reshaped the life of the Nation, and which will endure for many generations.

One by one he sounded the great themes of our time—peace and justice and the well-being of humanity. And many men will labor for many years toward the vision and the high purpose which was the generously-crafted outpouring of this great man's heart and skills.

He was an American. And he served America well. But what he saw, and what he spoke, and what he worked for, is the shared desire of all humanity. He believed in us, perhaps more than we deserved. And so we came to believe in ourselves much more than we had. And if we persevere, then on the foundation of that faith we can build the wondrous works of peace and of justice among all the nations.

He will not see that day. But it will be his day still.

So let us therefore, adversary and friend alike, pause for a moment and weep for one who was a friend and who was a guide to all mankind.

NOTE: The President read the statement at 3:17 p.m. in the White House Theater. On the same day he signed Executive Order 11233 ordering that the United States flag be flown at half-staff on U.S. buildings and facilities until interment (30 F.R. 8953; 3 CFR, 1965 Supp.).

Adlai E. Stevenson served as Governor of Illinois from 1949–1953, and as U.S. Representative to the United Nations from 1961 until his death. He was the Democratic candidate for President of the United States in 1952 and 1956.

See also Items 355, 359, 373, 504.

357 Remarks to the National Rural Electric Cooperative Association. July 14, 1965

Mr. Ellis and distinguished guests:

I am very happy to welcome to this Rose Garden and the White House such a fine group of taxpaying, economy-building, enterprising Americans.

It doesn't surprise me to find Clyde Ellis bringing you in here at this hour of the day. Last month our doorbell rang late one afternoon and when the policeman opened the gate, we found Clyde out there with 700 young people—just in time for supper.

Of course I think I ought to add I wanted all of you to stay to eat tonight, but Clyde told me he didn't think any of you liked barbecue. So we called off our plan. I'll let you settle that with Clyde after you leave.

Of all the work that I have been privileged to do in my public career, nothing has been more gratifying to me than my association with the rural electrification program. By many measurements, that program stands today as one of the most successful enterprises ever undertaken anywhere, at any time, by anyone.

There are many memories that I think we could share together of the years gone by. But we don't serve our country's interests, and we don't serve our program's interests, by reviving the past and talking now about who was right or who was wrong in some of those days when we had differences.

America and Americans, if they are going to continue to provide the leadership for the free world, must constantly look to the future.

So in our society today we serve no really useful purpose by keeping alive differences and divisions of yesteryear. We don't need to cling to the issues of the past. We do need to take hold of the issues of the future.

I am very proud to say that this is happening across the country. It is happening in the communities, and I am proud to tell you, above all, it is happening in the Congress. I think we are seeing today the strength, the talent, and the imagination of today's America being put to grips with the challenges of America's future and what to do about it. We see this in the very basic and the very important things that we have envisioned and we have dreamed and we have talked about—all my lifetime, at least, and I read where other people were talking about them before I discovered America.

We see this in education. We see it in health. We see it in regard to our beloved aged people—I signed the Older Americans Act early this morning. We see it in regard to our cities. We see it in every aspect of our national life. Quite frankly, and quite honestly, I am convinced that this is a period of sane and sensible but real, stirring progress, without parallel at any time in American history.

You will be proud to remember the day that you stood here in the garden of the White House during this period.

Now what does this mean to the rural electrification program, of which you are a part and which has filled a very vital role in the strengthening of this Nation and in the development of this Nation?

Well, you just cannot rest on the past. You must not just content yourselves with remembering old battles, or castigating old enemies, or parroting old slogans. None of us can do that and survive, whether we are business people, or laborers, or farmers, or politicians—but, least of all, men and women who are part of something that is as dynamic as the rural electric cooperatives.

So what do you need to do? You need to look far into the future—beyond 1965 or 1966 or 1970. And you really can't look far into the future, and you really cannot provide the leadership that you ought to provide, and you really cannot be a doer if you just ask yourself constantly, "What will I get out of this?" and "How does it serve me?" You have got to be selfless.

You have got to have a desire and an ambition to help people who can't help themselves if you are to provide the leadership that we need in the 20th century. You need to look to the America of 1980, and what it is going to be like, not just let it slip up on us—and 1990. You must look to the year 2000, when the clock turns and a new century begins. You must take the lead, therefore, in planning today for what is going to happen 35 years from now. You must take the lead in planning for a fuller utilization of rural America—providing the power and the services to meet your share of the future's demands.

If you don't do this, there is not going to be much rural America. They estimate in the year 2000, 80 percent of the people in America are going to be living in the cities, notwithstanding all of the things you are doing to try to keep them on the farm.

So you must, as I think you are at this meeting, give new attention to new responsibilities, to new management, to new planning. You must be concerned with developing the full water and power potential of this continent for the populations that are yet unborn.

I never go home for a weekend and look over a series of six beautiful lakes but what I remember when I was almost burned at the stake. I was investigated, I was condemned, and I was charged with everything under the sun. Right in the middle of all of it we had a big flood, and the dam hadn't been finished—and they said it was a man-made flood and I caused it.

Now you have to stand up to that kind of heat while you are doing this planning and this doing. And I think that you must also, as I know you are, turn your attention to horizons that are beyond your county, and your State, and your Nation, because you are living in a pretty big world.

There are 3 billion people in this world and America has less than 200 million of them. So for every American you find there are 15 others. And there is hardly a corner of this big earth, where 3 billion people live, where rural electrification is not needed now as much as it was needed when Roosevelt came to this town and issued an Executive order creating the REA.

So I am very grateful to all of you, and to Clyde Ellis, for the fine support that you are giving to our efforts to try to provide leadership, economic assistance, and rural electrification to southeast Asia.

Let me remind you of one thing in passing. The American people have invested more than any other people in history to preserve peace and freedom, not just for ourselves, but for all mankind.

Since World War II we have taken 100 billion of our treasury and spent it all over the world, to bring prosperity and peace to other parts of the world.

I was looking at one nation this morning—we spent over $8 billion in one country alone, made up of nearly half a billion people. Now we do not intend that this great effort that we have been going through since World War II shall have been in vain.

Where we have commitments, we intend to keep them. Now there are going to be some long debates, there are going to be some eloquent speeches, there are going to be some differences of opinion, and there is going to be some criticism of your President. But three Presidents—President Eisenhower, President Kennedy, and your present President—have made a commitment in the name of the people of the United States, and our national honor is at stake in southeast Asia. And we are going to protect it, and you just might as well be prepared for it, and we can do it better if we are united.

We have a good many generals in our own army, and we have a good many that are not in the army, that have their own individual programs. But you can follow whichever one you want to, but you better get ready to follow, because where our national honor is at stake politics stops. We have opportunities and we have challenges, and we have obligations and we intend to fulfill them, and we intend to help others to fulfill theirs, too.

And where we have a duty, we are going to meet it. We do not expect the road to be smooth, and you just be sure it is not going to be short. But we do intend that the end result shall be a better world where men of all lands and all colors and all cultures can enjoy in their lifetime something of the advance that we have known in our lifetime.

Think what would have happened in Korea if we had turned our back? What would have happened in Iran, in Greece, and Turkey if we had walked away? What would have happened if we would have been concerned with creature comforts in Lebanon or Formosa?

We have had our responsibilities around the world and we have lived up to them, and we expect to continue to. We love peace. We hate no man. We do not seek to bury any other people anywhere, but we are not going to be buried, either, and we are not going to ducktail and run from our responsibilities.

Now there are going to be some dark days and there are going to be some times when we may call on you for some help, and I don't think you will be found wanting.

I am sorry Clyde Ellis wouldn't let you stay for dinner. However, since Lady Bird is away, we might have had to eat out of the icebox anyway. So, I hope you will enjoy yourselves tonight and I hope you will come back again.

In the meantime, I want each and every one of you, from whatever State you come from, whatever party you belong to, to realize that your President is proud of the record that you have made and he is going to count on you in the days ahead.

Thank you very much.

NOTE: The President spoke at 6 p.m. in the Rose Garden at the White House. In his opening words he referred to Clyde T. Ellis, Executive Manager, National Rural Electric Cooperative Association.

During his remarks the President referred to Executive Order 7037 of May 11, 1935, which established the Rural Electrification Administration.

For the President's remarks upon signing the Older Americans Act of 1965, see Item 354.

358 Statement by the President on Requesting the Water Resources Council To Take Steps To Meet the Northeastern Drought. *July 14, 1965*

CONCERN is growing over the continuing drought in the Eastern United States. Rainfall in the Middle Atlantic and southern New England States has been between 35 and 45 inches short of normal precipitation over the past 4 years. Stream flows have been greatly reduced, water tables are lowered, and the major reservoirs are only partly filled. The Delaware River Basin Commission has recently taken emergency measures to deal with the problems in its region.

I come from a part of America where droughts are depressingly familiar. I know the anxiety they bring. I also know our water requirements will grow at an incredible rate in the years ahead, at the stimulus of expanding populations and new industries.

We must do whatever we can to help the people of the eastern seaboard in their plight.

Federal agencies are working with the States and local interests in attempting to devise measures for meeting the water shortage problems. These efforts will continue. However, I have requested the Secretary of the Interior, as Chairman of the Ad Hoc Water Resources Council, immediately to convene its members, together with other Federal agencies involved with water resources, to assess what further actions might be taken to assist the States in meeting the problems now confronting the New England and Middle Atlantic region.

The Council will obtain the views of the Delaware River Basin Commission. I have asked for a report to be submitted to me within a week, specifying how we can best mobilize the resources of the Federal Government to assist the States and local governments in meeting this urgent water problem.

It is going to require imaginative planning, a willingness to cooperate all along the line, and indeed some sacrifices on the part of all of us if we are to make the best use of our water resources. We must move quickly and firmly to preserve what we have and what we receive. An abundance of water is critical for the present generation of Americans and a vital legacy for the next.

NOTE: The Water Resources Council submitted the following reports to the President in response to his July 14 statement: "Drought in Northeastern United States," dated July 21, 1965 (22 pp., processed), and "Reappraisal of Drought in Northeastern United States," dated September 7, 1965, and released

September 10 (50 pp., processed). An additional interim report in the form of a memorandum to the President from the Secretary of the Interior, as Chairman of the Water Resources Council, was made public on August 7 (1 Weekly Comp. Pres. Docs., p. 60).

On July 20, 1965, the White House released a report to the President by the Secretary of Agriculture giving a résumé of steps being taken by his Department to provide aid to drought-stricken areas. The relief program included special loans to thousands of farmers throughout the United States.

On August 13, 1965, the White House announced that the President had asked Congress for additional appropriations to cover planning and construction of reservoirs and for further studies of water and land resources (1 Weekly Comp. Pres. Docs., p. 83).

See also Items 418, 434.

359 Exchange of Messages With the Secretary General of the United Nations. *July 14, 1965*

I AM deeply grateful for your message about Ambassador Stevenson. He was not only the Ambassador of the United States to the United Nations, but a wise and unwavering friend of the United Nations within the councils of the United States. Knowing how deeply he cared for the United Nations, I find it a comfort to know from you as Secretary General how highly he was esteemed by his friends and colleagues there. We shall miss him, but from his life and work we can take courage for the future.

LYNDON B. JOHNSON

[His Excellency U Thant, Secretary General of the United Nations, United Nations Headquarters, New York, N.Y.]

NOTE: Secretary General U Thant's message follows:
The President
The White House

I was so shocked and grieved to hear of the sudden and tragic death of Ambassador Stevenson. As the Representative of the United States of America, he had earned the respect, admiration and affection of all his colleagues at the United Nations for his extraordinary human qualities. I know that you must feel a sense of personal loss on the death of such a distinguished American who was also a member of your official Cabinet. Your grief is shared by all of us at the United Nations.

U THANT,
Secretary General

See also Items 355, 356, 373, 504.

360 Memorandum on Cost Reduction by Federal Agencies. *July 14, 1965*

Memorandum for the Cabinet and Heads of Agencies:

Maximum efficiency of Government has been a consuming interest throughout my

career and particularly since I have been President.

Such efficiency is no better illustrated than in the attached Annual Cost Reduction Report of the Department of Defense and the pamphlet, "The Challenge of Change", which describes the Department's efforts to meet its responsibilities to employees and communities affected by Defense changes.

I would like you to take the inclosed report and brochure home with you and read it carefully. Not only will you find it an illustration of a successful cost reduction program, but you may find it a source of ideas which can be put to use in your own Department or Agency.

I should be happy to have any plans of this nature that you may have brought to my personal attention.

LYNDON B. JOHNSON

NOTE: The two pamphlets, issued by the Department of Defense, are entitled "Department of Defense Cost Reduction Report" (July 12, 1965; Government Printing Office, 24 pp.), and "The Challenge of Change" (July 10, 1965; Department of Defense, 53 pp.).

See also Items 362, 387.

361 Remarks at the Signing of the Drug Abuse Control Amendments Bill. *July 15, 1965*

Members of Congress, ladies and gentlemen:

Over the years of this century, the American people have benefited greatly from the effective protection of their health and their well-being that has been provided by their Government.

The legislation before us today is in that proud and that respected tradition. The development of safe and effective drugs has brought more progress in the past few decades than in all the centuries before on reducing human suffering and on conquering human disease.

Drugs can, if properly used, protect our health, prolong our life, reduce much pain and suffering. Improperly used, drugs can cause great injury and do great harm.

The Drug Abuse Control Act of 1965 is designed to prevent both the misuse and the illicit traffic of potentially dangerous drugs, especially the sedatives and the stimulants, which are so important in the medicines that we use today.

Unlike narcotics, some of these drugs are very easily and very cheaply manufactured. Production has been rapidly increasing. Some of that production has been counterfeit. But more importantly, the Food and Drug Administration estimates that at least one-half the annual production of certain useful drugs is being diverted to criminal traffic.

Enough "goof balls" and "pep pills," for instance, are being manufactured this year to provide 2 dozen pills to every man, woman, and child in the United States.

We know all too well that racketeers in this field are making easy victims of many of our finest young people. The Congress hopes, and I hope, that this act will put a stop to such vicious business.

I cannot express too strongly my determination that this good and decent and law-abiding society shall not be corrupted, undermined, or mocked by any criminal elements, whether they are organized or not. I believe that most Americans share this hope and share this determination.

I think it is noteworthy that this legislation receive very widespread support from various citizens groups, from the drug industry, from organized medicine, and from others.

The values of our society and the security of our homes and communities can be protected by the law; and where the law is inadequate, or unjust, or obsolete, we have an obligation to cure what is wrong, and we can do it.

So, congratulations this morning are due the many Members of the Congress who made the determined effort to secure the enactment of this measure and bring it to the desk for signature.

The Chairman of the House Interstate and Foreign Commerce Committee, Oren Harris of Arkansas, did a most outstanding job. In the House he had very able and effective support from Congressman Delaney, and Congressman Boggs, and from Mrs. Sullivan.

Certainly, very special mention is due for the courageous public leadership offered to this cause by Senator Tom Dodd of Connecticut. He was the author of the forerunner of the present act, which passed the Senate last year.

I also want to thank Senator Hill and I particularly thank the manager of the bill, my friend, Senator Ralph Yarborough from my own State.

This is another step forward in the attack that we are making on crime and delinquency throughout the United States.

I hope this measure will be followed by the enactment of other important measures recommended in my message to the Congress on March 8, 1965.

NOTE: The President spoke at 12 noon in the Cabinet Room at the White House.

During his remarks he referred to Representative Oren Harris of Arkansas, Chairman of the House Interstate and Foreign Commerce Committee, Representative James J. Delaney of New York, Representative Hale Boggs of Louisiana, Representative Leonor K. Sullivan of Missouri, Senator Thomas J. Dodd of Connecticut, Senator Lister Hill of Alabama, and Senator Ralph Yarborough of Texas.

As enacted, the bill (H.R. 2) is Public Law 89–74 (79 Stat. 226).

---

362   Remarks to Members of Federal Agency Task Forces on Cost Reduction. *July 15, 1965*

I HAVE ASKED you to meet with me this morning because I am very deeply concerned about our budgetary outlook for the next year.

In the past 2 years we have made more progress in enacting progressive domestic legislation, I am told, than has been made at any time in this generation. We have gotten through the Congress—or will shortly have done so—the kind of forward-looking legislation which would have been regarded as all but impossible a few years ago.

This includes:

—$19 billions of reductions in income and excise taxes in 19 months—reductions which have helped to keep going the longest peacetime economic expansion in the Nation's history.

—Two major civil rights bills—helping to assure the American Negro his full rights as an American citizen.

—A medical care bill which provides far more in medical care for the elderly than even its original sponsors ever dared to suggest—involving some $7 billion.

—An antipoverty program which has already brought work and education, and above all, hope to millions of the desperately poor in our country.

—An education bill which, for the first time, clearly breaks through the barriers of tradition to assure much more adequate support for elementary and secondary education.

—A rent supplement proposal w h i c h

makes it possible to provide decent housing for low-income families on a large scale and in a dignified way. And that bill passed the House by half a dozen votes, and I hope it passes the Senate where it's being debated now.

I believe the reasons for unparalleled success, such as I just enumerated, are very clear:

First, because we, as a Government, have been able to demonstrate that these are sound, practical, and carefully developed programs which serve the best interests of all the people of this Nation.

Second, and equally as important, because we have made the effort—a very real and a very convincing effort—to guarantee the people and the Congress that they are getting full value for every dollar they spend. We have shown that compassionate Government does not mean imprudent Government—that we are just as interested in rooting out old and inefficient programs as we are in developing new programs.

Between fiscal 1964 and 1966 we will increase spending on the major Great Society programs by $4½ billion—and from 1964 to 1966, that is a rise on Great Society programs of over 60 percent. But our total budget will go up only $2 billion. Over half of the new spending is being financed from improved efficiency and by reductions that shrewd, and able, and discerning administrators have made in less essential programs.

Now this is a very sound and very progressive approach. It has paid off, as you can see, in terms of legislative success. And we certainly want to continue it.

But continuing in this direction is going to become increasingly difficult for three primary reasons:

First, we are all facing sharp increases in spending from programs that have been enacted during the last 2 years.

Second, for 2 years in a row now, the January Budget has been able to forecast substantial reductions in Defense spending. This will not be the case for next year—even before we take into account the rising costs of our Viet-Nam operations.

And third, we have sharply increased our sale of financial assets, thus freeing funds for use elsewhere. But we cannot count upon similar asset sale increases in future years.

You have all submitted your programs and your plans and proposals to the Budget Bureau, as a part of the summer budget preview. The Budget Director has estimated the 1967 costs of these programs. So if, between now and January, program requests are reduced by as much as they were in the same period last year, budget expenditures would still grow at a rate very substantially in excess of the rate of growth of our national economy.

Now I want to make it clear, first of all, that I intend to do whatever is necessary to always protect the security of this Nation—and that is number one priority; whatever is necessary to honor all the commitments that we have made abroad; and the commitments we have made to achieve the goals of the Great Society here at home.

But I also want you to know that I don't want a penny more than is necessary spent to do this, and I am absolutely certain that a growth in budget expenditures at the rate indicated is neither necessary nor inevitable.

At the last Cabinet meeting I asked each of the Cabinet members and agency heads to appoint a task force to identify areas where savings could be made that they thought would offset the increased spending for new and expanded programs.

So I have asked to meet with you today, and to talk with the members of these task forces, to impress upon each of you how very important I consider this special assignment that you have been given.

There are a number of principles that I think you ought to follow in your deliberations:

First, hold no program sacred. No program, no matter how long it's been established, should be free of a very cold and a very searching examination. Now let me worry about the political problems; I'll try to make those decisions and suffer the consequences. Some decisions may be unpopular for a time, but sanity and sense will be far more popular in the long run, as we have found with very few exceptions.

Second, the real savings are going to come from reducing or eliminating programs that can be reduced. While I do want you to find more efficient ways of running existing programs, I don't want you to concentrate so heavily on that aspect, that you refrain from asking whether this program is really essential to furthering the national interest.

Third, I want you to put your imagination to work. When it comes to proposing new programs, I find little want of imagination. We have some real dreamers and people that are quite idealistic. So I urge you to be equally ingenious in looking for imaginative ways to make savings, in examining alternatives that cost less.

So I want all of you to remember that the work you do is work that is being watched here in the White House. It's being supported here. It's being appreciated here, and we will be held responsible for it. It is creative work, vital work, and constructive work—and I think you can be proud of your contribution.

NOTE: The President spoke at 12:35 p.m. in the East Room at the White House. The group was composed of members of task forces appointed by every agency at the instruction of the President to identify areas where savings could be made.

See also Items 360, 387.

363   Letter to Mrs. Francis A. Cherry on the Death of Her Husband. *July 15, 1965*

Dear Mrs. Cherry:

With sadness and grief, I join all who mourn the death of Francis Cherry, respected judge, able Governor of Arkansas, and dedicated servant of the public good.

I particularly want to express my sympathy to his family and dear ones, and to the countless citizens of Arkansas who have lost in his passing a distinguished leader, and a native son whose devotion to constitutional principles and human dignity won for him the confidence and admiration of all who knew him.

His life has left for his State and nation a rich legacy of accomplishment.

Sincerely,

LYNDON B. JOHNSON

[Mrs. Francis A. Cherry, 5324 Albemarle Street NW., Washington, D.C.]

NOTE: Francis A. Cherry served as a member of the Subversive Activities Control Board from May 16, 1960, to January 31, 1963, and as Chairman of the Board from January 31, 1963, to March 4, 1965. He was Governor of Arkansas 1953–1955.

364   Statement by the President Following a Meeting on the
      Dominican Situation. *July 16, 1965*

AMBASSADOR BUNKER returned to Washington yesterday to attend to several official and personal matters. In the meeting this afternoon, which included Ambassador Bennett, there was an opportunity to examine all aspects of the Dominican situation. Tomorrow Ambassador Bunker will join with his colleagues on the OAS Ad Hoc Committee in reporting to the Meeting of Consultation on their activities to date in the Dominican Republic.

NOTE: In his statement the President referred to W. Tapley Bennett, Jr., U.S. Ambassador to the Dominican Republic, and Ellsworth Bunker, U.S. Representative to the Organization of American States.

365   Statement by the President Following a Meeting With the
      Advisory Committee on International Monetary Arrangements.
      July 16, 1965

I MET today with Secretary Fowler and his Advisory Committee on International Monetary Arrangements. We had a brief discussion of the United States balance of payments situation and the international monetary system.

There was complete agreement on the necessity for the United States to eliminate its balance of payments deficit quickly and to maintain payments equilibrium for a prolonged period.

While we were all pleased with the indications that my balance of payments program, announced February 10, seems to be taking hold, and that the business and financial community is doing a splendid job of voluntary cooperation, we are well aware that it is still much too early to get an accurate picture of just where we stand.

Secretary Fowler is moving ahead effectively to prepare for international agreement on solving any future problem of world liquidity which might arise after we have successfully maintained equilibrium for an extended period. He has put together an excellent committee and I am confident that, under the leadership of Douglas Dillon, they will provide him with the best talent and advice available in this area to supplement the resources in the Government on this vital subject.

NOTE: The statement was made public as part of a White House release announcing the President's meeting with the new Advisory Committee on International Monetary Arrangements. Establishment of the Committee by Secretary of the Treasury Henry H. Fowler was announced by the White House on July 3.

In addition to the President's statement the July 16 release contained statements by Secretary Fowler and by C. Douglas Dillon, Chairman of the Advisory Committee on International Monetary Arrangements.

In his statement Secretary Fowler said that the Committee was in unanimous agreement that the U.S. proposal for an international conference on the potential problem of world financial resources was an important step in the right direction. He added that he had set before the Committee the general framework of present U.S. policy including the following points:

"1. The importance of the United States eliminating its own deficit as promptly as possible as a necessary precondition to modification of the international monetary system.

"2. The importance of a flexible approach, not only by the United States but by other countries, in discussing international monetary arrangements.

"3. The need for thorough and careful preparation to promote fruitful negotiations on the international level.

"4. The need to build upon the existing system by making maximum use of present instruments of international financial cooperation which have served so effectively in the past.

"5. The necessity to maintain the dollar as the principal reserve currency in order to foster continuing stability in the international trade and pay-national level.

The release also included the names of the Government officials who attended the meeting, together with the following Committee members: Edward Bernstein, Kermit Gordon, Charles Kindleberger, André Meyer, David Rockefeller, and Robert V. Roosa.

366 Remarks on Crime Control at the Signing of the District of Columbia Appropriations Bill. *July 16, 1965*

Members of the Congress, Attorney General Katzenbach, Director J. Edgar Hoover, Judge Pine, General Duke, Chief of Police Layton, all those who care about the Capital City of Washington, ladies and gentlemen:

Thomas Jefferson once said of the city of Washington: "It has been the source of much happiness to me during my residence in the seat of government and I owe much for its kind disposition. I shall ever feel a high interest in the prosperity of the city and an affectionate attachment to its inhabitants."

In saying that, the third President spoke what, I am sure, have been the sentiments of all Presidents to follow—certainly those of the thirty-sixth President.

For myself, Mrs. Johnson, and our daughters, Washington is a city that we love and we cherish.

Today, throughout America, I believe all the people of this country want their Nation's Capital City to be the Nation's pride, a beautiful city, a city of good schools and good homes and good neighborhoods and good citizens. Above all, I believe Americans want Washington, D.C., to be an example of a clean and safe city where law is respected, where order prevails, and where every citizen is safe in his home or on the streets.

That is why I am this afternoon signing, within an hour from the time I received it,

the appropriation measure for the District of Columbia, just enacted by the 89th Congress. The scope of this measure is broad, covering, as it does, the full range of governmental services and programs serving the residents of the District of Columbia. For many of these activities, this bill will mean significantly improved support. In other areas we realize that still much more support is needed.

But this afternoon I want to emphasize one particular aspect of this legislation in which the Congress and the Executive are of one mind. That is, our determination that crime in the District of Columbia, like crime in all our cities, must and will be brought under control.

In our land today, no concern is more urgent to any of us than the increasing scope of crime and violence in the United States. There is no place where this malignant growth troubles us more than here in the Capital City of Washington, which should be the model city as well as the Capital of our Nation.

We know that Washington is not now a model for the preservation of peace and order. In fiscal year 1965, serious crimes in the Capital City rose 12.4 percent over 1964. Since 1957, housebreakings have tripled, auto thefts have more than tripled, and robberies have almost quadrupled. Serious offenses rose 26.3 percent in June

759

of 1965 over June of 1964. This June was the 37th consecutive month in which the incidence of local crimes exceeded that of the comparable month in the prior year.

And even these figures do not give full measure of the impact of crime in the District of Columbia, just as they do not in other cities. It is not possible to record in statistics the inconvenience and the alarm that is felt by thousands of residents and visitors who change the course of their daily lives for fear of becoming a victim and statistic of crime.

I say simply, but firmly, that this is not the way that Americans want to live, or need to live, or will live. We just must take effective measures against crime and criminals of all kinds, and that is why we are gathered here on this White House porch this afternoon.

The course of the last few years just must be reversed. The wave of crime must be met and it must be checked, and our citizens must be protected, and our streets must be made safe, and our Nation's Capital City must be a safe and secure showplace for visitors. Our efforts toward this goal must begin this afternoon without any further delay.

All that we do must be, and will be, done in a manner consistent with our society's cherished values of due process, and equal and even-handed treatment for every citizen. But we are not going to tolerate hoodlums who mug and rape and kill in this city of Washington.

Much is already being accomplished within existing institutions in Washington to reduce the crime and to erase the conditions on which crime feeds. The interim action programs which I have presented to Congress are essential additions, but all of this is not enough. There are other steps that we can take, and that we are beginning to take at this very hour.

First, this bill, when it is signed, will provide immediately for the equivalent of 250 additional policemen on the streets of our Washington neighborhood. This is not a long, slow, recruiting and training process. By authorizing additional overtime, this bill will permit Chief Layton and his fine men to increase police protection for District residents immediately.

Secondly, I am, this afternoon, signing an Executive order establishing the President's Commission on Crime in the District of Columbia. I am proud and privileged to announce that we have been fortunate in securing a blue-ribbon membership for this Commission—a group of distinguished persons intimately familiar with all aspects of District life which bear on crime and law enforcement, and criminal justice and rehabilitation.

To the chairmanship of the Commission I am appointing Herbert J. Miller, Jr. Mr. Miller is a noted Washington attorney, who has just completed more than 4 years of outstanding service as Assistant Attorney General in charge of the Criminal Division of the Department of Justice.

To the vice chairmanship I am appointing one of the District's most outstanding citizens, an admired and respected lady, Judge Marjorie Lawson. I am also accepting now Mrs. Lawson's resignation, effective on August the 20th, from her position on the Juvenile Court bench of the District of Columbia. I am very grateful to her for readily accepting this new and challenging assignment.

In addition to these, the other members of the Commission will be: Mr. Frederick A. Ballard, a former president of the D.C. Bar

Association; Mr. Donald S. Bittinger, president of the Washington Gas Light Company; Mr. Clarence C. Ferguson, the dean of the Howard Law School; Mr. Abe Krash, a prominent attorney with the firm of Arnold, Fortas, and Porter; David A. Pine, retired judge of the District Court; the Honorable William P. Rogers, former Attorney General of the United States; Patricia M. Wald, attorney and expert on the jail bail system.

This, I believe, is an experienced, understanding and, in every sense of the word, outstanding group of citizens. However, I am calling upon them to bring together the very finest expert knowledge that can be assembled from all over this Nation to support their efforts to meet the crime challenge in the Nation's Capital.

I want the Commission to lead the way— lead the way for all forces in the Washington community to act together against crime. Those who labor to correct social injustices must work together effectively in concert, and not in conflict, with those who have direct responsibilities in the detection and the prosecution of crime.

I anticipate the Commission will explore areas such as analysis of crime, its patterns, its causes in the District of Columbia, the most effective use of police services, and the improvements in law enforcement and training and methodology.

I want to make it clear that I want the best police force in the United States here in this Capital of our Nation, and I want to make it clear that we are going to have it or some fur is going to fly.

Treatment of offenders, particularly first offenders, from time of arrest to the time of rehabilitation and return to the community, possible revision of existing administrative and prosecution procedures, criminal laws, the rules governing criminal procedure, possible alternative methods of dealing with certain types of conduct that now process through criminal courts—all of this task is an enormous one.

But it must be comprehensive because too often in the past our approach to crime has been piecemeal; too many of those who study or work in the field feel alienated from others involved in the criminal law process.

From the frontlines of police action to the patient work of rehabilitation, the goals of protecting society, of erasing the causes of crime, of preserving justice, should be seen as a single foundation, all of which is essential to the support of a truly civilized society.

And finally, let me make a third announcement that I am proud to make. To succeed Judge Lawson on the Juvenile Court, the Government is most fortunate to be able to secure the services of a distinguished graduate of Cornell University, an outstanding member of the District Bar, who has agreed to accept this position, the Honorable Aubrey E. Robinson, Jr., who is here with us this evening.

Let me conclude now by saying this: the District of Columbia has meant much to me practically all of my adult life. As I cherish my own home country that is far away this afternoon, I love this Capital City, I love its beauty and simple dignity, and all the meaning that is present here in its past and that is present in its promise.

There are many things that I hope to accomplish during my alloted time in this office. But with all my heart, I hope that for generations to come these will be remembered as the years when Washington flowered into its finest age.

This bill that I am about to sign is only a

steppingstone, and all of us know that. There is more, though, much more, that is needed. What is needed will be done generously and fully.

We can all be proud to share in this work together, and I hope that the time is not too far-distant when this little group meeting on this porch this afternoon can reassemble and take inventory, and can point with great pride to the progress that began here this afternoon with the signing of this appropriation bill.

To the Members of the Congress who labored unselfishly long and hard to bring these results about, we say thank you for your understanding, and we will try to be worthy of your confidence.

NOTE: The President spoke at 5:27 p.m. from the portico overlooking the Rose Garden at the White House. In his opening words he referred to Attorney General Nicholas deB. Katzenbach, J. Edgar Hoover, Director of the Federal Bureau of Investigation, David A. Pine, retired Judge of the District Court for the District of Columbia, Brig. Gen. Charles M. Duke, Engineer Commissioner for the District of Columbia, and John B. Layton, Chief of Police for the District of Columbia.

During his remarks the President referred to Executive Order 11234 "Establishing the President's Commission on Crime in the District of Columbia" (30 F.R. 9049; 3 CFR, 1965 Supp.).

As enacted, the District of Columbia Appropriation Act, 1966, is Public Law 89–75 (79 Stat. 236). See also Item 381.

367   Letter Concerning the Issuance of a Commemorative Stamp Marking the 700th Anniversary of the Birth of Dante Alighieri. *July 17, 1965*

[Released July 17, 1965. Dated July 15, 1965]

Dear Chairman Re:

It gives me pleasure to join the millions of our citizens paying tribute to the immortal memory of Dante Alighieri on the 700th anniversary of his birth. A commemorative stamp in honor of this great Son of Italy is a fitting tribute to the universal contributions of an illustrious man who belongs to every age and to people of all ages.

Through his genius and creative achievement, Dante became forever a citizen of the world. Poet, philosopher, musician, political scientist and psychologist, Dante's renowned accomplishments are a lasting testament to his fully and richly rewarding life.

Dante's immortal *Divine Comedy,* with its sublime message of faith and hope, is his best known and most widely respected work.

But for those who are charged with administering their nation's affairs, his provocative political ideas, expressed in his other literary masterpieces, have enduring meaning and significance.

I am both proud and happy to express at this time my congratulations to our entire Italian American community for sustaining in their new home the revered ideals and traditions of the old. You have my personal good wishes on this memorable occasion.

Sincerely,

LYNDON B. JOHNSON

[Honorable Edward D. Re, Chairman, Foreign Claims Settlement Commission of the United States]

NOTE: The Postmaster General had requested Mr. Re to serve as chairman of a nationwide Italian-American Committee sponsoring the anniversary celebration.

368   Letter to the President of the Senate and to the Speaker of the House on the Proposed Teaching Professions Bill.
July 17, 1965

Dear Mr. President: (Dear Mr. Speaker:)

As I announced in my remarks before the National Education Association on July 2, I am proposing legislation to bring the best of our Nation's talent to its schools. This legislation—The Teaching Professions Act of 1965—will

—create a National Teacher Corps to serve in city slums and areas of rural poverty,

—establish a program of fellowships to prepare students for teaching careers in elementary and secondary education and to help experienced teachers enhance their qualifications,

—aid institutions of higher education to provide better programs for educating teachers.

The National Teacher Corps draws on that spirit of dedication of Americans which has been demonstrated time and again in peace and war, by young and old, at home and abroad. It will provide a challenge and an opportunity for teachers with a sense of mission—those best suited to the momentous tasks this Nation faces in improving education.

The National Teacher Corps can help improve the quality of teaching where quality is most needed and most often in short supply—in city slums and in areas of rural poverty. It will enroll experienced teachers, and, to work with them, students who intend to make teaching a career. They will teach in local schools at the request of local communities and will serve on the same terms as local teachers. They will be local, not Federal, employees.

The fellowships are essential if teaching is

to attract a higher proportion of our ablest young people, and if the best teaching is to prevail in the classroom. Students preparing for teaching in these days should have superior graduate training. Teaching is a difficult job at best; the more preparation for it, the better.

The desire of classroom teachers to replenish their skills and knowledge is not only to be applauded but aided. As revolutionary changes take place in all subjects and at all levels of learning, there is a limit to the sacrifice we can ask of our teachers in their efforts to renew their knowledge.

Finally, I propose a program of grants to help institutions of higher education offer first-rate programs to would-be teachers as well as to experienced teachers. This measure, coupled with the fellowship program and the National Teacher Corps, completes a program which is entitled to be called the Teaching Professions Act of 1965.

The Teaching Professions Act of 1965 is a composite of hard thinking about educational problems in the Congress, in the Executive branch, and in the teaching profession. It owes much to the proposals of Senators Gaylord Nelson and Edward Kennedy for a national teacher corps; to Senators Wayne Morse and Clifford Case and Representatives Carl Perkins and John Brademas for a program of fellowships for teachers; and to Representative Patsy Mink for a program of Federal grants to teachers for sabbatical leaves.

This bill will deepen the meaning and substance of the already impressive work of the 88th and 89th Congresses in the field of education. I have concluded that it is of sufficient urgency to justify action by this session of the Congress. The problems which face us in education do not grow smaller as time goes by; neither should our determination to attack and solve those problems. I commend to you the Teaching Professions Act of 1965, and hope that you will give it speedy consideration.

Sincerely,

LYNDON B. JOHNSON

NOTE: This is the text of identical letters addressed to the Honorable Hubert H. Humphrey, President of the Senate, and to the Honorable John W. McCormack, Speaker of the House of Representatives. A draft bill and a résumé of the proposed Teaching Professions Act of 1965 were made public by the White House along with the President's letter.

The National Teacher Corps was established by the Higher Education Act of 1965 which was approved by the President on November 8, 1965 (see Item 603).

For the President's remarks before the National Education Association on July 2, 1965, see Item 340. See also Item 369.

369 Remarks on the Proposed Teaching Professions Bill. *July 17, 1965*

MAN'S most noble enterprise is the work of education. In our Nation's classrooms, our future is being built. I believe that the chief architects of that future are the teachers of America.

Today I have completed work upon a legislative proposal which is a testament to those beliefs: the Teaching Professions Act of 1965. It is now on its way to the Congress.

Today in the United States there are nearly 2 million teachers in elementary and secondary schools. By this fall we will need almost 200,000 new teachers merely to accommodate growing enrollments and to replace teachers who retire and leave the profession. We will need nearly 2 million new teachers in the next 10 years alone.

Yet our needs cannot be expressed just in numbers. Tomorrow's teachers must not merely be plentiful enough, they must be good enough. They must possess not only the old virtues of energy and dedication, but they must possess new knowledge and new skill for the 20th century. If we are to have the best available teachers we must now attract to teaching the best available students in this country.

Today almost 5 percent of our teachers—

85,000—lack adequate qualifications. Almost 10 percent have less than a bachelor's degree. Only 25 percent of all of our teachers even have a master's degree.

Our Nation, whose needs are so immense and whose wealth is so great, really can do much better, and we must do better. This act offers us a way to do better.

The Teaching Professions Act of 1965 will establish, first, a National Teachers Corps. Members of the Corps—experienced teachers and students who plan to make teaching a career—will go together to the city slums and to the rural areas of our country, to poverty, to offer what these troubled regions need most—light and learning, help and hope.

Second, the act will create a program of fellowships to prepare superior students for teaching careers in elementary and secondary schools, and to help teachers renew their knowledge and skills. The Federal Government already assists men and women making their careers in college teaching, and now is the time to do the same for those who serve at the elementary and the secondary school levels.

Finally, this act will provide direct assistance to institutions—financial aid to institutions of higher learning so that they may develop better programs for teacher education.

The Teaching Professions Act of 1965 is a composite of hard thinking about educational problems in the Congress, in the executive branch, and in the teaching profession. We have with us this morning a number of the bright young men who have made material contributions to the formulation of this legislation. This legislation also owes much to the proposals of leaders in our country, like Senator Gaylord Nelson of Wisconsin and Senator Edward Kennedy of Massachusetts for a National Teachers Corps; to Senator Wayne Morse of Oregon, and to Senator Clifford Case of New Jersey, and to Representative Carl Perkins of Kentucky, and Congressman John Brademas of Indiana for the work that they have done on a program of fellowships for teachers; and to Representative Patsy Mink for her contributions in connection with a program of Federal grants to teachers for sabbatical leaves.

So, I am calling upon the Congress to make this beginning now—now—even though it is well along already in its present session. The problems confronting us in education will not diminish and do not diminish with the passage of time. Neither should our zeal for solving those problems diminish. This act will be just a beginning, but now is the time to begin.

Henry Adams said: "A teacher affects eternity; he can never tell where his influence stops." This act, I believe, will have an eternal influence on this Nation that we all love.

NOTE: The President spoke at 1:27 p.m. in the White House Theater. An advance copy of the President's remarks, entitled "Statement by the President," was also released.

See also Item 368.

370 Remarks Upon Announcing the Nomination of Arthur J. Goldberg as U.S. Representative to the United Nations. *July 20, 1965*

Mr. Justice, Mr. Secretary, ladies and gentlemen:

One week ago we, and the world, lost Adlai Stevenson.

For all who knew him, and for all whose lives were touched by his rare gifts of inspiration, the world will seem forever poorer for his death. Yet we know that the world will be forever richer for his life.

None can fill the void that his passing leaves in our hearts. But the vacancy left at the council tables of the United Nations must be filled.

Our yearning for peace and for justice on this earth, and our quest for the dignity of all mankind, are not the yearning and quest

of one heart but of 190 million. Where men and where nations come together to seek these goals, the voice of all America must be heard.

It is, therefore, my responsibility to select a successor to Ambassador Adlai Stevenson as the special Representative of the United States of America to the United Nations.

Since the birth of the United Nations 20 years ago, each President has faced the same responsibility. Each President has reflected the faith and the firmness of our commitment to the United Nations by always calling upon distinguished citizens of very high achievement to serve in this honored office.

As an example, President Truman called

upon Senator Warren Austin of Vermont.

President Eisenhower called upon an outstanding American, who serves his country faithfully and selflessly still, Henry Cabot Lodge of Massachusetts.

President Kennedy called upon the great Governor Adlai Stevenson of Illinois.

To assume these responsibilities now I have called upon a member of the Supreme Court of the United States, and a former member of the Cabinet—Justice Arthur Goldberg.

At the insistence of the President of his country, he has accepted this call to duty.

Justice Goldberg, like Governor Stevenson, is a son of Illinois. Where Governor Stevenson was descended from some of America's oldest settlers, Justice Goldberg was born of some of our newest. He rose from the city streets to Cabinet office, and then to the highest court in this land. His life embodies the story of our open and free society as a fulfillment of the opportunity that we want all mankind to share with us.

A counselor of the American trade union movement, Justice Goldberg won the esteem of both labor and business. His appointment to the Cabinet of the late, beloved President Kennedy drew bipartisan approval and drew praise from leaders of widely divergent philosophies. His nomination to the Supreme Court was warmly welcomed by all who knew him as a lawyer of exceptional ability, a student and a thinker of original and profound capacity, and, above all, a man of courage, and independence, and conviction, and generous humanitarian compassion.

But Justice Goldberg is a man of international reputation, too. Before entering public service he was an articulate and very forceful champion of the effort within the international labor movement to preserve and to extend the democratic institutions of the free world. In the Cabinet he represented the President on missions to Europe, and Africa, and Asia, and was continuously concerned with the affairs of the United Nations' International Labor Organization. Since becoming a member of the Supreme Court, he has traveled extensively in the world, speaking in many lands about the problems and the issues which all men share.

At different periods, over the past 20 years, we have had varying concerns in our constant and continuous efforts for world peace. But always—and really never more than now—we strive for a world where all men may live in peace with the hope of justice under the rule of law over the conduct of nations.

Committed as we are to this principle and this purpose, it is fitting that we should ask a member of our highest court to relinquish that office to speak for America before the nations of the world.

And finally, let me say that Justice Goldberg is an old and trusted friend of mine, a counselor of many years. He will sit in our Cabinet. He will always have direct and ready access to, and the full and respectful confidence of, the President of the United States and the Secretary of State. In this new office he will speak not only for an administration but he will speak for an entire Nation, firmly, earnestly, and responsibly committed to the strength and to the success of the United Nations in its works for peace around the world.

Now, if Justice Goldberg would say a word we would all be very pleased.

Thank you very much.

NOTE: The President spoke at 10:54 a.m. in the Rose Garden at the White House. In his opening words he referred to Justice Goldberg and to Secretary of State Dean Rusk. Later he referred to, among others, Henry Cabot Lodge, U.S. Ambassador to South Viet-Nam.

Following the President's remarks, Justice Goldberg spoke briefly. The text of his remarks, also released, follows:

Mr. President, Mr. Secretary, Mr. Bundy, my wife, Dorothy, my son, Bob:

Mr. President, with the death of Adlai Stevenson, a great voice of America in the world has been stilled, but the message of Adlai Stevenson to the world must go on.

That message is man's ancient supplication: Grant us peace, Thy most precious gift.

What has been prayer throughout the ages is a necessity today.

Adlai Stevenson was the voice of a great and powerful nation, at once dedicated to peace and implacable in its commitment to freedom.

The eloquence of his words no more than reflected the richness of his spirit and the righteousness of his cause.

We, and the world, are different because he lived.

Of Adlai Stevenson's departure and my appointment, I can only borrow words uttered on a similar occasion by Thomas Jefferson: I succeed him. No one could replace him.

I shall not, Mr. President, conceal the pain with which I leave the Court after 3 years of service. It has been the richest and most satisfying period of my career. And I shall have more to say about this in a letter I am sending to the Chief Justice and my brethren on the Court.

Throughout my life I have been deeply committed to the rule of law. The law gives form and substance to the spirit of liberty and to mankind's sacred stir for justice.

It now comes that the President has asked me to join in the greatest adventure of man's history—the effort to bring the rule of law to govern the relations between sovereign states.

It is that or doom—and we all know it.

I have accepted, as one simply must.

In my efforts at the United Nations, I shall do my best to carry on, in my own way, the work of my distinguished predecessors. I hope to help make real and manifest the assertion of the charter that social justice and better standards of life in larger freedom are indispensable to the achievement of world peace.

I am grateful to the President for judging me capable of the effort I now commence. I am grateful to the Secretary of State, my friend and my former colleague in the Cabinet, for welcoming me so warmly to this post.

It is with great humility that I undertake the role of our Nation's advocate of peace in the council of nations.

My wife, my son, my daughter—who is in Chicago, and cannot be with us today—my mother-in-law, all join with me in asking only the prayers of the American people that we shall succeed.

Thank you.

Justice Goldberg served as Secretary of Labor from January 21, 1961, through September 24, 1962, and as Associate Justice of the Supreme Court of the United States from September 28, 1962, through July 27, 1965.

See also Item 383.

371   Remarks at the Swearing In of Rear Adm. John Harllee and James V. Day as Chairman and Vice Chairman, Federal Maritime Commission. *July 20, 1965*

Members of the Congress, distinguished guests, ladies and gentlemen:

This is a very happy day here at the White House. We are glad you are present to join in these festivities with us and to share this pleasure.

For some years, the ideal of our country's policy has been that politics would stop at the water's edge. I am not always sure just which edge of what water, but it is a very fine sentiment to believe in. And I hope it is an idea that Americans will always practice as well as preach.

However, at the Federal Maritime Commission we want to take no chances. We have a Democrat as Chairman and a Republican as Vice Chairman and, between them, they have steered such a straight and steady course that we intend to keep them on the bridge together at all times.

Chairman John Harllee and Vice Chairman James Day, together with their very able colleagues, have done a fine job, and a difficult and demanding public responsibility. I am proud and very pleased that they have both accepted reappointment and that they will continue to efficiently serve in the posts that they now hold. We want—and we need—their experience and their leadership in the many challenges that we are going to face in the days ahead.

All through our Nation's history the prosperity of our people—as well as the safety of our people—has been tied very closely to the role that we play on the seas of the world. And that is a role that we can never wisely or never safely neglect.

Yet, I believe that we are all increasingly conscious of the fact that as a great Nation, we have been laggard and we have been neglectful in many areas of our transportation responsibilities and our transportation opportunities.

I am hopeful—greatly hopeful—that we can in the next few years shake off the effects of these neglected years and move forward to achieve the progress that we are so clearly capable of in every sector from the highways on which we travel to the high seas upon which we sail.

To do so will require much more than the answer of just money alone. So in all the fields of transportation, our future progress depends upon the willingness of many different groups and interests to cooperate in a manner to which they are not always accustomed.

Admiral Harllee, Vice Chairman Day, and their colleagues and staff have always placed cooperation ahead of control in their responsibilities, and the results have been most encouraging. As President, I very much welcome this type of approach.

The regulatory functions of the Federal Maritime Commission are unusually important to this Nation's economy and to this country's commerce, and they are now more so, perhaps, than any other time that we have lived in this century.

Expanding our overseas trade is a matter

that this Nation must give the highest priority. It is very important to all of our economic well-being.

You know we began this Nation as a world of traders, and we still are. It remains surprising and even shocking that about 80 percent of our business firms have never yet entered into foreign trade. I think this represents a great wasteland of unfilled opportunity that is open. I hope that over the next 10 years we can increase three- or four-fold the number of American shippers who send goods abroad.

In all that must be done, the great Maritime Commission has a key role to play—and I am looking to these men to continue to assume that challenge in their leadership at this great Commission.

The Commission has my strongest support for the continuing efforts to eliminate all the barriers to United States trade now presented by discriminatory freight rates. Likewise, the Commission has my support for its efforts to convince our allied trading partners that we welcome them to our shores to share in the prosperity that our commerce helps create for the free world.

In world trade, this country seeks no special favoritism. But we do seek equality of treatment. We do seek the elimination of unfair or unlawful discriminatory prejudices or predatory practices.

The roads we walk and the lanes we sail lead toward a more prosperous world. But we never forget that the goal we seek in the harbor toward which we all sail, the hope toward which our compass points, is peace—peace among all nations, peace for all mankind.

I, just a few moments ago, made an appearance here and I asked a distinguished member of the United States Supreme Court to relinquish his lifetime job to lead this Nation and other nations in the United Nations as successor to Ambassador Adlai Stevenson. I am proud to be able to realize that Justice Arthur Goldberg is the new Ambassador to the United Nations—a man who loves peace, who is concerned with the plight of the new independent nations, who is anxious to demonstrate our compassion and our cooperation.

We covet nothing of other nations. We seek, as our forefathers sought, only friendship and peaceful commerce with all nations of the world. And that will always be America's dream and America's goal until it is someday the world's ideal and the world's reality. And for the great contribution that you distinguished citizens will provide in your leadership, a grateful Nation will welcome and will applaud.

Thank you very much.

NOTE: The President spoke at 11:40 a.m. in the Rose Garden at the White House.

For the President's remarks upon announcing the nomination of Arthur J. Goldberg as U.S. Representative to the United Nations, see Item 370.

372 Remarks to the American Field Service Students on the Eve of Their Departure From the United States. *July 20, 1965*

Mr. Howe, our dear friend, Lindy Boggs, Mrs. Johnson, Luci, my young friends, ladies and gentlemen:

We are very proud to welcome you here to the White House today. This is the house of all of the American people.

You have made this a very memorable year and a happy year for the families with whom you have lived in the United States. I hope this year will live as a happy memory for all of you, too. You leave behind understanding of yourselves and the countries you have so well represented. I trust that is what you take away with you, as well as understanding of our people and our country.

We have no dogma, no doctrine, no discipline to impart to you. I hope none have tried to persuade you otherwise. We want you only to take with you a new vision and a new confidence in what you can be yourself and what you can help others to be in your own land.

While you have been here I am sure you have seen things that you don't like, things that you would like to change. If you have, then you can know that you have seen America as Americans themselves see it.

For we are a people who wake up every morning determined to go out and change what we may think is wrong, change what we believe should and could be better.

For all of our nearly 200 years as a Nation, America has been drawing her energy and her vitality and dynamic progress from this devotion to changing the conditions of man. If there is one secret to America's strength and success, I think it is the respect that we foster and try always to protect for the right of citizens to criticize what deserves criticism and to change what really needs changing.

I hope that you find that same spirit present in your own lands, for I think it is the spirit that is vital to the progress of all people in this dynamic and exciting century in which we are privileged to live.

The American people and their elected leaders are peaceful in their purposes always, but never forget of us, when you return to your homes, that we mean to win the wars that we have declared: the wars against poverty, the wars against ignorance, the wars against disease, the wars against discrimination and bias and bigotry.

We are fighting those wars in the development of our Great Society program, and already we have taken more legislative action in this session than one could expect almost in a century—certainly in a decade.

So, whatever your country, you may always know that we in the United States stand ready to work with you in these same endeavors so that some day all mankind may stand taller and may stand straighter in a world of peace, and a world of justice, and a world of equality among men.

In your time here you have come to know Americans as a people who are open and unguarded and, I hope, unafraid. We are not a formal people. We are not a people governed by tradition or custom. We are not a people so much concerned with the way things are done as by the results that we achieve. Since the frontier really opened we have been this way.

We have been concerned more with how our children shall live than with emulating how our fathers and our grandfathers lived. So this spirit of America, I think, is present in our policies and our purposes toward other peoples of other lands as we meet here this afternoon.

Some people believe that it is better if the peoples of the world hold each other at arms length and deal with each other in the most formal way. They sometimes ridicule informality. They like to believe that this prevents friction and misunderstanding and even the disillusionment that may come when people see each other's shortcomings.

That is the way people used to deal with each other back in the days of the clipper ships and the coach and the horse and buggy days. But I don't believe, and I am sure most Americans don't believe, this kind of relationship is what we want in the 20th century.

We really want all mankind to live together with purpose to accomplish the great things that are within the reach of us all. We believe that people must respect one another, respect each other's rights, respect each other's ways, respect their just dreams, and respect their honorable aspirations.

But we want such respect to be that of a lively and an affectionate family—open, frank, trusting, rather than the stiff, chilly, and even suspicious formality dictated by the protocol of ancient principalities.

So, in this America—this lively, stirring, exciting America of today—our hearts, as well as our homes, are open to you, open to you always.

We have been enriched by having you here this year. We hope that you will return many times through the many years ahead for you. And we hope that wherever you go you will work always, as we work, to try to change, to try to improve the life of mankind on this earth, and, most of all, to try to win peace for all peoples.

Thank you very much.

NOTE: The President spoke at 12:26 p.m. on the South Lawn at the White House. In his opening words he referred to Arthur Howe, Jr., President of American Field Service International Scholarships, Mrs. Corinne (Lindy) Boggs, wife of Representative Hale Boggs of Louisiana, Mrs. Lyndon B. Johnson, and Luci Baines Johnson, the President's daughter.

The group was composed of some 3,000 exchange students, representing 59 countries, who had completed one year in high schools in the United States and were preparing to return to their homes.

373   Letter to the Postmaster General Requesting the Issuance of an Adlai Stevenson Commemorative Stamp.   *July 20, 1965*

Dear Mr. Postmaster General:

Our Nation has lost one of its most rare and inspiring talents with the passing of Adlai E. Stevenson. In the generation since the Second World War, he touched the lives, the minds, and the hearts of his countrymen as few other Americans have done at any time. He called us to greatness—and we shall never forget either the man or his call.

As Governor, as a national leader, as an international statesman, Adlai Stevenson enlarged our horizons as Americans and helped to light the hopes of mankind all around the world. His place is secure in the hearts of all who knew him and in the history of these times. I believe it is fitting that we pay the honor that we can to this most exceptional man. So, I am, by this letter, requesting that you immediately undertake to develop and issue publicly a commemorative postage stamp appropriate to the life and works of Adlai Ewing Stevenson.

Sincerely,

LYNDON B. JOHNSON

[Honorable John A. Gronouski, Postmaster General, Washington, D.C.]

NOTE: On July 24, 1965, the White House released a letter to the President from Postmaster General Gronouski which stated in part, "I am pleased to notify you that plans are now under way to issue a five-cent memorial stamp in honor of Adlai E. Stevenson. . . .

"We are now making plans to issue the stamp on Saturday, October 23, in Bloomington, Illinois, where he is buried. I feel this will be an appropriate date of issuance, since it will coincide with the nation-wide observance of the 20th anniversary of the founding of the United Nations on October 24" (1 Weekly Comp. Pres. Docs., p. 4).

See also Items 355, 356, 359.

374   Remarks to the Delegates to the White House Conference on Education.   *July 21, 1965*

Mr. Gardner, distinguished members of the Cabinet, distinguished Ambassador to the United Nations, ladies and gentlemen:

I want to welcome all of you to the first White House teach-in.

I want to thank all of you for the work that you have done over the past 2 days on this most important of American problems—the education of the American people.

I have kept you waiting for some time, while I have listened to your panel chairmen review with me their impressions of the fruits of your labors for the past 2 days.

Education will not cure all the problems of society, but without it no cure for any problem is possible. It is high among my own concerns, central to the purposes of this administration, and at the core of all our hopes for a Great Society.

Belief in education is, of course, not a new belief. It is a faith as old as the Nation—the faith that the progress of America and the possibility of democracy depended really upon the education of our citizens. And so, through the generations, we have gone along investing our skill and our energy, and much of our resources, to build an educational system that is really broad enough to serve all the needs of all of our people. And I think no investment has ever been more wisely made and none has ever resulted in more abundant returns, either to a people or to a nation.

This central faith remains an unchallenged tenet of the American way of life. Your concern, and mine, is how can we remedy the serious defects of our present system, and how can we equip it to meet the new challenges which are already engulfing our Nation and engulfing the world.

Every aspect of our national life—from the office and factory to the doctors' offices and the halls of government—has become much more complex and intricate than ever before. Thus we must train more people in more skills if they are to really find fulfilling work and to make their proper contribution to this land that we love.

Many already spend more time not working than at their work, and the amount of leisure time is going to continue to rise in the days ahead. So we must open up new horizons of interest and creativity if periods of rest are not to become feared periods of sterile boredom.

Exploitation of the challenges, and escape from the perils of modern life demand new leaps of imagination and creativity. And thus we need education which will stimulate and which will energize the free spirit, rather than to crush it and dampen it, as is so often true.

Most of all we need an education which will create an educated mind. This is a mind not simply a repository of information and skills, but a mind that is a source of creative skepticism, characterized by a willingness to challenge old assumptions and to be challenged, a spaciousness of outlook, and convictions that are deeply held, but which new facts and new experiences can always modify.

For we are a society which has staked its survival on the rejection of dogma, on the refusal to bend experience to belief, and on the determination to shape action to reality as reality reveals itself to us. This is the hardest course of all for us to take. For without education it is really an impossible course, and all of this means not merely more classrooms and more teachers, although we need them—and we are going to have them—but it means a fundamental improvement in the quality of American education. It means an educational system which does not simply equip the students to adjust to society, but which enables the student to challenge and to modify, and at times reject, if necessary, the received wisdom of his elders.

We are far too easily satisfied when we know that a child has a desk in a classroom with a teacher to instruct him. But it is what happens inside that classroom that really counts, and that is finally what is really important. And far too often what does happen is sadly unequal to what we have a right to expect.

That is why I am so glad that this conference did not spend its time passing and mimeographing detailed resolutions and making a host of specific recommendations. We asked you to come here to stimulate some fresh thinking, not just talk about old ideas. I plan to take your proceedings and read them myself and to circulate them to every office of Government concerned with this subject. I want them to use your thinking as a basis for the evolution of new programs and new actions, and new legislative proposals wherever such proposals are appropriate.

In addition, I charge your Executive Committee to review the record and to constitute themselves a continuing task force on this most critical subject. So it will be their job to make sure that this conference does not come to an end today, that we have a continuing flow of new ideas from universities and private groups into the central processes of government.

For really we are quite busy catching up with our past failures, and we do not intend to fall behind again.

There is one specific proposal which I have mentioned and discussed with your leaders, and which I hope we can carry out. And that is the proposal to establish a series of Adlai Stevenson fellowships to enable a selected group of young men and women from all over the world to serve as interns in the organizations of the United Nations. This will not only be a great memorial to Adlai Stevenson, but it will be an indication of the interest of this Nation in the enlightenment of all mankind.

Of course this will not be the only memorial to Adlai Stevenson. It is just one of many. In fact, I have already asked Secretary Willard Wirtz, a former law partner to Governor Stevenson, to meet with members of the Stevenson family to discuss appropriate ways to pay adequate tribute to his memory. But there can be none more fitting, and I know you will agree, than the training of future leaders in the wondrous works of peace and compassion.

I had to go to the Supreme Court yesterday and ask one to leave that high tribunal to come and lead us down the road to compassion and to peace in the world, and I am so happy that he could be here with you today, and I want to ask him to stand just now so that we can all acknowledge his presence and his great sacrifice. Justice Goldberg.

I think most of you know the enveloping role which education has played in my own life. It really was the instrument which took a boy from the countryside of Texas and opened to him the boundless dreams and the opportunities of American life.

And I not only learned, but I taught, and

I saw for myself how the light of learning could brighten the path of the humble.

But my profound concern with education does not spring simply from the accidents of my youthful circumstances. It has, it is true, always existed. But the office that I now hold has deepened and widened and contributed greatly to the urgency of that concern. For it was only after I could become President of this country that I could really see in all its hopeful and troubling implications just how much the hopes of our citizens and the security of our Nation and the real strength of our democracy depended upon the learning and the understanding of our people.

A great public servant in the early days of the republic of my State said: "Education is the guardian genius of democracy. It is the only dictator that free men will recognize, and the only ruler that free men will accept."

This Nation has really always been an experiment—an experiment in the capacity of a whole people, ruling its rulers, to deal with changing peril and with shifting expectations. And every single time we think we have proved the success of that experiment, the scene changes, and America sets forth on a very different course.

And this is true again as we meet here today, but the stakes are really higher than they have ever been before, and I know now with greater certainty than I have ever known it before, that leaders can lead, they can set goals, they can make speeches and teach their people, but in our democracy, they cannot make people what they are not. They cannot exceed, in achievement or understanding, the best qualities of the American mind. And that, in turn, is the charge of those who teach the young, and who thus hold in their hands the possibilities of this President, and of many Presidents yet to come.

Thank you for coming.

NOTE: The President spoke at 6 p.m. on the South Lawn at the White House before a gathering of 700 participants in the White House Conference on Education, held in Washington July 20–21. In his opening words he referred to John W. Gardner, President of the Carnegie Corporation of New York who served as Chairman of the Conference, and to Associate Justice Arthur J. Goldberg of the Supreme

Court of the United States (newly designated U.S. Representative to the United Nations, see Item 370). During his remarks he referred to W. Willard Wirtz, Secretary of Labor.

On July 8, 1965, the White House had announced the names of 150 leaders in education, business, labor, and Government who were chosen by the President to lead, at the Conference, discussions of American educational problems. The White House release stated that the panelists would be joined by 500 other leaders who would participate in the discussions.

See also Item 291.

375 Remarks at the Signing of the Water Resources Planning Act. July 22, 1965

Distinguished Members of Congress and particularly the sponsors of this progressive legislation, Secretary Udall, my guests:

This is one occasion that I wish our outdoor signing could be rained inside.

If we could have had the kind of rain that we so desperately need throughout the East, I would be glad to sign this valuable bill outside—provided somebody would lend me one of those pens that writes under water.

I think, as all of you know, the deadline for signing this measure is still almost a week away. But I am signing it this morning because we just cannot overemphasize and we cannot overdramatize and we certainly cannot overreact to this Nation's growing problem of water supply and proper water management.

Over the years the Federal Government has made an investment of more than $50 billion in water resources projects. Our annual investment of some $1¾ billion is equal to the yearly investment outlay of the entire motor vehicle industry. So we spend roughly as much each year on water development as we do on our continental air and missile defense.

But the present drought in the Northeast is bringing home to us that we have done and are doing far less than enough to get the job done for this growing Nation.

Our capacity is overtaxed already—even without a drought. Yet only 15 years from now, in 1980, our water needs will more than double. And in 30 years, by the end of the century, our water needs will triple.

I was asked the other day what took most of my time as President, and I could answer without hesitation in one word: planning—planning—planning. We just don't realize keenly enough how pressing, and how urgent, and how critical it is for us to be planning today for America's future needs tomorrow—needs 10, 20, and 30 years hence, when this Nation will have three people for every two that we have today.

So, in this Water Resources Planning Act that we have before us this morning, Congress has given us a valuable tool for planning that we are going to have to do at every level—Federal, State, and local. Senator Anderson, who is beside me here, Senator Jackson, the very able chairman of the House Committee, Congressman Aspinall—all who supported S. 21—have made a very invaluable and very farsighted contribution to America's future. And I want to congratulate each Member of the Congress, who is invited here this morning, for their dedicated and patriotic and rather effective work in this field.

I think the day is past when the Nation can afford to listen to, or laugh smugly with, those who have gone about slandering our water resource projects throughout the years as pork barrel and boondoggle. Because we see very clearly in the East today the real boondogglers are those who oppose and who obstruct sensible, prudent, and long-range planning to meet our water needs.

It would be inappropriate on this occasion to talk about the future without speaking directly of the present problem that is plaguing the great Northeast—from Maryland to Maine.

The 4-year drought in this rich and populous region is the most severe in the history of the Nation. It is unequaled in the records dating back to the landing of the Pilgrims at Plymouth Rock.

Last night I received a comprehensive report on the situation that I had requested from the Water Resources Council, and I have asked that this report be released shortly. I hope I have a chance to review it with the Members of Congress from that area and then I will be able to make it public.

Water supply is, first of all, a great responsibility of our local governments—and, of course, we do not intend for the Federal Government to preempt this responsibility. But I have and I am directing every Federal agency with authority in this field to do all that should and can be done to contribute the maximum assistance in the present situation. I also am directing that Federal plans for future emergency action be made on the assumption that the drought will continue into the fifth year—and I hope that local planning will follow this same assumption.

The Council reports that there may be above-average rainfall the next 30 days in the Northeast, and more during the late summer and fall. Well, I hope so. But down where I come from, we don't run for umbrellas in July just because rain is predicted. In my country, sometimes you can't get a glass of water even out of the rivers—much less out of the restaurants.

And even with heavy rains, the Council informs me that it would take a year of normal rainfall to make much improvement in this great region's water shortage.

So we must—and we will—do all that we can under existing programs to assist in this growing emergency. For the longer-term, I believe it is imperative that we proceed toward the goal of "drought-proofing" our metropolitan areas, and their agricultural regions, through advances in the technology of desalting the waters of the sea. This has become a must, and we are giving it high priority in the executive department and in the Congress.

I met with a group of Ambassadors yesterday, who came in here for lunch with some of my associates, and I find that the entire world is vitally interested in the work that we are doing in the field of desalting. And while sometimes we are inclined to emphasize that more has been accomplished than really has, the interest is there, and the desire is there, and if we have the necessary determination, under sound leadership, we will have breakthroughs and we will get results. And Senator Anderson, Senator Jackson, Congressman Aspinall, and others who are pioneers in this field, all of the members of the Interior Committees of both Houses, have shown great imagination in the years past.

I have directed my Science Adviser, Dr. Donald Hornig, to coordinate all of the Federal efforts on desalting. We can do better. We must make certain that we proceed on the most effective and the most productive course. I am going to ask Dr. Hornig to talk to some of the leading Members of Congress in the next few days ahead to just see that we get the benefit of all the suggestions they have. I am asking the Secretary of the Interior today to see what can be done with interested cities to determine the feasibility of large desalting plants as sources of supplementary water supply for the future.

We must all remember the old wisdom that "willful waste leads to woeful want." Water has always been very precious to Americans, but it has never been more precious than now.

So this Nation can be grateful to this Congress for the responsible foresight that has been shown in this important response to our future needs. And the development of large parts of our Nation is limited only by water, and we must get ahead with the job, and this bill that I will shortly sign will be an important step in that direction.

Thank you very much.

NOTE: The President spoke at 10:53 a.m. in the Rose Garden at the White House. In his opening words he referred to Secretary of the Interior Stewart L. Udall. During his remarks he referred to Senator Clinton P. Anderson of New Mexico, Senator Henry M. Jackson of Washington, Chairman of the Senate Committee on Interior and Insular Affairs, Representative Wayne N. Aspinall of Colorado, and Dr. Donald F. Hornig, Special Assistant to the President.

For the reports of the Water Resources Council, see note to Item 358.

As enacted, the Water Resources Planning Act (S. 21) is Public Law 89–80 (79 Stat. 244).

376   Remarks to the British Ambassador at the Magna Carta Anniversary Ceremony. *July 22, 1965*

Sir Patrick:

I am most grateful to you. On behalf of the American people, I thank your Government and your countrymen for this most gracious and this very deeply appreciated act of yours this morning.

The Magna Carta has always meant much to all Americans.

The success of the lords who, shall we say, reasoned together with King John 750 years ago inspired the Americans who tried the same on King George III 189 years ago from Philadelphia. The outcome was good or bad—depending on the point of view, I think.

But more than that, the principles that are set forth in this Great Charter have inspired and guided all of us throughout our existence—and they do that today. All we do at home and all we do throughout the world, is meant to assure men the right to "freedom under law" and the right to expect impartial justice.

We never forget those great words of this Charter: To no one will we sell, to none will we deny or delay, right or justice.

Britain's sons, like America's sons, stand their guard today in many distant lands so that these promises may be fulfilled for all mankind, and that we may ultimately obtain our objective of a world that can live in peace together.

American families, like your families, Sir Patrick, devoutly want peace. We are extremely grateful in this country to your leaders, to your very able Prime Minister, for the courageous and their very willing initiatives and efforts that they have made seeking the peace. But we also know that you want, as we want, peace with honor, and peace with freedom, and peace with dignity.

So we are proud to stand with you this

morning, and to work with you, and to strive with you as friends and allies for a better world and for a peaceful world.

And while you are here, Sir Patrick, may I say this. I ask you to convey to your countrymen the appreciation of all the Americans for the very many thoughtful courtesies extended last week when death came in London to our beloved statesman, Adlai Stevenson. By birth and loyalty Ambassador Stevenson was an American, but in spirit he was at home really in both of our lands.

And when death came to him in the midst of your people, your gracious understanding touched all Americans, and I should like for you to say to them, on behalf of the people of the United States, we are so grateful that in this hour of trouble for us you were so understanding.

NOTE: The President spoke at 11:40 a.m. in the Rose Garden at the White House. In his opening words he referred to Sir Patrick Dean, British Ambassador to the United States. Preceding the President's remarks, Sir Patrick presented him with a copy of "Magna Carta" by James Clarke Holt (Cambridge University Press, 1965).

377 Message to the Congress Transmitting Annual Report of the Commodity Credit Corporation. *July 22, 1965*

To the Congress of the United States:

Thirty years ago, the Congress brought into being the Commodity Credit Corporation. In transmitting the report of this Agency for the fiscal year ended June 30, 1964, as provided by section 13 of Public Law 806, 80th Congress, I feel it is appropriate to view, in summary, the three decades of the Corporation operations.

Over the past 30 years, the Commodity Credit Corporation has:

1. Enabled farmers to hold their crops for fair market prices.

2. Minimized the depressing effect of surpluses by holding them off the market.

3. Assured a stable flow of food to consumers, deterring inflationary pressures.

4. Created a sound base for banks and other lending institutions which supply the credit needs of farmers.

5. Provided in wartime the means of supplying our allies with food and fiber, and in the postwar period became the instrument which insured that food could also help keep the peace.

6. Acted as the mechanism for executing the Food for Peace program, the Interna-

tional Wheat Agreement and other similar international programs.

7. Supported the rapid expansion of agricultural exports.

During fiscal 1964, the Commodity Credit Corporation reduced its investment in farm commodity inventories by more than $380 million. The wheat inventory was reduced by about 275 million bushels, and the supplies of dairy products were brought down to manageable levels.

The Commodity Credit Corporation is a creature of legislation. Its ability to fulfill our objectives for the future is no greater than the strength of legislation enacted by the Congress. It can function best when farm commodity programs are responsive to the conditions which exist in the agricultural economy. If these programs are in tune with the times, the Commodity Credit Corporation can perform its proper functions for farmers and for the public.

The legislation which I proposed this year, and which is now before the Congress, will help the Corporation to carry forward the objectives it should fulfill in the coming decade. These objectives are:

To continue the financial progress of our farmers;

To further reduce the Corporation's costs by bringing stocks of farm commodities down to more manageable levels;

To assure an abundant supply of high quality, reasonably priced foods without fear of severe price fluctuations for our consumers;

To cushion the forces of the revolution in farm productivity which enable output to far exceed our capacity for use by balancing the growth in farm output with our ever expanding food and fiber requirements;

To use our abundance as a force for peace and progress;

To rely more upon the market place as the primary source of fair farm returns.

Instruments of public policy can weight the scales of economic justice on the side of those who are disadvantaged, but they should enhance—not supplant—the equal opportunity for each person to obtain a decent livelihood from our economic system.

The Commodity Credit Corporation has an important place among the instruments of public policy:

Without the programs for which it acts as fiscal agent, the income netted by farmers would decline by half. Without adequate income, the family farm system which dominates our agriculture would die.

Without family farms the vast abundance of food and fiber we all have come to expect as a natural condition of a highly productive economy would no longer be assured.

The Commodity Credit Corporation as a visible expression of our commitment to abundance continues to be a servant of all people. What began 30 years ago as an experiment to provide economic justice for the farmer has now become a tested instrument in the continuing experiment each generation performs to demonstrate the vitality of our democracy.

LYNDON B. JOHNSON

The White House
July 22, 1965

NOTE: The report is published in "Summary of 30 Years' Operations of the Commodity Credit Corporation With Report of the President of the Commodity Credit Corporation, 1964" (Government Printing Office, 1965; 80 pp.).

The legislation before the Congress to which the President referred, the Food and Agriculture Act of 1965, was approved by the President on November 3, 1965 (see Item 597).

378   Remarks to the Members of the World Press Institute.
July 22, 1965

Mr. Fisher and members of the World Press Institute staff, outstanding young journalists:

It is a great privilege and pleasure to welcome all of you, especially Mr. Johnsson from Stockholm.

You come from continents and countries that I have enjoyed greatly in the past—from the Middle East, from South America, from Asia and Africa, from India and Italy, Switzerland and Sweden, England and France.

One of you has come in from Greece. Once I attended your Trade Fair and I asked my daughter to say a few words to your friendly citizens. She talked long and learnedly about the birthplace of Alexander the Great, and all the rich history of northern Greece and Macedonia. And when she had finished no one in attendance was even willing to listen to me.

I won't make that same mistake today. But I do wish that we could have a press conference, with me asking the questions and you giving the answers.

Americans have always been the respectors of the views of our visitors. Nowhere are views from other lands and other peoples more respected than in this White House.

Our country—our whole Nation—is, after all, the creation of peoples of all countries, and cultures, and colors, and creeds. In our veins flow the blood of all men. And that is why, in our hearts, we have for 189 years regarded America's cause as really the cause of all mankind.

The great meaning of America is that men of all nations can live together in understanding and in peace. That is the great challenge, and the great opportunity, and the great responsibility that is facing you and facing your profession—that is, to foster understanding among men so that there may be peace among nations.

Seventy percent of the world's peoples today lack the means of being informed about developments in their own countries, much less in other countries. Of Africa's 236 million people, less than 3 million actually receive newspapers. Nearly half the countries of the Middle East have no daily press at all. And so it goes on all around the world.

But we are so happy to observe that a new day is dawning, and you and I and all of us are living now the moment of one of history's great breakthroughs.

In the 18th century the world was altered by the political revolution. In the 19th century it was changed by the industrial revolution. Now, in this 20th century, the world is being changed as never before by the scientific revolution—the revolution of human knowledge.

It is no dim and distant dream to envision the day when men everywhere will be able to receive in their homes telecasts from satellites of sessions of the United Nations.

I was delayed for a moment in greeting you not by telecasts from the United Nations, but from a telephone call from what I hope will be the new United States Representative to the United Nations, who is going before the Foreign Relations Committee in the morning to be confirmed and, we hope, to be sworn in here at the White House as soon as he has been confirmed.

Yes, no technology is changing more rapidly or more dramatically than the technology of communications, which will permit communication between nations and people. And surely from these better communications will come better understanding between all of us.

But the meaning of this revolution, and the meaning of this breakthrough, runs far beyond the impact upon any one technology. The advances of science are rendering obsolete the old thinking, the old theories, the old doctrine and dogma about relations between nations.

Young and less developed nations have an opportunity today to bypass the hundred years of the industrial revolution and begin to enter the mainstream of the 20th century. New nations with a minimum of trained scientists can share, and can benefit, from the vast store of already existing scientific knowledge.

They can benefit from modern medicine to free their people of disease and of early death, and to extend life expectancy. They can benefit from advances made in agriculture and produce more food to feed their growing population. And we are trying so hard to encourage them and to help them and to get them to develop their agriculture better.

They have the hope nations never had before of building better lives for their people, regardless of their size or their power or their wealth or their past history.

779

So, it is a great and grand and thrilling vision that opens before mankind as we meet here this afternoon. And we of America are moved by that vision. We are moved by it in all that we do at home and all that we do in the world.

For if the dream is to become the reality, peace must be preserved for mankind, and peace is the purpose of all that we do.

There are those who would force human hopes and aspirations back into the darkness of the past by aggression, by terror, by oppression, by war. But we believe that mankind has outrun the darkness of those dogmas which subjugate man's body and which imprison man's soul.

We believe that mankind should have a choice, and we believe that mankind does have a choice today. We think he can choose the way of life, the way of peace, the way of freedom, the way of justice through the liberation of his mind and his soul.

And we believe that is the choice that men of all continents and of all cultures and all colors and creeds will really ultimately make if they are permitted to choose their way in peace.

The strength that we have and the success that we enjoy and the spirit that swells within the soul of America is mobilized and committed to one end—that end is to preserve the peace so that men everywhere can choose for themselves the way they want to go, in this dawning age of opportunity in which we are privileged to live.

I am glad that I am privileged to welcome you here and to make these observations. These are trying moments in our relations with other nations.

Yesterday I talked to a thousand brilliant leaders of the field of education in this country, not just about the programs that will involve advancement and adventure for our own citizens here at home, but about the great progress that we can make in the field of international education.

While we will be true to our commitments, we will keep our treaties, we will join in protecting freedom in the world. And we think that strength will be required to preserve that freedom.

At the same time, we will do everything within our power to see that, while strength is maintained on the military front to preserve freedom from aggression, there will be equal strength on the political, and on the diplomatic, and on the economic front that will try to find ways of avoiding contests. At the same time, we are prepared to deal with them, if we must.

I want to take a moment, if you will, before I return to my other appointments, to meet each of you individually. I want to ask you to convey to your leaders, and to your fellow men, our hopes and aspirations and best wishes for their success and their advancement.

We are not concerned just with 190 million people in this country. We are devoutly interested in all the 3 billion people of the world.

We are organizing, and planning, and mobilizing to win the wars that we have declared—and we will win them. And those wars are wars on poverty—it was being fought in the House of Representatives today, and we won a while ago by five votes. The wars on ignorance—we are making great advances there. The educational program this year has never been equaled in this country before. Wars on diseases—while our life expectancy has improved a great deal with the years, we are not at all satisfied with it. And we have a half-dozen far-reaching, comprehensive health measures that will not just confine our efforts to our own people but will help us to help others in the world, and provide leadership in improving the health and in some of the problems of population and other matters.

So, we are committed to win the wars that we have declared on the ancient enemies of mankind: ignorance, illiteracy, poverty, and disease.

And it will be a great day in the world when we can say that victory is ours against those ancient enemies in all lands.

Thank you very much.

NOTE: The President spoke at 5:43 p.m. in the Rose Garden at the White House. In his opening words he referred to Sterling W. Fisher, Chairman of the Board of Directors, World Press Institute, and Director of Public Affairs, Reader's Digest. During his remarks he referred to Hans-Ingvar Johnsson of the daily *Dagens Nyheter* of Stockholm, Sweden.

379   Memorandum in Response to a Report on the New Executive Seminar Center. *July 23, 1965*

Memorandum for Chairman Macy:

I found your report on the operation of the new Executive Seminar Center both interesting and encouraging. I congratulate you, your Civil Service Commission colleagues, and all who have worked to make this unusual interagency experiment in career development the success that it has been.

I am pleased by your report that the Center is making significant contributions to the excellence in the public service for which we strive. I am also pleased to find that the Center draws on the intellectual resources of the academic, business, labor, and Government communities to enrich the trainees' educational experience and broaden their perspectives by exposing them to the divergent ideas, views, and approaches the varied visiting faculty brings to the seminars. I hope, and I have confidence, that the performance of seminar participants in the years ahead will bear out your observation.

It is important that you continue to emphasize to agencies the need to make careful selections of seminar participants. They should be sure to nominate not those who can most easily be spared, but those who ordinarily can't be—the men and women who show real potential for assignment to career positions of greatest responsibility. Only in this way will the Seminar Center fulfill its high promise.

I will watch with continuing interest the course of the Seminar Center. I will be particularly interested in hearing more of your plans for establishment of similar centers in other areas. Please keep me advised of future developments and progress.

LYNDON B. JOHNSON

NOTE: The report, in the form of a memorandum from John W. Macy, Jr., Chairman of the Civil Service Commission, was made public by the White House on July 23, 1965. It stated, in part:

"Established by the Civil Service Commission under the Training Act of 1958, the Executive Seminar Center represented a significant new concept in career development when the first group of 35 mid-career executives began the first two-week seminar on 'Administration of Public Policy' in the fall of 1963. With the 31 subsequent seminar sessions, the soundness of the idea has proven itself to the Commission, the participants, faculty members and a distinguished Committee of Visitors. The consensus is that the Center constitutes a significant step forward in preparing promising executives for increasingly responsible assignments in the Federal service. . . .

"The curriculum is composed of ten related two-week courses designed to develop knowledge and understanding in three basic areas—public administration, Federal policies and programs, and management and organization. . . .

"Our experience so far leads me to believe that the Executive Seminar Center program has made and will continue to make a significant contribution

to the achievement of excellence in the public service. It will continue to aid in attaining more efficient and effective management and in development of executives who can understand and help to solve the complex problems our Government must meet in the years ahead."

380 Remarks at the Signing of the Coinage Act. *July 23, 1965*

Distinguished Members of Congress, ladies and gentlemen:

We are gathered here today for a very rare and historic occasion in our Nation's history.

Before I make some observations that I have made note of here, I want to say to the Congress again, as I do almost daily these days, in the words of the Navy—"Well done."

When I have signed this bill before me, we will have made the first fundamental change in our coinage in 173 years. The Coinage Act of 1965 supersedes the act of 1792. And that act had the title: An Act Establishing a Mint and Regulating the Coinage of the United States.

Since that time our coinage of dimes, and quarters, and half dollars, and dollars have contained 90 percent silver. Today, except for the silver dollar, we are establishing a new coinage to take its place beside the old.

My Secretary of the Treasury, Joe Fowler, is a little stingy about making samples, but I have some here. Joe made sure that I wouldn't put them in my pocket by sending them over here in plastic.

Actually, no new coins can be minted until this bill is signed. So these strikes, as they are called, are coins that we will never use. On one side is our first First Lady, Martha Washington. On the other, a replica of Mount Vernon.

The new dimes and the new quarters will contain no silver. They will be composites, with faces of the same alloy used in our 5-

cent piece that is bonded to a core of pure copper. They will show a copper edge.

Our new half dollar will continue our silver tradition. Eighty percent silver on the outside and 19 percent silver inside. It will be nearly indistinguishable in appearance from our present half dollar.

All these new coins will be the same size and will bear the same designs as do their present counterparts. And they will fit all the parking meters and all the coin machines and will have the same monetary value as the present ones.

Now, all of you know these changes are necessary for a very simple reason—silver is a scarce material. Our uses of silver are growing as our population and our economy grows. The hard fact is that silver consumption is now more than double new silver production each year. So, in the face of this worldwide shortage of silver, and our rapidly growing need for coins, the only really prudent course was to reduce our dependence upon silver for making our coins.

If we had not done so, we would have risked chronic coin shortages in the very near future.

There is no change in the penny and the nickel. There is no change in the silver dollar, although we have no present plans for silver dollar production.

Some have asked whether our silver coins will disappear. The answer is very definitely—no.

Our present silver coins won't disappear

and they won't even become rarities. We estimate that there are now 12 billion—I repeat, more than 12 billion silver dimes and quarters and half dollars that are now outstanding. We will make another billion before we halt production. And they will be used side-by-side with our new coins.

Since the life of a silver coin is about 25 years, we expect our traditional silver coins to be with us in large numbers for a long, long time.

If anybody has any idea of hoarding our silver coins, let me say this. Treasury has a lot of silver on hand, and it can be, and it will be used to keep the price of silver in line with its value in our present silver coin. There will be no profit in holding them out of circulation for the value of their silver content.

The new coins are not going to have a scarcity value either. The mint is geared to get into production quickly and to do it on a massive scale. We expect to produce not less than 3½ billions of the new coins in the next year, and, if necessary, twice that amount in the following 12 months.

So, we have come here this morning to this, the first house of the land and this beautiful Rose Garden, to congratulate all of those men and women that make up our fine Congress, who made this legislation possible—the committees of both Houses, the leadership in both Houses, both parties, and Secretary Fowler and all of his associates in the Treasury.

I commend the new coinage to the Nation's banks and businesses and to the public. I think it will serve us well.

Now, I will sign this bill to make the first change in our coinage system since the 18th century. And to those Members of Congress, who are here on this very historic occasion, I want to assure you that in making this change from the 18th century we have no idea of returning to it.

We are going to keep our eyes on the stars and our feet on the ground.

NOTE: The President spoke at 11:21 a.m. in the Rose Garden at the White House. During his remarks he referred to Henry H. Fowler, Secretary of the Treasury.

As enacted, the Coinage Act of 1965 is Public Law 89-81 (79 Stat. 254).

On October 30, 1965, the White House announced that circulation of the new 25-cent piece would begin on November 1. The White House release stated in part, "The new—nonsilver—quarter dollar will be added to the circulation of the traditional 90 percent silver quarter. Both the old and the new quarters are to circulate together.

"Approximately 230 million pieces of the new quarter will be distributed during the week beginning November 1. Initial distribution will be backed by production that will rise from 28 million to 60 million pieces a week during November, and will be still higher thereafter."

381 Letter to the Members of the President's Commission on Crime in the District of Columbia. *July 24, 1965*

Dear ——————:

I am pleased to appoint you as a member of the commission which I am creating to deal with crime and law enforcement in the District of Columbia.

The assignment of the commission is as broad as the problem of crime in the District. In my message to the Congress on February 15 I stated a number of areas which I believe warrant particular attention, but the commission should not regard these suggestions as in any way limiting its scope. Indeed, it is my hope that the commission, through the prompt organization of task forces, will find it possible to consider and make recommendations on every issue which it believes relevant to the central problem. I do not expect the commission, however, to duplicate the work already done in the District in the field of juvenile delinquency prevention under the auspices of the President's Committee on Juvenile Delinquency, although it doubtless will find useful the studies and data, as well as the results of the demonstration project now underway in the Cardozo area.

The task forces may include members of the commission, but in general should be selected from without as well as within the District, and from Federal and District Governments as well as from private life. Wide and varied membership in these groups will enable the commission to enlist particular skills and experience needed to reach sound conclusions. By way of suggestion, the following areas of study might be assigned to task forces:

(1) The best use of police services, including police selection, training, and improvement of police-community relationships.

(2) Causes of crime, and relationship to criminal activity of economic, educational, and social factors.

(3) Treatment of offenders, from arrest to conviction (e.g., uses and abuses of bail).

(4) Treatment of the convicted offender, particularly the first offender (e.g., treatment and ultimate disposition of those committed to mental institutions, supervision of convicted offenders after release, economic rehabilitation of offenders).

(5) Diagnosis and non-criminal treatment of socio-medical problem offenders (e.g., alcoholics, narcotic offenders, sex offenders, family quarrels, etc.).

(6) Examination of prosecutorial and judicial procedures, particularly juvenile court philosophy, organization, and procedures.

(7) Revision of D.C. criminal laws, other than those within the scope of other specific task force assignments.

It is my hope that the commission will work closely with the National Commission on Law Enforcement and Administration of Justice, which I am establishing. The District and National Commissions should immediately establish liaison, so that there will be neither duplication of effort nor failure to take advantage of mutually useful ideas, research, or results.

The commission, and the task forces, will be supplied with staff assistance, and I am instructing all departments and agencies of the Federal government to extend assistance to the commission in every way possible.

This commission should plan to report to me within a year, with specific recommendations. Indeed, I would welcome interim recommendations in any area as soon as the commission is prepared to make them.

The assignment you and the other members of the commission have accepted is one of major importance. Our goal, as I stated in my February 15 message, is no less than "the planning and establishment in the District of a model system which will best achieve fair and effective law enforcement." Achievement of that goal will of course benefit not only our Nation's capital, but every other city now grappling with similar problems.

Sincerely,

LYNDON B. JOHNSON

NOTE: This is the text of similar letters addressed to the Chairman and the members of the Commission. For the names of the Chairman and members see the President's remarks upon signing the District of Columbia appropriation bill (Item 366) in which he announced the establishment of the Commission. The letter to the Chairman was dated July 19; the remainder, July 22.

On May 14, 1965, the White House announced that the President had asked Congress for an additional $1,879,000 to enable the District of Columbia to increase its efforts against crime. The release stated that in a letter to the President of the Senate, transmitting the request in the form of an amendment to the 1966 budget, the President said:

"These funds will permit a significant effort to reverse the longstanding pattern of increasing crime in the District by increasing the effective strength of the Metropolitan Police during the next nine months to allow a substantial increase in police coverage at the times and places where it is most needed. With the additional police cars and two-way radios to be provided, this program should promptly improve the safety of the streets in the District. Moreover, since funds are also provided to permit careful evaluation of results, there will be a sound basis upon which to determine how much the size of the police force should be increased on a permanent basis. These appropriations will fund measures to fight crime that can be undertaken without delay. I hope that Congress can give early attention to this request for the needed funds.

"Additional measures, such as pistol registration, can also have an immediate impact. As other proposals are developed, particularly by the commission on District crime which I will appoint shortly, they will be promptly forwarded to the Congress. Prompt consideration of them by the Congress will demonstrate our mutual determination that crime can and will be brought under control."

The release further stated that the funds requested would provide for a demonstration—from July 1, 1965, to March 31, 1966—of the impact on criminal activity of a substantial concentration of police in areas of heavy crime and at critical hours of the day and night.

382 Statement by the President on Establishing the President's Commission on Law Enforcement and Administration of Justice. *July* 26, 1965

I HOPE that 1965 will be regarded as the year when this country began in earnest a thorough, intelligent, and effective war against crime. The present wave of violence and the staggering property losses inflicted upon the Nation by crime must be arrested. The time has long since arrived for this Nation to discard obsolete and unworkable methods of detecting and apprehending criminals. We must come to grips with the problems of punishment versus rehabilitation, of protecting society from criminals while, at the same time, working to prevent the development of potential criminals.

This national effort must begin with a systematic study of these fundamental problems. There is much we need to do. What are the basic causes of crime and delinquency? How can we increase respect for law and order? What are the optimum methods for preventing crime? As funda-mental as these questions are, we have never sought comprehensive nationwide answers. It will be the task of this Commission on Law Enforcement and Administration of Justice to seek these answers.

The significance I attach to this Commission is demonstrated by the fact that I have asked the Attorney General to serve as its Chairman. The Commission will have the benefit of expert assistance from professionals in a number of fields. I have ordered all relevant Federal agencies to cooperate fully in this enormous and unprecedented task. The Commission cannot obviously solve all the problems related to crime. I do ask it to commit wisdom, energy, and experience to the central need of this and any civilized society: the safety of its citizens.

NOTE: The statement was read by Bill D. Moyers, Special Assistant to the President, at his news conference held at the White House at 10:45 a.m. on

July 26, 1965. It was not made public in the form of a White House press release.

The President's Commission on Law Enforcement and Administration of Justice was established on July 23, 1965, by Executive Order 11236 (30 F.R. 9349; 3 CFR, 1965 Supp.). On July 26 the President named Attorney General Nicholas deB. Katzenbach as Chairman of the Commission and announced the names of the other 18 members (1 Weekly Comp. Pres. Docs., p. 7).

See also Items 422, 437, 500.

383   Remarks at the Swearing In of Arthur J. Goldberg as U.S. Representative to the United Nations.   *July 26, 1965*

Ambassador and Mrs. Goldberg, Members of the Cabinet, Members of Congress, distinguished guests:

The Vice President and I are delighted to have you here in the Rose Garden on this happy morning. This is a very delightful affair for Arthur Goldberg and his family, and for me, and for our country, and for the cause of all mankind.

Only a few days ago the great voice of a great and good American was stilled by the passing of Adlai Stevenson. Today another distinguished American comes forward to follow in his place. It is a symbolic and appropriate reminder to us, and to the world, of the continuity in the continuing purposes of this great Nation.

The voice of America is never one voice. The vision of America is never one man's vision alone. The will of America for a just and for a decent and for a peaceful world is never the will of just one citizen. But the continuing and constant will of 190 million citizens is the will that will be expressed by the distinguished Ambassador as the voice of America at the United Nations.

It is this constant, this unchanging, this unending will and resolve of our people that we ask our representatives to convey to all the peoples of the world through the forums of the United Nations.

Ours is a dynamic land and a dynamic so-ciety. Arthur Goldberg's own story testifies to this most eloquently. A son of immigrants, born to the most humble beginnings, he has risen from newsboy on the streets of Chicago to success in his profession, to serve in the Cabinet, to honor on the Nation's highest court, and now to a position where he will be the advocate of this Nation's policies before the world.

This personal story is a testament to the vigor, and the vitality, and the forward movement of our open and our restless and our questioning society.

But there is another side of America, a side which I hope the world will never forget or never underestimate.

We are a nation dedicated and committed to ideals and values about the worth of man and about the preciousness of his liberty. In support of our dedication and commitment, we are resolute and we have built great strength to manifest that resolve. But we are above all a patient Nation and a patient people, and we have the strength, and we have the stability and the success to permit us to be patient.

For 20 years or more we have manifested our patience around the world. Our sons, today, keep a vigil of peace and freedom on lines where they have stood now for more than a generation. We do not expect the world to change or to be changed either in a month, or a year, or a decade. But we have the patience and the resolve to pursue our purposes, for however long it may be necessary to assure for mankind the blessings of a world that is without terror, or without injustice, or without want.

So, let none abroad—and let none here at home—ever doubt or ever question that America has the patience or the perseverance to do what the cause of mankind requires, and what our many commitments around the world necessitate.

I know of no more gifted citizen, no more able individual, to express, and to interpret, and to explain the policies of the United States Government, as determined by the people and the President and the Congress,

than this most able and distinguished gentleman who will shortly take the oath of office—Arthur Goldberg.

This is a very proud moment personally, but it is also a very proud moment for all Americans.

I take particular pride in welcoming to this ceremony one of our most distinguished and most beloved Americans, the great humanitarian, the Justice of the Supreme Court, Hugo Black, who will now administer the oath of office.

NOTE: The swearing-in ceremony was held at 11:40 a.m. in the Rose Garden at the White House. The text of Mr. Goldberg's remarks is printed in the Weekly Compilation of Presidential Documents (vol. 1, p. 9).

See also Item 370.

384   Statement by the President Upon Announcing a White House Conference on Equal Employment Opportunities. *July 26, 1965*

BASIC to our national goal of equality of treatment and opportunity for all Americans is the assurance that employment will be on the basis of the applicant's ability and qualifications to do the job, rather than on irrelevant factors of race, religion, national origin, or sex. It is clear to all that economic strength is essential to achieving equality of housing, education, and public accommodation.

The genuine progress of the past few years in this field convinces me that American industry is anxious to assist in achieving equality of employment opportunity. I hope that the new Commission under the chairmanship of Franklin D. Roosevelt, Jr., will benefit by this recent change in national attitude. We expect to obtain from the Conference advice and guidance which will enable the Commission to discharge its re-

sponsibilities more effectively.

The Congress has indicated its belief that initial emphasis should be on securing the cooperation and support of the private sectors of our economy—both management and labor. Although every legal enforcement means available to the Commission should be employed when other methods fail, I strongly share the view that efforts to obtain voluntary compliance should receive priority.

In this period of great social change the Nation is at long last beginning to face the varied and complex problems of our minority groups. My interest in the employment problem is of many years standing and I am anxious that our progress continue. The Conference can and should be a useful instrument—I shall do everything possible to make it so, and we welcome the cooperation of all.

NOTE: The President's statement was made public as part of a White House release announcing that the first White House Conference to plan fair and effective administration of title VII of the Civil Rights Act of 1964 would be held at the Department of State Auditorium on August 19–20, 1965.

The release stated that title VII of the act, establishing the Equal Employment Opportunity Commission, of which the chairman was Franklin D. Roosevelt, Jr., had gone into effect on July 2, 1965.

The release also noted that the Conference would bring together in a series of workshops the EEOC Commissioners and key staff members with more than 300 representatives of employers, unions, employment agencies, public and private organizations, and of State and local fair employment commissions in order to discuss the various EEOC programs.

A White House release dated August 5, 1965, carried the tentative schedule of events for the forthcoming Conference and listed the topics to be covered in workshops together with the names of the workshop chairmen (1 Weekly Comp. Pres. Docs., p. 50).

For the President's remarks at the Conference on August 20, see Item 436.

385 Remarks on Announcing the Nominations of Anthony J. Celebrezze as Judge, U.S. Court of Appeals, Sixth Circuit, and of John W. Gardner as Secretary, HEW. *July 27, 1965*

Ladies and gentlemen:

I have a brief announcement that I think will be of interest to you. I intend to appoint the Secretary of Health, Education, and Welfare, the Honorable Anthony J. Celebrezze, to the United States Court of Appeals for the Sixth Circuit.

I have both a feeling of pride in Secretary Celebrezze's ascension to this high court, and a reluctance in seeing him depart the Department that he has guided so skillfully.

There is something much more powerful and remarkable in the American legend that directs a young immigrant of Italian birth who, as a baby, came to this country with his parents and, as a man, widened the dimensions of his adopted land.

As an Ohio State senator, as a fabled mayor of Cleveland—five times elected by his fellow citizens as their leader—and now as Secretary of Health, Education, and Welfare, Tony Celebrezze's first duty was always service to his neighbors.

With tolerance, with energy, with single-minded purpose, he presided over the greatest thrust for the future of American education and health that this Nation has ever known.

Today there is written, or there is about to be written into law, a plan for hospital and medical care for the elderly, and an elementary and secondary education bill that has dissolved an old and thorny debate and begins the towering task of educating our young people.

Though their families be poor or their future be bleak, this is an innovation in health that will transport the revealed genius of American doctors and scientists to those places in our land until now too far away from too many of our people. In all of these advances and adventures, Tony Celebrezze, with quiet, undisturbed, unruffled competence, played the role of a great leader and a hard worker.

So, he will go, with the advice and consent of the Senate, to his new duties with the gratitude of every child who now can learn but who might not have, of every older person who now can find care but who might not have, and of every man and woman who now survives cancer, heart disease, and stroke, but who might not have.

I am prepared today to announce to you Secretary Celebrezze's successor. I shall send to the Senate today, to become the new Secretary of Health, Education, and Welfare, the name of John W. Gardner.

He is regarded by his peers as one of the most knowledgeable men in the field of United States education in this country. For 10 years he has been the president of the Carnegie Corporation. He was born in Los Angeles, California. He's a holder of degrees from Stanford University and the University of California. He has been all of his adult life an explorer in the search for excellence.

So, as we near the outer edges of this century, the loss of quality and the discovery of excellence become the searing issues of the times in which we live. After a great deal of study and deliberation, I know of no one who is better suited by temperament, by experience, by commonsense intellectualism to confront these issues and to bend them to the national desire.

He is a Ph. D.; he's an ex-Marine; he's a former outstanding intelligence officer; he's a distinguished author and a Republican—though not necessarily in this order of importance or proportion of significance.

He was the leader of the President's special Task Force on Education last year that probed the Nation's need with a bold spirit of innovation and imagination. He helped to plant the seedbed of the educational harvest that has been produced by the 89th Congress.

I have just concluded a meeting with the leaders of that Congress and received their views and recommendations and report. Unless I miss my mark, this session of the Congress will go down in the history of this country as the best congress ever assembled from the standpoint of production, from the standpoint of understanding and compassion of our people, and from the standpoint of achievement. And that applies to members of both parties and to the entire Congress.

It has been successful because of the spadework and the thinking and the sacrifice of men like Mr. Gardner, and those thinkers and doers who had on the drawing boards months ahead of the assemblage of Congress the ideas and the programs that the Congress has evolved.

Just last week, Mr. Gardner was both the inspirer and the steward of a White House Conference on Education, which peered into the future and which found it full of promise and challenge.

Once he wrote in his excellent book on excellence these words:

"The society which scorns excellence in plumbing because plumbing is a humble activity and tolerates shoddiness in philosophy because it is an exalted activity will have neither good plumbing nor good philosophy. Neither its pipes nor its theories will hold water."

Any man who can believe that and write it is the kind of man who can and ought to become the President's leader of the fastest growing Department and the most comprehensive services in this Government.

If the Senate is willing, Mr. Gardner will shortly undertake his duties and start administering the program that this good Congress has, or is enacting, and will also have a farsighted, 20th century plan for the Congress that is to come in January.

Thank you very much.

NOTE: The President spoke at 10:30 a.m. in the Rose Garden at the White House. During his remarks he quoted from "Self Renewal; the Individual and the Innovative Society" by John W. Gardner (New York: Harper and Row, 1964).

See also Items 389, 433.

386 Message of Greetings to the Geneva Disarmament Conference Committee. *July 27, 1965*

I SEND my greetings to the members of the Disarmament Committee as they renew the most important task on earth.

The Bible describes "Death" as the fourth horseman of the Apocalypse, saying: "And Hell followed after him." Our genius has changed this from a parable to a possibility. For the wasting power of our weapons is beyond the reach of imagination and language alike. Hell alone can describe the consequences that await their full use.

Therefore, if we love man, nothing is more important than the effort to diminish danger—halt the spread of nuclear power—and bring the weapons of war under increasing control.

Many proposals to this end now sit on your Conference table. My delegation, and others, will make new proposals as the Conference continues.

I have instructed the American delegation to pursue the following objectives with all the determination and wisdom they can command:

First, to seek agreements that will limit the perilous spread of nuclear weapons, and make it possible for all countries to refrain without fear from entering the nuclear arms race.

Second, to work toward the effective limitation of nuclear weapons and nuclear delivery systems, so that we can diminish present danger as well as prevent expanding peril.

Third, to work for a truly comprehensive test-ban treaty.

Many nations will, and should, share in these discussions.

No difference among any of us, on any other issue, can be allowed to bar agreement in this critical area. This is not in any single nation's interest, nor is it in the interest of the multitude of nations and peoples whose future is so tied to the good sense of those at this Conference table.

My Nation is ready. If others are equally prepared, then we can move, with growing confidence, toward the light.

NOTE: The Conference of the 18-Nation Committee on Disarmament resumed meetings in Geneva on July 27, after a recess which began September 17, 1964.

387 Remarks at the Department of Defense Cost Reduction Awards Ceremony. *July 28, 1965*

Secretary McNamara, Secretary Vance, the Service Secretaries, General Wheeler, members of the Joint Chiefs, very valued employees of the Government of the United States:

I always come here to the Pentagon with a great sense of pride and a deep sense of gratitude. As a citizen, not as Commander in Chief, I am both proud and grateful for all of you who serve our country with such dedication—military and civilian alike.

This morning I came over here with something more—a slightly sore arm. Over the weekend Secretary McNamara and Mrs. McNamara and their son came up and visited with us at Camp David. And somehow some of the newsmen learned that I sometimes bowl up there. And the White House Press Office put out the word that my high score was 165. That was all right, but then they went on to say that no other score would be announced unless it was higher.

Now that is in the best Washington tradition—to take a great deal of pride in a figure only if it is higher than the last one. And that is a tradition we are trying very hard to change, and I came over here this morning to thank you for helping me. What happened at Camp David Saturday was this: I challenged Bob McNamara and I guess most of you know that was a mistake—for both him and me.

Under the McNamara influence, my bowling score was, shall we say, reduced considerably. But I took some comfort from the fact that it was 50 percent better than the Pentagon's leading tennis, squash, and ski enthusiasts.

A great deal has happened since I had the pleasure of coming and visiting with you here about a year ago. Among the many good things which have occurred are the benefits that we are enjoying as the result of your labors, and the savings and cost reduction actions that the Defense Department has taken. As a result of those achievements, our military strength has continued to increase faster than our Defense budget. And that is as it should be.

Last January, I told the Congress, and I quote:

"Defense expenditures in the years ahead must continue to be guided by the relentless pursuit of efficiency and intelligence of economy.

"There is no necessary conflict between the need for a strong defense and the principles of economy and sound management. And if we are to remain strong, then—

"Outmoded weapons must be replaced by new ones.

"Obsolete equipment and installations must be eliminated.

"Costly duplication of effort must be cut out.

"We are following this policy today, and so long as I am President, I continue to plan to follow that policy."

This is still our policy.

But I think I should tell you that I could not follow it successfully—and Secretary McNamara could not follow it at all—without your loyal and your energetic and your imaginative efforts.

So I have come here this morning first, to thank you, second, to congratulate you.

Secretary McNamara's report to me a few days ago tells an impressive story about your achievements. In the fiscal year 1964, you saved some $2½ billion. Last year, you nearly doubled that amount. In fact, your actual savings of $4.6 billion for fiscal 1965 were actually $2.1 billion more than he originally estimated.

Now this is a record of which all of you can be proud—and for which this country can be proud of you, and grateful to you.

But there is a good deal more to that story. You have proved the truth of my assurance to the Congress that economy and efficiency can go hand in hand with a strong defense. Side-by-side with our cost-reduction measures, our military strength has continued to mount.

Secretary McNamara reports to me that in the past 4 years you have achieved the following:

First, a 200 percent increase in both the number and total megatonnage of nuclear weapons in strategic alert forces.

Second, a 67 percent increase in the tactical nuclear weapons deployed in Western Europe.

Third, a 45 percent increase in the number of combat-ready Army divisions.

Fourth, a 51 percent increase in the number of tactical fighter squadrons.

Fifth, a 100 percent increase in air-lift capability.

Sixth, a 100 percent increase in general ship construction and conversion to modernize the fleet.

Seventh, a 1,000 percent increase in the special forces that are trained to deal with counterinsurgency threats.

Now without this magnificent record, we would be very ill-equipped to meet the situation that we have encountered in Viet-Nam, or the many other worldwide commitments we have to the cause of peace and freedom.

I just finished reviewing with the leading Members of Congress, the leadership, the chairmen of the House and Senate committees, the problems that face America in the world. And today the future of the whole society of free men depends to a very large extent upon the strength that you have built.

So you and your colleagues in the Defense Department are the men and women to whom America looks to provide that strength—and you are providing it.

So long as I am permitted to be your President, we will continue to spend whatever is necessary to spend for the security of our peo-

ple. We shall continue to maintain our military forces without regard to arbitrary budget ceilings. But, with your continued help, we will proceed to procure those forces always at the lowest possible cost. We will continue to operate them with the greatest possible economy and efficiency.

The first week I was in this Office I promised the people of this Nation that the country would get a dollar's worth of defense for every dollar spent, and now I wish to thank some of you for helping me to fulfill that promise.

We have 10 important departments in this Government. We have dozens of outstanding independent agencies that number their employees among the thousands. But I am proud this morning to acknowledge that you are the pacesetters. You are not only the leaders in protecting this Nation's security, but you are the leaders in protecting this Nation's solvency. And the work that the generals and the admirals and the secretaries and the stenographers have done together, by finding areas of agreement and uniting and following enlightened cost-conscious 20th-century practices, is now being emulated in every single department in this Government.

I have been a Government employee all of my adult life—for 35 years. I know the pride they take in their work and in their country. No person that ever served in uniform or ever served the men in uniform had more right to feel proud than those who are part of the Defense Establishment today.

Both in uniform and out, you have men of the highest caliber, of the highest integrity, the greatest quality of intelligence and dedication and leadership. I am proud of our Joint Chiefs of Staff. I am proud of their counselors. I am proud of our Service

Secretaries and their assistants and their associates. And I need not tell you how grateful I am for the sacrifice that you Americans are willing to make in order to continue to keep this the home of the brave and the land of the free.

And heading all that list to whom I am indebted, I am indebted to none more, and there is none that I have a greater affection or admiration for than the man who ranks you all in this Department—the great Secretary of Defense, Bob McNamara. He gave up a great deal of his hobbies and his pleasures and hundreds of thousands of dollars each year, and millions of investments to come here and serve his country. He has served it faithfully and well. And if he has made mistakes, they have been mistakes of the head and not of the heart. And in the days ahead we will face many trying moments. We will go through many periods when our authority and our position and our system will be challenged, but under the leadership of what this building houses, we will meet every challenge, we will respond to every challenge, and we will, God willing, bring to all the peoples of all the world peace and progress.

Thank all of you so much.

[*After the presentation of the awards the President resumed speaking.*]

I want to thank you again before I leave, for having me here. During the last 3 years you have trained one of the outstanding administrators in this Government, and I get so many calls from the Defense Department to make decisions that I have just come over to the Defense Department and got one of your outstanding administrators, Mr. Joseph Califano, to move over to the White House and kind of help take charge of it. So he has not only been helping run the Pentagon, but now he is helping run the White House. And I want to thank you for making him available to me.

I want to publicly thank General Wheeler, the Chairman of the Joint Chiefs of Staff, for his wise counsel during the period that I have been President.

There are many honored and hallowed names on the honor roll of the Chiefs of Staff and the Chairmen of the Chiefs of Staff, but there is none that is greater or has contributed finer service or more wisdom and understanding than the man who now occupies that high office, and if I weren't fearful that I would be charged with plagiarizing Jack Valenti, I would say that I sleep better every night when I sleep, because of General Wheeler.

NOTE: The President spoke at 11:05 a.m. on the concourse at the Pentagon building. In his opening words he referred to Robert S. McNamara, Secretary of Defense, Cyrus R. Vance, Deputy Secretary of Defense, and Gen. Earle G. Wheeler, Chairman of the Joint Chiefs of Staff.

During his remarks the President referred to Joseph A. Califano, Jr., Special Assistant to the President, who formerly served as Special Assistant to the Secretary of Defense, and to Jack Valenti, Special Assistant to the President.

At the ceremony 17 employees of the Defense Establishment were honored with Certificates of Merit in recognition of their efforts in achieving significant cost reduction in Government operations during the previous year.

See also Items 360, 362.

388   The President's News Conference of July 28, 1965

WHY WE ARE IN VIET-NAM

THE PRESIDENT. My fellow Americans:

[1.] Not long ago I received a letter from a woman in the Midwest. She wrote: "Dear Mr. President:

"In my humble way I am writing to you about the crisis in Viet-Nam. I have a son who is now in Viet-Nam. My husband served in World War II. Our country was at war, but now, this time, it is just something that I don't understand. Why?"

Well, I have tried to answer that question dozens of times and more in practically every State in this Union. I have discussed it fully in Baltimore in April, in Washington in May, in San Francisco in June. Let me again, now, discuss it here in the East Room of the White House.

Why must young Americans, born into a land exultant with hope and with golden promise, toil and suffer and sometimes die in such a remote and distant place?

The answer, like the war itself, is not an easy one, but it echoes clearly from the painful lessons of half a century. Three times in my lifetime, in two World Wars and in Korea, Americans have gone to far lands to fight for freedom. We have learned at a terrible and a brutal cost that retreat does not bring safety and weakness does not bring peace.

It is this lesson that has brought us to Viet-Nam. This is a different kind of war. There are no marching armies or solemn declarations. Some citizens of South Viet-Nam at times, with understandable grievances, have joined in the attack on their own government.

But we must not let this mask the central fact that this is really war. It is guided by North Viet-Nam and it is spurred by Communist China. Its goal is to conquer the South, to defeat American power, and to extend the Asiatic dominion of communism.

There are great stakes in the balance.

Most of the non-Communist nations of Asia cannot, by themselves and alone, resist the growing might and the grasping ambition of Asian communism.

Our power, therefore, is a very vital shield. If we are driven from the field in Viet-Nam, then no nation can ever again have the same confidence in American promise, or in American protection.

In each land the forces of independence would be considerably weakened, and an Asia so threatened by Communist domination would certainly imperil the security of the United States itself.

We did not choose to be the guardians at the gate, but there is no one else.

Nor would surrender in Viet-Nam bring peace, because we learned from Hitler at Munich that success only feeds the appetite of aggression. The battle would be renewed in one country and then another country, bringing with it perhaps even larger and crueler conflict, as we have learned from the lessons of history.

Moreover, we are in Viet-Nam to fulfill one of the most solemn pledges of the American Nation. Three Presidents—President Eisenhower, President Kennedy, and your present President—over 11 years have committed themselves and have promised to help defend this small and valiant nation.

Strengthened by that promise, the people

of South Viet-Nam have fought for many long years. Thousands of them have died. Thousands more have been crippled and scarred by war. We just cannot now dishonor our word, or abandon our commitment, or leave those who believed us and who trusted us to the terror and repression and murder that would follow.

This, then, my fellow Americans, is why we are in Viet-Nam.[1]

THE NATION'S GOALS IN VIET-NAM

What are our goals in that war-strained land?

First, we intend to convince the Communists that we cannot be defeated by force of arms or by superior power. They are not easily convinced. In recent months they have greatly increased their fighting forces and their attacks and the number of incidents.

I have asked the Commanding General, General Westmoreland,[2] what more he needs to meet this mounting aggression. He has told me. We will meet his needs.

I have today ordered to Viet-Nam the Air Mobile Division and certain other forces which will raise our fighting strength from 75,000 to 125,000 men almost immediately. Additional forces will be needed later, and they will be sent as requested.

This will make it necessary to increase our active fighting forces by raising the monthly draft call from 17,000 over a period of time to 35,000 per month, and for us to step up our campaign for voluntary enlistments.

After this past week of deliberations, I have concluded that it is not essential to order Reserve units into service now. If that necessity should later be indicated, I will give the matter most careful consideration and I will give the country—you—an adequate notice before taking such action, but only after full preparations.

We have also discussed with the Government of South Viet-Nam lately, the steps that we will take to substantially increase their own effort, both on the battlefield and toward reform and progress in the villages. Ambassador Lodge[3] is now formulating a new program to be tested upon his return to that area.

---

[1] Copies of a booklet, entitled "Why Vietnam" (Government Printing Office, 27 pp.), were distributed to reporters on August 23, 1965, by Press Secretary Bill D. Moyers. The President's foreword to the booklet, dated August 20, follows:

My fellow Americans:

Once again in man's age-old struggle for a better life and a world of peace, the wisdom, courage, and compassion of the American people are being put to the test. This is the meaning of the tragic conflict in Vietnam.

In meeting the present challenge, it is essential that our people seek understanding, and that our leaders speak with candor.

I have therefore directed that this report to the American people be compiled and widely distributed. In its pages you will find statements on Vietnam by three leaders of your Government—by your President, your Secretary of State, and your Secretary of Defense.

These statements were prepared for different audiences, and they reflect the differing responsibilities of each speaker. The congressional testimony has been edited to avoid undue repetition and to incorporate the sense of the discussions that ensued.

Together, they construct a clear definition of America's role in the Vietnam conflict:

—the dangers and hopes that Vietnam holds for all free men

—the fullness and limits of our national objectives in a war we did not seek

—the constant effort on our part to bring this war we do not desire to a quick and honorable end.

LYNDON B. JOHNSON

[2] Gen. William C. Westmoreland, Commander of U.S. Forces in South Viet-Nam.
[3] Henry Cabot Lodge, U.S. Ambassador to South Viet-Nam.

I have directed Secretary Rusk and Secretary McNamara to be available immediately to the Congress to review with these committees, the appropriate congressional committees, what we plan to do in these areas. I have asked them to be able to answer the questions of any Member of Congress.

Secretary McNamara, in addition, will ask the Senate Appropriations Committee to add a limited amount to present legislation to help meet part of this new cost until a supplemental measure is ready and hearings can be held when the Congress assembles in January. In the meantime, we will use the authority contained in the present Defense appropriation bill under consideration to transfer funds in addition to the additional money that we will ask.

These steps, like our actions in the past, are carefully measured to do what must be done to bring an end to aggression and a peaceful settlement.

We do not want an expanding struggle with consequences that no one can perceive, nor will we bluster or bully or flaunt our power, but we will not surrender and we will not retreat.

For behind our American pledge lies the determination and resources, I believe, of all of the American Nation.

Our Readiness To Negotiate

Second, once the Communists know, as we know, that a violent solution is impossible, then a peaceful solution is inevitable.

We are ready now, as we have always been, to move from the battlefield to the conference table. I have stated publicly and many times, again and again, America's willingness to begin unconditional discussions with any government, at any place, at any time. Fifteen efforts have been made to start these discussions with the help of

40 nations throughout the world, but there has been no answer.

But we are going to continue to persist, if persist we must, until death and desolation have led to the same conference table where others could now join us at a much smaller cost.

I have spoken many times of our objectives in Viet-Nam. So has the Government of South Viet-Nam. Hanoi has set forth its own proposals. We are ready to discuss their proposals and our proposals and any proposals of any government whose people may be affected, for we fear the meeting room no more than we fear the battlefield.

In this pursuit we welcome and we ask for the concern and the assistance of any nation and all nations. If the United Nations and its officials or any one of its 114 members can by deed or word, private initiative or public action, bring us nearer an honorable peace, then they will have the support and the gratitude of the United States of America.

Letter to U Thant

I have directed Ambassador Goldberg [4] to go to New York today and to present immediately to Secretary General U Thant a letter from me requesting that all the resources, energy, and immense prestige of the United Nations be employed to find ways to halt aggression and to bring peace in Viet-Nam.

I made a similar request at San Francisco a few weeks ago,[5] because we do not seek the destruction of any government, nor do we covet a foot of any territory. But we insist and we will always insist that the people of South Viet-Nam shall have the right of

---

[4] Arthur J. Goldberg, U.S. Representative to the United Nations.

[5] See Item 331.

choice, the right to shape their own destiny in free elections in the South or throughout all Viet-Nam under international supervision, and they shall not have any government imposed upon them by force and terror so long as we can prevent it.

This was the purpose of the 1954 agreements which the Communists have now cruelly shattered. If the machinery of those agreements was tragically weak, its purposes still guide our action. As battle rages, we will continue as best we can to help the good people of South Viet-Nam enrich the condition of their life, to feed the hungry and to tend the sick, and teach the young, and shelter the homeless, and to help the farmer to increase his crops, and the worker to find a job.

It is an ancient but still terrible irony that while many leaders of men create division in pursuit of grand ambitions, the children of man are really united in the simple, elusive desire for a life of fruitful and rewarding toil.

As I said at Johns Hopkins in Baltimore,[6] I hope that one day we can help all the people of Asia toward that desire. Eugene Black[7] has made great progress since my appearance in Baltimore in that direction— not as the price of peace, for we are ready always to bear a more painful cost, but rather as a part of our obligations of justice toward our fellow man.

THE PRESIDENT'S PERSONAL FEELINGS ABOUT WAR

[2.] Let me also add now a personal note. I do not find it easy to send the

---

[6] See Item 172.
[7] Eugene R. Black, adviser to the President on southeast Asian social and economic development and former President of the World Bank.

flower of our youth, our finest young men, into battle. I have spoken to you today of the divisions and the forces and the battalions and the units, but I know them all, every one. I have seen them in a thousand streets, of a hundred towns, in every State in this Union—working and laughing and building, and filled with hope and life. I think I know, too, how their mothers weep and how their families sorrow.

This is the most agonizing and the most painful duty of your President.

There is something else, too. When I was young, poverty was so common that we didn't know it had a name. An education was something that you had to fight for, and water was really life itself. I have now been in public life 35 years, more than three decades, and in each of those 35 years I have seen good men, and wise leaders, struggle to bring the blessings of this land to all of our people.

And now I am the President. It is now my opportunity to help every child get an education, to help every Negro and every American citizen have an equal opportunity, to have every family get a decent home, and to help bring healing to the sick and dignity to the old.

As I have said before, that is what I have lived for, that is what I have wanted all my life since I was a little boy, and I do not want to see all those hopes and all those dreams of so many people for so many years now drowned in the wasteful ravages of cruel wars. I am going to do all I can do to see that that never happens.

But I also know, as a realistic public servant, that as long as there are men who hate and destroy, we must have the courage to resist, or we will see it all, all that we have built, all that we hope to build, all of our dreams for freedom—all, *all* will be swept away on the flood of conquest.

So, too, this shall not happen. We will stand in Viet-Nam.

VOICE OF AMERICA APPOINTMENT; JOHN CHANCELLOR

[3.] Now, what America is, and was, and hopes to stand for as an important national asset, telling the truth to this world, telling an exciting story, is the Voice of America. I classify this assignment in the front rank of importance to the freedom of the world, and that is why today I am proud to announce to you the name of the man who will direct the Voice of America.

He is a man whose voice and whose face and whose mind is known to this country and to most of the entire world. His name is John Chancellor.

Mr. Chancellor was born 38 years ago in Chicago. For more than 15 years he has been with the news department of the National Broadcasting Company. During that time he has covered the world—in Vienna, London, Moscow, New York, Brussels, Berlin, and Washington.

Since 1964 he has been with you, one of the White House correspondents.

This, I think, is the first time in the history of the Voice of America that a working newspaperman, a respected commentator, an experienced, independent reporter, has been given the responsibility of leadership and direction in this vital enterprise. I think he understands the challenges that are present and the achievements that are possible.

I am satisfied that the Voice of America will be in imaginative, competent, reliable, and always truthful hands.

Stand up, John, will you please?

NOMINATION OF ABE FORTAS TO SUPREME COURT

[4.] The President has few responsibilities of greater importance or greater consequence to the country's future than the constitutional responsibility of nominating Justices for the Supreme Court of the United States.

I am happy today, here in the East Room, to announce that the distinguished American who was my first choice for the position now vacant on the Supreme Court, has agreed to accept this call to this vital duty. I will very shortly, this afternoon, send to the United States Senate my nomination of the Honorable Abe Fortas to be an Associate Justice of the Supreme Court.

For many, many years, I have regarded Mr. Fortas as one of this Nation's most able and most respected and most outstanding citizens, a scholar, a profound thinker, a lawyer of superior ability, and a man of humane and deeply compassionate feelings toward his fellow man—a champion of our liberties. That opinion is shared by the legal profession and by the bar of this country, by Members of the Congress and by the leaders of business and labor, and other sectors of our national life.

Mr. Fortas has, as you know, told me on numerous occasions in the last 20 months, that he would not be an applicant or a candidate, or would not accept any appointment to any public office. This is, I guess, as it should be, for in this instance the job has sought the man. Mr. Fortas agrees that the duty and the opportunity of service on the highest court of this great country, is not a call that any citizen can reject.

So I am proud for the country that he has,

this morning, accepted this appointment and will serve his country as an Associate Justice of the Supreme Court.

I will be glad to take your questions now for a period.

QUESTIONS

POSSIBILITY OF ESCALATION IN VIET-NAM

[5.] Q. Mr. President, in the light of the decisions on Viet-Nam which you have just announced, is the United States prepared with additional plans should North Viet-Nam escalate its military effort, and how do you anticipate that the Chinese Communists will react to what you have announced today?

THE PRESIDENT. I do not want to speculate on the reactions of other people. This Nation is prepared, and will always be prepared, to protect its national interest.

DURATION OF FIGHTING

Q. Mr. President, you have never talked about a timetable in connection with Viet-Nam. You have said, and you repeated today, that the United States will not be defeated, will not grow tired.

Donald Johnson, National Commander of the American Legion, went over to Viet-Nam in the spring and later called on you. He told White House reporters that he could imagine the war over there going on for 5, 6, or 7 years. Have you thought of that possibility, sir? And do you think the American people ought to think of that possibility?

THE PRESIDENT. Yes, I think the American people ought to understand that there is no quick solution to the problem that we face there. I would not want to prophesy or

predict whether it would be a matter of months or years or decades. I do not know that we had any accurate timetable on how long it would take to bring victory in World War I. I don't think anyone really knew whether it would be 2 years or 4 years or 6 years, to meet with success in World War II. I do think our cause is just. I do think our purposes and objectives are beyond any question.

I do believe that America will stand united behind her men that are there. I plan, as long as I am President, to see that our forces are strong enough to protect our national interest, our right hand constantly protecting that interest with our military, and that our diplomatic and political negotiations are constantly attempting to find some solution that would substitute words for bombs.

As I have said so many times, if anyone questions our good faith and will ask us to meet them to try to reason this matter out, they will find us at the appointed place, at the appointed time, in the proper chair.

GHANA-HANOI DISCUSSIONS

[6.] Q. Mr. President, there is now a representative of the Government of Ghana [8] in Hanoi talking with the Foreign Minister of North Viet-Nam about the war in Viet-Nam. Do you see any indication of hope that something good will come of these talks?

THE PRESIDENT. We are always hopeful that every effort in that direction will meet with success. We welcome those efforts as we welcomed the Commonwealth proposal, as we welcomed Mr. Davies' visit,[9] as we welcomed the Indian suggestion, as we have

---

[8] Kwesi Armah, Ghana's High Commissioner to London.

[9] See Item 347 [10].

welcomed the efforts of the distinguished Prime Minister of Great Britain and others from time to time.

As I just said, I hope that every member of the United Nations that has any idea, any plan, any program, any suggestion, that they will not let them go unexplored.

EFFECT ON THE ECONOMY

[7.] Q. Mr. President, from what you have outlined as your program for now, it would seem that you feel that we can have guns and butter for the foreseeable future. Do you have any idea right now, though, that down the road a piece the American people may have to face the problem of guns or butter?

THE PRESIDENT. I have not the slightest doubt but whatever it is necessary to face, the American people will face. I think that all of us know that we are now in the 52d month of the prosperity that has been unequaled in this Nation, and I see no reason for declaring a national emergency and I rejected that course of action earlier today when I made my decision.

I cannot foresee what next year, or the following year, or the following year will hold. I only know that the Americans will do whatever is necessary. At the moment we enjoy the good fortune of having an unparalleled period of prosperity with us, and this Government is going to do all it can to see it continue.

MISSILE SITES IN NORTH VIET-NAM

[8.] Q. Mr. President, can you tell us whether the missile sites in North Viet-Nam that were bombed yesterday were manned by Russians and whether or not the administration has a policy about Russian technicians in North Viet-Nam?

THE PRESIDENT. No, we have no information as to how they were manned. We cannot speak with any authority on that matter. We made the decision that we felt our national interests required, and as those problems present themselves we will face up to them.

REACTION OF FRIENDLY NATIONS

[9.] Q. Mr. President, I wonder if you have had any communications from Chiang Kai-shek that he is ready to go to war with you?

THE PRESIDENT. We have communicated with most of the friendly nations of the world in the last few days and we have received from them responses that have been encouraging. I would not want to go into any individual response here, but I would say that I have indicated to all of the friendly nations what our problems were there, the decision that confronted us, and asked for their help and for their suggestions.

ATTITUDE OF SOVIET UNION

[10.] Q. Mr. President, given the Russian military involvement, or apparent involvement on the side of Hanoi on the one side, and the dialog which Mr. Harriman has been conducting for you on the other,[10] as well as the disarmament talks in Geneva at the moment, could you tell us whether you believe this war, as you now call it, can be contained in this corner of southeast Asia without involving a U.S.-Soviet confrontation?

THE PRESIDENT. We would hope very much that it could and we will do nothing to provoke that confrontation if we can avoid

[10] W. Averell Harriman, Ambassador at Large, arrived in Moscow on July 15, 1965, for discussions with Soviet officials on the war in Viet-Nam.

it. As you know, immediately after I assumed the Presidency I immediately sent messages to the Soviet Union. We have had frequent exchange of views by letter and by conversation with Mr. Gromyko and Mr. Dobrynin.[11] We are doing nothing to provoke the Soviet Union. We are very happy that they agreed to resume the disarmament conference.

I went to some length to try to extend ourselves to make the proposals that I would hope would meet with acceptance of the peoples of the world. We would like to believe that there could be some success flow from this conference although we have not been too successful.

I know of nothing that we have in mind that should arouse the distrust or provoke any violence on the part of the Soviet Union.

ROLE OF SAIGON GOVERNMENT

[11.] Q. Mr. President, does the fact that you are sending additional forces to Viet-Nam imply any change in the existing policy of relying mainly on the South Vietnamese to carry out offensive operations and using American forces to guard American installations and to act as an emergency backup?

THE PRESIDENT. It does not imply any change in policy whatever. It does not imply any change of objective.

THE UNITED NATIONS

[12.] Q. Mr. President, would you like to see the United Nations now move formally as an organization to attempt to achieve a settlement in Viet-Nam?

THE PRESIDENT. I have made very clear in my San Francisco speech my hope that the Secretary General, under his wise leadership, would explore every possibility that might lead to a solution of this matter. In my letter to the Secretary General this morning,[12] which Ambassador Goldberg will deliver later in the day, I reiterate my hopes and my desires and I urge upon him that he—if he agrees—that he undertake new efforts in this direction.

Ambassador Goldberg understands the challenge. We spent the weekend talking about the potentialities and the possibilities, our hopes and our dreams, and I believe that we will have an able advocate and a searching negotiator who, I would hope, would some day find success.

CONSULTATION WITH THE CONGRESS

[13.] Q. Mr. President, what are the borders of your power to conduct a war? At what point might you have to ask Congress for a declaration?

THE PRESIDENT. I don't know. That would depend on the circumstances. I can't pinpoint the date on the calendar, or the hour of the day. I have to ask Congress for their judgments and for their decisions almost every hour of the day.

One of the principal duties of the Office of President is to maintain constant consultation. I have talked to, I guess, more than 50 Members of Congress in the last 24 hours. I have submitted myself to their questions, and the Secretary of State and the Secretary of Defense will meet with them tomorrow if they are ready, to answer any questions that they may need.

Up to now, we have had ample authority, excellent cooperation, a united Congress be-

---

[11] Andrei A. Gromyko, Soviet Foreign Minister, and Anatoly F. Dobrynin, Soviet Ambassador to the United States.

[12] See Item 390.

hind us, and—as near as I could tell from my meetings last night with the leaders, and from my meetings today with the distinguished chairmen of the committees and the members of both parties—we all met as Americans, united and determined to stand as one.

THE GOVERNORS' CONFERENCE

[14.] Q. Mr. President, in this connection, however, last night one of the leading Governors of the Republicans said some rather strong things. Governor Hatfield of Oregon said the most recent escalation of action in Viet-Nam is moving all the people of the world closer to world war III, and we have no moral right to commit the world and especially our own people to world war III unilaterally or by the decision of a few experts.

This seemed to imply rather strong criticism of present policies. Do you care to express any reaction?

THE PRESIDENT. Yes. I don't interpret it that way. I think that there are dangers in escalation. I don't think I have any right to commit the whole world to world war III. I am doing everything I know how to avoid it. But retreat is not necessarily the best way to avoid it.

I have outlined to you what I think is the best policy. I would hope that Governor Hatfield and the other Governors, when they understand what we are doing, and when I have a chance to submit myself to their questioning and to counsel with them, would share my view.

I know they have the same concern for the American people and the people of the world as I do. I don't believe our objectives will be very different.

As a matter of fact, I asked the Governors if they could, to come here at the conclusion of their deliberations. I will have my plane go to Minneapolis tomorrow, and I believe 43 of the 48 have indicated a desire to come here.

I will give them all the information I can—confidential, secret, and otherwise—because I have great respect for them, their judgments, their opinions, and their leadership. It is going to be necessary in this effort.

I will also have the Secretary of State and Secretary of Defense review with them all their plans, and answer any of their inquiries, and we hope resolve any doubts they might have.

THE PRESIDENCY

[15.] Q. Mr. President, after the week of deliberations on Viet-Nam, how do you feel—in the context of your Office? We always hear it is the loneliest in the world.

THE PRESIDENT. Nancy,[13] I am sorry, but because of the cameras and microphones, I didn't get your question. Raise the microphone up where I can hear, and you camera boys give her a chance.

Q. Mr. President, I said, after the week of deliberations on Viet-Nam, how do you feel, personally, particularly in the context we always hear that your Office is the loneliest in the world?

THE PRESIDENT. Well, I don't agree with that. I don't guess there is anyone in this country that has as much understanding and as much help, and as many experts, and as good advice, and many people of both parties trying to help them, as they are me. Of course I admit I need it more than anybody else.

Nancy, I haven't been lonely the last few days—I have had lots of callers.

---

[13] Nancy H. Dickerson of the National Broadcasting Co.

[16.] Q. Mr. President, would you be willing to permit direct negotiations with the Viet Cong forces that are in South Viet-Nam?

THE PRESIDENT. We have stated time and time again that we would negotiate with any government, any place, any time. The Viet Cong would have no difficulty in being represented and having their views presented if Hanoi for a moment decides she wants to cease aggression. And I would not think that would be an insurmountable problem at all. I think that could be worked out.

DEPARTMENT OF HEALTH, EDUCATION, AND WELFARE

[17.] Q. Mr. President, to shift the subject just a moment, does your appointment of Mr. Gardner [14] suggest that there will be less interest now in the creation of a separate department of education?

THE PRESIDENT. No, not at all. My appointment of Mr. Gardner suggests that I looked over America to find the very best man I could to lead us forward to become an educated nation where every child obtains all the education that he can take, and where the health of every citizen is his prime concern, and where the Social Security Sys-

---

[14] See Item 385.

tem is brought to the needs of the 20th century.

After canvassing some 40 or 50 possibilities, I concluded that Mr. Gardner was the best man I could get. I asked his board to relieve him of his duties and release him to the Government so that he could furnish the dynamic leadership officially that he has been furnishing unofficially to us.

He told me yesterday morning that he was prepared to do that. I remembered that I had not asked him what State he lived in, where his permanent residence was, so I could put it on the nomination paper, or what party he belonged to. And he rather— well, maybe somewhat hesitantly said, "I'm a Republican."

I don't mean that his hesitating meant any particular significance, but I was happy that he said that because a good many Republicans voted for me and I don't want to be partial or partisan in this administration. I like to see leadership of that kind come from the Republican ranks. So I told him if he had no objections, I would announce very promptly his appointment and I hoped that he would give us American leadership without regard to party. And that's what I think he will do. I believe all the Nation will be proud of him as we are of Secretary Celebrezze.

Reporter: Thank you, Mr. President.

NOTE: President Johnson's forty-seventh news conference was held in the East Room at the White House at 12:34 p.m. on Wednesday, July 28, 1965.

---

389 Letter Accepting Resignation of Anthony J. Celebrezze as Secretary of Health, Education, and Welfare. *July 28, 1965*

[Released July 28, 1965. Dated July 27, 1965]

My dear Tony:

You leave this Administration to sit on the bench of one of the highest courts in the land. I am aware that this new calling coincides with your own desires, and no man is more deserving.

You go with my reluctance. No Cabinet officer has worked longer, harder, with a more zestful spirit, than you. The results of what you have done are plainly evident in the Congress, and will leave even larger imprints in the objective scrutiny of history.

The legacy you bequeath, not merely to your successor, but to the succeeding generations of Americans is the mark of your achievement. Medical care for the aged; education for more young people too often disadvantaged; bold new pathways in combatting disease, particularly the unapprehended killers: cancer, stroke and heart disease; in all these adventures you were both leader and tireless worker.

You carry with you the gratitude of an advancing nation, and you take with you the appreciation and the friendship of your President.

Sincerely,

LYNDON B. JOHNSON

[Honorable Anthony J. Celebrezze, Secretary of Health, Education, and Welfare, Washington, D.C.]

NOTE: Mr. Celebrezze served as Secretary of Health, Education, and Welfare from July 31, 1962, through August 17, 1965. His letter of resignation, released with the President's reply, is printed in the Weekly Compilation of Presidential Documents (vol. 1, p. 19).

See also Item 385.

390 Letter to the Secretary General of the United Nations Expressing Confidence in Ambassador Goldberg and Emphasizing U.S. Willingness To Negotiate on Viet-Nam. *July 28, 1965*

Dear Mr. Secretary-General:

I want you to know from me directly of the very great personal confidence which I place in Ambassador Goldberg. His appointment as Permanent Representative of the United States to the United Nations—and his acceptance of this responsibility in the circumstances—is, I hope, strong evidence that this Government places the very highest importance on the work of the United Nations and will continue to give it our utmost support.

I have instructed Ambassador Goldberg especially to maintain close contact with you on the situation in Viet-Nam. Your efforts in the past to find some way to remove that dispute from the battlefield to the negotiating table are much appreciated and highly valued by my Government. I trust they will be continued.

Meanwhile, as I stated publicly last April, the Government of the United States is prepared to enter into negotiations for peaceful settlement without conditions. That remains our policy.

And as I stated in San Francisco last month, we hope that the Members of the United Nations, individually and collectively, will use their influence to bring to the negotiating table all governments involved in an attempt to halt all aggression and evolve a peaceful solution. I continue to hope that the United Nations can, in fact, be effective in this regard.

I hope that you will communicate to us, through Ambassador Goldberg, any helpful suggestions that may occur to you that can strengthen our common search for the road to peace in Southeast Asia.

Sincerely,

LYNDON B. JOHNSON

[His Excellency U Thant, Secretary-General of the United Nations, United Nations, New York]

NOTE: Secretary General Thant's reply to the President, released on July 29, follows:

Dear Mr. President:

It was my great pleasure yesterday afternoon to receive Ambassador Goldberg and welcome him to the United Nations, and at the same time to have from his hand the letter which you addressed to me, for which I thank you most warmly.

Your letter gives me much satisfaction and encouragement, not only as evidence of the very great personal confidence which you have in Ambassador Goldberg, but also as reassurance that your Government attaches highest importance to the work of the United Nations and will continue to give the United Nations its utmost support.

It is particularly gratifying to know that you have instructed Ambassador Goldberg especially to maintain close contact with me on the situation in Vietnam. For my part, of course, I will keep closely in touch with him on all important issues relating to international peace. Knowing the very great importance which I attach in the present circumstances to the question of Vietnam, you may rest assured that I look forward to continuous mutual consultation on this issue.

In this connection, Mr. President, please allow me to thank you for your kind words about my efforts in the past to find some way to remove the dispute over Vietnam from the battlefield to the negotiating table. I am heartened by your wish that my efforts should be continued, and I gladly assure you of my determination to pursue them by all the means at my disposal, since I believe most strongly that concerted efforts should be made to put an early end to all further hostile military activities.

I shall, of course, be pleased to communicate to you through Ambassador Goldberg, in accordance with your wish, any further suggestions which I would consider helpful in bringing peace to Southeast Asia.

Yours sincerely,

U THANT

[The President, The White House, Washington, D.C.]

391   Remarks Upon Viewing New Mariner 4 Pictures From Mars. *July 29, 1965*

Dr. Webb, Dr. Pickering, Dr. Leighton, Members of Congress, distinguished guests:

Unaccustomed as I am to welcoming men from Mars, I am very happy to see you gentlemen here this morning. As a member of the generation that Orson Welles scared out of its wits, I must confess that I am a little bit relieved that your photographs didn't show more signs of life out there.

I think I speak for every American when I tell you how very proud and how impressed, how grateful we are for what you and all the many members of your team have accomplished on the Mariner 4 mission.

The flight of Mariner 4 will long stand as one of the really great advances in man's unending quest to extend the horizons of human knowledge. In the history books of tomorrow, unlike the headlines of today, the project's name may be lost but the names of the men of vision, men of imagination and faith who made this enterprise such a historic success are going to be honored in the world for many generations to come.

This advance for mankind is awe-inspiring. It is all the more so when we realize that such capabilities have come into being within a short span of a very few years. As Director Webb observed a few moments ago, it was only 7 years ago that some could, and some did, say that none of this would ever be possible. In fact, some said a good deal more along that line, which I really don't want to repeat this morning because much of what they said was aimed directly at me.

What I believed in 1957 and 1958, when I was striving and searching and seeking to get our space program moving with hearings that almost went around the clock—what I believed then I believe even more strongly now because of what you have done.

Our Nation must live by its vision, must live by its faith, or we won't live at all. And where there is no vision the people perish.

For 189 years generations of Americans have had a vision and a faith that the world could somehow, someday live in peace. From 1776 to 1965 mankind has journeyed far toward the reality of that dream. And I am determined, and I believe the American people and their spokesmen in the great Congress are determined, that men and nations shall hold steady to that course toward the sun of sanity, and toward enlightenment and reason instead of war.

Mankind's progress toward the distant stars of peace and reason must not, and shall not, be either delayed or diverted by those who would cast the shadow of fear across its path and have it fall in the darkness of war.

This is the real purpose of all that we do on the earth around us and in the reaches of space beyond us. We are striving to shelter and to save the gains that man has made while, at the same time, we are seeking to help man fulfill the promise within him, to fulfill that promise in peace and in freedom.

I remain an optimist always about man and about man's future, and I have never been more optimistic than now. I believe it is very clear that in this day, when we are reaching out among the stars, the earth's billions will not set their compass by dogmas and doctrines which reject peace, and embrace force, and rely upon aggression and terror for fulfillment.

It may be—it may just be that life as we know it with its humanity is more unique than many have thought, and we must remember this.

In the works of space, as in the works of peace, this great Nation of ours stands always ready to join with any others—to join

with all others—and we are ready as I speak now.

So, today, it is my great pleasure to honor these outstanding Americans on behalf of all of their countrymen. They have brought the Mariner 4 from idea to reality and have kept the vigil with it now through 228 days of flight. So, this morning we all are very proud to salute them and to pay honor to their lasting contribution to the knowledge of all mankind, and to the men and women, the executives and the clerks, to the Congress—the House and the Senate—to the great industrialists and the forces of American labor, all of whom put their shoulder to the wheel and united to make it possible for these adventures and advances.

In the terms of the Navy, for which we all have such great respect, I say, "Well done."

Thank you.

NOTE: The President spoke at 10:45 a.m. in the East Room at the White House. In his opening words he referred to Dr. James E. Webb, Administrator of the National Aeronautics and Space Administration, Dr. William H. Pickering, Director of the Jet Propulsion Laboratory, Pasadena, Calif., and Dr. Robert B. Leighton, chief experimenter of the picture team at the laboratory. During his remarks the President referred to Orson Welles, actor, writer, and producer.

Following his remarks the President presented three National Aeronautics and Space Administration awards as follows: the Distinguished Service Medal to Dr. Pickering, the Outstanding Leadership Award to Oran Nicks, Director of the Lunar and Planetary Programs at NASA headquarters, and the Outstanding Scientific Achievement Award to Jack N. James, Acting Assistant Laboratory Director for Lunar and Planetary Projects at the Jet Propulsion Laboratory and former Mariner Project Manager.

The Mariner 4 spacecraft began its historic journey to the planet Mars on November 28, 1964. On July 15, 1965, it sent the first pictures back to the Jet Propulsion Laboratory at Pasadena.

392   Remarks on the Status of Women in America.
July 29, 1965

Mrs. Peterson, Mrs. Louchheim, distinguished delegates and friends:

Here at the White House I have many opportunities to speak to many distinguished visitors. But it is a very rare and very welcome pleasure to meet with a group which is both so distinguished and so attractive as this.

In this house where I live, women have a 3 to 1 ratio in their favor. And I don't mind—at least most of the time. But there are moments when, like most husbands and fathers, I wish there were a commission on the status of men to submit some of my grievances to.

I am glad that you could come here today. You represent the commission on the status of women that is created by the Governors of 44 States. When the Governors themselves are here at 5 o'clock this afternoon, I am going to congratulate them on your work which I have been observing.

You are carrying forward in your States and cities the work begun by the National Commission under that very great, grand, and lovely lady—Mrs. Eleanor Roosevelt. You are looking at the problems as they exist in your own areas; you are seeking solutions that are appropriate to the people of your own sections. The diversity of your outlook and approach is quite heartening and very helpful.

I could talk to you this morning about statistics—statistics on the status of women in the Federal Government. I am very proud that since becoming President, I have found it possible to, on the basis of merit, appoint 114 women to major positions in this Government, and almost 3,000 other women have received appointments or promotions to the highest grades in our career service.

But statistics are not our first concern. Our first concern must be, and is, people. And in our society, rich and strong and successful as it is, people—people, individual people—face increasingly complex and very severe personal challenges. And I am so glad that you are helping in the search for solutions to some of those challenges, especially those challenges which beset women who are both the breadwinners and the mothers.

While we seek to advance women to their rightful place at the top of the ladder of this society, we must never forget and never neglect those women who stand insecurely and uncertainly on the lower rungs. And I think especially of the mothers who face the uncertainties of the marketplace, the heartbreaking dilemmas of impoverished households, without training, often without motivation, very often without even the barest decencies of life, or even the emotional support of a husband.

Our society and its success is built around a family unit. And despite all of our advances and all of our gains, we must never neglect the fact that that unit—the family unit—has been attacked and has collapsed among too high a significant number of citizens in this country. This blight has hit a disproportionate number of individuals, particularly in our minority groups—especially the Negro. But it is not confined to one group. It is not confined to one income level. All through our society, in suburbia as well as in the slums, we are challenged to strengthen the family unit and to help our mothers, and especially find meaning for their lives and find answers for their burdening responsibilities.

A President must, in times like these, often weigh decisions that are great and that are grave—and most of the time they are grim. But I am always mindful and I never forget that in our complex and our changing, constantly challenging, society the most urgent human problem facing millions of our citizens is the matter of self, the matter of identity, the matter of purpose in his life. The answers that we help others find to such questions matter greatly to the kind of society that we are going to fashion, and matter greatly to the strength that we will have to meet the great tests of our destiny as a great people.

The American woman has a challenging responsibility to meet in this country, whether she puts her knowledge to use in her home community or in Washington, matters very little. What really does matter is that the collective wisdom of women never be lost and never be left unused as we face the serious tests and the soaring promises before us now.

And there are many sources of strength that a President must call upon and must summon in trying periods, and I am happy to say that in this great land of ours I have never found those strengths wanting, and I have never found them hesitant. But I know of no more inspiring and stimulating and confidence-building and tenacious contributions that have been made to me in the 20 months than those that have come from the women of our land—the grandmothers, the mothers, the wives, the daughters, the sweethearts, yes, even the babies.

I have on my desk a stack of letters that involve distress, depression, death, wounds—most of them relate to Viet-Nam where our men are out there trying to help other people have their freedom just as we obtained

ours almost 200 years ago. One lady told me, she said:

"We just had 7 months together, but, oh, what a beautiful 7 months it was, and I am proud that I picked the kind of a husband that loved his country enough that he would give his life to try to see that other peoples of other lands had the choice that we have in this country."

Another mother wrote me and said that her boy had lost his leg and had a little difficulty getting it replaced, where he could walk without great pain, but that he could endure that if I could only get him reassigned back to Viet-Nam where he could go and carry on with his boys against the problems that they face there.

Another lady wrote me the other day and said she is from a southern State, and she said:

"I want to tell you how proud I am of our country and our Government, and our Congress, and our President for standing up and facing the enemy and not appeasing and not putting off, and not letting happen to us what happened in World Wars I and II—going on until we almost lose before we decide what has happened." She said: "I have 3 boys and one of them died in Viet-Nam, the other one was wounded yesterday in the Dominican Republic, and the third one enlisted to be a paratrooper, to take his training in Texas. And I want to tell you how proud I am of the leadership that is coming." And that was just too much for me. I picked up the phone and said, "Get me that lady up here. I want to talk to her because she has something I need for the problems that I face."

She came, she saw, and she conquered. When she went away, I felt more equal to my responsibilities and more concerned and more compassionate about all of the people in this country.

I looked yesterday at a number of women that I would hope could serve on the highest Court of our land—where one has never served. I didn't select one because when I do, I want it to be absolutely without question the best person—male or female—available for that post. I have appointed some women to the Federal judiciary, some to high places in the executive department, some to the Atomic Energy Commission.

The one thing I need from you more than anything else, aside from your leadership in your local communities, is to take your eyes and your ears, and your head and your heart, and your heels, and try to develop for me the most outstanding women in this country that could be available to lead the people of this country. There are many places that we need to fill if we only could find the brilliant, the trained, the mind and

heart, that is out there that we just haven't been able to put our fingers on, and you can do that for me. If you don't get the kind of response from me, you take it up with Lady Bird, because she and Liz Carpenter mount that doorway all the time and put questionnaires to me nearly every day about what I have done for women lately.

Thank you for coming. God bless you all.

NOTE: The President spoke at 11:47 a.m. on the South Lawn at the White House to members of the Citizens' Advisory Council on the Status of Women and of the Governors' Commission on the Status of Women. In his opening words he referred to Mrs. Esther Peterson, Assistant Secretary of Labor for Labor Standards and Vice Chairman of the Interdepartmental Committee on the Status of Women, and to Mrs. Katie S. Louchheim, Deputy Assistant Secretary of State for Community Advisory Services. Later he referred to Mrs. Elizabeth S. Carpenter, Press Secretary and Staff Director for Mrs. Johnson.

The Citizens' Advisory Council on the Status of Women was established by Executive Order 11126 of November 1, 1963 (3 CFR, 1959–1963 Comp., p. 791).

393 Remarks at the Signing of an Agreement Providing for a Loan to the Central American Bank for Economic Integration. *July 29, 1965*

Distinguished guests, members of the diplomatic corps, Members of Congress:

I regret that these days and nights I am usually an hour late and a dollar short, but it is good to finally be here with you, and this house is honored today by the presence of such distinguished company. I am deeply privileged to extend to each of you a very warm welcome.

For all Americans of all the Americas, today is a very proud occasion. I believe we realize the real meaning of this moment as much more than just signing the papers that are before us. In a real sense, by what we have come to do, we really honor the spirit—

the new and the soaring spirit—that is stirring throughout the length of this young and this proud and this newly hopeful Western Hemisphere of ours. No cynicism can corrode the promise that is beginning to gleam so brightly in the sun of this New World's new day, for we are thinking as we have never had cause to really think before as Americans, as peoples, as nations, sharing not just a common history or even a common geography, but sharing a common vision and possessing common aspirations.

That spirit was brought to life here in this room 4 years ago when a good many of you heard President Kennedy speak his hopes, and speak the hopes of his countrymen, that the Americas could ally themselves together in peace to better the life of man in all the Americas.

We see that spirit gaining substance and reality now in a good many lands. But nowhere do we see it more than in the lands of Central America—Guatemala, Honduras, El Salvador, Nicaragua, Costa Rica. They have, in a series of acts of the highest statesmanship, embarked upon a process of integrating their economies which is one of the really most exciting undertakings of our world today.

Together these nations have created a common market. They have leveled their trade barriers. They have coordinated their efforts in higher education. They have done the same for their tax systems and their development planning. And they are all making an effort to cope with the problems created by the ancient enemies of all mankind—disease, poverty, and illiteracy.

And the results are already apparent and already gratifying. Trade among these nations has amounted to $20 million in 1958, but it reached $105 million last year, and the gross national product is rising at a rate of close to 7 percent a year. In support of these historic advances a key role is today being filled by the Central American Bank for Economic Integration. It is represented here today by its able and dynamic president, Dr. Delgado.

This Bank is capitalized by equal contributions from the five Central American countries. But as the governments have pledged mutual support to each other, so the members of the Alliance have pledged support to them.

In March 1963, in Costa Rica, our late beloved President John Kennedy pledged this country's support. And so today we have come here to fulfill that pledge by signing this loan agreement for $35 million.

Yes, great progress has been made in Central America, but the future offers greater promise, both there and throughout the hemisphere. The Central American Republics are providing all their neighbors and all the world what I would think is a very stirring example of what can be accomplished by free men with vision and with wisdom and with courage. And we of the United States are very proud to be fortunate enough to work with them in this very hopeful enterprise.

We are so grateful for your friendship, for your loyalty, for your cooperation in trying to solve the problems of this hemisphere and trying to be equal to the challenges of the 20th century. And we want you to know that, and we want your governments to know it.

And so this morning, to the distinguished representatives of Central America that may be present on this historic occasion, I would affirm again my country's deep respect and admiration and support for your efforts. And likewise, to the distinguished representatives of the Organization of American States, the CIAP, and the Inter-American Development Bank, I would reaffirm the interest and the support of the United States of America for economic integration throughout this hemisphere.

In all the world there are no dreams so stirring or so exciting or so inspiring as those that we can dream realistically and reasonably now in our own hemisphere. The day is no longer so dim and distant as once it seemed to be when those dreams begin to reach the lives of all our people, for we can truly believe that that day has already dawned and we are now working in its early morning. Long before the twilight of this century has come, we may believe that men and women of the Americas will come to know a much better life, a life of peace, a life of social justice, a life of liberty, a life of independence, a life where reason rules and where tyranny is vanquished.

And it is toward this happy hour that we work together now with a steady purpose and with a rising confidence and with a deep appreciation of what friendship and understanding really means.

I'm sorry I was late. Thank you so much for coming.

NOTE: The President spoke at 1:45 p.m. in the East Room at the White House upon signing the agreement under which the Agency for International Development loaned $35 million to the Central American Bank for Economic Integration. Following the President's remarks, Dr. Enrique Delgado, President of the Bank, addressed the group. The text of his remarks is printed in the Weekly Compilation of Presidential Documents (vol. 1, p. 23).

394   Remarks With President Truman at the Signing in Independence of the Medicare Bill. *July 30, 1965*

PRESIDENT TRUMAN. Thank you very much. I am glad you like the President. I like him too. He is one of the finest men I ever ran across.

Mr. President, Mrs. Johnson, distinguished guests:

You have done me a great honor in coming here today, and you have made me a very, very happy man.

This is an important hour for the Nation, for those of our citizens who have completed their tour of duty and have moved to the sidelines. These are the days that we are trying to celebrate for them. These people are our prideful responsibility and they are entitled, among other benefits, to the best medical protection available.

Not one of these, our citizens, should ever be abandoned to the indignity of charity. Charity is indignity when you have to have it. But we don't want these people to have anything to do with charity and we don't want them to have any idea of hopeless despair.

Mr. President, I am glad to have lived this long and to witness today the signing of the Medicare bill which puts this Nation right where it needs to be, to be right. Your in-

spired leadership and a responsive forward-looking Congress have made it historically possible for this day to come about.

Thank all of you most highly for coming here. It is an honor I haven't had for, well, quite awhile, I'll say that to you, but here it is:

Ladies and gentlemen, the President of the United States.

THE PRESIDENT. *President and Mrs. Truman, Secretary Celebrezze, Senator Mansfield, Senator Symington, Senator Long, Governor Hearnes, Senator Anderson and Congressman King of the Anderson-King team, Congressman Mills and Senator Long of the Mills-Long team, our beloved Vice President who worked in the vineyard many years to see this day come to pass, and all of my dear friends in the Congress—both Democrats and Republicans:*

The people of the United States love and voted for Harry Truman, not because he gave them hell—but because he gave them hope.

I believe today that all America shares my joy that he is present now when the hope that he offered becomes a reality for millions of our fellow citizens.

I am so proud that this has come to pass in the Johnson administration. But it was really Harry Truman of Missouri who planted the seeds of compassion and duty which have today flowered into care for the sick, and serenity for the fearful.

Many men can make many proposals. Many men can draft many laws. But few have the piercing and humane eye which can see beyond the words to the people that they touch. Few can see past the speeches and the political battles to the doctor over there that is tending the infirm, and to the hospital that is receiving those in anguish, or feel in their heart painful wrath at the injustice which denies the miracle of healing to the old and to the poor. And fewer still have the courage to stake reputation, and position, and the effort of a lifetime upon such a cause when there are so few that share it.

But it is just such men who illuminate the life and the history of a nation. And so, President Harry Truman, it is in tribute not to you, but to the America that you represent, that we have come here to pay our love and our respects to you today. For a country can be known by the quality of the men it honors. By praising you, and by carrying forward your dreams, we really reaffirm the greatness of America.

It was a generation ago that Harry Truman said, and I quote him: "Millions of our citizens do not now have a full measure of opportunity to achieve and to enjoy good health. Millions do not now have protection or security against the economic effects of sickness. And the time has now arrived for action to help them attain that opportunity and to help them get that protection."

Well, today, Mr. President, and my fellow Americans, we are taking such action—

20 years later. And we are doing that under the great leadership of men like John McCormack, our Speaker; Carl Albert, our majority leader; our very able and beloved majority leader of the Senate, Mike Mansfield; and distinguished Members of the Ways and Means and Finance Committees of the House and Senate—of both parties, Democratic and Republican.

Because the need for this action is plain; and it is so clear indeed that we marvel not simply at the passage of this bill, but what we marvel at is that it took so many years to pass it. And I am so glad that Aime Forand is here to see it finally passed and signed—one of the first authors.

There are more than 18 million Americans over the age of 65. Most of them have low incomes. Most of them are threatened by illness and medical expenses that they cannot afford.

And through this new law, Mr. President, every citizen will be able, in his productive years when he is earning, to insure himself against the ravages of illness in his old age.

This insurance will help pay for care in hospitals, in skilled nursing homes, or in the home. And under a separate plan it will help meet the fees of the doctors.

Now here is how the plan will affect you.

During your working years, the people of America—you—will contribute through the social security program a small amount each payday for hospital insurance protection. For example, the average worker in 1966 will contribute about $1.50 per month. The employer will contribute a similar amount. And this will provide the funds to pay up to 90 days of hospital care for each illness, plus diagnostic care, and up to 100 home health visits after you are 65. And beginning in 1967, you will also be covered for up to 100 days of care in a skilled nursing home after a period of hospital care.

And under a separate plan, when you are 65—that the Congress originated itself, in its own good judgment—you may be covered for medical and surgical fees whether you are in or out of the hospital. You will pay $3 per month after you are 65 and your Government will contribute an equal amount.

The benefits under the law are as varied and broad as the marvelous modern medicine itself. If it has a few defects—such as the method of payment of certain specialists—then I am confident those can be quickly remedied and I hope they will be.

No longer will older Americans be denied the healing miracle of modern medicine. No longer will illness crush and destroy the savings that they have so carefully put away over a lifetime so that they might enjoy dignity in their later years. No longer will young families see their own incomes, and their own hopes, eaten away simply because they are carrying out their deep moral obligations to their parents, and to their uncles, and their aunts.

And no longer will this Nation refuse the hand of justice to those who have given a lifetime of service and wisdom and labor to the progress of this progressive country.

And this bill, Mr. President, is even broader than that. It will increase social security benefits for all of our older Americans. It will improve a wide range of health and medical services for Americans of all ages.

In 1935 when the man that both of us loved so much, Franklin Delano Roosevelt, signed the Social Security Act, he said it was, and I quote him, "a cornerstone in a structure which is being built but it is by no means complete."

Well, perhaps no single act in the entire administration of the beloved Franklin D. Roosevelt really did more to win him the

illustrious place in history that he has as did the laying of that cornerstone. And I am so happy that his oldest son Jimmy could be here to share with us the joy that is ours today. And those who share this day will also be remembered for making the most important addition to that structure, and you are making it in this bill, the most important addition that has been made in three decades.

History shapes men, but it is a necessary faith of leadership that men can help shape history. There are many who led us to this historic day. Not out of courtesy or deference, but from the gratitude and remembrance which is our country's debt, if I may be pardoned for taking a moment, I want to call a part of the honor roll: it is the able leadership in both Houses of the Congress.

Congressman Celler, Chairman of the Judiciary Committee, introduced the hospital insurance in 1952. Aime Forand from Rhode Island, then Congressman, introduced it in the House. Senator Clinton Anderson from New Mexico fought for Medicare through the years in the Senate. Congressman Cecil King of California carried on the battle in the House. The legislative genius of the Chairman of the Ways and Means Committee, Congressman Wilbur Mills, and the effective and able work of Senator Russell Long, together transformed this desire into victory.

And those devoted public servants, former Secretary, Senator Ribicoff; present Secretary, Tony Celebrezze; Under Secretary Wilbur Cohen; the Democratic whip of the House, Hale Boggs on the Ways and Means Committee; and really the White House's best legislator, Larry O'Brien, gave not just endless days and months and, yes, years of patience—but they gave their hearts—to passing this bill.

Let us also remember those who sadly

cannot share this time for triumph. For it is their triumph too. It is the victory of great Members of Congress that are not with us, like John Dingell, Sr., and Robert Wagner, late a Member of the Senate, and James Murray of Montana.

And there is also John Fitzgerald Kennedy, who fought in the Senate and took his case to the people, and never yielded in pursuit, but was not spared to see the final concourse of the forces that he had helped to loose.

But it all started really with the man from Independence. And so, as it is fitting that we should, we have come back here to his home to complete what he began.

President Harry Truman, as any President must, made many decisions of great moment; although he always made them frankly and with a courage and a clarity that few men have ever shared. The immense and the intricate questions of freedom and survival were caught up many times in the web of Harry Truman's judgment. And this is in the tradition of leadership.

But there is another tradition that we share today. It calls upon us never to be indifferent toward despair. It commands us never to turn away from helplessness. It directs us never to ignore or to spurn those who suffer untended in a land that is bursting with abundance.

I said to Senator Smathers, the whip of the Democrats in the Senate, who worked with us in the Finance Committee on this legislation—I said, the highest traditions of the medical profession are really directed to the ends that we are trying to serve. And it was only yesterday, at the request of some of my friends, I met with the leaders of the American Medical Association to seek their assistance in advancing the cause of one of the greatest professions of all—the medical

profession—in helping us to maintain and to improve the health of all Americans.

And this is not just our tradition—or the tradition of the Democratic Party—or even the tradition of the Nation. It is as old as the day it was first commanded: "Thou shalt open thine hand wide unto thy brother, to thy poor, to thy needy, in thy land."

And just think, Mr. President, because of this document—and the long years of struggle which so many have put into creating it—in this town, and a thousand other towns like it, there are men and women in pain who will now find ease. There are those, alone in suffering, who will now hear the sound of some approaching footsteps coming to help. There are those fearing the terrible darkness of despairing poverty—despite their long years of labor and expectation—who will now look up to see the light of hope and realization.

There just can be no satisfaction, nor any act of leadership, that gives greater satisfaction than this.

And perhaps you alone, President Truman, perhaps you alone can fully know just how grateful I am for this day.

NOTE: The President spoke at 2:55 p.m. in the auditorium of the Harry S. Truman Library in Independence, Mo. In his opening words he referred to former President and Mrs. Harry S. Truman, Secretary of Health, Education, and Welfare Anthony J. Celebrezze, Senator Mike Mansfield of Montana, majority leader of the Senate, Senator Stuart Symington and Senator Edward V. Long of Missouri, Governor Warren E. Hearnes of Missouri, Senator Clinton P. Anderson of New Mexico, Representative Cecil R. King of California, Representative Wilbur D. Mills of Arkansas, Senator Russell B. Long of Louisiana, and Vice President Hubert H. Humphrey.

During his remarks the President referred to, among others, Representative John W. McCormack of Massachusetts, Speaker of the House of Representatives, Representative Carl Albert of Oklahoma, majority leader of the House of Representatives, Aime Forand, Representative from Rhode Island 1937–1939 and 1941–1961, Representative Emanuel Celler of New York, Senator Abraham Ribicoff of

Connecticut, former Secretary of Health, Education, and Welfare, Under Secretary of Health, Education, and Welfare Wilbur J. Cohen, Representative Hale Boggs of Louisiana, Lawrence F. O'Brien, Special Assistant to the President, John D. Dingell, Representative from Michigan 1933–1955, Robert F. Wagner, Senator from New York 1927–1949, James E. Murray, Senator from Montana 1934–1961, and Senator George A. Smathers of Florida.

As enacted, the Medicare bill (H.R. 6675) is Public Law 89–97 (79 Stat. 286).

On July 25, 1965, the White House released a report to the President from Secretary Celebrezze in response to the President's request for organizational changes in the Social Security Administration in preparation for administering the Medicare program.

The report stated that the reorganization would accomplish the following major purposes:

"It establishes new units in the Administration with special responsibility for hospital and supplementary medical insurance programs;

"It changes some existing units, giving them additional responsibilities under new programs;

"It centers data processing and transmission activities in a central headquarters in the Administration;

"It strengthens upper-level management in the Administration, makes the field service of the Administration more responsive to directions from headquarters, and improves coordination between Administration units."

The text of Secretary Celebrezze's report is printed in the Weekly Compilation of Presidential Documents (vol. 1, p. 6).

395   Remarks to Members of the Press at the LBJ Ranch.
August 1, 1965

WE'RE delighted you could come by. Joe [1] thought that you might enjoy stopping by for a few moments before you go back to Austin, and before we go back to Washington.

We plan to leave tomorrow evening late, unless something changes our plans, and we anticipate there will be no changes—sometime after the sun goes down tommorrow, so we have a chance to have a ride in a boat.

Appointment of Deputy Director, USIA

[1.] I have with me today, Bob Akers, who is being appointed Deputy Director of the USIA to succeed Don Wilson. It has been about a week trying to locate him in Europe. We traced him through Spain and finally located him in Greece, and brought him back Saturday. He's been interviewed by Mr. Macy [2] and the other appropriate people in Washington.

He's had 40 years in the newspaper business and 10 or more years as a commentator. He's traveled extensively and lectured at the USIA, on the Asian Continent, also in Europe. He's most recently been the managing editor of the Beaumont Enterprise and the Beaumont Journal, a commentator on KRIC–TV.

I had Mr. Laitin come down and he's going to give you some announcements a little later on in the day.

Effective Use of Military Personnel

[2.] I won't take your time now, but Joe Califano [3] and I have drafted a memorandum to Secretary McNamara,[4] which we have reviewed with him in the last few days following the appointment of our task forces on effecting economies.

The substance of the memorandum is that I asked him to set up some special people to recognize the need for deployment of addi-

---

[1] Joseph Laitin, an assistant press secretary.

[2] John W. Macy, Jr., Chairman of the Civil Service Commission.

[3] Joseph A. Califano, Jr., Special Assistant to the President.

[4] See Item 396.

tional military personnel in Viet-Nam, and to ask that they review the functions now being performed by all military personnel with the view to eliminating any unnecessary functions, or where functions are necessary but do not have to be performed by military personnel and can be accomplished in some other way.

I want him to be absolutely certain there is no waste or misapplication of American manpower in the Department of Defense effort. In other words, if we can save a few at this installation, and a few hundred at another, and a few thousand in another theater, we won't have such a serious drain on our manpower through the draft and other facilities.

We're getting some of our task forces reports back. I think maybe Joe told you yesterday some that we reviewed here. One bureau alone finds that they can reduce functions they had last year, this year by something like $300 million. So, we are making intensive reviews by these task forces.

The effect of this suggestion is to ask the Secretary of Defense to concentrate on personnel as he has done on contracts and as he has on other conscientious elements on his program.

MEETINGS WITH AMBASSADOR GOLDBERG

[3.] Mr. Goldberg [5] and I have reviewed the reaction that we have received from several dozen countries—some 40, and one group of about 30-odd in another—to our announcement on Viet-Nam. He has talked to me about conversations he's had at the United Nations. We talked about our plans in the days ahead, both in Washington and New York and other places in the

[5] Arthur J. Goldberg, U.S. Representative to the United Nations.

world.

We had a delightful, restful weekend, and he's returning to Washington this afternoon.

I think that is all we have to say. Mr. Peter Hurd [6] and Mrs. Hurd are here from New Mexico spending the weekend with us. They'll be going back when they have had enough of it.

As I said, we'll be leaving by dark tomorrow. If you have any questions—I don't want to get into a regular conference, but I don't mind answering anything that needs clearing up.

QUESTIONS

THE UNITED NATIONS

[4.] Q. Would you say, Mr. President, whether you went into the question of the financial crisis with Mr. Goldberg and what might be done to get the General Assembly back in operation?

THE PRESIDENT. We have talked about the problems of the General Assembly. We don't ever get into any crisis that we can avoid.

BREACH OF CONFIDENCE; VIET-NAM

[5.] Q. Mr. President, there is a story in some of the papers that you were dissuaded from taking a stronger line in Viet-Nam because of something that Senator Mike Mansfield said. Can you comment about that? [7]

THE PRESIDENT. Yes. That was the re-

[6] New Mexico artist who was painting a portrait of the President.

[7] On July 27, preceding his news conference of July 28, the President held a meeting with Democratic and Republican leaders. Reports circulated to the effect that Senator Mike Mansfield of Montana, majority leader of the Senate, had read a statement at the meeting dealing with the views of Congress on the Viet-Nam conflict, and that this statement had dissuaded the President from calling up the Reserves.

sult of a man who broke my confidence, and not only broke it but distorted it. I read Senator Mansfield's statement very carefully, following a backgrounder held by one of the prominent members of another party, and I found nothing to justify that statement. And I would brand it untrue and perhaps malicious. Fortunately it is untrue in writing. Senator Mansfield never mentioned Reserves, and it was not in any of his discussion, and the discussion did not have anything to do with the Reserves—and his paper will show it.

Most of the people you deal with—and we dealt with several dozen, perhaps a couple hundred, including the Governors—

all of them respect the confidence, but once in a while an inexperienced man, or a new one, or a bitter partisan has to play a little politics. I think they keep it to a minimum, generally speaking, but one or two of them will do it—and boys will be boys.

Q. Is this, Mr. President, going to throw a shadow on future bipartisan consultation?

THE PRESIDENT. No. I'm not going to provoke any fight. No b l o o d y noses. We're just going to answer your questions and give you the facts. Nothing to alarm and get your blood pressure up.

Reporter: Thank you, sir.

NOTE: The President met with the members of the press at the LBJ Ranch, Johnson City, Tex., at 1:05 p.m. on Sunday, August 1, 1965.

396 Memorandum to the Secretary of Defense on the Need for Effective Use of Military Personnel. *August 1, 1965*

Memorandum for the Honorable Robert S. McNamara, Secretary of Defense:

The need for deployment of additional military personnel to Vietnam, for the general augmentation of our active duty military strength, and for the increased readiness of our Reserve forces makes it imperative that all military personnel are assigned to duties for which there is a direct military requirement. To this end, I ask that you once again review the functions now being performed by military personnel with a view

to eliminating unnecessary functions, or where functions are necessary but do not have to be performed by military personnel, accomplishing them in other ways. At this time I want you to be absolutely certain that there is no waste or misapplication of America's manpower in the Department of Defense.

LYNDON B. JOHNSON

NOTE: The text of the memorandum was released at Austin, Tex.

397 Remarks to the International Platform Association Upon Receiving the Association's Annual Award. *August 3, 1965*

Mr. Pearson, delegates, and friends:

I am delighted that we could meet here together in the first house of our land this morning.

I am very indebted to you for this attractive silver bowl and I shall remember this occasion with a great deal of pleasure. I am sure through the years the folks that come to my little library will be reminded of your generosity and of the recognition of the International Platform Association Award.

I did have to travel until about 2:30 this morning to get back for this engagement, but I thought that the honor you would do me was great enough and the debt I felt to you was strong enough that I should be here.

Perhaps I should have come to listen instead of talk and, really, I haven't come to talk much. I did not anticipate that this would be an address. I came because Mr. Pearson, in passing the other day, asked me to his farm. And I just spent about all my life on a farm and I don't want to go back there until I have to, and I thought you would probably enjoy coming to the White House equally as much.

Your organization was founded by William Jennings Bryan, Bob LaFollette, William Howard Taft, and Paul Pearson, and I think it has a very special meaning for a former debate coach, like the one speaking to you this morning.

I only wish that my college teacher could be here to see what is happening now. Because in my first term in college, when I made the debating team as a freshman—which was slightly unusual—when I got my grade cards my teacher gave me the lowest grade I ever received in college—and in just the course that you would expect him to give it to me in. He gave me a "D" in argumentation!

We appreciate very much your coming here. Except for one of your members, as I stated, I might have come out to enjoy your air-conditioned hotel room with you today. But your former president, Drew Pearson, said that he believed in government being transacted out in the open, and if he does, why, you qualify out there in the sun this morning.

Drew, if you will pardon the expression, I predict—now I don't have an 83 percent prediction record—but I predict that some of your colleagues are going to get hot under the collar this morning out there in the sun. But I am proud to be associated with all of you on this occasion because you are the real champions of free speech. You believe in free and full discussion. You believe in the right to be heard.

President Eisenhower told me an interesting story after he returned from World War II. He said before he went out there, before he went to Europe to take command, they met at his mother's home out in Kansas. And some of his brothers were there, and his mother told him goodby, and his brothers told him goodby as he went away to war.

And he said, one day one of the Russian generals came in and complained to him about a story that an American newspaperman had written about him which he felt was not fully in keeping with the facts, and that he demanded that this newspaperman be punished, and that he be refused the privileges of a press correspondent.

President Eisenhower said he thought it over and told him to come back the next day. The next day he came back and he showed the Russian general a big scrapbook of unfair things and unkind things that had been said about him, because his plans went astray on occasion, too, and a lot of American soldiers had died.

And he said to the general, "Now let me tell you this story." He said, "Just before I came over here I met at my mother's home in Kansas with four of my brothers, and they were there to tell me goodby." And he said, "My father was a railroad man and he had married my mother as a young girl and out of this union had come these boys." And he said one of them was there and said he was a constitutional lawyer and a very conservative fellow, and nearly everything that came up he would quote the Constitution. Another one of them was a college professor—college president Milton Eisenhower of Johns Hopkins now—and, he said, he was very liberal. And he said, "Another one of my brothers is a conservative banker, and another is an engineer that is more liberal." And he said, "The fifth boy is General of the Armies."

And he said, "The real reason I'm over here, General, fighting this war is so that a railroad man can marry a little American girl and out of that union come five boys, two that are conservatives, two that are liberals, and one that is General of the Army."

That is what America stands for, and we want to keep it that way.

So, I think, that story rather well emphasizes that these are rights that we ought to keep sacred. These rights were not come by easily. They were hammered into our Bill of Rights, and they were put there by men who knew what it was to be jailed and to be beaten, and to be banished and to be ostracized for what they said or what they thought, or what they preached or what they published.

Our forefathers knew what these rights meant, and they exercised them. And we must exercise our rights, too. We must never allow ourselves to be cowed by conformity.

I don't think, from what I know about the fellow that introduced me, that he's likely to have that happen to him because I have never seen him conform very much. But all of us, collectively, must never be cowed by conformity. We must never be afraid to discuss or to challenge, or to innovate or to stimulate new ideas and new approaches.

This year, I sent to the Congress a rather novel and unique suggestion, and I must say that my prediction was wrong. It wasn't 83 percent wrong—it was 100 percent wrong. I thought the Congress would debate it 10 years before they acted on it—and we got it passed the first session. We're going to sign it this week.

It was a rent supplement that provides that when a fellow pays 25 percent of his rent—if he makes $200 a month and he pays $50 for rent, then the Government, if his rent is $60, can pay $10 of that $60. He pays $50 and the Government pays $10. If the Government paid $10 a month, that would be $120 a year, and that would be a lot cheaper than building big public housing that would cost $34,000 for him to live in. And it takes care of many more hundreds of thousands of families at less cost.

Now, we hope that it works out. We're going to try. But it is a new idea. And new ideas like that—at times passed in some States—just couldn't be suggested if they didn't conform. And in some places in the world today they can't be suggested.

It was not too many years ago that a midwestern newspaper circulated a petition at a Fourth of July rally. Now what do you think that petition contained? This is an interesting story. That petition was composed of extracts from the Declaration of Independence and the Bill of Rights. And every member but two in the entire crowd refused to sign it because they said it was too radical and they were too cowed to think for themselves.

So, free speech, free press, free religion, the right of free assembly, yes, the right of petition, the right to buy ads and to have teach-ins, and sit-ins, and parades and marches and demonstrations—well, they are still radical ideas. And so are secret ballots, and so are free elections, and so is the principle of equal dignity, and so is the principle of equal rights for all the sons and daughters of man.

But all of these things are what America stands for, and all of these things are what you and all other Americans need to stand up for today.

Now, it is a new idea, and a somewhat radical one, that the people of small nations have a right to live in peace without fear of their neighbors.

Today, the most difficult problem that confronts your President is how to keep an agreement that I did not initiate—I inherited it—but an agreement to help a small nation remain independent, free of aggression—the nation of South Viet-Nam. Now, in 1954 we agreed to that. We signed a solemn treaty, just as binding a contract as a sovereign nation can enter into, and it said we will help you to remain independent, free of aggression.

Now, I don't hear any people worrying much about this word aggression. They talk about the bombs. They talk about intervention. They talk about fighting a war in rice paddies. They talk about what sacrifices we are required to make. But during all of our history we have died in order to keep our contracts, in order to protect human beings.

The point I want to make is why—oh, why—oh, why don't people concern themselves sometimes with a country that is trying to maintain her independence from aggression, that is being invaded, that is trying not to be swallowed up, that is trying not to have an ideology imposed upon her?

Now, we saw it happen in Greece, we saw it happen in Turkey, and we saw it happen in Iran. We have seen it happen in other places in the world. And America has come and said, "We believe in a choice, in the right of people themselves to choose, and

we have agreed to help you resist aggression."

Now, my problem is how to help them resist aggression and keep them from being swallowed up, and still have peace in the world. If I resist them, if I deter them, if we keep our commitment that the Senate made in the treaty, 82 to 1, that three Presidents have made—President Eisenhower, President Kennedy, and the present President—then the people say, "Well, you should come on home. What happens there doesn't matter." If you stay there, there are some that say, "You ought to get it over with in a hurry."

So, some want to go and blow up everything. Some want to come and blow up nothing, and leave and get out, and forget them. We are trying to do the reasonable thing to see that power and brute force and aggression are not going to prevail. You can't do this thing by force. Now, let's sit down and reason it out, and let's try to allow these people a choice. That is what I'm trying so hard to do, and that is what I need your help on.

We don't want war with anyone. In 20 months we have agreed to 15 different approaches to try to bring peace, and each one of them has been turned down by the other side.

I was reminded this morning of something last week—I did not count it up—that said I left nine ways open to sit down and reason our problems out, to use words instead of guns, to use logic instead of bombs. But you can't have an agreement with just one man. You can't do it by yourself. We have said, "We will go anywhere, talk to any government at any time, and if you will just name the place we'll be in the right chair."

Now, I don't know what else you can do, how much further you can go. With the help of the Secretary of State, Ambassador Goldberg, and our diplomats around the world, we are going to do everything we can with our left hand to negotiate an agreement that will allow people to breathe free independently, independent of any ideology of ours or of anyone else—give them the right of choice. And if we do that we'll come home tomorrow.

We don't want an inch of territory. We don't want a single base. We don't want anything except to help those people do what we agreed to do. And this is an idea that we cherish and we champion, and that all through the years we have been willing to die to uphold for ourselves, and for other people throughout the world.

There are 114 nations in the United Nations and all the big powers can be counted on one hand. Now, if this little nation goes down the drain and can't maintain her independence, ask yourselves, what is going to happen to all the other little nations? So somebody must stand there and try to help the little nations protect themselves from the nations who would provoke aggression.

Now, the United States' strength rests not on our missiles. Our strength rests not on our men. Our strength rests not on our money, or our means. Our strength rests on the might of the ideas and the ideals which give America her meaning.

We hope, and we envision, and we plan, and we pray for the day when every child born in the world can have all the education that he or she can take; that they will be protected in their body and their mind from disease; that they will have a chance to rise out of the poverty that enslaves them and subjugates them; that under leadership of man they can throw off the yokes of the ancient enemies of mankind.

Now, America wins the wars that she undertakes. Make no mistake about it.

And we have declared war on ignorance and illiteracy, we have declared war on poverty, we have declared war on disease, and we have declared war on tyranny and aggression. We not only stand for these things but we are willing to stand up and die for these things.

We have been talking about them a long time in this country, but we are doing something about them today. This Congress has passed an education bill that is revolutionary, so comprehensive that in our fondest dreams we did not think that we could realize it this soon—$1.2 billion for elementary children.

This Congress this week will pass a voting rights bill that will give every American, regardless of his economic status, or where he lives, or what kind of a dress or suit he wears, or what his color is, or what his religion is— he will have that right that every free American ought to have of a secret ballot and to go and vote for his official, and it will be guaranteed to him by the United States flag in every precinct in this land.

This week we're going to have the most comprehensive housing bill in 50 years, to try to permit every person to have a roof over the head of his wife and his children.

Last week I sat down with that great humanitarian, Harry Truman, 81 years old, in Independence, Missouri. And with tears in his eyes, I saw his dream of 20 years ago come true when we signed the Medicare bill that not only provided hospital care and nurses' care and nurse home care and medicine, but also provided for doctors' bills that could be paid; and no longer made it necessary for a mother and a father, in the twilight of their career, to write their nephew or their niece or their son or their daughter and say, please come, send me some money so I won't starve, or so I can go to the doctor.

So, in the words of James Whitcomb Riley:

"Those days are gone and forgot,
The bridge of the railroad
Now crosses that spot;
And the old diving logs
Lay sunk and forgot."

Yes, education, poverty, housing, medical care, higher education, vocational education—all these things are just as necessary now as the three R's were when I was a child.

We cannot survive as leaders of this world, we cannot be first in the world if we are second in education, or health, or freedom. You have sent to Washington the best Congress I have ever seen. They have turned out more work on more far-reaching measures for more people. We have always had a Congress that could pass a bill for a few people if enough power got behind it—but these are for all the people.

I am so grateful that we have organizations such as yours upholding and encouraging free and unfettered debate that really supplies us the greatest source of our strength.

In these days we are all more responsible in what we say than Americans used to be. I remember one public figure once described another public man as, and I quote, "a mush-toed, spotted traitor to the Constitution and a political turkey buzzard."

Now, sometimes they try to get me involved in personalities. But we don't need name-calling and we don't need slander and we don't need libels and we don't need labels. You really don't gain much by getting into personalities and talking about a man or his wife or his dogs on a personal basis.

This is a great age. This is an age of knowledge. This is an age of ideas. And we don't respect ourselves unless we respect ideas and ideals. That is what makes our democracy live.

I want you to know that that is the first interest, that is the primary interest, that is the basic interest of all—all who live or work in that house, because that house is the house of all the American people, rich and poor, wise and learned, ignorant and illiterate.

If we have our way, and if we are successful, and if the American people will heed our call, the day will come in this century when we will have won our wars—wars against poverty and illiteracy, ignorance and disease. Then think about what a great and happy land it will be when all Americans are free and when all have equal rights and all have equal privileges, and there is no discrimination because of bank accounts or churches or voter restrictions or color or sex.

That is the kind of an America we look forward to.

Of course, we want to beautify it and plant some flowers—Mrs. Johnson does all along the way—but that is "America the Beautiful."

I hope that you of the IPA will go out into the hinterland and rouse the masses and blow the bugles and tell them that the hour has arrived and their day is here; that we are on the march against the ancient enemies and we are going to be successful.

Thank you very much.

NOTE: The President spoke at 10:40 a.m. on the South Lawn at the White House before 200 members of the International Platform Association, a group of lecturers and speakers devoted to improving the quality of public speaking. In his opening words he referred to Drew Pearson, newspaper correspondent and columnist and former president of the association.

During his remarks the President referred to, among others, Paul Pearson, father of Drew Pearson, Secretary of State Dean Rusk, and Arthur J. Goldberg, U.S. Representative to the United Nations.

398 Statement by the President Following House Judiciary Committee Action on the Immigration Bill.
August 3, 1965

TODAY, the House Judiciary Committee in an act of justice reported out the immigration bill. It is a breakthrough for reason, a triumph for fair play.

Since my first weeks as President, I have labored to bring realism and understanding to the immigration procedures of this Nation. Today, the House Judiciary Committee, in enthusiastic bipartisan concert, determined to redeem the pledge of this Nation to posterity—that free men have no fear of justice, and proud men have no taste for bias.

Families can now be united; skillful artisans whose trades are depleted here can now fill those voids—and we need no longer turn away from what is just to accept what has been alien to the American dream.

This bill does not signify that the floodgates are open. But it does say, without doubts, that the national origins procedure, which has since 1924 shamefully governed immigration in this country, will be forever abandoned. Now the country of a man's birth does not need to disbar him from our society.

Walt Whitman once sang his American saga in these words: "These states are the amplest poem; here is not merely a nation but a teeming nation of nations." This new immigration bill sings the same kind of melody.

I congratulate the House Judiciary Committee, Democrats and Republicans alike. I urge the prompt consideration of this reported bill by the House. I hope the Senate will report this bill swiftly and that both Houses of the Congress will wash away a stain on our national conscience and in its place engrave the mark of a just and hopeful country.

NOTE: The bill amending the Immigration and Nationality Act was approved by the President on October 3, 1965 (see Item 546).

399 Remarks at the Presentation of the Distinguished Service Medal to Maj. Gen. C. V. Clifton, Jr. *August 3, 1965*

General Clifton, Secretary Resor, Members of Congress, Secretaries of the services, members of the service, distinguished guests:

One of the oldest and one of the most honored offices of the Government of the United States is the Office of Military Aide to the President of the United States.

One of the most honored men to ever hold that office—but let me hasten to add, not one of the oldest—has been the officer that I have come here with you to join in saluting today.

It was 33 years ago that Gen. Ted Clifton entered West Point to graduate with the class of 1936. The members of that class could not know, as the Nation would not know, that so little time remained before the world would again be at war and they would be involved.

But it was not many years later, when in the European theater, that General Clifton was called upon to command the 1st Heavy Artillery Battalion there. And from Caserta to France and on through Germany, he supported the infantry and the armor of the 5th and of the 7th Armies, the British 8th Army, and those of the French forces. As an officer in combat he was outstanding.

When the war ended, his intelligence, his judgment, his demeanor, and his forthrightness led him to the councils of the highest leaders in his land.

In 1948 he joined the staff of the revered Gen. Omar Bradley, and from that day on, almost without interruption, Ted Clifton's career has been the valuable role of adviser and helper, and mediator and interpreter, and always friend.

You will always find him in the background but he's really never beyond reach.

General Clifton has been both an observer and a participant in the higher councils of our Government, and his influence—at least upon me—has been of the greatest value and, I think, the greatest worth to his country.

In 1961 he was chosen as the Military Aide to our late, beloved President, John F. Kennedy and, knowing him as I did, I asked Ted Clifton to continue as my Military Aide during the period that I have been Commander in Chief.

The services he has performed for me have been many and varied. They are services which have very often been quite tedious, usually demanding—although not so demanding as some would think—but rarely rewarding.

I shall always be grateful to him for the manner in which he has always met his responsibilities in the task entrusted to him throughout this period.

So, today, after this long career of loyal and dedicated and modern and imaginative service, I know that it is not without certain regret that General Clifton now leaves the service to which he has given his entire life. But I am happy and I am gratified that this exceptional man of rare talents will have a new and a broader horizon of opportunity as he enters civilian life.

Today, General Clifton, for myself and for Mrs. Johnson—and he's not unpopular with the ladies, I might add—for all of us here at the White House, as a matter of fact, I express to you our very deep and great appreciation for the dedication which you have brought to your profession, for the intelligence and the judgment with which you have inspired and have led the men who have served for you and with you.

And in appreciation for what you have done, and with the personal thanks for the support that you have given to both President Kennedy and to me, it gives me a great deal of personal pleasure in awarding you, this morning, here among your friends and the staff that you have led and served so well, your country's Distinguished Service Medal. You have earned this medal, and you have earned with it the respect and the gratitude of the entire Nation.

And to you and Mrs. Clifton and your family, I want you to know that wherever you go, whatever you do, we will be pulling for you, we will be remembering that the day was never too long, the night too dark, for you to do what the boss needed done.

Thank you.

NOTE: The President spoke at 12:22 p.m. in the Rose Garden at the White House. In his opening words he referred to Maj. Gen. C. V. Clifton, Jr., who retired on July 31 after more than 33 years of active military service, and to Stanley R. Resor, Under Secretary of the Army. During his remarks he referred to General of the Army Omar N. Bradley, first Chairman of the Joint Chiefs of Staff.

General Clifton served as Military Aide to the President from January 1961 until his retirement. His letter requesting release from his assignment and the President's reply granting the request were made public by the White House on July 10.

The text of the citation follows:

"Major General Chester V. Clifton, Jr., distinguished himself by eminently meritorious service while serving in positions of great responsibility from March 1957 to July 1965. During this period, General Clifton served concurrently as Deputy Chief of Public Information, Office of the Secretary of the Army and as Deputy Chief of Information, Office of the Chief of Staff, United States Army; and then as Military Aide to the President of the United States. General Clifton fulfilled sensitive, grave and difficult responsibilities with outstanding effectiveness during a period characterized by recurrent crises throughout the globe. In his highly sensitive and unique position as the Military Aide to the President, General Clifton demonstrated integrity, imaginative resourcefulness and an innate intellectual courage. General Clifton's performance of duty was char-

acterized by personal qualities of courtesy, consideration for others and cooperativeness. He carried out his important duties as Defense Liaison Officer with a most sensitive appreciation of the needs and viewpoints of the Secretary of Defense and of all the services. His mature judgment, basic knowledge and professional talents contributed to the achievement of results desired by the President. General Clifton's distinguished performance of duty is in the highest traditions of the United States Army and reflects great credit upon himself and the military service."

Also on July 10 the White House announced that General Clifton's successor would be Maj. James U. Cross, USAF.

400 Message to the Congress Transmitting First Annual Report of the Atlantic-Pacific Interoceanic Canal Study Commission. *August 3, 1965*

To the Congress of the United States:

By Public Law 88–609, I was authorized to appoint five men from private life to make a full study of the most suitable site for, and best means of constructing, a sea-level canal connecting the Atlantic and Pacific Oceans. On April 18, 1965, I appointed five distinguished American citizens to serve on the Atlantic-Pacific Interoceanic Canal Commission. They are: Robert B. Anderson, Chairman, Robert G. Storey, Vice-Chairman, Milton S. Eisenhower, Kenneth E. Fields and Raymond A. Hill.

The Commission immediately set about its difficult and complicated mission. The initial phase of its work has been to develop a program of investigations covering the many aspects of the construction of a sea-level canal. It has selected the Chief of Engineers, United States Army, to conduct the Engineering Feasibility Study under the direction of the Commission. The Commission will soon call upon other Government and private agencies to carry out additional studies to aid in assessing the broad

national and international implications of a sea-level canal. By early next year the Commission expects to begin on-site surveys of possible canal routes. The Commission is also contemplating a trip to Panama in the near future to study at firsthand the present Canal Zone and another possible canal route in Panama's Darien Province. I am highly gratified by the progress made by the Commission, under the able leadership of Mr. Anderson, during the short period that it has been working.

The Commission has requested the Congress to appropriate sufficient funds in Fiscal Year 1966 to initiate investigations on the most promising sea-level canal routes. On-site surveys would begin in January, with the next annual dry season on the Isthmus. I recommend prompt action on the request in order that the Commission be in a position to initiate this important aspect of its work during this four-month period of favorable weather conditions.

Under the terms of the authorizing legislation, the Commission is required to report to me on its progress for transmittal to the Congress on July 31 of each year and to make its final report not later than June 30, 1968. I take pleasure in submitting the first annual report of the Commission.

In forwarding this report to the Congress, I wish to reiterate the importance which I attach to pressing forward with plans and preparations for a sea-level canal. I think this is needed for the protection and promotion of peaceful trade, as well as for the welfare of the Hemisphere. It is needed in

the true interests of the United States and in fairness and justice to all.

LYNDON B. JOHNSON

The White House
July 31, 1965

NOTE: The report of the Commission (dated July 31, 1965, 9 pp., processed) is printed in the Weekly Compilation of Presidential Documents (vol. 1, p. 38).

The bill providing for the Atlantic-Pacific interoceanic canal study was approved by the President on September 22, 1964 (Public Law 88–609; 78 Stat. 990).

401   Remarks at the Signing of the Community Mental Health Centers Act Amendments of 1965.   *August 4, 1965*

Distinguished Members of the Congress, the Cabinet, guests, and friends:

If we had not already proclaimed so many other special weeks, I think I would be tempted this morning to designate this as Health Legislation Week at the White House and in the Nation.

The 89th Congress and Secretary Celebrezze are, between them, writing the greatest record in our Nation's history in the health field.

Only last week I was privileged to sign the landmark Medicare legislation at Independence, Missouri, completing the program that was begun 20 years ago by President Truman. This week I shall sign at least three major new legislative landmarks expressing America's broadening concern for the health of all of its citizens.

This measure before me now, we think, is especially important. While many do not realize it, mental illness is our number one health problem. One out of ten Americans need mental health care. Almost one half of all of our hospital beds in this country are filled by the mentally ill.

This bill, H.R. 2985, has two major purposes: first, to amend the Community Mental Health Centers Act to authorize Federal assistance in the initial staffing of personnel for these centers; secondly, to expand teacher training, and research and demonstration projects for the education of handicapped children. Both of these purposes are vital building blocks in the structure of our society.

Well over a century ago, Dorothea Dix took the mentally ill out of jails and dungeons and attics, and brought them into hospital asylums. And that was a major advance.

But today we know much more and we can do much more about these illnesses. We know that it helps mentally ill persons to remain close to their home. We know that many patients need only daytime care and therefore are able to return to their homes in the evening. We know others can be helped to stay on their jobs while receiving treatment at night. We know today that putting away the mentally ill in large isolated asylums is no longer either justifiable or useful. And that is why the focus of our efforts is upon strengthening community health resources.

The 88th Congress took a giant step forward by making it possible for local communities to secure Federal assistance in constructing mental health centers, and now it is time for another major advance. Now it is time to take more of our mentally ill out of the asylums, and bring them and keep them and care for them close to their homes, in their own familiar surroundings, and in their own communities.

And this legislation really gives us a very new, important tool to use in advancing this concept, by helping the communities staff their own local mental health centers. There is a second aspect of this legislation which is also equally important. Today at least 10 percent of our school-age population, a total of nearly 5 million of our children, need special educational services to help them overcome severe mental or physical handicaps. Of these, a quarter million children are too ill or too crippled to attend regular classes. Over 2½ million have sight or hearing or speech handicaps that require very special educational services. And more than 1 million children are mentally retarded, and almost a million more are emotionally disturbed.

These children cannot always be taught successfully by the usual teaching methods, but they can be taught and they do want to learn, and we should be able to provide them with the well trained teachers that they need.

The Office of Education estimates that 60,000 to 70,000 teachers of the handicapped are at work in our schools today. But you know what we need? We really need more than 60,000—we need 300,000.

The Elementary and Secondary Education Act that this wonderful 89th Congress passed made provisions to meet some of these special educational needs, and only 3 weeks ago I signed into law the act establishing a National Technical Institute for the Deaf. But the foundation on which we work is that laid down by the 88th Congress in the law that we are strengthening now.

Under this law our colleges, our universities, and our State education agencies are providing this year's traineeships and fellowships to 4,900 students that are preparing to become teachers of handicapped children. Six thousand new teachers will be in training this coming school year. But with these amendments we will now be able to double that number by 1967. In the years ahead, we shall be able to close the wide gap between the schooling needs of handicapped children and the services that we provide those children.

And I think it is a very fine commentary on this Congress and on this country that with all the responsibilities which we must meet around the world, that our society is still able and willing to show compassion for the mentally ill and for the children who face life under handicaps of nature.

I am glad to see so many familiar faces standing here with me this morning. They have been here several times during this session of Congress and the last session, each time taking an additional step forward in the field of improving the minds of our children, in the field of caring for the bodies of our people, in participating in the most laudable objectives that can come to government.

And I would like to feel that this particular group of men, of both parties, that this is a historic occasion, and that we could take a picture of these men and hang it in our living rooms, and over it put the roll of honor and teach our children to revere them for the advances that they are taking in this 20th century to give all the children all the education they can take, to give all the children all the care and treatment they need. What finer service could any legislator give to his country? What finer monument could he build?

So I feel that every American can and should take great pride in being part of a system that is so devoted and dedicated to justice and to decency, and to just plain old-fashioned simple goodness.

This measure and all the others in this field are going to live as a monument to a good many people, and I want to particularly point out Secretary Celebrezze, who is leaving in a short time to go to the court. They also stand as tributes to the specialized legislative leadership of skilled craftsmen in the Congress, men such as Lister Hill of Alabama, and Oren Harris, Congressman Fogarty, and I would like to call each one by name. I might miss a name though and I'd undo all the good; I'll just say all the men standing in front of you.

These men and all the Members in the Senate and the House who have made this progress possible deserve the gratitude of the American people. And I think it will just be a matter of time until our goals in health will be set and we will have new targets to shoot at.

We presently have a life expectancy of 70

years. I have a prediction—I am not in Drew Pearson's business and I don't want to compete with him—but I'm telling you now that we are going to raise that goal. It is not going to stay at 70; it is going to move up to 75 or on. We have an infant mortality that now runs at about 25 per thousand births. We are going to lower that.

We have heart disease, cancer, and stroke which now account for 70 percent of all the deaths in this country, and we are going to make a dent in that and reduce it. How we are going to do it, and when we are going to do it, and where we are going to do it is a little secret I will let you in on later this year.

Thank you.

NOTE: The President spoke at 9:40 a.m. in the Rose Garden at the White House. During his remarks he referred to, among others, Secretary of Health, Education, and Welfare Anthony J. Celebrezze, Senator Lister Hill of Alabama, Representative Oren Harris of Arkansas, and Representative John E. Fogarty of Rhode Island.

As enacted, the Mental Retardation Facilities and Community Mental Health Centers Construction Act Amendments of 1965 is Public Law 89–105 (79 Stat. 427).

For the President's remarks with President Truman at the signing of the Medicare bill, see Item 394.

The Elementary and Secondary Education Act of 1965 was approved by the President on April 11, 1965 (see Item 181).

The National Technical Institute for the Deaf Act was approved by the President on June 8, 1965 (see Item 305).

---

402 Letter to the Speaker Urging Consideration of the D.C. Home Rule Bill by the House of Representatives. *August 4, 1965*

[Released August 4, 1965. Dated August 3, 1965]

Dear Mr. Speaker:

On February 2, 1965, I transmitted to the Congress a home rule bill for the District of Columbia, with a special message urging its prompt and favorable considera-

tion. The Senate Committee on the District of Columbia, without a dissenting vote, recommended favorably, and on July 22 the Senate passed the bill by a vote of 63 to 29. A majority of the Senators on both sides of the aisle voted for its passage.

I cannot emphasize too strongly my conviction that this action by the Senate must not meet the fate of home rule bills passed by the Senate in previous Congresses. The House, too, must be given the opportunity, and promptly, to restore the basic rights of democracy at the very heart of the greatest constitutional system in the world.

For much too long this nation has tolerated in the District of Columbia conditions that our ancestors fought a revolution to eliminate. For much too long we have imposed on many hundreds of thousands of citizens who live in the District a badge of inferiority—the stigma of unworthiness to guide their own affairs. For much too long we have denied at our nation's capital the principles of representative government for which we stand throughout the world. The Congress has been aroused to redress denials of the right to vote in every part of this country—except the District. We affront its citizens and leave a significant part of our work unfinished by this unnecessary and invidious discrimination.

All of us cherish the heritage of our great charters of liberty. Yet in the District, with a population larger than that of eleven of our States, the governed have no voice and taxation is without representation. This is no less than a national disgrace.

The bill passed by the Senate will redeem our long neglect. It is not a partisan measure, nor should it be. Democrats and Republicans alike honor traditions of democracy and self-government. I feel confident that Members of the House, given the opportunity, will join with Members of the Senate to afford their fellow-citizens the full blessings of democracy and liberty. I know that you will do everything in your power to assure the Members that opportunity.

Sincerely,

LYNDON B. JOHNSON

[Honorable John W. McCormack, Speaker of the House of Representatives, Washington, D.C.]

NOTE: On September 29, 1965, the House of Representatives passed a bill providing for a charter commission to draft a plan for home rule for the District of Columbia. This differed from the Senate bill which provided for a mayor and city council. No further action was taken at the first session of the 89th Congress.

See also Items 39, 481, 486.

---

403 Remarks to College Students Employed by the Government During the Summer. *August 4, 1965*

Mr. Macy, my friends:

Unaccustomed as Lady Bird is to having 10,000 hungry young people drop in for lunch, I want you to know that Ambassador Taylor and I are delighted to see all of you.

I suppose that I should introduce myself first—I am the man who turns out the lights around this house. In fact, I am the only father in the country whose personal economy drive has the full and enthusiastic support of his daughters' boyfriends.

It is a great pleasure to have you here at the White House today. Out on these grounds where you now stand, great men have walked and relaxed, and made many very important decisions affecting this Nation and the world. I won't name all of them who have also held some news conferences out here, but Jefferson walked here, and Jackson, Abraham Lincoln, Woodrow Wilson, Franklin Roosevelt enjoyed this view, and so did Harry Truman and Dwight David Eisenhower and John Fitzgerald Kennedy. But no sight was ever more gratifying to any President than to see these grounds filled with bright, young, hopeful Americans keenly and vitally interested in their Government, and in their system of government and what makes it work.

If you like all that you have seen this summer, if you feel that the agencies where you work are doing the best possible job they can do, then your time in Washington this year has been wasted.

We must trust our system and we must respect it, but we must never, never be content with its performance. If you want to change what you have seen this summer, and if you want to improve upon it, and if you believe this Government can and should do a better job for all the people, then I am proud of you. I am proud to say welcome to the club.

America needs young people who want change, because America was conceived and America was brought into being by young people who believed the condition of man could be changed. And that is what we believe today.

We believe that the world can be made a safer and a saner and a more peaceful and a more principled place for men and women to live in dignity and to work. We believe that mankind can enjoy on this earth a finer and a fuller and a richer life of opportunity and fulfillment. And this is what we stand for, and this is what we work for, and this is what we fight for all around the world.

As it was 189 years ago, so today the cause of America is a revolutionary cause. And I am proud this morning to salute you as fellow revolutionaries. Neither you nor I are willing to accept the tyranny of poverty, nor the dictatorship of ignorance, nor the despotism of ill health, nor the oppression of bias and prejudice and bigotry. We want change. We want progress. We want it

both abroad and at home—and we aim to get it.

I am not disturbed by what some describe as the restlessness among young Americans today, because I share that feeling with you. I want to clear off and clear out the agenda of the past. I want to get ready for the works and the promises of tomorrow. And I know you want to, too.

What we make of tomorrow depends very heavily upon what we make of our Government today. As a Nation, we cannot fulfill our great promise if we allow government to grow unwieldy and uncontrolled and undisciplined, never permitting two employees to handle what three or four can do. Big government is not the end that we seek. Good government is. And good government requires of us self-discipline, self-control, and above all, self-respect.

So I want you to work in and with your Government, sharing your talents and your abilities and your skills with your people. But I do not want Government to monopolize these assets or to be their only outlet.

If Federal employment the last 10 years had gone up as fast as your population has grown, we would have almost 2,800,000 civilian employees instead of 2,400,000. If Federal payrolls had grown as fast as the State and local payrolls have grown, we would have 3,800,000 Federal job holders. For a free dynamic private society, that is too many.

Your Federal Government does not have to be fat to be faithful to its trust. It does not have to be loose in order to be liberal. And let me remind you, this year we are spending 64 percent more—$4.3 billion more—on health, on education, on housing, on the war on poverty, on manpower training, yet the total Federal budget is up only $2 billion more than last year. Why? Because we have, and we shall continue to weed out the outmoded and the obsolete and the outdated programs and costs to make room for your America, the America of the 20th century, the America of tomorrow. This we must continue—and we shall.

Robert Lowell, the poet, doesn't like everything around here. But I like one of his lines where he wrote "for the world which seems to lie out before us like a land of dreams." Well, in this great age—and it is a great age—the world does seem to lie before us like a land of dreams. We know more than man has ever known before. We know about the distant planet Mars, and the nearer worlds of man's own mind. And we think, as Emerson once put it, "that our civilization is near its meridian, but we are yet only at the cock crowing and the morning star."

Yes, this is a new day in America. A new day in the world. And we are only in the early morning of it. So I hope that you are even half so excited and thrilled and challenged by the opportunities before you as I am. I hope you believe, as I do, that this is a very rare and wondrous moment to make this great Government serve the cause of all humanity. And I hope that you feel as I do, that you will want to be a little part of that service.

It was back in World War I when a delegation from the American Chemical Society called upon the Secretary of War and offered the services of the Nation's chemists to the war effort. The then Secretary of War thanked them, and he asked them to call the next day while he looked into the matter. The next day the Secretary expressed appreciation for the offer, but he said it was unnecessary. He had looked into the matter and he found that the War Department already had a chemist.

That was just World War I. Today, your Government has quite a different attitude. We want, we need, we are eager to have the best minds and the best talents, and the best men and the best women. One out of ten Federal employees is now a professional: 75,000 engineers, 42,000 physicians or dentists or health technicians, 30,000 physical scientists, 24,000 biological scientists, and many more, including 10,000 lawyers.

So whatever your chosen pursuit or profession, we need you, and we need more like you. We are anxious to see you dedicate some of your life and time to the work of making this a better, and a stronger, and a more just, and a more decent, and a more livable society.

If you feel like protesting, I hope you will. I have been protesting all my life—protesting against poverty, protesting against illness, protesting against ignorance, protesting against injustice and discrimination, and against waste, and above all, against war. And I expect to continue, and I expect you to continue, until all of these evils are overcome in our land and around the world.

But I would commend to you a very fine thought expressed the other day by the son of Mayor Robert Wagner of New York, who advised young people on the campuses to remember, and I quote, "that there should not be a battle between themselves and society, but an attempt by individuals to overcome all that is stultifying and dehumanizing in society."

America has not been made strong and has not been made successful by generations of young puppets who did as they were told and who reacted as they were supposed to react, and who accepted just what was offered to them. So whether you enter Government service or private pursuits, I hope that you will always think for yourselves and act for yourselves, and seek change for yourselves and your generation, always honoring the rights of others as you respect the responsibilities of yourselves.

It is delightful to have been here with you this morning, and I want you to meet some of those who came with me, before I have to leave. First, I have been talking with a good and wise and dedicated public servant of this country and its ideals for more than 45 long years. He has gone through periods of crisis for this country at home and abroad, always faithfully discharging any responsibilities placed upon him. I consider him one of America's most outstanding, number one citizen—Ambassador Maxwell Taylor.

I think you know Mrs. Johnson, and our daughter Lynda Bird.

Thank you so much for coming. I hope you will stay as long as you like.

NOTE: The President spoke at 12:35 p.m. on the South Lawn at the White House before a group of 9,000 college students who had worked for the Federal Government in Washington during the summer. In his opening words he referred to John W. Macy, Jr., Chairman of the Civil Service Commission, who was in charge of the seminar. During his remarks he referred to, among others, Gen. Maxwell D. Taylor, former Ambassador to South Viet-Nam.

The annual White House Seminar for students working in Federal agencies for the summer opened on July 20 with the theme "Democracy's Challenge to Youth." The seminars are held each year to stimulate interest in careers in public service.

404   Letter to the Secretary of State on Social Science Research in Foreign Areas. *August 4, 1965*

[Released August 4, 1965. Dated August 2, 1965]

Dear Mr. Secretary:

Many agencies of the Government are sponsoring social science research which focuses on foreign areas and people and thus relates to the foreign policy of the United States. Some of it involves residence and travel in foreign countries and communication with foreign nationals. As we have recently learned, it can raise problems affecting the conduct of our foreign policy.

For that reason I am determined that no Government sponsorship of foreign area research should be undertaken which in the judgment of the Secretary of State would

adversely affect United States foreign relations. Therefore I am asking you to establish effective procedures which will enable you to assure the propriety of Government-sponsored social science research in the area of foreign policy. I suggest that you consult with the Director of the Bureau of the Budget to determine the proper procedures for the clearance of foreign affairs research projects on a Government-wide basis.

Sincerely,

LYNDON B. JOHNSON

[The Honorable Dean Rusk, Secretary of State, Washington, D.C. 20520]

405   Remarks to Members of the Bakersfield College Choir on the Creative and Performing Arts in America. *August 4, 1965*

Congressman Hagen, Mayor Karlen, members of the Bakersfield College Choir:

When I was your age, I think that if I could have ever made it from Monolith and

Tehachapi to Bakersfield I would have arrived, because at about your age I was out there in California working and Bakersfield was the place that I dreamed some day I would get to go and really upstage myself.

Here at the White House we are all very pleased to have young people and good music. Sometimes it seems to me that when Luci has a party, we have more of the former than the latter.

So we are happy now to have this excellent combination of both here today.

Over the years I have observed that public figures have a very suspicious habit; when they meet young journalists, public officials suddenly recall their own days when they were newspapermen. And if a football team comes to pay their respects, the officeholder suddenly remembers the days when he was a star quarterback.

I am sure this has happened to members of your organization, but in all candor and truth this afternoon, I have a confession. While I yield to no one in my enjoyment of harmony—you can take that any way you like—I do yield to nearly everybody in my ability to carry a tune. It may be refreshing to you to learn that your President was never asked or ever even encouraged to be a member of any choir.

This country can be very proud of you young people. You brought great honor upon yourselves and upon your country by winning the first-prize trophy for mixed choral groups at the recent international competition in Wales. We are extremely proud of you for that. We are also proud of you because you financed your own way and then won the competition over choral groups from 19 countries. This is a rather remarkable and rather splendid achievement.

I wish your example were not so exceptional in some respects. In this country, I regret to say, all too many of our talented individuals and groups are forced to struggle from day to day to survive, to maintain their existence. This includes t h e a t e r groups, dance and opera companies, sym-

phonies, m u s i c a l organizations, actors, writers. It also includes the solitary artist who seeks only the time to create his works.

I spent the weekend with a delightful friend who is an artist, and I have one of his pictures in there on my wall—it is pioneers going across the country in a covered wagon. His name is Peter Hurd, and he lives in New Mexico. But that picture that is hanging in the President's office is one he painted when he was on a WPA project. And of course that project permitted him to survive. And now he is painting one of the President of the United States for pay—much more than he got on WPA.

But for too long all the arts have had an uncertain footing in our society. There is, I think, a growing appreciation in America for the arts and a growing understanding and I think there is a growing demand among our people.

This is quite welcome and heartening, but the arts still lack a very sure and solid base on which to stand, and I believe, as they sometimes say in political years, I believe it is time for a change.

All societies that are remembered in history as great have been distinguished by a deep devotion to all the arts. Art is neither an indulgence nor a sanctuary. In more earthy terms, art that expresses the character and the aspirations of the people is really never a luxury or a frill. As a Nobel laureate once put it, art is a means of stirring the greatest number of men by providing them with the privileged image of our common joys and our common woes.

So I believe that in this young and creative and still emerging country of ours, we should realize that the creative and performing arts constitute a real national treasure, and as trustees of that treasure, we of this affluent and creative generation must answer to an especially demanding accounting.

So under times and conditions such as those in which we live, I believe it is imperative that America's arts be encouraged and be supported more actively. I particularly believe that the Federal Government can and should provide both leadership and resources to advance the arts so that the inner spirit and the life of our Nation and heritage may be continuously expressed and defined.

The Johnson administration now has a bill before the Congress to establish the National Foundation on the Arts and the Humanities. It will offer a realistic response to this opportunity and this challenge that I have been talking about. That legislation, I am very happy to say, has already passed the Senate, and—Congressman Hagen willing—I am hoping that it will soon pass the House of Representatives. I just have 434 more to go.

When this measure is signed, it will be one of the most historic enactments of any Congress in this century. Because in this land of such a highly diversified people the arts are really of the utmost importance. They are important as a unifying moral force. They also contribute to our awareness of who we are and where we are, and what we are and what we want to be as a people. And the arts are important as a celebration of the American experience which encourages and clarifies and points to the next direction in our continuing struggle to achieve the promise of our democracy.

So the campuses of our colleges across the Nation are producing many talents in many fields, and your country needs them all. And I am especially gratified that our colleges—the large ones, the small ones like I attended—are yielding so much talent to this national treasure in the arts.

So you from Bakersfield College are one example. You are a very fine example. I congratulate you, and on behalf of the Nation, I am privileged to commend each of you for your efforts and strivings which have won for you international recognition and honor.

I know Congressman Hagen, I know the other Members of the California delegation, all of them in the House, are very, very proud of you. Senator Kuchel has called and talked to me, to tell me of the pride that he feels and the great desire he had that I have a chance to say a word to you today.

So thank you for coming here to the White House. And if for any reason you should change your mind and extend me an invitation to become a part of your group, I would treasure membership.

NOTE: The President spoke at 5:18 p.m. in the Rose Garden at the White House. In his opening words he referred to Representative Harlan Hagen of California and Mayor Russel V. Karlen of Bakersfield, Calif.

During his remarks the President referred to his daughter, Luci Baines Johnson, Peter Hurd, artist from New Mexico who was painting a portrait of the President, and Senator Thomas H. Kuchel of California.

The Bakersfield Choir had just returned to the United States after winning an international music competition in Wales.

The National Foundation on the Arts and the Humanities Act of 1965 was approved by the President on September 29, 1965 (see Item 534).

406   Remarks at the Signing of the Community Health Services Extension Act. *August 5, 1965*

Distinguished Members of the Congress and sponsors of this legislation, friends who have supported it, my guests this morning:

Ordinarily, what is good for the Nation is good for Congress, too. The bills that we are signing here at the White House this week are certainly good for the health of all Americans. But, with these early morning signing ceremonies, I am not so sure this act is good for the health of Congress.

I have always been an early riser, but I remember my father used to pull me out of bed before daylight and say, "Lyndon, get up, every boy in town has already had an hour's start on you."

I hope that is not the case for me anymore. The older you get, the earlier you wake up, it seems like. And I am certain that is not the case for Congress, because there is no Congress in our history that has ever been ahead of the 89th Congress in the responsibility of meeting the health needs of the American people.

I was just telling my friend Senator Yarborough about the great Senator that preceded both of us in the United States Senate. One time he had some difficulties, in the days before we had direct election of senators in the Texas Legislature, and some of them voted for him and some against him. And he won out and they put him up on their shoulders, and they carried him up to the rostrum to make his speech.

His followers were all applauding and his detractors were kind of holding their heads down, and he made a very fiery speech. He said he was going to take two pictures of this legislature, this group of men. And over the picture of his detractors and those who had fought him, he was going to put the sign "The Rogues' Gallery." And over

those who had supported him in his hours of difficulties, he was going to put "The Roll of Honor."

And he said he was going to teach his children to love the one and to hate the other.

Well, now, I don't ever teach my children to hate anyone. We just don't hate around here. But we do love, and we are especially partial to "The Roll of Honor" that are here this morning—were here yesterday morning—and are going to be back here several times more this year.

Secretary Celebrezze just told me that they really had about 20 major measures that represent the greatest breakthrough in any century in the field of health and education. And I just can't think of anything that should amount to as much with the masses of this Nation, or the people of all nations, than the training of their children and the caring for their bodies.

We have recognized in this country for many, many years that public health is not divisible. An epidemic does not threaten just one of us alone; it endangers all of our people without regard to any political boundaries.

In more and more and more of our Government programs, this thought is being fully recognized. The Federal Government today is providing leadership, and we are using this pulpit here to say to the people of every State in the Union, and every nation in the world, that leadership is necessary and that financial assistance must follow it.

The States and local governments are being urged to provide administration and initiative and their own financial support as well. So, all together, the people of the United States are experiencing the fruitful and gratifying benefits of genuine cooperation between all their governments.

The law that we sign today is an outstanding example of this spirit.

Over the next 3 years it will provide $33 million to extend and expand the vaccination assistance program. I mentioned that briefly yesterday but I want to repeat it again, because it struck home with me. One of the heads of state that visited me this year said, "We may fall out with your men but our women will never let us fall out with your country." And I said, "Why?" He said, "Because one child out of every three in my country that was born died of measles."

Thirty-three and one-third percent! And the United States brought to us vaccination machines, and the drug people of the United States furnished this vaccine free of charge, and we vaccinated 750,000 little children against measles and we haven't lost a single life since. And he said every mother in that country will remember that as long as they live.

I just don't know of any greater foreign policy you can have than a policy like that.

So what we are saying is that we will continue to protect the people, especially our children, against things like polio—you remember the fear that every mother had just a few years ago; diphtheria—I remember as a child how frantic my mother was when my little sister had diphtheria; whooping cough; tetanus. Most importantly, we are going to begin a new program to protect all the children against measles.

Since 1962, when this program first came into being, locally conducted, but Federally assisted, vaccination programs have brought protection against polio to 58 million people. Now, today, more than two-thirds of all the children under the age of 5 have had their polio vaccination—two-thirds of every child under 5. Seven million children have been protected against diphtheria, tetanus, and whooping cough.

I think these figures may be a little boring to you sometimes, like they say about our foreign policy, but it is just about the most important thing we can deal with. And if it is necessary to bore you in order to get the job done, well, we are going to bore you.

So, I am very pleased and gratified this morning that this program will permit us to make an attack on the deaths and the defects and the disabilities caused each year by 4 million cases of measles.

Another provision of this very fine law that Congress has brought to me—this bill—allocates $24 million to continue the health services program for migratory workers.

I don't know whether you have ever seen a migratory worker or not. I don't know whether you have seen their families. I don't know whether you understand the conditions under which they live. But if you have seen, and if you have heard, and if you do feel, you have an impression that will last with you the rest of your life.

Migratory farm workers and their families are among our poorest people in our country. Their experiences are harsh ones. The advantages that most of us take for granted are unknown to them and their little children. They live on the far fringes of society. Most often, they have no voice whatever in the affairs of their community, their church, or no access to the facilities that are normally available to the rest of us.

Since 1962, 100 counties in the United States have received grants to provide public health services for these migrant families. And what a difference it makes in that family life. This has been a good and it has been a useful start. But there are not just 100 counties where these services are needed—there are 1,000 counties that we must reach.

So we are doing just 10 percent of what we ought to do, and this law is going to help us to accomplish that goal.

When you were here yesterday morning, I told Lister Hill, Ralph Yarborough, Oren Harris, and John Fogarty it looked like they were boarding down here. Every morning when I get up—they do come after breakfast, though—they are on the steps waiting with another bill, and I am made happier by it than they are, I assure you. But I said to them yesterday morning, the matter of raising health goals for the Nation is one that I want to throw out here and get all of you to thinking about, because I found out that some of the things we are signing today were thrown out 20 years ago—like medical care the other day. We worked on it 20 long years before it came into action. Of course, you're doing better as time goes on. I want to congratulate you.

I passed the housing bill this year and I estimated, when I sent it up, it would take 10 years to debate that one out, and they fooled me. It is down here this year and I am glad of it because we have a good Congress.

We are making long strides of social progress in America today—the longest that we have ever made in the history of this country. And we tend to measure progress in terms of quantity instead of quality. Over the next several months I am instructing those concerned with our programs— starting out here with Dr. Gardner, Under Secretary Cohen—to study and to develop for this Nation very ambitious, but obtainable, realistic goals and objectives for this

Nation in terms of improving the life of our people.

Some people have said to me, "Well, if you pass all these things this year, what are we going to do next year?" I said, "Don't worry about next year."

It's too early to specify all these goals or to say what is realistic and what is feasible, because they're studying them. But I want you to know what I'm thinking, and you may find some of my thinking somewhere in some of these task force reports and some of these recommendations to Congress.

I would like for America to have as goals, as a Nation:

Number one, that the first thing we do is our average life expectancy would jump up from 70 to 75 years. Adding 5 years onto your life expectancy means a lot to a fellow that is approaching 70.

Second, the infant mortality rate should be no greater than 16 per 1,000 births. It is now 25. And I'd just cut that into a third right quick. Take 8 off of that, move it from 25 that die out of a thousand to 16 that die, and 16 is too many. We can't do it all at once, though.

Third, the virtual elimination not only of all polio, diphtheria, and typhoid fever, but also of all tuberculosis, measles, and whooping cough, because as long as we have people dying from these things we are not doing the job that we ought to do.

Aside from the humanitarian thing, it is just awfully important that we keep these people here producing so that I can take half of their paychecks in taxes to do these other things. And we lose them when they get sick or they get crippled or they get disabled. From a purely selfish standpoint, it's good business.

Someone said to me, "Well, why are you talking about profits so much to these businessmen?" I said, "I just like to see profits."

Do you know that in the first 6 months this year, over the first 6 months last year, 1,100 corporations increased their profits 17 percent? The Federal Government increased its revenues, too, because every dollar they made, we took half of it. And we are going to take it and cure whooping cough and diphtheria, and educate their children.

Fourth, a reduction of one-fifth in the incidence of heart disease, cancer, and strokes which now account for 70 percent of all the deaths in the United States.

Now, we lose $32 billion a year just from people dying—what they would produce if they had lived—from heart disease, cancer, and strokes. Now, if we just put a stop to that and take $1 billion of that $32 billion, we'd have $31 billion to divide among everything else—if we just spend $1 billion to stop it. Now it is going to be stopped. It is a question of how soon. John Fogarty is going to want to stop it a little bit quicker than maybe even I do.

But that is just good business. Why should we go on losing $32 billion that these people could produce each year when we could take one or two or three and put a stop to it. Now that is what we have got to do.

So, I believe these goals are feasible for at least the next decade in this country. I believe the legislation that is now being enacted, the research that is now underway, the work that we are doing publicly and privately, and all the widespread public interest and support for improving our Nation's health will help us to reach these goals and, I think, really exceed them.

Such goals are not confined to the field of health alone because we can and we should establish targets for our efforts in every social field. And that is the work that we are devoting ourselves to now.

I just can't think that there is any man or woman present this morning that doesn't sometime think how they would like to be remembered, what legislation they would like to be identified with, and what they'd like for their little girls to think at night that their daddy has been doing all day long.

I don't know of anything that gives a man more satisfaction, and more pleasure, and more enjoyment than to be able to come home and say: "I improved the mind of the little children here today and I provided more education for more people. I made health better for more folks. I helped to care for the mind and the body, and I helped to protect them from suffering and things of that kind."

This group of men here that you see on this platform are the ringleaders. Down in our country, in the days before we had all these big trailer trucks and railroads, you would call them the lead horses, the ones that pull the load.

I am so proud of them and I am so grateful to them.

Thank you.

NOTE: The President spoke at 9:35 a.m. in the Rose Garden at the White House. During his remarks he referred to Senator Ralph Yarborough of Texas, Tom T. Connally, Senator from Texas 1929–1953, Secretary of Health, Education, and Welfare Anthony J. Celebrezze, Senator Lister Hill of Alabama, Representative Oren Harris of Arkansas, Representative John E. Fogarty of Rhode Island, Secretary-designate of Health, Education, and Welfare John W. Gardner, and Under Secretary of Health, Education, and Welfare Wilbur J. Cohen.

As enacted, the Community Health Services Extension Act is Public Law 89–109 (79 Stat. 435).

407 Statement by the President on the Proposed Korean Institute for Industrial Technology and Applied Science.
August 5, 1965

I AM very pleased and grateful for the enthusiastic and generous welcome given Dr. Hornig and his delegation by the people of Korea and by President Park. The interest there in the Institute for Industrial Technology and Applied Science project is most encouraging.

When President Park was here, we discussed the need and opportunity to bring the wealth of modern science and technology strongly to bear more effectively on the problems of Korea's growing industry. I believe the Institute idea which grew out of our conversations can set an example of excellence in Korea and in the world. It will provide opportunities at home for an able young generation of Korean engineers and scientists. Also, it will be a model for constructive cooperation with other developing countries.

We will work together with the Korean Government and Korean industry to build up the new Institute as rapidly as talented people can be assembled for the task. I have asked the Director of the Agency for International Development, in consultation with Dr. Hornig, to proceed as rapidly as possible with concrete steps to accomplish this goal.

I am grateful to Dr. Hornig, his wife, and the other members of the mission for the credit they have done their country by this outstandingly successful visit to Korea. I believe the language of science offers us new and still largely unstaffed opportunities for international understanding and cooperation. I am hopeful that we may develop an increasing number of joint programs in which the talents of our science and those of other countries can be united in constructive endeavors.

NOTE: The President's statement was made public as part of a White House release announcing his meeting with Dr. Donald F. Hornig, Special Assistant to the President for Science and Technology, and the group which had accompanied him to Korea (see Item 344).

The release stated that Dr. Hornig told the President that the proposed institute had aroused widespread interest in Korea and had been warmly supported by leaders in government, education, and industry.

See also Item 257.

408 Statement by the President on the Employment Record for July. *August 5, 1965*

EARLIER today the Department of Labor announced the employment and unemployment figures for July. I am extremely pleased that they showed an unemployment rate of 4.5 percent, the lowest rate since October 1957. We can all be gratified that fewer and fewer Americans have had to suffer unemployment in this past year, despite an extraordinarily rapid growth of the labor force.

From July 1964 to July 1965 the civilian labor force grew by 2.2 million people. This growth is

—more than twice as great as the 1 million increase in the preceding 12 months; and

—over 2½ times as large as the average yearly increase in the labor force from 1947 to 1964.

It is gratifying that employment opportunities grew even faster in the past year. Civilian employment rose by 2.4 million

—the largest year-to-year gain since the American economy was climbing out of the 1958 recession,

—more new jobs created in a single year than the total employment in a country such as Finland, or a great State like Massachusetts.

Teenagers and the long-term unemployed were special beneficiaries of expanding employment opportunities.

—Teenage employment in July was nearly 1 million higher than a year earlier, keeping pace with the large increase in the teenage labor force.

—Long-term unemployment (15 weeks or more) fell below 600,000, the lowest level in 7½ years. Most of the 270,000 decline from a year earlier occurred among persons out of work for 6 months or more.

These encouraging developments give us confidence and determination to seek further reductions in our national unemployment rate. Unemployment is still far too high among teenagers (13.2 percent) and among nonwhites (9.1 percent); this unnecessary waste of our manpower resources must be cut. Business, labor, and Government have worked together to create jobs and to strengthen our prosperity in the past year; we will continue to cooperate to widen employment opportunities in the months ahead.

409 Remarks in the Capitol Rotunda at the Signing of the Voting Rights Act. *August 6, 1965*

Mr. Vice President, Mr. Speaker, Members of Congress, members of the Cabinet, distinguished guests, my fellow Americans:

Today is a triumph for freedom as huge as any victory that has ever been won on any battlefield. Yet to seize the meaning of this day, we must recall darker times.

Three and a half centuries ago the first Negroes arrived at Jamestown. They did not arrive in brave ships in search of a home for freedom. They did not mingle fear and joy, in expectation that in this New World anything would be possible to a man strong enough to reach for it.

They came in darkness and they came in chains.

And today we strike away the last major shackle of those fierce and ancient bonds. Today the Negro story and the American story fuse and blend.

And let us remember that it was not always so. The stories of our Nation and

of the American Negro are like two great rivers. Welling up from that tiny Jamestown spring they flow through the centuries along divided channels.

When pioneers subdued a continent to the need of man, they did not tame it for the Negro. When the Liberty Bell rang out in Philadelphia, it did not toll for the Negro. When Andrew Jackson threw open the doors of democracy, they did not open for the Negro.

It was only at Appomattox, a century ago, that an American victory was also a Negro victory. And the two rivers—one shining with promise, the other dark-stained with oppression—began to move toward one another.

THE PROMISE KEPT

Yet, for almost a century the promise of that day was not fulfilled. Today is a towering and certain mark that, in this generation, that promise will be kept. In our time the two currents will finally mingle and rush as one great stream across the uncertain and the marvelous years of the America that is yet to come.

This act flows from a clear and simple wrong. Its only purpose is to right that wrong. Millions of Americans are denied the right to vote because of their color. This law will ensure them the right to vote. The wrong is one which no American, in his heart, can justify. The right is one which no American, true to our principles, can deny.

In 1957, as the leader of the majority in the United States Senate, speaking in support of legislation to guarantee the right of all men to vote, I said, "This right to vote is the basic right without which all others are meaningless. It gives people, people as individuals, control over their own destinies."

Last year I said, "Until every qualified person regardless of . . . the color of his skin has the right, unquestioned and unrestrained, to go in and cast his ballot in every precinct in this great land of ours, I am not going to be satisfied."

Immediately after the election I directed the Attorney General to explore, as rapidly as possible, the ways to ensure the right to vote.

And then last March, with the outrage of Selma still fresh, I came down to this Capitol one evening and asked the Congress and the people for swift and for sweeping action to guarantee to every man and woman the right to vote. In less than 48 hours I sent the Voting Rights Act of 1965 to the Congress. In little more than 4 months the Congress, with overwhelming majorities, enacted one of the most monumental laws in the entire history of American freedom.

THE WAITING IS GONE

The Members of the Congress, and the many private citizens, who worked to shape and pass this bill will share a place of honor in our history for this one act alone.

There were those who said this is an old injustice, and there is no need to hurry. But 95 years have passed since the 15th amendment gave all Negroes the right to vote.

And the time for waiting is gone.

There were those who said smaller and more gradual measures should be tried. But they had been tried. For years and years they had been tried, and tried, and tried, and they had failed, and failed, and failed.

And the time for failure is gone.

There were those who said that this is a many-sided and very complex problem. But however viewed, the denial of the right to vote is still a deadly wrong.

And the time for injustice has gone.

This law covers many pages. But the heart of the act is plain. Wherever, by clear and objective standards, States and counties are using regulations, or laws, or tests to deny the right to vote, then they will be struck down. If it is clear that State officials still intend to discriminate, then Federal examiners will be sent in to register all eligible voters. When the prospect of discrimination is gone, the examiners will be immediately withdrawn.

And, under this act, if any county anywhere in this Nation does not want Federal intervention it need only open its polling places to all of its people.

THE GOVERNMENT ACTS

This good Congress, the 89th Congress, acted swiftly in passing this act. I intend to act with equal dispatch in enforcing this act.

And tomorrow at 1 p.m., the Attorney General has been directed to file a lawsuit challenging the constitutionality of the poll tax in the State of Mississippi. This will begin the legal process which, I confidently believe, will very soon prohibit any State from requiring the payment of money in order to exercise the right to vote.

And also by tomorrow the Justice Department, through publication in the Federal Register, will have officially certified the States where discrimination exists.

I have, in addition, requested the Department of Justice to work all through this weekend so that on Monday morning next, they can designate many counties where past experience clearly shows that Federal action is necessary and required. And by Tuesday morning, trained Federal examiners will be at work registering eligible men and women in 10 to 15 counties.

And on that same day, next Tuesday, additional poll tax suits will be filed in the States of Texas, Alabama, and Virginia.

And I pledge you that we will not delay, or we will not hesitate, or we will not turn aside until Americans of every race and color and origin in this country have the same right as all others to share in the process of democracy.

So, through this act, and its enforcement, an important instrument of freedom passes into the hands of millions of our citizens.

But that instrument must be used.

Presidents and Congresses, laws and lawsuits can open the doors to the polling places and open the doors to the wondrous rewards which await the wise use of the ballot.

THE VOTE BECOMES JUSTICE

But only the individual Negro, and all others who have been denied the right to vote, can really walk through those doors, and can use that right, and can transform the vote into an instrument of justice and fulfillment.

So, let me now say to every Negro in this country: You must register. You must vote. You must learn, so your choice advances your interest and the interest of our beloved Nation. Your future, and your children's future, depend upon it, and I don't believe that you are going to let them down.

This act is not only a victory for Negro leadership. This act is a great challenge to that leadership. It is a challenge which cannot be met simply by protests and demonstrations. It means that dedicated leaders must work around the clock to teach people their rights and their responsibilities and to lead them to exercise those rights and to fulfill those responsibilities and those duties to their country.

If you do this, then you will find, as others have found before you, that the vote is the most powerful instrument ever devised by man for breaking down injustice and destroying the terrible walls which imprison men because they are different from other men.

THE LAST OF THE BARRIERS TUMBLE

Today what is perhaps the last of the legal barriers is tumbling. There will be many actions and many difficulties before the rights woven into law are also woven into the fabric of our Nation. But the struggle for equality must now move toward a different battlefield.

It is nothing less than granting every American Negro his freedom to enter the mainstream of American life: not the conformity that blurs enriching differences of culture and tradition, but rather the opportunity that gives each a chance to choose.

For centuries of oppression and hatred have already taken their painful toll. It can be seen throughout our land in men without skills, in children without fathers, in families that are imprisoned in slums and in poverty.

RIGHTS ARE NOT ENOUGH

For it is not enough just to give men rights. They must be able to use those rights in their personal pursuit of happiness. The wounds and the weaknesses, the outward walls and the inward scars which diminish achievement are the work of American society. We must all now help to end them—help to end them through expanding programs already devised and through new ones to search out and forever end the special handicaps of those who are black in a Nation that happens to be mostly white.

So, it is for this purpose—to fulfill the rights that we now secure—that I have already called a White House conference to meet here in the Nation's Capital this fall.

So, we will move step by step—often painfully but, I think, with clear vision—along the path toward American freedom.

It is difficult to fight for freedom. But I also know how difficult it can be to bend long years of habit and custom to grant it. There is no room for injustice anywhere in the American mansion. But there is always room for understanding toward those who see the old ways crumbling. And to them today I say simply this: It must come. It is right that it should come. And when it has, you will find that a burden has been lifted from your shoulders, too.

It is not just a question of guilt, although there is that. It is that men cannot live with a lie and not be stained by it.

DIGNITY IS NOT JUST A WORD

The central fact of American civilization—one so hard for others to understand—is that freedom and justice and the dignity of man are not just words to us. We believe in them. Under all the growth and the tumult and abundance, we believe. And so, as long as some among us are oppressed—and we are part of that oppression—it must blunt our faith and sap the strength of our high purpose.

Thus, this is a victory for the freedom of the American Negro. But it is also a victory for the freedom of the American Nation. And every family across this great, entire, searching land will live stronger in liberty, will live more splendid in expectation, and will be prouder to be American because of the act that you have passed that I will sign today.

Thank you.

NOTE: The President spoke at 12:05 p.m. in the Rotunda at the Capitol, prior to signing the bill. In his opening words he referred to Vice President Hubert H. Humphrey, President of the Senate, and Representative John W. McCormack of Massachusetts, Speaker of the House of Representatives.

As enacted, the Voting Rights Act of 1965 is Public Law 89-110 (79 Stat. 437).

Reports to the President on the implementation of the act, prepared by the Attorney General and the Chairman of the Civil Service Commission, were made public by the White House on August 5, August 14, and August 21. They are printed in the Weekly Compilation of Presidential Documents (vol. 1, pp. 51, 92, 125).

The determinations of the Attorney General are printed in the Federal Register of August 7 and August 10, 1965 (30 F.R. 9897, 9970).

410   Remarks at the Signing of the Health Research Facilities Amendments of 1965.   *August 9, 1965*

Secretary Celebrezze, Secretary Cohen, Dr. Shannon, Dr. Terry, Senator Hill, Senator Javits, Congressman Harris, Congressman Fogarty, Congressman Springer, the other distinguished Members of the Senate and the House, the staff, the employees of NIH, my fellow Americans, boys and girls:

Here on this quiet battleground our Nation today leads a worldwide war on disease. The experience of the past 10 years assures us that war can be won.

New vaccines have almost eliminated from our entire land the crippling curse of polio that sent shivers to the backs of every mother in this land just a few years ago. Measles vaccine today promises victory over disease which kills from 20 to 30 percent of all the people of other countries. A new vaccine may soon rid mothers of the fear that their unborn children could become the victim of German measles. Chemical treatment has already extended the lifespan of cancer victims and shows a very high promise of far greater successes. The artificial kidney gives invalids new hope for normal and productive life. Research is making it possible to renew and to rebuild the human heart.

Yes, a staggering era for medicine has begun. And you here at NIH are shaping it and you can be as proud of what you are doing as we are proud of you.

I want to say that you of the Congress, members of both of the great parties in the Congress, you are shaping it too. And you too can be proud of yourselves as we are so proud of you. Men like that veteran in this field who has devoted a long and honorable life to public service—Lister Hill, from the great State of Alabama; and Congressman Oren Harris, who will soon leave the legis-

lative to go to the judiciary—but not leave it until he gets those last five health bills passed out of his committee; and Congressman Fogarty from that progressive State of Rhode Island who, through the years, has furnished us statesmen who provided leadership; men like Aime Forand, who just the other day was out at Kansas City with us to sign the Medicare bill; and Theodore Francis Green in Foreign Relations; and John E. Fogarty is going to be around here for a long time making appropriations and making history for health; and Senator Javits, who is always to be found in the leadership of any progressive cause, is an eloquent voice for his party, and for his State, and his country, as is Congressman Springer who supports Oren Harris and the Members of the House in this very effective work; and as members of another party we salute them and recognize them this morning for their efforts here.

As we meet here this morning, our country is spending $1½ billion each year for health research. And this legislation that we will sign will enlarge greatly the program that NIH is running.

This bill that I will sign shortly, will provide the bricks and the mortar for the biomedical research laboratories throughout this entire Nation. This will will help foster new breakthroughs in our war on disease. This bill will accomplish the miracles of which today we only dream.

What are our goals? What do we hope to do? What are our objectives? What should be our targets? Well, the work you have done and the work that you are doing permits me this morning to give you some specific answers.

The American goal is to eliminate completely the disability and the death among children that is caused by rheumatic fever and rheumatic heart disease.

The American goal is to reduce substantially the tragic toll of heart disease.

Malaria and cholera were conquered in America a long time ago, but they still hold mortal fear for most of world humanity. The American goal is the complete eradication of malaria and cholera from the entire world.

And we are determined that the vital link between pure research and practical achievement will never be broken. We are determined that research and discovery yield results which not only increase man's knowledge but the strength of his body and the length of his life.

[*Quoting from the Bible*] "And Philip went down to the city of Samaria, and proclaimed unto them the Christ. And the multitude gave heed with one accord unto the things that were spoken by Philip, when they heard and saw the signs which he did. For some of those that had unclean spirits that came out crying with a loud voice, and many that were palsied and were lame were healed. And there was much joy in that city." [Acts 8: 5–8]

"And besides this, giving all diligence, add to your faith virtue, and to virtue knowledge, and to knowledge temperance, and to temperance patience, and to patience godliness, and to godliness brotherly kindness, and to brotherly kindness love. For if these things are yours and they abound, they make you to be not idle nor unfruitful unto the knowledge of our Lord Jesus Christ. Wherefore the rather, brethren, give diligence to make your calling and election sure, for if ye do these things, ye shall never fall." [2 Peter 1: 5–8, 10]

And as my minister said yesterday at Camp David: I am not here to ask any person to change their religion. I am not here to convert anyone from one faith to the other. I am here only to say to you, how does your religion serve you, and what does it do for you, and what do you do for other people?

And I hope that as we here on the grounds of NIH today, speaking with a voice that will heal the lame and will treat the palsied, and will add virtue and knowledge and temperance and patience and brotherly kindness and love, I am hoping that America can be worthy of all that flag stands for, and can provide that kind of leadership in all the world.

I said to Senator Hill coming out here this morning, with Congressman Harris and Senator Javits and some of the others, every night when I go to bed I look at the men that died that day and then I wake up in the morning and see the casualty reports. And the one thing that sustains me most is to see what we are doing for the lame and the palsied, what we are doing in adding knowledge in the field of education, what we are doing in conservation and beautification to make this a more beautiful land, and to make this not just "America the Beautiful," but the "World the Beautiful."

A distinguished British leader once observed that want is one of five giants on the road of reconstruction, and in some ways want is the easiest to attack. What are the others? Disease, ignorance, squalor, and idleness. And by measures like this one that we are signing today—and we are going to sign dozens more of them before we go home this year—we Americans—I didn't say we Democrats—we Americans are attacking these five giants. And I am here this morning to tell you we are attacking them successfully—and we are winning.

Now is not the time to tarry along by the roadside. Now is the time to say clearly where we mean to go. Now is the time to measure the distance that we can cover in the next year that is ahead of us, in the next decade that we face, and in what is left of this century.

And as the leader of this country, I plan to set some goals—some realistic, ambitious, farsighted goals—goals of vision. And so in the next few days I am going to announce a very special White House task force to report to the President, which will tell me and tell America where we are and where we are going and how we are going to get there.

The great experts of this Nation will be called together under the leadership of the President. And these experts, inside and outside Government—I want to pay due tribute to Secretary Marion Folsom who is here on the platform with us; Secretary, would you please stand up?—who, without regard to party or without regard to fear or favor, men of his type will advise us how best to reach these goals—the goals that we will set for education, the goals that we will set for health, the goals that we will set for happiness for all of the children of not only our land but what we can do to help others.

We do this because we have no choice, because we must advance daily or we will fail eternally. And we do it because we believe in Thomas Jefferson's words: that the care of human life and happiness is the first and the only legitimate object of good government.

Last night I was reading from a little book that I have read many, many times, but I get strength from it every time I read it. It is, "The Rich Nations and the Poor Nations," by Barbara Ward—Lady Jackson. And one brief passage appealed to me. I tried to get my speech writers to put it in my speech today but they wouldn't do it, so I am going to put it in myself:

". . . we have more resources at our dis-

posal than any group of nations in the history of man. And it is hard to believe that we have run out of the moral energy needed to make the change. Looking at our society I certainly do not feel that it already presents such an image of the good life that we can afford to say that we have contributed all that we can to the vision of a transfigured humanity. Our uncontrollably sprawling cities, our shapely suburbia, our trivial pursuits—our quiz shows, TV, the golf games"—I might add my bowling—"hardly add up to the final end of man. We can do better than this. We also have the means to do better. If we do not feel the need there is only one explanation: We no longer have the vital imagination for the task." [1]

Well, in the days ahead, under the leadership of NIH, we are not going to lack for imagination in this country. And we are not going to lack for vision, and we are not going to lack for leadership. One of our great leaders in the medical field, the Surgeon General of the Public Health Service, is leaving us to serve the great University of Pennsylvania as vice president. We owe a deep debt of gratitude to Dr. Luther Terry and to his family, and we deeply regret that he has seen fit to go on to other pursuits in the educational field but we are glad that we are not losing him in our attack on the five giants. Would you stand up, Dr. Terry?

And I said to the men coming out here with me this morning in the helicopter, Secretary Celebrezze and Secretary Gardner—who is one of the great successors to Secretary Celebrezze; it is going to take a great man to fill his shoes—Tony Celebrezze will bring to me this year 20 bills as important as this, or more, that represent adventurous

---

[1] Barbara Ward, "The Rich Nations and the Poor Nations" (New York: W. W. Norton & Co., Inc., 1962), page 141.

advances in the field of health and education before he goes on the court out there in Ohio. And John Gardner today is planning on what we are going to do in these days ahead.

And I said to Secretary Celebrezze and Senator Hill and Senator Javits, and Congressman Harris, and Congressman Springer and others, who will succeed Luther Terry?

I'll tell you who I want to succeed him— and this is not a surprise to the press. I don't want you folks to get surprised. I want the best, most adventurous, imaginative, best equipped doctor with vision in this country to succeed him. I don't know where he is, but we are going to start looking for him this morning, because in the days ahead in the field of health and education, illiteracy, ignorance, and poverty and all these things, your Government and you Americans are going to successfully conclude that war that you have declared on these ancient enemies.

And in the allotted time to us, each of us in our own way is going to make our maximum contribution to healing the lame

and caring for the palsied, and adding virtue and knowledge and brotherly love to this land.

Thank you very much.

NOTE: The President spoke at 12.13 p.m. at the National Institutes of Health, Bethesda, Md. In his opening words he referred to Secretary of Health, Education, and Welfare Anthony J. Celebrezze, Under Secretary of Health, Education, and Welfare Wilbur J. Cohen, Dr. James A. Shannon, Director of the National Institutes of Health, Dr. Luther L. Terry, Surgeon General, Public Health Service, Senator Lister Hill of Alabama, Senator Jacob K. Javits of New York, Representative Oren Harris of Arkansas, Representative John E. Fogarty of Rhode Island, and Representative William L. Springer of Illinois.

During his remarks the President referred to Aime Forand, Representative from Rhode Island 1937–1939 and 1941–1961, Theodore F. Green, Senator from Rhode Island 1937–1961, former Secretary of Health, Education, and Welfare Marion B. Folsom, and Secretary-designate of Health, Education, and Welfare John W. Gardner.

As enacted, the Health Research Facilities Amendments of 1965 is Public Law 89–115 (79 Stat. 448).

Dr. Terry's letter of resignation and the President's reply were made public by the White House on August 10. They are printed in the Weekly Compilation of Presidential Documents (vol. 1, p. 75).

For the statement by the President on announcing plans for the White House Conference on Health, see Item 424.

411   Letter Accepting Proposal for the Establishment of a Lyndon Baines Johnson Presidential Library in Austin. *August 9, 1965*

Dear Mr. Heath:

It is a pleasure to acknowledge and thank you for your letter of August 6, 1965.

I have been aware, of course, of the existence of the other Presidential Libraries and their contribution to history. It has been a source of satisfaction to know that through these institutions we are making certain that the full record of each presidential administration is being carefully kept

for study and use by all those interested in the history of our country.

Your letter has served as a suggestion that it is not too early for me to be giving thought to the planning of a similar institution for this administration. As you know, I am deeply committed to the preservation and safeguarding of our historical and cultural resources and have made an effort to preserve the papers of my own public career since

1937. I am, of course, particularly concerned that the generations that follow us should have the opportunity for detailed analysis of those historical records from which can be derived a full understanding of the momentous years through which we are passing.

Your letter has not only reminded me that it is time to give attention to this matter, but it has set my mind at rest as to how the whole question can best be dealt with. The fine public spirit and magnificent generosity that have prompted the University of Texas to make this unexampled offer of a site and structure on its campus for use as a Presidential Library should earn it the respect of the entire nation. I am pleased that you believe that placing the Library on the University of Texas campus will significantly strengthen and enrich the educational programs in which that great institution is engaged. I would also hope that your action would enhance the opportunity for improving the academic endeavors of all institutions of learning, and provide additional opportunities for scholarly research in public affairs.

It is with heartfelt gratitude, therefore, that I accept your proposal and join with you in this undertaking.

I have referred your proposal and a copy of this reply to Mr. Lawson B. Knott, Jr., Administrator of General Services, who is charged by existing law with establishing and operating Presidential Libraries as a part of our national archives system. Mr. Knott and I will cooperate in working out with you the detailed arrangements necessary to bring to actuality the benefits of this great national education asset which the University of Texas has undertaken to provide.

Sincerely yours,

LYNDON B. JOHNSON

[Honorable W. W. Heath, Chairman, Board of Regents, The University of Texas, Perry Brooks Building, Austin, Texas]

NOTE: Mr. Heath's letter follows:

Dear Mr. President:

It is our understanding that at an appropriate time you intend to donate your papers to the United States for ultimate deposit in a Presidential archival depository.

The University of Texas shares the belief of the academic world and others that the papers of a President constitute a vital part of our Nation's historical heritage. We likewise believe that the richness and fullness of the Nation's knowledge and understanding of that heritage depends in a large measure upon the completeness of a President's historical materials, the care with which they have been preserved, the adequacy of the archival and museum facilities in which they are housed, and their general accessibility and availability for scholarly research and study.

A university can only fulfill its total mandate by being sensitive to contemporary world affairs, the lessons of our national experience, and our Nation's constant effort to improve the processes of Government. The role of a university in bringing about an understanding of our times is affected adversely unless it can impart a knowledge of the conditions from which they arose; and it is equally clear that its responsibility to develop tomorrow's leaders, capable of making intelligent decisions for the future, can be greatly advanced when the inquisitive mind has available at the university the research collections from which a comprehensive view of the age in which we live can be obtained. It follows inevitably that convenient access to the rich resources of a Presidential Library, and the tremendous ancillary benefits which will follow will enable the University of Texas, in a most dramatic manner, to meet its responsibilities to expand its academic capabilities, especially at the graduate school level in the fields of history, government, economics, public administration and related disciplines. In furtherance of these objectives we intend to establish at the University of Texas a school to be known as the Lyndon Baines Johnson Institute of Public Service, at which we hope you will consent to teach or lecture after your retirement from the Presidency, devoting as much time thereto as you may find possible.

In view of the considerations set forth above, and the benefits which will thus accrue to the University of Texas in fulfilling its educational purposes and objectives as fixed by applicable law of the State of Texas, The University of Texas deems it an exceptional honor and privilege, consistent with its educational purposes and objectives, to make the following proposal:

1. The University, at its expense, will provide an

appropriate site comprised of fourteen (14) acres within the principal academic environs of the University at Austin, Texas, to be utilized as the site of a Presidential archival depository which will be known as the Lyndon Baines Johnson Library. The University warrants against encroachment on or use of such site for purposes other than the site of the Lyndon Baines Johnson Library and related parking areas except as otherwise expressly provided herein, or as may be later agreed by the University of Texas, you or your representatives, and the Administrator of General Services or successors in legal functions. The site selected will be subject to approval by you or your designee.

2. The University, at its expense, will design, construct, furnish and equip a building to be located on such site. The selection of the architect or architects and the design concept of the facility, including its orientation on the selected site and its physical relationship with other University facilities will be subject to approval by you or your designee. The building is to contain the following:

a. not less than 100,000 square feet of space to be dedicated to use as a Presidential archival depository for the housing and display of Presidential papers and other historical materials relating to and contemporary with your life and works as a fitting and lasting memorial to you and your long and distinguished years of service to our beloved Nation, and

b. additional space as the University deems appropriate for University purposes as detailed in paragraph 5–c, hereof.

3. The University will confer with the Administrator of General Services or his designee concerning site selection, design, construction, furnishing, and equipping the Library including its museum aspects.

4. The University will provide adequate, convenient parking facilities for the use of visitors to the Presidential Library.

5. The University of Texas, in expanding its teaching capabilities in history, government, economics, public administration, and related disciplines, expects:

a. To have access to the Presidential papers and other historical materials housed in the Lyndon Baines Johnson Library, recognizing, however, that the Presidential Library will be a national research institution and, therefore, officers, faculty, and students of the University, along with scholars and other interested persons everywhere, will be accorded access to the collections of Presidential papers and other Presidential historical materials housed therein. The University understands also, particularly since it is anticipated that great numbers of people will visit this Library on The University of Texas campus daily, that reasonable regulations must be provided to insure orderly use of the materials

and access to all such historical materials will be subject to such restrictions as may be imposed by the donors, or by statute, Executive Order, regulations, etc.

b. To offer and lend to the United States for deposit in the Lyndon Baines Johnson Library certain papers and other historical materials now held by the University relating to and contemporary with the life and works of Lyndon Baines Johnson, and,

c. In addition to the space dedicated to the Presidential archival depository to provide space and related facilities in the building contemplated in Paragraph 2, hereof, for University purposes to be used in furtherance of studies and research in history, government, economics, public administration and related disciplines.

6. Upon completion of the construction, furnishing, and equipping of the space and facilities to be occupied by the Presidential archival depository, the University hereby undertakes and agrees to turn over, dedicate, and make available the same, including the furnishings and equipment therein, to the United States for its use in perpetuity as the Lyndon Baines Johnson Library, but without transfer of title, pursuant to the provisions of Section 507(f) of the Federal Property and Administrative Services Act of 1949, as amended.

7. In consideration of the foregoing and upon acceptance by the United States, the Presidential Library and the space and facilities occupied by it will be administered, operated, protected, maintained, and staffed in perpetuity by and at the expense of the United States of America. It is also understood and agreed that the administering, staffing, maintaining, operating and protecting the site of the Presidential Library and such portion of the building as is used for activities of the University as contemplated by Paragraph 5–c, hereof, shall be borne by the University.

8. The space and facilities to be occupied by the Presidential Library will be completed and available for occupancy within two years after final working drawings are ready for marketing: Provided, however, that in no event shall said two year period begin to run until the Administrator of General Services has entered into an agreement, as provided for in Section 607(f)(1) of the Federal Property and Administrative Services Act of 1949, as amended, with The University of Texas, to maintain, operate, and protect said Presidential Library as a part of the National Archives system. It is understood that the said Administrator may not enter into such an agreement prior to the expiration of the first period of 60 calendar days of continuous session of Congress following the date on which a report of the proposed transaction is transmitted to the Congress as required by Section 507(f) of the Property Act,

supra. It is further understood that the time when such report may be submitted to the Congress is a matter entirely within the discretion of the President of the United States or his designee.

9. Upon your assent to this proposal The University of Texas will proceed with its implementation.

Respectfully,

THE UNIVERSITY OF TEXAS
W. W. HEATH
Chairman, Board of Regents

412   Meeting With White House Correspondents in the Office of the Press Secretary.   *August 9, 1965*

THE LYNDON BAINES JOHNSON LIBRARY

[*Bill D. Moyers, Special Assistant to the President, opened his regular afternoon news briefing at 4:15 p.m. on August 9, 1965. The President and Mrs. Johnson joined the group shortly thereafter, for the announcement of plans for the Lyndon Baines Johnson Library to be established at the University of Texas in Austin. Also present were Horace Busby, Jr., Special Assistant to the President, Dr. Harry Ransom, Chancellor of the University, and W. W. Heath, Chairman of its Board of Regents. The briefing was already in progress before a stenographic reporter arrived.*]

MR. BUSBY. [1.] . . . and the Franklin D. Roosevelt Library at Hyde Park, New York; the Harry Truman Library at Independence, Missouri—where the President visited week before last to sign the Medicare bill; the Eisenhower Presidential Library at Abilene, Kansas; and then the John Fitzgerald Kennedy Library at Cambridge, Massachusetts.

In the case of this news today, there are a couple of matters of interest to you. This is the first instance in which an institution of higher learning offered a living President the building and the facilities for this library, in conjunction with the operation of the university—the University of Texas.

Dr. Ransom won't say this himself, but the University of Texas is, and has long

been, distinguished for its overall library collection. It has done some fantastic work in recent years. Dr. Ransom, I will say, is the man most responsible personally, before he became chancellor, for the development and growth of this library.

This will be the first time in which there will be a library built around the papers of a man whose career has spanned such a long period of public service at so many different levels of office. The President has over the years maintained, at his own expense, very good records of all of his offices, beginning with the election to Congress in 1937, the Senate in 1948, and to the Vice Presidency in 1961. And there are many comprehensive civil records on all of those periods.

Q. Excuse me, Buzz, where are those papers now? In the Archives?

MR. BUSBY. Well, some of them are here. Some that we have the most immediate need for are within the White House, and I don't know where the storage is of some of the others.

THE PRESIDENT. Most of them are here. Several years ago I arranged, upon the recommendation of the Library of Congress, to get an outstanding lady with experience in this field to review all of the papers and extract those that were worthwhile. She's done that—papers dating from the time I came here in 1931. Mrs. Territo [1] had to

[1] Mrs. Dorothy P. Territo, Staff Assistant to the President.

leave that service, but has returned, working under the supervision of Mrs. Roberts [2] from my office.

Q. Busby, won't this be the first time that any university in another State established an institute for public service?

MR. BUSBY. You mean by the name?

Q. I mean by really training people for government service, I presume, under the auspices of that?

MR. BUSBY. It is the first of this kind, yes, in conjunction with the President's library. And this record spans a most valuable segment of our national history from 1937—actually, it goes back, as the President mentioned, to 1931—through World War II, the cold wars, and other periods.

Q. In the university letter there is a proposal that the President intends to teach after his retirement. Does this letter move that back?

THE PRESIDENT. I don't think, other than what the letter reflects, we ought to speculate on just what condition I'll be in when I retire, and what position I'll be able to take or assume. I would rather leave that down the road. I may tell you that it is an ambition of mine.

Q. Do you have any plans now about the beginning of construction and how much it might cost, and details like that?

MR. BUSBY. Those questions will be decided by the Board of Regents, and, of course, the design and the cost.

Q. Is this the first time that such a specific arrangement for a Presidential library has been made during the term of a President in question?

MR. BUSBY. It is the first time that this has been done in conjunction with the university, but I believe President Eisenhower's library agreements were made during his

term. President Truman's were not. They were made after his term.

Q. I assume that will include historical papers, radio and television, audio and visual?

MR. BUSBY. All of that. All things related to the life and times of the President will be available to the scholars, and the papers of his officers and others associated with him in the administration. They will all be collected in one place.

Q. Will Mrs. Johnson's papers be available, too?

MRS. JOHNSON. Anything that I have.

Q. Is there a cost anticipated?

MR. BUSBY. None contemplated. We couldn't anticipate costs.

Q. As I understand it, no contributions are anticipated?

Q. Is there a specific site of where the 14 acres are?

MR. BUSBY. The letter says the site is to be selected and approved by the President, or his deputy. That has not been done yet.

Q. Where are the 14 acres?

MR. BUSBY. The University of Texas has a rather substantial number of acres of land in several different places in Austin.

Q. When will the institute be put in operation, in conjunction with the library, or before that?

MR. BUSBY. That will be a decision of the Board and faculty.

Q. Is there a date for completion in mind?

MR. BUSBY. There is not now.

Q. Is this primarily for graduate study, following undergraduate degrees?

MR. BUSBY. Again, that would be a conjectural answer because the university faculty and the administration might want to make that answer.

Q. Will this consist of a series of buildings?

MR. BUSBY. I can't say. It depends on

[2] Mrs. Juanita D. Roberts, Personal Secretary to the President.

how the design comes out.

Q. At least there will be a complex of both the school and the library?

MR. BUSBY. It will be a complex of operations. Whether it will be one building or several buildings will depend upon the design.

THE PRESIDENT. Mrs. Johnson has done quite a bit of work visiting several libraries all over the country, and she has spent a good deal of time in joining facilities like the boyhood home, birthplace, and things of that kind. Maybe you want to ask her some questions.

Q. Would you like to see the President's library patterned after one of the three or four that you visited? Do you have any special ideas?

MRS. JOHNSON. No. My main desire is that it shall be a living thing that will be of use to a lot of young people who might want to learn about public service and governmental activities. I think that has been the story of my husband's life.

THE PRESIDENT. One thing I think you might be interested in is that we always find that you have less space than you need. That is why you have the minimum of 14 acres in there to us. Some find that after they started the space was totally inadequate. The university has guaranteed to us an amount for it, and other things. And we are anxious to have these facilities so that these papers and these documents, and even your questions and some of our answers, are available to the students of the future, and it will be available free, and the university has cooperated.

Q. Mr. President, have you made any decision about the accessibility of these papers? I presume that some of them will have to be kept closed for a period of time. Can you tell us when they will be opened up?

THE PRESIDENT. No, I have not gone into that. I think the next action will be by the university Board of Regents and the building and its physical details, and I assume by the time those things are finished we will have a little clearer insight into some of these questions that you are raising.

Q. Mr. President, have you personally visited the University of Texas site where this is to be constructed?

THE PRESIDENT. The Board of Regents will be determining where the site is and I am sure I'll be there a good many times.

Q. Have you designated members of your family to work on this?

THE PRESIDENT. I did not have to designate anybody. Mrs. Johnson appointed herself, and some people that have worked with other Presidents in connection with formulating policy of this kind, and the General Services people, and people in my office, and Mr. Busby, and Mr. Moyers are particularly interested in it. Busby was a former editor of the University of Texas in his younger days and was quite a crusading fellow around town. We're still going to maintain the right of the President to veto, and all of these details will be worked out later. This is the first step—to go from here to the Regents. And I would anticipate before the end of this term—to which I have been elected—that we would hope to see the building completed.

MR. BUSBY. Let me add one other thing. We mentioned two names here. You know Mrs. Juanita Roberts, the President's personal secretary, who has been very instrumental in not just this but in maintaining these archives through the years. And the lady who is in direct charge of the President's archives, Mrs. Dorothy Territo. They are both back in the corner there, and they both have been not only of enormous help in this but of help to us at all times around the White House in tracing things back that we want to learn from the distant past.

THE PRESIDENT. To give you an illustration of the details, another prominent fellow came into my office and said he was impressed that I had spent several hours with a news magazine the other day, and one of them just told me how I wasted a complete afternoon. And I asked Mrs. Roberts to give me the facts. She was there. And she came back in 30 seconds. "They checked in at 2:10. They left at 5:04. You had two lunches. This is the schedule. This is what they discussed. These are the questions you were asked. These are the replies you made." And so on. I guess the other fellow won't exaggerate much next time. All of this time, every minute that your President is doing something, is accounted for. They account for whatever you're doing, how many discussions you've had. And, in addition, including this meeting today.

Q. Mr. President, you said the building will be completed——

THE PRESIDENT. I said it would be hoped to be completed by the end of this term, that means by January 1969, we hope.

MR. MOYERS. Are there any other questions concerning this particular subject? Mr. Heath and Dr. Ransom will be available later.

Q. Can I ask one other question? The building will be completed by the end of the term?

THE PRESIDENT. I would say we hope.

Q. Whenever it is completed, will it then immediately go into operation?

THE PRESIDENT. You don't build a big building and then lock the doors.

MR. BUSBY. In regard to that, all of these libraries, from the time the President's papers go into it until they are opened for use of any scholars, is usually a rather long period of time. The FDR Library was opened more quickly than any others, but that was 10 years.

MR. MOYERS. I think Mr. Heath and Dr. Ransom will be available in the Fish Room after this briefing is over, in the event that you have specific, technical questions that you would like to address to them and talk to them about. That can be done informally. Three or four members of the Texas press asked to see them individually, so we decided to have this little session in the Fish Room immediately after this. You are all invited.

THE PRESIDENT'S REMARKS IN RESPONSE TO AN EARLIER QUESTION ON A BRIEFING WITH SENATORS

[2.] MR. MOYERS. I think that while the President is here, now is the best time for the answer to be given to the question asked earlier of what went on this morning at the briefing with the Members of the Senate who were present in the State Dining Room.

I was prepared to give you some of the details of that, but the President is here and, if he is willing—and he is a more direct source than I am—he can give you the details.

THE PRESIDENT. Not to close the library discussion, but Mrs. Johnson holds three degrees from the University of Texas and I hold one honorary degree and we compromised to build the library at the University of Texas.

At the briefing this morning we had a 15-minute report from Gen. Maxwell Taylor[3] that involved the military and diplomatic situation in South Viet-Nam and his experiences in the last year, his views concerning our involvement there, the progress

---

[3] Gen. Maxwell D. Taylor, former U.S. Ambassador to South Viet-Nam.

there, and our problems there, a good deal of which must necessarily be kept off the record.

We had a report from Ambassador Taylor that I found very interesting and I asked him to pass it on to the Members of the Senate and to the Members of the House, and no doubt he will meet with other groups in the days to come around the country, as he did over television yesterday.

Ambassador Harriman,[4] just returned from the Soviet Union, Yugoslavia, England, and other places, reviewed some of the discussions that he had with world leaders—Mr. Kosygin, Marshal Tito, and others.

He was followed by Eugene Black,[5] who discussed the proposal I made in my Johns Hopkins speech [6] concerning the Asian Bank, and the progress that the Asians themselves had made in connection with that plan, the various countries they had visited. He reviewed the commitment of the Japanese, of various Asian countries, the commitment of the United States—all of those based on the formation of the Bank.

He discussed his visits in Western Europe, his hopes of obtaining cooperation with other nations, and he expressed the hope that it was close to the day when we could anticipate to move forward on the Asian Bank, involving $1 billion capital to be subscribed by the various nations—$200 million by the United States, $200 million by the Japanese, and $200 million by other Asian nations and other countries yet to make a commitment.

He was followed by the distinguished Ambassador to the United Nations, who reviewed the various conversations he had with the Secretary General, with the representatives of many other countries, letters he had

presented to the Secretary General from the President and letters which were delivered to me from the Secretary General concerning our various proposals through the years and our specific invitation extended the other day in my press conference to any country who had any idea to make, any suggestions they could think of. And he went into some detail. He expressed his views and his hopes.

He was followed by Secretary McNamara, who reviewed the military strength there, what we are doing, what their plans are, what the conditions are, as he sees it, today. And he went over the maps with them, picked out certain locations where our boys are located, where they had certain establishments.

He was followed by Secretary Rusk, who indicated the political situation as he saw it there, the efforts we had made in the past, the efforts that were now going on in connection with an attempt to go carry out my request to engage in unconditional discussion, and that we would be willing to meet with any people, or any government of any kind, anywhere who offered a reasonable hope for peace.

That took a little less than an hour. And the next hour was devoted largely to questions. Those questions were free and forthcoming from many members of both parties. There was a fine exchange, very constructive—no argument or debating, but there were searching and penetrating questions.

Senator Aiken made an observation, as the ranking member of the Foreign Relations Committee that was present, about the briefing itself and the efficiency of it and the fullness of the information.

Senator Mansfield also made a comment as the leader of the Senate and we adjourned.

We'll have a meeting similar to that this afternoon. I will be meeting the leaders

---

[4] W. Averell Harriman, Ambassador at Large.

[5] Eugene R. Black, adviser to the President on southeast Asian social and economic development and former President of the World Bank.

[6] See Item 172.

personally at 5 o'clock in the House to talk over a legislative program. We have some bills that are still pending there. Some will be reported out of committees, and we want to check on the status of them.

And then we will meet the balance of the Senate. Tomorrow we will meet with the Senate leaders—Democratic leaders— concerning the schedule of certain bills, how they are getting along. Then we will meet with the Members of the House of Representatives.

I anticipate around the 17th of August that we will meet with 100 business, labor, and professional leaders at the White House, and we will have this same type of exchange. I pointed out this morning that we have a policy here that we want to be as accessible as possible, but at the same time it must be measured, and any of them that wanted to do so could ask questions and make observations, and those that did not have time to, I would be glad to receive their views in writing. And we will do that with the leaders that meet with us on August 17th for dinner, as we did the last meeting we had with them.

We have these meetings periodically. We will pass the cigar box. From 15 to 20 of them will draw out of it—all of them will draw a slip—15 to 20 of them will be talkers, the rest of them will be writers. The ones that draw the talking slip will get up and make an observation of from 2, 3, or 4 minutes, and some questions. The ones that draw the writing slip will write us their views.

All of those that attended the last meeting that drew writing slips have written us letters, very constructive letters. We had them evaluated by the Secretary of State, the Secretary of Defense, USIA.

General Taylor was present this morning to answer any questions that they wanted to ask him.

The first meeting of the business, labor, doctors, educators, and the professional representatives will be on the 17th. We will finish Congress this week.

This is not unusual or unique for this Administration. We have already met with the Senate twice this year, every Member of it in this session. We have met with all of the Members of the House, and we are going on the second round with them. We have 9:30 coffee and I guess we will have 5:30 coffee. I think we will wind up our meetings Wednesday.

I did not come in for a press conference. I don't want you to stay too long but I don't want to avoid any questions if you have some that are pertinent to the briefing. Everything I have said to you is on the record.

I think there was a good deal that was said that I don't want to go into. You can understand the reasons for it. I believe that these meetings are very, very helpful, as was the appearance of General Taylor this morning, and television yesterday. Without your feeling that you are getting too much information, I want to encourage the leaders in Government to be accessible and to give you their thoughts, and to tell you all they can about your Government without violating security.

I have asked Secretary Rusk and Secretary McNamara to be available to Congress at any time, any group that asked them to come to put that high on the list. Secretary McNamara testified last week over 20 hours. We hope next week he will be available to give some of his talents to Viet-Nam. He explained to the H o u s e Appropriations and Senate Appropriations. House Foreign Affairs will be Wednesday. Secretary Rusk did the same thing.

They are speaking tonight on television and I would invite your attention to it at 10 o'clock.

Are there any questions?

QUESTIONS

THE SITUATION IN VIET-NAM

[3.] Q. Mr. President, could you characterize, without violating security, how things are going in Viet-Nam now?

THE PRESIDENT. Well, General Taylor this morning outlined the things that he considered optimistic and made him optimistic—a long list of them; and the things where he is pessimistic. I would say that these are well-balanced. There are serious problems there, but also things that are better in a good many situations than we anticipated.

Q. Mr. President, do you draw any conclusions from the apparent dropoff in the Viet Cong incidents in recent weeks?

THE PRESIDENT. No. I don't want to speculate on those. Everything I say here is being read by them. They have swung rather wildly and they have suffered some substantial reverses, as you know. On the other hand, I don't want that statement to indicate—and I wouldn't want it thought—that I spoke very glowingly here today, and so forth, because I don't intend to do that.

I think you must understand what I said the other day that I don't want to get into figures anymore. One of the most noted leaders of this country said to me the other day that I must constantly be aware when I am talking to you that everything about our Government is not bad, and I am not necessarily on trial, and we are not criminals here to have to argue and reply on every course of action, and that we need not explain any more of the details than is necessary to see the public has a reasonable knowledge.

Because when you overdo it, when you go further than you should—as this experienced man said to me in a report I received—you give the enemy information they shouldn't have, and that includes the numbers and the dates and the hours that we are doing certain things. And I spent a long time talking to Mr. Zorthian,[7] the Chairman of the USIA Advisory Committee, Mr. Moyers, and Mr. Chancellor[8] today about how we could make the truth—all the truth—available as quickly as we could here and there without endangering Merriman Smith's[9] boy, who is out there. We have a joint obligation. We are trying to do that. And General Taylor might say it is generally more encouraging than it would be if one just followed the news dispatches each day. He went into that.

I think that there are a good many things happening out there that would give you pride, and we try to point them up, although the more dramatic things are the bombs, the number of planes, and the weight of the bombs, and things of that kind; and not the number of children that are in school—there are five times as many as there were—and not the number of lives that have been saved, and not the success that our specialization program is having in certain areas.

So, we are trying to see that all of those things are balanced but it is difficult, as you know.

Bill Moyers gave me an illustration. The other day, with Mr. King and Mr. Farmer[10] and others, we reviewed the personnel problem, and the employment of Negroes earn-

---

[7] Barry Zorthian, Minister-Counselor for Information at the U.S. Embassy in Saigon.

[8] John W. Chancellor, Director of the Voice of America.

[9] Merriman Smith of United Press International.

[10] Martin Luther King, Jr., President of the Southern Christian Leadership Conference, and James Farmer, National Director of the Congress of Racial Equality.

ing $10,000 a year had increased 8 percent. And there have been 20 major acts signed in just the last 2 weeks—19 supplementing the Civil Rights bill, and things of that type that we have reported on, and that they have reported, but those things don't make the news that one demonstration makes outside of the gate.

Ambassador Lodge[11] will be with us again this afternoon and will meet with us in all of these meetings, and the economic and political phases of it are going to be stressed and increased every way we can, as I outlined in my speech before the cartoonists and as Ambassador Goldberg[12] has outlined the last few days.

EXTENT OF CONGRESSIONAL APPROVAL OF
VIET-NAM POLICY

[4.] Q. Mr. President, there have been various reports that there are members of your own party in Congress who disagreed privately with the Viet-Nam policy. You just had these congressional meetings today. You will be having another this afternoon. Just what is your finding?

THE PRESIDENT. I find that there are members of my party, and the other party, and my country, that frequently disagree with me on a good many things. I don't think that it is private. I have not found anything that told me something that they have not told you first. I would say that we don't seek uniformity in this country, and we don't ever reach unanimity on matters that are as difficult as the situation we have in Viet-Nam.

We have asked Congress for an expression and a delegation of authority, which we have,

and which we are exercising as Commander in Chief. We asked them in August for it and they debated it and they acted, and we did not ask it for 3 weeks, or 3 months, or 3 years. We asked it to cover the situation there.[13]

It is very comprehensive. I did not go into it with you. I am prepared, if you want to, but I referred to it this morning. It goes just as far as we know how to go in investing the authority which the President already has. It says that the Congress approved and supports the determination of the President to repel any armed attack. I guess it could have said any and all, but it says any, and to take all necessary measures. And then it says the United States is prepared, as the President determines, to take all necessary steps, including the use of Armed Forces, to assist any member—that is, South Viet-Nam—in the defense of freedom.

And there is a very good clause that I want to remind you of. Again, I don't want to encourage anybody, or excite anybody, but we carefully put it in. The resolution expires when we find the solution to it, or it may be terminated by concurrent resolution any time the Congress desires, without the President's approval, if somebody wanted to do it.

Now, we had the leaders in and asked them when we needed some additional money whether we should ask for that money or whether we should use our transfer authority. This was some time ago. It involved $70 million or $80 million of economic and military aid. And the leadership was of the opinion that it was good to have it debated then and brought up then and to have hearings at that time and considered.

---

[11] Henry Cabot Lodge, U.S. Ambassador to South Viet-Nam.
[12] Arthur J. Goldberg, U.S. Representative to the United Nations.

[13] The joint resolution to promote the maintenance of international peace and security in southeast Asia was approved by the President on August 10, 1964 (Public Law 88–408; 78 Stat. 384).

And we said it was immaterial to us, that we would follow their guidance. So we submitted it again and it was debated, and some said we submitted it for the purpose of involving somebody, to put them on the spot. We just followed the leadership's—both parties—suggestion. And that was done.

We did not need to go to Congress this time for additional authority. But we have gone to the Armed Services Committee. We will go to the Foreign Relations Committee and explain what we are doing and subject ourselves to their cross-examination.

But the votes that we have had were 504 to 2 and 500-something to 10. And I would say that I have no indication that there will be a great deal of difficulty now. And I would warn any would-be hopeful enemy of the United States that they must not make the miscalculation that other people have made in the past to believe this country is divided, and that the course of action that has been established by three Presidents is going to be affected by dissent here or there.

Our policy has been enumerated. It has been established with Congress. It has been established by President Eisenhower, President Kennedy, and President Johnson, and we are there to stay. We are going to do what we need to do in order to resist aggression. The moment that aggression ceases, our resistance will cease. And I don't want any of them to say, because somebody makes a speech that questions this or questions that, or suggests a different method or different idea—that is the freedom of democracy and we welcome it—that there is any substantial division in our country. And, in my judgment, there is no substantial division in the Congress, and it is not confined to one party.

I pointed out this morning that Secretary Rusk had said to me, from one of his testifying periods before the Foreign Relations Committee, that if a foreign citizen had walked in and listened to that hearing with Senator Aiken, the ranking Republican there this morning, and Senator Fulbright, that he would have difficulty determining which party which one belonged to. Because they are not Democrats or Republicans in matters like this. They are Americans.

Reporter: Thank you, Mr. President.

413 Remarks at the Signing of a Bill Establishing a Five-Day Week for Postmasters. *August 9, 1965*

Mr. Speaker, Mr. Majority Leader, Mr. Postmaster General, Senator Monroney, Senator Carlson, Senator Yarborough, Chairman Dulski, Congressman Corbett, other distinguished Members of the Congress, the summer Government interns from Mount Holyoke College who are witnessing this ceremony, my employees, members of the press, boys and girls, ladies and gentlemen:

The bill that I will shortly sign culminates 15 years of effort by this Nation's postmasters to secure what most people have enjoyed all along—a 5-day week.

It is a just bill. And it is a bill that I am going to take a great deal of pleasure in signing.

I tried to get it amended. I talked to the majority leader and I talked to my own Senator to include Presidents. But I learned that I didn't have as much influence as John Gronouski had.

My only regret is that my cherished friend, the late, beloved Olin Johnston, is not here with us to see this bill that he authored become law. But he is well represented by one of the great Senators of our time—Senator Russell of South Carolina—who I am happy is here.

For more than 30 years most employees in the postal field service have had the benefit of a 40-hour week. But up until now, the postmasters had to mind the store without regard to hours. Postmasters, like Presidents, must be responsible for the function of their office 24 hours a day, 7 days a week. And that responsibility is in no way changed.

But the new law places a 5-day maximum on the number of days that postmasters will have to be physically present in their offices. And that will help some.

I am glad that I don't have to physically be present here 7 days, even though when I go to Camp David, most of the time I spend there is on Government business.

This bill has another feature which is important to clerks who, from time to time, must substitute for the postmasters who happen to be on leave. Present law regulations allow postmasters to delegate responsibility to assistant postmasters when the postmaster takes a Saturday off. Now, as any second or third class postmaster could readily tell you, clerical funds are not that easy to come by, and as a result it has been quite difficult in the past for postmasters in the small offices throughout the country to ever take a Saturday off, even if it's to go fishing, or spend it with the family, or to watch the local ball game.

And there was always another little problem. When the clerks took over for their boss, their hourly pay always dropped, so the clerks preferred to do the fishing and let the bosses do the fretting.

I suppose I ought to make one thing clear: This does not mean that post offices will be closed on Saturday while the postmaster is taking the day off. In other words, it simply establishes a long overdue system to permit postmasters to obtain some of the privileges enjoyed by most of their fellow Americans since the 1930's.

This bill will become effective the first day of the first pay period beginning on or after January 1, 1966. Even though after that date no postmaster will be required to work more than 40 hours a week, I am sure that being conscientious public servants, they will quite often put in more than 40 hours, considering the magnitude of their civic and their social responsibilities.

I know that Postmaster General Gronouski is as happy as I am that this bill has been enacted.

I want to again commend my own fine Senator, my friend, Senator Ralph Yarborough of Texas, Congressman Dulski, and all of their colleagues in both the House and the Senate, for their leadership in getting this bill enacted.

This will cost the Federal Government some money. We have some recommendations before the Congress that will add some more to our budget. We have made recommendations for pay raises, and I think there is even some talk that you might want to spend more money in that regard than we have recommended. And I shouldn't be surprised that you don't take some action along that line.

I do want to say to all of you that it is going to be pretty difficult for the President of the United States to be the first person to be the chief wrecker of a noninflationary wage and price policy. President Kennedy established some guidelines, and I have signed two military pay bills since I have been President, in 20 months. We had a substantial bill last year. We recommend one this year. And I am going to recommend one next year.

But I do hope that I am not confronted

with a request from the unions and from the employers of this country that say to me: Well, now, Mr. President, you are an employer and you decided that you could give *x*-percent increase and we think we ought to be allowed to have the same privilege that you have. Because if you do that, you are going to promote inflation, and our whole noninflationary price policy is going by the wayside. And I hope that the postmasters who will benefit from what we are doing today, and the other Federal employees who will benefit from the recommendations that we have made on all this legislation this year, will not ask for any special privileges over and above what we ask the rest of the country to follow.

It is wonderful to have you here in the White House. We are going to have the signing of the housing bill tomorrow. We had the signing of the National Institutes of Health bill today. It is glorious that we can be here in this peaceful attitude and be making so much progress with, I think, the best Congress that has ever assembled. And I see friends of mine like Senator Carlson, that I have known for many years, Senator

Fong and other members of the Republican Party here today. I almost hesitate to mention Republican Party—I wouldn't mention it except that I want to point out that they are here not as Republicans, and Senator Yarborough not as a Democrat—that we are all Americans and that is what has made this Congress so outstanding. Most of our votes have been based not on party, but what is good for the country. And I commend every person who has participated in this fine program.

Thank you very much.

NOTE: The President spoke at 5:45 p.m. in the Rose Garden at the White House. In his opening words he referred to Representative John W. McCormack of Massachusetts, Speaker of the House of Representatives, Senator Mike Mansfield of Montana, majority leader of the Senate, Postmaster General John A. Gronouski, Senator A. S. Mike Monroney of Oklahoma, Senator Frank Carlson of Kansas, Senator Ralph Yarborough of Texas, Representative Thaddeus J. Dulski of New York, and Representative Robert J. Corbett of Pennsylvania.

During his remarks the President referred to Olin Johnston, Senator from South Carolina 1945–1965, Senator Donald Russell of South Carolina, and Senator Hiram L. Fong of Hawaii.

As enacted, the bill (H.R. 1771) is Public Law 89–116 (79 Stat. 449).

414 Telegram to General Eisenhower on the 91st Anniversary of the Birth of Herbert Hoover. *August 10, 1965*

ON THIS 91st anniversary of the birth of President Hoover, may I ask you to convey my warmest personal good wishes to the members of his family, friends and all others assembled today to pay tribute to this great and good American.

Like yourself, Mr. President, Herbert Hoover was a man larger than party and partisanship. It is gratifying to me, as I know it is for you, to see history recognize and honor this President whose life and works so well epitomized the humanitarian-

ism, dignity, love of freedom and devotion to peace of the American people.

Over the years of my friendship with him, I found President Hoover to be one of the wisest and most inspiring men I have been privileged to know. As a Nation we have much to profit from remembering the uncomplaining selflessness of Herbert Hoover's life of service as well as from the memory of the words he so wisely spoke.

For it was President Hoover who told Americans 35 years ago that, "Peace requires unremitting, courageous campaigns, laid with strategy and carried on successfully on a hundred fronts and sustained in the spirit and from the hearts of every individual in every town and village of our country."

This is the essential spirit with which we must and do face the challenges confronting us now in keeping from administration to administration the sacred honor of our Nation pledged to those peoples around the world willing to defend the treasure of human liberty.

As you know, there is now on my desk legislation designating the birthplace of Herbert Hoover as a national historical site. I am not signing it on this anniversary because

of the attendance of so many of those closest to President Hoover at the ceremonies in West Branch. But it is my hope that you, members of the family and others identified with his service and with his party will shortly join me at the White House to honor President Hoover still further when this measure is signed into law as a symbol of affection and respect for him.

LYNDON B. JOHNSON

[General Dwight D. Eisenhower, West Branch, Iowa.]

NOTE: An act to establish the Herbert Hoover National Historical Site in the State of Iowa was approved by the President on August 12, 1965 (see Item 420).

415   Remarks at the Signing of the Housing and Urban Development Act.   *August* 10, 1965

Mr. Vice President, distinguished Speaker McCormack, Senator Mansfield, Senator Sparkman, Congressman Patman, distinguished Members of the Congress, distinguished Governors and mayors, and friends:

This is a very proud and very gratifying occasion. I am very proud and I am very privileged to welcome you today to the first house of the land—the house that belongs to all of the American people. I am gratified, as you are, that we could come together to sign into law a measure which will take us many long strides nearer the goal that has been the dream and the vision of every generation of Americans. That is the goal of honoring what a very great President, Franklin D. Roosevelt, 21 years ago expressed as "the right of every family to a decent home."

From Plymouth Rock to Puget Sound, the first priority of the men and women who settled this vast and this blessed continent was, first of all, to put a roof over the heads

of their family. And that priority has never, and can never, change.

I am so happy this morning to see the great and distinguished Mayor of New York here because it was his father who pioneered the housing legislation in this country. And here on the platform with me is one of those who joined with him—the very able and distinguished Senator from Louisiana. It took a lot of courage for him to stand on some of those bills. He got in with Bob Wagner and Bob Taft and he got in the middle between those two, and it did take courage to stand there.

Many elements mattered to the success and the stability of our great American society. Education matters a great deal. Health matters. Jobs matter. Equality of opportunity and individual dignity matter very much.

But legislation and labors in all of these fields can never succeed unless and until every family has the shelter and the security, the integrity and the independence, and the dignity and the decency of a proper home.

For me, this is not a belief that comes recently. It is a conviction, and it is a passion, to which I was born 57 years ago this month in a humble home on the banks of a small river in Central Texas.

Men may forget many memories of their childhood. But many of you know—as I know—that no man and no woman ever grows too old or too successful to forget the memory of a childhood home that was without lights, and that was without water, and that was without covering on the floor. And I have never forgotten.

The first great effort, the first great reward of my public service was to secure for my little congressional district, as a young Congressman, the Nation's first public housing project that President Roosevelt signed in the 1930's. And Bob's father was there at that allocation. What I sought then for the people of one city—Austin, Texas—I am determined as President that we shall seek and we shall obtain for all the people of all the Nation.

We have the resources in this country. We have the ingenuity. We have the courage. We have the compassion. And we must, in this decade, bring all of these strengths to bear effectively so that we can lift off the conscience of our affluent Nation the shame of slums and squalor, and the blight of deterioration and decay.

We must make sure that every family in America lives in a home of dignity and a neighborhood of pride, a community of opportunity and a city of promise and hope.

This legislation represents the single most important breakthrough in the last 40 years.

Only the Housing Act of 1949 approaches the significance of this measure. And in years to come, I believe this act will become known as the single most valuable housing legislation in our history.

The Housing and Urban Development Act of 1965 retains, and expands, and improves the best of the tested programs of the past.

It extends and gives new thrust to the FHA mortgage insurance program so that millions of Americans can come toward attainment of new homes in the future, as millions already have under that program in the past.

It opens the way for a more orderly and cohesive development of all of our suburbs; and it opens the door to thousands of our veterans who have been unable to obtain the benefits of a Federal housing program.

It extends and enlarges and improves the urban renewal program so that we can more effectively challenge and defeat the enemy of decay that exists in our cities.

It faces the changing challenge of rural housing. It continues the loan programs to assure the needed dormitories on our college campuses, and decent housing at decent costs for the elderly and the handicapped and those of lower income.

But the importance of the bill is not only that it retains and improves the best of good and traditional programs; it is a landmark bill because of its new ideas.

Foremost and uppermost of these is the program of assistance for the construction and the rehabilitation of housing for the elderly and for families of low income—the people who live in the most wretched conditions in our slums and our blighted neighborhoods.

The conception of this fine program, endorsed by this fine Congress, calls for the best in cooperation between Government and free enterprise. I am so happy to see so many members of the building industry and the trade unions and our free enterprise system—that has made us the strongest nation in all the world—here to honor us with their presence this morning.

This imperative housing will be built under the sponsorship of private organizations. It will make use of private money, and it will be managed by private groups. With supplements paid by their Government, the private builders will be able to move into the low-income housing field which they have not been able to penetrate or to serve effectively in the past.

Furthermore, this legislation responds to the urgent needs of our cities. It offers Federal assistance to the cities and communities of our Nation to help pay the cost of essential public works.

And finally, this legislation meets our compelling responsibility for giving attention to the environment in which Americans live. Grants are provided for the acquisition of open spaces, for the development of parks, for the construction of recreational facilities, and for the beautification of urban areas.

This measure votes "no" on "America the Ugly"—and it votes "yes" on preserving, for our posterity, "America the Beautiful."

The promise and the portent of this legislation cannot be justly described in the limited time we have this morning. But there is embodied in this legislation that generosity of vision, that breadth of approach, that magnitude of effort, with which we must meet all of our challenges here in America.

So, I am very proud to congratulate and to salute those outstanding Members of Congress whose influence and whose leadership have helped to achieve this landmark today. There is Senator John Sparkman—the son of a tenant farmer, and still the tenant farm-

ers' friend, as this bill reflects—who has done perhaps as much or more in America than any living legislator.

There are others whose study and understanding of housing has helped us much. I would like to name all of them but that would take too long. But I must not overlook Senator Paul Douglas of Illinois who is here, Senator Edmund Muskie from Maine, Senator George Aiken of Vermont. On the House side there was the great leader of my delegation in the Congress, my longtime friend and the cherished friend of my father ahead of me, Congressman Wright Patman. He has always been a champion and always been faithful to the people. There is Congressman Barrett, whose services have meant so much. There is Congressman Widnall, who has worked now years in a row with Congressmen Patman and Barrett to try to give this Nation good bills.

I would like to express my appreciation to the Governors and the mayors, especially the great mayor of New York, Bob Wagner; the great mayor of Chicago, Dick Daley; and all of the others who have been of so much help to me.

And I just cannot overlook being grateful to the constructive role of the Nation's home builders, under the leadership of the patriot, Bernie Boutin.

And last, but certainly not least, foremost is the leader of us all in this field—the modest, retiring, and able administrator, Bob Weaver, who finds not much satisfaction in the compliments paid him, or even the recognition accorded him by his superiors, but who finds ample satisfaction in the achievements that come his way. And, this bill is a monument to him.

Now, this is not the last housing bill that we shall need and it is not going to be the last that we shall pass.

For I pledge to you that we shall do all that must be done to fulfill our commitment—and the Vice President and I have made it in every State in this Union. And he is going to stand by my side here and throughout the States of the Union to see that we do our best to try to get every American in every family living his life not with the haunted memory of a dilapidated and degraded hovel that he must call home, but with a happy memory of a decent and a dignified home worthy of a free and just society, where a man can enjoy the privacy of his family and can help to build a stronger America, a more profitable and peaceful America, and, finally, something we all want—a more beautiful America.

Thank you very much.

NOTE: The President spoke at 12:02 p.m. in the Rose Garden at the White House. In his opening words he referred to Vice President Hubert H. Humphrey, Representative John W. McCormack of Massachusetts, Speaker of the House of Representatives, Senator Mike Mansfield of Montana, majority leader of the Senate, Senator John Sparkman of Alabama, and Representative Wright Patman of Texas.

During his remarks the President referred to, among others, Mayor Robert F. Wagner of New York City and his father, Robert F. Wagner, Senator from New York 1927–1949, Senator Allen J. Ellender of Louisiana, Robert A. Taft, Senator from Ohio 1939–1953, Representative William A. Barrett of Pennsylvania, Representative William B. Widnall of New Jersey, Mayor Richard J. Daley of Chicago, Bernard L. Boutin, Executive Vice President of the National Association of Home Builders and former Administrator of the General Services Administration, and Robert C. Weaver, Administrator of the Housing and Home Finance Agency.

As enacted, the Housing and Urban Development Act of 1965 is Public Law 89–117 (79 Stat. 451).

416 Statement by the President in Response to Reports on the Federal-State Program of Vocational Rehabilitation. *August* 10, 1965

I AM making public the attached reports from Secretary Celebrezze and Commissioner Switzer so that the public may be fully familiar with the valuable work being done in this country to help our disabled citizens become active and useful citizens.

I can think of no better example of what this administration is trying to accomplish for the American people than the Federal-State program of vocational rehabilitation.

However difficult the circumstances, whatever the burdens of poverty, whatever the deficiencies in educational opportunity that exist today, we must and we will find ways to offer full opportunity for a useful and satisfying life for all Americans.

If we can do this for 135,000 of our people who, along with other problems, face the obstacle of a serious physical or mental handicap, then we can do it for other people as well. That is our goal.

NOTE: The reports of Secretary of Health, Education, and Welfare Anthony J. Celebrezze, dated August 5, and of Commissioner of Vocational Rehabilitation Mary Switzer, dated August 4, were made public by the White House on August 10. They stated that in fiscal year 1965 almost 135,000 men and women had been rehabilitated, an increase of nearly 13 percent over the previous year. The reports noted that the total represented 4,000 more disabled people than the States had previously estimated.

The reports are printed in the Weekly Compilation of Presidential Documents (vol. 1, pp. 73, 74).

417   Remarks at the Signing of the Saline Water Conversion Act.   *August 11, 1965*

Senator Anderson, Senator Jackson, Senator Kuchel, Congressman Aspinall, Congressman Saylor, Governors Hughes, Scranton, Terry, and Rockefeller, Members of the Cabinet, Members of Congress, my friends:

I am very delighted to see so many Members of the House and many of my friends in the Senate come here this morning.

There is always a certain amount of cynicism among members of the executive branch and, I guess, sometimes among even members of the press about the productiveness of the Congress. I will measure my words when I say that over the past several weeks Congress has sent to the executive department, to my desk for signature, what appears to me to be an unprecedented procession of legislative measures which can only be described as truly historic and which I think is a tribute to every Member of both the House and Senate, of both parties.

It is my own studied and considered judgment, however, that this bill that you are witnessing being signed this morning will be the most historic of all of them: not for what it provides but rather for what it promises, not for what it accomplishes but rather for what it symbolizes.

True, this is a research and development bill—and it is only that. This legislation will not, by itself, build a single desalting plant in this country. But this is a commitment—the step across the threshold toward the breakthrough that must and will come, in my judgment, during the last half of the 1960's.

I may or may not be the most optimistic person in America about the progress we can make on desalting the seas, but I am, and I intend to remain, the most determined man that we shall make the great breakthroughs before the calendar turns to 1970.

I believe today what I believed in 1957 about space: that the greatest mistake the political system of a nation can make is to underestimate the pace of this century's advance of human knowledge and of this century's changing capabilities.

We need this research. We need this study. We need the experimentation that this bill provides—but we need to do more than spend all our time just learning.

So what does that mean? It means the time has come to set our sights, to pick our targets, and to act. For if we succeed, our success could well change the condition of man all around the world.

We have lingered too long under the impression that desalting sea water is a far out and a far distant goal. Since the dawn of time, every drop of water that man has drunk or used has been desalted in Nature's own still.

Nature's system has been erratic—and we have spent and we are spending billions to overcome many costly and many cruel uncertainties.

What can we do? What must we do? Well, now, the thing we can do is to free mankind from Nature's tyranny by setting out to produce water when and where we need it at a price that we can afford.

And in doing that we are going to need all the skill and all the ingenuity of modern science and modern industry. But I think the time has never been so ripe to get going on this kind of a job. We have new resources of abundant energy that can provide the power that this will require. And what was impossible and inconceivable yesterday is very near to reality today. And I want this Nation to lead the effort to close this gap—not in the next 50 years but in the next 5 years.

I would, therefore, lay out before the talents of our industry and science and institutions of higher learning, and our leaders of this Nation, these challenges this morning and these goals:

1. That plans be developed for constructing by 1970 desalting plants that will bridge the gap between the 1 million gallon per day plants that we have and the 100 million gallon per day plant that we must have.

That is first.

2. That we aim at having by 1968—or sooner—plants from 1 to 10 million gallon daily capacity to meet the needs of all of our smaller towns and cities. And I would add that, hopefully, such small, efficient plants may someday be economical for individual farms to use in desalting brackish water from their own wells.

3. That we realize that the seas are not our only recourse and that we aim to make it feasible to mine, desalt, and put to productive use the brackish groundwater which underlies more than 2 million square miles of the United States—all the way from the Appalachians to the Rockies.

4. That as rapidly as we develop economic desalting plants, we be prepared to share our technology with other countries where desalting offers the best answer to their local water problems.

Now desalting is not a dream. Three of our cities, ships at sea, the oil fields of other lands already depend upon desalting plants. We have only to learn to do these things at a price that we can afford—and I am convinced that we can learn them before this decade ends.

The program authorized by this bill will help us to learn—first for our thirsty cities and industries, and then someday for agriculture.

A millenium ago, in what is now the great State of Arizona, there were Indians who built extensive water works, as we ourselves build them now. They irrigated the lands that are now desert. But when the drought came and their works were of no value, the Indians disappeared, remembered in history only as "the people nobody knows."

Well, in our Nation, water has long been treated by many as the concern only of the farmer and the rancher. But we are beginning to learn better. In our complex and concentrated urban economy and society, water today, as we meet here, has never had more meaning. The drought being experienced now in our most populous region reminds us anew that we cannot and must not rely alone on building bigger reservoirs and longer pipelines, or grander schemes of waterworks to supply this essential of life.

I remember a few years ago when we had had a great drought in the Southwest for some 5 or 6 years, and the then great President, President Eisenhower, was very concerned about it. And he flew to the south plains of Texas, and Amarillo, and the Oklahoma area, and he traveled over it and showed his concern, and called together people as we are calling our people together here. There weren't many of our metropolitan leaders very interested in that situation. It was just the cowman that couldn't get water for his stock. But since then there is not a city in that State that hasn't awakened—and the sleeping giants are now on the move. So we can, and because we can, we really must develop the capacity to produce water and to produce it when and to produce it where we need it at a price we can afford.

I believe that we will succeed. I have a vision that such success could be one of history's most vital contributions to the cause of peace among nations. Our water policy will greatly influence our foreign policy.

Many share the credit for this landmark legislation that is before us—Senators Anderson, Jackson, and Kuchel, all of whom serve with distinction on the Interior Committee of the Senate, Congressman Aspinall, the distinguished chairman of the House committee and an authority in this field himself, Congressman Rogers, Congressman Saylor, Secretary Udall, Chairman Seaborg of the Atomic Energy Commission, and my own Science Adviser, the very able Dr. Hornig.

I am proud now to sign this bill into law to mark the beginning of what I hope will be a new era of national effort and national achievement. And I particularly welcome the distinguished chief executives of other States who are here to help us start on this new program this morning and, a little later in the morning, to help us explore ways and means for facing up to an emergency that we have now. And to the mayors and to

the Governors and to the other officials who have come here to meet with us, I say thank you. You are mighty welcome.

NOTE: The President spoke at 11:45 a.m. in the Rose Garden at the White House. In his opening words he referred to Senator Clinton P. Anderson of New Mexico, Senator Henry M. Jackson of Washington, Senator Thomas H. Kuchel of California, Representative Wayne N. Aspinall of Colorado, Representative John P. Saylor of Pennsylvania, Governor Richard J. Hughes of New Jersey, Governor William W. Scranton of Pennsylvania, Governor Charles L. Terry, Jr., of Delaware, and Governor Nelson A. Rockefeller of New York.

During his remarks the President referred to Representative Walter Rogers of Texas, Secretary of the Interior Stewart L. Udall, Glenn T. Seaborg, Chairman of the Atomic Energy Commission, and Donald F. Hornig, Special Assistant to the President for Science and Technology.

As enacted, the Saline Water Conversion Act is Public Law 89-118 (79 Stat. 509).

A report by Secretary Udall and Jack Valenti, Special Assistant to the President, following a tour of the Demonstration Plant of the Office of Saline Water at Freeport, Tex., was made public by the White House on August 5, 1965. The text of the report is printed in the Weekly Compilation of Presidential Documents (vol. 1, p. 48).

418 Remarks at a Meeting of the Water Emergency Conference. *August 11, 1965*

Secretary Udall, distinguished Governors, Members of the Cabinet, Chairman Seaborg, Mr. Ackley:

First, I am happy that I have been able to hear some of the discussion. I deeply regret that I have not heard more, and I do want to have you share with me some of your private thinking. If it is agreeable, and you don't mind the quality of the lunch, why, we'll just have lunch together when we get through.

You may be a little late to your next meeting, but the folks over in the other wing are accustomed to having guests on short notice—as I know they are in your capitals—and so if you will bear in mind anything

that you want to raise, we will do it during the lunch hour.

Second, apropos of the very excellent suggestion made by Governor Rockefeller, who has talked to me about this a number of times, I followed his atomic plant with great interest. He's discussed that with me, and I hope our people can be helpful in connection with the matching that he's been discussing. I rather doubt that there will be any comprehensive appropriations possible, in the next few weeks that we will be here, to carry out suggestions that you have made, although I will ask the Director of the Budget and the Secretary of the Interior and the head of the Corps of Engineers to get any very specific ideas you have, after these teams make their visits, and be available for our budget hearings, which will begin September, October, and November in anticipation of the Congress' return in January.

I called you here today in the face of a 4-year drought that is unequaled in the Northeast section of our country. As I said earlier, I have known drought in the Southwest and I have seen what it can do, and I still have a grateful heart for what our then President Eisenhower did to help us in that emergency. And I want to do everything that the White House can do to work with you in this one.

In other sections of this Nation, in times past, the challenge of the drought has been met. The Northeast, though, is facing a serious drought for the first time, really, in its history. And I am confident that the steps that we can take together in the challenge that does face us, that we will somehow meet the test and that the challenge will be overcome.

Now, this is a time for action. It is a time for Federal action, but that never substitutes for State or local action, as you all point out when the mayors meet and the Governors meet and we talk about States' rights and local rights, and so forth. And it is not any substitute for private action.

So, the big thing we must start out with is that we must act together, if that is possible, and I know with this group we can. We must act together, first, to solve the immediate crisis that is facing us. We must act together to prepare for a possible fifth year of drought—as you just said.

We must act together to assure our citizens of the Northeast, and their children, that the supply of water that they need for their industry, and their health, and their recreation is assured and guaranteed so far into the future as we can see now.

So, as a result, I have already tried to mobilize the Federal Government into action. The Department of Agriculture, the Department of Health, Education, and Welfare, the Department of the Interior, the Federal Power Commission, the Corps of Engineers, the Office of Civilian Defense, the Office of Emergency Planning—headed by one of your most popular and able former Governors, Governor Ellington—are already focusing their efforts on the problems in the Northeast.

To continue to fulfill that responsibility, I am directing the Secretary of the Interior today to dispatch, tonight, water crisis teams to the five cities that are represented here today.

I have asked Secretary Udall to make hard and fast decisions immediately and on the spot to assist each affected community.

I have directed the Secretary of the Army and the Chief of Army Engineers to move as rapidly as possible on all vital water supply projects in the area.

And how does that happen?

Number one, we're going to add $400,000 to the Tocks Island reservoir project in the Delaware River Basin immediately, and this will quicken the construction of that project by at least a year.

Second, we're going to add $400,000 to the Beltzville, Pennsylvania, project, and that will greatly expedite construction there.

Third, we're going to add $100,000 to the reservoir project at Blue March, Pennsylvania, so we can speed up the planning and design there.

Fourth, we're going to add $150,000 to planning a $5 million water supply addition to the Prompton Reservoir project.

Fifth, we're going to begin planning a new $11 million water supply project at Trexler Reservoir.

I have asked my Water Resources Council to consult with each of you on a daily basis and to report to the President on any additional action that they think can be taken. Should the Council find that additional White House action is required, I want you to know that I am prepared to do whatever is necessary and to do it immediately.

Now, water problems are no longer limited to manmade State or municipal boundaries. These problems are regional and we recognize them as such.

Many years ago, I had a study made—one of the first in the Nation—of a regional water problem we had. We had to take into consideration the effect on many sections, many regions, many States, and some dozen rivers, before we could have a real comprehensive water plan. And as a result of that survey, we have developed one. So, I am, therefore, initiating a $4 million comprehensive water resource planning survey for the entire Northeast—all the way from Virginia to Maine.

Now, for the long range, I have directed Secretary-designate Gardner of Health, Education, and Welfare, and my very able and imaginative—I hope he did not get me out on these goals too far; I hope they are realistic—Science Adviser, Dr. Hornig, to start to work with you, within 6 months to have a plan of action for pollution control.

I am asking Secretary Udall to work with Dr. Hornig and Dr. Ackley, of my Council of Economic Advisers, and Dr. Seaborg to examine the potential of desalting for the Northeast, and to give me a complete report on the potentialities and possibilities there within 6 months.

As Nelson told you—as you have observed—I have just signed a bill—I hope you still have that pen to take home with you. I am increasing the funds for the desalting program by $185 million—that's 175 more than it was last week. They had me down to $10 million for a period there.

I know you are really interested in this whole field, but in the field of conservation, in the field of highway improvement—sometimes called beautification—in the field of pollution, we need all the leadership we can get. We don't need it here at the White House. We need it in the House and the Senate and in the committees that have those matters under their control.

I hope that you will take a look at that situation. We have a stronger pollution bill in the Senate than we had in the House. We have it in conference now, and it is in conference, and we want it to come out of that conference, and I beseech you and I implore you and I invite you to render me the same kind of effective assistance in that field that Governor Scranton did when Appalachia was pending.

The pollution bill, this highway improvement bill, the conservation measures that apply to your States—those decisions are being made right this session. They are going to be decided in the next 3 weeks. And I think they will all be decided favorably, but maybe more expeditiously and maybe a little more favorably if your views are known to your people from your States.

Now, top priority is going to be given to every one of these problems that exists in the Northeast. You are in trouble and when you are in trouble we're in trouble. And we are going to be there to help.

I have told you that this is what we can do and this is what we will do.

But water supply really is a local responsibility. Only you are going to be able to conserve the water that you now have. There is not much I can do about the third of Bob Wagner's water that we don't know where it is going.

You must devise and you must enforce the necessary procedures to avoid the waste of water by leakage or by unnecessary use. And you can do a good deal about the unnecessary pollution. The pollution that is taking place in this country, and the effect that a few industrial plants are having on the future of our country, is absolutely disgraceful. I don't want to put it on your doorstep. I'm putting it on mine here—right here on the Potomac, where George Washington threw his dollar. It is disgraceful.

I was out on it last night and you can hardly go down the river without reflecting and wondering why we have been so short-sighted these years. And it has got to stop. We have got to do something about it. And good men, and great men, and wise men, and good Americans, like you, can do something about it.

You can do it in your leadership in your States, and you can do it in your speeches, and you can do it here in Washington. I need all the help I can get in that field.

I have been getting a lot of it. Your brother is giving a lot to it. I want to give you at lunch a book that he has had published in that very field, showing some of the beauties of America and also some of the shame.[1]

So, as leaders of your States, and as leaders of your cities, I think that if you do nothing else out of this White House Conference except go back and urge your citizens to use the water they now have, but use it with prudence, and use it wisely, and use it without contaminating it and without polluting it—and to say to these giants and titans, who may not have had the appreciation of all the conservation angles that some professor would have, that you take a new look at

what you are doing to the water that belongs to all the people. It is not your private water to do what you want to do with it.

So, no one will solve this problem by himself. No one single program is going to solve it. But the expertise of the Federal Government is available to you, and it is going to help you and it is going to try to provide what leadership it can.

Comprehensive planning is available to you and it can help you, and we are going to use it. Antipollution and desalting programs can help. And if you will help me get the pollution bill through the Congress, the desalting bill and the appropriation bill to supply it, well, we will give you some matching—we can and we will help.

The Senate passed $200 million and the House was ready for $10 million, and we compromised with them for $185 million—but you understand those things. That one is behind us. But this Conference might have had something to do with helping along a little bit on that.

These programs must be welded together by men working together. And they must work together into an effective weapon to end the current crisis, and to prevent any such crises from developing again.

Now there are some much more ambitious programs that could be developed. Where they are realistic I will ask our people, within the limits of our resources, to try to help match you on a local and State basis to meet them.

We are going to have severe drains because of the new programs we are passing in other fields this year. I have signed at least 40 major bills in this session—more major bills have been signed, I think, than in any other period in the history of the Congress.

That is the work of the Congress. It is not

[1] Laurance S. Rockefeller, Chairman of the White House Conference on Natural Beauty held in Washington May 24–25, 1965. The book is entitled "Beauty for America—Proceedings of the White House Conference on Natural Beauty" (Government Printing Office, 1965, 782 pp.).

the work of anyone else. And you have sent these men to Congress. And they have acted as Americans.

I heard Dean Rusk say the other day he was going to the Foreign Relations Committee, and you could not tell when you were hearing Fulbright and Aiken—if you were a foreigner—which one was the Republican and which one was the Democrat. All you knew was that both of them were good Americans. And the Congress is pretty well functioning that way this year.

Some of our people don't always see things as we do, but we expect that. But these 40 bills are the fruits of their labor—and we still have 40 more to come. They are coming every day, right down the line.

We're going to have an Urban Affairs Department this afternoon. We're going to have a public works and area redevelopment bill this afternoon—I hope—unless I'm disappointed. They're voting in the House and Senate now.

But we do want, before we leave here, something that is important to you. Do you know that the tourist trade has picked up unbelievably abroad? And if you travel over some of our country you can see why people want to get away from it. Yet a few men are coming in and insisting that we keep these dirty little old signs up in these dirty little old towns, and that *this* is going to affect free enterprise, and *this* is going to do this and do that—while our tourist trade is picking up, and picking up, and picking up.

When I leave this meeting I'm going out to talk to the "See the U.S.A." group that is traveling the U.S.A., and try to see that we point up the glories of this country.

My wife has been going in one direction, my daughter has been going in another direction, and I hope, before the summer is over and Congress leaves, that I can go in another direction to illustrate "America the Beautiful."

And you Governors can contribute a great deal, not only by helping us with this present program that we are considering—how to make Pennsylvania and New Jersey and New York and Delaware and Texas more beautiful—but to conserve our resources and to help us conserve some of our dollars here at home, too.

Our net loss this year is going to be nearly $2 billion on tourists abroad—almost $2 billion—and that has got to be made up somewhere. It is one of our major problems. I know of no problem I have that is as important as the balance of payments problem.

I just wish that these States could evolve and develop their water supply and their rivers in such a way—their scenery and their parks and their concessions and their affairs, and other things—so as to be able to compete successfully with their sister States and their sister countries.

We don't want to ban any travel. We're *for* people traveling. We are not against them traveling abroad. We want them to see all the world. But we want to make our place so beautiful that we want them to see it, too.

So, if you will collect your papers and indulge me about 5 minutes—until I appear before the "U.S.A." group—we will explore this further at lunch. And I hope the Senators have returned by that time, if they have passed the bill. If they haven't, I hope they stay there until they do.

NOTE: The President spoke at 1:08 p.m. in the Fish Room at the White House before a conference of Governors and other officials from the drought-stricken Northeastern States. In his opening words he referred to Stewart L. Udall, Secretary of the Interior, Glenn T. Seaborg, Chairman of the Atomic Energy Commission, and Gardner Ackley, Chairman of the Council of Economic Advisers.

During his remarks the President referred to Governor Nelson A. Rockefeller of New York, Director of the Bureau of the Budget Charles L. Schultze, Director of the Office of Emergency Planning Buford Ellington, former Governor of Tennessee, Lt. Gen. William F. Cassidy, Chief of Army Engineers, Secretary of the Army Stephen Ailes, Secretary-designate of Health, Education, and Welfare John W. Gardner, Donald F. Hornig, Special Assistant to the President for Science and Technology, Governor William W. Scranton of Pennsylvania, Mayor Robert F. Wagner

of New York City, Secretary of State Dean Rusk, Senator J. W. Fulbright of Arkansas, and Senator George D. Aiken of Vermont.

For the President's remarks upon signing the Saline Water Conversion Act, see Item 417.

The Water Quality Act was approved by the President on October 2, 1965 (see Item 543).

The Highway Beautification Act of 1965 was approved by the President on October 22, 1965 (see Item 576).

See also Items 358, 434.

419 Remarks to the Members of the See the U.S.A. Committee.
August 11, 1965

OUT HERE in the Rose Garden our meetings are both happy and hot, and at this time of day it is more the latter than the former.

The Vice President told me that he had informed Bob Short that this job that he had would take a lot of toil and sweat, and it looks like today, at least half of that prophesy is being fulfilled.

I came out here for just a moment to say primarily that I thank you and I appreciate what you have done, and what you are willing to do, and what those that you speak for and represent—your stockholders and your management, and your employees—have tried to help us do. I am most grateful to each of you and for that matter, all of our travel industry in the United States, for your cooperation and for the support that you have given the See the U.S.A. program.

All Americans are really heirs of travelers who originally came here from far across the seas to cast their lot in this great country of ours. What we want now is for that tradition to be honored. We want Americans to travel. We want our friends from other lands to travel. Now we aren't trying to discourage travel anyplace—we never have. There have been some misconceptions in that regard. But we are trying to encourage more travel to see more of the wonders and

the beauties of this vast and marvelous land of ours.

And we feel in doing that we will not only build a better country and a better people, but we will also make great contributions to our own industry and to our own system.

We must, and we do, recognize that there is a great gap between what Americans spend on travel abroad and what visitors from other lands spend here. Most of us are rather competitive and I just hate to see us do so poorly from a competitive standpoint. I hate to see the balance weighed so heavily the other way.

Since you started talking about travel in the U.S.A., Mrs. Johnson hasn't been home a full week!

MRS. JOHNSON. And I have only just whetted my appetite.

THE PRESIDENT. And that is bad. I don't like that, but it is even worse when she's got my daughters traveling too. And Luci is enjoying it so much that she is going to some places for repeat performances, and now she's having to get a blonde wig in order to go.

Lynda started out at Grasshopper, Arizona, and went to Wyoming, Utah, and Colorado and all those beautiful scenes of the West. Luci has almost taken up residence in a good part of the Midwest that she has made her travels. Mrs. Johnson has been doing a good deal of it.

And I hope before the year is out, when Congress gets out of here, I can travel some, too.

This gap that I was talking to you about, where they were doing a better job competitively than you are doing—and I don't know why a travel bureau, airline, hotel, or a different kind of chef can make their things look so much better to our people than you can make them to look to our people—but that gap amounted to $1.6 billion last year, and it is going to be considerably larger this year. You are going to lose almost $2 billion more than comes this way, and that is something that you are going to have to face up to and cope with.

This Cabinet task force that is headed by our popular and very able Vice President has done a great deal to help us put this problem in focus. I don't know how many other people he has got traveling, but I told you he has got all the folks around the White House traveling. He has a secretary out in New England this week, going up to see that area. But the most striking fact and the most significant fact is that we have grossly neglected the potential of our tourism and our travel here at home. We have concentrated on selling tickets all right—we have done a good job of that—but I don't think we have concentrated enough on being sure where those tickets are being sold to, and where they are going, especially places that our growing families and the families abroad could really afford.

I believe this is being rectified by what you are doing here today, by this meeting, and by the Vice President's task force. I think you are awakening the realization of the opportunities that we have here in our 50 States.

I have been meeting with some of the Governors of the States, but the States and many cities and many elements of the travel industry are working together much more effectively than they did just a few months ago. And I want to assure you the resources of this Government that I head are all-out, fully committed to support this effort.

America is truly, I think, "America the Beautiful." And it is difficult to begin cataloging the wonders of nature or even the wonders of man, but they are here to behold, and they are here to enjoy, and I hope that you can contribute to both the beholding and the enjoying.

Only the poets, I guess, could do them justice—and I am not going to quote any poetry here today—but a friend of mine sent me a line the other day from an ancient Greek writer who advised: "If for the sake of a crowded audience you do wish to hold a lecture, your ambition is no laudable one; and at least avoid all citations from the poets, for to quote them argues feeble industry."

And I am taking that advice. I am going to be brief because I want to give Bob Short all the time he needs to report on progress and to get some progress.

And all else aside now—balance of payments, fiscal factors, economic growth, or whatever—I regard it as a matter of first importance. Your President feels that we should encourage our own citizens and the citizens of other nations to get better acquainted with what we have here in America.

We think America is a beautiful land. We think it is going to be more beautiful. We think we have fine highways. We think we are going to improve them more. We think we have a strong land. We know we have a young land. It is alive with change, excitement, and constant newness.

Ours is really an open land, an open society with no walls around it, nothing to hide within it, and we want the world and we want Americans themselves to see the U.S.A. For to see it, I think, is to understand better why we Americans all love peace and why we love freedom so much, and why we would like for all the people of the world to love it as we do.

So I would hope that when we take a look at the ledger at the first of the year, that this competitive operation of trying to stimulate and arouse interest in various forms of travel and various sections to travel in, various points of beauty—that we will find that our

efforts have been helpful and have been successful.

Thank you very much.

NOTE: The President spoke at 1:40 p.m. in the Rose Garden at the White House, following an introduction by Vice President Hubert H. Humphrey. During his remarks he referred to Robert E. Short of Minneapolis, Chairman of the See the U.S.A. Committee, which had been established to encourage tourism throughout the United States. The group included 60 representatives of the transportation and hotel industries in the Nation who supported the Committee's program.

Following the President's remarks, Mrs. Johnson spoke briefly. The text of the Vice President's and Mrs. Johnson's remarks is printed in the Weekly Compilation of Presidential Documents (vol. 1, pp. 79, 80).

420   Remarks at the Signing of the Bill Establishing the Herbert Hoover National Historic Site.   *August 12, 1965*

Mr. Allan Hoover, President Milton Eisenhower, Senator Miller, Senator Hickenlooper, Congressman Schmidhauser, distinguished Members of the Congress and the Cabinet, guests, and friends:

I have a wire from one of our most distinguished and beloved Americans that I would like to read on this occasion. It says:

Dear Mr. President:

For a matter of weeks I have assured many friends that I would be present at the opening of the PGA at Ligonier. Upon receipt of your kind invitation to be present at the signing of the Hoover legislation, I asked my brother to act as representative for both of us at the ceremony. And I send this telegram with my regret that I could not be present in Washington tomorrow. Appreciation for your thoughtfulness.

Sincerely,

DWIGHT D. EISENHOWER

Last October, the Nation—and the world—were deeply saddened by the passing of

Herbert Hoover, our former President, at the age of 90 years.

When he died, we felt the loss of something good and something honest and something uniquely American. And we still feel that loss.

Men of Herbert Hoover's caliber come all too seldom in public life. But today, here in the Rose Garden, we welcome the opportunity to pay to Herbert Hoover a tribute that his life most richly deserves, and that we most respectfully give.

The Congress has passed, and I shall sign today, a bill to establish the Herbert Hoover National Historic Site in West Branch, Iowa, the scene of his birth and the site of his burial.

This 28-acre park has been donated to the Federal Government by the Herbert Hoover Birthplace Foundation. There are the graves of the late President and his beloved wife. There also is the restored cottage in which Herbert Hoover was born. There is also a duplicate of his father's blacksmith shop, and a beautiful, modern library in which the papers of his Presidency are kept.

The visitors to this historic site will sense the essence of this land of opportunity. For out of those humble origins, this young man found his way to greatness in this land—and, yes, greatness in this world.

Herbert Hoover was truly a remarkable man. He was self-made. He was a great engineer. He was a world traveler. He was a humanitarian who helped to feed the millions of starving Europeans after two World Wars. He was a great and efficient Secretary of Commerce under two Presidents of the United States. He was the 31st President of the United States. He was adviser to two Presidents on Government reorganization, and he was adviser to a third one, yours truly, on other things, including Government reorganization.

He reminded me the last time I saw him that he didn't believe any of my Cabinet had read his reorganization reports except Secretary McNamara, and he wanted to call it to my attention and to the other members of the Cabinet. I told Secretary McNamara that and he flew to New York to talk to him and he put some of them into effect, and some of you fellows are still protesting them out there. But they saved the Government a good deal of money.

He was chairman of the Boys Clubs of America. He was a writer, a fisherman of some note, and above all, always—always— he was an American patriot, ready at any time to answer any call of his Government.

Herbert Hoover was President when I first came to Washington in 1931. In later years, one of the rich and rewarding inspirations of my life was to know him when I was Vice President, and Senator, and later as President, to visit with him, to talk to him, to sit in his apartment at the Waldorf. I shall always cherish his wisdom and his insights, but most especially I shall cherish the inspiration of his character.

I am sure that all his life, both before and after his Presidency, Herbert Hoover never had any petty instinct or never had any mean impulse to do other than place the national interest of his country above his party and above himself.

He knew—as every man knows who occupies the highest Office of this land—that once you become President you want to be President, and you should be President, of all the people. And in the rich and in the satisfying later years of his life, President Hoover answered the calls of Democratic as well as Republican Presidents.

One of the things that interested me most, when I visited Mr. Truman's Library, was to see a letter that Herbert Hoover had written him responding to his call to be of help when Mr. Truman needed him.

So, as we gather here this morning to reflect upon his career, it is to really remind ourselves that this house and this Government and this society, of which we are members, really belong to no party, because the partisan spirit is an alien spirit to America.

In my lifetime, two Presidents from the Republican Party have raised higher the standards of nonpartisanship of this office— Herbert Hoover and Dwight David Eisenhower. And to those here today, from both of our parties, may I observe that it is my hope for myself that some way, somehow, I can justly follow in their footsteps and have the same thing said of my service. And it is my hope for our country that the same can always be said for all who come here in times to come.

Public life can be a cruel life and President Hoover experienced that cruelty. But I never observed, in my associations with him, that he was ever embittered by it in the least. He took it like the great statesman that he was.

His wit and his humor seemed to grow with the years. I shall never forget the passage in his memoirs that were dealing with the 1932 Presidential election, when he wrote very simply: "You will expect me to discuss the last election. Well, as nearly as I can learn, we did not have enough votes on our side."

He was a big man, and he was a dedicated man. He was a good man and, above all, he was a devout and honest and compassionate man.

So today, I think it is quite appropriate that we set aside for posterity this memorial on the soil from which came an uncommon man and an uncommon American.

By this act, that soil from which he came, and where he returned, becomes a permanent part of our American heritage.

There were a good many regulations against doing this, and a few rules that prevented it. But when Mr. Cowles and the distinguished Governor of the State of Iowa—Mr. Gardner Cowles brought him in here one day—told me the problems they had at Interior, I said that one of the prerogatives of the President is to repeal and remove some of those obstructions—which I promptly set about to do, and it was changed somewhat, and this bill is before us.

I think we are all richer for it, just as we are richer for having had Herbert Hoover with us in this country for 90 years.

Our gratitude goes to Congressman Schmidhauser for introducing this legislation and working so tirelessly for its passage, and the entire Iowa delegation, both House and Senate.

I am especially glad that we can have with us today, not only so many members of President Hoover's party, but so many of those who were associated with him—Mr. Allan Hoover; Admiral Strauss, once his personal secretary; Mr. J. Harold Stewart, the Director of the Budget in the Hoover administration; Mr. William Anderson, former president of the Herbert Hoover Birthplace Foundation and a close personal friend; our own beloved friend of many years, a great public servant, Congressman Joe Martin.

I am also privileged to welcome many distinguished members of President Hoover's party, from both public and private life. For us all it is an honor to share together this moment of tribute to a man that we all admire and we all respect and, for those who knew him, we all had deep affection.

NOTE: The President spoke at 11:41 a.m. in the Rose Garden at the White House. In his opening words he referred to Allan Hoover, son of former President Herbert Hoover, Milton Eisenhower, President of Johns Hopkins University and brother of former President Dwight D. Eisenhower, Senator Jack Miller of Iowa, Senator Bourke B. Hickenlooper of Iowa, and Representative John R. Schmidhauser of Iowa.

During his remarks the President referred to, among others, Secretary of Defense Robert S. McNamara, Gardner Cowles, President of Cowles Publications, Governor Harold E. Hughes of Iowa, Adm. Lewis L. Strauss, former Chairman of the Atomic Energy Commission, J. Harold Stewart, Chairman of the Task Force on Budget and Accounting of the Commission on Organization of the Executive Branch of the Government (Hoover Commission), and Representative Joseph W. Martin, Jr., of Massachusetts.

The President signed the bill on the desk used by President Herbert Hoover while he was in the White House.

As enacted, the bill (H.R. 8111) is Public Law 89–119 (79 Stat. 510).

See also Item 414.

421 Remarks at the Swearing In of Henry Cabot Lodge as Ambassador to South Viet-Nam. *August 12, 1965*

Mr. Vice President, the Ambassador and Mrs. Lodge, Secretary Rusk, Secretary Mc-Namara, Ambassador Taylor:

This is a very proud occasion for all of us here. But in a larger and more important sense, I think this is an occasion to make all the Nation proud.

What America is, and all that America will ever be, is built on the willingness of her most able citizens to serve their country in times of need without regard either to their personal comfort or sacrifice. The duties of freedom today call many of our finest young Americans to the jungles of Viet-Nam, half a world away—and we are deeply proud of those young men and we are proud of the services they are rendering as we meet here in this very small ceremony, by special request of Ambassador Lodge. But it is a very great cause for special pride and reassurance that seasoned and able Americans like Maxwell Taylor and Henry Cabot Lodge are willing to respond voluntarily and unselfishly to the same call that our young men have responded to out there in the rice paddies.

Last year when Ambassador Lodge asked to return from his post, I was thrilled and I was somewhat moved, as President, by the many who came to me and who volunteered to accept this assignment, to take up the duties as Ambassador to Viet-Nam—men like Dean Rusk, Bob McNamara, McGeorge Bundy, and a member of the Cabinet at that time, now Senator Robert Kennedy, as well as the Chairman of the Joint Chiefs of Staff, Maxwell Taylor.

I selected General Taylor for this most important of our diplomatic assignments with the understanding that I would ask him to serve for a period of a year.

And the search for the best man to succeed Ambassador Taylor was neither very long nor very difficult, for the search led first to Ambassador Lodge. I thought he was the best equipped by training and by experience and by knowledge of conditions there. And when he was first asked, his first and immediate answer was "Yes, Mr. President."

So America can be very proud of both of these distinguished sons.

Ambassador Lodge is just that. He is one of the truly distinguished Americans of our time. He is a Senator. He gave up his Senate seat to go into the Army in World War II. He was a soldier. He is a diplomat. He was the nominee of his party for the second Office of the land. He is a son of an honored American family. He served his country and his times with very rare ability and effectiveness. His return to Saigon is a characteristic act of a man that is motivated only by a great sense of duty to his people and to his country. It inspires the respect and the confidence of all of his countrymen and the leaders of other nations in the world.

I have known Cabot Lodge as both personal friend and as a political opponent. Whether ally or adversary, his wisdom, and his courage, his decency and patriotism have always had my admiration. I understand the yearning within him that leads him to seek again not the easy life, not the quiet life, but the active and useful life, the dangerous life of the duty to which he returns.

Ambassador Lodge and I have spent many hours together these past few weeks. In the review of our Viet-Nam policies and the shaping of the decisions announced on July 28, he had a very full part as a participant and I am glad to say he is in full agreement with those decisions.

Ambassador Lodge and I are fully agreed on the underlying principle that in Viet-Nam we are there to help the people and their Government to help themselves. We are not there to substitute our effort for theirs. We are there to supplement their own brave and gallant and continuing effort of defending themselves.

Our determination is built on their determination. The United States would never undertake the sacrifice these efforts require if its help were not wanted and requested.

Ambassador Lodge remembers, as I remember, the tragic road of weakness and expediency that led this world to war a generation ago. He remembers, as I remember, when the appetite of aggressors was allowed to feed on small and defenseless nations. He is determined, as I am and as I believe the American people are, that the world shall not walk that tragic road toward darkness again.

We have made commitments around the world. And those who seek our support against aggression are going to have it. In Viet-Nam the credibility of our commitment everywhere is challenged. We did not choose the time or the place of testing. But we do choose to meet that test and to keep our trust and to keep that word that has been given by three Presidents.

At the same time, we of this Nation have made, and for 189 years we have kept, a higher commitment to all mankind: the commitment to use our resources and our strength and our will to support the end of peace. The defense of peace is the very purpose of our power, and peace for the people of Viet-Nam is the purpose of our

presence in Viet-Nam. And I would remind all in the world that that is our only purpose.

Our effort to assure peace for the Vietnamese people is an effort that proceeds on many fronts. Ambassador Lodge and General Westmoreland will continue to work as a team, doing what is necessary militarily so that what is desirable politically and economically can be done to secure and strengthen peace for the people of Viet-Nam.

Let these leaders and all Americans there know that they have the support of a Nation that is united, and a people that is undivided.

So, today, I am very proud to publicly express to Maxwell Taylor our country's gratitude for a fine and faithful service, and to wish him well, and to urge him to stay close by our side in the days ahead. And to say to Ambassador Lodge that I express our country's admiration and appreciation for his willing return to the duties of this great effort—this great effort for freedom—and to wish him Godspeed.

NOTE: The swearing-in ceremony was held at 12:25 p.m. in the Rose Garden at the White House. In his opening words the President referred to Vice President Hubert H. Humphrey, Ambassador and Mrs. Henry Cabot Lodge, Secretary of State Dean Rusk, Secretary of Defense Robert S. McNamara, and Gen. Maxwell D. Taylor, Ambassador to South Viet-Nam June 1964–July 1965.

During his remarks the President referred to Mc-George Bundy, Special Assistant to the President, Senator Robert F. Kennedy of New York, former Attorney General of the United States, and Gen. William C. Westmoreland, Commander of U.S. Forces in South Viet-Nam.

Following the administration of the oath of office, Ambassador Lodge spoke briefly. The text of his remarks is printed in the Weekly Compilation of Presidential Documents (vol. 1, p. 82). Mr. Lodge previously served as Ambassador to South Viet-Nam from July 1963 to June 1964.

422 Excerpt of Letter to the Members of the President's Commission on Law Enforcement and the Administration of Justice.
August 13, 1965

[Released August 13, 1965.   Dated August 11, 1965]

THE COMMISSION'S primary assignment is to conduct the first systematic, nationwide study of the entire spectrum of crime problems. The mounting crime rate and the unprecedented increase in the incidence of juvenile delinquency are matters of deep concern to me and to most Americans. As you know, I sent a special message concerning these problems to the Congress on March 8, 1965, and have recommended the enactment of certain new legislation designed to combat those problems.

However, that new legislation is but a beginning and there is still much to be done. I am convinced that you and your distinguished colleagues on the Commission can and will make significant contributions to this drive to devise means to eradicate lawlessness, disrespect for the law, and the causes thereof.

NOTE: The excerpt from the letter was read by Bill D. Moyers, Special Assistant to the President, at his news conference at Austin, Tex., at 4 p.m. on Friday, August 13, 1965. It was not made public in the form of a White House press release.

The letter was sent to the Chairman of the Commission, Attorney General Nicholas deB. Katzenbach, and to the following members: Mrs. Genevieve Blatt, former Deputy Attorney General of Pennsyl-

vania; Judge Charles D. Breitel, Justice of the New York State Supreme Court, Appellate Division; Kingman Brewster, Jr., President of Yale University; Garrett Byrne, District Attorney, Suffolk County, Mass.; Thomas J. Cahill, Chief of Police, City of San Francisco; Otis Chandler, publisher of the Los Angeles Times; Leon Jaworski, Houston, Tex., attorney, and former President of the American College of Trial Lawyers; Thomas Lynch, Attorney General of California; Ross L. Malone, Jr., Roswell, N. Mex., former Deputy Attorney General of the United States and former President of the American Bar Association; William P. Rogers, Washington, D.C., attorney and former Attorney General of the United States; United States District Judge James B. Parsons, Chicago; Lewis F. Powell, Jr., Richmond, Va., President of the American Bar Association; Robert G. Storey, Dallas attorney and former President of the American Bar Association; Mrs. Robert J. Stuart, Spokane, Wash., President of the League of Women Voters; Mayor Robert F. Wagner of New York City; Herbert Wechsler, professor of law at Columbia University and Director of the American Law Institute; Whitney M. Young, Jr., New Rochelle, N.Y., Executive Director of the National Urban League; United States District Judge Luther W. Youngdahl of Washington, D.C.

For the President's statement on establishing the Commission, see Item 382.

For the President's message to Congress of March 8, 1965, on law enforcement and the administration of justice, see Item 102.

The Law Enforcement Assistance Act of 1965 was approved by the President on September 22, 1965 (see Item 526).

See also Items 437, 500.

423 Message to the President of Korea on Learning of Plans To Dispatch Korean Troops to South Viet-Nam.
August 13, 1965

I WAS deeply gratified to learn that the National Assembly of Korea, at your request, has approved the dispatch of a Korean division to join the Korean troops already as-

sisting the Vietnamese people in their fight to preserve the freedom of the Republic of South Viet-Nam.

The American people welcome this further demonstration of the devotion of Korea to the spirit of liberty and independence.

I know how much this contribution owes to your leadership and I want to express to you my personal gratitude.

LYNDON B. JOHNSON

[His Excellency Chung Hee Park, President of the Republic of Korea]

NOTE: The message was read by Bill D. Moyers, Special Assistant to the President, at his news conference at Austin, Tex., at 4 p.m. on Friday, August 13, 1965. It was not made public in the form of a White House press release.

424 Statement by the President on Announcing Plans for the White House Conference on Health. *August 13, 1965*

WE MUST constantly protect and improve the health of our people. The time has come to call upon our best scientific and administrative talents to help chart the future in this critical area. I hope that this Conference will formulate guidelines for developing creative programs that will bring better health to every American. The mandate of this Conference will not stop at the water's edge. I will call upon it to help develop international goals in the field of health.

NOTE: The statement was read by Bill D. Moyers, Special Assistant to the President, at his news conference at Austin, Tex., at 4 p.m. on Friday, August 13, 1965. It was not made public in the form of a White House press release.

In making the announcement Mr. Moyers added that the Conference would be held November 30–December 1, 1965. He stated that Dr. George W. Beadle, President of the University of Chicago, would serve as Chairman, and that Boisfeuillet Jones, President of the Woodruff Foundation of Atlanta and former Special Assistant to the Secretary of Health, Education, and Welfare, would serve as Executive Vice Chairman.

425 Statement by the President Commemorating the 30th Anniversary of the Signing of the Social Security Act. *August 15, 1965*

THIRTY YEARS ago yesterday—August 14, 1935—President Franklin D. Roosevelt signed into law the Social Security Act—an act which was to bring a better life to many millions of Americans then living and to countless generations yet unborn.

For millions of Americans the enactment of this legislation meant the beginning of a new era of hope and confidence, and the end of an era of bleak and bitter despair.

We pause now to remember that moment of great social renewal and to honor the memory of the man whose moral and political leadership brought this act into being, and who committed the Nation to the prop-

osition that the man or woman who had labored over a lifetime was entitled to the grace and dignity of self-support in old age.

This anniversary is one of deep significance in the history of this country. For the act that was created on that August day, 30 years ago, became the foundation of a great new social structure built by all the people of this country for the protection of all the people.

—Here was the beginning of the world's largest social insurance program which today pays out benefits to more than 20 million people—the aged, the disabled, the widowed, and orphaned.

—Here were the social insurance programs which now provide a base on which our people can build, through their initiative, thrift, and hard work, the elements of a good life.

—Here was the start of our nationwide unemployment insurance program—a partnership of Federal and State Governments to protect workers and their families during periods of temporary joblessness.

—Here were the first threads of today's broad network of State and local public welfare agencies which, with the help of Federal funds, serve the blind, the destitute, the aged, and especially the needy children of this land.

The 1935 law laid the foundation for all of these measures which are so vital to the strength of American society.

We are still building, still improving that great social structure that was started three decades ago.

Two weeks ago, in Independence, Mo., in the presence of President Harry Truman, another social pioneer, I signed the amendments that this Congress—the great 89th Congress—has fashioned for this law to help shield our elderly people from the economic burdens of illness and to update our social security programs in many other ways.

But we know, as President Roosevelt knew and said 30 years ago, that this structure is not yet complete. It will continue to grow as our needs grow—a living monument to the American ideal of health, prosperity, and happiness for all.

Some of these needs are clear to us today, and have been translated into national goals. Among these are:

—first, the assurance of a level of income for every citizen of this Nation who is too young or too old to work, or has become physically or mentally disabled, or who is unable to find work that is sufficient to assure health and decency.

—second, the rehabilitation for gainful employment of every disabled person for whom such rehabilitation is possible.

—third, opportunity for the pursuit of meaningful civic, cultural, and recreational activities in the retirement years.

These are immediate national goals for improved social well-being. We are working to fulfill them today. At the same time we know there will be other needs tomorrow.

This great, living law allows us to respond, as a Nation, to meet those needs. It is the instrument of a democratic society, engaged in a great and historic effort to secure the well-being and happiness of all of its people.

NOTE: The Social Security Act, approved August 14, 1935, is printed in the United States Statutes at Large (49 Stat. 620).

For the President's remarks with President Truman at the signing in Independence of the Medicare bill, see Item 394.

The statement was released at Austin, Tex.

426   Statement by the President Following the Restoration of Order in Los Angeles. *August* 15, 1965

THE PEOPLE of the Nation, as well as the city of Los Angeles, feel a deep sense of relief as order is being restored to the frightened streets of that city.

The action of Governor Brown and other California officials is another vindication of the principle of local responsibility for maintaining law and order. The Federal Government, by word and act, has offered any help that might be required.

But it is the State of California and the city of Los Angeles which are meeting the crisis. And, in so doing, demonstrating again the wisdom of our Federal principles.

However, the riots in Los Angeles are more than State concerned. It is not simply that what happened there can happen elsewhere. It is also that the Los Angeles disorders flow from a violent breach of rooted American principles.

The first is that injustices of our society shall be overcome by the peaceful processes of our society. There is no greater wrong, in our democracy, than violent, willful disregard of law. If men live decently it is because obedience to legal process saved their lives and allowed them to enlarge those lives.

To resort to terror and violence not only shatters the essential right of every citizen to be secure in his home, his shop, and in the streets of his town; it strikes from the hand of the Negro the very weapons with which he is achieving his own emancipation.

Those who strike at the fabric of ordered liberty also erode the foundation on which the house of justice stands.

The enforcement of this central truth is the responsibility of all Americans, and is a special challenge to the Negro community and those who are its leaders.

But it is not enough simply to decry disorder. We must also strike at the unjust conditions from which disorder largely flows. For the second great American principle is that all shall have an equal chance to share in the blessings of our society.

As I have said, time and time again, aimless violence finds fertile ground among men imprisoned by the shadowed walls of hatred, coming of age in the poverty of slums, facing their future without education or skills and with little hope of rewarding work. These ills, too, we are working to wipe out.

We must not only be relentless in condemning violence, but also in taking the necessary steps to prevent violence. We must not let anger drown understanding if domestic peace is ever to rest on its only sure foundation—the faith of all our people that they share, in opportunity and in obligation, the promise of American life.

NOTE: On August 15 Governor Edmund G. Brown of California extended the 8 p.m. curfew to 50 square miles of Los Angeles and stated that he did not believe that the help of Federal forces would be necessary. On the following day he declared that order had been restored in the predominantly Negro district of Watts.

During the 5-day riot, 35 persons were killed and over 900 were injured. See also Item 453.

The statement was released at Austin, Tex.

427 Statement by the President on the Ratification by Korea of the Basic Relations Treaty With Japan. *August* 15, 1965

THE United States Government has for many years believed that the establishment of normal relations between the Republic of Korea and Japan would be a historic step that would bring important and durable benefits to both nations and to the free world.

I was pleased to learn that the Korean Government has just ratified the Basic Relations Treaty with Japan and its associated

agreements. The establishment of normal relations between these two countries will be welcomed by all friends of the Republic of Korea and Japan.

NOTE: The statement was read by Joseph Laitin, an assistant press secretary, at his news conference at Austin, Tex., at 2:15 p.m. on Sunday, August 15, 1965. It was not made public in the form of a White House press release.

428   Statement by the President on the Need for Industry-Wide Procedures To Settle Manning Disputes on Automated Ships. *August 16, 1965*

THE KEY ISSUE in the present controversy between the American Merchant Marine Institute and the Marine Engineers Beneficial Association involves procedures for handling manning disputes on automated ships.

This difficulty has arisen repeatedly in other situations in the shipping industry.

It is clear that an industry-wide procedure, or a uniform pattern of procedures, for the handling of manning and related issues in the maritime industry has become an absolute necessity.

Such a procedure cannot be developed in a single set of negotiations and a settlement of the present controversy should not be held up while the necessary broader procedures are established.

I have today asked the Secretary of Labor and Mr. George Meany, President of the AFL–CIO, to undertake the development, with the participation of all unions and associations in the maritime industry, and with such assistance as they find necessary, of effective procedures for resolving manning and related issues arising from the mechanization and retrofitting of ships.

A general charter for the establishment of such procedures is contained in the unanimous Automation Report of the President's Advisory Committee on Labor-Management Policy:

1. Automation and technological progress are essential to the general welfare, the economic strength, and the defense of the Nation.

2. This progress can and must be achieved without the sacrifice of human values.

3. Achievement of technological progress without sacrifice of human values requires a combination of private and governmental action, consonant with the principles of a free society.

The contemplated procedures to be effective must provide the fullest practicable assurance that manning and related issues be settled without interruption of operations.

Such procedures must be made on the concurrence and participation of all private parties whose interests are affected, and must achieve a parity of procedures insofar as interrelated interests are affected.

I have asked Secretary Wirtz and Mr. Meany to report the results of their undertaking to me, with accompanying recommendations if this is appropriate, at the earliest possible time. I will then take or propose such action as appears appropriate in the light of their report.

I propose to see to it that this problem, which involves public and private interests alike, is met fully and effectively.

It will be essential to the working out of these procedures that while they are being developed there be no interruption of operations resulting from disputes over manning or related issues on automated ships, and that there be no action taken which will make the development of such procedures more difficult. If particular manning issues arise in the interim, Secretary Wirtz and Mr. Meany will be in a position to propose procedures for their handling which will not be inconsistent either with existing contract provisions or with the carrying out of their responsibility under this statement.

I request and will expect the full cooperation of all shipping associations and unions in the development of such procedures, recognizing existing contract provisions and also the desirability of establishing a parity of manning dispute procedures.

I urge that the manning dispute procedure issue between the AMMI and the MEBA be quickly resolved in reliance upon the establishment of procedures under the auspices indicated in this statement, and in general conformance with the recommendation made to them by the Secretary of Labor on July 30, 1965.

It is imperative that negotiations between the AMMI and the Masters, Mates and Pilots Association, and those between the Institute and the American Radio Association and other officer unions, also be quickly concluded.

I recommend that if it is necessary, any remaining issues in any of the three cases be submitted to settlement procedures to be

prescribed by the Secretary of Labor.

I have asked Secretary Wirtz to report to me regarding this situation by 5 p.m., Wednesday, August 18.

It is the intent of this action and these proposals that they will result in the speedy resumption of operation of the ships which are now idle.

My broader intent is that there be established in this industry an effective and fair method of disputes settlement which is essential to the future of the American merchant marine.

NOTE: The report of the President's Advisory Committee on Labor-Management Policy, entitled "Automation," is dated January 11, 1962 (Government Printing Office, 11 pp.).

Secretary of Labor W. Willard Wirtz and George Meany, President of the AFL–CIO, reported orally to the President on August 18, 1965.

See also Item 463[3].

The statement was released at Austin, Tex.

429 Remarks at a Ceremony Commemorating the Fourth Anniversary of the Alliance for Progress. *August 17, 1965*

Mr. Vice President, Secretary Rusk, distinguished Ambassadors, members of the Cabinet, my distinguished friends in the Congress, my fellow citizens of the Americas:

Four years ago this hemisphere embarked upon a great adventure—the greatest perhaps since an unknown Italian mariner first touched these shores almost five centuries ago.

It was nothing less than to transform the life of an entire continent.

It was to reach into the homes and the villages of more than 200 million people, touching each with great hope and expectation.

It was to replace privilege with social justice, and unchanging poverty with economic

progress. Where there was disease we would bring health. Where there was ignorance we would bring learning. We would feed the hungry and we would shelter the homeless, and we would do all of this as free men making liberty the companion of progress.

The adventure began in a dozen scattered spots. In Columbia the Act of Bogotá was signed. In Caracas, Rómulo Betancourt moved a nation from dictatorship to a very living and a very hopeful democracy. In Costa Rica and Mexico, and in many other places, new standards were being shaped and old dreams were taking on fresh meaning. Across the hemisphere revolution was in the air, promising these three things: freedom, justice, and progress.

And then all these growing, resistless

forces converged on this room where a brilliant new President of the United States addressed himself to his fellow citizens of this hemisphere. And with unmatched spaciousness of vision John Fitzgerald Kennedy called for "a vast cooperative effort unparalleled in magnitude and nobility of purpose, to satisfy the basic needs of the American people. . . ."

And 5 months later—4 years ago today—on the coast of Uruguay, 20 American Republics solemnly resolved to establish and to carry forward the Alliance for Progress.

That act was a turning point, not only in the history of the New World, but in the long history of freedom itself.

The goals were towering, almost beyond achievement. The hopes were soaring, almost beyond fulfillment. The tasks were immense, almost beyond capacity. But entire nations are not stirred to action by either timid words or narrow visions. The faith and the will of millions do not take fire from the brands that are muffled in reluctance and fear. And if the reality of progress was to be slow, the radiance of ultimate achievement must be bright enough to compel the effort and the sacrifice of generations.

If our Alliance was suffused with compassion and idealism, it also responded to the most real and the most urgent necessities of our time. Our continent is in ferment. People long oppressed demanded their share of the blessings and the dignity which the modern world can offer to man. The peaceful democratic social revolution of the Alliance is not the alternative to tranquility and changelessness. It is the alternative, and the only alternative, to bloodshed and destruction and tyranny. For the past is really gone. And those who struggle to preserve it enlist unawares in the ranks of their own destroyers.

We will shape the future through the principles of our Alliance or we will find it swallowed up in violence that is bred of desperation.

How fortunate we are to live in such a time when justice so mingles with necessity, and faith mingles with opportunity.

Almost from the moment of birth, the Alliance for Progress was beset by doubt. But men of rooted faith in every country held firm to the purpose. And if we have not really reached the farthest limit of expectation, we have done much more, indeed, than many ever believed we could do.

FOUR YEARS OF PROGRESS

This 4 years has been the greatest period of forward movement, progress, and fruitful change that we have ever made in the history of this hemisphere. And that pace is now increasing.

Last year Latin America as a whole exceeded the Alliance for Progress target of 2½ percent per capita growth rate. Our experts tell me that we will do the same this year. And in the Central American Common Market the growth is almost 7 percent.

A large and swelling flood of resources contributes to this progress. In 4 years the United States alone has contributed almost $4½ billion in grants, in loans, in goods, and in expert assistance. The nations of Latin America have channeled $22–24 billion into development. And more than an extra billion dollars has come from other countries and other international agencies.

At the heart of the Alliance are the twin urgencies of planning and reform. Ten nations have already submitted development programs, and others are on the way. Fourteen nations now have major tax reforms underway, and their rate of tax collection is steadily increasing. Fourteen nations have now instituted land reform programs.

Others are confronting the growing importance of population control. One government after another is determined to reconcile reform and economic growth with the struggle against destructive inflation. And this morning I salute those—the people of Brazil—who have helped to lead the way.

AMERICA HELPS

In my own country we have constantly worked to improve the speed and the usefulness of our own participation in the Alliance, and we have made remarkable progress.

I hope you will listen to this.

In the last year and a half we have loaned over $847 million—and that is almost $150 million more than was loaned in the entire 2 full preceding years combined. The number of loans is increasing. The amount of investment guarantee is on the rise. Housing guarantees alone have gone up 20 times in the last 2 years.

So you see in both the United States and Latin America we are moving more and more swiftly to meet the obligations and to reach the goals that we set in the Alliance for Progress.

HOPE IS BORN

And behind the statistics lie the countless stories of human needs that have been met, human suffering that has been relieved, and human hopes that have been fulfilled.

Twenty-five million people—13 million of them little children—are today, as we speak, receiving food from the Alliance programs.

More than 1½ million people already have new homes. A million children now have new classrooms, and 10 million textbooks have already been produced.

Hundreds and hundreds of thousands now can find relief from suffering in more than 850 hospitals and health centers and health units that have been placed into operation already.

More than 100 million people today are protected from malaria. And all across the face of the hemisphere new roads are being constructed. Electric power lines are going up. And institutions for saving and credit and development are already opening new doors.

Yes, these are very important gains. But, perhaps more importantly, the banners of reform, of social justice, of economic progress have been seized by governments and by leaders and by parties throughout this hemisphere. Elections are fought and elections are won on the principles of the Alliance. And where once the light of hope flickered in very few places, today it burns in many nations. In the oppressed countryside and in the desperate slums, growing numbers of people know that far away in distant capitals—under different slogans and with varying success—their leaders are working to brighten their days and to ensure their dignity.

For the fact is, even though the forces of injustice and privilege and tyranny still hold many fortresses, they are actually on the defensive today. And we can say, far more surely than we once could, that their final day is coming.

But whatever we have accomplished, we all know that the road ahead is longer and it is more steep than the way behind. If many have been helped, then there are many more that are still untouched. If some are newly free, there are millions that are still shackled by poverty and disease and ignorance and malnutrition. If we have made more progress than before, as we have, we have made far less than we should and than we must.

Toward A Brighter Future

So, to this end, we must all increase the efforts that we are now making: first, to build modern industry and the structures on which it rests; to attract a growing flow of private investment and technology to Latin America; to speed up the process of social reform.

But it is not just enough to continue doing what we are doing. From the experience and the achievement and the failures of the first 4 years, we can now shape new directions.

Recently, I received—as did the other American Presidents—a letter from CIAP suggesting changes and new departures. The leadership of this organization is itself one of our very healthiest developments. And I pledge that my Government will review this letter with great care and sympathy.

But from this letter—and from our own experience—we can already see the shape of future emphasis.

First, we must step up our efforts to prevent disastrous changes in the prices of those basic commodities which are the lifeblood of so many of our economies. We will continue—as we did this week in London—to strengthen the operation of the coffee agreement and to search for ways to stabilize the price of cocoa.

We will try to maintain a regularly expanding market for the sugar that is produced by Latin America. And consistent with the CIAP recommendations, I will propose this afternoon that Congress eliminate the special import fee on sugar so that the full price will go to the Latin American producers.

Second, we must try to draw the economies of Latin America much closer together. The experience of Central America reaffirms that of Europe. Widened markets—the breakdown of tariff barriers—leads to increased trade and leads to more efficient production and to greater prosperity.

The United States will, as CIAP suggests, contribute from its Alliance resources to the creation of a new fund for preparing multinational projects. By building areawide road systems, by developing river basins which cross boundaries, by improving communications, we can all help to dissolve the barriers which have divided the nations.

In addition, I hope the American nations will consider the establishment of a program—patterned after the European Coal and Steel Community—for the production and trade, on a continental basis, of fertilizer, pesticides, and other products that are needed to increase agricultural production. My country stands willing to help in such a venture.

And thus, in ways that he never imagined, we can move much closer to the dream of Bolívar.

Third, we must emphasize the needs of rural Latin America. Here is the scene of the most abject poverty and despair. Here half the people of Latin America live. And it is here, in the countryside, that the foundation of a modern economy will finally be built. Through the diversification of crops, we can decrease dependence on a few export products. Through increasing production, the countries of Latin America can feed their own people. Through increasing farm income, we can provide growing markets for new industry.

And we must, as CIAP also suggests, direct more of our efforts toward those things which directly touch the lives of individual human beings—housing, education, health, and food. And it is not enough simply to say that a growing economy will ultimately meet those needs. Misery and pain and despair exist in the present, and we must fight them in the present with all we have and the best way we can. This is not only the command of compassion. It is, as we all recognize, the counsel of wisdom. For factories and banks and dollars do not alone build a nation. People build a nation. And on those people, on their health and their knowledge and their faith, their participation and their sacrifice, really rests the future of all of us and the future of all nations.

This is the common thread which runs through the Great Society in my country and the Alliance for Progress in all countries.

These are a few—and only a few—of the many tasks which lie before us as we meet here this morning to labor to complete the second revolution of the Americas.

DIGNITY FOR ALL

The task of development is a practical process. Development d e m a n d s skilled leadership. It demands careful judgment. It demands initiative, ingenuity, and imagination that is firmly tempered by possibility. But it also demands something more. For our progress is not its own end. It is an instrument to enlarge the dignity of man. And so we must build on faith and on belief and on those values which are the resistant and enduring mark of our civilization.

This means that each man should have the chance to share in the affairs of his nation. This means that each man should participate in that liberating process of self-

rule that we know as democracy. It is fundamental to our Alliance that all of our nations should be free and that all of our people should be a part of that freedom. We have not yet achieved that for all of our countries, indeed for all the people of even my own country. But that is our goal for this entire continent. And, however we build, the Alliance will not be a success until that is accomplished.

It is to protect that right of self-determination that the OAS today works in the Dominican Republic. I know that all of you share the wish that the future government, chosen by the Dominican Republic and by the Dominican people themselves, will be devoted to the principles of liberal democracy and social justice; and that you share as well the intention of my country to try to help them rebuild that memory and to help rebuild that strife-scarred land.

This also means that each man's nation, whether it is great or small, must walk as an equal with all others—free to shape its society, free to select its institutions and free to find its own way to the future so long as it respects the rights of its fellows. And, from that enriching diversity of custom and tradition—practice and the conduct of affairs—I think we will all draw strength and, perhaps even draw wisdom.

This also means that each man must have a chance to share in present benefits and to share in future progress. God did not create any man to live in unseen chains, laboring through a life of pain in order to heap the table of a favored few. No farmer should be enslaved to land that he can never own. No worker should be stripped of reward for toil. No family should be compelled to sacrifice while others escape the obligations of their society. "Indeed," said Thomas Jefferson, "I tremble for my country when I reflect that God is just." We must surely tremble for our continent as long as any live and flourish protected by the walls of injustice.

Progress Will Fulfill Dreams

If we follow these commands in all our lands, then progress will fulfill our dreams. But if we sacrifice them to weakness, or interest, or to false promise, then the hand that builds will become the hand of desolation.

I am, as best I can, and best I know how, trying to follow them in my own country. This year new laws will help the old in my country to find health, will help families to supplement the cost of their homes, will help the Negroes to share in democracy, will help the poor to find an exit from poverty, and will help little children to seek learning. For in my Nation, like yours, we are still struggling to find justice for all of our people. And because we are fortunate in abundance, we feel that morality requires that we must also try to help others who seek it for their own people, too.

And there is also something more. The process of development is still an unknown process. Although we mask our uncertainty with charts and tables, calculations and intricate theories, we are all still very uncertain. But one thing we do know. Development is not just a matter of resources, or trade, or production, or even crops. Rather, in some mysterious way, a people—because they have great leaders and because they have great hopes and because they themselves are great—an entire people begin to stir, and to sacrifice and to work. And when they do, a nation begins to move.

And today in this country and, I believe, throughout this continent, this is really beginning to happen.

It is this—not the numbers or reports—which tells us these have been fruitful years, prosperous ones, and that with luck and with skill and with intransigent resolve we will clear away the thousand barriers that lie ahead. But if enough hands grasp them, then all will be allowed to make the journey.

To all that was pledged that momentous August day 4 years ago—and everything promised since then—I here, on this anniversary today, again pledge my administration and my personal life in office.

As for the future, let's leave that to the New World. It will be ours, as it was promised so many years ago.

Thank you.

NOTE: The President spoke at 10:25 a.m. in the East Room at the White House. In his opening words he referred to Vice President Hubert H. Humphrey and Secretary of State Dean Rusk. During his remarks he referred to, among others, former President of Venezuela Rómulo Betancourt.

The Alliance for Progress was established in August 1961 by the Charter of Punta del Este. The text of the Charter is printed in the Department of State Bulletin (vol. 45, p. 463).

A report to the President by Jack H. Vaughn, Assistant Secretary of State for Inter-American Affairs and United States Coordinator, Alliance for Progress, was made public by the White House on September 10, 1965. The text of the report is printed in the Weekly Compilation of Presidential Documents (vol. 1, p. 242).

The Sugar Act Amendments of 1965 (H.R. 11135) was approved by the President on November 8, 1965 (Public Law 89–331; 79 Stat. 1271).

430 Statement by the President on the Draft Treaty To Prevent the Spread of Nuclear Weapons. *August 17, 1965*

THIS MORNING, on my instructions, the United States Delegate to the Geneva Disarmament Conference, Mr. William C. Foster, has presented a draft treaty to prevent the spread of nuclear weapons.

President Kennedy gave voice to international concern over this gravest of all unresolved human issues. He urged the disarmament conference to find ways to both the understanding of urgent needs, and the undertaking of prompt action. For he knew, as each individual citizen senses, the time to halt nuclear spread is before its contagion takes root.

It was in that spirit that he constructed the nuclear test ban treaty, the first hopeful, helpful step in the long journey toward peace.

Now we continue that journey today in Geneva.

This draft treaty would bind its signers in a pledge to refrain from actions which would lead to any further increase in the number of nations having the power to unleash nuclear devastation on the world. This United States draft is an important step forward. It plainly demonstrates that a treaty can be drawn which meets the legitimate interests of nuclear and nonnuclear powers alike.

Our draft treaty is now open for discussion and negotiation. The United States is pre-pared to move forward with promptness and determination to make this proposal a reality. We call upon all those at Geneva to join in this effort.

I speak for all my countrymen in reaffirming our conviction that the peace of the world requires firm limits upon the spread of nuclear weapons.

This has been the policy of the United States for 20 years. The policy is still as right as ever.

In this great issue the interests of the people of the United States are at one with the interests of all people everywhere. The threat to peace—and to human life itself—is universal. If the response is universal, the threat can be met.

President Eisenhower and President Kennedy sought, as I seek now, the pathway to a world in which serenity may one day endure. There is no sane description of a nuclear war. There is only the blinding light of man's failure to reason with his fellow man, and then silence.

The time is now. The hour is late. The fate of generations yet unborn is in our hands. And "humanity with all its fears, with all the hopes of future years is hanging breathless" on that fate.

NOTE: The draft treaty is printed in the Department of State Bulletin (vol. 53, p. 474).

431   Exchange of Messages With the President of Chile Concerning
      U.S. Assistance in the Chilean Flood Disaster.
      August 17, 1965

[Released August 17, 1965. Dated August 15, 1965]

Mr. President:

My deep sympathy and that of the people of the United States goes out to you and the Chilean people as you move to relieve human suffering following in the wake of the second natural catastrophe which has struck your country this year.

I am proud to tell you that the people of the United States through the various U.S. private relief agencies, church world service, Catholic relief services (Caritas), CARE and others in cooperation with various public agencies are responding rapidly to the emergency in Chile.

An initial shipment of blankets, clothes and medicines will be arriving in Chile on Tuesday to be followed by other supplies in the coming days.

We are anxious and our hearts are saddened this Sunday at the disaster which has struck your country but with God's help and fraternal assistance we are confident that the Chilean people will overcome these difficulties.

LYNDON B. JOHNSON

[His Excellency, Eduardo Frei Montalva, President, Republic of Chile]

NOTE: President Frei Montalva's letter, dated August 16, 1965, follows:

Mr. President:

I have just this moment received your letter in which you express the solidarity of the people of the United States before the new test which faces the Chilean people. Your words of encouragement and solidarity are deeply appreciated by our people and by me.

Once again, Mr. President, the United States Government and nation, through their institutions, are expressing their effective and generous solidarity in the face of the catastrophies which are affecting us. The Chilean people do not forget and will not forget that on every occasion you have contributed unhesitatingly to alleviate the sufferings of many thousands of affected families, whether it be the result of an earthquake or in this case, a rainstorm.

I wish to tell you that despite these two great difficulties which we have experienced during the course of the year, the will and determination of the people and government are unbroken and we are confident that we shall overcome them, and that they will even serve as a stimulus for our will and will secure the unity and solidarity of all Chileans.

Once again I reiterate to you, Mr. President, in the name of my country and in my own, the expressions of our appreciation together with my most cordial greetings.

EDUARDO FREI MONTALVA

[His Excellency, Lyndon B. Johnson, President of the United States of America]

432   Exchange of Messages With Prime Minister Pearson on the 25th
      Anniversary of the Canada-U.S. Permanent Joint Board
      on Defense. *August 18, 1965*

THE Canada-United States Permanent Joint Board on Defense has played an invaluable role in developing the close and effective cooperation of Canada and the United States in our common defense. I am confident that it will render equally signal service to the defense of our two countries in the years ahead. On this twenty-fifth anniversary of the Board, I am happy to extend my congratulations and best wishes.

LYNDON B. JOHNSON

NOTE: The message from Prime Minister Pearson follows:

Throughout its quarter century of dedicated service, the Canada-United States Permanent Joint Board on Defense has symbolized the spirit of friendly cooperation which characterizes relations between our two countries. Created to meet the requirements of wartime, it has continued to fullfill a valuable role in North American defense. On this, its twenty-fifth anniversary, I congratulate the Board and wish it continued success.

LESTER B. PEARSON

The Permanent Joint Board on Defense was established by President Franklin D. Roosevelt and Prime Minister W. L. Mackenzie King at a meeting in Ogdensburg, N.Y., on August 17 and 18, 1940. The establishment of the Board marked the beginning of the close cooperation of Canada and the United States in their common defense.

433 Remarks at the Swearing In of Dr. John W. Gardner as Secretary of Health, Education, and Welfare. *August 18, 1965*

Mr. Vice President, Dr. and Mrs. Gardner, Secretary Wirtz, Secretary Rusk, Members of the Cabinet, Members of the Congress, friends:

I want to observe this morning that the 89th Congress has constructed more beneficial measures for the good of our land and has placed more legislation on the statute books to improve the lot of all of our citizens, than any other of the previous 88 Congresses. All this has been done during the last 6 months, and all of it, both in design and purpose, aims to lift the level of living for 200 million Americans.

Nothing that we have done excels in durability of its benefits the far-reaching vocational, elementary, secondary and higher education bills that this Congress has acted on, or the monumental health legislation, including the long-sought, too long denied, health care for older Americans that helps to pay hospital bills, and doctors' bills, and nurses' bills, and extended care facilities, and drug bills, and other expenses.

I am very happy that Members of the House and Senate could be here this morning, particularly the architect of so many of these measures, that legislative craftsman, Lister Hill, the Chairman of the Labor Committee and the Chairman of the Appropriations Committee that implements all of these fine measures.

Also the man who is largely responsible for the passage of all of this legislation is today off the payroll as Secretary of Health, Education, and Welfare, but the Nation owes a great debt of gratitude to Tony Celebrezze and his very helpful wife, Ann.

So we come here today to mark ceremonies and to herald a new beginning. We have come this morning to the Rose Garden to welcome into the family of the Cabinet and to the stewardship of the Department of Health, Education, and Welfare a most eminent American, an extremely talented, a superbly qualified man to take over this leadership.

Dr. John Gardner was told by the President that the cause of public welfare in this country, the health care, and the education of the young minds needed the excellence of leadership that he could provide. He was told that, and he is here. He is a Republican, but that doesn't make much difference. He really provides a desirable balance of the four Cabinet members that I have appointed. Two were Democrats—Secretary Fowler and Attorney General Katzenbach; one was Republican—Secretary Connor; and now Dr. Gardner evens the score and makes it two and two.

I hope that these men get along as well working together as my Democratic Secretary of State, from Cherokee County, Georgia, and my Republican Secretary of Defense from California.

The job that Dr. Gardner has to do doesn't have much to do with party politics—and it just mustn't have. It does have to do with American people and American ideas and the greatness of the American Nation and of our American children. That kind of work involves all of us.

Dr. Gardner is a man of action. He knows how to achieve. He knows how to get things done. But he is also a philosopher and an educator, and this country and this Government needs those assets.

"We shall renew neither ourselves, nor society, nor a troubled world," Dr. Gardner once wrote, "unless we share a vision of something worth saving." Well, this administration, Dr. Gardner, intends to share that vision and to have it chart the course of this administration that will mark the 20th century as the century that fought the war and won the victory over mankind's ancient enemies—poverty, and ignorance, and bigotry, and disease.

This week we hope the Congress will act upon the administration's bill that will permit us to launch an all-out assault against the three major killers of human life in our country today—heart disease, and cancer, and stroke—to track them down, to isolate them, and to destroy them. And we are not going to stop there.

This administration intends to bring the healing miracle of modern medicine to everyone in this country, no matter how remotely they live from the city. If we could just reduce the sick leave of every American worker by one day a year we would be adding $10 billion annually to our gross national product. The savings in human suffering are beyond measure, and if we could have saved the lives of those who died last year alone from heart disease, in that year from cancer and from stroke, they would have earned $5 billion, and the Government would have gotten almost half of it. Now, from that income your Government, as you can see, would have received in excess of $2 billion.

So think of the advances that we could have made on problems that plague us if we had saved that money instead of letting it go down the drain, but both lives and incomes were lost—and they are gone now forever—last year.

We are trying to look ahead to next year. This administration is seeking new ideas and it is certainly not going to discourage any new solutions to the problems of population growth and distribution.

This administration hopes to provide the leadership for an environment that is free of the contamination which pollutes the water that we drink and the air that we breathe.

So I am glad this morning to see one of the most effective and inspirational former leaders of the Department of Health, Education, and Welfare—Abe Ribicoff—working at his post to help us continue in the Congress the work that he so ably started when he was in President Kennedy's Cabinet. I know that he would echo what I have said today if he could be out of that committee meeting, for he knows what there is to do and how urgently we need to do it, and I expect the Ribicoff-Gardner team to be heard from more in the days ahead.

So I just want to observe finally, in closing, that we will, as long as I am President, Dr. Gardner, try to provide an educational opportunity for every youngster in this country, regardless of the condition of his birth, the section he comes from, the poverty of his family, the color of his skin, or his religion.

These are our goals. They are the goals of John Gardner. John Gardner has made excellence his goal and the search for excellence his life. Now, the philosopher, the teacher, and the writer today becomes the active leader in the greatest Government in the world in a great march toward national excellence.

Today, Mr. Secretary, I want to assure you that I will reenlist in your army of excellence, and we all stand ready to march with you under your guidance.

NOTE: The President spoke at 11:47 a.m. in the Rose Garden at the White House. In his opening words he referred to Vice President Hubert H. Humphrey, Dr. and Mrs. John W. Gardner, Secretary of Labor W. Willard Wirtz, and Secretary of State Dean Rusk, who administered the oath of office.

During his remarks he referred to Senator Lister Hill of Alabama, Anthony J. Celebrezze, outgoing Secretary of Health, Education, and Welfare, Secretary of the Treasury Henry H. Fowler, Attorney General Nicholas deB. Katzenbach, Secretary of Commerce John T. Connor, Secretary of Defense Robert S. McNamara, and Senator Abraham Ribicoff of Connecticut, former Secretary of Health, Education, and Welfare.

Following the administration of the oath of office, Secretary Gardner spoke briefly. The text of his remarks is printed in the Weekly Compilation of Presidential Documents (vol. 1, p. 105).

See also Item 385.

434 Remarks at a Conference on the Water Crisis in the Northeastern States. *August 18, 1965*

Secretary Udall, distinguished Governors and mayors, my fellow Americans:

It was a week ago today that I called you here together in the face of a 4-year drought that has been unequaled in the Northeastern United States.

I said then that this was a time for action—a time for action to meet and to overcome the challenge of this great drought. That action is being taken.

Last Wednesday I sent water crisis teams under the direction of Secretary Udall and the Chief of Engineers into the Northeast. These teams, with the full support and with the help of all the Governors—Governors Hughes, Rockefeller, Scranton, and Terry, and Mayors Wagner, Tate, Pierce, and Addonizio—have forged a plan of action. The Congressmen and the Senators are on Capitol Hill voting on important legislation today and could not be here with us, but they have made valuable contributions. And while they cannot be here, I particularly and especially want to thank each of them for their interest and for their constructive help.

This morning the Delaware River Basin Commission ratified this plan. It has already been reviewed by the top water experts in the Federal Government. There is universal agreement that we should proceed at once. Under the plan, the States and the local communities, with the help of the Federal Government, can begin immediately to combat this unprecedented drought.

First, at the request of the Governors of the drought-stricken States, I am today writing to Governor Ellington, the Director of the Office of Emergency Planning, declaring certain portions of New Jersey, New York, Pennsylvania, and Delaware as disaster areas.

Second, to ease the critical water crisis in northern New Jersey, I am directing the Chief of Engineers to install an emergency pump-pipeline system at Lake Hopatcong, New Jersey. We have obtained the approval of New York State to release water stored in the Greenwood Lake to the Newark reservoirs. I am directing the Secretary of Interior to drill emergency wells in the underground Passaic Lake to develop standby water supplies.

Third, to resolve the water problems between New York and Philadelphia we have reached an agreement to establish a "strategic waterbank" with the 200 million gallons of New York reservoir water now released daily into the Delaware River as a "salt water buffer" for Philadelphia. This water will now be held for use by New York or Philadelphia, as determined by the Delaware River Basin Commission.

Fourth, to assure Philadelphia a continuing water supply, construction of the Torresdale intake will be speeded up to completion and full operation by December the 1st.

Finally, and in many ways most important, the Governors and the mayors of the drought stricken areas have agreed to increase their efforts to conserve their existing water supplies.

Our experts believe these measures are sufficient, if they are accompanied by aggressive conservation measures at the same time.

Now, if additional action is necessary your Federal Government will be prepared to act. In northern New Jersey, for example, we are prepared to provide an emergency pump-pipeline system from the Passaic Lake wells. If indeed it is needed, we are also prepared to provide an emergency supply system on the Delaware River to insure that the water needs of Philadelphia are met.

Now, these are strong steps. But they are wise steps, and they must be taken together.

For only if we work together can we overcome the water shortage threat now facing 25 million citizens in the most populated section of our Nation.

This has been a very commendable American effort. We have associated with us in these endeavors members of both parties, Republican Governors and Democratic Governors, mayors of both parties, and they have worked together not determining for a moment what is best for their party but what is best for their country and their areas.

I have been stimulated by the opportunity I have had to work with them and to cooperate with them, and I want to commend each Governor present, and each mayor present, and each head of Federal agency present, for the nonpartisan way they have attacked this matter, the diligence that they have demonstrated, and the results that they have achieved.

Whatever needs to be done in the future, so far as the Federal Government is concerned, will be done. I thank each Governor and each mayor for their true public-spirited leadership.

Thank you very much.

NOTE: The President spoke at 12:30 p.m. in the Cabinet Room at the White House. In his opening words he referred to Secretary of the Interior Stewart L. Udall.

During his remarks the President referred to Lt. Gen. William F. Cassidy, Chief of Army Engineers, Governor Richard J. Hughes of New Jersey, Governor Nelson A. Rockefeller of New York, Governor William W. Scranton of Pennsylvania, Governor Charles L. Terry, Jr., of Delaware, Mayor Robert F. Wagner of New York City, Mayor James H. J. Tate of Philadelphia, Mayor Alfred R. Pierce of Camden, N.J., Mayor Hugh Addonizio of Newark, N.J., and Buford Ellington, Director of the Office of Emergency Planning and former Governor of Tennessee.

The text of elements of the agreement on Federal, State, and municipal action in the water crisis, also made public on August 18, is printed in the Weekly Compilation of Presidential Documents (vol. 1, p. 107).

See also Items 358, 418.

435 Letter to the President of the Senate and to the Speaker of the House on Earthquake Recovery Assistance to Alaska. *August 20, 1965*

Dear Mr. President: (Dear Mr. Speaker:)

I have the honor to transmit herewith a report of activity under authority of Public Law 88–451 which covers actions taken by five Federal departments and agencies to assist in the recovery of Alaska following the earthquake of March 27, 1964.

The Act, entitled, "1964 Amendments to the Alaska Omnibus Act", was designed to speed additional aid to Alaska following the earthquake.

This report covers the period from January 1, 1965, through June 30, 1965. During the period covered in the report, more than $30 million in grants and loans were furnished Alaska under Public Law 88–451. During the twelve-month period since the amendments have been in force, $52 million have gone to Alaska. This assistance is only a fraction of the total recovery programs that the Federal Government has provided. Submission of this report to the Congress, as required by Public Law 88–451, also affords an opportunity to review briefly the total assistance to Alaska and its meaning to the State.

As of this date, more than $336 million in grants and loans have been made to the State, its communities and its people. Of this amount, nearly $163 million has been in the form of direct grants and still another $91 million in loans to individuals, business concerns, and other organizations. The remainder is for the repair of damaged Federal facilities in Alaska.

This means that $1,360 per citizen has gone to Alaska since the earthquake.

Today, Alaska has substantially recovered from the earthquake. Scars remain, but the worst effects have been overcome by the stamina, courage and resources of Alaska's people aided by speedy and significant Federal assistance of many kinds.

Repairs to Alaska's highways are virtually complete. Damage to airports has been repaired. The Alaska railroad is running again on a full schedule and with new equipment. Most schools have been repaired or rebuilt. Docks and harbors are being repaired and expanded to meet the growing needs of the populace. Lifeblood industries have fully recovered from the devastating blow. The fishing industry was put back on its feet at such a rapid rate that it was able to increase its catch by 100 million pounds during 1964, for an increased value of $11,600,000.

The per capita income of the Alaskan citizen has increased from $2,850 at the time of the earthquake to $3,154 today, an increase of 11 percent.

At no time in recent years has an individual State suffered such a catastrophe and at no time was such a massive and effective program of Federal assistance carried out. It is a tribute to the individual citizens of Alaska, to the Congress, and to the thousands of State and Federal personnel who worked tirelessly in the hours and months that followed this tragedy.

The future of Alaska is one of great potential and immediate fulfillment. The damage and dislocation left by the earthquake are gone and the destiny of our forty-ninth State is once again bright with promise.

Sincerely,

LYNDON B. JOHNSON

NOTE: This is the text of identical letters addressed to the Honorable Hubert H. Humphrey, President of the Senate, and to the Honorable John W. McCormack, Speaker of the House of Representatives.

The text of the report was not made public by the White House.

The 1964 Amendments to the Alaska Omnibus Act was approved by the President on August 19, 1964 (Public Law 88–451; 78 Stat. 505).

436   Remarks at the White House Conference on Equal Employment Opportunities.   *August* 20, 1965

Chairman Franklin D. Roosevelt, Jr.:

I always feel stimulated and inspired a little bit just to repeat that name—Franklin D. Roosevelt, Jr. And I know that your father and your mother would be very happy if they could observe how your talents are being used in this critical hour in our national history.

I think they would feel the same way about my fellow workers in the cause of equal opportunity, and I know you don't want me to salute you very long—in view of that sun out there—but I do salute you, one and all.

I commend you for coming here, in the heat of a Washington August, to give us your insights into one of America's most critical problems. We asked you to come here for your country's sake—because we believe that it is a problem beyond the capacity of any single one of us in this Capital, or any single group of us, to ever solve alone. We need your help—and I am glad that you have responded out of a sense of duty to both your country and to humanity.

Last year we were given the indispensable legal means for solving this problem. Title VII of the Civil Rights Act of 1964—guaranteeing equal employment opportunities—is a key to hope for millions of our fellow Americans. With that key we can begin to open the gates that now enclose the ghettos of despair.

But I would remind you this morning that it is just a key. It will open the gates only for those who are willing to shoulder the responsibilities, as well as the rights that it offers. The key itself cannot provide the skills and the determination that the economy of this Nation requires. It cannot reverse at once those melancholy currents by which millions are swept along—in slum houses, in crowded schools, in the desolate streets where unemployment and boredom lead hopeless men to crime and to violence.

But none of that solemn history could ever be changed without this key.

If there is one thing I think we have learned from the civil rights struggle, it is that the problem of bringing the Negro American into an equal role in our society is more complex, and is more urgent, and is much more critical than any of us have ever known. Who of you could have predicted 10 years ago, that in this last, sweltering, August week thousands upon thousands of disenfranchised Negro men and women would suddenly take part in self-government, and that thousands more in that same week would strike out in an unparalleled act of violence in this Nation?

Our conscience cries out against the hatred that we heard last week. It bore no relation to the orderly struggle for civil rights that has ennobled the last decade. Every leader in that struggle has condemned this outrage against the laws of the land. And during the few days that preceded it, I had spent all week at the White House visiting individually with Dr. King, Mr. Farmer, Dr.

Roy Wilkins, Mr. Philip Randolph—all talking about the great meeting that we had to have here later in the fall, because the cities of this Nation and the Negro family in this Nation are two of our most pressing, most important problems. Well, the bitter years that preceded the riots, the death of hope where hope existed, their sense of failure to change the conditions of life—these things no doubt led to these riots. But they did not justify them.

I hope that every American who believes in equal opportunity for his fellow men, understands this distinction that I have made. For we shall never achieve a free and prosperous and hopeful society until we have suppressed the fires of hate and we have turned aside from violence—whether that violence comes from the nightriders of the Klan, or the snipers and the looters in the Watts district. Neither old wrongs nor new fears can ever justify arson or murder.

During the past decade more of my energy has been spent on protecting and preserving and writing into law, through the legislative halls, the rights of all Americans than I have spent on any single subject or any half-dozen subjects.

The Civil Rights Act of 1957—night after night after night, I slept in my Senate chair. I did not see my family for weeks. The Civil Rights Act of 1960, the Civil Rights Act of 1964, the Voting Rights Act of 1965—these were the advances in whose cause were enlisted men of goodwill from every part of the country. A good many of them sacrificed their political life in this cause. I see some of them out there now. The road to passage of all of these bills was a long one, and a winding one, and a tortuous one. But they were conceived and they were enacted, the first in almost a century. Lincoln signed the Emancipation Proclamation 100 years ago,

but it was a proclamation and never a fact. And these measures, one by one, were conceived and enacted to protect the rights of American citizens that were set forth in the American Constitution, and in the minds and the hearts and the spirits of our Founding Fathers.

But I must remind you, and all the world, this morning, that with these rights comes responsibility.

And with responsibility there goes obligation.

We cannot, and we must not, in one breath demand laws to protect the rights of all of our citizens, and then turn our back, or wink, or in the next breath allow laws to be broken that protect the safety of our citizens. There just must never come the hour in this Republic when any citizen, whoever he is, can ever ignore the law or break the law with impunity.

And so long as I am your President I intend to preserve the rights of all of our citizens, and I intend to enforce the laws that protect all of our citizens—without regard to race, religion, region, or without fear or favor.

A rioter with a Molotov cocktail in his hands is not fighting for civil rights any more than a Klansman with a sheet on his back and a mask on his face. They are both more or less what the law declares them: lawbreakers, destroyers of constitutional rights and liberties, and ultimately destroyers of a free America. They must be exposed and they must be dealt with.

It is our duty—and it is our desire—to open our hearts to humanity's cry for help. It is our obligation to seek to understand what could lie beneath the flames that scarred that great city. So let us equip the poor and the oppressed—let us equip them for the long march to dignity and to well-being.   But let us never confuse the need for decent work and fair treatment with an excuse to destroy and to uproot.

Ours is an open society.   The world is always witness to whatever we do—sometimes, I think (results of the cooperation of some of my friends) to some things we don't do. We would not have it otherwise.   For the brave story of the Negro American is related to the struggle of men on every continent for their rights as sons of God.   It is a compound of brilliant promises and stunning reverses.   Sometimes, as in the past week when the two are mixed on the same pages of our newspapers and television screens, the result is baffling to all the world.   And it is baffling to me, and to you, and to us. And always there is the danger that hours of disorder may erase the accumulated goodwill of many months and many years.   And I warn and plead with all thinking Americans to contemplate this for a due period.

Yet beneath the discord we hear another theme.   That theme speaks of a day when Americans of every color, and every creed, and every religion, and every region, and every sex can be trained for decent employment, can find it, can secure it, can have it preserved, and can support their families in an enriching and a rewarding environment.

For those who have been denied equal access throughout the years to public facilities, I am proud to say that this administration has led the way in ripping down the barriers of discrimination.

To those who have been denied the precious right to vote that ought to go with American citizenship, this administration is opening the polling booths again and is registering them by the thousands so they can exercise that right.

For those who have been denied an equal opportunity to learn, through Head Start, through elementary, secondary, vocational, and higher education, the Johnson administration is trying to turn hope into reality.

And to those who have been trapped in the dark ghettos that are barren of playgrounds for their little children, and barren of decent homes for their families, eroded by the monotony of each day's existence, I promise them that as long as I am here every day I am going to be working to see that that, too, is changed.

In education, in housing, in health, in conservation, in poverty, in 20 fields or more, we have passed, and we will pass, far-reaching programs heretofore never enacted that are rich in hope and that will lead us to a better day.

We will do all this through the work of men and women like you—men and women who believe both in equal opportunity and equal responsibility and obligation.   And unless this work wins the day, and unless we are successful in what we are trying to do, we may all be consumed, without discrimination, by the fires of hate and bigotry.

You have been asked to come here because you are already enlisted in this—what I consider the most important cause of our time.

I welcome you.   I am grateful for your energy and your purpose.   For our cause is the liberation—the liberation of all of our citizens in all of our sections in all of our Nation through peaceful, nonviolent change.

And we shall overcome, and I am enlisted for the duration.

Earlier in the spring, I asked the very able and dedicated Vice President, who has given his life to promoting equality among all races and religions and regions, to head up a blue-ribbon Cabinet task force to see what we could do about 2 million youngsters,

899

most of whom came from broken homes, a good many of whom slept with the rats every night—if they slept at all—all of whom were without jobs, without education, without food, to see if he couldn't, with the help of the Cabinet and with the help of the businessmen and labor men of this country, find jobs for these men, so that they could wipe away this monotony and have useful work, constructive work for their talents this summer.

We were ambitious. Perhaps not as ambitious as that great man of vision, Franklin Roosevelt, when he said, "We will build 50,000 planes a year." And they ridiculed him. But we said we must get 500,000 jobs for these young people this summer.

Our late beloved President, John Fitzgerald Kennedy, started programs that brought thousands and thousands of youngsters into private and into public employment and made them closer to their country and to their Government. And so, in his memory, and faced with this crisis, the Vice President, at my direction, undertook this assignment.

Before his target date approached, he said, "We have reached the goal already." That is what every United Fund head in the country likes to hear, every Red Cross drive. He had reached the goal. And I said, "Well, let's just get a better goal—750,000."

Now, he's coming home tomorrow. This is supposed to be a secret. And I guess we'll get a little publicity on it, if I tell it off the record. But I do want to observe that he's already placed 800,000, and I am going to raise the goal on him tomorrow, although we're in mid-August, and tell him, "Let's go to 1 million."

So, the unemployment of young people has taken a nosedive. The employment has skyrocketed. But if we reach our goal of 1 million, that we never dreamed of a few weeks

ago, we will have done only 50 percent of our job, because we started out with 2 million to deal with.

Our unemployment is at the lowest it has been for 7 years. But we can't sit back in our rocking chairs and be happy and satisfied as long as there is 1 million, or 100, who have energy and are willing to work, that are denied work.

So to you who have given your time and talents to come here, on behalf of this country I thank you.

We have problems of foreign policy. But the foreign policy of this country is going to be: Do unto others as you would have them do unto you. And I said to Secretary Rusk and his staff yesterday, every one of them, the foreign policy of this country is to educate all of our people to give every child all the education he can take; find work for every human being that is willing to work; find medical care so that we will preserve their bodies and keep them on the payroll and on the taxroll as long as we can.

Education, health, move them out of the slums and the poverty, provide housing, and beautify the land and make it something that is truly symbolic when we say "America the Beautiful," because we want this to be a good world.

And when other nations look at us and see what we are doing at home, they must know that people that do those things with their own folks are not going to treat other people very badly.

Now, the African continent, the Western Hemisphere, the European continent—we reviewed each one of them one by one, the hundred-odd nations that we have relations with. And those relations, I am glad to say, are better than one could really expect under all the problems that face a complex world.

We do have a serious situation in VietNam. We need to get to a negotiating table.

We need, in the words of Isaiah, to "reason together." And I pray every night that the day will come when others will be willing to accept our proposals and join us in our hope of satisfying these problems and dealing with these difficulties by talking instead of fighting.

There are some that will use this problem in Viet-Nam to lock the door of opportunity on housing, and on education, and on space, and on health, and on conservation. But they are singing an old song. They're living in another century. The people of America are progressive, prudent folks that are on the march and they know that we cannot lead the world if we lead them in ignorance, and illiteracy, and poverty, and disease.

While on the one hand we are going to protect our liberties and defend our convictions and plead for an opportunity to live in peace, we are never going to neglect the education of our little ones, or the salvation of our lame or our halt or our palsied, or even

forget the countryside, because people work better, longer, faster, produce more in a land that we like to call "America the Beautiful."

Thank you for what you are doing for it, thank you more for what you are going to do.

NOTE: The President spoke at 12:23 p.m. on the South Lawn at the White House. In his opening words he referred to Franklin D. Roosevelt, Jr., Chairman of the Equal Employment Opportunity Commission. During his remarks he referred to Martin Luther King, Jr., President of the Southern Christian Leadership Conference, James Farmer, National Director of the Congress of Racial Equality, Roy Wilkins, Secretary of the National Association for the Advancement of Colored People, A. Philip Randolph, President of the Brotherhood of Sleeping Car Porters, and Dean Rusk, Secretary of State.

On August 5, 1965, the White House announced the program for the White House Conference on Equal Employment Opportunity which was held in Washington on August 19–20 (1 Weekly Comp. Pres. Docs., p. 50).

For the President's statements following the riots in the Watts district of Los Angeles, see Items 426, 453.

437   Remarks on Announcing Appointment of James Vorenberg and Dr. Ralph Huitt. *August 20, 1965*

THE PRESIDENT. Nick, you want to tell them why you're here?

MR. KATZENBACH. I'm here today because the President just appointed Mr. James Vorenberg to be Executive Secretary of the Crime Commission. With the meeting of the Commission scheduled for the 8th and 9th of September, we expect to be well on our way.

Mr. Vorenberg has already done considerable planning as to the activities for the Crime Commission to go into. You are all aware, as I am, of the President's deep interest in doing something effective about this problem, which is one of our major problems

domestically. And we hope to accomplish that with Mr. Vorenberg and the staff of the Commission which we already have, and with the work of the Commission to do something really significant in terms of proposing solutions, concrete solutions, to deal with the rising crime rate in this country.

THE PRESIDENT. This is going to be one of the three or four or five principal subjects with which this administration will be dealing, and I am very proud of what the Attorney General has been able to do in attracting the very high quality personnel, and not only members of the Commission but members of the staff. It is one of the most difficult problems that faces our country and hasn't any easy answers. We want to get into the innermost recesses and make a study in depth, and we will come up with the best recommendations that this study indicates.

I have with me the Secretary of Health, Education, and Welfare. He has brought with him Dr. Ralph Huitt from the University of Wisconsin, to be Assistant Secretary for Legislation of the Department of Health, Education, and Welfare. He was on some kind of grant up there. How long were you up there?

DR. HUITT. Six months.

THE PRESIDENT. And he was on Senator Proxmire's staff for a year. He was on a destroyer escort during the war and later instructed at the University of Texas. He joined the faculty of the University of Wisconsin in 1949, and became associate professor and full professor in 1959; he received a Rockefeller Research Foundation Award in 1960 for the advancement of education. He is Director of the Wisconsin Center for Education in Politics, member of the Advisory Board of the Committee for Economic Development and Committee for Improvement of Management in Government; he was selected in 1964 by the American Political Science Association to direct a far-reaching study of congressional reform—that is a bad word to use in this announcement—under a Carnegie Corporation grant.

So here he is and he is going to try to reform the HEW.

We are going to have a number of top staff people over there and Dr. Gardner is in the process now of selecting them, and I want to help him.

Thank you, gentlemen.

NOTE: The President spoke to a group of White House correspondents in his office shortly after the opening of the Press Secretary's news briefing at 11:17 a.m. During his remarks he referred to, among others, John W. Gardner, Secretary of Health, Education, and Welfare.

As printed above, the remarks follow the text of the Press Secretary's briefing; they were not made public in the form of a White House press release.

A progress report from the Attorney General on the President's Commission on Law Enforcement and the Administration of Justice was made public by the White House on August 20, 1965. The report stated that the Attorney General had called the first formal meeting of the Commission to be held in Washington on September 8–9, 1965. The Commission was to be divided into subcommittees, the report continued, each supported by a panel of experts, which would study the following subjects: public safety, administration and organization of police forces, corruption in public life, administration of criminal justice, youth crime, and correctional institutions. The text of the report is printed in the Weekly Compilation of Presidential Documents (vol. 1, p. 115).

438   Remarks With the Vice President on the Youth Opportunities Campaign.   *August 21, 1965*

Mr. Vice President, Secretary Wirtz, members of the Council, my friends:

On behalf of the entire Nation, I want to thank the Vice President and his very special task force on Youth Opportunity. The material that you have presented to me is much more than a statistical report; it is a passport to the future for hundreds of thousands of young Americans.

In this all-out effort, Mr. Vice President, that you and members of your group have made in an attempt to help these young men and women, you enlisted the willing support of the various groups that you have just listed, and we all owe a very special thank you to them, particularly to the employers who were willing to open their arms and accept new people to their ranks.

Your goal was set deliberately high, at half a million in the public and private sector. We thought we might not reach it, but at least it was a daring adventure, and you always like to undertake assignments of that kind.

But what we did was really underestimate what the task force could do under your leadership, and what the Americans of this country would do for their fellow man.

I thought, as you were speaking, I guess if we had a man-of-the-year poll—that type of poll in the Government—that the Vice President would be voted the one person in the Government that is everybody's best friend. If the Secretary of State, Defense, or Labor or any of them had a peculiar and particular and delicate situation on their hands, I imagine they would want to talk to him—and they usually do—to get not only sympathy and understanding, but to get some energy and some effort and some constructive leadership. I know that is true of the Cabinet. It is particularly true with me. In a very wide range of fields and complex subjects, I find the Vice President specializes in practically all of them.

But what is quite appealing to me about him and what always has been, is that he could get so wrapped up in the individual boy—the Negro boy that is 16 years old, that lives down in Podunk, x State, who comes from a broken home, who sleeps in a room at night where rats are known to roam, and who doesn't really have much opportunity ahead for him. And the Vice President goes out with the help of Secretary Wirtz and others, and shows up here not with 500,000 jobs but 820,000—maybe 880. I heard him give the figure 880—they told me 820—and I shouldn't be surprised if he hasn't gotten 60,000 extra ones since my speech was written.

But I think that in this day and time when we have specialists who concentrate on really what we do wrong and point up the little errors that their country makes, or their leaders make, or their Government makes—always constructive, but they do, on occasions I observe, have some comments about some mistake that was made or how it could have been done better. I think this is a rather astonishing record of performance, and I just don't know how to tell the Vice President and Secretary Wirtz and the other members of the Council here how much I appreciate it or how much I want to tell industry, the businessmen, the power company, the transportation company, the paper factory, the folks that really had some compassion and then were willing to listen and were willing to extend themselves a little to do something about it.

I think the leaders in this Nation, in industry and in labor and in Government, should be thanked for their unstinting support. And that is what I want to emphasize this morning. If they had not listened to the recommendations it never would have gotten off the ground.

Now what we have done this summer is more than just a matter of finding summer jobs for youngsters. We have added a real new dimension to these youngsters' lives. So we are going to raise that goal that we set before. It has been exceeded a couple of times. I guess this is August 21—that is at least 6 days before my birthday—that is the way I keep things now. I am going to hold it off as long as I can.

I want to say this morning that we are not only going to continue this vital program, but I am going to charge the Vice President, on August 21, with finding a million jobs before the summer ends. Now if he has 880,000, as he said, that is just 120,000. If he has 820,000, that is 180,000. But that is a sizable undertaking and I am going to ask him to shoot at that, and I am going to ask the business people of this country to come in kind of like the United Fund drive. We are just close to going over the top and let's get a million jobs for these young people before the school term starts.

I have another assignment I want to give him. At the start of the school term last fall there were 3,100,000 young people who left school without a high school diploma. Their unemployment rate was almost 17 percent. It was four times the rate of the entire balance of the labor force. Now, during the coming school year, we face the prospect again of another three-quarters of a million youngsters dropping out. Many of them will never even begin the new term. So the decision for many people to remain in school must be given the highest priority.

Therefore, I am going to ask the Vice President this morning to call some people together in Government, and the leaders out in the country, to take immediate steps to try to mobilize nationwide support behind a back-to-school drive, and let's get everybody in school in September that we can.

I know he will be calling on each of you in this room a little later, but I want to call on you now to try to do your bit, put in your nickel's worth and help the Vice President get this campaign underway, because it is a very laudable goal.

I ask employers, the unions, the civic, the trade, the religious organizations, the State and local governments, to exert every influence that they can command to bring these young people the facts about how important it is to stay in school. Because once the importance of education is impressed upon them, this administration will do everything in its power to see that they get it.

One of the real bright spots in the world

today—and it is bright in most of the continents—but the bright spot in our continent, in our area, is the lack of jealousy and envy and hate and fear that exists between business and labor, and employer and employee; associations and organizations that used to put out these mimeographed handouts every other day predicting that the country was going to pot, are now spending that great reservoir of energy and talent on finding jobs for young people, helping them get back to school, helping us develop better health programs and things of that nature, and providing more jobs, making extra capital investments.

I am just so proud that our gross national product is growing, that the depth of our hatreds are being minimized, and that there is a minimum of actual hate between our business and labor groups existing. And this is a good demonstration of it.

We have a rather low unemployment figure—the lowest unemployment rate in 8 years. If any of you in here have any jobs to pass out, we welcome them, and we will try to make it the lowest in 10 years if you will help us a little bit.

Thank you very much.

THE VICE PRESIDENT'S REMARKS

I am pleased to report to you, Mr. President, that your Youth Opportunities Campaign, launched earlier this year, produced over 880,000 work and training opportunities for young Americans between the ages of 16 and 21 in less than 3 months from May 23, when you announced the Youth Opportunities Campaign.

The business community, the labor movement, service and religious organizations, Federal, State, and local governments rallied to your call to produce this success.

The impact of the Youth Employment Opportunity Campaign is illustrated clearly in the Department of Labor's unemployment figures for July. Unemployment among the 16- through 21-year-old group dropped to 12.3 from 18.5 percent in June. At the same time, employment for this group rose by 800,000.

The Youth Opportunity Campaign contributed to the improvement of the national employment figures for July. Unemployment in June stood at 4.7 but fell to 4.5 percent in July—the lowest level since October 1957.

As you recall, Mr. President, your message was direct and to the point. Unless Federal, State, and local governments, business and civic and religious leadership collaborated in the Youth Opportunity Campaign, more than 2 million 16- through 21-year-olds, as you reminded us, would be unable to find work this summer.

The work in the training opportunities that were produced not only gave the Nation's youth money to continue in school or to contribute to the family budget, but also to serve as gateways to future careers. These job opportunities produced the self-confidence and self-respect which is the vital byproduct of steady employment.

The Youth Opportunity Campaign task force mounted a massive cross-country push that produced jobs at the rate of 10,000 daily. Within the Federal Government over 26,000 young men and women were placed in jobs, another 50,000 were enrolled in the Neighborhood Youth Corps. But in the large majority of the jobs, the large majority came from private industry—labor, service and religious organizations, State and local governments. Almost 300,000 jobs were reported in 7,000 letters from American businessmen to the Secretary of Commerce. Hundreds of thousands of additional job openings were offered by over 80,000 employers who communicated with the State employment service offices.

Mr. President, we are indebted to the U.S. Conference of Mayors, the National League of Cities, and the National City Managers Association that worked closely with the Cabinet task force in organizing support for the program through their local communities.

The Youth Opportunity Campaign depended on employers offering jobs, but it also needed the help of the communications industry, trade associations, and national organizations. Radio and television stations across the country were asked for and readily contributed hundreds of hours of public service time to bring the campaign and the need for it across to the American public.

Through regular reporting and editorial comment, newspapers supported the campaign, offering free of charge the want ad column to young people who wanted a job.

Five thousand AM and FM radio stations and 700 television stations received the original campaign kit as the campaign progressed and they were blanketed with up-to-date fact sheets and releases. Four hundred trade and civic organizations also cooperated.

The U.S. Chamber of Commerce, American Legion, Veterans of Foreign Wars, National Federation of Independent Businessmen, the National Council of Churches, and many others endorsed the program and your message, Mr. President. Still many others included the National Association of Manufacturers, the National Urban League, the AFL–CIO, Lions International, Big Brothers of America, the National Council of Jewish Women, and the Young Presidents' Organization—all these people helped do the job.

I am happy to report to you, Mr. President, that despite the fact there was still much more to do, through the energetic work of your Cabinet officers who worked day and night to launch this effort we can give you at least some reasonably reassuring report of progress in the matter of youth employment opportunities.

Mr. President, I am sure that our people would like to hear from you, and it is my privilege to present the President of the United States.

NOTE: The President spoke at 12:10 p.m. in the Cabinet Room at the White House. In his opening words he referred to Vice President Hubert H. Humphrey and Secretary of Labor W. Willard Wirtz.

On the same day the White House made public a summary of a task force report on the President's Youth Opportunities Campaign (1 Weekly Comp. Pres. Docs. 129).

439   Statement by the President Upon Signing the Military Pay Raise Bill.   *August* 21, 1965

I AM TODAY signing into law H.R. 9075, substantially raising the pay for all the members of our Armed Forces.

As I said last January in my Message to the Congress on Defense: "The success of all our policies depends upon our ability to attract, develop fully, mobilize and retain the talents of outstanding men and women in the military services."

This has been the policy of the Kennedy-Johnson administration since its inception.

Since January 1961 the President has submitted and approved military pay increases totaling $1.7 billion per year.

This year, after reviewing the findings of an expert pay panel, I sent to the Congress a request to increase military pay by $500 million.

The Congress, after carefully considering our proposal, voted for more than a 100-percent increase over our recommendation. The bill of the Congress will add $550 million per year to our expenditures beyond what we had planned or believed necessary at this time.

In this critical period, however, in light of the alternatives available to me, I have con-cluded that the public interest will best be served by signing the bill.

First, because the bill contains many provisions recommended by the administration to make certain that the pay of our men and women in uniform is ample, on a continuing basis, to provide a standard of living commensurate with the goals of the Great Society, and is sufficient to attract and retain outstanding men and women in the military services.   The bill provides—

—A regular 4-year review of the military pay structure.

—An annual review to assure that military pay stays in line with the cost of living.

—Increased combat pay for American servicemen in Viet-Nam.

—Special bonuses to help us retain highly skilled servicemen, such as electronics specialists, whose training is especially costly.

Second, because the bill recognizes the importance of the nearly 3 million Americans who wear the uniform of our country's Armed Forces.   For it is the soldiers, sailors, airmen, and marines—not the weapons or the ships and planes—who are the real bulwark of our military might.   Their bravery and dedication is the reason America is the land of the free today.

NOTE: The bill (H.R. 9075) is Public Law 89–132 (79 Stat. 545).

On August 31, 1965, the White House announced that members of the Armed Forces stationed in Viet-Nam and contiguous waters would be able to send post cards and letters free to any place in the United States and to any military post office in the world.

On November 1, 1965, the President signed Executive Order 11255 "Designation of Vietnam and Waters Adjacent Thereto as an Overseas Combat Area for Purposes of Armed Forces Mailing Privileges" (30 F.R. 14135; 3 CFR, 1965 Supp.).

440   Veto of the Military Authorization Bill.
August 21, 1965

To the House of Representatives:

I regret that I must return H.R. 8439 without my approval.

I have been advised by the Attorney General that certain provisions of the bill are repugnant to the Constitution. Its enactment would represent a fundamental encroachment on one of the great principles of the American Constitutional system—the separation of powers between the Legislative and Executive branches.

The bill authorizes a military construction program. The objectionable provisions appear in Section 611 which applies to all military installations in the United States and Puerto Rico. The only exceptions are the movement of men and equipment solely for tactical purposes and minor posts manned by less than 250 people.

Section 611 provides that no military camp, post, station, base, yard, or other installation or facility shall be closed, abandoned, or substantially reduced in mission until 120 days after reports of the proposed action are made to the Committees on Armed Services of the Senate and House of Representatives. A further restriction is that such reports can be submitted only between January 1 and April 30 of each year. If Congress adjourns sine die before 120 days pass, the report must be resubmitted to the next regular session of the Congress.

These limitations could seriously interfere with and adversely affect the administration of our military program and our continuing efforts to improve our defense posture.

We cannot commit ourselves, for the prolonged period required by this bill, to delay action necessary to meet the realities of the troubled world in which we live.

By the Constitution, the executive power is vested in the President. The President is the Commander in Chief of the armed forces. The President cannot sign into law a bill which substantially inhibits him from performing his duty. He cannot sign into law a measure which deprives him of power for eight months of the year even to propose a reduction of mission or the closing of any military installation, and which prohibits him from closing, abandoning or substantially reducing in mission any military facility in the country for what could be a year or more and must be 120 days. The times do not permit it. The Constitution prohibits it.

The limitations upon the Commander in Chief and the executive branch of the government here sought to be imposed are a clear violation of separation of powers. The Attorney General has so advised me. The Congress enacts the laws. Their execution must be left to the President. The President must be free, if the need arises, to reduce the mission at any military installation in the country if and when such becomes necessary.

The legislative and executive branches share responsibility for the security of the nation, and each has a vital role to play. But under the separation of powers decreed by the Constitution, the responsibility of each is distinct and each must avoid interfering in the proper sphere of the other. Under the Constitution Congress has the power to enact laws to "raise and support" armed forces, and only Congress can provide the necessary appropriations for maintaining our fighting forces. In turn, the President is responsible for the direction and operation of those forces, for the faithful execution of the laws enacted by Congress, and for the most effective use of appropriated funds.

In our history, the Congress has occasionally passed bills which have required, in various circumstances, that executive action must be deferred until the proposed action has been reported to specified Congressional committees, and the Congress has provided a waiting period during which the Congress may, if it sees fit, enact appropriate legislation. Some of these bills received Presidential approval. Others have been vetoed.

For example, Attorneys General in unbroken succession since at least the time of President Wilson have advised their Chief Executives that so-called "come-into-agreement" clauses, requiring approval of executive action by legislative committees, are unconstitutional. Although Section 611 is not literally a "come-into-agreement" clause, its limitations upon effective executive action, in the critical area of national defense, go substantially further than any bill heretofore enacted and approved by any President.

In addition to the constitutional principle involved, effective national defense in this nuclear age requires flexibility in the management of our defense installations, including the assignment of their respective missions.

Further, the American people are entitled to a dollar's worth of defense for every dollar spent. The base closure program is a vital element in effecting important economies within the military establishment. Actions have been taken under it to reduce or close more than 600 bases with an estimated ultimate saving of more than $1 billion annually. At the same time that these savings have been realized, we have been strengthening and modernizing our military program. Also we have done much to soften the effect on the communities and individuals involved. I deem it to be of primary importance that our base closure program not be impaired.

Also a President, under his oath of office, must be concerned about the cumulative erosion of the executive power by legislation such as Section 611 of this bill. The power of the Congress in which I served for nearly two dozen years, is not served by assuming executive functions. The need for wise legislative action, and the dependency of our welfare upon it, was never greater. The legislative burdens of the Congress were never greater. Not only does separation of powers fail when Congress impairs the executive function, but the sheer inability of the Congress to deal meaningfully with the multitudinous details of execution of its laws weakens government.

By my action here, I do not mean to imply that a reasonable reporting provision, consistent with the legislative powers of the Congress, would warrant a veto.

We should recall James Madison's words

spoken on the floor of the House of Representatives in the first session of the first Congress in 1789:

"If there is a principle in our Constitution, indeed in any free Constitution, more sacred than another, it is just that which separates the Legislative, Executive and Judicial powers."

For these reasons, I am compelled to return this bill without my approval.

LYNDON B. JOHNSON

The White House
August 21, 1965

NOTE: The Congress reenacted the bill as the Military Construction Authorization Act of 1966. In its revised form it was approved by the President on September 16, 1965 (see Item 518).

441 Statement by the President on the Death of Representative Clarence J. Brown of Ohio. *August 23, 1965*

I AM distressed to learn of the death of Representative Clarence Brown, a distinguished public servant and my longtime colleague in the Congress.

Representative Brown was a principal sponsor of the Commissions on the Organization of the Executive Branch of the Government, known as the Hoover Commissions. To the work of those Commissions he devoted his great energies and his dedication to good Government.

He was a strong partisan, in the best tradition of American politics. He was also a patriot who served his country faithfully during the quarter century of his tenure in Congress.

NOTE: Representative Brown served in the House of Representatives from January 3, 1939, until his death.

The President's statement was released by Bill D. Moyers, Special Assistant to the President, at his news conference at 4 p.m. on Monday, August 23, 1965. It was not made public in the form of a White House press release.

442 Telegram to Mrs. Philip Daniels on the Death of Her Son Jonathan, a Theological Student. *August 23, 1965*

I GRIEVE with you in the death of your son. We labor towards the day when the cause of brotherhood may prevail, and the violence that sometimes scars the face of America may be ended. May God comfort you and strengthen you in this hour.

LYNDON B. JOHNSON

[Mrs. Philip Daniels, 67 Summer Keene Street, Keene, New Hampshire]

NOTE: The telegram was read by Bill D. Moyers, Special Assistant to the President, at his news conference at 4:25 p.m. on Monday, August 23, 1965. It was not made public in the form of a White House press release.

Jonathan M. Daniels was killed by a shotgun blast on August 20, in Hayneville, Ala., shortly after his release from jail where he had been held for civil rights activities. His companion, Rev. Richard F. Morrisroe, was injured (see Item 444).

443 Remarks at the Swearing In of Judge Thurgood Marshall as Solicitor General. *August 24, 1965*

Judge and Mrs. Marshall and your two attractive young boys, Mr. Justice Black, Mr. Justice Clark, distinguished Attorney General Katzenbach, Honorable J. Edgar Hoover, Members of Congress, my distinguished guests and friends:

Since assuming the Presidency more than a year and a half ago, I have made a total of 370 major appointments to the Federal Government. In each of these appointments it has been my goal and my determination to seek out the best qualified man or woman in the nation for the job, regardless of their party or their race or their sex.

That goal is fulfilled today as we meet here for the installation of Justice Thurgood Marshall as the 33d Solicitor General of the United States, and by this act we pay honor to a high office in the American Government, to a man, and, most of all, to the law.

Thurgood Marshall symbolizes what is best about our American society: the belief that human rights must be satisfied through the orderly processes of law.

At the pinnacle of our system of law is the great Supreme Court of the United States, and the Solicitor General is our first advocate before that great court. So it is a cause of profound satisfaction to me that in Judge Marshall we shall have an advocate whose lifelong concern has been the pursuit of justice for his fellow man.

For although his client will always be the United States of America, his interest does not always rest in triumph. As Mr. Justice Sutherland once observed, the Government's paramount interest "is not that it shall win a case, but that justice shall be done." And that is the interest that we vest in the Solicitor General. In performing it he serves not only the executive branch but he serves the Court itself, for traditionally it has relied on him to set the standard for all the American bar in the country to follow. The position of Solicitor General is one of tremendous responsibility, and it is also, as that able scholar Archibald Cox, President Kennedy's Solicitor General, said, "the finest lawyer's position in all the world."

I want to say at this point that few men have served more forcefully or more successfully as Solicitor General of the United States than Archibald Cox. And as I noted when I accepted his resignation, Mr. Cox has argued more cases before the Supreme Court than any other living man—and he will hold that record at least until Thurgood Marshall. And he has argued those cases with remarkable effectiveness. His return to private life has left a void that can only be filled by a great professional from among the highest ranks of the American bar.

The life and the accomplishments of Thurgood Marshall testify that he is such a man. As chief counsel to the National Association for the Advancement of Colored People, he represented his clients not as Negroes, whose cases were special and different, but he represented them as Americans, with the same rights and the same responsibilities that the Constitution is supposed to give to every citizen.

The cases in which Judge Marshall became involved are already part of the social and legal history of our time. From 1940 on, Thurgood Marshall was in the vanguard of the legal effort against discrimination in higher education, against discrimination in housing, against discrimination in voting.

And then in 1954 came the climax toward which this good man had labored so brilliantly for so long.

The Supreme Court's school desegregation decision launched the great movement to end the injustice that's too often inflicted on our Negro citizens. And I have asked our Cabinet officer, Mr. Gardner of HEW, to have his men work around the clock to make the desegregation decision of the Supreme Court a reality and a fact. I am glad that we are approaching it with such effectiveness, and I hope we will complete the job between now and the time the school term opens.

A decade later some may have forgotten how much courage and how much work and how much faith in the Nation those efforts demanded, but I think all of us remember his vision and his unyielding pursuit of justice.

In 1961 he was appointed by our late beloved President, John Fitzgerald Kennedy, to one of the Nation's highest courts, and in the past 4 years he has written a distinguished record there. No one who knew this man expected it to be otherwise. No one who knew him thought that he would say "no" when a new and an even more compelling challenge was presented to him by his President. He accepted this assignment for one reason—because he knew that he was needed, and because he has always responded when he has been needed.

I think it might be observed that Thurgood Marshall is the first Negro in the history of the United States ever to become the Solicitor General. Thurgood Marshall is already in the front ranks of the great lawyers of this generation. He has argued 32 cases before the Supreme Court; he has won 29 of them. And that is a batting average of .900. It is likely that should he continue in his present assignment for the next 3 years, that he could very well argue 50 more cases before the highest Court in the land—and that would make him try more cases before the Supreme Court than any man in history had ever presented to that body.

But what is more relevant is that his Nation has now progressed to the point—in large measure because of some of the things that he has done—that race really no longer serves as a bar to the exercise of experience, or as a bar to the exercise of one's skills.

And so with gratitude for what he has done for all the people of America, and with confidence in his leadership to come, this morning we gather here in the Cabinet Room in the great Capital of the United States—where we hope very shortly we will have home rule and select our own officials—to salute Thurgood Marshall, the great American, the new Solicitor General of the United States of America.

NOTE: The President spoke at 10:53 a.m. in the Cabinet Room at the White House. In his opening words he referred to Judge Marshall and his wife and sons, Associate Justice Hugo L. Black of the Supreme Court of the United States, Associate Justice Tom C. Clark of the Supreme Court of the United States, Attorney General Nicholas deB. Katzenbach, and J. Edgar Hoover, Director of the Federal Bureau of Investigation.

During his remarks the President referred to George Sutherland, Associate Justice of the Supreme Court of the United States 1922–1938, and John W. Gardner, Secretary of Health, Education, and Welfare.

444   Telegram to the Reverend Richard Morrisroe Expressing Hope for His Recovery.   *August 24, 1965*

OUR HEARTS are with you this evening and we pray for your complete recovery. God grant you peace in your distress. God grant us all an end to violence and a renewed commitment to human brotherhood.

LYNDON B. JOHNSON

[Reverend Richard Morrisroe, Baptist Hospital, Montgomery, Alabama]

NOTE: The telegram, dated August 23, was read by Bill D. Moyers, Special Assistant to the President, at his news conference at 11:28 a.m. on Tuesday, August 24, 1965. It was not made public in the form of a White House press release.

Rev. Richard F. Morrisroe, a Catholic priest, was critically wounded by a shotgun blast on August 20 in Hayneville, Ala., shortly after his release from jail where he had been held for civil rights activities. He later recovered. His companion, Jonathan M. Daniels, was killed (see Item 442).

445   Remarks at the Signing of the Bill Extending the Peace Corps Act.   *August 24, 1965*

WE ARE delighted to have with us our very popular and beloved Vice President, the very able and personable Director of the Peace Corps, the dedicated Members of Congress who have worked so faithfully through the years to make this great adventure a success, and we are particularly pleased to have the Peace Corps trainees and the returned volunteers here with us this morning in the Rose Garden.

Those of you here from at least parts of this hemisphere may find it equally as hot here as you have in some of your assignments out there.

I hope that you will come in and pay your respects before you leave the Rose Garden. Bill Moyers has had me up since about 6:30, and about every 15 or 20 minutes he reminds me to be sure to invite all of you in my office before you leave to tell you how wonderful you are, and how wonderful the Peace Corps is. I could say—he did not tell me to say this, but—how wonderful Bill is.

I sometimes wonder whether Bill is really working for the Peace Corps or for the President. I guess the answer is that he is working for both of us all the time and we are very fortunate.

A few weeks ago I announced that conditions in the world—particularly in Viet-Nam—required us to increase the number of American soldiers and Marines in Viet-Nam. I made that decision very regretfully. I did it for a reason. The most awesome burden that any President bears is the responsibility for making a decision that sends the pride of our young manhood—our American boys—to foreign battlefields. But no other course lay open to me in the light of our long-standing commitment to the people of South Viet-Nam. Yet the knowledge that some of our boys would not return rested very heavily on my heart—and still does.

Today I have come here to this beautiful setting, to these very dedicated public servants. Today I shall sign into law another kind of authority that will send Americans abroad. And I pray—I pray—in the years to come only this kind of authority will ever be required by an American President, because it is an authority not for joining a conflict but for continuing the works of peace throughout the world.

The Peace Corps began as a dream. It was the dream of many of us. It was born with the great vision and leadership of that very remarkable man whom we all love and honor—President Kennedy.

I remember the many speeches—that first dozen or so I listened to with great enthusiasm—that Senator Humphrey made on the subject. Then, as the years went on, I kind of wished we would hurry up and pass the bill so we would not have to listen to those speeches every day in the Senate, late in the evening, on the Peace Corps.

I even talked about it myself out at the University of Nebraska in 1960 before the legislation was ever passed. But it began as a dream and it is now a great reality.

So great have been its achievements, such hope that it has given to millions of men and women, such a challenge for useful endeavor has it presented our own young people, that it is really difficult to remember that it was 5 years ago that it was only an idea in the minds of a very few thoughtful men.

But it was a part of the pledge of President John F. Kennedy, that he and I made, to the American people in the campaign of 1960, to lead with imagination and vigor, to constantly search for ways to better the conditions of life on this planet.

Today, under the rather dynamic, personable, and I think very farsighted leadership of Sargent Shriver, and the very unusual, highly qualified people that he has brought to his vicinity, 12,500 Americans are part of the Peace Corps. More than 8,000 are overseas serving their fellow men, and 4,700 of them are in Latin America, 3,800 of them are in Africa, and thousands more are in the Near East and in Asia.

In 45 countries—almost half the countries of the world—they are out teaching school, and they are healing the sick, and they are bringing new methods of farming to the remote areas of the world. They are calling human beings together in a hundred ways to cope with the problems of the city and the village life.

One of the most challenging assignments, and one of the great honors of my career in public life, was when Sargent Shriver and President Kennedy asked me to serve as chairman of the advisory committee for this group, and I had just a little slice of it.

I'll bet you that—I'll venture the assertion—that is a better way to put it—that Vice President Humphrey considers this one of his most noble contributions to Government is his connection with the Peace Corps. And I know you feel that way.

Because there are professors out there in all these countries. There are carpenters. There are plumbers. There are farmers. There are engineers. There are lawyers, nurses, teachers, social workers. The youngest I observed is 18 years old. The oldest is 76 years old. And in between are thousands of men and women who will be able to say to their grandchildren that they answered the call when it came. They ventured forth to an unknown land to give of themselves the very best they had.

I always, when I think of the Peace Corps, think of my high school motto. A little class of six that graduated from my high school said, "Give to the world the best you have and the best will come back to you."

That is what the Peace Corps is doing every place I have been, where I have seen it. That is what your great leader, one of the most remarkable young men in this Nation—you can count among the fingers of your two hands and he rates right up at the top—that is what he is doing and what the people associated with him are doing, from that 18-year-old to that 76-year-old.

913

I have been in your training camps. I have seen where you have to climb a tree and stay under water and all of those things, and I thank goodness that I did not have to qualify.

But this is a priceless heritage for the generations to come. History is going to be written about your movement, about what you have done, about the contributions you have made to save the world, what you have done to defeat the ancient enemies of mankind—disease, hunger, poverty, illiteracy, bigotry, hatred, and racial prejudice.

You will have kept afire the torch of service that has been a part of America's tradition from the time we were born. You will have reached out across the oceans with more than words and a great deal more than dollars. You will have given your skills and your talents and your understanding to those who really need them, not in condescension, not in a paternalistic way, but in a spirit of sharing what you have with others—leading, and guiding, and counseling, and cooperating, and in a spirit of brotherly love and the Golden Rule: "Do unto others as you would have them do unto you."

Your lives and the lives of your grandchildren will have been enriched beyond measure because for a time they were willingly very poor.

So, I think it is a privilege for me, this morning, to have this very special audience, these contributors. You know we have campaign contributors that buy tickets to the Jefferson-Jackson Day dinners. I don't think many of these people buy them—they sell them—but we have contributors to these things, and you are a very special group of contributors to the betterment of humanity and the world.

And it is a great privilege for me to be here to sign this bill, and by doing so make it possible for a larger and a more successful Peace Corps of men and women who carry America, and who carry America's dream of peace and well-being for all men, to the four corners of the globe.

You have done your job so well that every place I have gone, and every ambassador I have talked to, and I have talked to 218 this year—that is about twice as many countries that are represented, but I have seen several of the ambassadors four and five times—but I have never yet had any of them say anything but the finest things about your work.

And now one little personal note to each of you. I appreciate the fact that you have carried on as you have when I had to borrow from your ranks to permit me to carry on. After that terrible tragedy in Dallas I had that night to pull Bill Moyers in here to help us carry on in this house.

And day after day I have had to get Sargent Shriver to come over and take a little of my load off of me—not for the Peace Corps, but in education, and in health, and work assignments, and speaking engagements. No one has helped me more than he.

The Vice President, Mrs. Johnson, and I thank you for sharing a little bit with us. I know you are envious. I know you are jealous. I know you want him full time all by yourself. But you are going to learn, as you go through life, that you just can't have everything you want.

So I do hope that you will understand if I say, "Thank you very much for sharing with us."

NOTE: The President spoke at 12:12 p.m. in the Rose Garden at the White House. During his remarks he referred to Vice President Hubert H. Humphrey, R. Sargent Shriver, Director of the Peace Corps, and Bill D. Moyers, Special Assistant to the President.

As enacted, the bill extending the Peace Corps is Public Law 89–134 (79 Stat. 549).

446 Statement by the President Upon Signing Bill Amending the Atomic Energy Act. *August 24, 1965*

I HAVE today approved H.R. 8856, which clarifies the authority of the Atomic Energy Commission with respect to the generation, sale, or transmission of electric power.

It is, of course, essential that AEC possess the authority to perform its mission and especially to advance nuclear research. Although programs must not be jeopardized by State or local requirements, there is the most compelling need for AEC, and all other agencies, to cooperate with and work with State and local authorities, and private organizations as well. Every effort must and will be made to adapt Federal practices to State and local requirements. H.R. 8856 is general legislation in that it clarifies AEC's authority with respect to all of its programs, and the bill confers no powers on the AEC not presently possessed by other Federal agencies with similar responsibilities.

The particular problem that created the need for clarifying the AEC authority is the proposed transmission line to be located in San Mateo County (California) to supply the new linear accelerator facility under construction at Stanford University. The town of Woodside, through which a portion of the line will pass, has indicated in many ways its strong desire that the transmission line be placed underground rather than in the conventional overhead fashion. Putting aside all questions of legal authority and the views of the various parties involved, it is clear than the preservation of our Nation's scenic beauty merits very high priority. There is, however, in this particular situation a compelling need to have power available to the accelerator in order to maintain the research program on schedule and to keep intact the scientific team that has been put together to operate the program.

Faced with this dilemma, I asked Mr. Laurance Rockefeller, one of the Nation's outstanding conservationists and the Chairman of the White House Conference on Natural Beauty, to visit the site and to make such recommendations as he thought appropriate.

In response to my request, Mr. Rockefeller has made such a study and has recommended the following course of action:

1. The AEC should be instructed to construct overhead transmission lines to meet the immediate power needs for the Stanford project, with the line to be designed and built with the maximum concern for the natural environment of the area.

2. The town of Woodside should be requested to use any funds earmarked for the undergrounding of the accelerator transmission line to bury existing distribution lines in the community.

3. The Federal Government should immediately undertake a program of accelerated research into the technology of placing high voltage transmission lines underground.

4. The AEC should agree to replace the overhead transmission line with an underground line when full power is required for the project—estimated to be sometime between 5 and 7 years—assuming that the local area has made reasonable progress in its own efforts to underground the powerlines in the community.

It seems to me that Mr. Rockefeller's suggestions make the best of a difficult situation. This administration is firmly committed to preserving and protecting natural beauty and welcomes a role of leadership in encouraging others to do so. However, the practical considerations involved in this instance and our admitted need for improved technology in handling underground high voltage transmission lines argue strongly for constructing the line by conventional procedures, with appropriate assurances to the community that the question will remain under constant review.

To those who argue that failure to locate this line underground at this time would be a severe blow to our natural beautification program, we can sincerely say that construction of this line is not an irrevocable or irreversible act. I earnestly hope that our technology will move swiftly forward and that this particular line can be undergrounded not too far in the future.

In the meantime, attention to aesthetic considerations will continue to be stressed throughout the Federal Government. By the same token, it is my hope that the action of the Federal Government will spur State and local governments, as well as private organizations, to give equally strong emphasis to aesthetics in these and similar situations.

I have instructed the AEC to give great weight to the natural environment in constructing the line, including not only the design of the poles but to their location and to the clearing operations. In addition, I have instructed my science adviser, Dr. Donald Hornig, to work with the appropriate Federal departments and agencies to speed our research into the technology of placing high voltage lines underground.

Preserving our Nation's bountiful heritage of natural beauty is not a cheap nor an easy matter. Strengthened efforts are necessary if we are to pass on to future generations a Nation that enjoys the benefits of both industrialization and of unspoiled natural scenery.

NOTE: As enacted, the bill (H.R. 8856) is Public Law 89-135 (79 Stat. 551).

447   Statement by the President to Cabinet Members and Agency Heads on the New Government-Wide Planning and Budgeting System. *August 25, 1965*

I HAVE ASKED you to meet with me this morning to discuss the introduction of a new planning and budgeting system throughout the Government.

The objective of this program is simple: to use the most modern management tools so that the full promise of a finer life can be brought to every American at the least possible cost.

This program is aimed at finding new ways to do new jobs faster, better, less expensively; to insure sounder judgment through more accurate information; to pinpoint those things we ought to do more, and to spotlight those things we ought to do less; to make our decision-making process as up-to-date as our space-exploring equipment.

In short, we want to trade in our surveys for automobiles, our old cannon for new missiles.

Everything I have done in both legislation and the construction of a budget has been guided by my deep concern for the American people—consistent with wise management of the taxpayer's dollar.

In translating this principle in action, and with the help of an outstanding Congress, we have passed more progressive legislation than in any comparable period in history.

We have been compassionate. We have also been prudent.

But we can and must do better if we are to bring the Great Society closer to all the people.

Good government demands excellence.

It demands the fullest value for each dollar spent. It demands that we take advantage of the most modern management techniques.

This is what I want to introduce today— a new planning-programing-budgeting system developed by our top management experts led by Budget Director Charles Schultze. Once in operation, it will enable us to:

(1) Identify our national goals with precision and on a continuing basis

(2) Choose among those goals the ones that are most urgent

(3) Search for alternative means of reaching those goals most effectively at the least cost

(4) Inform ourselves not merely on next year's costs, but on the second, and third, and subsequent year's costs of our programs

(5) Measure the performance of our programs to insure a dollar's worth of service for each dollar spent.

This system will improve our ability to control our programs and our budgets rather than having them control us. It will operate year round. Studies, goals, program proposals, and reviews will be scheduled throughout the year instead of being crowded into "budget time."

To establish this system and carry out the necessary studies, each of you will need a central staff for program and policy planning accountable directly to you. To make this work will take good people, the best you now have and the best you can find.

I intend to have the 1968 budget and later-year programs presented in this new form by next spring.

With these programs will go the first studies produced by your planning and policy staffs.

It is important to remember one thing: no system, no matter how refined, can make decisions for you. You and I have that responsibility in the executive branch. But our judgment is no better than our information. This system will present us with the alternatives and the information on the basis of which we can, together, make better decisions. The people will be the beneficiary.

The Budget Director has already talked to most of you about the need for this new approach. He is now preparing plans for setting it up. He is ready to help you in any way he can.

Within the next several weeks he will send out detailed instructions for incorporating fiscal year 1968 and later-year programs into this system. But to make this new plan a success, he will need your full support. I know that you will give him that support.

NOTE: The President discussed the new system with members of the Cabinet and heads of Government agencies at a breakfast meeting at 8 a.m. at the White House. See also Item 448 [3].

448   The President's News Conference of *August 25, 1965*

THE PRESIDENT. Good morning, ladies and gentlemen.

MANNED ORBITING LABORATORY

[1.] After discussion with Vice President Humphrey and members of the Space Council, as well as Defense Secretary McNamara, I am today instructing the Department of Defense to immediately proceed with the development of a manned orbiting laboratory.

This program will bring us new knowledge about what man is able to do in space.

It will enable us to relate that ability to the defense of America.

It will develop technology and equipment which will help advance manned and unmanned space flight.

It will make it possible to perform very new and rewarding experiments with that technology and equipment.

The cost of developing the manned orbiting laboratory will be $1.5 billion.

Unmanned flights to test launchings, recovery, and other basic parts of the system, will begin late next year or early 1967. The initial unmanned launch of a fully equipped laboratory is scheduled for 1968. This will be followed later that year by the first of five flights with two-man crews.

The Air Force has selected the Douglas Aircraft Company to design and to build the spacecraft in which the crew of the laboratory will live and operate. The General Electric Company will plan and develop the space experiments. The Titan III–C booster will launch the laboratory into space and a modified version of the NASA Gemini capsule will be the vehicle in which the astronauts return to earth.

The Rule of Law in Outer Space

[2.] Even as we meet, Gemini 5, piloted by two very gallant men, backed by hundreds of dedicated space scientists and engineers and great administrators, now orbits the earth as a dramatic reminder that our American dream for outer space is a dream of peace and a dream of friendly cooperation among all the nations of the earth.[1]

We believe the heavens belong to the people of every country. We are working and we will continue to work through the United Nations—our distinguished Am-

bassador, Mr. Goldberg, is present with us this morning—to extend the rule of law into outer space.

We intend to live up to our agreement not to orbit weapons of mass destruction and we will continue to hold out to all nations, including the Soviet Union, the hand of cooperation in the exciting years of space exploration which lie ahead for all of us. Therefore, I have—today, in fact—directed Mr. James Webb,[2] the administrator of our civilian space program, after conferring with the Secretary of State and our Ambassador to the United Nations and others, to invite the Soviet Academy of Science to send a very high level representative here next month to observe the launching of Gemini 6.

I hope that he will find it convenient to come. We will certainly give him a warm welcome in America.

New Government-wide Planning and Budgeting System

[3.] This morning I have just concluded a breakfast meeting with the Cabinet and with the heads of Federal agencies.

I am asking each of them to immediately begin to introduce a very new and a very revolutionary system of planning and programing and budgeting throughout the vast Federal Government, so that through the tools of modern management the full promise of a finer life can be brought to every American at the lowest possible cost.[3]

Under this new system each Cabinet and agency head will set up a very special staff of experts who, using the most modern methods of program analysis, will define the goals of their department for the coming

---

[1] See Item 462.

[2] James E. Webb, Administrator of the National Aeronautics and Space Administration.

[3] See Item 447.

year. Once these goals are established, this system will permit us to find the most effective and the least costly alternative to achieving American goals.

This program is designed to achieve three major objectives:

It will help us find new ways to do jobs faster, to do jobs better, and to do jobs less expensively.

It will insure a much sounder judgment through more accurate information, pinpointing those things that we ought to do more, spotlighting those things that we ought to do less.

It will make our decision-making process as up-to-date, I think, as our space exploring program.

Everything that I have done in both legislation and the construction of a budget has always been guided by my own very deep concern for the American people—consistent with wise management, of course, of the taxpayer's dollar.

So this new system will identify our national goals with precision and will do it on a continuing basis. It will enable us to fulfill the needs of all the American people with a minimum amount of waste.

And because we will be able to make sounder decisions than ever before, I think the people of this Nation will receive greater benefits from every tax dollar that is spent in their behalf.

APPOINTMENT OF MEMBERS OF U.S. MISSION TO THE UNITED NATIONS

[4.] On July the 20th, I named as United States Ambassador to the United Nations a man to whom the sacred cause of peace is an obsession—Justice Arthur Goldberg.

So I am happy this morning to reinforce the United States team at the United Nations with four Americans who also share a passion for peace:

—As Ambassador Goldberg's principal Deputy, I am naming a career Ambassador with a distinguished record of more than 20 years in diplomacy—Mr. Charles Yost.

—As Representative to the Security Council, with the rank of Ambassador, I am naming the noted president of Howard University—Dr. James Nabrit, Jr.

—As Representative to the Economic and Social Council of the United Nations, a famous American who is giving up his seat in Congress to become our new Ambassador—Mr. James Roosevelt, the eldest son of the late beloved Franklin Delano Roosevelt. Mr. Roosevelt is with us this morning. Will you please stand, Mr. Roosevelt?

—As Representative to the Trusteeship Council of the United Nations, also with the rank of Ambassador, a vibrant, attractive American woman who has already served as the Nation's chief diplomat in both Denmark and Bulgaria—Mrs. Eugenie Anderson of Minnesota.

OTHER APPOINTMENTS

[5.] Tomorrow I will sign into law one of the most important bills enacted by Congress this session: the Public Works and Economic Development Act of 1965.[4] To direct this far-reaching program of promise for the distressed areas all across America, I intend to nominate as Assistant Secretary of Commerce and as Director of Economic Development one of our most brilliant young public servants, the outstanding Administrator of the Small Business Administration—Mr. Eugene P. Foley. Please stand, Mr. Foley.

---

[4] See Item 452.

[6.] I am also pleased to announce this morning the appointment of Mr. Hobart Taylor, Jr., as a member of the Board of Directors of the Export-Import Bank. Mr. Taylor has been Associate Special Counsel to the President since May 1964. He was previously Executive Vice Chairman of the President's Committee on Equal Employment Opportunity and has largely directed our efforts with the large corporations and institutions of this country in our plans for progress. Will you please stand, Mr. Taylor?

He will be succeeded as my Associate Special Counsel by another talented young lawyer who holds degrees from both Harvard and Yale and now serves as Deputy Special Assistant to the President—Mr. Clifford Alexander, Jr. Mr. Alexander has recently reached the tired old age of 32. Will you please stand, Mr. Alexander?

[7.] It is also a pleasure to announce the nomination this morning of the new United States Attorney for the District of Columbia—it may interest some of you people who live here in the District of Columbia—Mr. David G. Bress. Mr. Bress has not only carried on a very vigorous private practice and civic life but he has taught in the field of law at American University, at Georgetown Law Center, the University of Virginia Law School, and has been head of the Bar Association of the District of Columbia. Will you stand, Mr. Bress?

The Sovereignty of Self-Governing People

[8.] Fifty years ago, President Woodrow Wilson asked, "Just what is it that America stands for? If she stands for one thing more than another, it is for the sovereignty of self-governing people."

So I am very proud of the progress that we are making toward that principle on one front—and I am disappointed at the lack of progress that we are making on another.

Registration Under the Voting Rights Act

[9.] The Attorney General and the Chairman of the Civil Service Commission have just reported to me what I think is a truly remarkable story: In the 19 days since I signed into law the Voting Rights Act of 1965,[5] which I recommended to Congress and they promptly enacted, already a total of 27,385 Negroes in 13 counties in 3 Southern States have qualified to vote. And they represent nearly one-third of the potential applicants in all those 13 counties.

Only this morning a team of Federal examiners will begin to list voters in the 14th county that has been designated by the Attorney General. That new office will be opened in the town of Prentiss in Jefferson Davis County, Mississippi.

I am equally encouraged by the high level of acceptance and I am very pleased with the compliance that we have had in scores of other Southern counties throughout the country.

—A check of 45 counties in Georgia shows already that 99 percent of 2,000 Negro applicants have been registered without any difficulty.

—In 50 Louisiana counties, not a single Negro has been rejected.

—In Mississippi, nearly 12,000 Negroes have been registered by local registrars—over and above those that we mentioned that were registered by Federal examiners. The number of Negro citizens registered in Mississippi has increased 100 percent in the last 6 weeks.

---

[5] See Item 409.

Obedience is always preferable to enforcement. Where enforcement is necessary, we will not hesitate to meet our responsibilities under the law. But the very clear and the very heartening lesson of this wonderful report is that obedience to the law is a fact of life to so many men and women of good will throughout the South.

HOME RULE IN THE DISTRICT OF COLUMBIA

[10.] On another front—here in our lovely Nation's Capital City—"the sovereignty of self-governing people" is still unresolved.

The people of the District of Columbia, I think deserve and I think must and will have home rule. It is an irony and disgrace that having extended self-government already to the Philippine Islands and to Puerto Rico, having enthusiastically recommended democratic principles to nations around the world, nation after nation, after having welcomed Alaska and Hawaii as new States, that somehow some people seem to be afraid to trust almost a million American citizens with the management of their own affairs here in the District of Columbia.

Congress is moving to redeem this disgrace. The Senate—as on at least five different occasions in the past—has acted to pass a good home rule bill containing a solid and a workable charter for home rule.

That bill should come before the House of Representatives very shortly. The limits of reasonable delay have long since been reached and passed.

No one doubts the outcome once that bill finally gets to the floor of the House and the Members are permitted to vote on it. But what is needed this morning is a commitment by the leadership and by the members of both parties, if you please, to the only practical means of getting the bill on the floor, and that seems to be the petition to discharge the House District Committee from further delay of the bill.

Bills have been pending before that committee for year after year after year. So I have, as President, urged the Speaker of the House of Representatives, Mr. McCormack, and the other leaders and members of my own party to lead the way in this movement. But to all of those who believe in our two-party elective system, to all of those who believe in taxation with representation, to those who believe in keeping faith with our own people, I express the hope that you, too, will join us in this effort.

I am now ready to take any questions that you may have to ask.

QUESTIONS

THE STEEL NEGOTIATIONS

[11.] Q. Mr. President, the steel negotiators still seem to be considerably apart on an agreement, and a strike is threatened within a week. Would you care to comment on that situation?

THE PRESIDENT. Yes. I think that the steel situation is on almost every citizen's mind in this country. The decisions which will be made in Pittsburgh this week are of vital importance to every person in this country and to people in other parts of the world. There must be continued cost and price stability in our American economy and I expect full and complete responsibility in the current wage negotiations and I expect continued stability in steel prices.

As we meet here today, we are troubled with many questions, but we must never forget that our boys are still fighting in

South Viet-Nam and that our economic strength is the keystone of free world peace. It is extremely important to the security that we hold very dear. So the decisions that will be made this week by steel management and by labor in the days that are ahead must certainly take into account the overall greater national interest which is involved.

The Director of the Federal Mediation Service, one of my most trusted public servants, Mr. William Simkin, is in Pittsburgh; and he is there for the purpose of making every contribution he can to assist the parties in reaching a responsible agreement. The eyes of this country are on the leaders of both management and labor. We are expecting and we believe we will receive the responsibility which the national interest requires.[6]

VIET-NAM

[12.] Q. Mr. President, in World War II there were notable air strikes which completely knocked out, in single raids, vast industrial complexes and transportation facilities, yet in the war in Viet-Nam we read from over there of repeated cases of where it takes several raids to demobilize or deactivate certain industrial installations. I am thinking of the powerplants they were hitting yesterday over and over, and such things as bridges.

Is our current inability to knock out some of these big industrial complexes or railroad staging areas or bridges—is this a purposeful thing to avoid saturation bombing, or is there any other explanation?

THE PRESIDENT. No, I think that our operations have been up to our expectations. I think a review and evaluation of them will reflect that they have been rather effective,

and I think that they are in keeping with the planned purpose of their mission.

Q. Mr. President, do you think the so-called white paper issued by House Republicans under the leadership of Congressman Ford [7] has injected undue partisanship into the Viet-Nam situation?

THE PRESIDENT. Well, I don't want to get into any personalities in the matter. I think the issues of war and peace in Viet-Nam are far greater than any personal differences that one might have—for that matter, far greater than any party's.

I have said on many occasions, and I should like to repeat to the American people, and to Hanoi also, that I am very pleased with the support the American people are giving to the policies of their Government, both at home and abroad. While our men are fighting and dying for freedom in South Viet-Nam, I am going to do everything that I can to support those men and to unite the country behind them.

I think that, generally speaking, the country is united behind them and I think this will be a source of strength to our boys out there. I have received excellent cooperation from the leadership of both parties in the past, and I expect to continue in the future. The boys that are fighting the war are not divided between Republicans and Democrats. The men directing the strategies involved— I don't know what party they belong to.

The distinguished Secretary of Defense, before coming into Government, was a member of a party different from mine. The President with whom I counsel often and who has had the greatest experience in not only political and diplomatic matters, but in matters of a military nature, President

---

[6] See Item 483.

[7] Representative Gerald R. Ford of Michigan, minority leader of the House of Representatives.

Eisenhower, has been a tower of strength to me, to the Joint Chiefs of Staff, to the Secretary of Defense, and to the leaders of the Congress.

So I would say that we welcome expressions of viewpoint from the leadership in both parties. There will be times when we don't see everything alike, but that may contribute strength to our system.

I don't think that Hanoi should ever for a moment entertain the illusion that the people of this country are not united in the work of this Government.

THE IMMIGRATION BILL

[13.] Q. The congressional session is almost over and what are the prospects of the immigration bill passing, and could you assess for us some of the long-range effects of it if it passes?

THE PRESIDENT. I don't know how good a prophet I am. I had put this legislation very high in our list. I think it is extremely important. I have continually urged the leadership to proceed with this consideration. The House has it under study now. I have talked to the Speaker at length, yesterday and again today.

I am sending him a letter later today expressing very strongly the views of the executive branch of the Government again.[8] I am hoping that that bill will pass as reported by the House Judiciary Committee without crippling amendments. It has not been acted upon yet by the Senate Judiciary Committee.

I believe that it should be acted on before the Congress gets out of here. I favor the House bill. I think it will result in a great improvement not only in our relations with other nations but will be very satisfying to large segments of our own people. I believe

it will pass. I would like to have the help of all of you, though, in that connection.[9]

THE CIVILIAN PAY RAISE BILL AND WAGE-PRICE GUIDELINES

[14.] Q. Mr. President, do you believe that the guidelines of your administration and Mr. Kennedy's administration laid down on wage and price stability apply to Federal employees, and if so, do you believe that the civilian pay raise bill now reported out of the House committee violates those guidelines?

THE PRESIDENT. I would think that the Federal Government has a different situation from what we have in certain segments of our private sector, but I would hope that we would never ask for privileges for ourselves in Government that we would not expect private industry to share in.

Therefore, when you make allowances for the difference in public and private employment and the various policies and fringe benefits, I would hope that we could keep our civilian pay structure in line with the guidelines that we recommend for private industry.

I do think the House bill goes too far. I do think that it would violate the guidelines. I do hope that the Congress will carefully and thoroughly consider the destructive effect it would have if we should pass the bill in its present form.

We had a most distinguished panel of most distinguished Americans study this whole subject. They made recommendations.

We would hope that the Congress would enact those recommendations with certain

---

[8] See Item 449.

[9] An act to amend the Immigration and Nationality Act was approved by the President on October 3, 1965 (see Item 546).

modifications that they thought were required, but certainly not go anywhere near
the overall recommendations made by the
House committee, because we think that
would be very disastrous to our price-wage
stability policy in this country and we
think it would violate the guidelines.[10]

VIET-NAM—OUR DESIRE FOR PEACE

[15.] Q. Mr. President, getting back to
Viet-Nam for a moment, the other night on
television some of your top advisers spoke in
a way that seemed rather pointed about the
1954 agreements [11] as a possible basis for a
new agreement.

Does this reflect an administration emphasis and does it reflect a feeling that perhaps
somebody is listening to you now, sir?

THE PRESIDENT. I think that we are
always hopeful that all the world is aware
of our desire for discussions and our desire
for negotiations and our desire for peace. I
don't think it is really important how much
extra you get an hour in your steel contract,
or what the increase of Federal pay is, if
your boy is going to be drafted tomorrow
and going to be called upon to give his life
in Viet-Nam.

So peace—peace, that simple little 5-letter
word—is the most important word in the
English language to us at this time and it
occupies more of our attention than any
other word or any other subject. We do
expect they are listening; we do hope they
are listening.

Secretary Rusk, Ambassador Goldberg,
Secretary Ball,[12] and all of the other trained
diplomats that we have in this country are
going to constantly be searching for ways
and means to substitute words for guns, and
to bring men from the battlefield to the conference table. Our every waking hour is
going to be spent trying to find the means
for doing this.

REPEAL OF SECTION 14(B) OF THE TAFT-
HARTLEY ACT

[16.] Q. Mr. President, do you still
consider the repeal of section 14(b) of the
Taft-Hartley Act a major legislative goal
in this session of the Congress? There
seems to be some question in the Senate,
sir.

THE PRESIDENT. I don't know of any
question. I certainly do.

LOS ANGELES TASK FORCE

[17.] Q. Sir, have you been in contact
with Governor Collins [13] about the situation in Los Angeles?

THE PRESIDENT. Yes.

Q. Do you have in mind any action
which might avert further tension?

THE PRESIDENT. Yes, sir. We have detailed action planned that we worked on
until late in the evening last night. Mr.
Moyers [14] will have a release available for
you. We didn't want to take the television
time and further time from your questions,
but it will be available later in the week.[15]

---

[10] The Federal Employees Salary Act of 1965 was
approved by the President on October 29, 1965 (see
Item 589).

[11] The Geneva Accords of 1954, which ended the
war in Indochina, were signed by the Government
of France and by the government of Ho Chi Minh of
North Viet-Nam. The United States was not a
party to them.

[12] George W. Ball, Under Secretary of State.

[13] LeRoy Collins, Director, Community Relations Service, Department of Commerce, and
former Governor of Florida.

[14] Bill D. Moyers, Special Assistant to the President.

[15] See Item 453.

We are appointing a top-flight task force, headed by Deputy Attorney General Ramsey Clark, and they will proceed to Los Angeles at a very early date. The details of their work and their program will be announced as soon as they are available.

THE DOMINICAN REPUBLIC

[18.] Q. Mr. President, have we come to any closer solution to the problem in the Dominican Republic?

THE PRESIDENT. Ambassador Bunker [16] has done a very exceptional job there. We are very hopeful that we can obtain agreement on provisional government, and that we can set up the guidelines that will result in an election at an early date where the people of that area can have self-determination and can make the selection of their own government officials. We have felt very close to a solution several times, and we never are quite sure when it will come, but we expect it shortly.

PENDING LEGISLATION

[19.] Q. Mr. President, you said yesterday that what you really wanted for your birthday tomorrow were several bills out of committee, but you didn't say what the bills are. Would you care to tell us, sir?

THE PRESIDENT. I don't have the time to review all of my messages. But as I remember it, there are about four bills still in House committees that have not been reported, that are being worked upon.

They include the highway improvement bill, beautification bill, and the heart, cancer, and stroke bill. Larry O'Brien [17] is a much better authority on this than I am. He will be glad to be helpful in that respect. There are some eight bills in Senate committees that still need to be reported.

There are a dozen or so bills that have been reported that need to be scheduled. They are either awaiting a rule or awaiting schedule in one body or the other.

There are about six bills in conference, one of which has emerged recently, much to our satisfaction—the foreign aid bill. We are hopeful that all of those measures can be moved. There are relatively few to be reported. There are a good many more to be scheduled. There are only half a dozen in conference.

We think that in a reasonable time, by diligent work—not around the clock, but a full week in the next several weeks—we can complete our program. If we could, we would like to do that, so that the Members could go home and have some rest before coming back in January.

There will be some important messages for them, awaiting them, when they return in January, but we would not expect anything like the volume of substantive legislation next year. We would expect several substantive bills like a transportation policy and like some refinements in our foreign policy, that we will be submitting messages on food and health and things of that nature. But we look forward to the Congress being able to get out of here early next year—I would say certainly far ahead of the end of the fiscal year in June—so that the Members could be at home and could report to the people.

We like for the Republicans and the Democrats all to be home and report to the people what is going on here, what is going on in the world, so they can be fully informed, and we think that it makes for a more united country.

---

[16] Ellsworth Bunker, United States Representative to the Organization of American States.

[17] Lawrence F. O'Brien, Special Assistant to the President.

PROGRESS IN VIET-NAM

[20.]   Q.   Mr. President, of late, sir, have you been able to detect any military advantages in Viet-Nam? Have we turned the corner there after it has gone apparently so bad for so long?

THE PRESIDENT.   I am always hesitant to make a prophecy about how good things are or how bad they are, because you fellows have a way of remembering what a public official says way back there and feeding it up to him from time to time.

But I think it must be evident to you that your Marines and your other soldiers in the Army, and the men in the Navy and the Air Force have been giving a good account of themselves. And working very closely with the dedicated and patriotic and determined South Vietnamese, always associated with them and working with them, they have been quite effective in the last few weeks.

As I told you, in our last meeting, I plead with my Cabinet every time I see them. I say to Secretary McNamara, "You be sure that our men have the morale, and have the equipment, and have the necessary means of seeing that we keep our commitments in Viet-Nam, and we have the strength to do it."

I say to Mr. Rusk, while he is working with his right hand on strength and stability there and doing the job we are committed to do, "You and Mr. Goldberg and the rest of you, use that left hand and be sure that you do everything to get us away from the battlefield and back at the conference table, if that is possible."

So we are like a man in a ring. We are using our right and our left constantly.

INDONESIA

[21.]   Q.   It seems increasingly possible, Mr. President, that the conflict between Indonesia and Malaysia could erupt into an earthquake that would affect southeast Asia far more gravely than anything that is going on in Viet-Nam today.

Would you assess that danger for us, including the point as to whether you think it is possible to keep Indonesia from completely going into the Communist Chinese orbit?

THE PRESIDENT.   I would agree that the whole situation there is very delicate, a matter that requires constant watching. Our Secretary of State is doing that. The President is doing it. We have recently sent to Indonesia one of our most trained and trusted diplomats.[18] We are going to make every contribution that we can to try to preserve peace in that area.

We think that what we are doing in South Viet-Nam has a very important bearing on the whole sector of that part of the world. I would not want to make any prophecies as to what the final outcome would be, other than we will be hopeful and we will be continuing in our efforts to contribute anything we can to a peaceful solution.

VETO OF MILITARY CONSTRUCTION BILL

[22.]   Q.   Mr. President, sir, you vetoed the military construction bill the other day [19] and said you did it because it was repugnant to the Constitution. Some people disagree with you. They think that very clearly, while your powers are limited by the Constitution, the powers of Congress are extensive.

I would refer you to section 8 of the Constitution, where it says that Congress will make all the rules for government and regulation of the land and naval forces. Don't

---

[18] Marshall Green, U.S. Ambassador to Indonesia.
[19] See Item 440.

you think you might reconsider that?

THE PRESIDENT. Well, first I reviewed that veto message very carefully late in the evening of the last day with most of my best legal advisers. The statement as I remember it said that the Attorney General informed me that it was repugnant to the Constitution. So I would refer you first to the Attorney General, and I know he would be glad to give great weight to any observations you might have.

I, myself, agree with the Attorney General. I hope the Congress will share that view. I think that we do owe the Congress a reasonable reporting procedure. I indicated in my message that I would willingly make those reports if it could be worked out where it would not adversely affect our military posture or my duties as Commander in Chief.

I genuinely believe that the bill, in the form that I vetoed it, did considerably restrain the Commander in Chief and was not in the national interest.

Merriman Smith, United Press International: Thank you, Mr. President.

NOTE: President Johnson's forty-ninth news conference was held in the East Room at the White House at 10 a.m. on Wednesday, August 25, 1965.

There was no text of the transcript of the President's forty-eighth news conference, held on August 19, 1965.

---

449   Letter to the Speaker Urging House Action on the Immigration Bill. *August 25, 1965*

Dear Mr. Speaker:

As you suggested I write you, more fully and formally, the view I expressed in our conversations earlier yesterday and today.

There is no piece of legislation before the Congress that in terms of decency and equity is more demanding of passage than the Immigration bill. Four Presidents have urged this kind of legislation. Four decades have been witness to this kind of need. Countless Americans with ties of family and heritage reaching beyond the seas have cried out for this kind of action.

Our present restrictions say that Italians, Greeks, Spaniards, all the Southern European countries in particular, are not as desirable as others. What a shameful declaration.

By what distorted principle do we assert that Enrico Fermi, or Conrad Huber, or David Sarnoff, or Marconi, or George Christopher, or I. M. Pei, Benjamin Cardozo, John Philip Sousa or Senators Fong and Pastore, and Congressmen Mink, Brademas, and Pucinski have not added to the culture and achievement of our land? All these men and women, and millions more whose forebears were immigrants, are stained by a national commitment to restriction, isolation and indifference.

You and I, Mr. Speaker, and the great majority of the Congress know this is wrong. The vast majority of our fellow citizens know this is wrong.

I hope the Congress will act speedily on the Immigration bill as reported by the House Committee, free of any crippling amendments.

Sincerely,

LYNDON B. JOHNSON

[The Speaker, The House of Representatives, Washington, D.C.]

NOTE: The letter was read by Bill D. Moyers, Special Assistant to the President, at his news conference at 4:15 p.m. on Wednesday, August 25, 1965. It was not made public in the form of a White House press release.

An act to amend the Immigration and Nationality Act was approved by the President on October 3, 1965 (see Item 546).

450   Remarks in Response to a Report by the Advisory Committee on Private Enterprise in Foreign Aid.   *August 25, 1965*

IN THE YEARS since World War II, this Nation has undertaken the most ambitious— and effective—foreign assistance program in the history of civilization.

Our efforts have taken many forms, from the Marshall plan aid of the 1940's to the Peace Corps of the 1960's. But whatever the form, our objective has remained the same: to assist our fellow men in their struggles to achieve a healthier and more meaningful life.

We have taken this responsibility upon ourselves because we know it is right. But we also know that, ultimately, it is the alternative to chaos.

In a very real sense, our foreign aid programs are an indispensable part of our quest for world peace.

But Government assistance alone will never bring about the better world we seek. We need the help of all facets of our society: of business, labor, agriculture, the universities, the foundations, the churches, and other private organizations.

That is why your Committee was established by the 88th Congress: to seek new ways of enlarging the role of the private sector in foreign economic assistance.

I welcome your report today. It points up the progress we have already made. It brings into focus the problems and challenges we still face. And it gives us a number of valuable recommendations to meet those problems and challenges.

Our accomplishments to date have been many:

—Specific risk investment guarantee contracts have been sharply increased. Total coverage issued now stands at over $2.5 billion. Since 1962 the number of developing countries with which we have investment guaranty agreements has been increased from 43 to 67.

—Our technical assistance contracts with American universities and private organizations total nearly a half billion dollars and include 143 contracts with some 106 universities in 39 different countries.

—American engineering and construction firms are at work in more than 50 countries, helping to design and construct AID-assisted capital projects worth more than $4 billion.

—AID is helping the American labor movement to run a very successful Institute for Free Labor Development in Latin America and has recently organized an African-American labor center.

—Ninety-three savings and loan associations have been organized in 11 Latin American and African countries and have already attracted more than 318,000 savers and more than $85 million in savings. They are funding homes for more than 35,000 people.

—AID is helping 61 private voluntary associations, like CARE, Church World Services, and Catholic Relief Services, to distribute clothing, medicines, tools, and food overseas.

Despite this record of achievement, we know that more and stronger measures are needed to increase the flow of private capital and the technical knowledge that goes with it. We have already made certain recommendations—both in tax treaties now before the Senate and in my foreign aid message—for using tax measures to encourage private investment in the developing countries. I am certain that the Congress, in its consideration of this subject, will give weight to the views of this Committee.

Despite other restrictions brought on by balance of payments considerations, we will continue to encourage the flow of private capital to the developing countries. Not to do so—as your report points out—would defeat our purpose of encouraging the development of these countries, particularly the development of their private sectors.

To you, Mr. Watson, and to your Committee, I would like to offer congratulations for a splendid job. Following the wishes of Congress, we are sending copies of your report to all its Members and are otherwise distributing it widely. We intend to give most careful consideration to your recommendations and to seek ways of carrying them out.

I thank you sincerely for your help in this most vital area of our foreign policy.

NOTE: The President spoke at a noon meeting in the Cabinet Room at the White House. During his remarks he referred to Arthur K. Watson, Chairman of the Advisory Committee on Private Enterprise in Foreign Aid.

The report of the Committee, dated July 1965, was published by the Agency for International Development (57 pp.).

As printed above, this item follows the prepared text released by the White House.

451   Statement by the President on Efforts To Improve the International Monetary System.   *August 25, 1965*

LAST MONTH I authorized Secretary Fowler to announce that the United States stands ready to participate in an international monetary conference that would consider what steps might be taken to secure substantial improvements in international monetary arrangements.

Secretary Fowler very properly specified in his July 10th speech that such a conference must be preceded by careful preparation and international consultation. He has been meeting with the financial and monetary officials of other nations as opportunities to do so became available in Washington, including, to date, representatives of Japan and Canada. The trip he and Under Secretary of State Ball are about to take will extend and broaden these consultations.

The international monetary system, as it has existed since World War II, has functioned with commendable flexibility and resourcefulness in the rebuilding of monetary reserves and in their enlargement and distribution in keeping with the tremendous and widespread economic rehabilitation and growth that has characterized the free world.

We want to determine through our own studies and in consultation with others, what may be needed to assure the satisfactory future performance of that system.

The United States is not wedded in this enterprise to any particular procedure, nor to any rigid timetable. The point to be kept in the forefront is that we are determined to move ahead—carefully and deliberately, but without delay—because we are convinced that not to act when the time is ripe can be as unwise as to act too soon, or too hastily.

I believe that government and monetary officials everywhere are prepared to join with us in the earnest search upon which we have embarked for ways to assure continued sound and stable growth of the free world's international monetary system, which is fundamental to the continued economic progress of the nations of the free world whatever their stage of economic development.

We must press forward with our studies and beyond, to action—evolving arrangements which will continue to meet the needs of a fast growing world economy. Unless we make timely progress, international monetary difficulties will exercise a stubborn and increasingly frustrating drag on our policies for prosperity and progress at home and throughout the world.

NOTE: The President's statement was made public as part of a White House release announcing that the President had met at noon with Secretary of the Treasury Henry H. Fowler and Under Secretary of State George W. Ball, who were about to leave for Europe for discussions with governmental and financial authorities of seven nations.

Secretary Fowler's report to the President, following his exchange of views with European leaders on international monetary matters, is printed in the Weekly Compilation of Presidential Documents (vol. 1, p. 264).

452   Remarks at the Signing of the Public Works and Economic Development Act. *August 26, 1965*

Members of the Congress, Mr. Vice President, members of the Cabinet, and friends:

Years from now the historians will settle on a term to describe the decade of the sixties, in which we are now living. I envision and I hope, and I genuinely believe, the term that will be used will be—"the decade of opportunity."

For all that we have tried to do for America in our time of leadership is encompassed in that word.

Under the guidance and with the support—many times, the heartaches and the backaches—of you men and women out there in the Congress, we have really begun to open the gates of opportunity for the very poor people of this country.

Every time we try to do that, there are many obstacles. There are suggestions made as to why this is unconstitutional, we are doing it too fast, we are doing it the wrong way. I have never seen a real comprehensive effort made to help the very poor that there weren't apostles of greed who would find reasons why it couldn't be done.

But what is important is that we are now doing it—we are doing it, and you are doing it.

We have struck down the legal barriers that have denied opportunity to men that were born with dark skins.

We have commenced a great education program—elementary, secondary, vocational, higher education—that offers all of our children a chance and a share in the world of tomorrow.

We have opened up new avenues of training and retraining for the unskilled, and for those whose skills have become obsolete.

We have reduced our taxes—$19 billion in 19 months—so that commerce and industry might make new job opportunities available for millions of people who want to work.

But still for some of our fellow Americans, the gates are still closed. These folks live in the fishing villages and the old textile towns of New England; they live in the railroad centers of Pennsylvania where the coal trains no longer run; they live in the small areas of Arkansas and Oklahoma and east Texas; they live in the mountain towns of Utah and Idaho, in the timber settlements of the Far West.

For them the laws of economic change have been rather harsh and unyielding. Industry has moved away, the mines and the timber that once provided the livelihood are gone, they have been depleted. The farm costs have risen faster than farmers could meet them. There are many, many reasons *why* these communities have suffered in the past, but there is a common result, I think, among all of them: and that is the slow decay of hope among the old who remain, and the anxiety of the young to get away.

I go back to my hometown and I find difficulty locating anyone under 21 years of age that has finished high school. They have moved on. I see the men sit around under the shade playing dominoes—but they are in the late sixties and early seventies.

Now two courses of action are open to us in the face of these conditions. One is to do nothing. That is the thing we have been doing for a good many years, and we just let these little towns die. Their schools and their churches will grow empty each year. The "For Rent" signs will appear with depressing frequency before their stores and their little, modest cottages.

If we take that course, we do more than just write off small town life as unimportant to America. We make certain that thousands upon thousands of families will be compelled to move away and go into the great cities. And when they get there, they are going to be concentrated in slums, they are going to live on the edge of poverty, they are going to be separated from all that would give them security and give them confidence if they could stay back home.

Now the other course is the course of opportunity. If we choose that, we say that empty fatalism has no part in the American dream. Like the lawmakers in our past who created the Homestead Act, some of them who wrote the Land-Grant Act, some of you out there who helped write the Farmers' Home Act, we say that it is right and that it is just, and that it is a function of government, and that we are going to carry out that responsibility to help our people get back on their feet and share once again in the blessings of American life. We say that we are not helpless before the iron laws of economics, that a wise public policy uses economics to create hope—and not to abet despair.

That is the course we are taking today under the leadership of you men that sit there in that front row and all those other rows. We are embarking this morning on a new program of grants and loans to those cities and those towns where too many men have been out of work too long. And we think that is the proper function of government. We want them, in these little towns, to put their men to work, to improve their water systems, to stop the pollution of their streams and their lakes—and I do hope that some of you can help Senator Muskie and the members of the House Public Works Committee, Congressman Blatnik, to get that pollution bill out—let's not get it tied up in conference. I know it is difficult and I know we have some disagreements, and I know we will have some other disagreements, too— I have been observing them—but if we could, we could pass that bill now and make a great contribution to our country. We could develop our harbors and our channels, control our rivers, and lay out roads and provide utilities for new industry. We want them to do whatever it takes to bring hope back to the people of these smaller towns.

The question has really never been how to do these things. The question has always been, where do we find the means to do them? In my judgment this new act—the Public Works and Economic Development Act of 1965—gives us the authority and gives us the vision that we need. And under the leadership of these substantial numbers of progressive Congressmen and Senators who are here this morning, the fine Secretary of Commerce and that brilliant new Assistant Secretary of Commerce, Gene Foley, who is going to be Assistant Secretary for Economic Development, I believe we are going to open the gates of opportunity for yet another body of this people.

So this morning, I sign it into law with gratitude to each of you in the Congress that passed this bill, and I am confident in the future that you and your posterity will remember being participants here in the East Room in this forward-looking step to try to save people, save human beings, save the small towns that are really the backbone of our country. We can always put off these things, and we have had a habit of doing that in bygone years, but we are facing up to most of our responsibilities—sometimes we face up to them a little late.

I was up early this morning trying to arrange for a top man in the Federal Government to take a plane and take a program to Los Angeles. That is a fine, sprawling, building, progressive city of millions of Americans. But they are going there too late, really. The tragedy has already occurred, the damage is done, the dead cannot be revived, the scars of years of inaction reflected themselves. And when people feel that they don't get a fair shake, when they feel that justice is not open to them, you always see these things occur. They occur in different sections at different times.

Those of you here in the District of Columbia, I want to warn you this morning, that the clock is ticking, time is moving, that we should and we must ask ourselves every night when we go home: Are we doing all that we should do in our Nation's Capital, in all the other big cities of the country where 80 percent of the population of this country is going to be living in the year 2000?

Now, if you don't ask yourself that question and you don't answer it, and you find year after year after year you can't get a committee to act, or if the committee acts you can't get some other committee to act, or if it acts, you get something else happening, and so forth, then you are going to have problems that we are trying to solve.

We got excellent cooperation from the people in a good many States in the Union. I am so proud of the progress we have made in giving men the right to vote and registering in the last few days. I am so proud in the respect for law that such a substantial number of our people have. But remember, when people feel mistreated and they feel injustices, and when they have to move from their homes and they have no jobs, and they have no vote, and they have no voice—well, there is not one place to go if you can't go up. Just any adventure, any danger, you can't do much worse than you are doing now. And I asked myself last night, what can I do to see that we don't have any more incidents as occurred in Los Angeles in this country.

So, let's act before it is too late. And you have done that in this bill. I commend you and I thank you. And if Gene Foley and Jack Connor can do their job of good, solid, prompt administration as well as you have done yours, we will have at least provided part of the answer, and I hope to see Senator Muskie and Bob Jones and the rest of you back in another ceremony on that pollution bill.

Thank you.

NOTE: The President spoke at 9:34 a.m. in the East Room at the White House. In his opening words he referred to Vice President Hubert H. Humphrey. During his remarks he referred to Senator Edmund S. Muskie of Maine, Representative John A. Blatnik of Minnesota, Secretary of Commerce John T. Connor, Eugene P. Foley, Administrator of the Small Business Administration and newly designated Assistant Secretary of Commerce for Economic Devel-

opment, and Representative Robert E. Jones of Alabama.

As enacted, the Public Works and Economic Development Act of 1965 is Public Law 89–136 (79 Stat. 552).

On November 13, 1965, the White House announced a new program for the economic development of qualified distressed areas which would emphasize planning and coordination across county and State lines in order to create permanent new jobs in areas suffering from high unemployment and low family income (1 Weekly Comp. Pres. Docs. 501).

The Water Quality Act of 1965 was approved by the President on October 2, 1965 (see Item 543).

---

453   Statement by the President Upon Announcing a Program of Assistance to Los Angeles.   *August 26, 1965*

WE HAVE all felt a deep sense of shock and dismay at the riots last week in Los Angeles. I have expressed my conviction that there is no greater wrong in our democracy than violent or willful disregard of law.

At the same time, we cannot let the actions of three or four thousand rioters stay our compassion for the hundreds of thousands of people in the city of Los Angeles—of every race and color—who neither participated in nor condoned the riots. Many suffered at the hands of the rioters. Many are in need of help.

We must eliminate the deepseated causes of riots such as those we witnessed. Recent studies paint a stark picture. The Watts district is in the center of an area in Los Angeles marked by:

—the largest number of school dropouts.

—the highest crime rate.

—the highest population density.

—the lowest median family income.

There are complex problems and the solutions are neither quick nor easy. Long-term answers must and will be found. The White House Conference on Civil Rights this fall should help us. The work of Gov-

ernor Brown's special commission should help us.

But now is a time for immediate action.

There are men and women without work.

There are children without homes.

There are hundreds upon hundreds of school dropouts.

There are citizens whose businesses have been destroyed and must be rebuilt.

I am today sending a team of Federal officials under the leadership of Ramsey Clark, the Deputy Attorney General, as my personal representative to Los Angeles to develop with Governor Brown, Mayor Yorty, and other officials a combined program to restore and rehabilitate the damaged areas of Los Angeles. This program will be aimed at helping those citizens affected by the riots to help themselves. In short, the team's charter is to make available the best programs now known to wipe out the causes of such violent outbursts.

Among the matters to be considered are:

1. A special employment program with emphasis on work in the devastated areas.

2. Stepped-up youth training programs.

3. Establishment of pilot child care

centers, to provide care for parentless children and to give needy mothers training and employment opportunities.

4. Establishment of a small business development center to aid business in the area.

5. Increased health and medical service—emphasizing the children.

6. A vigorous back-to-school program.

7. An expanded surplus food distribution program.

8. An expedited program for placing surplus property such as clothing, medical equipment, and mobile buildings in these stricken areas.

9. Setting up more neighborhood facilities.

10. Accelerating planning and construction of low-income housing.

Mr. Clark will be accompanied by Jack Conway, Deputy Director of the war against poverty, and Andrew Brimmer, Assistant Secretary of Commerce. Other Federal agencies, including the Department of Health, Education, and Welfare, the Housing and Home Finance Agency, and the Small Business Administration, will be represented on the team.

NOTE: In his statement the President referred to, among others, Governor Edmund G. Brown of California, Mayor Samuel W. Yorty of Los Angeles, and Jack T. Conway, Deputy Director of the Office of Economic Opportunity.

On September 2, 1965, the White House announced that the President had received an interim progress report from Mr. Clark. The announcement stated that, based on the recommendations in the report, the President had ordered approximately 45 individual and community self-help projects to be expedited in order to assist all sections of Los Angeles in need of help (1 Weekly Comp. Pres. Docs., p. 192).

See also Item 426.

454 The President's News Conference of *August 26, 1965*

THE PRESIDENT. I guess you all want to get your lunch, but I wanted to tell you what I knew about my plans and I had a statement that I ought to make to you that you may want to file before lunch.

STEEL NEGOTIATIONS

[1.] I have had a very friendly conversation this morning with Mr. R. Conrad Cooper, the Executive Vice President of the United States Steel Corporation, and Mr. I. W. Abel, President of the United Steel Workers of America.

I communicated with them separately over the telephone. I said the same thing to each of them, the substance of which was that I pointed out the question I had received at the press conference yesterday, and my reply to it,[1] and I asked them to read it and review it, which they had done. I told them that I had relied upon them, in these troubled times, to negotiate peacefully a decent and responsible settlement. I was sure that neither the company nor the union wanted the disruption of work or an inflationary situation in our country; that I regarded both the industry and the union to be my friend, and I did not in any way want to try to dictate details of what settlement should be negotiated.

I felt, very briefly, that this was a matter for them to settle by collective bargaining; that I did believe that the President of the country had an extreme responsibility for proclaiming the national interest and serving the national interest; that I had a right

[1] See Item 448 [11].

934

to ask their complete cooperation; that I was asking for that and I expected to receive it, and I believed I would. Both of them assured me that they would be glad to be helpful in any way they could, consistent with their view of what the national interest was and the needs of their respective constituents.

They wished me a happy birthday, and I told them I sure would have one if they carried out my hopes.[2]

[2.] I am going to shoot for a departure of between 3 and 4:30. I would like to meet with a group of ladies that Mrs. Johnson is having at the house between 4 and 6 in Texas. I expect I will miss it, but she is having a group that has been working on a library, on our little boyhood home, and things of that kind, and I would like to visit with them if I can get through with my schedule.

I am running behind. I have some Members of the Congress to see, and some meetings with State Department people, and Mr. Bundy,[3] and the staff, and I have a Quadriad meeting that is just beginning, so I can't tell. I'd like to be precise, but I can't tell you at this moment. It depends on how long they talk and how much rebuttal I have to make.

Q. Mr. President, can I ask you a question?

THE PRESIDENT. If it's in relation to the trip, I want to get off.

[3.] Q. I just wondered if there was any discussion from these men that they would be willing to extend that deadline?

THE PRESIDENT. They did not mention deadline. I told you all that happened.

---

[2] See Item 483.
[3] McGeorge Bundy, Special Assistant to the President.

[4.] Q. It is now on the record you are going to Texas?

THE PRESIDENT. Yes.

TENSION IN THE CITIES

[5.] Q. Mr. President, one question that is bothering a lot of us this morning since the bill signing [4]——

THE PRESIDENT. Just one? You don't mean this is just something that bothered you this morning?

I'll tell you a story. Bill White [5] came in one time and he said, "You know, I'm bothered and I'm confused." The first 3 years he did that to me I really took it at face value until I found out how many times I had made mistakes and all the headlines I had made. So I just quit trying to clear up confusions or to clear up people bothering. What is the problem?

Q. It has to do with your statement this morning about the dangers of increasing tension in the cities, and you also mentioned the District of Columbia. I wondered if you thought it would be at all useful for you to restate or amplify, or try to help us out, on exactly what you meant?

THE PRESIDENT. I meant just what I said. And that was that we ought to try to face up to these problems that we have, such as the one we are facing up to this morning, before we had to suffer more serious problems and create additional problems.

Every little town in this country that you can see has problems. The young are leaving and the old are staying there, and the town is drying up, businesses are folding, and all of those things. We are trying our best through area redevelopment,

---

[4] See Item 452.
[5] William S. White of United Feature Syndicate.

through public works, by trying to solve our water problem, the housing problem, trying to solve the urban renewal problem, and to recognize the economic facts of life and meet them while there is time to do it.

Now, some of these places we don't get to until it already happens and we have to do the very thing we would have to do anyway, plus some additional things. And in Los Angeles we found that we could not contain disappointments and the frustrations, and it took rather drastic action to get that situation back into focus, and now we have all the problems we had before, plus all that were created by this situation.[6]

But the Congress, recognizing our ability of meeting these things head on in this particular instance, had rather wisely acted. There are other places I want them to act on, other fields I want them to act on. And they are acting. They are turning out a good volume.

So, my purpose was twofold. One, was to caution and to point up the desirability of facing up to the problems before they increased in nature; and, two, was to commend them, in this specific instance, for having done a rather effective job.

And, three, to fully recognize the interest of the great State of Minnesota in this field. I saw a good many of them there. Mr.

[6] See Items 426, 453.

Foley [7] has spent a good part of the last 2 or 3 days talking to me about the great opportunity in this field, and I wanted to enlist the aid of all the Members of Congress present.

I don't have the privileges of the floor anymore. That's about the only chance I have to appeal to them. I just did this the best way I could.

I did not want to bother anybody or create more problems than I have. I want to solve them before additional ones come along—in Johnson City, New York City, Washington, D.C.—what town were you born in?

Q. Boston.

THE PRESIDENT. Boston.

Q. Do you think it's bad up there?

THE PRESIDENT. I don't say it's bad. We are going to face up to those problems while we can before additional ones develop. That is what they are doing.

This is a rather revolutionary bill, a far-reaching one, a bipartisan one. I pointed that out.

Reporter: Thank you, Mr. President.

NOTE: President Johnson's fiftieth news conference, an informal meeting with White House correspondents, was held in his office at the White House at 12:17 p.m. on Thursday, August 26, 1965.

[7] Eugene P. Foley, Administrator of the Small Business Administration and newly designated Assistant Secretary of Commerce for Economic Development.

455 Statement by the President Following House Passage of the Higher Education Bill. *August 26, 1965*

THIS is a great night for higher education in America. The House of Representatives has added a major building block to our college system by passing the Higher Education Act of 1965. More than a million students can benefit in the next year by guaranteed low interest loans—a program I have

urged for the past 15 years. More than a quarter million needy students can get part-time jobs to help them continue their college studies. More than one hundred thousand students of exceptional promise and great financial need can receive opportunity grants.

The bill passed by the House also strengthens our colleges by providing books and trained personnel to enrich college libraries and funds to assist our less developed institutions of learning.

Finally, the House has challenged our universities to face the problems of the city through community service programs.

This bill not only strengthens higher education; it adds to the mental might of the Nation.

NOTE: The Higher Education Act of 1965 was approved by the President on November 8, 1965 (see Item 603).

---

456   Statement by the President Upon Signing Bills Providing Additional Benefits for Disabled Veterans.   *August 27, 1965*

I HAVE today approved two bills that bring a greater measure of justice to our veterans who suffer from service-connected disabilities.

The first bill provides a 30 percent increase in the basic subsistence allowance paid to such veterans. This amount is comparable to increases in living costs since April 1, 1948, when the current rates were established. It is fair and right that these adjustments be made.

The second bill provides a longer period of time during which service-connected disabled veterans may receive vocational rehabilitation training. Under present law

that period is 9 years. Hereafter a disabled veteran whose disability becomes more grave, and who requires additional training because of his misfortune, may receive it during an additional 10-year period.

America owes these new laws to the men who have been injured or wounded in her service. I am proud to sign them into law.

NOTE: The statement was read by Bill D. Moyers, Special Assistant to the President, at his news conference at the White House at 11:50 a.m. on Friday, August 27, 1965. It was not made public in the form of a White House press release.

As enacted, the first bill (H.R. 206) is Public Law 89–137 (79 Stat. 576); the second bill (H.R. 208) is Public Law 89–138 (79 Stat. 577).

---

457   Statement by the President Following Senate Committee Action on the Higher Education Bill.   *August 27, 1965*

I AM delighted at the bipartisan and overwhelming support that the House gave to the higher education bill yesterday. This brings us closer to the moment when every young man and woman in America can be assured of an education on the basis of his talent rather than on the basis of his ability to pay.

I am also very pleased at the swift action by Senator Morse and his Subcommittee on Higher Education in unanimously reporting the Senate bill this morning. Our colleges

by 1970 must be prepared to add 50 percent more enrollment to their presently overcrowded facilities. This bill is a major step toward the meeting of the demands of the next decade.

NOTE: The statement was read by Bill D. Moyers, Special Assistant to the President, at his news conference at the White House at 11:50 a.m. on Friday, August 27, 1965. It was not made public in the form of a White House press release.

The Higher Education Act of 1965 was approved by the President on November 8, 1965 (see Item 603).

458 Exchange of Messages With H. H. Cheeley of Iuka, Ill., on the President's Birthday. *August 27, 1965*

MANY happy returns on your birthday. I am proud to share the day with you and am heartened by your warm expressions. I wish you the best in health and happiness until our next birthday.

LYNDON B. JOHNSON

[Mr. H. H. Cheeley, Iuka, Illinois]

NOTE: The text of Mr. Cheeley's letter follows:

Mr. President, Dear Sir:

Your birthday is the same day as mine, on the 27th day of August. I am 102 years old. I am a Democrat and voted my first vote for Grover Cleveland on November 4, 1884. I have voted for every Democrat since then for 20 Presidents. For 80 years I voted at the same place in Iuka Township, Marion County, State of Illinois.

I back your way of doing business—less talk and more doing good.

Truly.

H. H. CHEELEY

The President called White House correspondents into his office in the afternoon of August 27 and read the foregoing exchange. It was not made public in the form of a White House press release.

459 Remarks at the Presentation of Plans for a Park in Johnson City, Texas. *August 27, 1965*

Lady Bird, Mr. Linen, my beloved friends of Johnson City:

This is a very proud moment for me and I deeply appreciate, Mr. Linen, what you are doing for this wonderful little city that is made up of so many good people.

It is going to be through public-spirited citizens and public-spirited businesses that we make this great land of ours a more beautiful land in the years ahead.

I have heard a lot of talk during my 35 years in public life about the power of the press, and particularly the power of Life, Time, Fortune, and a few other publications associated with you. But as I look out this afternoon at this vacant lot and I see this beautiful sketch of what it is going to be a few months from now, I am made aware for the first time of the real power of the press to make the trees grow and the flowers bloom. And we welcome it, Mr. Linen.

I guess I shouldn't tell this story, but a friend of mine many years ago was indicted for buying poll taxes down in San Antonio. And they put the witnesses on the stand, and

they produced the women that went to the table to pick up their half dollar pieces, they produced the taxicab fellow that took him to the bank where he got the money in a sack, they produced the banker that distributed the half dollars in return for a check from David Dubinsky in New York. And it was about that time that my friend Mayor Maverick sent for me and asked to borrow my lawyer, and the testimony was already in.

The case was made and it was just a matter of moments until the jury rendered its verdict, and my dear, beloved friend Senator Wirtz was called upon to make the argument of defense without ever having heard all the testimony. But he read it quickly, and he said the Mavericks had made a great contribution to Texas. They fought at the Alamo. They had served in our various governments for many years. The then mayor had been a distinguished Member of Congress, and here he was on trial. On trial for what? For being the first man in Texas that could go north and meet this Yankee, David Dubinsky, and get some of that money that we have been sending up there all these years, and bring it back to Texas. And not use it for himself, not appropriate it to his own comforts, but rather to take it and permit poor women to have their very first vote and to have the right of franchise. And he said, "I would think instead of trying him and committing him to a penitentiary that we ought to build a monument to him out here in front of the Alamo!"

Now, I don't know how Mrs. Johnson has gone to New York and got you to come down here, but it is a great tribute, I think, to both of you—one, that she would want to go up there and get you, and, next, that you would want to come. And I just can't think of anything that makes me more pleased on my birthday.

Birthdays are a time for reflection, and I have been reflecting all day—with the maritime workers, and with the steelworkers, and the steel companies, with the boys out in Viet-Nam, and some people down in the Dominican Republic, with the spacemen that are circling the globe, and a good many other things—and I have been reflecting all day just how I was finally going to get here to spend the evening with Lady Bird. Because, in case you have not heard it yet, she is rather interested in beautification. And it appears that she not only wants people to say it with flowers, she wants them also to say it with trees. I hope when we meet here again that we'll have more trees and more flowers here on this somewhat rather sacred spot.

I have been trying to see Ohlen Cox out here. I don't know whether he is here this afternoon or not. But I remember—about where that boy is with that orange shirt on there—Ohlen chasing me from in front of that garage and catching me there. He was wrestling with a fellow and they were trying to put each other's shoulders to the mat, and I ran up and kicked both of them while they were down. And he took off after me, and he said, "I'm going to spank you all the way from the garage to your house"—which is right up there.

And he started out, and I was showing the effects of his spanking in a rather loud voice, and my dear old friend, Bud Winters' home was here then—right over there—and as we crossed his front yard and he heard this yelling, he came out on the porch and he stopped Ohlen, and he separated us. And while he and Ohlen were continuing their conversation, I excused myself and went on home.

And little did I recognize then that some day, through the generous spirit and the prosperity of the Time and Life publications, that they would come here and build a beautiful park where the good people—the young people who are here could enjoy it in the daytime, and those in the twilight of their career could come here and sit under its trees on comfortable benches amidst beautiful surroundings and enjoy it in the twilight of the evening of their lives.

It is a great day, and thank you very much.

NOTE: The President spoke at 4:45 p.m. at the site of the future park in Johnson City, Tex. In his opening words he referred to Mrs. Johnson and James A. Linen, president of Time Inc. During his remarks he referred to David Dubinsky, president of the International Ladies Garment Workers Union, Maury Maverick, mayor of San Antonio 1939–1941, and Alvin J. Wirtz, Texas State senator 1922–1930 and Under Secretary of the Interior January 1940–May 1941.

The park, located one block from the President's boyhood home, was a gift from Life magazine. It was presented to the town of 611 people as a part of Mrs. Johnson's beautification program.

460   Statement by the President Upon Signing Bill Authorizing
Apportionment of Funds for the Interstate Highway System.
August 28, 1965

WITH the signing of this legislation, we are authorizing the largest single year apportionment of Federal aid to the States for highways.

The highways to be built and improved under the Federal-aid highway program will save time, save money, and save the lives of motorists. They will strengthen our national economy and our national defense. They will increase the markets for the products of our farms and they will give flexibility to the movement of people and goods in our growing urban areas. They will broaden the travel and recreational opportunities for all Americans. They will permit everyone to see the beauty and grandeur of America conveniently, comfortably, and safely.

This legislation also provides for the study of the orderly continuation of the Federal-aid highway program. Congress has asked that it be provided with regular estimates of the future highway needs of the Nation. This administration, through the Department of Commerce and its Bureau of Public Roads, has a study underway of our future highway needs. On the basis of that study, I will, in January 1968, consider legislation for a program of Federal aid to the States for highways to continue after the expiration of the present program in 1972.

This legislation also provides the tools for a coordinated national attack on highway accidents. It provides that the Secretary of Commerce shall develop uniform standards for State highway safety programs. The death of over 48,000 persons on our highways last year and the prospect of an even greater total this year give urgency to a national safety effort. The approach provided for by this legislation is in keeping with the traditional Federal-State relationship through which the Federal-aid highway program has operated so successfully. It recognizes the primary responsibility of the States for highway safety and at the same time acknowledges the Federal Government's responsibility to lead and coordinate.

This legislation, however, is but part of what is needed to insure that our highways will be able to meet the increasing demands placed upon them. I have proposed to Congress legislation to insure that the Highway Trust Fund will receive the revenue it needs so that the States might receive Federal aid sufficient for the timely completion of the Interstate Highway System. I have also submitted to Congress legislation that will insure that the enormous public investments in highways will be protected from roadside blight and that highways will serve the increasing public demand for the beautiful as well as the merely utilitarian. The everyday driving of Americans provides the greatest opportunity to see and enjoy the beauty of our Nation. The higher standard of living and the increased leisure time of Americans have created a demand for scenic and recreational roads. I anticipate that the Congress will shortly act on these needs.

This proposed legislation meets a public need, in reality a public necessity, and is going to be pursued with all the vigor of the executive department until acted upon.

We are a Nation of almost 100 million drivers and 90 million vehicles. By 1970 we will be driving a trillion miles a year in

America. We cannot depend on the roads of yesterday to carry the motor traffic of today and tomorrow. The life and pocketbook of every American are affected by the efficiency of our motor transportation system. The legislation now before Congress is necessary if we are to meet the new needs essential to the progress of our motor transportation system.

I appeal to all patriotic citizens interested in the improvement and continued develop-ment of our highway system to unite to the end of making that system adequate, superior in construction, and most important, attractive and beautiful.

NOTE: As enacted, the bill (S.J. Res. 81) is Public Law 89–139 (79 Stat. 578).

On the same day the White House released a summary of the provisions of the bill (1 Weekly Comp. Pres. Docs., p. 167).

The Highway Beautification Act of 1965 was approved by the President on October 22, 1965 (see Item 576).

The statement was released at Austin, Tex.

461   Statement by the President Announcing Program in Aid of Elderly Citizens of Low Income.   *August 28, 1965*

PRESIDENT JOHNSON today announced a Federal program aimed at lifting 5½ million elderly citizens out of poverty.

The first stage—$41 million in four projects—will open a new front in the war on poverty.

The President pointed out that a third of all Americans over 65 are living in poverty; the average income of these people is under $1,150.

"The aged poor have maturity and experience to offer," he stated. "They are eager to help themselves and others. We are going to use this rich, untapped human resource to help others less fortunate. In turn, it will enable these elderly people to find the dignity and usefulness they seek."

The initial five-point program will employ 17,600 elderly Americans of low income. They will help attack the poverty of 140,000 of the Nation's most cruelly deprived—neglected babies, retarded children, the homebound sick, and the bedridden and isolated elderly.

One of the new projects is a "Foster Grandparents" program in which the elderly will be "substitute parents" for neglected children in institutions. Within a year it will reach into all 50 States at a total cost of $10 million. It has two parts:

—2,000 of the elderly poor will work with 5,000 neglected infants living in institutions. Twenty-two projects in 20 States are starting immediately with $2.7 million in grants.

—Another 2,000 will help care for 2,000 older children in institutions. These projects will be funded in about a month.

The remaining three projects are:

—10,000 will be trained as home health aides to bring help and comfort to the bedridden sick and disabled.

—1,800 will start work this fall in both urban slums and rural hollows, caring for children from broken homes.

—2,400 will be trained this fall to meet the needs of mentally retarded children.

Additional programs recommended by a task force on problems of the aged and under consideration include: employment services for the elderly with skills, work opportunity centers for the elderly who are unable to compete in the labor market, home maintenance service, employing the elderly poor to assist in repair of substandard dwellings inhabited by the elderly; a food program; special services to the elderly poor in rural areas; and an "outreach" service to help the elderly understand and use the assistance available to them.

The new and future programs will be funded by the Office of Economic Opportunity. They will be operated by local community agencies and institutions in close cooperation with the Department of Health, Education, and Welfare.

The $41 million will be distributed as follows:

—$10 million total to the Foster Grandparents programs,

—$6 million for services to mentally retarded children,

—$5 million for the project to help children from broken homes, and

—$20 million for the home health aides.

NOTE: The statement was released at Austin, Tex.

462 Remarks by Telephone to Astronauts Cooper and Conrad Following Completion of the Gemini 5 Mission. *August 29, 1965*

THE PRESIDENT. Good morning, gentlemen. For myself and all of your countrymen, I want to say congratulations and well done.

I am sure that all people in all lands are greatly thrilled by what you have shown that man can do. And we are all so thankful for your safe return.

After listening to you and your wives all week, I feel somewhat out of step this morning, not having a poem to read to you. If Luci were here, I'd borrow one of hers, but she has gone to church.

I do want to salute you both for the very calm and cool courage that you have shown throughout these last 8 days. In the face of disappointment and discouragement you have conducted yourselves nobly. You have certainly proved, I think, once and for all that man has a place in the exploration of the great frontier of space.

Gordon, when are you going to be ready to go up again?

ASTRONAUT COOPER. I think it will be a day or two again, sir——

THE PRESIDENT. Well, that is fine. Astronaut Conrad, after you see that family of yours, would you like to see some of the world at ground level for a change?

ASTRONAUT CONRAD. I'm sorry, sir, I couldn't hear you.

THE PRESIDENT. I say, after you see that family of yours, how would you like to see some of the world at the ground level for a change?

ASTRONAUT CONRAD. Oh, I'd like to very much, sir.

THE PRESIDENT. Well, you are going to get the chance. We want you to take a good rest and work with your doctors and follow out Mr. Webb's and Dr. Seamans' instructions. But afterwards, we hope that both of you, along with the other astronauts, can accept some of the invitations to share your achievements with the peoples of other lands because the one thing that we are all working for, and really our only purpose in space, is peace in the world.

We want all mankind to be the beneficiary of what you have done and I know that you can continue to communicate America's message on earth as in the skies.

We spent a good part of last evening working out some plans for you. Now Gemini 5 will long be remembered and long honored for the courage of the crew, the competence of the team on the ground, and

942

the vision of all who dared conceive this great enterprise. We can only hope that your achievement will encourage all other nations to accept more fully what great accomplishments can be wrought by cooperating together in these new realms of infinity.

So I just want to say, God bless you both. We are glad you are back. We shall be everlastingly proud of you, and we are so thankful for all the blessings that are ours.

Do either of you have any observations you want to make?

ASTRONAUT COOPER. Well, sir, it was certainly a wonderful trip and we saw a lot of the whole world and a lot of countries, and a lot of places that were extremely interesting, and it makes one really realize how small and insignificant . . . country or world and how we all should work together to further peace in the whole world.

THE PRESIDENT. Well, Gordon, I wish you could be out here with us this morning.

ASTRONAUT COOPER. (Response inaudible.)

THE PRESIDENT. Gordon, do you read me?

ASTRONAUT COOPER. Yes, sir, I read you.

THE PRESIDENT. Are you just reluctant or did you not hear me?

ASTRONAUT COOPER. We're reading you; are you reading us?

THE PRESIDENT. I sure am. I wish you could go to the Scharnhorst with me this morning as we did, not long ago.

ASTRONAUT COOPER. That would be nice.

THE PRESIDENT. So we will be looking forward to seeing you, and congratulations again. I know your families are going to be mighty happy to see you again.

ASTRONAUT COOPER. Thank you very much for calling us.

THE PRESIDENT. Over and out.

ASTRONAUT CONRAD. We'll see you. Bye.

NOTE: The President spoke with Lt. Col. L. Gordon Cooper, Jr., and Lt. Comdr. Charles Conrad, Jr., at 9 a.m. from the LBJ Ranch at Johnson City, Tex. During his remarks he referred to James E. Webb, Administrator, National Aeronautics and Space Administration, and R. C. Seamans, Jr., Associate Administrator.

The astronauts had landed in the North Atlantic that morning just 1½ hours short of completing their original 121-orbit, 8-day mission.

463   The President's News Conference at the LBJ Ranch.
August 29, 1965

THE PRESIDENT: Good afternoon ladies and gentlemen:

[1.] I want to first of all congratulate the press on their new record today. You have just completed a new record of orbits between Johnson City and the LBJ Ranch. I want to congratulate you on your successful reentry.

We have had a very happy and busy birthday weekend. I am very grateful for all the thoughtful expressions which have reached us from so many families across the land and from leaders in other parts of the world.

From the way it has begun I anticipate

that this 57th year may be one of the best years, and that is a very happy thought for me. The weekend has been made especially happy by the presence here of so many good and old and trusted, cherished friends.

I am especially happy to have one of my very favorite couples—Mr. and Mrs. Larry O'Brien.[1] Many of you have been writing about Larry's departure from the White House and I can confirm that this afternoon. But I did want him to spend a weekend here in Texas before he departed. I also

---
[1] Lawrence F. O'Brien, Special Assistant to the President.

want to say a word or so about Larry's future in a few moments.

The Postmaster General and his lovely wife came down to check on the White House ZIP code. Secretary Rusk and Mrs. Rusk wanted to check up on our relations between the United States and Texas. And I think they have found them generally good the last 24 hours.

Ambassador Goldberg, of course, was eager to come back because he is just naturally more at home in cowboy country.

Seriously though, I do have a statement that I want to make to you before we go back to Washington this afternoon, and that is this:

THE GEMINI 5 ACHIEVEMENT

[2.] This is a moment of very great achievement not only for Astronauts Gordon Cooper and Charles Conrad but for everyone whose hopes have ridden with Gemini 5.[2]

I am so happy that Mr. Webb and Mr. Seamans,[3] who had so much to do with directing this very successful venture, are here to share with us the pride we all feel today. And I deeply regret that our late, beloved President Kennedy, under whose leadership all of this work was so carefully planned and thought out, can't be here to enjoy the fruits and success of his planning and his forethought.

The successful completion of the 8-day, 3-million-mile flight of the Gemini 5 proves, I think, not only man's capacity for endurance in space but it proves that man is in space to stay.

We can be, and we are, enormously proud

of every member of our space team—that means all the scientists and the technicians and the controllers and the trackers. To everyone who contributed in any way, as President of this country, I want, this afternoon, to extend the thanks of the entire Nation for a job well done. To Gordon Cooper and Charles Conrad, and to their wonderful families, I want to simply repeat again: We are all very deeply proud of you.

The difficulties and disappointments of this flight have served to increase our appreciation and our respect and our trust for the skill and the ability of all the men involved. We can face the challenges and the opportunities with far greater confidence and certainty in the future, and I think this is an unmistakable gain for all of us.[4]

Only 7 years ago we were neither first nor second in space—we just weren't in space at all. And as we meet here this afternoon, the capacity of this country for leadership in this realm is no longer in valid question or dispute anyplace in the world. Openly, proudly, we are proceeding on our course, willing always to share our knowl-

---

[2] See Item 462.

[3] James E. Webb, Administrator, National Aeronautics and Space Administration, and R. C. Seamans, Jr., Associate Administrator.

[4] On August 31, 1965, the White House announced that the President had approved the following policy on the promotion and decoration of astronauts:

1. Each military astronaut will receive a one-grade promotion as a direct result of the first successful space flight, but not beyond the grade of colonel in the Air Force and Marine Corps or captain in the Navy. Promotions to general officer rank will be accomplished through usual military selection board process.

2. Each Gemini astronaut will be awarded the NASA Medal for Exceptional Service (or Cluster) after completion of a successful space flight. The NASA Medal for Distinguished Service, the highest award which can be given by that agency, will be awarded for exceptional accomplishments in the Gemini program including, but not limited to, accomplishments in actual flight.

3. Military decorations associated with space flights, such as awards for exceptional heroism or other distinguished service, will be determined on an individual basis consistent with general policy governing the award of traditional military decorations.

edge and our gains with all of mankind. So, I would repeat and I would renew again this afternoon America's invitation to all nations to join together to make this adventure a joint adventure.

This globe seems much smaller today than it has ever seemed before.

Somehow the problems which yesterday seemed large and ominous and insoluble today appear much less foreboding. As man increases his knowledge of the heavens, why should he fear the unknown on earth? As man draws nearer to the stars, why should he not also draw nearer to his neighbor?

As we push ever more deeply into the universe—probing its secrets, discovering its way—we must also constantly try to learn to cooperate across the frontiers that really divide earth's surface.

No national sovereignty rules in outer space. Those who venture there go as envoys of the entire human race. Their quest, therefore, must be for all mankind. And what they find should belong to all mankind. And that is the basis of the program of which our proud astronauts Cooper and Conrad are a part today.

For, as the great Woodrow Wilson said of this country half a century ago, "We ask nothing for ourselves that we do not also ask for all of humanity."

And we ask peace. Peace—and the real opportunity to help our neighbors, to improve the quality of all of our lives, to enlarge the meaning of liberty for all, and to secure for all the rights and dignities intended for man by his Creator.

This flight of Gemini 5 was a journey of peace by men of peace. Its successful conclusion is a noble moment for all mankind, and it is a very fitting opportunity for us today to renew our pledge to continue our search for a world in which peace reigns and in which justice prevails.

To demonstrate the earnestness of that pledge, and to express our commitment to the peaceful uses of space exploration, I intend to ask as many of our astronauts as possible—when Mr. Webb thinks their schedule and program will permit—to visit the various capitals of the world. Some, I hope, will be able to journey abroad very soon.

Secretary Rusk and Director Webb and I spent a good part of last evening going over the anticipated problems that will arise and the schedules that will have to be worked out. But Gemini is really just the beginning. We resolve to have many more such journeys—in space and on earth—until man at last is at peace with himself.

The End of the Shipping Strike

[3.] I am glad, also, to announce to you today that the eight east coast and gulf shipping companies and three licensed officer unions have reached agreement. So the normal operation of the merchant marine will now be resumed again.

The losses from the 75-day tie-up of a hundred ships can never be recovered. It took too long to settle these cases. We all know that.

But this was very constructive bargaining. More was done during this period than simply putting new patches on the leaky hull of maritime labor relations.

A firm basis has already been laid in these agreements to resolve manning disputes resulting from automation, without interruption of future operations.

New principles of parity have been built into the pattern of these three contracts.

The economic terms are built around specific recognition of established stabilization policies.

Provision has been made for taking a clear

look at the questions which really must be faced if the pension plans in this industry are to be found.

These settlements are steps toward a new and a responsible maritime policy for the United States of America. They will give the rule of good sense a much better chance to work in the future. No man has done more to bring about this important settlement—the one that was reached in the wee hours of this morning—than the very able and distinguished Secretary of Labor, Willard Wirtz. He has worked patiently, he has worked tirelessly, he has worked reasonably around the clock. And all of America owes him an enormous vote of thanks.

THE DOMINICAN REPUBLIC

[4.] The Secretary of State and I spent yesterday afternoon and last evening and this morning reviewing various matters of interest around the world.

Secretary Rusk reported that in the Dominican Republic the OAS committee is continuing its very patient and determined work for peace.

It is clear now that this work corresponds to the real hopes of the Dominican people and to the hopes of the whole Western Hemisphere. It is also clear that the OAS committee is right in its belief that the time for agreement is now.

We have followed the negotiations closely and we will support the changes which the OAS committee has proposed in its Act of Reconciliation.[5] We believe that these changes strengthen the document by making clearer provisions for the procedure of dis-

armament, and by reinforcing the authority of what will be a fully sovereign provisional government.

I am confident that the Dominican people and the members of the OAS are one in their belief that any who continue to oppose the OAS solution are serving no true interest of their country or peace in the world. And it is greatly to the credit of the Organization of the American States that all members of its committee and all officers of the Inter-American Peace Force are doing their dead level best to bring all sides to agreement on the OAS proposal in its present form.

THE KASHMIR ISSUE

[5.] The Secretary and I also discussed the tense and difficult situation in Kashmir. We are naturally greatly concerned over any flareup involving India and Pakistan. Our longstanding and our very consistent stance has always been that the Kashmir issue must, and should be, solved by peaceful means. The U.N. is already involved, and we hope that the constructive efforts of the Secretary General may be successful there.

I might add that we are also always acutely interested in the course of affairs in the subcontinent in general. This is an area to which the United States has provided truly massive assistance and to whose people the United States is deeply attached.

THE YEMEN AGREEMENT

[6.] In the Middle East, we are happy to see the statesmanlike agreement between King Faisal and President Nasser,[6] which seems to offer great promise of a peaceful settlement in Yemen. This crisis has long been a very disruptive element in the rela-

---

[5] On August 31, 1965, the Act of Dominican Reconciliation, proposed by the ad hoc committee of the Organization of American States, was signed at Santo Domingo (OAS doc. 281). A summary of the terms is printed in the Department of State Bulletin (vol. 53, p. 478).

[6] King Faisal of Saudi Arabia and Gamal Abdel Nasser, President of the United Arab Republic.

tions between our two friends. We share their confidence that this long-festering issue is on the road to settlement by negotiation rather than force, and that is most encouraging.

THE NEGOTIATIONS IN GENEVA

[7.] In Geneva today, our negotiators are continuing their efforts to make progress toward a sound international agreement to stop the spread of nuclear weapons. The cause of peace has no more urgent task.

We regret very much that some are still unwilling to join in serious negotiations on the false grounds that our proposals would permit nuclear proliferation in Europe.

In the same way, we regret that these proposals have been misunderstood by others as if they interfered with the legitimate defensive interests of any of the NATO allies. They do nothing of the sort, and I am glad to say that we have had full consultation and understanding with such outstanding leaders as Chancellor Erhard [7] on this point.

APPOINTMENT OF AMBASSADOR TO POLAND

[8.] Early in 1964, speaking at VMI, I pledged my administration to a policy of building bridges across the gulf which has divided us for more than two decades from the people of Eastern Europe.

I said then, "They will be," I said, "bridges of increased trade, of ideas, of visitors, and of humanitarian aid."

Our hopes for the people of these countries are identical to their own aspirations for their own future. We want to strengthen their ability to shape their own society. And we seek to bring every European nation closer to its neighbors in the ties of peace.

And so today I am very pleased to announce one of the most important steps that this Nation has yet taken to implement that policy: I am asking a member of my Cabinet, a vigorous, intelligent, highly trained, and deeply committed public servant—Postmaster General John Gronouski—to serve as United States Ambassador to Poland.

I have discussed this assignment at great length with Secretary Rusk and other top key officials in the Department of State. And we believe that Mr. Gronouski's appointment reaffirms our strong desire for increased trust and friendly cooperation between Poland and the United States.

Mr. Gronouski is going to Warsaw to do everything in his power to further increase understanding and goodwill between Poland and our country. He is a grand and a very warm human being who enjoys people. His background and his experience uniquely qualify him to translate American ideals to Poland and Polish ideals to America.

I have asked Mr. Gronouski to say to the peoples and to the leaders of Poland that a deep and historic bond exists between Poland and the United States. Let, therefore, trust grow between us. Let us strengthen that bond, and let us work together for the peace and the liberty that we all seek for all peoples everywhere.

John Gronouski is the man, I think, that can carry that message.

America is in his blood, but so is Poland.

He was born the grandson of a Polish immigrant. He is a member of the Polish Institute of the Arts and Sciences of Chicago, a director of the Pulaski Foundation, the honorary chairman of the Committee for an Endowed Chair in Polish Studies at the University of Chicago. In 1963 he became Postmaster General by selection of President Kennedy. He was the first American of Polish descent to ever serve in the Cabinet.

[7] Ludwig Erhard, Chancellor of the Federal Republic of Germany.

947

And it was my great pleasure to reappoint him to the Postmaster Generalship last February.

But John Gronouski is more. He is one of the very few men with a doctor of philosophy degree ever to sit in the Cabinet. And as an expert on international economics and on government finance, he established a most outstanding record as commissioner of taxation for one of the great, progressive States in the Union—Wisconsin. He is a talented administrator who has opened up new paths of progress for the postal service of the United States.

Just as another very extraordinary American—who I am delighted to see with us today—Ambassador Arthur Goldberg, left the Supreme Court to accept a very extraordinary and highly significant diplomatic assignment, John Gronouski is now leaving the Cabinet with a distinguished record and high honor to serve his President and his country.

And he is, by the way, enhancing a noble and unique tradition. For the man who really set up our postal service, our first Postmaster General, also went on to later serve his country as Ambassador. His name was Benjamin Franklin.

APPOINTMENT OF POSTMASTER GENERAL

[9.] Now to succeed John Gronouski as Postmaster General, I have chosen a man widely recognized as a very talented and ardent practitioner of government, a very skilled manager and organizer whose endless capacity for work and clear vision of the greater public good have earned him immense respect and affection among all who know him. He has been Special Assistant to the President for Congressional Relations; his name is Lawrence F. O'Brien.

Larry O'Brien's credentials are as impressive as the job of Postmaster General is demanding. His appointment recognizes merit and recognizes demonstrated ability in government. He is a veteran of 3 years in the Army. He was for 17 years a businessman in Massachusetts. In 1960 he served as national director of organization in the late beloved John F. Kennedy's campaign for the Democratic nomination for President, and later as national director of organization for the Kennedy-Johnson campaign.

He came to the White House in 1961 as President Kennedy's Chief Assistant for Congressional Relations. He became the key legislative architect of the New Frontier. After the tragedy of November 22, 1963, he stayed on—at the President's request—to help enact legislation that meant so much to President Kennedy and to the Kennedy-Johnson administration.

I know of no single individual who has contributed more to the enactment of legislation that touches the lives of more Americans than Larry O'Brien.

From voting rights to medical care, from the tax cut to the war on poverty, from the Peace Corps to education, Larry O'Brien has expressed his compassion for people in the enactment of major legislation.

He enjoys the high regard of Congress and the executive branch of Government. He will be warmly welcomed into the Cabinet by his new colleagues. I have conferred with the leadership of the Congress and they expressed their great pleasure also. We all know him to be a man concerned not only with the process of government but with the philosophy of government.

Wise counselor, gifted strategist, efficient manager, warm humanitarian, he is a man who—as the respected Business Week magazine pointed out last April—has earned the title of "the 11th Cabinet member."

So I am very proud this afternoon to make him a member of the Cabinet in fact as well as in the magazine and in reputation. He will continue to be a very strong right arm to the President. Don't be surprised if you see him on the Hill occasionally.

But let me caution you, Larry—just because Ben Franklin went to Paris and John Gronouski is going to Warsaw, that doesn't mean that you are ever going to Dublin.

I'll be glad to take any questions you may care to ask, and after the television time is over Secretary Rusk and Ambassador Goldberg and Administrator Webb will be glad, for a few minutes before you leave, to give you any material on background that you would like to have.

QUESTIONS

STEEL MEDITATION EFFORTS

[10.] Q. Mr. President, what do you hear from the steel strike?

THE PRESIDENT. We had a very lengthy report this morning. And the special mediators I asked to go up yesterday were meeting again, first, with the steel management, and later with the steel union. They have really made no progress since they went there yesterday. They have been going into the facts of the situation and we have carefully evaluated the factual report they have brought us. We are asking them to get back in touch with us after lunch this afternoon and we will give further attention to it during the day and the evening.

VIET-NAM

[11.] Q. Mr. President, the Russians are reported to be saying that North Viet-Nam might be willing to start negotiations if there is another cessation of U.S. bombing. Do you credit these reports and, if so, are there any plans for another temporary halt on the bombing?

THE PRESIDENT. I don't know where the reports are. I have not seen them, and we hear a lot of reports but so far as I am aware there is nothing official about them, and I expect some newspaperman is speculating.

Q. Mr. President, there have been a lot of published reports this week about new initiatives, perhaps on the fringe of Hanoi. Are we measurably any closer to peace talks? Can you discuss these reports and give us some background on it?

THE PRESIDENT. I would say that reports come and go but there is not anything that I can add to what I have said in my last press conference. The word "peace" is a great word in our vocabulary. We are searching for it. We are doing everything we can to prevail on all parties concerned to leave the battlefield and go to the conference table. But I have nothing official, or nothing reliable, that would indicate that any of the parties of interest are ready to do that at this time.

EFFECT OF A STEEL STRIKE

[12.] Q. Mr. President, what would the steel strike do to the national economy? [8]

THE PRESIDENT. Well, it would be very damaging. It would depend on how long it went on, to say the least. It is something we don't want to happen. I have appealed to both management and labor to let collective bargaining work, and I hope that it will be successful. We are going to do everything we can to ask both parties to be responsible,

---

[8] See Item 483.

and to act in the national interest, and I hope and believe they will.

SCHEDULE FOR A FLIGHT TO THE MOON

[13.] Q. Mr. President, in light of the success of the Gemini 5 flight, where do we stand in our schedule to get a man on the moon? Can we do it in this decade, sir?

THE PRESIDENT. Yes, I think that our schedule is going along very well. That's been our hope. Director Webb can go into further details with you in the backgrounder following this conference, but I don't want to be overoptimistic. A lot of hard work is ahead of us. It is going to be very costly in both time and resources. But I know of no project our Government has ever undertaken that has been better managed, that received more cooperation from the 20 thousand-odd business companies in this country, and all the workers belonging to labor, and the fine management team of Webb, Dryden,[9] and Seamans. And I think that we will continue to advance and make progress and meet our goals.

STEEL MEDIATION EFFORTS

[14.] Q. Mr. President, is there anything further you can do to put off the steel strike?

THE PRESIDENT. Well, I'm going to do everything I can to avoid it. We have to take one step at a time and see what progress is made, but I have no doubt but what management wants to avoid a strike if it can. I know that the workers want to avoid the costly price that the strike would bring. And we are trying to work it out in the American way, and I hope we'll be able to. If not,

we'll have to look to the national interest and see what it requires and then carry it out.

ALLEVIATION OF RACIAL TENSIONS

[15.] Q. Mr. President, the other day, in the wake of what happened in Los Angeles,[10] you warned against further violence and lawlessness in the city streets, and afterward the Republican leader of the House [11] suggested that by your remarks you might tend to incite the very thing that you are trying to prevent. Do you have any comment on this?

THE PRESIDENT. I would certainly hope not. I don't want to incite anything. I think we recognize that we have very serious problems in this area. And I think the Congress has acted very forthrightly and very effectively—at least most of the Congress—to find the answer to this problem.

The higher education bill passed with only 22 votes against it last week. The poverty bill passed with an overwhelming vote. Both of those measures will be helpful to us. The elementary education bill passed by a rather substantial vote.

I think this Congress has done a great deal in the way of voters' rights. And what I said at the White House, I would remind you all, is something that I think every American recognizes is a fact. We have a good many of these problems that we need to face up to, and I don't think any Congress has ever faced up to them better than this Congress.

We have not concluded our work, but we are rapidly approaching the end. And if we can get the legislation we have asked, we can do our planning, we can make some mass as-

---

[9] Hugh L. Dryden, Deputy Administrator of the National Aeronautics and Space Administration.

[10] See Items 426, 453.
[11] Representative Gerald R. Ford of Michigan, minority leader of the House of Representatives.

saults on these conditions, where 35 or 40 percent of the young people in a given area are unemployed, and can get them back to work, or get them back to school, or get them back in better housing and better living conditions.

I think that we will find an answer to these problems, and that is what I am trying to get the country to do. Housing, poverty, education, medical care, home rule—all of these are measures that I would hope the Congress would carefully consider and act upon, and they have done that in most fields.

Reporter: Thank you, Mr. President.

NOTE: President Johnson's fifty-first news conference was held at the LBJ Ranch, Johnson City, Tex., at 12:30 p.m. on Sunday, August 29, 1965.

464 Letter to Secretary General U Thant at the Second United Nations World Population Conference in Belgrade. *August 30, 1965*

My Dear Mr. Secretary General:

The United States Government recognizes the singular importance of the meeting of the second United Nations World Population Conference and pledges its full support to your great undertaking.

As I said to the United Nations in San Francisco, we must now begin to face forthrightly the multiplying problems of our multiplying population. Our government assures your conference of our wholehearted support to the United Nations and its agencies in their efforts to achieve a better world through bringing into balance the world's resources and the world's population.

In extending my best wishes for the success of your conference, it is my fervent hope that your great assemblage of population experts will contribute significantly to the knowledge necessary to solve this transcendent problem. Second only to the search for peace, it is humanity's greatest challenge. This week, the meeting in Belgrade carries with it the hopes of mankind.

Sincerely,

LYNDON B. JOHNSON

[His Excellency U Thant, Secretary General of the United Nations]

465 Statement by the President on the Role of the National Export Expansion Council. *August 30, 1965*

I HAVE asked former Secretary of Commerce Luther H. Hodges to meet with key officials of the Department of Commerce tomorrow to map plans for a renewed effort to increase the sale of U.S. goods abroad.

The National Export Expansion Council is being enlarged and revitalized with the assistance of Governor Hodges and Fred C. Foy, chief executive officer of the Koppers Company of Pittsburgh, Pa., who will serve as chairman, and Robert F. Dwyer, a Portland, Oreg., lumber executive, vice chairman.

Despite the long dock strike during the early part of this year, exports in the first 6 months were running at an annual rate of $24.8 billion—nearly $200 million greater than exports for the same period in 1964. However, with imports rising at a much faster pace in the first half of the year— climbing 13 percent—to an annual rate of

$20.3 billion, the need for intensifying the Nation's export expansion effort is evident.

The contribution which the National Export Expansion Council and its 42 regional councils have already made is reflected in the sharp growth in U.S. exports in the past 4 years—growing from $19.6 billion in 1960 to $25.6 billion last year—an increase of 31 percent. In the past 3 years the 1,200 business and professional leaders volunteering their services through these councils have also played a large role in our helping some 4,000 American companies become exporters for the first time.

Increasing numbers of American companies are taking a look at trade opportunities in the world market as a result of the administration's program. Through the voluntary efforts of the Council and the work of this department:

(1) officials of 10,000 companies were contacted;

(2) more than 1,200 seminars on selling abroad were organized throughout the country;

(3) numerous trade missions were sent to distant lands; and

(4) the Government moved to eliminate trade barriers and other obstacles to our foreign commerce.

In strengthening the National Export Expansion Council we have asked the chairmen of the 42 regional councils to serve on the national body so local problems affecting the growth of U.S. exports can be more effectively presented in Washington. The Council, which is being expanded from 33 to 66 members, will also include 11 prominent business and professional leaders and the heads of 10 national associations.

466   Televised Statement by the President Announcing Postponement of a Shutdown in the Steel Industry.   *August 30, 1965*

My fellow Americans:

I have been meeting with Mr. I. W. Abel, president of the United Steel Workers of America, and Mr. R. Conrad Cooper, the executive vice president of the United States Steel Corporation, Secretary of Labor Willard Wirtz, and the Secretary of Commerce, the Honorable John Connor.

This morning I requested that there be no shutdown of operations and that production by the steel industry continue during the negotiations by the parties.

In response to my request, the union and company representatives have agreed to postpone the imminent shutdown for 8 days. During this period they will continue their negotiations in Washington. The next meeting will be held at 10 o'clock tonight.

I am confident that all Americans appreciate this response by the union and by the company representatives. Their decision has certainly been made in the public interest. I am sure that as they return to their negotiations this evening, they will be aware of the importance of their efforts to every man and woman in this country of ours, and to the health and the vitality of our economy and the security of America all around the world.

Gentlemen, this postponement will serve your country's national interest, and I am very proud of each of you for the contribution that you and your organizations have made.

Thank you very much.

NOTE: The President read the statement at 9 p.m. in the White House Theater. See also Item 483.

467   Remarks on Announcing Plans To Extend Project Head Start. *August 31, 1965*

Director Shriver, Dr. Richmond, ladies and gentlemen:

First of all, I want to thank you, Mr. Shriver, for all the good that you are doing in this country and throughout the world in providing humanity some of the most dynamic and intelligent leadership that we have ever seen in this country.

I want to thank Dr. Richmond for his great contribution to our efforts in Head Start, and to every person that has come here this morning to attend this ceremony.

This summer some hope entered the lives of more than 500,000 youngsters, and those half million youngsters needed that hope the most.

Before this summer, they were on the road to despair. They were on the road to that wasteland of ignorance in which the children of the poor grow up and become the parents of the poor.

But today, after the first trial of Project Head Start, these children are now ready to take their places beside their more fortunate classmates in regular school.

Nearly 560,000 preschoolers attended 13,400 Head Start centers in 2,500 American communities. In each of those communities this program generated a new and a neighborly spirit. Nearly a million parents of Head Start children participated. Half a million volunteers 100,000 teachers and doctors and dentists and neighborhood workers joined hands in preparing these children for school—and for life.

Through Head Start, children who had never spoken learned to talk. Parents who were suspicious of school authorities came to see the centers—and they stayed on to help the teachers. Volunteers gave millions of hours to children and proved to these chil-

dren that somebody, after all, really cared. Teachers tried new approaches and they learned new techniques.

All the workers lived—lived time and again—through an infinitely rewarding moment: seeing a child open his eyes and his mind to the wonders of this world in which we live, seeing a child who had never seen a book, a child who had never held a pencil, a child who had never tasted a banana or one who had never even heard a fairy tale.

In New York City, where the Spanish-speaking population is hemmed in by the language barrier, 95 percent of the Head Start children learned enough English to fit them for school.

In San Saba, Texas, Head Start reached beyond the children to touch their homes, and two-thirds of the parents of Head Starters attended classes designed to make them better parents and better homemakers.

In Staten Island, New York, a 16-year-old girl made a tiny Head Starter her very special project. This little girl would not talk, would not eat, would not react. But through the care and through the patience of just one volunteer, the child made such progress that now she is able to take her place in school. Without Head Start that child might well have been classified as mentally defective—and condemned to life in a dark and a very narrow world.

Project Head Start was concerned with the physical health of the child as well as with his mental growth. And through medical checks of 1,055 Head Start children in Jacksonville, Florida, the volunteers discovered that 52 percent of the children were anemic, 42 percent needed dental care, 31 percent had hearing defects, 25 percent had eye trouble, and 5 percent were partially blind.

Volunteers for Vision, an auxiliary of the American Optometry Association, examined the eyes of nearly 50,000 children. I know quite well the success of this group, because its chairman is a very special friend of mine— a young lady whom I left asleep on her bed this morning when I got up, Luci Baines Johnson.

These are only a very few of the many victories, though, that Head Start has finally won.

Project Head Start, which began as an experiment, is now battle tested and it has been proven worthy.

And I am very happy to announce today that I have instructed Sargent Shriver and Frank Keppel to carry out plans for extending Head Start, with the hope of making it a continuing part of the American educational system.

This fall, a three-part extension of the program will be launched.

First, year-round centers for 3-year-olds and up. We expect to enroll 350,000 needy children in the first session, and many more within the next 5 years.

Second, summer programs for those not included in the year-round classes. These programs could involve over 500,000 children next summer.

Third, follow-through programs for children limited to summer sessions. These will begin with this year's Head Starters: There will be special classes; there will be home visits; there will be field trips; and other ways of sustaining the headstart that these children have made.

And so today, we have reached a land-mark—not just in education, but in the maturity of our own democracy. The success of this year's program—and our plans for years to come—are symbols of this Nation's commitment to the goal that no American child shall be condemned to failure by the accident of his birth.

So, on behalf of a very grateful Nation, I welcome you here this morning, under the leadership of a man whom I trust a great deal, and of whom I am very fond, and to whom all the Nation and, yes, the world is indeed indebted to his leadership—Sargent Shriver.

I congratulate each of you, too, and I offer to him and to Dr. Richmond, and to each of you, my thanks and my very deep appreciation for what you have done for human beings.

Thank you.

Besides all you are doing for the Head Starters, you bring me some good news from the Hill. While I was talking, the Senate Labor Committee unanimously reported the higher education bill. So, if you'll start them right, we'll finish them right.

NOTE: The President spoke at 10:34 a.m. in the Rose Garden at the White House before a group of officials of the war on poverty program. In his opening words he referred to Sargent Shriver, Director of the Office of Economic Opportunity, and Dr. Julius B. Richmond, Program Director of Project Head Start. During his remarks the President referred to his daughter, Luci Baines Johnson, and to Francis Keppel, Commissioner of Education.

Following the President's remarks, Mr. Shriver held a meeting with reporters and distributed copies of a report entitled "Project Head Start" (17 pp., processed).

The Higher Education Act of 1965 was approved by the President on November 8, 1965 (see Item 603).

468   Remarks at the Swearing In of Leonard Marks as Director, United States Information Agency.   *August 31, 1965*

Mr. Justice Clark, Mr. and Mrs. Marks, Members of Congress, the Cabinet, my friends:

This is a particularly happy and gratifying occasion for us. In this Government, at this time in our national life, few offices carry such weight of responsibility and opportunity as that of the Director of the United States Information Agency.

Last year, shortly after coming to the Presidency, I was presented with the very sad and sorrowful duty of accepting the resignation from that office of one of our most distinguished and respected Americans—the late Edward R. Murrow.

Fortunately, at that time, I was able to call upon another honored son of this land, known and respected in lands around the world—my friend, Carl Rowan.

Carl's tour meant for him, and his family, an extension of the time that he had intended to devote to public service. But he knows of my gratitude and the gratitude of the country for the outstanding service that he has rendered so ably, so very effectively, these past 18 months.

Today, another very able and respected, internationally-known American takes the reins of this vital agency. His name is Mr. Leonard Marks.

He is a leader of his profession. He is eminently qualified for any of many positions of the very highest trust. But both professionally and personally he has devoted much of his life, both at home and abroad, to the field with which the USIA is most concerned: the field of communications.

Mr. Marks has been a moving force behind the development of educational television in this country. He has also been a leader in such efforts all around the world. In 1962 President Kennedy recognized Mr. Marks' tireless efforts in the public interest and appointed him as one of the first directors of the Communications Satellite Corporation. Over that same period, he has served as chairman of the International Communication Committee of the American Bar Association. In all his work, Mr. Marks has been concerned not merely with the legal aspects of communications but with the purposes and philosophy of this great instrument of international understanding.

If he won't object to my quoting him, I would like to read one paragraph from some of Mr. Marks' writings:

"Communications is the lifeline of civilization. Without it, people live in small tribal societies, suspicious of strange and different customs. With improved communications comes better understanding and a removal of the barriers of suspicion and distrust. When we know our neighbors, we are more likely to become friends, philosophically and socially, and from this relationship may evolve a world dedicated to the preservation of law in an atmosphere of peace. When that millennium is reached, the tribal boundaries will extend beyond the village and encompass the world."

Today the advancing technology of communications presents all of the human race the first real opportunity to encompass the world with the understanding that will finally assure peace for all mankind. This is an opportunity, and this is a challenge from which America cannot and must never turn away.

This Nation, and this Government, have no propaganda to peddle. We are neither advocates nor defenders of any dogma so fragile or a doctrine so frightened as to require propaganda. But we are, as our forefathers were 189 years ago, respectful of the opinions of mankind. And our devotion to the course of freedom requires of us a like devotion to the course of truth—so the opinions of mankind may really be informed and may be responsible.

Truth wears no uniform and bears no flag. But it is the most loyal ally that freedom knows. It is the mission, therefore, of the USIA to be always loyal and always faithful and always vigilant to the course of the truth.

The USIA now has an opportunity, I think, without parallel in its entire history. The truth about America today, I believe, if you tell it, is stirring and exciting. This is a country that is succeeding. This is a country that is moving forward. This is a country that is confident of its course, a country more devoted than it has ever been to the cause of mankind everywhere.

But truth about America is essentially the truth about freedom—and the story of freedom is the story that we want to tell the world.

So I believe this is a new era in the affairs of man and the relations between nations. It is an era of greater maturity, and I hope that our own goals and standards may also mature. I hope that we shall not expect quick answers to ancient questions, that we shall not expect simple solutions to complex problems. I especially hope that we may not strive foolishly and vainly for the world's love and affection when what we really seek is the world's respect and the world's trust.

In this era the USIA has the most valuable role to fulfill. It is a most important arm of our Government. It is a great arm of our society. There is no partisanship associated with it because the success of the USIA is success for all Americans.

The Director of USIA sits as a member of our National Security Council, along with our beloved and distinguished Vice President. And under this administration, he also will participate in meetings of the President's Cabinet. For we recognize the value and the importance and imperative of this Agency's success as the champion of truth in the great and the continuing course of freedom everywhere.

So today, I want to extend my own personal gratitude and my warmest wishes to Carl Rowan and his charming wife Vivian and their son for every success and for every possible happiness, to which they are duly entitled. Likewise, I am very grateful and proud that Leonard Marks, his wife Dorothy, and their sons, are now today joining our official family. Leonard Marks has my every confidence. He will have my fullest support to do the job which must be done now for freedom, for truth, for America—and to do it here and do it all around the world.

Thank you very much.

NOTE: The President spoke at 11:35 a.m. in the Rose Garden at the White House. In his opening words he referred to Associate Justice Tom C. Clark of the Supreme Court of the United States, who administered the oath of office to Mr. Marks.

The text of Mr. Marks' remarks is printed in the Weekly Compilation of Presidential Documents (vol. 1, p. 182).

Outgoing Director Carl T. Rowan's letter of resignation and the President's reply were made public by the White House on July 10.

469   Statement by the President Following a Meeting With Dr. Howard Rusk on Health and Welfare Needs in South Viet-Nam. *August 31, 1965*

I HAVE had a most profitable discussion with Dr. Howard Rusk about the immense health and welfare needs of the people of South Viet-Nam.

Dr. Rusk has agreed to go to Viet-Nam at my request to survey the situation and to report to me his recommendations as to how we can best strengthen and expand our efforts to relieve human suffering there. The needs of the Vietnamese people are intensified today by the distress of hundreds of thousands of refugees who have been driven from their homes by the Viet Cong.

Dr. Rusk will look into the several successful programs that are being undertaken by our American private welfare organizations in cooperation with the Vietnamese Government. And he will explore with all relevant people and agencies the opportunities that exist for a new and mighty people-to-people effort by Americans in our time-honored tradition of humaneness and compassion.

Dr. Rusk is a great patriot of wide experience in advancing human welfare, both at home and abroad. I am deeply grateful that he is willing to undertake this assignment.

NOTE: On August 30 the White House announced that the President had asked Dr. Howard Rusk, Director of the Institute of Physical Medicine and Rehabilitation at New York University, to go to Viet-Nam to survey the possibilities for expanding and strengthening the work of private agencies in helping the Vietnamese people. The release stated that Dr. Rusk's experience in organizing the American-Korean Foundation made him highly qualified for the mission.

470   Statement by the President Reviewing Progress in the Desegregation of Schools. *August 31, 1965*

THE OPENING of schools this week and next is a hopeful time for this Nation. It brings heartening evidence of the efforts of Governors, school officials, and other citizens to assure that respect for law remains a vigorous force everywhere in the country.

In accordance with the letter and spirit of the Civil Rights Act, your Government has sought to bring about voluntary compliance with its provisions. The results have been deeply encouraging.

Of the more than 5,000 school districts in 17 Southern and Border States, 4,463—88 percent—are making preparations to comply. This represents an increase of 291 school districts since 1 week ago.

In the 7 Southern States of Alabama, Georgia, Louisiana, Mississippi, North Carolina, South Carolina, and Virginia, 538 school districts today are in compliance, compared to 317 a week ago.

A staff of 117 men and women in the U.S. Office of Education, working around the clock and over weekends, is assisting local school districts in achieving acceptable plans.

One week ago there were 172 school districts which had taken no action to meet the requirements of the Civil Rights Act. Today the figure is 135—and it is shrinking rapidly.

The adoption of an acceptable desegregation plan, of course, is only a beginning. The coming weeks—and years—will demand of local officials and concerned citizens much patience and dedicated effort if change is to be achieved successfully and if plans are to be translated into performance.

I have directed the Office of Education to stand ready day and night to work toward solutions in the remaining communities which have not submitted plans or whose plans have not yet been accepted.

I strongly urge every responsible State official, school officer, and local official who cherishes the future of our children to lose no time in working for progress where prog-

ress is needed. There is still time—and the results of your labors can mean the difference, in many cases, between full educational opportunity for all and the tragedy of lost opportunity. Certainly none of us wants to see this Nation's educational future clouded by delay, indifference, or neglect.

I congratulate all who have had a part in this effort. Their thanks will come, ultimately, from a generation of hopeful young Americans—and from a Nation with a deep reverence for the rule of law.

---

471   Remarks at the Signing of a Bill Establishing the Delaware Water Gap National Recreation Area.   *September 1, 1965*

Ladies and gentlemen, Secretary Udall, Governor Hughes, Governor Scranton, distinguished Members of the Senate and the House, my friends, members of the press:

Since the dawn of civilization, man has been the unwilling pawn of the forces of his natural environment. Even when he has come to terms with those forces, the terms have really never been his own. So today, we possess the tools to reach out into our own environment. We have the skills to bend the forces of nature to our own will. We have the knowledge to become the masters of all that we survey.

We can extract fresh water from the sea, and we can eliminate drought and famine from the face of the earth. We can tame our rivers and never again suffer the ravages of flood. We can unleash unlimited electric power for the growth of commerce and industry. We can wipe out epidemics for all times to come. And even as exciting as these prospects are, they represent only half of our new-found potential. For if we can control man's surroundings for his physical

well-being, we can also control them for his spiritual well-being.

In short, we can build a new America where our people can live in peace and harmony with nature, drawing strength from its beauty and wisdom from its variety. And that is the meaning and the potential of the bill that we have come here today to act upon and that I will shortly sign.

The Delaware Water Gap National Recreation bill authorizes the creation of a 72,000-acre national park in the great State of Pennsylvania—halfway between New York and Philadelphia. And this will be much more than just a piece of American wilderness that we have reclaimed for public use. The wilderness in the East has really all but disappeared. This will be a man-made project, the second of its kind in this entire Nation.

At Tocks Island we will build a dam, and behind that dam there will form a lake 37 miles long, for every kind of water sport imaginable—and I hope to have something to do with imagining some of them. And surrounding that lake will be an area of very exceptional natural beauty, consisting of mountains and waterfalls and trails and camping areas.

A full 15 percent of this Nation's entire population, almost 30 million people, will live within 100 miles of this reservation. Confined within the discomforts of noise and ugliness, surrounded by decaying buildings and despoiled landscapes, these people of ours yearn for beauty and hunger for the opportunity to find refreshment in nature.

These yearnings have their roots deep in our American dream: an almost mystical dream of virgin forests and rich, deep soil, and a place where a man could try to discover the meaning of his life.

The Delaware Water Gap National Recreational Area will be just such a place. Here will come as many as 150,000 visitors in 1 day. Here will come more than 10 million people in 1 year. Here they will come and they will swim and they will fish and they will camp out, and their lives will be infinitely richer because they came this way.

A President really never knows how history is going to catalog him. But I would hope that I might find some small place in history as a President who cared and a President who tried and a President who, in some small measure, succeeded in preserving and in enriching the natural beauty of our land, and thus making more beautiful the lives of all of our people.

Thank you.

NOTE: The President spoke at 12:12 p.m. in the Rose Garden at the White House. In his opening words he referred to Secretary of the Interior Stewart L. Udall, Governor Richard J. Hughes of New Jersey, and Governor William W. Scranton of Pennsylvania.

As enacted, the bill (H.R. 89) is Public Law 89–158 (79 Stat. 612).

472 Statement by the President on the Agreement To Form a New Government in the Dominican Republic. *September 1, 1965*

I AM deeply gratified that agreement was reached last night on a new government in the Dominican Republic. While there are still grave problems to be faced by the Dominican people, the way has been opened for an end to strife and for the choice of leaders through the process which all free men cherish. The hopes of democratic and peaceful men the whole world over have taken new strength and nourishment from these events today.

The road to peace and freedom is always hard, and wherever this road is being traveled successfully, there can always be found many men and women who have given of themselves and of their talents in great measure. The Dominican Republic is no exception, and there have been many who have done just this. All democratic elements in the hemisphere are indebted to the Dominican leaders who have worked for this agreement, to Ambassadors Penna Marinho, Clairmont Dueñas, and Bunker for their outstanding statesmanship, and to the many others who contributed so much in order that this achievement could be made possible.

NOTE: In his statement the President referred to Ilmar Penna Marinho, Brazilian Representative to the Organization of American States, Ramón de Clairmont Dueñas, representative from El Salvador to the Organization of American States and Ambassador to the United States, and Ellsworth Bunker, U.S. Representative to the Organization of American States.

See also Items 473, 482, 484.

473 Statement by the President on the Contributions Made by the Organization of American States to the Dominican Agreement. *September 1, 1965*

Your Excellencies:

I have been meeting this morning with the Secretary General of the Organization of American States, Dr. José Mora, to express my very deep appreciaton and the gratitude of the people of the United States for the very important contributions that were made by the OAS—the Organization of American States—to the agreement reached last night on a new government in the Dominican Republic.

I want to take this special opportunity now to thank Dr. Mora for his own very excellent and fine work as well as the performance of his fine Organization. Special thanks must go to Ambassador Penna Marinho, Ambassador Clairmont Dueñas, and our own Ambassador Ellsworth Bunker.

There are still very grave problems facing the Dominican people. But the way has finally been opened for an end to strife and for the choice of leaders through the process which all free men cherish. I am certain that the hopes of men who really love peace and the democratic process have taken new strength from these developments and these events.

In a very short time there will be a provisional government in the Dominican Republic. This government will need the energetic support of the whole Western Hemisphere as it sets about the work of restoring peace and trying to rebuild the entire Dominican economy. The United States and the Organization of American States will work together in these new tasks—shoulder to shoulder—as we have worked together in these recent months. We all have the same objective. We all seek the same goals—peace and prosperity for the hemisphere.

Thank you very much.

[*After reading the foregoing statement the President made the following remarks.*]

I have the very great honor of having the distinguished Ambassador from Argentina, Dr. Mora, the Ambassador from Bolivia, and the Ambassador from Colombia. They happened to be having lunch over in the White House—off the Fish Room; they serve much better food there than in the mansion—with some of my associates. I asked them to join me here.

Ambassador Mora, would you like to say something?

AMBASSADOR MORA. Thank you very much, Mr. President. I am very happy on this occasion to express my recognition to all the government members of the Organization of American States for their participation in this great effort for the establishment of peace and democratic procedures in the Dominican Republic.

This is a demonstration of the capacity of the Organization of American States to obtain a solution to such a delicate situation. And I want also to express my deep appreciation to President Johnson for his personal interest in the cause of peace in the Dominican Republic.

Thank you very much.

NOTE: The President spoke at 1:33 p.m. in the White House Theater. In his statement he referred to José A. Mora, Secretary General of the Organization of American States, Ilmar Penna Marinho, Brazilian Representative to the OAS, Ramón de Clairmont Dueñas, Representative from El Salvador to the OAS and Ambassador to the United States, Ellsworth

Bunker, United States Representative to the OAS, Norbert M. Barrenechea, Argentinian Ambassador to the United States, Julio Sanjines-Goytia, Bolivian Ambassador to the United States, and Eduardo Uribe, Colombian Ambassador to the United States.

See also Items 472, 482, 484.

474 Telegram to Dr. Albert Schweitzer.
September 1, 1965

THE PRAYERS of millions of the world's people are with you. Our hope is that your recovery will be quick and complete.

With kindest regards.

LYNDON B. JOHNSON

[Dr. Albert Schweitzer, Lambaréné, Gabon Republic]

NOTE: The telegram was read by Bill D. Moyers, Special Assistant to the President, at his news conference at 4:12 p.m. on Wednesday, September 1, 1965. It was not made public in the form of a White House press release.

Dr. Albert Schweitzer died on September 4 at his jungle hospital in Lambaréné at the age of 90.

475 Statement by the President on the Signing of the Labor, HEW, and Related Agencies Appropriations Bill. *September 1, 1965*

THE SIGNING of H.R. 7765 was a moment of particular pleasure for me, and, I believe, an event of profound significance for this country.

Too often when we talk about rising productivity and growing prosperity, when we compile and analyze statistics, the truly significant concerns are clouded over in the process of counting up.

I think it important, therefore, that we make clear just what the true meaning of this bill is.

This bill is more than a routine appropriation measure.

It is more than a symbol of the patient work done by the Congress on complex and detailed legislation.

It is a symbol of our commitment to fulfill through common effort some of the deepest hopes of our people: the desire for a better job, richer educational opportunities, better health protection and care.

The $8 billion committed through this measure will make possible activities from cancer research to vocational education to the fight against juvenile delinquency.

It extends the programs of the National Institutes of Health which are seeking the causes and the cures for epilepsy, arthritis, muscular dystrophy, cystic fibrosis, mental illness, and hundreds of other diseases.

This bill will assist in reducing the number of mentally ill in State institutions; it will make possible better facilities, care, and rehabilitation for the mentally sick all over the Nation. It promises hope to 5 million mentally retarded persons through research centers and modern medical and educational services.

It makes possible such simple and easily attainable accomplishments as better care for newborn babies—but it also reaches into the future and promises such developments as an artificial heart and the successful transplant of human organs.

By the signing of this bill we advance the fight against polluted air and water, unsafe drugs and food.

We expand vocational education and manpower training programs; loan programs to 340,000 college students; educational assistance to teachers, librarians, physicians, dentists, nurses, and social workers. We help build schools, libraries, hospitals, nursing homes, and other facilities throughout the Nation.

The Congress which passed this measure is building more than a record of statistics: it

is building a monument to hope—and showing that hope can become reality, that national problems can be alleviated through creative Government programs.

NOTE: As enacted, the bill (H.R. 7765), approved by the President on August 31, 1965, is Public Law 89–156 (79 Stat. 589).

476 Statement by the President on the Appointment of Gen. Maxwell D. Taylor as Special Consultant to the President. *September 1, 1965*

I AM HAPPY to announce that Gen. Maxwell D. Taylor has accepted appointment as Special Consultant to the President. General Taylor will take up his new duties on or about the 15th of September. He will have an office next door in the Executive Office Building and we expect that he will be giving about half his time to special assignments for the President.

I naturally expect that General Taylor will play a continuing role in our work in support of the people and the Government of Viet-Nam. I have also asked him to under-

take a review of all the practices and policies of our Government in the broad field of assistance to free peoples who are threatened by Communist terror and subversion. I expect that from time to time he will have other important assignments.

I am delighted that General Taylor has been willing to accept this new assignment. It will give his country the benefit of his extraordinary experience and wisdom while permitting him at the same time to meet his personal and family obligations.

477 Remarks at the Signing of a Bill Authorizing the Auburn-Folsom Project, California. *September 2, 1965*

WE ARE DELIGHTED this morning to have our distinguished and very progressive Secretary of the Interior here with us, and some of the responsible Members of Congress, who have been very helpful to us in our endeavors during the past 8 months that the Congress has been here.

Those months have been marked by some savage and tragic contrasts in our water problems across the Nation.

In the West and the Midwest the raging floods have swept through town after town, claiming lives, destroying millions of dollars worth of property.

And while that was happening in the West and Midwest in our great country, here in the East we were in the grip of an unprecedented and deepening drought.

And when these emergencies arise, the Government is pledged to do what has to be done and what can be done. Let me make it clear that I do not like emergencies.

First, because they are expensive. In the past 12 months the flood damages in the United States alone have amounted to a billion and a quarter dollars.

Second, because they are wasteful. Last year's floods in northern California alone carried enough water into the sea to meet the domestic and municipal and complete industrial demands of the entire Nation for a whole year—16 trillion gallons.

Third, because they are really unnecessary. We now have the capability to plan ahead and to build together so that these disasters can be prevented. Our generation is challenged to really make a steady, determined, and, I hope, successful effort to eliminate drought and flood from this land.

In the last few months we have had challenges equally as important that have been met. And if our astronauts can do what they did the other day—spend 8 days in space—we have got enough ingenuity, imagination, and determination here to get the job done with drought and floods.

Now, the 89th Congress has responded more to this challenge than any Congress in our history. It has compiled the greatest 8-month record of conservation since the Nation was born.

And today, as part of that record, we have gathered here in the White House to sign into law the Auburn-Folsom South Project for California's Central Valley. (I saw Carl Hayden here and I was wondering if this was that billion dollar Arizona bill.) But in every sense, this is really a modern answer to an age-old problem.

The city of Sacramento, California, has been living under the perennial threat of floods from the American River. Now we are going to eliminate that threat with the construction of the massive Auburn Dam.

The water that is stored behind that dam will drought-proof the entire Central Valley. If this dam had been in existence last year, when the American River rampaged, we could have saved enough water to serve the city of Sacramento for more than 5 years.

New homes and townsites, of course, will result and be developed. Industry and agri-culture will be assured of the water they need.

The reservoir itself, located on the western slope of the Sierras, will provide wholesome outdoor recreation for millions of nearby citizens.

And, finally, the water of the American River soon will be spinning huge turbines, generating cheap electric power for the farm and for the city.

Thus, we add to the legacy of America—a legacy of protection, of growth, of recreation, of electric power, and we do it all with one single project.

Governor Pat Brown, the very able and progressive Members of the California congressional delegation, have worked long and have worked hard for the Auburn-Folsom South.

I am glad that I can be a small part of their diligence and their success, and I am happy to be able to participate in making their dreams come true.

I have never seen a dollar invested anywhere in this Nation in water conservation, in multiple-use projects, that in a period of even a decade didn't prove that it was a good investment, and would pay very high returns on what we had spent for it.

So, this is not the last conservation project that we will approve. It is not the last legislation in this field. We are going to continue it until we have stopped the floods, we have prevented the drought, and we have the kind of conservation program that is worthy of the 20th century, and worthy of the foresight of the American people.

Thank you very much.

NOTE: The President spoke at 11:10 a.m. in the Rose Garden at the White House. During his remarks he referred to Secretary of the Interior Stewart L. Udall, Senator Carl Hayden of Arizona, and Governor Edmund G. (Pat) Brown of California.

As enacted, the bill (H.R. 485) is Public Law 89-161 (79 Stat. 615).

478 Remarks at the Swearing In of Charles R. Simpson as Judge, Tax Court of the United States. *September 2, 1965*

Mr. and Mrs. Simpson, Justice Clark, Senator McClellan, Chairman Mills, Mr. Cohen, my old friend Judge Trimble:

I found it possible to exchange views with the steel negotiators at a particularly appropriate moment today. I had to go order their lunch and have it sent over to the Executive Office Building. And they kind of had a press conference with me and asked a few questions back and forth, and I was delayed. But I know that Judge Simpson and Justice Clark and all of you good folks out there would hardly find any subject that is more important to the country than the steel negotiations, and I am sorry that it has given you a little extra suntan by having to wait. I am very proud that you are here.

There are few appointments that I have made in my term of office since I became President that have really given me as much inner satisfaction as this appointment. The reason for that, I think, is that it has given so much satisfaction to other people also.

Soon after I announced my intention to nominate Jim Simpson to the Tax Court, I received a great number of letters from all throughout this country.

Some of them were from his colleagues in the Internal Revenue Service. Some of them from those who had worked with him professionally through the years. But a great many were from men and women throughout all of America who find themselves, like Jim Simpson, suffering from disabling handicaps.

Now most of the professional letters did not even refer to Jim's handicap. They didn't mention it. Instead, they spoke of a man whose brilliance of mind and whose fairness of judgment made him the natural

and, I would say, almost the inevitable choice for elevation to this high court.

From the letter of Sheldon Cohen, the brilliant young Commissioner of Internal Revenue, one who did not know Jim Simpson would have learned nothing about his sightless eyes. The letter didn't mention it. But what Sheldon Cohen, the Commissioner, said—and what all of his colleagues said—was that great ability and deep integrity had finally been recognized in a highly deserved appointment.

The other letter writers expressed their appreciation of the fact that here in this America of ours, it was possible for a man that is crippled by fate to rise to one of the most responsible positions in the powerful Government of the United States, not because of his misfortune, but in spite of his misfortune. And I share their satisfaction, and I rejoice in the example that Jim Simpson has provided for all those in this Nation and elsewhere—the blind, the deaf, the crippled, those who cannot talk, and those who cannot hear—who aspire to conquer their disadvantages and to fulfill the promise of life.

Judge Simpson's career is illustrious by any standard. His academic marks at the University of Illinois Law School were the highest there in 25 years. He has taught at Harvard Law School. He has served in the Illinois General Assembly, and he was until today the Director of Legislation and Regulations in the Office of General Counsel of the Internal Revenue Service.

His preparation for this new task is beyond dispute. His courage is an inspiration—not only to the handicapped, but to every American, including the President of the United States. His colleagues and millions of disabled people proudly salute him. He did not apply for this job, he didn't even know he was being considered. He was appointed for one reason and one only—men whose judgments I rely on, including my own, knew him to be the best equipped man that we could find in the 50 States to occupy this high office.

So it is with great pride that we welcome you here today to participate in recognizing some of the unusual achievements of this good and modest man. It is with great pride that we in the Government welcome him to the Tax Court of the United States of America.

NOTE: The President spoke at 12:45 p.m. in the Rose Garden at the White House. In his opening words he referred to Judge Simpson and his wife, Mrs. Ruth Simpson, who serves as his secretary, Associate Justice Tom C. Clark of the Supreme Court of the United States, who administered the oath of office, Senator John L. McClellan of Arkansas, Representative Wilbur D. Mills of Arkansas, Sheldon S. Cohen, Commissioner, Internal Revenue Service, and Representative James W. Trimble of Arkansas, formerly judge of the fourth judicial circuit of that State.

Following the administration of the oath of office, Judge Simpson spoke briefly. The text of his remarks is printed in the Weekly Compilation of Presidential Documents (vol. 1, p. 191).

---

479 Statement by the President Following Passage by the Senate of the Higher Education Bill. *September 2, 1965*

THE SENATE'S passage of the Higher Education Act is a triumph for Congress and for millions of students and teachers upon whose achievements our destiny largely depends.

This legislation is the most comprehensive program for higher education in our history. It will provide opportunity grants for 140,000 talented young Americans who want—and should—go to college but cannot afford it. It will assure loans for more than a million students to ease the burden on their families.

This legislation offers grants for less developed colleges to improve their faculties and teaching programs, and funds for enriching college library programs.

I am particularly glad that the Senate added provisions for a 6,000-member National Teacher Corps and for fellowship grants to elementary and secondary schoolteachers. These programs will mean much to schools in areas of poverty whose students have been the victims not only of impoverished homes but of impoverished schools.

This act has many provisions, but it has only one purpose: to nourish human potential today, so that our Nation can realize its rich promise tomorrow.

NOTE: The Higher Education Act of 1965 was approved by the President on November 8, 1965 (see Item 603).

---

480 Statement by the President on the Employment Record for August. *September 3, 1965*

I AM very pleased that the reports on unemployment in August confirm this summer's gains. This afternoon the Department of Labor announced that, in August, the national unemployment rate was at 4.5 percent
—matching the level of July and
—maintaining the lowest rate since October 1957.

The number of employed persons has grown by 2 million since last August. And the ranks of the unemployed have been reduced by

—400,000 over the past year,

—600,000 since August 1963, and

—1,300,000 since August 1961.

It is particularly gratifying to see the especially good gains made by our Negro workers, who have so long suffered from high unemployment. The unemployment rate for Negroes was down to 7.6 percent in August, matching May of this year as the lowest Negro rate since May 1957. We are making progress toward equality of opportunity in a prosperous economy. We still have a long road to travel before equality has been achieved, but we are well on our way.

The teenage unemployment rate fell to 12.4 percent, compared with 15.0 percent a year ago. Although 12.4 percent is still far too high, it is remarkable that this rate has improved despite the enormous increase in the number of young workers seeking jobs.

—It shows that our young people of today, better educated and healthier than ever before, can find their way to jobs.

—It demonstrates the benefits of an expanding economy.

—It reflects the nationwide cooperation that made our Youth Opportunity Campaign such a success.

—It means that the hands and minds of our young people are being better used to build our society.

The uninterrupted progress of our economy continues in its 55th month, still strong and well-balanced. As it continues, as our new investments in human resources pay dividends, and as our manpower programs help increasingly to match workers and jobs, our expanding labor force will find new job opportunities. We look forward to ever wider participation in the benefits of a prosperous economy by those workers who have suffered most from unemployment—the less skilled, the Negroes, and the inexperienced members of our labor force.

481   Televised Statement by the President Concerning the Signing of the D.C. Home Rule Petition by a Majority of House Members. *September 3, 1965*

TODAY the last major Federal territory on this American Continent has taken a decisive step toward full membership in the American Union.

A majority of the House of Representatives has signed a petition requiring consideration of home rule for the District of Columbia.

Thus, we near victory in the final battle of the American Revolution—a revolution that was fought so that men might govern themselves.

A majority of the Members of both parties in the Senate have this year approved self-

government for the District—as the Senate had five times before. But until today a small group of men in the House of Representatives have kept the Congress from exercising its will. Now the House of Representatives is going to vote. And I am confident that the House will affirm the right to democracy for the almost 1 million citizens of the Capital City.

In so doing, they will redeem a pledge that is older than the Nation itself.

It was in 1783 that the Continental Congress pledged that the future seat of government—the capital of a nation yet un-born—would govern itself.

In obedience to this promise, James Madison wrote—in the Federalist Papers—that under the new Constitution citizens of the District would elect their own representatives and would frame their own laws.

Now for almost two centuries history and circumstance, indifference and hostility, have conspired to deny this historic pledge.

But now the time of fulfillment is at hand.

This is not a revolutionary bill. It does not make fundamental and far-reaching changes in the structure of the Nation. It simply extends the most elementary rights of democracy to almost a million of our fellow Americans—the right to choose their own leaders, frame their own laws, and manage their own affairs. It is a right which those in every State and community have long assumed, and cherished, and fought to keep. Now that same mantle of democracy will cover the entire land.

This Congress has already passed a law protecting the right of all to govern themselves whatever their race or color. And now it prepares to yield that same right to Americans wherever they live. And in so doing, it links itself in honor with those who founded this country and with the ideals that they proclaimed before an amazed world.

This is truly the Congress of democracy. Its acts add luster to the great Nation which it governs. For it is proving once again that if the search for justice is unending, our vitality in that pursuit does not diminish.

And let me add that there have been few, if any, achievements that have given me personally greater pleasure. I came to this Capital almost 35 years ago. I have spent a good part of every year since that time as a resident of Washington. Here I brought my bride. Here my children were born. Here I have lived with my family. Here, also, I have made many lasting friends and we have enjoyed the manifold beauties and the opportunities of this great beautiful city. Therefore, not only as President, but as a resident, I feel very deeply the obligation to help liberate the people of this city—to extend to them the same democracy which is part of the life of the citizens of my other home in Texas.

Now that obligation is going to be fulfilled. And history, I think, will honor the leaders of the Congress and the many others whose work and sense of justice has brought us to this day.

NOTE: The President spoke at 2 p.m. in the White House Theater. See also Items 39, 402, 486.

482 Letters to Participants in the Dominican Republic Negotiations. *September 3, 1965*

Dear Dr. Mora:

I extend to you the warmest thanks for your extraordinary efforts for peace in the Dominician Republic in the last four months. Your energetic and imaginative work in Santo Domingo helped to lay the basis for the later efforts of your colleagues in the OAS Committee, and your persistent devotion to peace and to democratic institutions has been a continuous force for good, in the best tradition of the Americas.

I send thanks also, through you, to the whole Organization of American States, which you serve so ably as Secretary General. The OAS has met a major challenge, and it has been strengthened by the success of its patient effort for peace.

With warm personal regards

Sincerely,

LYNDON B. JOHNSON

[Dr. José Mora, Secretary General, Organization of American States, Pan American Union, Washington 6, D.C.]

Dear Ellsworth:

This brings my warmest thanks and congratulations on your superb performance in Santo Domingo. Your patience and skill and determination have once again been of the greatest value to your country—and a source of great strength for me. I am afraid you have put yourself right in line for more impossible assignments like this last one, but you must be sure to get a well-earned rest first.

Sincerely,

LYNDON B. JOHNSON

[Hon. Ellsworth Bunker, U.S. Representative to the

Council of the Organization of American States, Department of State, Washington, D.C.]

Dear Tap:

At this moment of hope, I want to send you a word of thanks for all that you have done in the hard months since April. I know that this has been a most testing time for you, and you must be in no doubt that you have the full confidence of your Government, and our lasting gratitude for your prompt, courageous and correct advice at the critical moment last April.

Sincerely,

LYNDON B. JOHNSON

[Hon. W. Tapley Bennett, Jr., American Ambassador, Santo Domingo, Dominican Republic]

NOTE: Letters from Dr. Mora, Mr. Bunker, and Mr. Bennett, replying to the President's letters, were made public by the White House on September 4 (1 Weekly Comp. Pres. Docs., p. 209).

See also Items 472, 473, 484.

483 Televised Statement by the President Announcing Settlement of the Steel Dispute. *September 3, 1965*

My fellow Americans:

The representatives of labor and management in the steel industry have reached essential agreement.

After the details are worked out, including some noneconomic issues, and once the agreement has been ratified by the union wage policy board and the company presidents, the danger of a steel strike will be gone.

We can now say tonight with confidence that the grim threat of thousands of men out of work, of idle plants, of declining production for our economy and declining prosperity for our people—that threat has

been met head-on, and has been overcome.

All America is grateful to these men that you see beside me: Mr. Cooper, and the representatives of the steel companies; and Mr. Abel, and the representatives of the steelworkers.

They bargained hard. They represented their interests with great skill and conviction—but they always put the interest of their Nation first. To them, the welfare of the American people, the needs of freedom in Viet-Nam and in every continent, took precedence over any other consideration or interest or desire.

And so they worked long and sleepless

hours—not so the union would win, not so the companies would win—but so their country would win.

And the American Nation has won.

The settlement is a fair one. It is designed to prevent the inflation which would damage our Nation's prosperity. It is also within the guiding spirit of free collective bargaining in a free country.

Management and labor have fought many battles in the long history of American industry; yet tonight, I believe that most Americans share my own view—that cooperation and mutual trust bring greater rewards than unreasoning hostility and distrust.

Ever since the first day that I became President of this country I have asked labor and management to work together with me to try to enrich the lives of all Americans. I am glad to report to the American people that they have never let me down. They have fully responded.

Companies and unions alike have come here to the White House to discuss their problems openly and honestly and to seek solutions. After almost 8 months of negotiations the men of the steel industry did the same.

When I received a report from my mediators, Senator Wayne Morse of Oregon and Governor LeRoy Collins, Under Secretary of Commerce, I requested an extension of negotiations last Monday. Both sides agreed. In a week they were here in Washington working, and at the end of that week they have found a solution.

The members of the union wage policy committee from all over this Nation will soon be gathering in Pittsburgh, and I hope and I expect that they will swiftly ratify this agreement.

And then they can continue the job of making the steel on which American abundance and power, on which the prosperity of our people and the prospect of freedom so largely rest.

I cannot praise too highly the quality of work and the patience and the skill given in these meetings by Secretary Connor and Secretary Wirtz. They never slept, and they never lost heart or purpose. This Nation is truly in their debt.

What does this settlement mean?

To the steelworkers it means continued uninterrupted work. It means a steadily improving life for all the families of these steelworkers.

To the steel companies, it means continued production and growth and reasonable profits.

To the American people, it means a continued rise in the production which is the greatest foundation upon which this Nation is based. It means abundance in our history.

To the world, it is another proof that the home of liberty is mighty and it is founded upon the rock of conviction.

To our soldiers out tonight in the jungles of Viet-Nam it means a continued uninterrupted flow of the goods that are so essential to freedom and to his life, and even more, the assurance that those at home will never forget his sacrifice in the pursuit of their narrow and selfish ends.

The steel industry is a great industry. It has raised great cities, it has brought forth abundance beyond belief. It has forged the weapons of war as well as the products of peace. Its achievements are the marvel and the model of all the world. But I believe that in all of its long history it has never had a prouder moment than this.

And so tonight I am going to leave the White House and go away to the hills of home, with my heart full of gratitude for the great progress that a united America has made this week.

Thank all of you.

NOTE: The President spoke at 6:30 p.m. in the White House Theater. In his statement he re-

ferred to R. Conrad Cooper, Executive Vice President of the United States Steel Corp., I. W. Abel, President of the United Steelworkers of America, Senator Wayne Morse of Oregon, Under Secretary of Commerce LeRoy Collins, former Governor of Florida, Secretary of Commerce John T. Connor, and Secretary of Labor W. Willard Wirtz.

484 Statement by the President Announcing U.S. Recognition of the New Dominican Government. *September 4, 1965*

THIS PAST WEEK, Dominican leaders, with important assistance from the OAS, agreed on the establishment of a provisional government under the leadership of Dr. Hector García-Godoy. This action marked the end of an impasse which had brought danger and hardship to the Dominican people during 4 long and difficult months.

Last night, the provisional government, officially installed, announced its adherence to the Dominican Republic's international obligations, pledged its allegiance to the high purposes of economic, social, and democratic progress, and requested recognition by the nations of the world. This action marked the beginning of a new road to peace, freedom, and hope for the Dominican people.

Today, after consultation with other OAS States, the U.S. Government is extending recognition to the new provisional government.

On behalf of the people of the United States, I extend best personal wishes to the distinguished new President and to the brave Dominican people.

President García-Godoy's government will face many great and hard tasks over the coming months—as he leads his country to free elections and as he moves to rebuild his country's economy.

In the difficult but promising days ahead,

I want President García-Godoy and the Dominican people to know that they have our full support.

We are already discussing on an urgent basis the resumption of certain projects which have been interrupted since the tragic days of last April.

We are ready to participate fully with the OAS, its committee on the Alliance for Progress and international financial institutions in the important rehabilitation effort that lies ahead. We earnestly hope that, on request of the Dominican Government, the OAS will take the lead in this great enterprise.

Meanwhile, preliminary discussions have established an immediate need for approximately $20 million in assistance and we hope that arrangements can soon be concluded with the provisional government to make this amount available. These funds will help to defray some of the immediate needs of economic reconstruction, which include the rehabilitation of private industry, a program of public works, and temporary financing of some of the essential operating expenses of the government and key public enterprise.

While no one knows better than the Dominican people how much work it will take to clear the road to peace, progress, and democracy, they should also know that the whole hemisphere shares their hope for a bright future and will work shoulder to shoulder with them to make this hope a reality.

NOTE: The statement was released at Austin, Tex. See also Items 472, 473, 482.

485 Statement by the President on Appointing Dr. Francis Keppel as Assistant Secretary, Department of Health, Education, and Welfare. *September 4, 1965*

MY APPOINTMENT of Dr. Keppel recognizes his outstanding performance over the past 3 years in helping meet the greatest education tasks of the Nation. His promotion to the new position of Assistant Secretary will enable him better to serve the needs of the Department and to stimulate education activities that do not lie strictly within the jurisdiction of the Office of Education.

This leadership is made even more necessary by the new legislation for elementary, secondary, and higher education passed by the 89th Congress. The programs of the Office of Education have expanded 25-fold over the past decade. The total activities of the Federal Government in the field of education have tripled during the past 4 years. I am determined that these programs shall be administered wisely and well. This has highest priority for Dr. Francis Keppel.

NOTE: The statement was read by Bill D. Moyers, Special Assistant to the President, at his news conference at Austin, Tex., at 10:40 a.m. on Saturday, September 4, 1965. Mr. Moyers stated that Dr. Keppel would serve as both Assistant Secretary and Commissioner of Education. The statement was not made public in the form of a White House press release.

486 Letter to the Chairman, House Committee on the District of Columbia. *September 4, 1965*

[Released September 4, 1965. Dated September 3, 1965]

Dear Mr. Chairman:

This will acknowledge the letter dated September 2 and signed by you and several other members of the House of Representatives Committee on the District of Columbia.

Your letter states that under H.R. 4644, the District of Columbia Charter Act shortly to be considered by the House of Representatives, "the Mayor and Council are authorized to levy annual taxes on such property" (of the United States Government). Your letter further states that the provisions in the bill for a Federal payment to the District would be in violation of the appropriations provisions of the Constitution.

These arguments were made during consideration of the bill by the Senate Committee on the District of Columbia. The Chairman of that committee, Senator Alan Bible, requested an opinion of the Justice Department on the merits of the contentions. Deputy Attorney General Ramsey Clark replied that the bill does not authorize the District of Columbia to tax Federal property and therefore does not raise a constitutional question in that regard. Further, General Clark stated, the bill does not propose an unconstitutional delegation of the appropriation power of Congress. The Senate Committee accepted this opinion, and, as you know, the Senate itself passed the measure by a heavy, bipartisan majority.

I am enclosing a copy of General Clark's reply to Senator Bible, and a detailed memorandum giving the basis for his conclusions.

Very truly yours,

LYNDON B. JOHNSON

[Honorable John L. McMillan, Chairman, Committee on the District of Columbia, House of Representatives, Washington, D.C.]

NOTE: The letter was released at Austin, Tex. The enclosures referred to in the last paragraph were not made public as part of the White House release.

The letter, dated September 2, from the members of the House Committee on the District of Columbia is printed in the Weekly Compilation of Presidential Documents (vol. 1, p. 211).

---

487 Statement by the President on Approving a Program To Assist El Paso, Texas, in Adjusting to the Chamizal Treaty. *September 4, 1965*

ON January 14, 1964, we concluded the Chamizal Treaty with Mexico. Certain lands in the city of El Paso, Tex., were ceded to Mexico and certain Mexican lands ceded to the United States. This historic event removed a long-standing irritant from our warm and friendly relations with our neighbors to the south.

To carry out the provisions of the treaty, the Congress subsequently enacted legislation to acquire property, relocate the river channel, and provide relocation costs. This work is now underway and is progressing well.

Today I have approved recommendations for a complementary program to be undertaken by the Department of Commerce, the Department of the Interior, and the Department of State. It will assist the city of El Paso in adjusting to the change necessitated by the treaty. We have been working on this program for some time. It involves expenditures of $14.5 million and has the enthusiastic support of the Federal Government and city officials. There are three elements:

—Construction of a 4-lane, limited access Chamizal Memorial Highway costing $12 million. The highway will run along the Rio Grande from downtown El Paso to a suburban point 12 miles eastward.

—Construction of a $2.2 million, 40-acre Chamizal Memorial Park with an auditorium, a reflecting pool, and a monument.

—Relocation and enlargement of the irrigation canal adjacent to the new river channel. The enlargement will cost $325,000.

I am confident that this complementary program will proceed without delay. I congratulate the many people who have worked very hard to bring it to fruition.

NOTE: For the President's remarks upon signing the ratification of the Chamizal Convention on December 20, 1963, see 1963–64 volume, this series, Item 58. It was proclaimed by the President on January 16, 1964.

On April 29, 1964, the President approved the American-Mexican Chamizal Convention Act of 1964 to facilitate compliance with the convention (Public Law 88–300, 78 Stat. 184).

The statement was released at Austin, Tex.

488   Statement by the President Urging Safe Driving During the Labor Day Weekend.   *September 4, 1965*

MILLIONS of Americans will be motoring on our national highways this Labor Day weekend.

Each year the travel on our highways results in needless accident, injury, suffering, and death for growing numbers of people.

Last year alone Americans killed some 47,000 of their fellow citizens in traffic accidents. That is more than 300 times as many Americans as our enemies were able to kill in all the fighting in South Viet-Nam during that same year.

American highways are unsurpassed in the world. Our traffic experts and safety engineers ceaselessly work to increase the pleasure and safety of driving. But, in the last analysis, the only person who can guarantee true driving safety is the safe driver. When you drive this weekend, drive safely.

NOTE: The statement was released at Austin, Tex.

489   Statement by the President: Labor Day.   *September 4, 1965*

ON THIS Labor Day, let us renew our dedication to a system of democracy in which each individual is guaranteed the opportunity to share fully in the benefits and responsibilities of our society.

Together, we in the United States have reached new heights in our quest for individual rights and for general prosperity.

Employment is at an alltime high as more people are working at better jobs for higher wages than ever before.

The record of achievement is impressive.

—Employment this summer rose to an alltime high of nearly 75 million, almost 2½ million more than the year before.

—Unemployment is down substantially from 1964.

—Per capita spendable income, up 3 percent over the previous year, is at a record high of $2,343 in current prices.

—The average take-home pay of a factory worker registered an alltime high of $108.21 in June, nearly $5 more than a year before.

—The economy, setting new marks month after month, is driving upward in the longest unbroken peacetime expansion in more than a century.

The unparalleled progress we have witnessed is the result of the concerted energies and talents of each individual American working together to build a better tomorrow. In this effort no one has taken a more active, more effective role than the working men and women in this country and the free trade union movement.

Since last Labor Day, we have witnessed the enactment by the Congress of landmark legislation to:

—provide medical and hospital care and increased social security benefits for older Americans.

—assure every American, without regard to race, the right to vote and thereby seek to better his lot in life.

—improve educational opportunities for millions of disadvantaged American children.

—extend and expand the Manpower Development and Training Act of 1962 to increase the employability of more citizens.

—promote economic development of Appalachia and to assist the region's large body of poor and jobless residents.

But, in spite of our progress, a large segment of our citizens remain untouched by our prosperity. They still remain the victims of poverty, racial and age discrimination, inadequate education, and technological change.

Our promise of a better America will become fact only when all citizens—not just most—have the opportunity to enjoy the benefits of our free society.

To accomplish these goals, our national purpose must be to:

—expand the employment opportunities of the impoverished and the undereducated.

—open more job opportunities for minorities and older citizens.

—expand the opportunities of our young people for education, training, and constructive work experience necessary for our highly-specialized society.

—lessen the impact of technological change for displaced workers and disrupted communities.

—develop and fill new jobs and continue measures to spur our economic growth.

We have the means, as never before, to extend the full benefits of our society to all and to build the Great Society we envision. We have only to exercise the will.

490 Statement by the President in Response to a Report on the Nation's Employment Record. *September 4, 1965*

SECRETARY of Labor Wirtz today reported to me on a remarkable record of achievement in reducing unemployment in the Nation's major labor areas.

At the recession low point of spring of 1961, 101 of 150 population centers surveyed regularly by the Department of Labor were classified as areas of substantial unemployment.

By summer of this year, that number had been cut to 19, an 81 percent reduction.

In many of the 82 areas which have left the substantial unemployment list, the improvement in the job situation has been truly dramatic. In a little over 4 years, Birmingham's unemployment rate declined from 12.9 percent to 3.5 percent, South Bend's 12.9 to 3.5, Detroit's 15.2 to 4.6, Johnstown, Pennsylvania's 20.6 to 4.0, Philadelphia's 8.1 to 4.8, and Pittsburgh's 12.7 to 3.1. Many other labor areas have had similar experiences.

These figures reflect at the community level—where it is most meaningful—the

fruits of the 6.4 million new jobs the Nation created between summer of 1961 and summer of 1965. They also reflect our national reduction in unemployment by 1.6 million during the same period.

The overall record provides satisfying and encouraging evidence of the job-creating power of a free economy assisted by positive governmental actions and programs at Federal, State, and local levels. It clearly demonstrates that unemployment is not something we have to learn to live with, and it points the way to the development of a truly full employment economy in our society.

That task still remains an imposing one. Despite our steady improvement in recent years, 3.3 million Americans were looking for jobs in August and couldn't find them. Many of these come from the ranks of our hard-core unemployed—the school dropout, the poorly educated adult worker, the displaced farmworker, the low-skilled worker, and others. Many of these Americans need and will get special assistance through specially designed programs such as the Manpower Act and the Economic Opportunity Act.

Whatever is required must be done. With all of its worldwide commitments to the defense of freedom and to the pursuit of peace, America simply cannot afford the waste of a man's potential not fully developed or the economic loss that that waste brings about.

NOTE: The statement was released at Austin, Tex.

491 The President's Message of Greeting for the America Days Celebration in Turku, Finland. *September 5, 1965*

MY FRIENDS of Finland, this celebration of America Days in Turku recalls an occasion 2 years ago when I had the privilege of opening the America Days in Helsinki. I was to make a few remarks, then cut a ribbon to open the celebration. But as the crowd pressed close I found part of the job done for me: the ceremonial ribbon had snapped in the rush and, as good friends, we had all cut it together.

During our visit to Finland, Mrs. Johnson and I spent one sunny day in Turku. We saw your modern university, the handsome cathedral, and the ancient castle. We heard your mayor describe Turku as a city still small enough for neighbors to know one another. We met many of those neighbors, and we have warm memories of their kindness.

I have asked my old friend and Ambassador at Large, Averell Harriman, to represent the United States in your America Days celebration this year. I know he is going to fall under the spell of Turku's graciousness, just as we did.

I have asked him to tell you how much America esteems the great Finnish people. We here know very well how great they are, for they helped create America itself, and we shall never forget that.

My very best wishes to you all.

NOTE: Ambassador Harriman delivered the President's message of greeting at the America Days ceremonies sponsored by the Finnish-American Society in Turku. In his message the President referred to his visit to Finland as Vice President in 1963.

The announcement of the message was released at Austin, Tex.

492 Statement by the President Announcing Extension of the Food Stamp Program. *September 5, 1965*

WHEN these new programs are in operation, low-income families in 206 areas in 39 States and the District of Columbia will be able to use food coupons to buy more and better food.

Our goal is to extend the benefits of this important food program to a million people by June 30, 1966.

When I signed the Food Stamp Act of 1964 about a year ago, I directed Secretary of Agriculture Orville L. Freeman to extend this program as quickly as possible to as many areas requesting it as the budget would permit. Since then, Secretary Freeman reports the Department of Agriculture has increased the number of food stamp areas by more than 2½ times—from the 43 pilot operations of last August to 116 counties and cities in 30 States and the District of Columbia currently.

Another 16 areas approved to enter the food stamp program earlier will begin operation in the coming months. Two counties in Mississippi will start this week. Latest reports show that in July nearly 640,000 people were taking part in the program, gaining an average of $6.30 a month per person in more food buying power. For many of these people it is the first time they have ever been able to go into a store and buy the food their families need.

This kind of progress all over the country makes the food stamp program a vital part of our work to break the cycle of poverty among our less fortunate citizens. They have a chance to help themselves by investing their own money in food coupons worth more than they paid. The coupons are spent like cash at authorized local food stores. Experience and research show that farmers sell more food, grocers get more business, and the entire economy of the area gets a boost from the added food buying power of food stamp customers.

We designed the food stamp program to expand or contract as economic and employment conditions warrant. A steady increase in available jobs during the past year has enabled many families to find work and move off the program.

Thus, we have been able to plan an expansion of the program into several more areas, largely less populous rural areas which have not felt the impact of the continuing improvement in the national employment picture.

The Department of Agriculture has more requests for the food stamp program than can be honored right now. During the year we will carefully evaluate all progress reports and move quickly to extend the program where possible within available funds. Over the next few years we expect to bring the food stamp program to all parts of the country that request it.

NOTE: The President's statement was made public as part of a White House release announcing extension of the food stamp program to an additional 74 counties in 24 States. The release stated that Secretary of Agriculture Freeman had reported to the President that officials of the 74 areas indicated that they would move promptly towards the earliest possible opening of coupon sales, some as soon as October 1965.

For the President's remarks upon signing the Food Stamp Act on August 31, 1964, see 1963–64 volume, this series, Item 546.

The statement was released at Austin, Tex.

---

493   Letter in Response to Report of the Committee on the Economic Impact of Defense and Disarmament.   *September 5, 1965*

Dear Dr. Ackley:

I want to thank you and your colleagues for the first report of the Committee on the Economic Impact of Defense and Disarmament.

I established this committee at the end of my first month as President. It has devoted itself for a year and a half to studies which affect two of the greatest issues our Nation faces. The first is to provide for national defense in ways that bring no unnecessary hardship to any American community. The second is to keep every road open for rapid progress toward disarmament as soon as others will join with us.

Your report gives a comprehensive account of the extensive efforts which our government is making to ensure that changes in our defense needs are brought about in ways that are fair to all affected groups and individuals. You rightly note our achievements in community assistance, and you rightly conclude that our work in this field must be improved still further. I agree with you that we must strengthen our aids to workers. I agree also that this is a task for state and local agencies and for private groups working in harmony with the Federal government.

What I find most encouraging of all in the report is your conclusion that our heavy current commitment to defense is not a bar to rapid progress toward disarmament. All Americans will welcome your clear conclusion that "there is no economic reason for the Nation to undergo a major economic decline or a slow stagnation if and when defense outlays are reduced."

The American people will continue to be determined that our great industrial effort for national defense is their servant and not their master. This is the tradition of the armed forces themselves, and it is the conviction, I am sure, of those who serve in the national defense industries, too.

This country will therefore go forward with renewed courage and conviction to provide the defenses that freedom demands and at the same time to press along the hard road toward the disarmament mankind must have.

Finally, your report gives eloquent restatement to the basic principle that sound decisions in a free society must be built on the best possible information. I strongly endorse your recommendation that your studies be continued, just as I strongly endorse your reaffirmation of the need for a constant growth in the basic research which can enlarge the opportunities for peaceful progress throughout our society.

Sincerely,

LYNDON B. JOHNSON

[Dr. Gardner Ackley, Chairman, Council of Economic Advisers]

NOTE: The Committee on the Economic Impact of Defense and Disarmament, chaired by Dr. Ackley, was established by the President on December 21, 1963 (see 1963–64 volume, this series, Item 62).

The report of the Committee, dated July 1965 (Government Printing Office, 92 pp.), expressed confidence in the ability of existing Federal programs to sustain economic growth and to minimize any adverse effects of changes in defense procurement, although it recognized that such shifts could create serious economic problems requiring special action by Federal, State, and local governments.

The principal recommendations of the Committee were that a permanently constituted Federal Task Force on Community Assistance be organized; that this Task Force and the existing agencies in the Department of Defense and AEC should quickly bring to communities affected by defense changes the whole array of Federal programs that can ease the economic impact and speed readjustment; that policies and procedures for advance notice of impending changes in defense programs be reviewed; that prime contractors be required to supply information on the impact of contract changes on subcontractors; that the Federal-State employment service be strengthened; that interarea recruiting services be rapidly expanded; that Federal agencies take more initiative in mortgage forbearance in emergencies created by changes in defense programs; that continued study be given to relocation assistance; that community needs continue to be given highest priority in disposal of surplus Federal property; and that Federal agencies should review policies governing use of Government-owned, contractor-leased facilities.

The report concluded that neither the recent shifts in defense procurement nor those likely in the future would pose major problems for the national economy.

A summary of the Committee's report is printed in the Weekly Compilation of Presidential Documents (vol. 1, p. 217).

The text of the letter was released at Austin, Tex.

494 Statement by the President on Announcing the Selection of Panel Chairmen for the First International Symposium on Water Desalination. *September 6, 1965*

A DEPENDABLE supply of fresh water is an absolute requirement for a world seeking peace and prosperity. Water is needed to grow food, to permit basic development in emerging nations, to allow industrial expansion in others, and to increase living standards for an increasing world population. The Symposium chairmen can lead the way toward new paths of achieving this goal.

The developing technology of water desalting has received enthusiastic and universal support by nations, large and small, again demonstrating that international coopera-

tion is the key to humanity's advancement.

NOTE: The President's statement was made public as part of a White House release announcing the selection of 19 leading scientists and engineers from 11 nations, the United Nations, UNESCO, and the United States to act as session panel chairmen of the First International Symposium on Water Desalination to be held in Washington October 3–9, 1965. The release also stated that five additional countries would send delegations to the meeting, bringing the total to 63 nations. The names of the session panel chairmen and the days on which they were to serve were included in the release (1 Weekly Comp. Pres. Docs., p. 221).

See also Items 325, 547, 558.

The statement was released at Austin, Tex.

495 Statement by the President Upon Signing the Foreign Assistance Act. *September 6, 1965*

TODAY I am signing into law the Foreign Assistance Act of 1965, which provides authority to carry forward our programs of economic and military assistance in fiscal year 1966.

These programs have been a vital part of U.S. foreign policy in four administrations of both parties since the end of World War II.

We have had great successes. We have made some mistakes. Foreign assistance is always and everywhere a limited instrument and no cure-all. But, I am convinced that without the American foreign aid program, without this expression of our humanity and our highest goals, hundreds of millions of people would have had no escape from the chaos, frustration, and despair on which tyranny grows and wars ignite.

Instead, these people look to the future with hope. Much remains to be done to

make the hope a reality. The work of building modern economies and new societies is difficult. It requires patience, strength, and knowledge. We cannot eradicate the injustice and deprivation of centuries in a matter of a few years.

It also requires a sense of adventure, of challenge, and of dedication on the part of all Americans, not just those who serve us so valiantly—normally without recognition—in the quiet battle against poverty, ignorance, and disease that goes on everyday around the world.

The hope can become reality only if the people and governments of the developing nations do their part—make the hard choices, carry forward with new legislation, push for internal reform. We will continue to base our assistance on the sound principle that self-help and reform on the part of recipients is the key to success.

We will also continue to base our program on the principle that other developed nations should provide more aid, on softer terms. The resolutions adopted at the recent meeting of the Development Assistance Committee of the OECD in Paris marked an important step in this direction. I urge all free world nations to continue in these efforts, particularly in bringing the terms on which aid is given within the targets established by the Development Assistance Committee.

I should like to express my appreciation to Chairman Fulbright and Chairman Morgan and the Members of the House-Senate conference on the foreign aid authorization for the hard work devoted to reaching agreement on the legislation. The matters at issue in the conference involved the future content and direction of the foreign aid program. This is also a matter of major concern to me.

The conference report and the two chairmen have urged "a review of the aid program as presently constituted, seeking to direct it more effectively toward the solution of the problems of the developing countries." The executive branch will, this fall, undertake appropriate studies of the program. It is my expectation that these studies will provide the basis for recommendations as to the future course of U.S. assistance policy.

I also expect to request that the multiyear principle approved by the Congress in 1961 and 1962 for development loans be extended to the other categories of assistance.

I am confident that next year's legislation will mark a renewal of our long-term commitment to assist those people who want to live in peace and independence; a renewal of the program which has been vital to U.S. interests around the world; and a renewal of the cooperative relationship between the executive and the Congress which has shaped the great foreign policy decisions of the postwar world.

NOTE: In his statement the President referred to Senator J. W. Fulbright of Arkansas, Chairman of the Senate Foreign Relations Committee, and Representative Thomas E. Morgan of Pennsylvania, Chairman of the House Foreign Affairs Committee.

As enacted, the Foreign Assistance Act of 1965 is Public Law 89–171 (79 Stat. 653).

The statement was released at Austin, Tex.

---

496 Letter to the Nation's First Social Security Beneficiary Informing Her of Increased Benefits. *September* 6, 1965

[Released September 6, 1965.   Dated September 3, 1965]

Dear Miss Fuller:

My best wishes to you on your 91st birthday.

Since you became the first Social Security beneficiary in January, 1940, the size of the program—and of the more than 300 monthly checks you have received—has grown steadily. That growth means increased well-being for older people, widows and orphans everywhere in the Nation.

On July 30, I had the pleasure of signing an act which increased monthly benefits by seven per cent. As a major new advance, it added health insurance protection for the aging to the social security law.

This increase is retroactive to January—and so this month you are receiving an extra social security check for the amount of the increase due you for the months of January through August.

I am happy that you can receive this "bonus" check on your birthday; I hope that you receive it—and many others—in good health.

With kindest regards,

Sincerely,

LYNDON B. JOHNSON

[Miss Ida Fuller, 33 Pleasant Street, Ludlow, Vermont]

NOTE: On September 6 the White House announced that Raymond E. Bender, Social Security District Manager in Rutland, Vt., had that day delivered to Miss Fuller a check for the retroactive increase in her social security benefits. The release stated that retroactive checks would be mailed to 20 million other social security beneficiaries beginning September 15, and that the amount paid out would total $885 million.

For the President's remarks upon signing the Social Security Amendments of 1965, see Item 394.

The letter was released at Austin, Tex.

497 Statement by the President on Cost Reduction Programs by Civilian Agencies.   *September 7, 1965*

I THINK you all know one of my most insistent goals is cost reduction. Ever since November 1963, I have instructed the heads of every department and agency to be imaginative and relentless in their pursuit of savings. I have required them to report to me periodically on cost reduction actions underway and planned.

I have just received a report from the Budget Bureau on civilian agency accomplishments during the 18-month period from January 1964 through June 1965. I am most impressed and pleased with the results. I think they show what happens when cost reduction becomes the personal goal of each Federal employee—from the President on down.

From January 1964 through June 1965, the civilian agencies of the executive branch took actions that saved over $1.1 billion. These savings have been achieved through thousands of separate cost reduction actions over the entire 18-month period. They have involved many agencies. Some were large savings; many more were small. But in total they add up to a major dividend for the American taxpayer—both in terms of his pocketbook and better program quality.

Let me give you three recent examples of what makes up this total. They are typical of what is being achieved in hundreds of cases throughout the Federal establishment:

—By doing some shopping in the excess property catalog, the Forest Service of the Department of Agriculture has avoided spending $28 million on equipment required for its various programs. By maintaining a sharp lookout for equipment no longer needed by other Government agencies, Forest Service managers have been able to put to work excess road graders, tractors, portable buildings, bedding, cooking utensils, and similar equipment.

Many other agencies are doing the same thing.

—By improved processing procedures, the Patent Office was able to increase its productivity by 35 percent in 1965 over 1964.

—The Census Bureau, by saving $1.8 million in its 1963 censuses of business, manufacturers, mineral industries, and transportation, will not need to request funds for these censuses in 1966.

These civilian agency efforts are in addition to the impressive results Secretary McNamara has achieved in the Department of Defense. As you know, he has announced savings in his budget of $4.6 billion in fiscal year 1965—$2.1 billion more than previously estimated.

Although we can take pride in what we have accomplished, we have much more to do. There is always room for further improvement. I mean to step up our current

efforts. I think we have only seen the beginning of what we can achieve.

NOTE: The statement was released at Austin, Tex.

---

498   Statement by the President on Announcing Progress in the Development of the Herbert Hoover National Historic Site. *September 7, 1965*

HERBERT CLARK HOOVER was not only a dedicated President, but he was a truly great humanitarian. He placed service to his country, and to the cause of humanity throughout the world, above all else. His outstanding contributions to the operations of our Government and the wise and generous counsel he gave to leaders of both national parties who followed him in office exemplify the highest traditions of public service. They make his birthplace a deeply significant part of our Nation's history, a part that will now be preserved and made accessible to all Americans.

NOTE: The President's statement was made public as part of a White House release reporting that rapid progress was being made in converting former President Herbert Hoover's birthplace at West Branch, Iowa, into a national shrine.

The release continued as follows:

"President Johnson signed the act establishing the area as a national historical site on August 12. He requested the Department of the Interior to move quickly to implement the legislation.

"Since then, plans have been drawn for a visitor center and parking area, as well as the rerouting of city traffic from in front of the cottage where the 31st U.S. President was born. In addition, provision is being made for restoring some of the older buildings near the cottage to preserve the atmosphere of the site.

"The Department of the Interior's National Park Service will arrange as soon as possible for transfer to the Service of some 200 acres now being administered by the General Services Administration. This will include the cottage, a number of other buildings, and the graves of the former Republican President and his wife, Lou Henry Hoover. GSA will continue to administer the modern Herbert Hoover Library.

"When the transfer has been completed, physical preparation of the site can begin immediately. Selection of supervisory staff is now underway, and the interim appointment of an acting superintendent for the area will be announced shortly."

See also Items 414, 420.

The statement was released at Austin, Tex.

---

499   Remarks at the Signing of the National Capital Transportation Act. *September 8, 1965*

Governor Tawes, Members of the Congress, my friends:

Over the years, I have found two distinct schools of thought around Washington in regard to Senators. One holds that Senators should be treated like people. The other school is somewhat more revolutionary and holds that people should be treated like Senators.

The bill I am about to sign today represents a victory for the second school of thought.

So, henceforward, the people—including the House Members—will have what only Senators have enjoyed until now: high-speed subways to take them to and from their work.

Here in the District of Columbia, justice has been long delayed and long denied on many matters, although I am proud the pace of progress is picking up somewhat this year.

I believe this legislation means justice and progress at long last for the residents of our great National Capital.

On an average weekday more people enter and leave downtown Washington than visit Manhattan Island in New York City. Unless we want to pave the Potomac with bridges, there is little more that we can do to ease the congestion until we have properly balanced our transportation system. And that is what this bill permits us to do.

The metropolitan area's highway system has been planned on the assumption that it would be balanced by a rapid rail system. And I congratulate the Congress on following through to make this balance feasible.

Our goal must be to make the suburbs of Maryland and Virginia a part of this system. The Maryland Legislature has already approved the compact to make that possible— and we hope that Virginia will do the same in 1966.

We all realize the significance of this measure reaches beyond the Federal City itself. If we are to realize the full promise of tomorrow's urbanized America, we must all— across our land—meet today the pressing challenge of urban transportation.

Today there are 75 million automobiles in use in this country. In only 15 more years, by 1980, that number will exceed 106 million.

Over the next 10 years, by 1975, the total vehicle miles traveled in the Nation's urban areas will increase by more than 64 percent.

Our great interstate highway program is meeting the needs for intercity and cross-country travel in this highly mobile Nation of ours. But we must not forget that of the 150 million automobile trips made each day in our metropolitan areas—60 percent of them are for distances of less than 5 miles.

Our most acute transportation problem— one that costs us billions of dollars each year now—is that of local traffic. In a day when our astronauts can circle the globe in less time than many Americans spend driving to and from work, our challenge is real, and it is serious, and it is urgent.

This bill will help us to fulfill our goal of making the District of Columbia the model city for the Nation that Washington ought to be. So I want to express my very deep appreciation, my personal thanks. I want to congratulate all in the Congress for the enthusiastic bipartisan support which made possible its passage.

As one who still remembers the years of fighting the traffic in Rock Creek Park— when they still let me do my own driving— I am personally pleased to be able to sign this very important and this very long-needed piece of legislation.

Thank you very much.

NOTE: The President spoke at 10:04 a.m. in the Rose Garden at the White House. In his opening words he referred to Governor J. Millard Tawes of Maryland.

As enacted, the National Capital Transportation Act of 1965 is Public Law 89–173 (79 Stat. 663).

500   Remarks to the Members of the President's Commission on Law Enforcement and Administration of Justice. *September 8, 1965*

Attorney General Katzenbach, Director Hoover, members of the Crime Commission:

I want to welcome you to the White House this morning as you undertake a most important assignment.

Crime is a sore on the face of America. It is a menace on our streets. It is a drain on our cities. It is a corrupter of our youth. It is a cause of untold suffering and loss. But just saying this does not solve the problem that we have before us. We must bring it under control, and then we must root out the cause.

So let the Nation know that today we have taken a pledge not only to reduce crime but to banish it.

The first steps have already been taken. This year we passed major legislation on juvenile delinquency and drug control. This week I will sign another bill on prisoner rehabilitation. I soon hope to sign an important new law enforcement assistance act.

Further, we have launched new programs aimed at poverty, disease, illiteracy, discrimination, unemployment, housing, and slums. All these are the breeding grounds of crime. But much, much more remains to be done and that is why I have asked you to come here to serve as members of the President's National Crime Commission.

So let us together spearhead a new war against crime in this country. Among those of you who are members of this Committee are lawyers, judges, law enforcement officials, educators, social workers, and Government officials. The Nation wants you to put this collective valuable experience to work.

We know that the problems of crime do not yield to easy answers. But today I am challenging you to try to find these answers.

I want to know why—why one-third of all parolees revert to crime. I want to know why one man breaks the law and another living in the same circumstances does not. I want to know why drug addiction is increasing among our youth. I want to know why organized crime continues to expand despite our best efforts to prevent it. I want to know why juvenile delinquency knows no

economic or educational barriers.

And when you find the "whys" I will try to see that corrective action is taken. So I ask this Committee to be daring and be creative, be revolutionary in your recommendations.

Mark Twain once said that loyalty to a petrified opinion never yet broke a chain or freed a human soul. So I would hope that you would ignore the petrified opinions.

I pledge to you and I pledge to this Nation the full resources of this great Government, and they will all be behind you. I think you understand the importance of your task.

Under the very effective leadership of the able Attorney General, Mr. Katzenbach, the Nation and I know you will give us the blueprints that we need for effective action to banish crime.

I have looked over the 50 States in this Union and we have brought together here in the Cabinet Room this morning the outstanding citizens from those States, who have graciously agreed to serve their country in this connection. We look forward with great hope to the results of their labors.

Thank you very much.

NOTE: The President spoke at 11:25 a.m. in the Cabinet Room at the White House. In his opening words he referred to Attorney General Nicholas deB. Katzenbach, Chairman of the President's Commission on Law Enforcement and Administration of Justice, and J. Edgar Hoover, Director of the Federal Bureau of Investigation.

On September 7 the White House announced that a 2-day session of the 19-member Commission had been called by the Chairman and that Attorney General Katzenbach and Mr. Hoover would welcome the members at the opening session which would be followed by a meeting with the President.

The release also stated that all Federal investigative agencies were continuing to contribute to the war on crime, and were submitting reports regularly on racketeers, their associates, and their activities, under the general supervision of the Organized Crime and Racketeering Section, Criminal Division, Department of Justice.

See also Items 382, 422, 437, 526.

501 Statement by the President Upon Making Public a Report on Benefits Available to Young People Under the Social Security Amendments of 1965. *September 8, 1965*

THE Social Security Amendments of 1965, which provide urgently needed health insurance plans for the aged, reflect this administration's concern for the well-being of our more than 18 million older citizens.

Just as importantly, this historic legislation provides significant new and improved services and benefits for millions of our young people, from neglected infants to the sons and daughters of low-income families who are working their way through college. Most importantly, it can do much to help eliminate sickness and disability as causes of lifelong poverty.

Because, as I have often said, our children are our most precious national resource, I want to call special attention to the many services and benefits available to young people—especially the children of the poor—under the new amendments. The Secretary of Health, Education, and Welfare has provided the attached summary of these provisions.

As Secretary Gardner has emphasized in a letter to the Governors of all the States,

many of these additional benefits and services can be made available to those who need them only if the States take advantage of the Federal assistance offered by this legislation for the improvement of State health and welfare programs. I want to urge State and local officials in every part of the Nation to take prompt action to bring these benefits to the young people who hold in their hands the future well-being of our society.

NOTE: The summary report to the President from Secretary of Health, Education, and Welfare John W. Gardner was released by the White House along with the President's statement.

The report enumerated the newly available benefits and services for young people under the following headings: medical care for children, special project grants for needy children, expansion of child health and welfare services, training of personnel to assist crippled children, increased monthly social security benefits, increased public assistance payments, part-time jobs for children under 18, and liberalized payments to students.

The text of the report is printed in the Weekly Compilation of Presidential Documents (vol. 1, p. 234).

For the President's remarks on signing the Social Security Amendments of 1965, see Item 394.

The statement was released at Austin, Tex.

502 Statement by the President Following Passage by the House of the Foreign Assistance Appropriation Act. *September 8, 1965*

PASSAGE of the Foreign Assistance Appropriation Act by the House of Representatives, coming so swiftly after the authorization bill enacted last week, reflects a welcome and healthy understanding between the executive and legislative branches on this important program at a critical moment in history.

The bill passed by the House provides the

smallest reduction ever made below the administration's original authorization request. It is $175 million below the request I submitted early this year, and $75 million below the appropriation request.

I commend the Members of the House for the prudence and promptness of their action today. It is heartening news to those here and abroad who look to this program for help in liberating men from tragic want, disease, and oppression.

NOTE: The Foreign Assistance and Related Agencies Appropriation Act, 1966, was approved by the President on October 20, 1965 (see Item 570).

503 Remarks at the Signing of Bill Establishing a Department of Housing and Urban Development. *September 9, 1965*

Mr. Vice President, Members of the Congress, most distinguished mayors, ladies and gentlemen:

This is a very rare and a very proud occasion. We are bringing into being today a very new and needed instrument to serve all the people of America.

This legislation establishes the 11th department of our Federal Government—the Department of Housing and Urban Development.

When our Nation was born, the only departments of Government were State and Treasury and War. Our country and our Government have grown greatly since that time. But we have been sparing in creating new and additional departments except when the need has been clear and compelling and continuing. That is clearly the case for this, the newest department.

The America of our Founding Fathers was, of course, a rural America. The virtues and values of our rural heritage have shaped and strengthened the American character for all of our 189 years. Our debt to this heritage is deep and abiding, and we shall honor it always.

When Thomas Jefferson spoke of rural virtues, cities were insignificant on the countryside of this continent. Only 5 percent of our people lived then in cities or villages. America was the land of the farmer, the woodsman, the hunter and mountaineer. Even a century ago when Abraham Lincoln asked the Congress to create a Department of Agriculture, fewer than 20 percent of our people then lived in cities.

Now that day is gone. It never will return.

In less than a lifetime—in less than my own 57 years—America has become a highly urbanized Nation, and we must face the many meanings of this new America.

Social change in our country is often faster than the mind of a generation can comprehend. But the pace of our urbanization has been stunning. It will move still faster in the immediate years ahead.

Between now and the end of this century our urban population will double. City land will double.

In the next 35 years we must literally build a second America—putting in place as many houses, schools, apartments, parks, and offices as we have built through all the time since the Pilgrims arrived on these shores.

The physical challenge is awesome. But there is a challenge to the spirit that is even greater and more demanding.

It is not enough for us to erect towers of stone and glass, or to lay out vast suburbs of order and conformity. We must seek and we must find the ways to preserve and to perpetuate in the city the individuality, the human dignity, the respect for individual rights, the devotion to individual responsibility that has been part of the American character and the strength of the American system.

Our cities and our new urban age must not be symbols of a sordid society. The history of every civilization teaches us that those who do not find new means to respond to new challenges will perish or decay.

Unless we seize the opportunities available now, the fears some have of a nightmare society could materialize.

Unless we match our imagination and our courage and our affluence, we could fail both our past and our posterity.

So the enactment of this legislation, and so many other measures of this Congress, represents the unified determination of this generation to preserve the best of the past by preparing to make the future better still.

With this legislation, we are—as we must always—going out to meet tomorrow and master its opportunities before its obstacles master us.

In the days of our population's westward movement, we created the Department of Interior. The rise of great industry brought the response of a Department of Commerce and a Department of Labor. The growth of our world responsibilities made it necessary to unify our security forces in a Department of Defense. President Eisenhower saw that the magnitude of our health and education and welfare programs required a new department devoted to their fulfillment.

So today we are taking the first step toward organizing our system for a more rational response to the pressing challenge of urban life. This is a historic action and this is a historic occasion. All who have been a part of it can forever be proud of it.

I am grateful, particularly to those Members of the Congress whose energies and efforts have made this ceremony possible today: the distinguished Vice President; Senator Ribicoff; Senator Muskie; Senator Clark; the dedicated Chairman of the House Committee, Congressman Bill Dawson; his colleagues, Congressman Fascell and Congressman Reuss; and a dozen more Congressmen and Senators I do not have time to mention. They all, the Congress, all of them, had a vital bipartisan support from a host of their fellow Members.

This is a wise and this is a just and this is a progressive measure for all America, and I am honored to sign it this morning.

Thank you.

NOTE: The President spoke at 10:06 a.m. in the Rose Garden at the White House. In his opening words he referred to Vice President Hubert H. Humphrey.

During his remarks he referred to Senator Abraham Ribicoff of Connecticut, Senator Edmund S. Muskie of Maine, Senator Joseph S. Clark of Pennsylvania, Representative William L. Dawson of Illinois, Chairman of the House Committee on Government Operations, Representative Dante B. Fascell of Florida, and Representative Henry S. Reuss of Wisconsin.

As enacted, the Department of Housing and Urban Development Act is Public Law 89–174 (79 Stat. 667).

504   Remarks at the Unveiling of the Design for a Commemorative Stamp Honoring Adlai Stevenson. *September 9, 1965*

Members of the Stevenson family, Mr. Vice President, the distinguished leadership and Members of the Congress, Postmaster General Gronouski, friends and associates of Adlai Stevenson, ladies and gentlemen:

We meet here today to share an act of remembrance. Less than 2 years ago, Adlai Stevenson took part in a ceremony honoring the memory of Eleanor Roosevelt with a commemorative stamp. He said of her that she was a symbol of man's humanity to man.

So, today, in honoring him we honor another whose life speaks to us of the brighter side of man's nature—the side of service and the love of our fellows.

I will not now add to the many words

which have been said in his praise. It is sufficient to know, as Winston Churchill once said, that he has left a lonesome place against the sky.

For almost two decades, Adlai Stevenson skillfully and beautifully helped shape the dialog of 20th century democracy. The possibilities that he revealed, the horizons that he opened, and the dangers of which he warned are today the central concern of the United States of America.

I know they are my concern.

Above all, he taught that the goals of America, and the road we must travel to reach them, could be followed consistently with the most noble of our ideals. Indeed, there could be no other way.

What more can be said of a public man

than this: He believed in man. He revealed the prospects of peace. And in his own life he served the cause of mankind just as he so eloquently proclaimed it.

NOTE: The President spoke at 11:32 a.m. in the Rose Garden at the White House. In his opening words he referred to Vice President Hubert H. Humphrey and Postmaster General John A. Gronouski.

The ceremony was attended by Mr. Stevenson's sons, Borden and Adlai E. Stevenson 3d, and by his sister, Mrs. Ernest Ives.

The stamp, a picture of Adlai Stevenson with the United Nations emblem in the background, was issued by the Post Office Department on October 3, 1965, at Bloomington, Ill., where Mr. Stevenson is buried.

For Mr. Stevenson's remarks on October 11, 1963, at the ceremony marking the issuance of the Eleanor Roosevelt Commemorative Stamp, see "Public Papers of the Presidents, John F. Kennedy 1963," Item 408.

See also Items 355, 356, 359, this volume.

505 Statement by the President on Receiving Report on Federal Taxes Collected During Fiscal Year 1965. *September 9, 1965*

I AM advised by the Internal Revenue Service that gross collections of Federal taxes in the year ending June 30 reached an all-time high of $114.4 billion.

That represents an increase of $2.2 billion over fiscal 1964.

In addition, the individual income tax collections in the second quarter of this year were running 13 percent ahead of those in the second quarter of 1964, and so far through August this trend is holding up.

I think that these figures are one more indication of the wisdom and effectiveness of the tax programs carried out in recent years.

These record tax collections result despite the fact that we have enacted a record income tax cut and a substantial excise tax cut.

As a result of these two measures alone, the Federal income tax burden next year

will be lighter by $17.5 billion than it would have been without them. And that figure does not include the investment tax credit for business which was part of the Revenue Act of 1962, nor does it include the depreciation tax reform of 1962 which was liberalized early this year.

When these measures are taken into account, the total tax reduction effective in 1966 comes to more than $20 billion.

I am happy to report that, even with such massive tax reduction, we anticipate that Federal revenues for the 5-year period, fiscal 1961 to 1966, will have increased by over $18 billion—almost twice the increase over the previous 5 years when there were no tax cuts at all.

NOTE: On the same day the White House made public the preliminary figures on Federal taxes for fiscal year 1965. The release stated that the largest part of the increase was accounted for in corporation income taxes which yielded $26.1 billion, that income tax collections from individuals (reflecting a full year at reduced tax rates) had declined $930 million to a total of $53.7 billion, and that excise taxes totaled $14.8 billion, an increase of $848 million (1 Weekly Comp. Pres. Docs., p. 238).

506 Memorandum Requesting a Study of Means of Financing Federal Loan Programs Through Private Capital. *September 9, 1965*

Memorandum to the Director, Bureau of the Budget:

At the July 27 Cabinet meeting, I asked for an evaluation of the Federal Government's direct loan programs and its portfolio of financial assets. To make the best use of scarce budgetary resources we should seek the substitution of private for public credit wherever this is compatible with the achievement of the basic purposes of our various Federal credit programs. This should be done in the most economic way possible.

The evaluation I have requested should be available in time to assist in the formulation of the fiscal 1967 budget. To reach this objective, I request:

1. That you prepare, in cooperation with the Federal departments and agencies involved, an inventory of those Federal loan programs which might appropriately be financed through the private capital market. You should specify the financial techniques by which private finances can be secured, indicate how the basic objectives of the various loan programs can be preserved, and state any changes in legislation which would be required. In addition, you should specify which loan programs cannot appropriately be financed through the private capital market and provide an explanation, in each instance, of the reasons.

Include in this inventory a statement of existing and projected Federal holdings of financial assets, specifying the amounts which can be prudently sold to private investors.

2. That this review encompass a broader reexamination of difficulties in existing procedures for the sale of financial assets and the financing of Federal loan programs, including any problems in coordination or direction and any inefficiencies or excessive costs resulting from present procedures. All possible improvements in the financial techniques by which private financing can be secured should be explored with the Secretary of the Treasury, such as the conception of centralized financing for all Federal loan programs.

3. That you consult with the Secretary of the Treasury and the Chairman of the Council of Economic Advisers in the development of this inventory and in the broader review of techniques and problems, and in the evaluation of its monetary and financial implications.

4. That you present to me, in our deliberations on the 1967 budget, the results of this evaluation, together with specific recommendations for administrative action and legislative proposals. Your report should, of course, include the views of the Secretary of the Treasury, the Chairman of the Council of Economic Advisers, and the heads of the departments and agencies involved.

I believe that we should seek, wherever possible, to encourage the participation of the private capital market in those Federal programs whose primary objective is the extension of credit. While there are some programs whose very nature makes this impossible, I believe that wider private participation in Federal credit programs is a highly desirable objective.

First, it economizes on scarce Federal budgetary resources.

Second, by bringing private lenders into contact with individuals and groups whose major source of credit is now the Federal Government, it can substantially increase the availability of credit for these individuals and groups.

I am confident that this careful and de-tailed evaluation will substantially improve our Federal credit programs and I trust that you will begin the evaluation at once.

LYNDON B. JOHNSON

NOTE: On April 20, 1966, the President sent a letter to the President of the Senate and to the Speaker of the House of Representatives, transmitting the proposed Participation Sales Act of 1965, which was designed to forward the objective of substituting private for public credit (2 Weekly Comp. Pres. Docs., p. 550).

507 Statement by the President Following a Meeting With the U.S. Representative to the NATO Council. *September 9, 1965*

[Excerpt from the Press Secretary's news briefing]

MR. MOYERS. The President met this afternoon, following his weekly session with Secretary McNamara, Secretary Rusk, and Mr. Bundy,[1] with Mr. Harlan Cleveland, the recently appointed Ambassador to NATO. He asked Mr. Cleveland to concentrate especially on three tasks which are of "enduring importance to this country and to our partners in the Western Alliance."

Q. Is there a statement on this?

Q. Is this the statement that Secretary Rusk referred to?

MR. MOYERS. That is correct.

Q. Bill, before you go ahead, is this a White House statement or a Presidential statement?

MR. MOYERS. This is a Presidential statement. I'll put in the statement, and when it is the President's I'll quote it.

The first task, he told him, is to strengthen, of course, the North Atlantic alliance organization as an organization.

Now, let me read from the President's statement:

---

[1] Robert S. McNamara, Secretary of Defense, Dean Rusk, Secretary of State, and McGeorge Bundy, Special Assistant to the President.

"This alliance is the centerpiece of the worldwide system we have been building for 20 years to protect the free world. NATO has succeeded in its deterrent role. A strong NATO remains essential if we are to reach a solid agreement with the Soviet Union that reflects the common interest of each of the allied nations in peace and security.

"Naturally, each member of NATO sees the alliance and the international organization that serves it from its own perspective. But this alliance of the West is bigger than any of its members. We must maintain its strength and we must continually update it to serve the common aspirations of all of us."

Q. Bill, is that a statement that the President made to Mr. Cleveland?

MR. MOYERS. This is a statement that I'm making to you in the President's name.

Q. Is that the end of the quote?

MR. MOYERS. Yes. I'm paraphrasing now.

The second task is to continue to develop NATO—the President wanted Mr. Cleveland to develop NATO as an instrument of political cooperation.

Now, as part of the President's statement,

this is a direct quote:

"I have asked Ambassador Cleveland, working with his colleagues in the Department of State, to examine the ways in which all members can continue, within the North Atlantic alliance, to strengthen the process of political consultation on a wide variety of world issues."

The third task the President assigned to Mr. Cleveland was to work out improved ways of organizing our collective nuclear defense.

"This will be high on the agenda in the months ahead. I have asked Ambassador Cleveland to make clear to our friends in NATO the continuing desire of the United States to find more satisfactory means of dealing with this central problem.

"The partnership of Atlantic nations is not the only center of power in our world of diversity, but it is the most free and the most powerful. Our continuing purpose is to work with our friends to see that this power is managed responsibly in the larger service of freedom on every continent."

NOTE: The foregoing appears on the first two pages of the news conference held by Bill D. Moyers, Special Assistant to the President, at 4:25 p.m. on Thursday, September 9. It was not made public in the form of a White House press release.

508 Veto of Bill "To Incorporate the Youth Councils on Civic Affairs, and for Other Purposes." *September 10, 1965*

To the House of Representatives:

I return herewith, without my approval, H.R. 3329, a bill "To incorporate the Youth Councils on Civic Affairs, and for other purposes."

The Committee reports indicate that this organization had its origin in Jacksonville, Florida, in 1962 and that it was incorporated under Florida law in March 1963. Its general purposes are to promote youth activities for the good of the community and to make youth aware of their civic responsibilities. Obviously, these worthwhile purposes are not the basis of my concern with this bill.

For some time I have been concerned with the question of whether we were granting Federal charters to private organizations on a case-by-case basis without the benefit of clearly established standards and criteria as to eligibility. Worthy civic, patriotic, and philanthropic organizations can and do incorporate their activities under State law. It seems obvious that Federal charters should be granted, if at all, only on a selective basis and that they should meet some national interest standard.

Other questions indicate the desirability of further study of this matter. For example, does the granting of Federal charters to a limited number of organizations discriminate against similar and worthy organizations and possibly stifle their growth? Should federally chartered corporations be more carefully supervised by an agency of the Federal Government? Does Federal rather than State chartering result in differences in the legal or tax status of the corporation, and are any differences appropriate ones?

I note that last year Congress enacted Public Law 88–504, at the recommendation of the General Accounting Office, to provide common standards of auditing and reporting for federally chartered corporations covered by Title 36 of the United States Code. This reflected a concern similar to mine that proper standards and criteria be established in this area.

I hope that the Judiciary Committees will find it possible to make a comprehensive study of the questions I have outlined above. I am asking the Department of Justice and the Bureau of the Budget to explore these questions also and to make appropriate recommendations to me.

In the light of these concerns and without reflection in any way on the worthy purposes of the organization which would be incorporated by this bill, I feel constrained to withhold my approval from H.R. 3329 at this time.

LYNDON B. JOHNSON

The White House
September 10, 1965

509   Statement by the President Upon Signing Bills Providing Rehabilitative Techniques for Adult Offenders.
September 10, 1965

FOR the first time, the Attorney General of the United States has the authority to apply a full range of rehabilitative techniques to adult offenders. H.R. 6964, which I have today signed into law, allows him to (1) commit or transfer adult prisoners to residential community treatment centers (more popularly known as "halfway houses"), (2) grant prisoners leave for emergency purposes or to contact prospective employers, and (3) permit them to go into a neighboring community to work at paid employment or to obtain training.

One or more of these techniques have been used successfully by the Federal Bureau of Prisons in dealing with youthful offenders, by several States and European nations, and by the military services. We expect similar success with adult Federal prisoners.

This measure has been described as one of the most important pieces of legislation affecting the Federal prison system in the past 30 years. It is a beginning in the search for improving a correctional system that today sees one out of three parolees revert to crime.

I have also signed today H.R. 2263, the Correctional Rehabilitation Study Act of 1965. If we are to find new and better ways to help parolees return to society and to a good and useful life for themselves and their families, we must have highly trained specialists at our disposal. The studies to be financed under this bill will tell us the kind of specialists we need, the number we must have, and what training we must provide for them.

With these bills, with the Drug Abuse Act I have previously signed, and with the Law Enforcement Assistance Act just passed by the Congress, we take the first steps toward fulfilling our solemn pledge to the Nation not only to reduce crime but ultimately to drive it from our society.

NOTE: As enacted, H.R. 6964 is Public Law 89–176 (79 Stat. 674); H.R. 2263 is Public Law 89–178 (79 Stat. 676).

510 Letter to the Recipient of the First Home Improvement Grant Under the New Housing Act. *September 13, 1965*

Dear Mrs. Whelan:

You are the first in the Nation to receive one of the new housing rehabilitation grants, authorized for urban renewal areas only a month ago when I signed the landmark Housing and Urban Development Act of 1965.

While your city is arranging a special ceremony to award this grant to you, I want to add the congratulations of your President on this signal occasion.

Our urban renewal program is a cooperative effort by the city and the national government, and by the citizen and the private enterprise contractor, to renew and rehabilitate our urban environment. Because of the new law, the Congress has made it possible for many more residents of urban renewal areas to pay for necessary home improvements without having to move.

I hope you will soon be seeing and enjoying the results of the rehabilitation work that now gets underway on your home. And I hope that those of your fellow citizens in the "West End" area, in other parts of St. Louis, and across the United States, who could not previously participate in urban renewal in this direct way, will follow your example.

Sincerely,

Lyndon B. Johnson

[Mrs. Annie Laurie Whelan, 944 Laurel Avenue, St. Louis, Missouri 63112]

note: The Housing and Urban Development Act of 1965 was approved by the President on August 10, 1965 (see Item 415).

511 Message to the Members of the Urban Development Seminar. *September 13, 1965*

I EXTEND to you my heartiest welcome to the United States of America and wish you every success in your studies.

Your task for the next 4 weeks will be to examine the urban programs and institutions we have developed in the United States—not with a view of copying them, because you cannot transplant techniques from one culture to another—but to explore ideas and principles which can be adapted to your social and economic environments.

In particular you should carefully look at the accomplishments of private profit and nonprofit enterprises, such as cooperatives, which stimulate capital formation so essential to housing construction. And do not overlook the vast contributions American labor has made towards raising our living standards, for no amount of money can develop the best laid plans without the trained workers necessary to implement a program.

You will be interested to know that last Thursday I signed legislation establishing a Department of Housing and Urban Development. This new department, the eleventh in our Federal Government, will draw together the programs and personnel formerly scattered through several agencies to provide a more effective means of solving this country's problems of growth and urbanization.

The creation of this department is an important step in our national effort to achieve a Great Society. But let me assure you that I earnestly hope and pray that the time will come when all your nations also achieve the goal of a Great Society. Our Agency for International Development, working closely with the new department, will continue to develop new tools to help the developing countries solve their urban problems.

I am looking to this Seminar to generate the ideas necessary to stem the tide of urban deterioration and to develop the guidelines for providing decent housing and suitable environments for people everywhere.

I wish you Godspeed in your important task.

NOTE: The President's message was read to the members of the Seminar, meeting in the State Department Auditorium, by Robert C. Weaver, Administrator of the Housing and Home Finance Agency. The group was made up of more than 60 housing experts from 25 underdeveloped nations.

The Department of Housing and Urban Development Act was approved by the President on September 9, 1965 (see Item 503).

---

512   Statement by the President to the Cabinet on Cost Reduction Programs by Civilian Agencies.   *September 13, 1965*

LAST MONDAY I announced the results of cost reduction actions taken in the 18-month period from January 1964 through June 1965. The civilian agencies effected savings of more than $1.1 billion. Added to the results achieved in the Department of Defense, this record shows what can be done when a willing effort is made. Impressive as these results are, they are only a beginning of what we can and must achieve in the year ahead.

On March 25, I requested each agency to establish an organized program for cost reduction, to prepare and submit formal cost reduction targets for fiscal 1966, and to make progress reports to me.

I have now received these reports from each of you. By trimming back or dropping marginal or out-of-date programs and by more efficient operating procedures, the civilian agencies have established a further savings goal of $1.5 billion this fiscal year.

You have identified savings in the next 12 months substantially higher than in the prior 18 months. This represents real progress.

But the fact that we are making progress doesn't mean that our efforts can be eased.

I have said before, and I shall continue to repeat, that the willingness of Congress and the American people to support the legislation we have requested stems, in part, from their recognition and trust that this administration will carry out Federal programs at the minimum possible cost.

I have instructed the Budget Director, in reviewing your 1967 budget requests with me, to present me with a list of possible savings through

—greater efficiency in operation,

—elimination or reduction of obsolete programs, and

—substitution of private for public credit totaling at least $3 billion.

I want to outline for you some of the specific areas in which I believe you ought to concentrate your attention:

1. *A relentless review of marginal or lower priority programs.* The task forces on budgetary savings which you earlier established, at my request, must continue their efforts during the preparation of your 1967 budget requests. With their help you must extend and enlarge upon the savings already identified in your cost reduction reports.

In the longer run, the planning-programing-budgeting system which the Budget Director outlined to you at the last Cabinet

993

meeting provides a good basis for a continuing search for lower priority programs. Where legislation is required to drop or reduce these programs, we will seek such legislation. The national interest must be our test of whether a program is continued.

2. *A renewed effort to hold down Federal employment.* In the next year there will be increasing upward pressure on Federal employment. We must redouble our efforts to economize on personnel costs.

Don't fill a single vacancy until you are sure it is absolutely necessary. Aggressively seek out labor-saving techniques—and don't be hesitant in introducing them. I personally watch each agency's employment figures and how well you are living within the ceilings we have established. I expect you to give this matter your personal attention.

3. *A renewed program to reduce travel costs.* At my request, the Budget Bureau issued, on August 23, a directive suggesting nine specific areas where travel costs might be reduced. I want you to get out this directive and read it again. We must be sure that every trip is necessary.

4. *We can all make do with a little bit less if we try.* The moratorium on the purchase of file cabinets has hurt no one. We can find other areas where we can postpone or reduce our purchases.

Shortly after assuming the Office of President, I announced that cost reduction would be a major role of my administration. I have reiterated this objective several times; I expect to reiterate it in the future. It will take persistent efforts by all of us to accomplish our objective of weeding out the old programs that need to make way for new and more urgent ones—to find ways of doing things cheaper and better. It must be the goal of every Federal official and employee. The objective will be accomplished as the product of hundreds of actions. We have demonstrated that it can be done and we must try much harder to do much more.

NOTE: On the same day the White House made public a list of examples of cost reduction actions in six Federal agencies, as follows:

Department of Agriculture, rate reduction under the Uniform Grain Storage Agreement—estimated first year savings of $15 million. Conversion of direct Federal rural housing loans to insured private loans—estimated first year savings of $273 million; savings in later years of $100 million.

Federal Aviation Agency, improved efficiency in the airways system—estimated savings of $11 million in air traffic control operations and $4 million in airways maintenance costs.

Department of Commerce, improved engineering of Tiros weather satellites—estimated savings of $15 million per year.

Department of the Treasury, Coast Guard vessel replacement—estimated savings of $2.9 million annually over the next 10 years.

Department of Housing and Urban Development, reduction of public housing expenses—estimated savings of $10 million.

Veterans Administration, mortgage loans to veterans—estimated savings of $40 million in 1966 (1 Weekly Comp. Pres. Docs., p. 264).

The Bureau of the Budget directive of August 23, 1965, on reduction of travel costs in Government (3 pp., processed), is in the form of a memorandum to heads of all executive departments and agencies and is signed by Elmer B. Staats, Acting Director of the Bureau of the Budget. See also Item 497.

513   Remarks at the Signing of the State Technical Services Act. *September* 14, 1965

Mr. Vice President, Secretary Connor, distinguished Members of the Congress and Governors, ladies and gentlemen:

The test of our generation will not be the accumulation of knowledge. In that, we have surpassed all the ages of man combined. Our test will be how well we apply that knowledge for the betterment of all mankind.

We are responding to this challenge.

Today we sign into law the State Technical Services Act. We are committing ourselves to an intelligent and an orderly application of the great technical and scientific breakthroughs of our time. We are recognizing that this Nation can no longer afford economic development on a helter-skelter basis.

Not very much has been written about this bill. But 20 years from now, Americans will look back on it as the "sleeper" of the 89th Congress.

This bill will do for American businessmen what the great Agricultural Extension Service has done for the American farmer. It will put into their hands the latest ideas and methods, the fruits of research and development.

It will result in the creation of new industries and the expansion of old ones.

It will speed the development of cheaper and better consumer products.

It will reduce the impact of technological changes on local economies.

It will help to diversify local industry.

It will assist in the retraining of workers whose skills are outmoded.

If we had had this legislation 25 or 30 years ago, we might have prevented the economic depression that today exists in Appalachia.

And if we use this bill effectively in the future, we can prevent more Appalachias from ever occurring.

But I want to make it clear this morning that the Federal Government does not want to run this program. We will provide matching grants. We will act, through the Department of Commerce, as a clearinghouse for the latest scientific developments.

But this must and will be a local program, spearheaded by local initiative and local imagination.

The vehicles for success will be 250 colleges and technical schools throughout the land. They will distribute the information. They will serve as the economic planning centers for their areas.

And the success or the failure of this program is therefore in the hands of the States and the local officials. I challenge you to take those tools of progress and to make them work.

I welcome those of you who have come here this morning to participate in this ceremony, and I thank those of you who helped make it possible.

NOTE: The President spoke at 9:50 a.m. in the East Room at the White House. In his opening words he referred to Vice President Hubert H. Humphrey and Secretary of Commerce John T. Connor.

As enacted, the State Technical Services Act of 1965 is Public Law 89–182 (79 Stat. 679).

514 Statement by the President to the Cabinet and Memorandum on Strengthening Academic Capability for Science.
September 14, 1965

THROUGHOUT the postwar years, it has been my abiding and actively-supported conviction that the policies of this Nation in support of the advance of science would have a decisive role in determining the extent to which we fulfill our potential as a Nation—

and a free society.

On occasion, during these years, there have appeared attitudes almost medieval in their myopia toward the meaning and promise of the growth of human knowledge. Happily, these attitudes have not prevailed and our national policies have been guided by reason, light, and faith in the future of man. As a result, American science today leads the world—free, unfettered, and devoted to the ends of bettering the condition of man in every land.

I say this, by way of preface, because I am proud of the part I have been privileged to play—in the Congress and as Vice President—in opening the doors through which we have moved to some of our most significant scientific gains. Now, in this Office I am determined that we shall marshal our resources and our wisdom to the fullest to assure the continuing strength and leadership of American science and to apply the information yielded by its inquiry to the problems which confront our society and our purposes in the world.

Our policies and attitudes in regard to science cannot satisfactorily be related solely to achievement of goals and ends we set for our research. Our vision in this regard is limited at best. We must, I believe, devote ourselves purposefully to developing and diffusing—throughout the Nation—a strong and solid scientific capability, especially in our many centers of advanced education. Our future must rest upon diversity of inquiry as well as the universality of capability.

This is very much a concern and a responsibility of the Federal Government and all the departments and agencies of the executive branch.

Today the Federal Government is spending $15 billion annually on research and development activities. Nine percent of this—$1.3 billion—is being spent in our universities on research grants and contracts. Additional sums are spent for educational purposes such as fellowship or training grants and the programs provided by the Higher Education Facilities Act or the National Defense Education Act.

The impact of these Federal funds is significant. They account for about two-thirds of the total research expenditures of colleges and universities. The manner in which such funds are spent clearly has a most important effect upon advanced education in this country and upon the future of our Nation's universities.

Almost all of the Federal research money is provided to produce results that are needed now and in the future to achieve our many national goals in health, in defense, in space, in agriculture, and so on. Of the total provided to universities, 34 percent comes from the National Institutes of Health, 23 percent from the Department of Defense, 9 percent from NASA, 6 percent from the AEC, and 4 percent from Agriculture. Only 13 percent is provided by the National Science Foundation—the only agency which supports science and science education as such.

The purpose of the new policy statement I am issuing today is to insure that our programs for Federal support of research in colleges and universities contribute more to the long-run strengthening of the universities and colleges so that these institutions can best serve the Nation in the years ahead.

At present, one-half of the Federal expenditures for research go to 20 major institutions, most of which were strong before the advent of Federal research funds. During the period of increasing Federal support since World War II, the number of institutions carrying out research and providing advanced education has grown impressively. Strong centers have developed in areas which were previously not well served. It is a particular purpose of this policy to accelerate this beneficial trend since the funds are still concentrated in too few institutions in too few areas of the country. We want to find excellence and build it up wherever it is found so that creative centers of excellence may grow in every part of the Nation.

Under this policy more support will be provided under terms which give the university and the investigator wider scope for inquiry, as contrasted with highly specific, narrowly defined projects. These and many more actions will increase the capacity of our universities to produce well-trained scientists and to serve as a source of the ideas on which our national welfare depends.

By adopting this policy, I am asking each agency and department with major research responsibilities to reexamine its practices in the financing of research. I want to be sure that, consistent with agency missions and objectives, all practical measures are taken to strengthen the institutions where research now goes on, and to help additional institutions to become more effective centers for teaching and research.

Memorandum for Heads of Departments and Agencies:

A strong and vital educational system is an essential part of the Great Society. In building our national educational system, we must bear in mind all of the parts, and all of the levels—from Head Start for preschool children to the most advanced university levels. At the apex of this educational pyramid, resting on the essential foundation provided for the lower levels, is the vital top segment where education and research become inseparable. The Federal Government has supported academic research in agriculture for over a half century and in the physical sciences, life sciences, and engineering since World War II; the returns on this national investment have been immense.

Of the $15 billion which the Federal Government is spending in research and development activities this year, $1.3, or about 9 percent, is spent in universities. The $1.3 billion, which includes only Federal research grants and contracts, accounts for about two-thirds of the total research expenditures of our American colleges and universities. Over 25,000 graduate students in engineering, mathematics, physical and life sciences are supported indirectly by employment under these research grants and contracts. Plainly the Federal expenditures have a major effect on the development of our higher educational system.

The strength of the research and development programs of the major agencies, and hence their ability to meet national needs, depends heavily upon the total strength of our university system. Research supported to further agency missions should be administered not only with a view to producing specific results, but also with a view to strengthening academic institutions and increasing the number of institutions capable of performing research of high quality.

The functions of the Federal agencies in relation to the strengthening of academic institutions are as follows:

a. The National Science Foundation continues to have responsibility for augmenting the research capabilities of academic institutions in all fields of science through the support of basic research and research facilities and through measures for improving the quality of education in the sciences;

b. The Department of Health, Education, and Welfare will contribute to the overall development of colleges and universities and to the development of health professional schools, particularly through programs of the Office of Education and the Public Health Service;

c. All Federal agencies with substantial research and development programs have an interest and need to develop academic capabilities for research and scientific education as a part of their research missions.

To the fullest extent compatible with their primary interests in specific fields of science, their basic statutes, and their needs for research results of high quality, all Federal agencies should act so as to:

a. Encourage the maintenance of outstanding quality in science and science education in those universities where it exists;

b. Provide research funds to academic institutions under conditions affording them the opportunity to improve and extend their programs for research and science education and to develop the potentialities for high quality research of groups and individuals, including capable younger faculty members;

c. Contribute to the improvement of potentially strong universities through measures such as:

—Giving consideration, where research capability of comparable quality exists, to awarding grants and contracts to institutions not now heavily engaged in Federal research programs;

—Assisting such institutions or parts of institutions in strengthening themselves while performing research relevant to agency missions, by such means as establishing university-administered programs in specialized

areas relevant to the missions of the agencies.

Funds for these purposes should be provided on a scale and under conditions appropriate to the mission of an agency and in accordance with any Government-wide policy guidelines which may be established.

Departments and agencies should carefully assess the degree to which and the manner in which their existing programs support this policy, and when indicated, should use a larger proportion of their research funds in accordance with the intent of the policy. The means for attaining this objective will be determined by each department and agency. In carrying out the policy, the various Federal agencies supporting research at a university should act in concert to a greater degree in making decisions, so as to make the university better able to meet the collective needs of the agencies and to make the Federal support most effective in strengthening the university.

My Special Assistant for Science and Technology, Dr. Donald Hornig, with the help of the Federal Council for Science and Technology, will follow the response of the departments and agencies to this policy. I have asked him to obtain monthly progress reports and submit them to me.

515   Remarks at a Meeting With the Congressional Fellows.
September 15, 1965

Chairman Macy, Congressional Fellows, and friends:

Since assuming the Presidency nearly 2 years ago, I have made 370 appointments to the executive branch of the Government. About half of those selected for these positions were career Government employees. This will continue to be the trend for the future. Where talent and imagination and experience exist in this Government, we are

going to seek it out.

You are such a group. You have been sought out on the basis of your achievements. Your horizons have been broadened. Your future is one of opportunity. It is entirely possible that among you today are Cabinet officers and heads of agencies for tomorrow.

The year's experience that you have just received in the Congressional Fellowship program represents an invaluable addition to your careers. No high Government official can be completely effective if he does not understand the role of Congress in our democracy.

Too often in our history the executive and the legislative branches have been reduced to suspicion and to petty bickering. And too often the cause of progress has suffered because of it.

Although our Constitution divides us into separate branches, it charges all of us with the same mission—that is, to serve the American public. Some disagreement between the branches of Government is quite natural. But cooperation between the branches of Government is quite imperative.

I expect every member of my administration to understand this and to apply this to the day-to-day operations of the Government.

I am not just talking about congressional relations, I am talking about understanding the job that the Congress has to do. And I am talking about trying to help the Congress do that job that it has to do.

We have entered a new era, I think, of respect and good will between the executive and legislative branches of the Government. I intend to do everything I can to encourage this respect and to promote this good will.

Because of the experience that you have gained in the Congressional Fellowship program, I am charging each of you with the responsibility of helping me in this important task. You have gained new insights and new attitudes. So your task now is to pass them to the Federal executives and the managers with whom you work.

Further, I am today placing renewed emphasis upon the Congressional Fellows program. I want every department and I want every large agency of the Government to have at least one of its most promising young executives in this program next year. And next year when I address the group of Fellows, I want to be able to look out and I want to see some pretty faces out there. There hasn't been a woman enrolled in the 4-year history of the program. I don't like that and I don't really see any reason for it. In fact, I deplore it.

I am glad you are here. You cheer me with your zeal and with your purpose. I have not the slightest idea but what you will find in the years to come that this has been a great experience for you and for your country. And next year's program is going to be better even than this year's.

Thank you very much.

NOTE: The President spoke at 11:45 a.m. in the Cabinet Room at the White House. In his opening words he referred to John W. Macy, Jr., Chairman of the Civil Service Commission.

In announcing the meeting Joseph Laitin, an assistant press secretary, stated that the Congressional Fellows, a group of approximately 30, were career civil service employees detailed for a short period to Members of Congress and congressional committees to learn about the legislative branch of the Government.

---

516 Remarks to the Delegates to the Conference on World Peace Through Law. *September 16, 1965*

Mr. Rhyne, Chief Justice Warren, Mr. Thompson, Attorney General Katzenbach, delegates, my fellow Americans:

I need not here reaffirm my Nation's con-

tinuing dedication to the rule of law. We will work to extend it to the relations between countries. For we believe that is the surest road to a fruitful and a secure peace.

Therefore, we who seek a world of law must labor to understand the foundation on which law can rest. We must set to work to build it. For if the rule of law is an ideal, the establishment of that rule is the practical work of practical men. We must not let the difficulties of this task lead us into the twin dangers of cynicism or unreasoning faith.

For the fact is that if law cannot yet solve the problems of a tormented earth, it is steadily growing in importance and in necessity.

The first condition of law is justice. That law which oppresses the weak, or denies the fair claims of the poor, will prove a flimsy barrier against the rising storm of man's demand for justice.

Law must not be the prisoner of plunder or privilege.

Law is not the soothing keeper of the status quo. Law is an instrument in the battle for the hopes of man. And if it is not fashioned as such an instrument, then no matter how beautifully and logically framed, it will yield to violence and to terror.

So if we, the fortunate of the earth, would ask other people to submit to law, then we ourselves must assume some responsibility for peoples' liberty and peoples' well-being.

International law has been primarily concerned with relations between States. In pursuit of justice, it must now concern itself more than in the past with the welfare of people.

So I look forward to the day when the relief of hunger and misery and ignorance in all parts of this world will be fixed in legal obligation—as it now is in my own country.

When our world law embodies the right of the despairing to hope, and the responsi-bility of the fortunate to help, then it will be strengthened a thousandfold in the cause of peace.

If world conditions were largely satisfactory it would not be difficult to evolve a rule of law. But we do not live in a satisfactory world. It is stained with evil and injustice, by ruthless ambition and passionate conflict. Only by fighting these forces do we help build a base on which the temple of law may rest.

The second condition of law is institutions. Through them law receives meaning and force. And institutions themselves, through their own actions, help to make new law. The United Nations General Assembly has done this in peacekeeping.

The past 20 years have seen an abundant flowering of new international structures. From the Common Market and NATO, to the IBRD and the Asian Development Bank, order and legal process have been imposed upon spreading segments of the affairs of countries.

Some of these institutions have played a large role in the prosperity of the West and in the keeping of the peace.

Others contribute to the progress of the developing countries.

The United States has helped to build many of these organizations. Their strength represents a victory for the cause you represent—a legal order contributing to the prosperity of each and to the peace of all. My country intends to protect and strengthen those institutions, sharing the task with all who share our common purpose.

Central to the hope of world peace through law is the United Nations. Since its beginning, dozens of disputes, many laced with violence, have come before the world assembly. Some have remained unsolved. Many have found a settlement sufficient to allow mankind to move forward in peace. And in some places the United Nations was able to prevent conflict and bloodshed.

I hope we can strengthen the United Nations—not simply as a forum for debate, but as an arena for the solution of disputes.

That is why I asked a great Justice of our Supreme Court, Arthur Goldberg, to become America's Ambassador to the world body. The life of Ambassador Goldberg has been devoted to resolving disputes between those who at first believed that they could not yield one iota from their positions, and who came at last to sign a common agreement.

And my country will fully support the efforts of the Secretary General to bring peace between the great nations of India and Pakistan.

And perhaps in the United Nations, and with the patient effort of individual countries, we can also halt the terrible arms race which threatens to engulf the earth. Perhaps we can succeed through an effective treaty preventing the spread of nuclear weapons, through extending the test ban treaty, by obtaining an agreement halting production of fissionable material for use in nuclear weapons and allocating substantial portions of this material to peaceful uses, by agreeing to reverse the arms race in strategic nuclear weapons and delivery vehicles, and by working toward general and complete disarmament under effective international controls, which must be the world's goal.

The third condition of law is acceptance. World law, if it is to bring world order, must reflect the judgment and the felt desires of men and of nations. When law ignores this—as we have seen in our own history—it itself is ignored.

I think that we may be evolving a world consensus on which law can stand. The mass of mankind is slowly realizing the dangers of conflict and the futility of war. They are accepting their responsibility to relieve their own poverty and the misery of their fellow inhabitants of the earth. They are finding—in knowledge and fear and pain—that their common interest lies in common acceptance of their own obligations and the rights of others.

We can see this in a hundred small ways. During the past year the United States was present at 629 international conferences. In the short time since I became President the United States has participated in more such conferences than during the entire first 150 years of our history.

Of course, the great issues and the great dangers are not resolved. In the past 12 months there is not a single continent that has been spared violence. In the past 2,000 years there has hardly been a decade without war.

If this was all, the future would look dark indeed. But there is another and a brighter thread which runs through the history of the race. It is man's drive to create and to live in harmony with his fellows. And that is what we call civilization.

Law is the great civilizing machinery. It liberates the desires to build and it subdues the desire to destroy. And if war can tear us apart, law can unite us—out of fear or love or reason, or all three.

World peace through world law will not come quickly. We must work, in a variety of ways, to create the vital conditions which may bring us to that day, to build the justice which forms it and the institutions which give it life, and to find the understanding acceptance which will make it work. This means we must be willing to accept small advances and limited goals. But the final objective is the largest and the most elusive that man has ever known: peace. Peace which is not simply the absence of conflict or even of fear—but peace which is the framework for the fulfillment of human possibility.

How can we dare to hope for that which has always escaped mankind? Perhaps it is because our invention draws us together to the point where any war is civil war. Perhaps the vastness of our destructive power makes us shrink from conflict. Perhaps, under the horror and the murder of this carnage-filled century, civilization has been slowly flowering, leading us toward victory in the endless battle between man's love for his fellow and man's desire to destroy him.

Law is the greatest human invention. All the rest give him mastery over his world, but law gives him mastery over himself.

There are those who say the rule of law is a fruitless and utopian dream. It is true that if it comes, it will come slowly. It will come through the practical and the wise resolution of numberless problems. But to deny the possibility is to deny peace itself and to deny that flowering of the spirit which we must believe God meant for man.

I do not deny it. I believe in it. And so do you. And if others will join us, then the time may yet come when you and your colleagues will be honored as pathfinders toward the final armistice in man's war against himself.

NOTE: The President spoke at 10:30 a.m. in the Washington Hilton Hotel. In his opening words he referred to Charles S. Rhyne, President of the World Peace Through Law Center and former President of the American Bar Association, Earl Warren, Chief Justice of the United States, William S. Thompson, Secretary General of the World Peace Through Law Center, and Attorney General Nicholas deB. Katzenbach.

The conference was held in Washington September 12–18, 1965.

517   Message to the Shah of Iran on the 25th Anniversary of His Reign. *September 16, 1965*

Your Imperial Majesty:

In the quarter century since Your Majesty ascended the throne of Iran, the world has lived through times of cataclysmic and destructive war and of hopeful and, I sincerely pray, enduring peace. The friendship between Iran and the United States, strong and enduring, has been enriched by the shared experiences of our two nations. The program of reform and renewal which you have initiated in your country has demonstrated your wisdom and compassion, your perception and statesmanship. The United States is proud to have been associated in your efforts to maintain the freedom of your people and to establish for your country an honored place in the world community of peace-loving nations.

Your Majesty can take great pride from the record of dangers met, obstacles overcome, and progress achieved during this turbulent period of world history. The people of the United States of America join me in expressing to Your Majesty our friendship and high regard and our warm personal wishes to you and your family on this most auspicious occasion.

Sincerely,

LYNDON B. JOHNSON

[His Imperial Majesty, Mohammad Reza Shah Pahlavi, Shahanshah of Iran, Tehran, Iran]

NOTE: The message and a gift for the Shah were presented by the President to His Excellency Khosro Khosrovani, Iranian Ambassador to the United States, shortly before noon in the President's office.

518 Statement by the President Upon Signing the Military
Construction Authorization Act. *September 16, 1965*

I HAVE today signed into law the Military Construction Authorization Act for fiscal year 1966.

Few measures I have signed this year have so refreshed my faith in our institutions of government. Men of reason and good will in the legislative and executive branches have fashioned an acceptable bill, one that will strengthen the national security and contribute to the defense of freedom.

Less than a month ago I returned a similar measure to the Congress without my approval, because I felt that one of its provisions was repugnant to the Constitution. That provision required a lengthy waiting period, limited to one period of the year, before an economy could be achieved by the closing, or substantial reduction in mission, of a military base.

In my message of disapproval I said, "I do not mean to imply that a reasonable reporting provision, consistent with the legislative powers of the Congress, would warrant a veto."

The Congress has speedily enacted a new bill, containing such a reasonable reporting provision. I am happy to approve the bill, and I congratulate the Members of the Congress on the promptness with which they adopted this perfected measure.

NOTE: As enacted, the Military Construction Authorization Act of 1966 is Public Law 89-188 (79 Stat. 793).

For the President's veto of a similar measure on August 21, 1965, see Item 440.

519 Remarks at the Smithson Bicentennial Celebration.
September 16, 1965

Mr. Chief Justice, Secretary Ripley, Dr. Carmichael, Bishop Moore, Reverend Campbell, ladies and gentlemen, distinguished scholars from 80 nations:

Amid this pomp and pageantry we have gathered to celebrate a man about whom we know very little but to whom we owe very much. James Smithson was a scientist who achieved no great distinction. He was an Englishman who never visited the United States. He never even expressed a desire to do so.

But this man became our Nation's first great benefactor. He gave his entire fortune to establish this Institution which would serve "for the increase and diffusion of knowledge among men."

He had a vision which lifted him ahead of his time—or at least of some politicians of his time. One illustrious United States Senator argued that it was beneath the dignity of the country to accept such gifts from foreigners. Congress debated 8 long years before deciding to receive Smithson's bequest.

JAMES SMITHSON'S LEGACY

Yet James Smithson's life and legacy brought meaning to three ideas more powerful than anyone at that time ever dreamed.

The first idea was that learning respects no geographic boundaries. The Institution bearing his name became the first agency in the United States to promote scientific and scholarly exchange with all the nations of the world.

The second idea was that partnership between Government and private enterprise can serve the greater good of both. The Smithsonian Institution started a new kind of venture in this country, chartered by act of Congress, maintained by both public funds and private contributions. It inspired a relationship which has grown and flowered in a thousand different ways.

Finally, the Institution financed by Smithson breathed life in the idea that the growth and the spread of learning must be the first work of a nation that seeks to be free.

These ideas have not always gained easy acceptance among those employed in my line of work. The Government official must cope with the daily disorder that he finds in the world around him.

But today, the official, the scholar, and the scientist cannot settle for limited objectives. We must pursue knowledge no matter what the consequences. We must value the tried less than the true.

To split the atom, to launch the rocket, to explore the innermost mysteries and the outermost reaches of the universe—these are your God-given chores. And even when you risk bringing fresh disorder to the politics of men and nations, these explorations still must go on.

IDEAS, NOT ARMAMENTS

The men who founded our country were passionate believers in the revolutionary power of ideas.

They knew that once a nation commits itself to the increase and diffusion of knowledge, the real revolution begins. It can never be stopped.

In my own life, I have had cause again and again to bless the chance events which started me as a teacher. In our country and in our time we have recognized, with new passion, that learning is basic to our hopes for America. It is the taproot which gives sustaining life to all of our purposes. And whatever we seek to do to wage the war on poverty or to set new goals for health and happiness, to curb crime or try to bring beauty to our cities and our countryside—all of these, and more, depend on education.

But the legacy we inherit from James Smithson cannot be limited to these shores. He called for the increase and diffusion of knowledge among men, not just Americans, not just Anglo-Saxons, and not just the citizens of the Western World—but all men everywhere.

The world we face on his bicentennial anniversary makes that mandate much more urgent than it ever was. For we know today that certain truths are self-evident in every nation on this earth; that ideas, not armaments, will shape our lasting prospects for peace; that the conduct of our foreign policy will advance no faster than the curriculum of our classrooms; that the knowledge of our citizens is the one treasure which grows only when it is shared.

It would profit us little to limit the world's exchange to those who can afford it. We must extend the treasure to those lands where learning is still a luxury for the few.

Today, more than 700 million adults—4 out of 10 of the world's population—dwell in darkness where they cannot read or write. Almost half the nations of this globe suffer from illiteracy among half or more of their people. And unless the world can find a way to extend the light, the force of that darkness may ultimately engulf us all.

A NEW BEGINNING

For our part, this Government and this Nation are prepared to join in finding the way. During recent years we have made many hopeful beginnings. But we can and we must do more. That is why I have directed a special task force within my administration to recommend a broad and long-range plan of worldwide educational endeavor.

Secretary of State Dean Rusk has accepted my request to chair this task force. Secretary John Gardner of the Department of Health, Education, and Welfare has agreed to serve on it. Both these men have proved, in their past careers, how great is their devotion to international education.

I intend to call on leaders in both public and private enterprise to join with us in mapping this effort.

We must move ahead on every front and at every level of learning. We can support Secretary Ripley's dream of creating a center here at the Smithsonian where great scholars from every nation will come and collaborate. At a more junior level, we can promote the growth of the school-to-school program started under Peace Corps auspices so that our children may learn about—and care about—each other.

AN INTERNATIONAL EFFORT

We mean to show that this Nation's dream of a Great Society does not stop at the water's edge: and that it is not just an American dream. All are welcome to share in it. All are invited to contribute to it.

Together we must embark on a new and a noble adventure:

First, to assist the education efforts of the developing nations and the developing regions.

Second, to help our schools and universities increase their knowledge of the world and the people who inhabit it.

Third, to advance the exchange of students and teachers who travel and work outside their native lands.

Fourth, to increase the free flow of books and ideas and art, of works of science and imagination.

And, fifth, to assemble meetings of men and women from every discipline and every culture to ponder the common problems of mankind.

In all these endeavors, I pledge that the United States will play its full role.

By January, I intend to present such a program to the Congress.

Despite the noise of daily events, history is made by men and the ideas of men. We—and only we—can generate growing light in our universe, or we can allow the darkness to gather.

De Tocqueville challenged us more than a century ago: "Men cannot remain strangers to each other, or be ignorant of what is taking place in any corner of the globe." We must banish the strangeness and the ignorance.

In all we do toward one another, we must try—and try again—to live the words of the prophet: "I shall light a candle of understanding in thine heart which shall not be put out."

NOTE: The President spoke at 4:33 p.m. on the south side of the Mall in front of the Smithsonian Institution. In his opening words he referred to Earl Warren, Chief Justice of the United States, Dr. S. Dillon Ripley, Secretary of the Smithsonian Institution, Dr. Leonard Carmichael, Vice President of the National Geographic Society and former Secretary of the Smithsonian Institution, the Right Reverend Paul Moore, Jr., Suffragan Bishop of Washington (Episcopal), and the Very Reverend Gerard J. Campbell, President of Georgetown University.

The group was composed of more than 500 scholars and scientists representing 90 countries. After the President's remarks they moved in formal academic procession across the Mall to an area behind the Museum of Natural History where some 3,000 spectators listened to other speeches and to music provided by the U.S. Marine Band.

The ceremony marked the beginning of the celebration of the 200th anniversary of the birth of James Smithson for whom the Institution is named.

The report of the task force, chaired by Secretary of State Dean Rusk, was not made public by the

White House. Its recommendations were embodied in the President's message to Congress of February 2, 1966, on international education and health programs (2 Weekly Comp. Pres. Docs., p. 158).

The Smithson bicentennial celebration was proclaimed by the President on August 13, 1965 (Proc. 3667; 1 Weekly Comp. Pres. Docs., p. 96; 30 F.R. 10281; 3 CFR, 1965 Supp., p. 53).

520 Message to Chancellor Erhard on His Victory in the German Elections. *September 20, 1965*

HEARTIEST congratulations on your great victory. I look forward to an early chance to meet with you again and to discuss our great common tasks in working for the peace of Europe, the reunion of Germany, and the steady growth of the Atlantic community.

LYNDON B. JOHNSON

NOTE: The message was read by Joseph Laitin, an assistant press secretary, at the 4:35 p.m. news briefing on Monday, September 20, 1965, in the Press Secretary's office at the White House. It was not made public in the form of a White House press release.

521 Remarks at the Signing of a Bill Establishing the Assateague Island Seashore National Park. *September 21, 1965*

Mr. Secretary of the Interior, Senator Jackson, Chairman Aspinall, Governor Tawes, Members of Congress, ladies and gentlemen:

We are living in the century of change.

But if future generations are to remember us more with gratitude than with sorrow, we must achieve more than just the miracles of technology. We must also leave them a glimpse of the world as God really made it, not just as it looked when we got through with it.

Thanks to this bill that I will sign this morning, we can now do that with Assateague Island. It stretches some 33 miles along the Maryland and Virginia coastline. This is the last undeveloped seashore between Massachusetts and North Carolina.

One-fifth of all the people in our Nation live within an easy day's drive of Assateague. And now as the result of your labors—you, the farsighted Members of Congress—these wide sandy beaches will be the people's to enjoy forever.

They were almost lost. The National Park Service, as Secretary Udall will testify, first recommended an Assateague National Seashore 30 years ago, back in 1935. Many Congressmen and Senators have come and gone since that time. Many bills were introduced in the Congress. Many proposals were made. But few proposals were acted upon and it took us 30 years to make this dream a reality.

Sometimes I think we must learn to move faster. Our population is growing every year, but our shoreline is not. Of the more than 3,700 miles of shoreline along our Atlantic and gulf coasts, only 105 miles—really less than 3 percent—are available to us today for the public to use.

What the Good Lord once gave in greatest abundance have now become rare and very precious possessions. Clear water, warm sandy beaches are a nation's real treasure.

For the rest of this century, the shoreline within reach of the major cities of this country just must be preserved and must be maintained primarily for the recreation of our people. This cannot be done by the Federal Government alone. Conservationists, State governments led by men like Governor Tawes, municipalities led by my good friend Mayor McKeldin and others, the States and the cities working with the Federal Government—all of us must put the bit in our teeth and act, and we must begin to act now if this basic heritage is to be preserved for future generations.

We have already accomplished much. Last year we acquired Fire Island National Seashore in New York—and it is within easy reach of one out of every four Americans in this country. Like Assateague, which we acquire today, Fire Island symbolizes the new philosophy we have in this country of conservation. We are going to acquire our places of recreation where they will do the greatest good for the greatest number of people.

The year I was born, 57 years ago, President Theodore Roosevelt held a great conference on conservation here in the White House. He was a member of another party. He is remembered as the conservation President, and he and the other great conservationist, Gifford Pinchot, rescued millions of acres of Western wilderness from commercial exploitation.

Well, I grew up in that West. I know what that heritage means. And I pledge you that so long as I am your President, I mean to preserve and I mean to extend that heritage for all of our people, East as well as West, North as well as South. I intend to seek out what can still be saved, and with your help, will try to preserve it for unborn generations. I intend to find those oases of natural beauty which should never have been lost in the first place, and to reclaim them for all the people of this country.

Conservation has been in eclipse in this country ever since Theodore Roosevelt's day. Members of the House will listen with care because conservation had barely gotten off the ground when Uncle Joe Cannon, the Speaker of the House in those days, issued one of his many ultimatums, and he said: "Not one cent for scenery."

Well, those days are gone and forgotten, and we are going to start repealing Cannon's law here today. We are declaring a new doctrine of conservation. And I hope—before my allotted time has run out—I hope to see the best and the fairest regions of America a matter of daily concern among the leaders of both parties and among the representatives of all this Government.

I hope to see the preservation—or the reclamation—of those areas become an annual concern of the Congress.

I hope that we will be here several times each session, adding to our treasure and to our national assets. I want to see our unrivaled power to create matched by America's equal power to conserve.

We have already gone far in that direction. We have almost doubled the portion of our precious shoreline in our national park system. And every Member of the Congress that has had a part in that can take great pride this morning. Almost 320,000 acres of sand dunes and beaches are now a perpetual possession of all our people.

Nearly 27 million acres of the most beautiful land in America have been set aside for the joy and the pleasure of present and future generations. I have asked the conservation and park and seashore people to put under the microscope every acre that has been declared surplus by our great Defense Department to see if somehow, somewhere the little people of America might not be able to enjoy this in the few hours of relaxation that is theirs on a weekend.

Most of this would have been impossible except for a conservation-minded Congress led by competent, able, and thorough men. And that is the kind of Congress that we have. The 88th Congress passed more than 30 major conservation bills. And I salute the Senate and the House, and the Secretary of Interior for his leadership in that field. The 89th Congress is already adding magnificently to that record. And we haven't finished it yet.

These, yes, have been memorable years in the history of conservation. But the work is unfinished. We have shown what can be done. And if we can continue the same superb record which we have already begun, then the day will soon come when we can say to our people, "Your heritage is secure."

It was over a hundred years ago that Henry David Thoreau looked out upon the beauty of America and wrote: "It is a noble country where we dwell, fit for a stalwart race to summer in."

So it remains for us, who live in the summer of our greatness as a Nation, to preserve

both the vision and the beauty which gave it rise.

And I hope the picture of those of you who have made this possible, who are gathered here for this event this morning, will be hung in prominent places in this land where those who come after you can see the wisdom of your vision and your efforts.

Thank you very much.

NOTE: The President spoke at 9:50 a.m. in the East Room at the White House. In his opening words he referred to Secretary of the Interior Stewart L. Udall, Senator Henry M. Jackson of Washington, Representative Wayne N. Aspinall of Colorado, Chairman of the House Interior and Insular Affairs Committee, and Governor J. Millard Tawes of Maryland.

During his remarks the President referred to, among others, Mayor Theodore R. McKeldin of Baltimore and Joseph G. Cannon, Representative from Illinois 1873–1891, 1893–1913, and 1915–1923, who served as Speaker of the House of Representatives 1903–1911.

As enacted, the bill (S. 20) is Public Law 89–195 (79 Stat. 824).

522 Statement by the President on Federal Grants for Academic Research. *September* 21, 1965

THE PARTNERSHIP of the Federal Government and the Nation's universities in carrying forward man's quest for knowledge has produced enormous dividends in the past two decades.

It has been an enlightened partnership. It must remain so. Creative research through free inquiry is the working way to new greatness in our society. It can open roads to

—man's mastery of his environment,

—sufficient food, water, and energy to sustain the massed population that is making ours a crowded planet,

—the building of corridors linking the earth to the stars,

—ultimate victory over the tragedy of mental and physical afflictions, and

—progress in helping man live in peace with his neighbor.

So as a Nation we are committed to strengthen and nourish what Vannevar Bush once called "Science, the Endless Frontier."

Federal grants for academic research perform an indispensable role in strengthening science education in our colleges and universities.

I am happy to see that the Congress is acting on my recommendation to remove the statutory restrictions which have restricted us in reimbursing colleges and universities for the indirect costs of doing research under Federal grants. The Congress is acting wisely. The Government and the research community both owe thanks—to the men and women in the Congress who are making this progress possible and to citizens like yourselves who have helped your Government to understand the needs of the academic institutions.

The universities will, under the new legislation, share to some extent in the cost of research projects. We intend to see that this requirement is administered—as I know the Congress meant it to be—in a constructive and reasonable way.

Our hopes demand new excellence in academic science. It must have the talent, the resources, the faith, and the freedom to prosper.

Government's part in meeting this challenge is of critical importance. We will help

—to bring educational opportunities to our gifted young people,

—to build the new facilities that higher education needs,

—to create new centers of excellence, and

—to meet the costs of creative scientific research.

I know that America's colleges and universities, which you gentlemen represent, will continue to help your country in every possible way.

NOTE: The President's statement was made public following a meeting with the following representatives of university boards of trustees: Juan Trippe, Yale; Arnold Beckman, California Tech; Arthur Dean, Cornell; R. Keith Kane, Harvard; Marion Folsom, Rochester; Maurice P. Moore, Columbia; Bryant Leeb, Princeton; and David Packard, Stanford.

The White House stated that the purpose of the meeting was to discuss the removal of the ceilings that had heretofore been applied on overhead. In the past, because of stipulations in appropriation bills, the Government had been restricted to paying 15 (later 20) percent of overhead costs. The last of these stipulations had been removed that day by the conference committee dealing with the military appropriations bill. Now that the restrictions had been removed, the universities would no longer find it necessary to take funds from administrative sources or faculty salaries to pay overhead costs, which had been as high as 35 to 40 percent of the cost on some projects.

---

523 Message to the Ninth General Conference of the International Atomic Energy Agency. *September 21, 1965*

I WELCOME this opportunity to speak, through Chairman Seaborg, to the delegates to the Ninth General Conference of the IAEA. I believe it is significant that you are meeting this year in Tokyo, the capital of a nation whose people have made such remarkable progress through the peaceful development of science and technology.

Today we realize, more than ever before, the power of science. We also realize that the mighty force of science is not the domain of any one nation. Its great knowledge springs from sources in many lands. Its fullest development demands international responsibility and the cooperation of all men. This is the reason for the existence of the International Atomic Energy Agency. You are directing the atom, the greatest source of power which man has ever wrested from nature, towards peace, towards the fulfillment of human need.

Since its inception in 1957, the IAEA has made noteworthy progress. In organizing and implementing international programs of scientific and technological cooperation, it has shown the world that men gain far more by sharing their knowledge and tools than by using them alone in secrecy and isolation. The IAEA has offered the advanced countries and their lesser developed neighbors and friends opportunities to work together and to share the scientific developments of many nations.

But the IAEA also has the solemn duty—and the unique opportunity—to assure the world that materials and equipment employed for peaceful uses of atomic energy are not used for any military purpose. Prevention of the spread of atomic weapons is one of the most important tasks of our times. It is my deep conviction that the IAEA, through its safeguards system, can make a crucial contribution to achievement of this goal. The United States Government is pledged to do all in its power to assure the success of the Agency's system. I urge every member state to give its support to the Agency system in principle and in practice.

There must be no resting. The work which you have been doing must be carried on with increasing effort and support. There is no standing still in your twofold task of keeping the peaceful atom peaceful and directing its enormous energy toward productive uses.

I take this opportunity to renew my country's pledge to assist the International Atomic Energy Agency in the full pursuit of those benefits which the peaceful atom can bestow.

With gratitude for your past accomplishments, I send you the best wishes of the people of the United States for your future endeavors.

NOTE: The President's message was read to the conference on September 22 by Glenn T. Seaborg, Chairman of the Atomic Energy Commission, who served as U.S. representative at the conference. The conference was held in Tokyo September 21–30, 1965.

524 Statement by the President on the Cease-Fire Agreements by India and Pakistan. *September 22, 1965*

I SPEAK for every American when I commend the statesmanship and restraint shown by the leaders of Pakistan and India in their acceptance of the cease-fire call of the United Nations Security Council. The leadership shown in both nations thus takes us a long step away from the terrible dangers which have threatened the subcontinent of Asia.

On behalf of the American people, I want to express our deep appreciation and gratitude to Secretary General U Thant for his fairness and firmness in the service of peace in these last weeks. I am especially proud of our own gifted Ambassador Arthur Goldberg and members of his new U.N. team. As President of the Security Council he has given his able and untiring support to the efforts of the Secretary General.

We now hope that both nations, in the spirit of the Security Council resolution, will move forward to peaceful settlement of their outstanding differences. The job of the U.N. has just begun. We will fully support it every step of the way by our actions and our words.

NOTE: The statement was read by Bill D. Moyers, Special Assistant to the President, at his news conference at 11:30 a.m. on Wednesday, September 22, 1965, in his office at the White House. It was not made public in the form of a White House press release.

The longstanding dispute between India and Pakistan over Kashmir led in August 1965 to increasing violations of the 1949 Kashmir Cease-Fire Line—crossing of armed personnel from Pakistan into Indian-held Kashmir, Indian retaliation against the other side of the line—and the conflict escalated in September into 3 weeks of open warfare in Kashmir and the Punjab. Working through the U.N. Security Council, the United States and other powers sought a cease-fire. U.S. Ambassador Goldberg, who was President of the Security Council, played an important role in ensuing diplomatic efforts, and U.N. Secretary General U Thant himself went to the subcontinent on a peace mission which resulted in the cease-fire of September 22.

525 Memorandum to Federal Agencies on Voluntary Blood Donations. *September 22, 1965*

[Released September 22, 1965. Dated September 17, 1965]

Memorandum for the Heads of Executive Departments and Agencies:

In recent times we have made great progress through the enlightened legislation passed by Congress to provide better health and medical programs for the American people. In this we are waging a relentless fight on many of the nation's health problems such as cancer and heart disease.

One of the essential elements in the practice of modern medicine is the continuing availability of whole blood and blood derivatives in adequate amounts throughout the nation. I, therefore, urge all Federal employees to fulfill their citizenship responsibility by serving as voluntary blood donors through their Red Cross blood centers and community blood banks. In this way, they will be materially assisting the crusade for better health and medical care for the nation.

I will appreciate your personal cooperation by urging continuing participation of your department personnel wherever assigned.

LYNDON B. JOHNSON

526 Statement by the President Following the Signing of Law Enforcement Assistance Bills. *September 22, 1965*

THE CONTROL of crime is a major target of this administration.

The Great Society we are striving to build cannot become a reality unless we strike at the roots of crime, and strike again until we have brought it under our control.

We labor for that day when every man can satisfy his basic needs and those of his family; when every child has a chance to develop his mind and enlarge his spirit to the limits of his being; when the slow killers—want, ignorance, and prejudice—are finally contained.

But if we reach that day, and still walk in terror through the public streets, our labors will have been futile. The taste of affluence would soon sour with fear. The common criminal would come to dominate our affairs, as no malign power, foreign or domestic, has ever done.

No more bitter irony could be imagined than this—that a people so committed to the quest for human dignity should have to pursue that quest in trembling behind locked doors.

We are determined that this shall not happen.

Yet the crime rate continues to rise. Our parks are deserted. Our storekeepers weigh the dangers of arming themselves against the dangers of attack. Crime and violence in the suburbs increase even more rapidly than in the central cities.

Until every woman in this land can walk the streets of her city at night, unafraid and unharmed, then we have work to do in law enforcement.

Out of this conviction, I submitted last March to the Congress a message on law enforcement. Yesterday and today I have signed into law two important instruments in our search for better ways to insure the supremacy—not of fear but of the law.

One authorizes funds for the Commission

on Law Enforcement and the Administration of Justice. That Commission has been appointed to evaluate the many elements and types of crime—and their causes.

Its mission is to delve into the alarm, the terror, the human and financial cost that makes up 20th century crime. Its purpose is to develop facts, and having done so, to translate facts into active programs that attack the springs of criminal behavior.

It will consider the problems of crime prevention; the needs of law enforcement; the tasks of administering criminal justice in our courts; the effectiveness of our systems of corrections and rehabilitation.

The members of the Commission are among our most dedicated citizens. They have already begun their momentous work. At their first meeting in Washington 2 weeks ago, they demonstrated their seriousness of purpose.

While the life of the Commission is 18 months, its Chairman, Attorney General Katzenbach, has reported to me that the members are determined to make specific proposals during the course of their work and expect to make the first such recommendation in a few months.

Our efforts against crime must not, however, be limited to developing long-range programs. We must also take prompt, direct action to halt the immediate suffering which lawlessness brings to our citizens. It is my devout hope that the Law Enforcement Assistance Act I have signed today will give us the means to accelerate the fight against crime now.

This act will make funds available to States, localities, and private organizations to improve methods of law enforcement, court administration, and prison operation. For years we have provided Federal assistance in the fields of housing, employment, mental health, education, transportation, and welfare. Because the anchor of society must be an abiding respect for law and order, it is appropriate that the Federal Government provide material aid to resist crime and promote the rule of law on the local level.

We are not dealing here in subsidies. The basic responsibility for dealing with local crime and criminals is, must be, and remains local. But the Federal Government can provide an infusion of ideas and support for research, for experiments, for new programs.

The policeman is the frontline soldier in our war against crime.

He bears a burden which increases each day. We must give him modern training, organization, and equipment if he is to succeed in saving our cities from the malignancy of crime. This is a major objective of the Law Enforcement Assistance Act.

We recognize that speedy justice is both an essential of fairness and a meaningful deterrent to crime; yet we have permitted our criminal courts to flounder in delay, lack of dignity, and the tortuous disposition of criminal cases. Swift, fair, and effective justice is an objective of the Law Enforcement Assistance Act.

We believe rehabilitation is indispensable if we are to break the cycle of crime by convicted offenders. Yet, too often, we offer only four walls of a prison containing no opportunity for learning a trade, maintaining family ties, or preparing to return to the community. Too often prisoners do not leave their confinement as law-abiding men. They leave, rather, as released criminals. Rehabilitation is an objective of the Law Enforcement Assistance Act.

These are necessary goals. But it is not enough to appoint a crime commission. It is not enough to sign a Law Enforcement Assistance Act. We must move forward with the same commitment and conviction we have given our attack on every other social evil that besets our people.

The local policemen, the local district attorneys, city and State judges can know this President will support them, without hesitation, in their efforts to fight crime in their towns.

I will not be satisfied until every woman and child in this Nation can walk any street, enjoy any park, drive on any highway, and live in any community at any time of the day or night without fear of being harmed.

I have directed the Attorney General of the United States to prepare a legislative program with this objective:

To strengthen the partnership of the Federal Government with our States and local communities in performing the first and most basic function of government—the preservation of law and order and the protection of every citizen.

NOTE: As enacted, the joint resolution to authorize funds for the President's Commission on Law Enforcement and Administration of Justice and the President's Commission on Crime in the District of Columbia, approved September 21, is Public Law 89–196 (79 Stat. 827); the Law Enforcement Assistance Act of 1965, approved September 22, is Public Law 89–197 (79 Stat. 828).

See also Items 382, 422, 437, 500.

527   Remarks After Signing Bill Providing Funds for Programs Under the Elementary and Secondary Education Act. *September 23, 1965*

TWENTY-ONE years ago, President Franklin Roosevelt issued an urgent call to Congress for Federal assistance to education in this country. He called this "our national obligation to all of our children." "This country," he said, "is great enough to guarantee the right to education adequate for full citizenship."

So today we are helping to write the answer to that historic challenge. I have just signed into law a bill providing supplemental appropriations for the Departments of Labor and Health, Education, and Welfare. And more than $1 billion will go for programs that are authorized by the Elementary and Secondary Education Act of 1965, which we signed a short time ago.

Today, we reach out to 5½ million children held behind their more fortunate schoolmates by the dragging anchor of poverty:

—This act provides funds to pay for the teachers and the services to help overcome handicaps that cause our bright young minds

to shut out the joy of learning.

—Today, we take a giant step forward—increasing the learning of the world by greatly enlarging the libraries of the schools.

—This act contains funds for school libraries, for school textbooks, and for school teaching aids.

So today, we strengthen the foundation of each school in every community of this Nation:

—This act will help finance supplemental educational centers and regional educational laboratories in order to bring new ideas and new techniques into the classrooms of our children.

And finally, today, we preserve an education system that is based on local and on State leadership:

—This act has funds to help State departments of education to develop and to strengthen their services.

I have directed Secretary Gardner and Commissioner of Education Keppel to do everything in their power, starting now, to speed the flow of funds to all State and all local education agencies.

But the Office of Education here in Washington cannot do this job alone. The main task now lies with the local school boards, with the parents, with the teachers, with the State school superintendents, with the State education commissioners.

You bear the responsibility for translating the vision of this law into the vitality of our country's education system.

And so to you, I have this to say: Act now. Get your plans made. Open your schools to the promise of these new programs.

I hope that not a single day will be lost. For in education, the time we waste today can mean a life wasted tomorrow.

We have always believed that our people can stand on no higher ground than the schoolground, or can enter any more hopeful room than the classroom. We blend time and faith and knowledge in our schools—not only to create educated citizens, but also to shape the destiny of this great Republic.

NOTE: The President spoke at 11:04 a.m. in the White House Theater. During his remarks he referred to Secretary of Health, Education, and Welfare John W. Gardner and Commissioner of Education Francis Keppel.

As enacted, the bill (H.R. 10586) is Public Law 89-199 (79 Stat. 831).

The Elementary and Secondary Education Act of 1965 was approved by the President on April 11, 1965 (see Item 181).

On December 30, 1965, the White House made public an interim report to the President from Commissioner Keppel on the first 100 projects established under title I of the Elementary and Secondary Education Act, designed to improve the schooling of children of low-income families. The report stated that these projects were benefiting 347,047 children in 12 States and that these were only the first of thousands of educational projects which would be established as a result of the legislation. The report summarized details of projects in Kayenta, Ariz., Minneapolis, Minn., Hatch Valley, N. Mex., Alton, Maine, and Houston, Tex. The text of the report is printed in the Weekly Compilation of Presidential Documents (vol. 1, p. 628).

528   Statement by the President Upon Signing Bill Extending the Incentive Awards Program to Members of the Armed Forces. *September 23, 1965*

I HAVE today signed Public Law 89-198, which authorizes the establishment of an incentive cash award program for members of the Armed Forces. Under this program, cash awards of up to $25,000 will be made to military personnel for suggestions, inventions, or scientific achievements which contribute to the efficiency and economy of Government operations. The law extends the cash incentive concept already in force in the Federal civil service to our men and women in uniform.

The cost saving program of the Department of Defense has already reached an annual level of savings of $4.6 billion each year.

On the basis of experience with the cash incentive programs elsewhere in the Government this new program can be expected to produce additional savings of more than $180 million a year at an approximate annual cost of less than 4 percent.

This Nation is a nation of peace, but there is one war to which I am committed, which we will wage on every front with every possible weapon—that is the war on waste and inefficiency. I am asking our men and women in uniform to join me in this effort.

I have today instructed the Secretary of Defense personally to bring this campaign to the attention of every member of our Military Establishment, at home and around the world. He will designate one of his principal assistants to conduct this special program.

NOTE: The statement was read by Bill D. Moyers, Special Assistant to the President, at his news con-ference at 4:20 p.m. on Thursday, September 23, 1965, in his office at the White House. It was not made public in the form of a White House press release.

As enacted, the bill (H.R. 8333) is Public Law 89-198 (79 Stat. 830).

529 Remarks to Members of the Board of Directors of the International Association of Lions Clubs. *September 23, 1965*

Dr. Campbell and directors of Lions International, and your charming wives:

This is a great pleasure for me to welcome you to the Rose Garden at the White House this afternoon.

For some time, I have been telling my assistants that if we are going to get our work done what we needed was "a tiger in our tank."

They told me this afternoon that they had something better—they had a hundred Lions out here in the Rose Garden.

There is more truth than humor in that remark. You, and your fellow Lions, and members of all of the great service organizations are helping to do the work that must be done to strengthen our land—to strengthen all lands—and help us secure peace in the entire world.

The volunteer spirit is vital to America's spirit.

Where poverty dwells, where despair thrives, where ignorance is king, and illness is dictator, there the decision lies about the America of tomorrow.

I remember a great general once testified before a committee that I was chairing when I was a Member of the United States Senate. And he expressed as his personal motto in peace as well as in war this thought: "Go to the heart of the battle for it is there that the decision lies."

So, we must go to the heart of the battle if we are to have a better life—for it is there that the decision lies. It is in the slums. It is in the less privileged neighborhoods of our cities. It is in the pockets of want across rural America. It is there—yes, and there is more. I believe that we must strive to preserve and to perpetuate the beauty of America, to reach out for excellence, to labor long for dignity and decency in the lives of all of our people.

So you and the members of your organizations have great opportunities in every community, and you also have great responsibilities. I want you to know that your efforts are not only welcomed by your President, but they are respected and they are applauded. And I hope, through you, to recognize in the talents and the efforts of every individual Lion in the world that we commend them for their contribution and for their service. You are trying to give more than you get. And I think that is the spirit that will assure American success in the years to come.

There are many things that we want. We would like to see the enemies of mankind—wherever they exist—driven underground and exterminated.

Disease—oh, what a great world it would be if everyone was healthy!

Ignorance—what a different atmosphere and environment we would have everywhere if people had the benefits of education that they should have, and every child had all the education that he could take.

Poverty—if every naked body could be clothed and every growling stomach could be fed this would be a much more reasonable and much more sane world.

And finally, and uppermost, and something that takes priority over everything else, is peace—a five-letter word—the most important word to all of you in any language. Because it doesn't make any difference how many hours you work, or when you get off, or when you finish your payments on your car, or you get a new refrigerator or a laundry machine, or what kind of recreation you have, or how many honor rolls your children make, or what kind of steel contracts you get, or what your fringe benefits are— those things don't amount to anything if your boy is going to get killed in Viet-Nam tomorrow, or we're going to have a war spread over Asia, or a world war III with all of its horrors is knocking at the door.

So, we have a lot to be thankful for. We have a lot, though, yet to do.

As we meet here in this peaceful, serene atmosphere of the White House this afternoon, we are all grateful for the statesmanship that President Ayub Khan and Prime Minister Shastri exhibited yesterday when they were willing, for the moment, to agree to the cease-fire. And we are all deeply in the debt of that great Secretary General of the United Nations for his courage and for his leadership in helping to bring this about.

It was only a few days ago when some unthinking and, I thought, rather selfish people remarked to me, "Why would a man like Arthur Goldberg, who had spent his life in the law and ultimately had risen to the greatest position of power and influence and leadership and honor that any lawyer can have in this country—the Supreme Court of the United States—why would he walk off of that bench and take the job up here in a debating forum called the United Nations where they resolute from day to day?"

And I thought of an expression that my mother—with the Bible in her lap—used to say to me: "God forgive them, for they know not what they do."

What was more important than anything else in the world was what Arthur Goldberg was then doing. There is not a court anywhere, any time, that has more far-reaching influence than that voice, speaking for the most powerful Nation in the world, had last week when he helped bring about this cease-fire.

So we must all engage in a little introspection and ask ourselves: Are we being tolerant? Are we being understanding? Are we being judicious? Are we being fair? Are we doing everything that we know how to do to try to save this mother's boy from death that came to a good many of them yesterday, and could come to thousands and millions of them if we are just not successful?

We know how to circle the globe. Our electronics and our modern inventions, and everything, have taught us how to do everything better than almost anybody can do it— except we have not learned a simple little thing: How to get along with each other.

And until we do that, there is going to be hovering over us constantly that thought that we might not wake up the next morning in this nuclear world in which we are living.

So, I implore you and I beseech you to look back upon the past, where you have concerned yourself so much with yourself, and look ahead to the time when you can contribute and devote some of these talents and some of this good fortune that has come to you, trying to be your brother's keeper and look out for all the world.

Thank you very much.

NOTE: The President spoke at 5:43 p.m. in the Rose Garden at the White House before about 100 members of the board of directors of the International

Association of Lions Clubs and their wives. In his opening words he referred to Dr. Walter Campbell of Miami, president of the association.

During his remarks the President referred to President Mohammed Ayub Khan of Pakistan and Prime Minister Lal Bahadur Shastri of India, whose countries agreed to a cease-fire on September 22 (see Item 524).

530   Memorandum on Reassignment of Civil Rights Functions. *September 24, 1965*

Memorandum to the Vice President:

I concur in your recommendations to streamline and strengthen the civil rights effort of this Administration.

I share your conviction that it is of paramount importance to attach responsibility for effective civil rights programs to each and every official of the Federal government.

Those who are responsible for our programs in education, in the development of our cities, in employment—indeed, in every area—must also bear the responsibility for administering those programs without discrimination on the basis of race, creed or color. Each official of the government must understand that every program for which he is responsible must be administered to insure equal opportunity for all Americans.

I know that there is no cause to which you have been more devoted than the cause of equal opportunity. The energy and dedication which you have brought to this difficult problem of governmental organization will make even more effective our important civil rights program.

LYNDON B. JOHNSON

NOTE: The memorandum from the Vice President recommending reassignment of civil rights functions, also made public on September 24, follows:

"As you will recall, last February and on many occasions since, we discussed the desirability of a careful review of the activities of the various Federal agencies involved in the field of civil rights. It was clear then that there were many functions that might well be consolidated. In every field of governmental

activity, it is essential to eliminate duplication or undesirable overlap—and that principle is equally applicable to civil rights programs.

"I have just completed an intensive review and am pleased to propose a number of changes which, in my view, will strengthen the operation and direction of our civil rights programs and at the same time eliminate confusion and duplication.

"A cardinal principle underlying these recommendations is that whenever possible operating functions should be performed by departments and agencies with clearly defined responsibilities, as distinguished from interagency committees or other interagency arrangements. That principle is particularly applicable to civil rights programs where it is essential that our objectives be pursued vigorously and without delay that frequently accompanies a proliferation of interagency committees and groups.

"Thus, one of the prime considerations running through my study and these recommendations is that each officer and employee of the Federal Government who administers a Federal program recognizes that he is responsible for making certain that the program is administered without discrimination on the basis of race, creed, and color and with full consideration of our objective of equal opportunity for all Americans.

"Every employee responsible for the administration of our vast education programs must recognize that he is also responsible for enforcement of equal opportunity and nondiscrimination.

"Every individual responsible for the administration of our labor programs must recognize that he is also responsible for compliance with our civil rights laws as they affect his programs.

"Every person who contracts on behalf of the Government with private parties must recognize that he is responsible for nondiscrimination in Government contracts.

"Every individual who hires any Federal employee must recognize that he is responsible for equal opportunity for all Americans to serve in the Federal Government.

"In short, I believe the time has now come when

operating functions can and should be performed by departments and agencies with clearly defined responsibility for the basic program, and that interagency committees and other interagency arrangements would now only diffuse responsibility.

"The President's Committee on Equal Employment Opportunity, which you served as Chairman during your tenure as Vice President, has made a valuable and lasting contribution to the elimination of discrimination in employment. As Chairman of that Committee, I have had the opportunity to observe its operation and I am convinced that its functions can be even more effectively administered if transferred to existing agencies.

"The responsibility for insuring that the Federal Government, in its employment, promotion, and other personnel policies, does not discriminate, can best be handled by the Civil Service Commission which has overall program responsibility for Federal personnel policies. The record of the Federal Government in this field in the past 4½ years has been one of steady progress, but much remains to be done, and I believe that transferring these functions to the Chairman of the Civil Service Commission will place them in an operating agency where they logically belong.

"The Secretary of Labor, as Vice Chairman of the Committee, has had primary responsibility for reviewing complaints and, through the contracting departments and agencies, insuring compliance by Government contractors with nondiscrimination requirements. With all the experience gained over a period of years by the personnel involved in this program, responsibility should now be vested directly in the Department of Labor, and I so recommend.

"The Plans for Progress program, under which hundreds of the Nation's leading business and labor organizations have pledged to promote employment policies free of any racial, religious, or national origins bias, rests on a voluntary basis. Its continued operation on a private voluntary basis is essential to the achievement of the objectives of the Equal Employment Opportunity Program of the Federal Government. The support which it has received from our Federal Government should continue.

"The reassignment of these functions of the Committee on Equal Employment Opportunity to existing agencies which can be accomplished by Executive order will eliminate the need for the Committee's continuation. I realize the deep personal attachment you have for the work of the Committee because of your long and successful association with it—and, of course, I share this attitude—but nevertheless I am convinced that these changes will result in more effective operation.

"The Community Relations Service was located in the Department of Commerce by the Congress when it enacted the Civil Rights Act of 1964 on the assumption that the primary role of the Service would be the conciliation of disputes arising out of the public accommodations title of the act. The acceptance of the public accommodations provisions by businesses—even in those areas of the country where they constituted a reversal of generations of custom and practice—exceeded our most optimistic predictions. I believe, therefore, that the basis for the original decision to place this program in the Department of Commerce, while appropriate at the time, no longer exists.

"With the disappearance of its primary function, the conciliation service has undertaken a number of productive efforts in the field of race relations. Many of these should be continued. But the Secretary of Commerce agrees with me that they could be more effectively and efficiently carried on within agencies which have responsibility for substantive programs which can help eliminate racial disputes and bias. Thus, disputes which involve school problems should be handled by the Commissioner of Education and his staff; disputes which involve housing should be dealt with by the Department of Housing and Urban Development; disputes which involve employment should be dealt with by the Equal Employment Opportunity Commission; etc.

"The Department of Justice has had deep and broad experience in racial matters and possesses information on a nationwide basis. I recommend, therefore, that the Community Relations Service be transferred to the Attorney General so that when necessary he can call upon the appropriate department with expert knowledge and positive programs to conciliate disputes.

"The clearinghouse and data gathering functions which are currently being performed by the Community Relations Service should be undertaken by the Civil Rights Commission which already has similar responsibilities.

"I understand that the changes proposed above will require a reorganization plan, and I urge such a plan be prepared for submission at the commencement of the next session of Congress. I believe that such a plan will not only prevent duplication of effort, make civil rights responsibilities an integral part of operating responsibilities; it will also result in substantial savings.

"During this period of evaluation and adjustment to the Civil Rights Act of 1964, it has been essential to have had the Council on Equal Opportunity which was established by Executive order earlier this year. In line with our goal of reducing the number of governmental bodies in this field, I have examined the role of the Council and have concluded that the reasons for creating the Council no longer exist, and I recommend, therefore, that it be terminated. I am satisfied that the working relationships between departments and agencies have advanced to the point where the formal organizational structure of the Council is no longer essential, and should be terminated by Executive order. The coordination of Title VI policies and practices within the Federal agencies has been most encouraging. Now that this significant program of insuring that Federal funds are not used to support State and local programs administered on a discriminatory basis has moved to the phase in which hearings and possible judicial action is involved, the Justice Department which has the ultimate responsibility for enforcing Title VI should be assigned the task of coordinating the Federal Government's enforcement policies in this area.

"Those of us who have seen new agencies come into being throughout the years recognize how difficult it is to bring them to a close even when the need for them no longer exists. I am especially pleased and proud, therefore, to recommend these consolidations and terminations to you. If you should act favorably upon these recommendations, I hope it will be perfectly clear to all that they do not represent a determination that civil rights problems in this country are resolved or eliminated, for indeed, the more difficult and complicated part of the journey to our national goal of a prejudice-free society lies ahead of us. Rather our effort has been to eliminate separate agencies where possible and to locate essential functions where they can be performed properly and most efficiently.

"Under your leadership as President, the executive branch of the Federal Government—in a partnership with the Congress that is essential to progress in this field—and the American people have made greater strides in the area of civil rights than ever before in our history. I believe that the actions I have recommended will continue the tremendous steps forward and bring us closer to fulfillment of one of the most important objectives of the Great Society—equal opportunity and full freedom for all men."

On September 24, 1965, the President signed two Executive orders on civil rights functions: Executive Order 11246 "Equal Employment Opportunity" (1 Weekly Comp. Pres. Docs., p. 305; 30 F.R. 12319, 12935; 3 CFR, 1965 Supp., p. 167); and Executive Order 11247 "Providing for the Coordination by the Attorney General of Enforcement of Title VI of the Civil Rights Act of 1964" (1 Weekly Comp. Pres. Docs., p. 310; 30 F.R. 12327; 3 CFR, 1965 Supp., p. 177).

531   Remarks on Announcing Intention To Nominate
Dr. William H. Stewart as Surgeon General, Public Health
Service. *September 24, 1965*

THIS ADMINISTRATION has committed itself to a historic effort to advance the health of the American people—and of peoples in other lands. The 89th Congress is providing farsighted legislation that will enable us to move forward in many areas:

—In the care of our young people and our older citizens,

—In the acceleration of research aimed at combating heart disease, cancer, stroke and other diseases which take such a tragic toll in disability and death,

—In meeting our national need for more physicians, more nurses, more professional and technical personnel in all of the health fields, and for more hospitals and other health facilities so that the benefits of our research and the skills and dedication of our professional people can be made more readily available to all who need them.

At this time in our history it is essential that the Public Health Service be led by a man of high intellectual capacity with a proven gift of leadership. This is a combination found in few candidates. I am convinced that Dr. Stewart is such a man. He is young, imaginative, energetic, devoted to his profession and dedicated to the great work which this Government is determined to carry out for the betterment of all mankind.

NOTE: The President spoke shortly after noon outside the West Lobby on the White House grounds before a group of White House correspondents.

His remarks were made public as part of a White House release which stated that Dr. Stewart, Director of the National Heart Institute, National Institutes of Health, would succeed Dr. Luther L. Terry who had resigned to accept an appointment as vice president of the University of Pennsylvania.

532 Statement by the President on the Progress of Treaty Negotiations With Panama. *September 24, 1965*

I HAVE today an announcement of especial importance regarding the progress of treaty negotiations with Panama.

In the past 18 months, representatives of the United States and the Republic of Panama have been conducting negotiations concerning the Panama Canal.

On December 18th, I told the American people that the United States sought fair play and justice, with a decent respect for the rights of all. The fact that we are large and that Panama is small would have no bearing on these discussions. We were determined then, as we are determined now, to do what is fair and what is right.

I asked our representatives to sit down and to seek answers. I pledged that we would reason together to find solutions that would be reasonable and right—right for our own people and right for the good people of Panama.

Today, I am happy to announce that areas of agreement have been successfully reached. I am very proud of Ambassadors Robert Anderson and Irwin, who spoke for the United States of America. I am very grateful to Ambassadors Arias, de la Rosa, and Aleman, who spoke for Panama.

They have proven again the truth of our deepest conviction—that nations can resolve their differences honorably and reasonably, without violence and conflict.

At this very moment, President Robles of Panama is anouncing to his own people the areas of agreement which our two countries have now reached. They are the following:

"In order to meet their present and future needs the two countries are negotiating separately a new and a modern treaty to replace the 1903 treaty and its amendments— a base rights and status of forces agreement— and a treaty under which there might be constructed across Panama a new sea level canal.

"The two countries recognize that the primary interest of both countries lies in ensuring that arrangements are provided for effective operations and defense of the existing Panama Canal and any new canal which may be constructed in Panama in the future.

"With respect to the status of the negotiations on a new treaty to replace the 1903 treaty and its amendments, general areas of agreement have been reached. The details of these areas of agreement are the subject of current negotiations.

"The purpose is to ensure that Panama will share with the United States responsibility in the administration, management and the operations of the canal as may be provided in the treaty. Panama will also share with the United States in the direct and the indirect benefits from the existence of this canal on its territory.

"The areas of agreement reached are the following:

"1. The 1903 treaty will be abrogated.

"2. The new treaty will effectively recognize Panama's sovereignty over the area of the present Canal Zone.

"3. The new treaty will terminate after a specified number of years, or on or about the date of the opening of the sea level canal, whichever occurs first.

"4. A primary objective of the new treaty will be to provide for an appropriate political, economic and social integration of the area used in the canal operation with the rest of the Republic of Panama. Both countries recognize that there is a need for an orderly transition to avoid abrupt and possibly harmful dislocations. We also recognize that certain changes should be made over a period of time. The new canal administration will be empowered to make such changes in accordance with the guidelines in the new treaty.

"5. Both countries recognize the important responsibility they have to be fair and helpful to the employees of all nationalities who are serving so efficiently and well in the operation of this very important canal. Appropriate arrangements will be made to ensure that the rights and the interests of these employees are safeguarded.

"The new treaties will provide for the defense of the existing canal and any sea level canal which may be constructed in Panama. United States forces and military facilities will be maintained under a base rights and status of forces agreement.

"With respect to the sea level canal, the United States will make studies and site surveys of possible routes in Panama. Negotiations are continuing with respect to the methods and the conditions of financing, constructing and operating a sea level canal,

in the light of the importance of such a canal to the Republic of Panama, to the United States of America, to world commerce and to the progress of all mankind.

"The United States and Panama will seek the necessary solutions to the economic problems which would be caused by the construction of a sea level canal.

"The present canal and any new canal which may be constructed in the future shall be open at all times to the vessels of all nations on a nondiscriminatory basis. The tolls would be reasonable in the light of the contribution of the Republic of Panama and the United States of America and of the interest of world commerce."

So, today, I take great pleasure in congratulating the negotiators for the very fine progress that they have made. I want to express my confidence in their ability to negotiate the details of these treaties, within the guidelines that have been agreed upon. All that we do is in the mutual interest and the welfare of the United States, Panama, and, we believe, the world at large.

Thank you very much.

NOTE: The President read the statement at 1:35 p.m. in the White House Theater. In the statement he referred to Robert Anderson, former Secretary of the Treasury, and John N. Irwin, United States delegates at the negotiations; Ricardo Arias Espinosa, Panamanian Ambassador to the United States, Diogenes de la Rosa, and Roberto Aleman, Panamanian delegates; and Marco A. Robles, President of Panama.

533 Statement by the President Following the Signing of the United Nations Participation Act Amendments. *September 28, 1965*

IN RECENT WEEKS the United Nations has once again proved its critical value to mankind. Because it is the principal forum to which all nations may bring disputes that threaten world peace, it is vital that the organization of the United Nations reflect its

high purposes. Each nation therefore has an obligation to strengthen and support the delegation representing it in the world today.

I am happy to sign into law today a measure that will enhance the effectiveness of our delegation to the U.N. In the past, only the chief representative of the United States and his deputy could represent this country before the Security Council and certain other major agencies of the U.N. This has proved unduly restrictive on the work of our delegation.

Under the new law, other members of our U.N. team may represent this country before any organ or commission of the United Nations. This will provide Ambassador Goldberg with the flexibility he needs to make use of the rich and diverse talents of those who now serve on the American delegation—Representative James Roosevelt, Ambassador

Eugenie Anderson, and Dr. James Nabrit.

In my experience we have never had a stronger delegation to the United Nations than we have today. The outstanding men and women who represent us there have demonstrated that they possess those qualities of mind and spirit that will serve, not only American interests in the U.N., but the interests of all mankind in its quest for peace. By this act we hope to make the fullest use of those qualities in every facet of the U.N.'s work.

NOTE: As enacted, the United Nations Participation Act Amendments (S. 1903) is Public Law 89–206 (79 Stat. 841).

534   Remarks at the Signing of the Arts and Humanities Bill. *September 29, 1965*

Mr. Vice President, Mr. Speaker, Senator Mansfield, distinguished Members of the Congress:

In the long history of man, countless empires and nations have come and gone. Those which created no lasting works of art are reduced today to short footnotes in history's catalog.

Art is a nation's most precious heritage. For it is in our works of art that we reveal to ourselves, and to others, the inner vision which guides us as a Nation. And where there is no vision, the people perish.

We in America have not always been kind to the artists and the scholars who are the creators and the keepers of our vision. Somehow, the scientists always seem to get the penthouse, while the arts and the humanities get the basement.

Last year, for the first time in our history, we passed legislation to start changing that situation. We created the National Council on the Arts.

The talented and the distinguished members of that Council have worked very hard. They have worked creatively. They have dreamed dreams and they have developed ideas.

This new bill, creating the National Foundation for the Arts and the Humanities, gives us the power to turn some of those dreams and ideas into reality.

We would not have that bill but for the hard and the thorough and the dedicated work of some great legislators in both Houses of the Congress. All lovers of art are especially indebted to Congressman Adam Clayton Powell of New York, to Congressman Frank Thompson of New Jersey, to Senator Lister Hill of Alabama, to Senator Claiborne Pell of Rhode Island, to many Members of both the House and Senate who stand with me on this platform today—too many names to mention.

But these men and women have worked long and hard and effectively to give us this bill. And now we have it. Let me tell you what we are going to *do* with it. Working together with the State and the local governments, and with many private organizations in the arts:

—We will create a National Theater to bring ancient and modern classics of the theater to audiences all over America.

—We will support a National Opera Company and a National Ballet Company.

—We will create an American Film Institute, bringing together leading artists of the film industry, outstanding educators, and young men and women who wish to pursue the 20th century art form as their life's work.

—We will commission new works of music by American composers.

—We will support our symphony orchestras.

—We will bring more great artists to our schools and universities by creating grants for their time in residence.

Well, those are only a small part of the programs that we are ready to begin. They will have an unprecedented effect on the arts and the humanities of our great Nation.

But these actions, and others soon to follow, cannot alone achieve our goals. To produce true and lasting results, our States and our municipalities, our schools and our great private foundations, must join forces with us.

It is in the neighborhoods of each community that a nation's art is born. In countless American towns there live thousands of obscure and unknown talents.

What this bill really does is to bring active support to this great national asset, to make fresher the winds of art in this great land of ours.

The arts and the humanities belong to the people, for it is, after all, the people who create them.

NOTE: The President spoke at 9:50 a.m. in the Rose Garden at the White House. In his opening words he referred to Vice President Hubert H. Humphrey, Representative John W. McCormack of Massachusetts, Speaker of the House of Representatives, and Senator Mike Mansfield of Montana, majority leader of the Senate.

As enacted, the National Foundation on the Arts and the Humanities Act of 1965 is Public Law 89-209 (79 Stat. 845).

535   Special Message to the Senate Transmitting Income Tax Protocol, U.S.-Germany. *September 29, 1965*

To the Senate of the United States:

With a view to receiving the advice and consent of the Senate to ratification, I transmit the protocol between the United States of America and the Federal Republic of Germany, signed at Bonn on September 17, 1965, modifying the convention of July 22, 1954 for the avoidance of double taxation with respect to taxes on income.

I transmit also for the information of the Senate the report of the Secretary of State with respect to the protocol. The protocol has the approval of the Department of State and the Department of the Treasury.

Modification of the 1954 convention in certain respects has been made advisable by reason, not only of experience in the application of the convention since its entry into force, but also of some relevant changes in the tax system of the Federal Republic of Germany. The protocol to effect certain desirable modifications has been formulated as a result of a long period of technical discussions between officials of the two countries.

Some of the modifications are designed to effect improvements in the provisions of the convention and bring them more nearly into line with corresponding provisions in the more recent income-tax conventions concluded by the United States. The convention would be expanded, for some purposes, to cover certain Federal Republic taxes which are not taxes on income as such, thus increasing the tax relief available to American enterprises. United States residents and companies would also derive special benefit from new provisions, unilateral in application, that would exempt them from Federal Republic capital taxes with respect to certain forms of property. American non-profit institutions would be accorded exemption from Federal Republic tax comparable with that accorded Federal Republic nonprofit institutions under United States law.

The protocol would make various other important amendments or would insert in the convention important new provisions relating to the taxation of industrial and commercial profits, the withholding tax rate on dividends, an extension of the tax exemption of interest to cover interest on debts secured by mortgages, an extension of the tax exemption of royalties to cover payments for "know-how" and gains from the disposition of property or rights which give rise to royalties, a clarification of the provisions dealing with income from real property, the

granting of reciprocal exemption with respect to capital gains other than gains on real property, a broadening of the exemption with respect to personal service income, a broadening of the provisions dealing with governmental salaries, wages, and pensions to cover injury or damage sustained as a result of hostilities or political persecution, a modification of the credit article of the convention as applied to shareholders other than Federal Republic parent companies of United States subsidiaries, the disclosure of tax information to courts or administrative bodies concerned with tax assessment and collection, and an improvement in the convention provisions dealing with taxpayer claims in order to prevent double taxation contrary to the convention.

Upon entry into force, the protocol would become in effect an integral part of the 1954 convention.

LYNDON B. JOHNSON

The White House
September 29, 1965

NOTE: The protocol and the report of Acting Secretary of State George W. Ball are printed in Senate Executive I (89th Cong., 1st sess.).

The convention of July 22, 1954, is printed in the United States Treaties and Other International Agreements (5 UST 2768).

---

536 Remarks at the Signing of the High-Speed Ground Transportation Act. *September 30, 1965*

Mr. Vice President, Members of the Congress, distinguished guests:

Last March I suggested to the Congress that the time has come to do something about improving the speed and the convenience of ground travel in this United States of ours. I requested authorization for the Commerce Department to undertake a program of research and development.

Many suggestions of this nature had emanated in the Congress itself and I had spent weeks reviewing and giving thought to these proposals.

The Congress responded to that suggestion by passing the High-Speed Ground Transportation Act, which I will sign this morning in the presence of the men who are really responsible for it.

I am pleased to observe that we are indebted for this bill to the hard working, intelligent Members of what is, in my opinion, one of the best Congresses in the history of this country. The names of those who devoted long hours and hard thought to this legislation are obviously too numerous to mention. But history could be recorded and preserved if the cameras would take pictures of all of them sitting out here this morning.

I do personally want to thank each and every one of you for your contribution in this field, particularly Senator Pell, who harassed me week after week until he got me to take some action.

In recent decades, we have achieved technological miracles in our transportation. But there is one great exception.

We have airplanes which fly three times faster than sound. We have television cameras that are orbiting Mars. But we have the same tired and inadequate mass transportation between our towns and cities that we had 30 years ago.

Today, as we meet here in this historic room where Abigail Adams hung out her washing, an astronaut can orbit the earth faster than a man on the ground can get from New York to Washington. Yet, the same science and technology which gave us our airplanes and our space probes, I believe, could also give us better and faster and more economical transportation on the ground. And a lot of us need it more on the ground than we need it orbiting the earth.

So I hope this meeting this morning will provide a platform for us to get that kind of transportation. We must do it. We must start getting it now. In the past 15 years, travel between our cities has more than doubled. By 1985—only 20 years away—we will have 75 million more Americans in this country. And those 75 million will be doing a great deal more traveling.

So, we must find ways to move more people, to move these people faster, and to move them with greater comfort and with more safety.

This bill is a first step toward accomplishing some of those objectives.

It will help us to determine what kind of high-speed ground transportation people want, what kind of transportation they will use if it is available. The Secretary of Commerce, in cooperation with private industry, is now authorized to test the public response by making trial improvements in existing passenger systems.

Today, I announce the first of those tests.

Secretary Connor informs me that he has already received scores of designs and operating suggestions for a new railroad passenger car which he wants to try out. These suggestions have come to him from private industry. They are produced at no cost to the Government. And as a result of the enthusiastic cooperation, the Department of Commerce and the participating railroads expect to have completed their final specifications sometime within the next 2 weeks.

Thus, we can begin taking bids for the construction of these new experimental rail passenger cars just as soon as we can make the funds available. The first of these cars are expected to be delivered by the fall of 1966. At that time, the Pennsylvania Railroad will begin providing rail service between New York and Washington, and between New York and Boston, at speeds up to 125 miles an hour.

Now, a similar experiment will be conducted on the New Haven Railroad, using gas turbine engines. That test will also begin in the fall of next year, or very shortly thereafter.

Research and development work under this program is not going to be limited to rail traffic alone. We will be investigating all the new and the promising concepts of high-speed ground travel. We may find that meeting the transportation needs of the coming decades requires some radical new techniques as yet unknown.

And I don't think that any of you who are participants in this Congress will ever earn the title of the "Status Quo Congress," because it hasn't been that kind of a body. You are thinking to the future, you are moving ahead, you are anticipating the problems of the 20th century, and you are finding solutions to them.

This High-Speed Ground Transportation Act of 1965 really gives us, for the first time in history, a coordinated program for improving the transportation system that we have today, and making it a better servant of our people.

So we begin this morning to really plan the revolutionary advances of tomorrow.

And again, I think that each of you, members of both parties, Members of both Houses, who made your contribution to the passage of this legislation, in the years to come will be proud of the part you played.

I told Chairman Harris, who provided leadership in this movement, that we weren't going to let him leave the Congress and go back to put on the judicial robes in Arkansas until we had a rail system that would permit us to get to see him faster than we are now—and we are about to get it.

NOTE: The President spoke at 9:45 a.m. in the East Room at the White House. In his opening words he referred to Vice President Hubert H. Humphrey. During his remarks he referred to Senator Claiborne Pell of Rhode Island, Secretary of Commerce John T. Connor, and Representative Oren Harris of Arkansas, Chairman of the House Interstate and Foreign Commerce Committee.

As enacted, the High-Speed Ground Transportation Act of 1965 is Public Law 89–220 (79 Stat. 893).

537 Message to the Congress Transmitting Eighth Annual Report on U.S. Participation in the International Atomic Energy Agency. *September 30, 1965*

To the Congress of the United States:

The Third International Conference on the Peaceful Uses of Atomic Energy, which was held at Geneva, Switzerland, from August 31 to September 9, 1964, yielded much evidence that the world is on the threshold of an exciting new era of nuclear power. The work of the International Atomic Energy Agency at Vienna, since its establishment in 1957, has contributed to the development of the capabilities of many countries to cross this threshold. The programs of the International Atomic Energy Agency, as they were carried forward during 1964, gave promise that the Agency will contribute in growing measure over future years to the

application of the atom to the constructive works of man.

Particularly noteworthy was the progress made by the International Atomic Energy Agency during 1964 in laying the foundations for restricting the use of nuclear energy exclusively to peaceful purposes. In February 1964 the Agency adopted a system of safeguards, applicable to all nuclear reactors, designed to guard against the diversion of nuclear materials to military use. In September 1964 the Agency's Director General reported that agreements had been negotiated with 17 of the 38 countries of the world possessing nuclear reactors, whereby some or all of their nuclear facilities would be placed under the safeguards of the Agency.

The United States has supported these activities, and looks to the Agency to play an increasingly significant role in developing the use of atomic energy for the benefit of the peoples of the world. United States participation in the International Atomic Energy Agency during the year 1964 is the subject of this eighth annual report which

I am transmitting to the Congress pursuant to the provisions of the International Atomic Energy Agency Participation Act.

LYNDON B. JOHNSON

The White House
  September 30, 1965

NOTE: The report is printed in House Document 297 (89th Cong., 1st sess.) and in Department of State Publication 7946 (Government Printing Office, 23 pp.).

---

538   Letter to the President of the Senate and to the Speaker of the House on the Pennsylvania Avenue National Historic Site. *September* 30, 1965

Dear Mr. President: (Dear Mr. Speaker:)

I am transmitting to the Congress herewith a proposed Joint Resolution "To provide for the administration and development of Pennsylvania Avenue as a National Historic Site".

Increasing concern with the shabby condition of Pennsylvania Avenue—the Nation's most distinguished and historic thoroughfare—led to the appointment by President Kennedy of the Council on Pennsylvania Avenue, which devoted almost two years to the preparation of plans for its rejuvenation. The work thus started has been carried forward by a Temporary Commission on Pennsylvania Avenue, created by Executive Order No. 11210 on March 25, 1965. The Temporary Commission recommended as the next appropriate steps the designation of the Avenue as a National Historic Site and the proposed Joint Resolution.

The proposed Joint Resolution will provide for the administration and development of the Avenue as a National Historic Site through a Commission on Pennsylvania Avenue. The Commission is to carry forward the work of the Temporary Commis-

sion and to coordinate activities along the Avenue, including Federal or District projects in the area.

That Pennsylvania Avenue will be redeveloped is inevitable. We must be sure that this development will be of a character worthy of this historic axis, which has from the beginning linked the Capitol and the White House. The proposed Joint Resolution will be a substantial step toward this goal. I hope it will have favorable consideration from the Congress.

Sincerely,

LYNDON B. JOHNSON

NOTE: This is the text of identical letters addressed to the Honorable Hubert H. Humphrey, President of the Senate, and to the Honorable John W. McCormack, Speaker of the House of Representatives.

The President's letter was made public as part of a White House release which announced that the President had approved an Order of Designation, signed by Secretary of the Interior Stewart L. Udall, and made under the Historic Sites Act of August 21, 1935 (49 Stat. 666).

The release stated that the designated portion of the Avenue would extend from the edge of the Capitol grounds to the boundary of the White House grounds and would include the Federal Triangle, Judiciary Square, the Lincoln Museum, the Treasury Building, and portions of downtown Washington's commercial district. The release pointed out that congressional action would be required to provide funds to develop the area as a national historic site. The release included a resolution of the Advisory Board on National Parks, Historic Sites, Buildings and Monuments adopted in August 1965 (1 Weekly Comp. Pres. Docs., p. 331).

The President referred to Executive Order

11210 of March 25, 1965, entitled "Establishing a Temporary Commission on Pennsylvania Avenue" (30 F.R. 4051; 3 CFR, 1965 Supp., p. 117).

The proposed joint resolution is printed in House Document 296 (89th Cong., 1st sess.).

The Council on Pennsylvania Avenue was established by President Kennedy on June 1, 1962.

539   Remarks Upon Accepting the Charles B. Stillman Award for Outstanding Service to Education. *September 30, 1965*

President Cogen, Mr. Meany, Mr. Bates, Secretary Gardner, Commissioner Keppel, distinguished educational leaders all:

I thank you so much for the undeserved and extremely generous statements that you have made, and particularly these two awards that you have presented to me. I value them more highly almost than any other that I might receive.

Their purpose is to, as I understand it, recognize and honor an educator, and I still think of myself as one, though my classroom career was momentarily interrupted about 35 years ago.

I wouldn't ever want the teachers to believe that my teaching experience was limited to high school in Houston, because that, in our State, is usually regarded as where the big city boys live, and I started my teaching at the little town of San Marcos in a high school there. Then I was promoted as principal of a grade school at Cotulla, down in south Texas near the Mexican border, where I earned the magnificent and munificent salary of $125 a month. Then I advanced to a position of greater responsibility as a principal at Pearsall, Texas, and there I made $175 a month. From there I went to Houston, and made the great mistake of leaving the teaching profession and coming on to Washington.

But I value this award, particularly because it bears the name of the dedicated public servant, Charles Stillman, who, as you said, was your first president.

When President Stillman organized your American Federation of Teachers in 1916, the responsibility for teachers was very high, but, as I have just indicated, the rewards were quite low. But his vision and his energy and his leadership brought a great many of his fellow teachers into your very fine organization. And today, when the teachers' salaries are still unequal, in my judgment, to the great load of responsibility that they bear, that energy, that vision, those hopes of his leadership continue to be felt.

Your founder would be the first, I think, to say, if he could be here with us this morning, that we have much unfinished work yet to do in the field of education. I do think that he would share our pride in the progress that we have made and to which you have alluded.

I would like for all of us to try to remember that more than 54 million Americans— one out of every four in this country—are in school today.

Total American expenditures for education have more than doubled in the past 10 years, from $15.9 billion to more than $32.6 billion.

The number of Americans graduating from high school has doubled in the last decade, from 1,351,000 to 2,567,000. And we are trying to work out arrangements where practically every one of those graduates that needs financial help to go to college will have it made available to them in one form or another—grants, loans, or some type of thing. That's a great breakthrough since my day.

The number of college graduates each year has risen 85 percent—think of it—85 percent, from 388,843 to 746,124 in the last 10 years.

In the last 2 years, we have enacted—the last 22 months since I have been President—we have passed through the House and the Senate and this President has signed 24 major measures to improve education in America. We have appropriated more than $5 billion for education, and we have established or enlarged 70 programs which brighten the educational future for more than 54 million Americans.

I think that Mr. Meany deserves very special recognition. A lot of measures that labor is interested in, you just read about them in the paper these days, but every single one of these 24 measures, no one has done more to help bring them to the attention of the American people than the leader of this great organization. And it is not only true of education, but it is true of health, it is true of social security, and it is true of conservation, it is true of beautification. It is true of everything that makes this a better land to live in.

These things that I have alluded to, I think, could be termed a very proud record. We are not going to rest upon it either. What we are going to do is take this record and we are going to build upon it—and we have just begun.

This year, with the help of your organization and many other friends of education, Congress enacted its crowning achievement in education—the Elementary and Secondary Education Act of 1965.

Under the provisions of this legislation, more than 5½ million schoolchildren in areas of poverty throughout this Nation from coast to coast will be helped; teacher training and educational research is going to be materially improved; State education departments in every State in the Union are going to be substantially strengthened. Supplementary education centers will be established in all the communities throughout the land.

Now, through all the years of your existence as a union, I am proud to say that you have never abandoned faith in the future that teachers can really build for America, and, thank goodness, you have never abandoned each other, either.

You have won better salaries for your people, you have helped to improve the working conditions for the teachers, and you have made real progress for your profession. And, I'm glad to say, you haven't stopped there. You have gone to the school boards, you have gone to the State legislatures, yes, you have even come to Washington on behalf of America's schools and America's students.

When the AFT was organized in 1916, I was an 8-year-old schoolboy back in the hills of Texas. Since then, both you and I have moved along some. I think, though, we have really been traveling the same road—the road toward a chance for all Americans to enjoy better education, better housing, better health, better conservation. And all of it just adds up to one thing—a better future for our children who will come after us. I don't know of any higher road that man could desire to travel.

So it is with a great deal of pleasure and a real honor to me that I welcome you here today. I would be less than human, I think, if I didn't tell you that I appreciate very much the honor that you have paid me by your visit.

In conclusion, I want to say that the thing that I would like to do perhaps most of all, in the allotted time that the Good Lord has given me here; and particularly in this position of leadership, I would like to feel in my own heart that I had been deserving, and that I had not failed in the eyes of at least my fellow teachers, who have helped me along with their encouragement and with their faith every step of the way along the long, long, winding road.

Thank you very much.

NOTE: The President spoke at 12:10 p.m. in the Cabinet Room at the White House following the presentation of the first annual Charles B. Stillman award for outstanding service to education. In his opening words he referred to Charles Cogen, president of the American Federation of Teachers, who presented the award, George Meany, president of the AFL–CIO, Harry C. Bates, president emeritus of the Bricklayers, Masons and Plasterers International

Union of America, John W. Gardner, Secretary of Health, Education, and Welfare, and Francis Keppel, Commissioner of Education.

Along with the award the President received a scroll which reads as follows:

"To Lyndon B. Johnson, who taught school in Houston, Texas, during those desperate depression years, who kept aglow his burning dedication to education throughout a long and distinguished career as a Congressman, who remains a teacher at heart as he serves in the highest office in the land, and who, as President of the United States, has sponsored the most far-reaching educational legislation in our Nation's history, we proudly present this first annual Charles B. Stillman award for educational leadership.

"The American Federation of Teachers, September 30, 1965.

"Charles Cogen, President."

The text of Mr. Cogen's remarks on presenting the award and scroll to the President is printed in the Weekly Compilation of Presidential Documents (vol. 1, p. 333).

The Elementary and Secondary Education Act of 1965 was approved by the President on April 11, 1965 (see Item 181).

540 Statement by the President in Response to Report on the Federal Incentive Awards Program. *September 30, 1965*

THIS unparalleled record of cost consciousness and alertness to improvement on the part of our career civil servants deserves the heartiest plaudits of the American people. Each individual, each supervisor, each manager who contributed to this record has my gratitude.

NOTE: The President's statement was made public as part of a White House release giving highlights from a report by John W. Macy, Jr., Chairman of

the Civil Service Commission. The release stated that 133,449 Federal employee suggestions had been adopted during fiscal year 1965, resulting in Government savings of more than $95 million, the greatest dollar savings ever achieved. Awards to employees for adopted suggestions, the release noted, had set a record at $3.9 million, with an additional 67,099 employees receiving superior performance awards for work achievements which returned more than $150 million in benefits to the Government. These employees shared $8.7 million in awards, with the average award amounting to $145 (1 Weekly Comp. Pres. Docs., p. 335).

541 Remarks at the Annual Meeting of the World Bank and the International Monetary Fund. *October 1, 1965*

Mr. Chairman, President Woods, Managing Director Schweitzer, Mr. Secretary, distinguished governors of the Bank and Fund:

It is a great pleasure to meet with you, the leaders of international finance, and to bid

you Godspeed on your labors for another year.

This year marks the 21st birthday of both the International Monetary Fund and the World Bank. It is a milestone that many never expected to see. They were the skeptics—those with little faith that institutions of order could long exist in a troubled world. But those skeptics did not understand that, amid the idealism, a new and urgent sense of reality was being born. They failed to see, as others did see, that institutions of order had to prevail—because without them, civilization itself could not prevail.

And so, from what Woodrow Wilson once called the "fountains of enthusiasm" soon came the foundations of achievement.

Today, your two great organizations stand at the center of a remarkable system of international cooperation. They have fostered the unprecedented economic growth of the free world.

The international monetary system merits a new and an imaginative look—not because its past performance has been faulty, but because a new situation faces us.

For nearly 20 years the United States spent and invested more money in foreign lands than it earned from its own exports and investments. The gold and dollar reserves of our friends, particularly in the developed world, were strengthened, even while their economies grew and prospered.

When a nation's reserves are good and growing it can trade with confidence. The nations of the free world have been doing just that, trading with confidence and in ever-increasing volume.

American dollar deficits have been one of the important factors in this greatest and best-sustained period of prosperity that the world has ever known. The United States deficit made it possible for many nations to develop their own currencies as strong and convertible sources of international finance.

It is no longer appropriate or possible for one country alone, through its deficits, to be largely responsible for the creation of world reserves. Moreover, the erosion of United States reserves could not go on indefinitely.

Thus, the United States has taken firm action to arrest the dollar drain. Should further action be necessary in the future, such action will be taken.

I want to be very clear about this, because we must, in our own interest and in the interest of those who rely on the dollar as a reserve currency, maintain our payments in equilibrium. This we will do.

The world not only expects but the world requires that the dollar be as good as gold.

The long period of large United States deficits has come to an end. If growth is to continue and trade is to expand, we must provide an effective and an adequate substitute.

This is not a matter of an immediate crisis. But it is a matter on which we must begin to act—and to act now. We must begin now to provide machinery for the creation of additional reserves. Gold alone will not be enough to support the healthy growth which the entire world demands. It will not be enough in the future any more than it has been in the past.

There is no shortage of plans for reforming the world's monetary system.

But let us try to choose the best. Let us remember the best is sometimes the enemy of the possible. Let us not become so preoccupied by questions of mere detail that we end up doing nothing. Ours is a large and a growing world. It has a large and growing trade. So let us provide for this growth.

Men who manage money are usually conservative. They should be. No one wants a banker who is careless with other people's money. But let us be clear about what it means in this case to be conservative. It does not mean inaction. Nor does it mean inadequate action.

Twenty-one years ago at Bretton Woods it was not the course of conservatism to cling to the monetary system which we then inherited. The men who were meeting on the slopes of Mount Washington knew that they had to move ahead. And they were proven right.

And so it is today.

The job of building sound and effective institutions for financing world trade is never finished.

On February the 10th of this year, in announcing a new program to bring the United States balance of payments into equilibrium, I said:

"We must press forward with our studies and beyond, to action—evolving arrangements which will continue to meet the needs of a fast growing world economy. Unless we can make timely progress, international monetary difficulties will exercise a stubborn and increasingly frustrating drag on our policies for prosperity and progress at home and abroad."

Now, during your meeting this week, you have taken a major action to assure the continued sound and stable growth of the international monetary system. I refer to the procedural undertakings of the managing director of the Fund and the finance ministers and central bank governors of the 10 leading industrial nations. There begin immediately negotiations to seek basic agreement on plans to ensure, among other things, that the free world's future reserve needs are adequately met.

So I want to congratulate the managing director and the ministers. I look forward to the results of the work of their deputies next year. Their later collaboration with the executive directors of the International Monetary Fund, representing all of the 103-nation members of the Fund, will have my

consuming interest. Meanwhile, I think it important that the International Monetary Fund, under the able leadership of Pierre-Paul Schweitzer, continue its important work on international monetary arrangements and cooperate actively with the Group of Ten.

I am proud of the role played in the discussions that preceded the ministers' decision by United States representatives, including my own Secretary of the Treasury, Henry Fowler.

Earlier this week the farsighted president of the World Bank, George Woods, spoke on another subject of great importance—international development. And I hope that the leaders of all the other free nations of the world paid as close attention to Mr. Woods' views as I did. He spoke with eloquence and with directness of the problem of development, and of the growing impatience of both developed and developing nations over the pace of progress.

One important way to help accelerate this pace, in my judgment—and it is a matter that bankers ought to be as interested in as they are in money—is education, the opportunities of education. Education is the guardian genius of all the liberties of all of us, including our money supply.

Earlier this month, I announced the establishment of a new task force to chart a worldwide educational endeavor for all peoples.

At that time, I noted that today, as we meet here, more than 700 million adults—4 out of 10 of the world's population—cannot even read or write. And that is a matter that ought to concern every human being in the world. Almost half the nations of the globe are crippled by illiteracy among half or more of their people.

This task force will prepare a course of action and recommend to me ways and means to lighten the burden of ignorance and illiteracy throughout the world, and what at least our Nation can do in participating in that advance.

I would presume to suggest and ask you to consider how the World Bank and the International Monetary Fund, and the great leaders associated with these endeavors, might contribute your might to this effort.

Perhaps the Bank and the Fund could expand and diversify the concept embodied in the Bank's Economic Development Institute and the IMF Institute.

I began my career as a public schoolteacher working with the boys and girls in the high school back in my home State. But I spent my evenings teaching bankers. And the thing that gave me the greatest satisfaction was that the men that dealt with dollars all day would spend their evenings coming to learn about people, because there is a direct relationship.

So I would hope that such an expanded program might draw upon the educational facilities of all the member nations of the World Bank and the Fund, including the United States of America. Where necessary, it would meet not only the educational expenses but also the living expenses of its students.

Such a program would increase the flow of teachers and engineers and economists and administrators and technical experts and men who create and produce wealth and dollars and money and gold in those countries which really need them most.

Because increasing educational opportunity is only one of the ways that we human beings must meet the pressing demands of the times and the demands upon human beings for development and for advancement and for progress—as opposed to *laissez-faire* and the *status quo*.

In all of the areas of development—wherever you look, whatever you see in the areas of development—the needs are urgent.

In my country we knew no such urgency in the course of our development. In the early days attendant to our birth, we were an underpopulated nation. Beyond the villages and the towns were virgin forests and deep rivers and wild game and rich and fertile soil. In this environment, a man's life was what he chose to make of it. The opportunity was there. The opportunity was seized.

But there is no such cushion of time among the developing nations of the world today as we meet here.

In many of these nations, the land is overcrowded. The people are poor. The soil is already worn out and tired. There is only the relentless crush of human needs—and a flickering of hope. Well, we need to nourish that hope if we are worthy of the title that we bear of leaders of the world. We need to nourish and preserve and advance and bring to fulfillment that hope.

And in this I am not speaking solely to the nations represented in this room.

I have found, in my 35 years of public life, that it is usually governments who find it difficult to communicate with each other. Little trouble in finding pathways to friendship is found among the people themselves.

In this world that is shrunk by the jet and frightened by the atom, the peoples of every country must urge and demand their governments to join together in dealing with the problems that really concern people and that really matter in the lives of human beings.

There is so much to be done in the world to develop minds and to preserve bodies. And no one nation alone is going to be able to do it. No one group of nations can succeed—either in Viet-Nam, where as the terror of aggression finally ends, the healing hand of reconstruction must begin—or anywhere men set out to win a better life.

This is work that must challenge and should challenge us all—every industrial country, including the countries of Eastern Europe, and including the Soviet Union.

So this is our task.

The world of t o m o r r o w—peaceful, healthy, beautiful, educated—all this awaits us if only we, led by bankers, stir ourselves to move forward toward it.

NOTE: The President spoke at 11 a.m. at the Sheraton Park Hotel in Washington. In his opening words he referred to Yilma Deressa, Minister of Finance of Ethiopia and chairman of the 19th annual meeting of the World Bank and the International Monetary Fund, George D. Woods, President of the World Bank, Pierre-Paul Schweitzer, Managing Director and Chairman of the Board of Executive Directors, International Monetary Fund, and Henry H. Fowler, Secretary of the Treasury.

542 Statement by the President Upon Signing Bill Increasing War Orphans' Educational Assistance Allowances. *October 1, 1965*

I HAVE SIGNED a bill which will provide an increase in the rates of war orphans' educational assistance allowances to some 20,000 deserving sons and daughters of veterans who lost their lives, or were totally and permanently disabled, defending our freedom around the world. This bill will also liberalize the eligibility requirements so as to provide benefits for all children whose veteran-parent was killed, or permanently and totally disabled, as a result of service after the end of the Korean conflict.

This is the first rate increase afforded under the War Orphans' Educational As-

sistance Act since it was enacted in 1956. This amendment will increase the monthly allowance payable to those who are presently pursuing education under the program, or who will do so later, from $110 to $130 per month for full-time educational training.

It is fair and right that this rate adjustment, and liberalized eligibility criteria, should be provided. Our obligation to these children is clear. I am proud to sign this bill into law.

NOTE: As enacted, the bill (H.R. 205) is Public Law 89-222 (79 Stat. 896). It was approved on September 30, 1965.

543 Remarks at the Signing of the Water Quality Act of 1965. *October 2, 1965*

Members of the Cabinet and Members of Congress, ladies and gentlemen:

Happy birthday, Mr. Hayden. I sent you a little note last night and I had intended to come to see you today, but since you are here, I hope you will stay over and just visit with me a little bit after the ceremony.

This moment marks a very proud beginning for the United States of America. Today, we proclaim our refusal to be strangled by the wastes of civilization. Today, we begin to be masters of our environment.

But we must act, and act swiftly. The hour is late, the damage is large.

The clear, fresh waters that were our national heritage have become dumping grounds for garbage and filth. They poison our fish; they breed disease; they despoil our landscapes.

No one has a right to use America's rivers and America's waterways that belong to all the people as a sewer. The banks of a river may belong to one man or even one industry or one State, but the waters which flow between those banks should belong to all the people.

There is no excuse for a river flowing red with blood from slaughterhouses. There is no excuse for papermills pouring tons of sulphuric acid into the lakes and the streams of the people of this country. There is no excuse—and we should call a spade a spade— for chemical companies and oil refineries using our major rivers as pipelines for toxic wastes. There is no excuse for communities to use other people's rivers as a dump for their raw sewage.

This sort of carelessness and selfishness simply ought to be stopped; and more, it just must be reversed. And we are going to reverse it.

We are going to begin right here in Washington with the Potomac River. Two hundred years ago George Washington used to stand on his lawn down here at Mount Vernon and look on a river that was clean and sweet and pure. In our own century President Theodore Roosevelt used to go swimming in the Potomac. But today the Potomac is a river of decaying sewage and rotten algae. Today all the swimmers are gone; they have been driven from its banks.

Well, with the signing of the Water Quality Act of 1965 this morning, I pledge you that we are going to reopen the Potomac for swimming by 1975. And within the next 25 years, we are going to repeat this effort in lakes and streams and other rivers across this country.

I believe that with your help and your continued cooperation, water pollution is doomed in this century.

This bill that you have passed, that will become law as a result of a responsive Congress, will not completely assure us of absolute success. Additional, bolder legislation will be needed in the years ahead. But we have begun. And we have begun in the best American tradition—with a program of joint Federal, State, and local action.

The ultimate victory of reclaiming this portion of our national heritage really rests in the hands of all the people of America, not just the Government here in Washington. But much of the money, some of the imagination, much of the effort must be generated at the local level. And then, and really only then, will this blueprint for victory become victory in fact.

Thank you for coming this morning.

NOTE: The President spoke at 10:04 a.m. in the East Room at the White House before a group composed of United States Senators, Representatives, and members of the Cabinet. At the beginning of his remarks he referred to Senator Carl Hayden of Arizona, President of the Senate pro tempore, who was celebrating his 88th birthday.

As enacted, the Water Quality Act of 1965 is Public Law 89–234 (79 Stat. 903).

On November 10, 1965, the President signed Proclamation 3688 "Water Conservation Month" (1 Weekly Comp. Pres. Docs., p. 489; 30 F.R. 14349; 3 CFR, 1965 Supp., p. 75).

544 Letter Authorizing the Secretary, HEW, To Undertake a Joint United States-Japan Medical Research Program. *October 2, 1965*

Dear Mr. Secretary:

Pursuant to the authority vested in the President by section 5(f) of the International Health Research Act of 1960 (PL 86–610), you are authorized to undertake a joint United States-Japan medical research pro-

gram. This program, designed to pool the knowledge and resources of the two countries in fighting major diseases affecting the people of Asia, results from the discussions which I had with Prime Minister Sato in January. It is known as the United States-

Japan Cooperative Medical Science Program.

The program responsibility assigned to you hereby will be administered within the limits of foreign policy as prescribed by the Secretary of State.

I am pleased with this opportunity for the United States to participate with Japan in the joint solution of health problems which will have worldwide benefits.

Sincerely,

LYNDON B. JOHNSON

[Honorable John W. Gardner, Secretary of Health, Education, and Welfare, Washington, D.C. 20201]

NOTE: On the same day the White House announced the beginning of the program. The release stated that, following the President's discussions with Prime Minister Sato in January 1965, initial plans for the program were made at a preliminary meeting of United States and Japanese scientists in April. A Committee for the United States-Japan Cooperative Medical Science Program was to meet in October, the release stated, and annually thereafter. The Committee planned to use panels of scientific experts from both countries in research efforts to control or eradicate cholera, tuberculosis, leprosy, certain virus and parasitic diseases, and malnutrition (1 Weekly Comp. Pres. Docs., p. 355).

For the joint statement of the President and Prime Minister Sato following their discussions in January 1965, see Item 15.

545 Statement by the President Making Public a Joint Report on Natural Beauty in America. *October* 2, 1965

I AM TODAY releasing the results of the first 8 months of the Federal Government's efforts to preserve and improve the beauty of America. These efforts are of particular concern to me, because they will determine the kind of America my daughters—and all the children of America—will inherit.

Last February I sent to the Congress a message on natural beauty. I pointed out, as emphatically as I knew how, the threat of eventual blight to our God-given heritage of natural beauty.

In that message I called specific attention to the fact that our growing population is swallowing up areas of natural beauty with its demand for living space.

I noted with concern that the increasing tempo of urbanization is already depriving many Americans of the opportunity to live in decent surroundings.

I said that a new conservation would be required to deal with these new problems if we are to protect the countryside, save it from destruction, and restore what has been destroyed.

And I also said that this conservation must be not just the classic conservation of protec-

tion and development, but a creative conservation of restoration and innovation.

That message was only one of several instances in which I have attempted to convey my interest in preserving and renovating our heritage of beauty.

I spoke of my concern in the State of the Union Message.

I reiterated my concern at the White House Conference on Natural Beauty.

I have since reemphasized it in other messages, in speeches, and in great detail in much of my correspondence.

My administration has made a number of proposals to bring the full resources of this Government to bear on the problem of dwindling beauty.

I am pleased to issue the first fruits of these proposals—a report from the Secretaries of Interior; Agriculture; Commerce; Health, Education, and Welfare; the Director of the Office of Economic Opportunity; and the Administrator of the Housing and Home Finance Agency.

This report summarizes the major efforts of the Federal Government to lead the way in keeping America beautiful. It is an encouraging report because it indicates that concrete progress is being made.

Among other things, it reflects the plans to make this Capital the Nation's showcase.

It outlines what is being done to beautify locations that range from such diverse areas as New York City to the great open spaces of the West.

It indicates in strong fashion that research and training are important tools to be used in giving natural beauty a foothold in both urban and rural environments.

It sums up what we have done thus far to promote natural beauty in the countryside, to retain and improve our scenic and historic sites, and to preserve our wildlife.

It notes the action we have taken to offer improved outdoor recreation to more of our people.

It details our activities to improve our water and waterways as useful and yet beautiful natural resources, and our plans for controlling pollution of streams and rivers.

It points up what we have done and what we intend to do to make our vast network of highways not only useful but beautiful.

There is much more.

This report reflects action that ranges from schools and classrooms to local neighborhood projects, from the disposal of refuse and waste products to the use of trash and garbage as fuels for operating desalting plants.

And yet it is only a beginning. It is a first step.

I have asked those who prepared this report to continue to report to me, on a regular basis, the progress which they have made in this all-important area. These reports will be available as they are made.

But I want you to know that this is more than just a report on action taken and action contemplated.

It is also a request for help.

The task of creating a more beautiful America, of making it a more pleasant place in which to live, is not and cannot be the job of the Federal Government alone. We must have the enthusiasm, the concern, and the cooperation of every level of government—States, counties, cities, and precincts.

I believe that the American people share our feelings. I believe that they want a beautiful country. And I believe that they will respond to the challenge which we have set—to make this the most beautiful nation on earth.

NOTE: The text of the report is printed in the Weekly Compilation of Presidential Documents (vol. 1, p. 357).

For the President's message to Congress of February 8, 1965, on the conservation and restoration of natural beauty, see Item 54.

For the annual message to Congress on the State of the Union, see Item 2.

For the President's remarks to the delegates to the White House Conference on Natural Beauty, see Item 277.

546 Remarks at the Signing of the Immigration Bill, Liberty Island, New York. *October 3, 1965*

Mr. Vice President, Mr. Speaker, Mr. Ambassador Goldberg, distinguished Members of the leadership of the Congress, distinguished Governors and mayors, my fellow countrymen:

We have called the Congress here this afternoon not only to mark a very historic occasion, but to settle a very old issue that is in dispute. That issue is, to what congressional district does Liberty Island really belong—Congressman Farbstein or Congressman Gallagher? It will be settled by whoever of the two can walk first to the top of the Statue of Liberty.

This bill that we will sign today is not a revolutionary bill. It does not affect the lives of millions. It will not reshape the structure of our daily lives, or really add importantly to either our wealth or our power.

Yet it is still one of the most important acts of this Congress and of this administration.

For it does repair a very deep and painful flaw in the fabric of American justice. It corrects a cruel and enduring wrong in the conduct of the American Nation.

Speaker McCormack and Congressman Celler almost 40 years ago first pointed that out in their maiden speeches in the Congress. And this measure that we will sign today will really make us truer to ourselves both as a country and as a people. It will strengthen us in a hundred unseen ways.

I have come here to thank personally each Member of the Congress who labored so long and so valiantly to make this occasion come true today, and to make this bill a reality. I cannot mention all their names, for it would take much too long, but my gratitude—and that of this Nation—belongs to the 89th Congress.

We are indebted, too, to the vision of the late beloved President John Fitzgerald Kennedy, and to the support given to this measure by the then Attorney General and now Senator, Robert F. Kennedy.

In the final days of consideration, this bill had no more able champion than the present Attorney General, Nicholas Katzenbach, who, with New York's own "Manny" Celler, and Senator Ted Kennedy of Massachusetts, and Congressman Feighan of Ohio, and Senator Mansfield and Senator Dirksen constituting the leadership of the Senate, and Senator Javits, helped to guide this bill to passage, along with the help of the Members sitting in front of me today.

This bill says simply that from this day forth those wishing to immigrate to America shall be admitted on the basis of their skills and their close relationship to those already here.

This is a simple test, and it is a fair test. Those who can contribute most to this country—to its growth, to its strength, to its spirit—will be the first that are admitted to this land.

The fairness of this standard is so self-evident that we may well wonder that it has not always been applied. Yet the fact is that for over four decades the immigration policy of the United States has been twisted and has been distorted by the harsh injustice of the national origins quota system.

Under that system the ability of new immigrants to come to America depended upon the country of their birth. Only 3 countries were allowed to supply 70 percent of all the immigrants.

Families were kept apart because a husband or a wife or a child had been born in the wrong place.

Men of needed skill and talent were denied entrance because they came from southern or eastern Europe or from one of the developing continents.

This system violated the basic principle of American democracy—the principle that values and rewards each man on the basis of his merit as a man.

It has been un-American in the highest sense, because it has been untrue to the faith that brought thousands to these shores even before we were a country.

Today, with my signature, this system is abolished.

We can now believe that it will never again shadow the gate to the American Nation with the twin barriers of prejudice and privilege.

Our beautiful America was built by a nation of strangers. From a hundred different places or more they have poured forth into an empty land, joining and blending in one mighty and irresistible tide.

The land flourished because it was fed from so many sources—because it was nourished by so many cultures and traditions and peoples.

And from this experience, almost unique in the history of nations, has come America's attitude toward the rest of the world. We, because of what we are, feel safer and stronger in a world as varied as the people who make it up—a world where no country rules another and all countries can deal with the basic problems of human dignity and deal with those problems in their own way.

Now, under the monument which has welcomed so many to our shores, the American Nation returns to the finest of its traditions today.

The days of unlimited immigration are past.

But those who do come will come because of what they are, and not because of the land from which they sprung.

When the earliest settlers poured into a wild continent there was no one to ask them where they came from. The only question was: Were they sturdy enough to make the journey, were they strong enough to clear the land, were they enduring enough to make a home for freedom, and were they brave enough to die for liberty if it became necessary to do so?

And so it has been through all the great and testing moments of American history. Our history this year we see in Viet-Nam.

Men there are dying—men named Fernandez and Zajac and Zelinko and Mariano and McCormick.

Neither the enemy who killed them nor the people whose independence they have fought to save ever asked them where they or their parents came from. They were all Americans. It was for free men and for America that they gave their all, they gave their lives and selves.

By eliminating that same question as a test for immigration the Congress proves ourselves worthy of those men and worthy of our own traditions as a Nation.

ASYLUM FOR CUBAN REFUGEES

So it is in that spirit that I declare this afternoon to the people of Cuba that those who seek refuge here in America will find it. The dedication of America to our traditions as an asylum for the oppressed is going to be upheld.

I have directed the Departments of State and Justice and Health, Education, and Welfare to immediately make all the necessary arrangements to permit those in Cuba who seek freedom to make an orderly entry into the United States of America.

Our first concern will be with those Cubans who have been separated from their children and their parents and their husbands and their wives and that are now in this country. Our next concern is with those who are imprisoned for political reasons.

And I will send to the Congress tomorrow a request for supplementary funds of $12,-600,000 to carry forth the commitment that I am making today.

I am asking the Department of State to seek through the Swiss Government immediately the agreement of the Cuban Government in a request to the President of the International Red Cross Committee. The request is for the assistance of the Committee in processing the movement of refugees from Cuba to Miami. Miami will serve as a port of entry and a temporary stopping place for refugees as they settle in other parts of this country.

And to all the voluntary agencies in the United States, I appeal for their continuation and expansion of their magnificent work. Their help is needed in the reception and the settlement of those who choose to leave Cuba. The Federal Government will work closely with these agencies in their tasks of charity and brotherhood.

I want all the people of this great land of ours to know of the really enormous contribution which the compassionate citizens of Florida have made to humanity and to decency. And all States in this Union can join with Florida now in extending the hand of helpfulness and humanity to our Cuban brothers.

The lesson of our times is sharp and clear in this movement of people from one land to another. Once again, it stamps the mark of failure on a regime when many of its citizens voluntarily choose to leave the land of their birth for a more hopeful home in America. The future holds little hope for any government where the present holds no hope for the people.

And so we Americans will welcome these Cuban people. For the tides of history run strong, and in another day they can return to their homeland to find it cleansed of terror and free from fear.

Over my shoulders here you can see Ellis Island, whose vacant corridors echo today the joyous sound of long ago voices.

And today we can all believe that the lamp of this grand old lady is brighter today—

and the golden door that she guards gleams more brilliantly in the light of an increased liberty for the people from all the countries of the globe.

Thank you very much.

NOTE: The President spoke at 3:08 p.m. on Liberty Island in New York Harbor before a group of several hundred guests who had crossed to the island by boat for the ceremony. In his opening words he referred to Vice President Hubert H. Humphrey, Representative John W. McCormack of Massachusetts, Speaker of the House of Representatives, and Arthur J. Goldberg, U.S. Representative to the United Nations.

During his remarks the President referred to Representative Leonard Farbstein of New York, Representative Cornelius E. Gallagher of New Jersey, Representative Emanuel Celler of New York, Senator Robert F. Kennedy of New York, Attorney General Nicholas deB. Katzenbach, Senator Edward M. Kennedy of Massachusetts, Representative Michael A. Feighan of Ohio, Senator Mike Mansfield of Montana, majority leader of the Senate, Senator Everett M. Dirksen of Illinois, minority leader of the Senate, and Senator Jacob K. Javits of New York.

As enacted, the immigration bill (H.R. 2580) is Public Law 89–236 (79 Stat. 911).

In late September Cuban Premier Fidel Castro had announced that Cubans with families in the United States would be permitted to emigrate. The first of these refugees began arriving in Florida by small boat on October 7, and by October 18 the number had exceeded 700.

On October 31, 1965, the President approved the Supplemental Appropriation Act, 1966, which included an additional sum of $12,600,000 for the Department of Health, Education, and Welfare for assistance to refugees in the United States (Public Law 89–309, 79 Stat. 1133).

On February 15, 1966, the White House made public a report to the President from Attorney General Katzenbach which stated in part, "Although the Act has been in effect only two months, it has already reunited hundreds of families through its preferential admissions policy for aliens with close relatives in the United States. . . . Another 9,268 refugees from Cuba arrived in the United States during 1965. Of these, 3,349 came in December via the airlift arranged by the United States and the Cuban governments. Some 104,430 resident aliens were naturalized as American citizens during the year." The text of the report is printed in the Weekly Compilation of Presidential Documents (vol. 2, p. 220).

See also Items 601, 618.

547   Statement by the President Welcoming the Delegates to the First
International Symposium on Water Desalination.
October 4, 1965

I WELCOME YOU to this International Symposium. You represent more than 60 nations. You have come here from all parts of the world. And you have come to search—together—for a common solution to a common problem.

Even while you deliberate, men are without water. Land lies untilled which should produce food for the hungry. People around the world are impatient for the results of your efforts. And I am the most impatient of all.

Techniques to desalt water have been used in many places for many years—on ships at sea, among the islands of the Caribbean, in desert lands along the Persian Gulf. But if our vision for the future is to be realized—the vision of an inexhaustible supply of pure, drinkable water—then the cost of desalting must be drastically reduced.

With this objective, the United States began a program of research and development over a decade ago. It has already yielded heartening results. We have built five plants capable of testing new technologies. Their daily capacities range from a few hundred thousand gallons to more than 2 million gallons. We have built and operated a score of pilot plants. We have witnessed the cost of desalted water cut in half and then halved again. To accelerate this work, we have recently launched a new 5-year, $200 million program of research and development.

We have concrete goals in view: by 1968, to construct plants with the capacity of 10 million gallons a day; by 1970, to extend the range to 100-million-gallon plants. We are also at work on smaller plants varying in size from less than 1 million gallons to 15 million gallons per day, employing many different processes.

From the creative work you perform in your laboratories and on your drawing boards, and from conferences like this one, we will gain new freedom from the harsh accidents of geography. Brackish wells will nurture crops—and the oceans, pure and clear, will flow from our faucets.

The need is worldwide, so must be the effort. Knowledge, like thirst, belongs to all men. No country can be the sole possessor. We in this country are ready to join with every nation—to share our efforts, to work in every way. We cannot wait—for the problem will not wait.

NOTE: The President's statement was read at 9:30 a.m. by Dr. Donald F. Hornig, Special Assistant to the President on Science and Technology, at the opening session of the Symposium in the Department of the Interior auditorium. Although copies were made available to correspondents at the White House press office, the statement was not made public in the form of a White House press release.

See also Items 325, 494, 558.

548 Statement by the President Concerning the White House Conference "To Fulfill These Rights." *October* 5, 1965

LAST JUNE, in addressing the graduating class of Howard University, I announced that a White House Conference would be held this fall and with this theme: "To Fulfill These Rights." I described its object to be "to help the American Negro fulfill the rights which, after the long time of injustice, he is about to secure."

I am pleased to announce the Conference will be held in Washington on November 17 and 18. To provide leadership and guidance for those who participate in the Conference, I have asked a most distinguished American, Mr. A. Philip Randolph, president of the Brotherhood of Sleeping Car Porters, and a vice president of the AFL–CIO, to serve as honorary chairman. Working with him as cochairmen of the Conference will be Mr. Morris Abram of Atlanta and New York City, and Mr. William Coleman of Philadelphia. Both Mr. Abram and Mr. Coleman have earned widespread respect as men of the law and as men of deep personal commitment to the cause of civil liberty.

We are entering a new and far more difficult phase of our national effort to ensure that all Americans participate fully in the benefits and responsibilities of this most prosperous of nations.

It is, therefore, especially fortunate that we have men with such impressive credentials willing to devote their time, energy, resourcefulness, and creativity to the Nation's most difficult domestic problem.

Because of the gravity, scope, and importance of this issue, it is apparent that it cannot be considered in an effective way without more extensive preparations. The November Conference will draw together men and women with long experience in the fields of housing, employment, education, social welfare, and the like. They will point the way toward new efforts to include the Negro American more fully in our society. In the spring of next year, a larger conference of concerned Americans will convene in Washington to consider the conclusions and recommendations of the November meeting.

We look forward to these deliberations with high hope and confidence—hope that through the vision of dedicated men and women in both private and public life, we may find the new avenues of opportunity for Negro Americans—confidence that those for whom we labor will one day walk down those avenues toward full participation in a Great Society.

NOTE: On October 23, 1965, the White House made public a progress report to the President from the Cochairmen, Morris B. Abram and William T. Coleman, concerning the November planning session of the Conference. The report stated that Berl I. Bernhard, former Staff Director of the United States Civil Rights Commission, had accepted the position of Executive Director for the session. The report added, "We have sought the advice of knowledgeable persons in the fields of civil rights, labor, religion, business, and social welfare, as well as scholars and experts. Aided by these discussions we have developed plans for a November session which will explore in depth and in their interrelationships issues and proposals in such areas as employment and economic security, education, housing, family stability, administration of justice, and government and private resources for change." (1 Weekly Comp. Pres. Docs., p. 428).

On February 26, 1966, the White House announced the formation of a Council to make preparations for the Conference scheduled to be held in Washington June 1–2, 1966. The membership of the Council is printed in the Weekly Compilation of Presidential Documents (vol. 2, p. 283).

For the President's commencement address at Howard University on June 4, 1965, see Item 301.

For the President's remarks at a reception for participants in a planning session for the White House Conference, see Item 613.

549   Statement by the President Announcing That He Would Undergo Surgery.   *October 5, 1965*

AT THE RANCH on September 7, I felt some pains in my stomach which seemed to be the result of something I had eaten. The White House Physician, Dr. Burkley, examined me early that morning and, because of the location of the pains, suspected gall bladder trouble. He suggested that X-rays be taken after my return to Washington.

The X-rays were made that week. Dr. Burkley informed me that they indicated a poorly functioning gall bladder. A thorough examination showed this to be the only trouble. A second series of X-rays was taken. The films were forwarded to my family physician of many years, Dr. James Cain, at the Mayo Clinic. After thorough study by Dr. Cain and Mayo radiologists, they confirmed Dr. Burkley's initial judgment of a poorly functioning gall bladder with stones.

After further consultation, the doctors recommended that the gall bladder be removed. I will, therefore, enter Bethesda Naval Hospital Thursday night for surgery Friday.

I have discussed this with the Vice President, members of the Cabinet, my White House staff, leaders in Congress, and General Eisenhower. I have informed them that the doctors expect there will be minimal time during which I will not be conducting business as usual.

As you know, the Vice President and I shortly after the election agreed to adhere to certain procedures in the event of Presidential inability. These procedures are identical with those which President Eisenhower and Vice President Nixon and President Kennedy and I adopted. Bill Moyers will give you copies.

While I do not anticipate the need for Presidential decision, or actions during the short time that I shall not be available for the purpose, the Cabinet, and particularly the Secretary of State and the Secretary of Defense, as well as my White House staff, will always be in contact with the Vice President. The Vice President will be here in Washington Friday. These men have been a party to and participated thoroughly in all major policy decisions. They are fully and currently informed.

The public will, of course, be kept fully and currently advised of my progress.

NOTE: The President entered the Bethesda Naval Hospital on October 7. The operation was performed the next day by Dr. George Hallenbeck and Dr. Ormond Culp, both of the Mayo Clinic. Five hours later the President was able to stand. The next morning the President walked about his room. He returned to the White House on October 21.

On November 19, 1965, the White House made public a statement signed by the President's physicians, Dr. James C. Cain and Dr. George G. Burkley, following an examination of the President. The statement said in part, "We feel the President to be recuperating in a very satisfactory manner. It is now six weeks since the date of the operation and he has been out of the hospital for a month. . . .

"We suggested that the President continue to follow a graduated exercise program trying to obtain adequate rest and limit his activities until the first of the year. His physical examination at this time was satisfactory in every way. There remains some sensitivity in the scar area which is to be expected at this time following an operation." (1 Weekly Comp. Pres. Docs., p. 522).

550 Statement of Procedures for Use in the Event of Presidential Inability. *October 5, 1965*

THE following procedures, which are identical to the procedures adopted by President Eisenhower and Vice President Nixon as well as President Kennedy and Vice President Johnson, have been agreed upon by President Johnson and Vice President Humphrey:

(1) In the event of inability the President would—if possible—so inform the Vice President, and the Vice President would serve as Acting President, exercising the powers and duties of the Office until the inability had ended.

(2) In the event of an inability which would prevent the President from so communicating with the Vice President, the Vice President, after such consultation as seems to him appropriate under the circumstances, would decide upon the devolution of the powers and duties of the Office and would serve as Acting President until the inability had ended.

(3) The President, in either event, would determine when the inability had ended and at that time would resume the full exercise of the powers and duties of the Office.

NOTE: For the President's special message to the Congress on Presidential disability and related matters, see Item 34.

551 Remarks at the Signing of the Heart Disease, Cancer, and Stroke Amendments of 1965. *October 6, 1965*

Secretary Gardner, Members of Congress, distinguished health leaders, members of the press:

Before this year is gone, over a million productive citizens will have been killed by three murderous diseases. Seven out of ten Americans who lose their lives this year will be the victims of heart disease or cancer or stroke.

Now these are not dry statistics; these are deadly facts whose anguish touches every single family in this land of ours.

This year, in this Nation, at least 25 million people are going to be crippled by heart ailment.

More than 2 million citizens are survivors of strokes.

The economic cost of this death and disease is staggering beyond one's imagination—an estimated $45 billion last year alone; more than $4 billion annually just in direct medical expenses.

And the cost in human agony is far too great to ever tell.

With these grim facts in mind, and at the insistence of that lovely lady, Mrs. Mary Lasker, I appointed a commission to recommend national action to reduce the toll of these killer diseases.

"Unless we do better," I said to the commission, "two-thirds of all Americans now living will suffer or die from heart disease or cancer or stroke." And further speaking to the commission, I said, "I expect you to do something about this."

Well, they did something. And that is why I have asked you to come here this morning.

One of the world's great surgeons and teachers, Dr. Michael DeBakey of Houston, Texas, headed this commission. Their report last December set forth a series of extremely bold and daring proposals—the seed which will grow and flower into a much healthier America.

Chairman Lister Hill, that warrior of so many health battles, and Oren Harris, the chairman of the House committee, met with us, applied their talents, lent their support to this dedicated effort to do something in this field. So did men who have given their lives to the health program in this country, like John Fogarty particularly, who gets every dollar he can and channels it into this field, Bill Springer, who compliments us this morning with his presence. And then the careful deliberation of both committees of both Houses produced this measure—the heart disease, cancer, and stroke measure of 1965.

Its goal is simple: to speed the miracles of medical research from the laboratory to the bedside.

Our method of reaching that goal is simple, too. Through grants to establish regional programs among our medical schools and clinical research institutes, we will unite our Nation's health resources. We will speed communication between the researcher and the student and the practicing physician.

Our Nation desperately now needs more medical personnel. Under this act, we will make the best use of existing medical personnel in these critical diseases, and then we will start improving the training of other specialists.

Our Nation desperately needs better medical facilities and better medical equipment. And under this program we will get them— and we will use them—to help the victims of these killer diseases.

Our Nation desperately needs to help physicians and health personnel continue their education. This act will make that help possible.

We cannot close the dark corridor of pain through which sufferers must pass. But we can do all that is humanly possible to increase the knowledge about these diseases—to lessen the suffering and to reduce the waste of human lives.

It has been written: "Men who are occupied in the restoration of health to other men are above all the great of the earth. They even partake of divinity, since to preserve and renew is almost as noble as to create."

That is true of our great doctors—our great doctors whose healing hands are going to give meaning to this act that you farsighted legislators have carved. But I think it is true of others, too. I think it is true of all the citizens who have worked for this measure. And it is particularly true—I want to say to Senator Mansfield and the other members of the leadership of both parties— it is particularly true of this fabulous 89th Congress.

There is no partisanship in educating the child or preserving his health, and this Congress has demonstrated that. You in the Congress have given us more than leadership: you have given our people a gift of hope—hope for a much longer and a much happier life, not just for ourselves, but for all the little ones that look up with their trusting faces and expect us to do right by them.

We have so many things to be thankful for this morning as we meet here in this historic East Room where Abigail Adams used to hang out her washing, where Theodore Roosevelt gave his daughter away, and where people came to pay their last respects to Abraham Lincoln and John Fitzgerald Kennedy.

DR. HOWARD RUSK'S MISSION TO VIET-NAM

Just before I sign this bill, or while I'm signing it, I am going to ask you to take an extra 5 minutes—and it won't be longer than that—to hear a message from a great man who wears a great name. The name of Rusk is revered in this country, and Howard Rusk is always where the doctors need him, in brain and heart and soul.

He has just come back from Viet-Nam, and he sat here last night with 150 tycoons from business and talked to them about the health problems out there. I am going to ask him, while I'm unpacking these pens and trying to get this thing started, to come up here and just talk frankly to you about our problem, because I have an airplane on the way, going out there this morning at his request.

Dr. Howard Rusk.

[*At this point Dr. Rusk addressed the group. The President then resumed speaking.*]

I am going to ask Dr. Rusk and those associated with him to meet with Members of the House, and particularly with the Senate group that is planning to visit Viet-Nam, Senator Kennedy and the others, on the refugee problem, so that we can work very closely together, because I know your deep interest in that field.

Again, I want to thank all you Members of Congress who are here this morning— Senator Prouty and Senator Mansfield, Congressman Fogarty and Mr. Springer, Senator Hill and Chairman Harris, and others of you who have contributed to helping make this day possible.

I congratulate all of you.

NOTE: The President spoke at 10:03 a.m. in the East Room at the White House. In his opening words he referred to John W. Gardner, Secretary of Health, Education, and Welfare.

During his remarks the President referred to Mrs. Albert D. (Mary) Lasker, cofounder of the Albert and Mary Lasker Foundation for medical research, Dr. Michael E. DeBakey of Houston, Tex., former Chairman of the President's Commission on Heart Disease, Cancer and Stroke, Senator Lister Hill of Alabama, Chairman of the Senate Committee on Labor and Public Welfare, Representative Oren Harris of Arkansas, Chairman of the House Committee on Interstate and Foreign Commerce, Representative John E. Fogarty of Rhode Island, Representative William L. Springer of Illinois, Senator Mike Mansfield of Montana, majority leader of the Senate, Dr. Howard Rusk, Director of the Institute of Physical Medicine and Rehabilitation, New York University, Senator Edward M. Kennedy of Massachusetts, and Senator Winston L. Prouty of Vermont.

As enacted, the Heart Disease, Cancer, and Stroke Amendments of 1965 is Public Law 89–239 (79 Stat. 926).

For the President's remarks of December 9, 1964, upon receiving the report of the President's Commission on Heart Disease, Cancer and Stroke, see 1963–64 volume, this series, book II, Item 798.

In his remarks Dr. Rusk described his recent visit to Viet-Nam in September to observe the health and welfare needs of the population and to study what was being done by the volunteer agencies and by the U.S. military to alleviate conditions there and to improve understanding on a people-to-people basis. He reported on the living conditions of Vietnamese orphans, students, and disabled veterans, and he announced that President Johnson had ordered an airplane to bring Vietnamese amputees to the United States for training and rehabilitation.

Dr. Rusk revealed that the U.S. aid program had distributed 1½ million books to Vietnamese children who would have schoolbooks for the first time in their history. The text of his remarks is printed in the Weekly Compilation of Presidential Documents (vol. 1, p. 371). See also Item 469.

---

552   Message to the Congress Transmitting Annual Report on the International Educational and Cultural Exchange Program.
October 6, 1965

To the Congress of the United States:

Pursuant to the provisions of the Mutual Educational and Cultural Exchange Act of 1961 (Public Law 87–256), I am transmitting the annual report on the International Educational and Cultural Exchange Program for the Fiscal Year 1964.

This report suggests something of the

experience of life in other lands which students, teachers, professors, lecturers, research scholars, performing artists, athletes and coaches, foreign leaders, writers, judges, doctors—indeed the whole company of the adventurous, the skilled, the searching—have shared with their counterparts abroad, since the exchange programs began two decades ago.

In those twenty years they have become an established part of our commitment to international understanding. That commitment is expressed through Congressional action, through the voluntary efforts of thousands of individual citizens, through our universities and colleges, and through national and local community organizations all across the country.

I commend the report to the thoughtful scrutiny of the Congress.

LYNDON B. JOHNSON

The White House
   October 6, 1965

NOTE: The "Annual Report to the Congress on the International Educational and Cultural Exchange Program, Fiscal Year 1964" was issued by the Bureau of Educational and Cultural Affairs, Department of State (Government Printing Office, 1964, 160 pp.).

553   Message to the Congress Transmitting Second Annual Report on Special International Exhibitions.   *October 6, 1965*

To the Congress of the United States:

I am transmitting the Second Annual Report on Special International Exhibitions, for the fiscal year 1964, pursuant to section 108(b) of Public Law 87–256, the Mutual Educational and Cultural Exchange Act of 1961.

This program is designed to reveal to peoples abroad the true nature and broad extent of our economic, social, and cultural attainments. These exhibitions are also designed to advance mutually profitable trade relationships.

This American know-how is presented to show how it harmonizes with the host country's own aspirations and capabilities. This is done by presenting major U.S. exhibitions at selected international fairs and expositions, or as special events, in support of American foreign-policy objectives.

This program concentrates mainly in Eastern Europe and the developing countries. Hundreds of American business and industrial firms, private institutions, and individuals cooperated with government agencies and contributed materials, time, and talent to help insure the success of these exhibitions.

For people who yearn to learn more about us, the American pavilion is like a large picture window through which they can look and see for themselves. The steady stream of young and old, from all walks of life, flocking to our exhibitions to improve their knowledge of what America is and means is a sight not easily forgotten.

These exhibitions are a vital adjunct to our country's unceasing pursuit of peace, freedom and human dignity for men everywhere. I am gratified by the support the Congress has given this program since it began a decade ago.

LYNDON B. JOHNSON

The White House
   October 6, 1965

NOTE: The "Second Annual Report, Special International Exhibitions, July 1, 1963–June 30, 1964" (47 pp.) was issued by the Bureau of Educational and Cultural Affairs, Department of State.

554 Remarks to Officials and Chambers of Commerce Representatives of the Appalachian Region of Tennessee. *October 6, 1965*

Governor Ellington, and my beloved friend, Joe Evins, Mr. Johnson, distinguished guests:

Lady Bird and I are most grateful for these beautiful carvings, for this lovely rug, for these other examples of the craftsmanship and the artistry for which Tennessee, that great State, is so justly famous.

I thank you also for this very splendid scroll expressing your support for the Appalachia program.

We will treasure these presentations, we will remember them, and we have a very special place for memories of this kind. We are going to have an exhibit in the memento room at the University of Texas Library, where we will have these on display for children of Tennessee and other States who may from time to time visit that library.

I remember how much pleasure I received when President Eisenhower took me on a tour of the Oval Room—now what we call the Yellow Room—in the White House, which President Roosevelt once used for his office, and I saw all the mementos that President Eisenhower had received when he was our European Commander.

And I am keeping these pictures and mementos that are brought to me from time to time.

I want to thank you for what you have said about the Appalachia program, because, as you have presented from the people of Tennessee, your President accepts these little items in behalf of all the people of our land who have made the Appalachia plan really possible.

Now we are moving behind the planning stage.

I have just been receiving in the next room some of the cartoonists who take care of

our military boys, and who are being honored today over at the Press Club. I hope that I can go over there and join them. They presented me with a cartoon, which I will put in this room with your presents. Bill, if you will get it. It is in my room in there, that chart, the cartoons they presented me.

They also presented Mrs. Johnson one, and since you referred to beautification, I thought you would enjoy this.

This is almost a prize-winning cartoon. I'm not sure that either Lady Bird or Liz Carpenter would approve of this display, but our good friend Bill Mauldin has this beautiful interstate highway. We signed a bill the other day involving billions of dollars in the years ahead that we will spend on interstate highways through the country, and here is the highway, with its very carefully designed, its winding beautification scheme here. And then, here are the signs along it: "Smoke El Smello," "Drink El Fizzo," "Eat Here," "Gas Here," "Try Here," and "Use Here."

And then, most prominent, is found one little spot left for a billboard there on the curve before you go over the divide, and that one says: "Impeach Lady Bird"!

Here is one they drew in the office this morning. They have put a Navy cap on me, that is supposed to represent all the services, though. These were done by the cartoonists who were here.

But with our Appalachia program, we have charted our course with care and with vision. We are so happy that it has attracted your cooperation, and we just must make that vision come true.

To do this, we are going to need the cooperation of your spokesmen in public life, particularly your Representatives in Congress, your able Governor, your mayors, your Senators; all of your public officials, particularly your teachers, your doctors, your nurses, and all public-spirited groups represented here today.

I want to thank the State of Tennessee for furnishing me one of the best minds, one of the most able men in this administration, and certainly one of the closest friends I have—Governor Ellington. He has been a tower of strength to me, and in the days and hours ahead when I'll be out of pocket for a little bit, I am going to rely on men like Buford Ellington to be sure that the Government continues to operate at a high state of efficiency. And to you people in Tennessee who lent him to me temporarily, I want to say thank you.

This job cannot be done, however, just by the Government alone. Only the toil and the efforts of all the people in all the 373 counties of the Appalachia area can produce the miracles that we need.

So, the future in that area of the country rests in your hands. I have seen what you can do with the great Tennessee Valley, and I have seen the pioneering leadership that the great State of Tennessee has always supplied.

You know, it's just a common garden variety expression in my State that every schoolboy has at the end of his tongue: There never would have been a Texas if there hadn't been a Tennessee. You gave us Sam Houston, you gave us Sam Rayburn, and you have given us the men who fought at the Alamo and San Jacinto. You have given us our independence, and you are still supporting us. And what you have given us today in these little tokens are representative symbols of the spirit of the people of Tennessee, and the kind of hard work that you believe in.

They will be memorials to you in our little memorial room.

Americans have always been dedicated to the proposition that tomorrow can be whatever we wish it to be, and for millions in the Appalachia area, tomorrow is going to be better.

We are planting trees by the rivers of water, and in the words of the Psalm, "They will bring forth fruit in their season."

We are going to have a big test tomorrow—a test whether the Federal Government, that spends the money in building the roads of the country, will have any right to determine what kind of places and how the scenery on those roads will be preserved.

We believe that the people are going to win.

We believe that we are going to take the necessary precautions to preserve the scenery of our land for the enjoyment of our children.

You don't know how happy I am that the people of Tennessee would come here today and share their generosity with me and their vision with me, and I am going to look forward to the day when I can come back to your great State, and Joe Evins' district, and see some of your people building and working and making the things that will make life happier for all of us.

Thank you so much.

NOTE: The President spoke at 12:20 p.m. in the Cabinet Room at the White House. In his opening words he referred to Buford Ellington, Director of the Office of Emergency Planning and former Governor of Tennessee, Representative Joe L. Evins of Tennessee, and William Johnson of Sparta, Tenn.

During his remarks the President referred to, among others, Bill D. Moyers, Special Assistant to the President, Mrs. Elizabeth S. Carpenter, Press Secretary and Staff Director for Mrs. Johnson, and Bill Mauldin, political cartoonist.

The group included representatives from the Upper Cumberland area of Tennessee, among them members of the Upper Cumberland Development Association, who came to the White House to express their appreciation for the President's interest in and action on behalf of the Appalachian region.

Shortly before the President spoke, Mr. Moyers announced that the President was about to meet with the following cartoonists who were to be honored that day at the National Press Club: Milton Caniff, George Wunder, Roy Crane, Mort Walker, and Don Sherwood. Mr. Moyers added that Mr. Mauldin would accompany the cartoonists.

555   Remarks at the Signing of the Water and Sanitation Systems in Rural Areas Bill.   *October 7, 1965*

Senator Aiken, Congressman Poage, Mr. Chairman Cooley, Secretary Freeman, Governor Hoff, Members of Congress, Senator Ellender, Senator Mansfield, ladies and gentlemen:

Mark Twain once described a place as, "This poor little one-horse town." But that was 90 years ago, and things haven't gotten any better since. Our cities have been growing and prospering, while our little dusty rural communities have just stood still.

At the turn of the century, more than half of our population still lived out in the country—or at least in the country towns. Today, as we meet here in the East Room of the White House, nearly three-quarters of our population has become urban.

The rural life doesn't have anything to offer our young people any more—or at least they think it doesn't—and so our young people have been drifting away, moving into the big cities.

I don't think this is a very desirable situation. Every year hundreds of thousands of unskilled and undereducated people pour into our cities searching for opportunities that are just not there. And in a very short time, they find themselves much worse off than they ever were before: unemployed and trapped in a web of utter despair.

I also think that if we allow our small towns and our villages to die on the vine, something good and something essential to the America that we know and that we love is going to die along with them. Much

of our national character and our national philosophy was molded in the small town life, and I am one that thinks we ought to preserve that.

But we can't preserve it and we can't encourage it among our young people, we can't get them to remain there unless we do something to improve the quality of rural life.

One of the pressing needs for rural America is the establishment of adequate water systems. This is vital for food processing; it is vital for preparing vegetables for the market; it is necessary for adequate fire protection; it is very desirable for almost every household use. And it is also a very powerful force for economic development. Land values go up. Homes are remodeled. New industries spring up. Existing industries expand.

So the bill that we are signing into law today is, we think, going to help bring these new water systems into being.

Another pressing need for rural America is for the construction of modern sewage treatment systems. Too many of these communities are pouring untreated wastes into their rivers and their streams—and the result is not only a pollution problem but a very serious health hazard as well. This bill will provide us with a major tool to correct that situation.

What the bill promises, then, is *clear* water, *constant* water for all of our rural America. It is long overdue, but it is never too late.

And I believe that we just must give a spur and an incentive and a desire for people to embrace rural life in America. We are indebted to Senator George Aiken of the State of Vermont, Congressman Bob Poage, the chairmen of both the Senate and House Agricultural Committees, and the leadership in the House and Senate for helping us take this very important step, this first step.

Some people have implied on occasions— that it varies, depending on which election you refer to—in the election of 1952 the people were worried about the two-party system, and in the election of 1962 or 1964 they were worried about it going the other way. We are a nation of worriers sometimes. But I am concerned with the two-party system. I do want it preserved. I do want both parties to be strong, virile, healthy, imaginative, positive, and affirmative. And I hope that they will be.

This is an example of what I think the leadership of both parties can embrace. This, I think—what Senator Aiken has done with his bill—might be an example for Democrats if we ever get in a minority, or might be an example for Republicans, if they would just quit trying to recommit everything and really stand for something positive instead of just being against and critical, and finding wrongs and mistakes that we make. If they would just say, "Now this is what needs to be done and this is how we are going to do it."

A President belongs to a party and the party has to help him get elected. But once he is elected, my conception of the institution is that—he is President of all the people and he ought to try to be the servant of all the people. And I am just looking for good Republican ideas, and if they will present alternatives, if they will present affirmative programs, if they will present positive programs for the good of all the people, this Democratic President will be the first to embrace them and sign them. And this is a classical example of what a member of a minority party can do, and how quickly a Texan will join him and bring the bill down here to the White House.

And so I hope that between now and the time we gather here in January, if we want to preserve the two-party system, the members of both parties can make a survey of what we are going to need for the next few years and then try to evolve the best solutions, the best program to meet those needs, and then try to approach it in a bipartisan spirit as you have done with this legislation.

I want to commend each of you that have had a part in formulating it, and I want to thank you for your understanding and your consideration of the executive department in working with us and bringing it to where it is today.

Thank you very much.

NOTE: The President spoke at 10:05 a.m. in the East Room at the White House. In his opening words he referred to Senator George D. Aiken of Vermont, Representative W. R. Poage of Texas, Representative Harold D. Cooley of North Carolina, Chairman of the House Committee on Agriculture, Secretary of Agriculture Orville L. Freeman, Governor Philip H. Hoff of Vermont, Senator Allen J. Ellender of Louisiana, Chairman of the Senate Committee on Agriculture and Forestry, and Senator Mike Mansfield of Montana, majority leader of the Senate.

As enacted, the bill (S. 1766) is Public Law 89-240 (79 Stat. 931).

556 Remarks at the Signing of Proclamation "White Cane Safety Day, 1965." *October 7, 1965*

Good morning, ladies and gentlemen:

The blind poet Milton once asked, "Doth God exact day-labor, light denied?" And he answered, "They also serve who only stand and wait."

This morning, America's blind citizens—nearly a half million of them—stand and wait. But now they wait for us. It is no longer the physical condition of blindness that rules their fate. It is our attitude toward that condition.

Too many blind people are condemned to a life of frustration because we have been willing to accept as fact that they can do no more. Well, I have not been willing to accept that fact, and as long as I hold this Office of the Presidency I am going to try not to accept that fact. Because today we know from experience that blind people can master such diverse occupations as teaching, sales, computer work, public relations, journalism, and law.

I just recently appointed to one of the highest legal assignments in this country—a member of the Tax Court—a person who is blind. He will serve with great distinction on that Federal bench and by so doing, I think, will open many other opportunities to blind people, not only on the bench but in other places in Federal service. Notwithstanding this, too many of these blind people today are making brooms and wicker furniture because no one has really given them a chance to do anything else.

And we are going to move forward in this area. We just must understand that blind people want to live normal, productive lives—and we believe they have the ability to do so.

So, today, we have come here to proclaim October 15th as "White Cane Day." In so doing we hope to remind all the American people, and through the generous services of all the media, remind the American people that the blind are dependent on them. So let us respond as the kind and the compassionate people that I believe we really are.

When we see a blind person on the street, let us try to be a little extra courteous and helpful. Let us give him the right of way. If we are on foot, let us speak to him. Let us offer our assistance at the crossings.

Above all, let us light the world of our blind citizens with opportunity. The white cane is not a symbol of uselessness. I think it is a symbol of determination. But it is up to us, all of us—everyone in this room and everyone in this country—to open the way.

If there was ever a time for us to apply the Golden Rule, let us set an example and engage in a little introspection this morning and ask ourselves if we do unto others as we would have them do unto us.

The blind need no longer stand and wait in order to serve. It is my judgment that now they are just awaiting our call and awaiting an equal opportunity.

Thank you very much.

NOTE: The President spoke at 12 noon in the Cabinet Room at the White House just prior to signing Proclamation 3679 "White Cane Safety Day, 1965" (1 Weekly Comp. Pres. Docs., p. 378; 30 F.R. 12931; 3 CFR, 1965 Supp., p. 65).

For the President's statement at the swearing in of Charles R. Simpson, who is blind, as Judge of the Tax Court of the United States, see Item 478.

557   Remarks Upon Signing Proclamation "National Day of Prayer, 1965." *October 7, 1965*

Distinguished clergy, ladies and gentlemen:

Today I am signing a proclamation, setting aside Wednesday, October 20, as the National Day of Prayer of 1965. In so doing, I remind all Americans of the line from "The Star-Spangled Banner": "In God is our trust."

Those are not just ringing words of poetry. They reflect the very soul of our great Nation: our purpose as well as our source of greatness.

In putting my name to this paper, I cannot proclaim that all Americans will pray on October 20th. Nor would I do so even if I could. But I do hope by this action that we will remind our citizens of the blessings that God has bestowed upon them. I do ask them to remember that our reliance upon Divine Providence is a far greater force for freedom in the world than all of our wealth combined.

And in remembering, let each man pray, according to the dictates of his own conscience, that we may continue to be worthy of God's blessings. And let us remember those words from our own great, late, beloved President, John Fitzgerald Kennedy: "Here on earth, God's work must truly be our own."

[*At this point the President signed the proclamation. He then resumed speaking.*]

Now I will read the proclamation that I have just signed.

NATIONAL DAY OF PRAYER, 1965

By the President of the United States of America a Proclamation

Even as they deliberated the conception of this Nation, our forefathers, mindful of the frailties of mortal men, turned for guidance to Almighty God.

Their humble and sincere prayer, delivered in their belief that all good things are the gift of God, established a reliance that remains unbroken.

As did our founding fathers, our people continue to place their trust in God.

Time and time again we have turned to Him for succor, and time and time again He has answered with manifestations of abundance.

In our own times, the Congress by a joint resolution of April 17, 1952, provided—that the President "shall set aside and proclaim a suitable day each year, other than a Sunday, as a National Day of Prayer, on which the people of the United States may turn to God in prayer and meditation at churches, in groups, and as individuals."

Now, THEREFORE, I, LYNDON B. JOHNSON, President of the United States of America, do hereby set aside Wednesday, October 20, 1965, as National Day of Prayer, 1965.

Few nations have been so favored by Almighty God, and it is altogether fitting that a day be set aside for this purpose.

Thus it is in the same spirit of humility and conviction demonstrated by our forefathers that I urge each citizen, according to his own conscience to pause on that day to acknowledge our dependence upon God.

In these days of peril and uncertainty, I urge that each of us plead for wisdom, strength and courage.

I urge that we pray for God-given vision and determination to make the sacrifices demanded by our responsibilities to our fellow men in our own Nation and in other lands of this world.

IN WITNESS WHEREOF, I have hereunto set my hand and caused the Seal of the United States of America to be affixed.

DONE at the City of Washington this seventh day of October in the year [SEAL] of our Lord nineteen hundred and sixty-five, and of the Independence of the United States of America the one hundred and ninetieth.

LYNDON B. JOHNSON

By the President:
GEORGE W. BALL
Acting Secretary of State

NOTE: The President spoke at 2:06 p.m. in the Cabinet Room at the White House.

558 Remarks to the Delegates to the First International Symposium on Water Desalination. *October 7, 1965*

Distinguished Members of the Congress, Secretary Udall, distinguished signatories, symposium delegates, members of the press, ladies and gentlemen:

We are very pleased that you could join us here this afternoon.

You represent more than 60 nations. You have come here from all parts of the world. You have come to search—together—for a common solution to a very common problem.

I think that no event could hold more promise for the peace and progress of man. No international gathering ever met anywhere for a more important purpose.

If science can unlock the door to an unlimited supply of pure and drinkable water, I think it will be an event in human history as significant as the harnessing of the atom.

Since the beginning of time, fresh water has always been one of humanity's most precious needs. For it, many wars have been fought throughout the years. Without it, whole civilizations have vanished from the earth.

Now, we of this generation have an opportunity to put an end to all of that. Our generation realizes that we have the power. It is the power which you at this conference really represent. That power is the power of science. But if we are to use that power effectively we must use it together.

Nature is not impressed by the lines that we draw on these little maps. The clouds above us refuse to stop for border guards and so the rain falls upon the just and the unjust alike.

The earth's water belongs to all mankind. Together we just must find ways to make certain that every nation has it in full share and that there is really enough of it for all nations.

Now, that is the central purpose of the International Symposium that you have been attending here in Washington. Since that is also the purpose of the agreement that we are about to sign, it seemed appropriate to me to ask you to come here and join us in this ceremony.

The United States of America and our good neighbor to the south, Mexico, share much in common—including great areas which are very short of water. Together, with the help of the International Atomic Energy Agency, we are now going to explore a promising answer to a very difficult but a very mutual problem.

This agreement will help us discover whether nuclear power can be applied, in a practical and in an economical way, to convert sea water and generate electricity for the great arid region which joins our two countries.

President Diaz Ordaz and I are equally determined that every effort possible must be made to find new water for this thirsty part of this continent. We are going to look to the oceans and to the modern technology that you have been studying at your conference. We hope that this study will be a model for future cooperation among neighbors in all the regions of the world that are suffering from water shortage.

We have barely left the shore for the start of a very long journey. None know better than you how difficult is the task before us. But we cannot, we will not, we just must not delay it any longer.

Over vast areas of the world today water is the key to man's prosperity or man's poverty—a key to his comfort or to his misery.

Every 24 hours there are nearly 200,000 more people on this earth. A billion human beings already live on the ragged edge of starvation. Water is a prime necessity, for only if we have water can our growing populations ever be fed. Only water can give future generations a chance to escape wholesale misery and wholesale starvation.

My country, as you know, supports with enthusiasm a continuing Food for Peace program. We support an Atoms for Peace program, committed to harnessing the awesome power of nuclear energy for the betterment of humanity.

And today I want to announce the beginning of a Water for Peace program. Under this new program we will join in a massive, cooperative, international effort to find solutions for man's water problems.

As I have already announced, the United States has launched a new 5-year, $200 million program of research and development to lower the cost of desalted water. But the time has now come to move beyond research and development.

Therefore, I shall present to the next session—I repeat, next session—of the United States Congress a plan and a program with proposals and recommendations (realizing that the Executive makes proposals and you make disposals) for constructing practical prototype plants to make the fullest use of our technological discoveries. Those discoveries already promise plants that are capable of producing up to 10 million gallons of fresh water a day by 1968, and 100 million gallons a day by 1970.

But the need is worldwide—not limited to any one country, not even ours. And so should be our effort in trying to meet that need.

Therefore, today I call upon all the nations of the world to join us in the creation of an international fund to bring the fruits of science and technology to all the corners of a parched and thirsty world.

The United States is prepared to contribute its share of the resources needed for an international crash program to deal with world water resources. We ask other nations to join us in pursuit of a common objective.

That objective is water for all humanity.

In pursuit of that objective, the United States—in addition to efforts that I have just described—is prepared: to build upon the achievements of this desalting conference by announcing now that we would convene within a year another great conference to deal with all the world's water problems, and by announcing now to increase our support for the scientists of more than 70 nations that are now working on water problems for the United Nations, and to announce now that we are willing to send our own best experts abroad, when requested, to establish a program of grants or fellowships to bring scientists from other lands to our own United States to engage in further study and additional research.

All this, I think, marks the beginning and not the end, by any means, of our efforts.

I earnestly believe that desalting is the greatest and is the most hopeful promise that we have for the future. I have believed it for a long time. It was more than 10 years ago, as a United States Senator, that I warned:

"We have reached a point . . . where very serious consideration must now be given to the pressure of individual, industrial, agricultural needs upon the water resources of this Nation. We have already passed the time when we can afford to be complacent."

Well, the problem is far greater today than it was 10 years ago. There are more people in the world for one thing. They need a great deal more to eat. They need a great deal more to drink. They need more industry to clothe them, and more houses to house them. But they can really never have any of these things without water.

And in the decade ahead we must accomplish more—much more—than in the decade past.

And I pledge to you that as far as I am concerned the United States is going to accomplish much more.

So the occasion which brings us together here this afternoon is testimony to the sincerity of our purpose.

The agreement that we are about to sign is just one more example of the joint efforts that are going forward every day under the Alliance for Progress program. Under that program last year we dispensed $159 million more than the combined allocation of the previous 2 years.

The 19 independent republics of Latin America and the United States of America have a partnership. We are all working to bring to all the peoples of the Western Hemisphere the fruits of modern science and modern technology.

So let us then extend that partnership. Let all of us—East and West—apply our science and our technology to this, the greatest of problems.

Let future generations remember us as those who freed man forever from his most ancient and dreaded enemies—drought and famine.

And now our efforts to free him from the enemies of draught and famine will be extended to free him from ignorance by an international education program, free him from disease by cooperative health adventures together.

And what a great satisfaction it would be to everyone in this room if at some future date we can point back to this year when the United States of America was willing to put forth leadership to free humanity from the ancient enemies of mankind—poverty, illiteracy, ignorance, disease, thirst.

NOTE: The President spoke at 2:30 p.m. in the East Room at the White House. In his opening words he referred to Secretary of the Interior Stewart L. Udall. During his remarks he referred to President Gustavo Diaz Ordaz of Mexico.

The delegates to the First International Symposium on Water Desalination had been invited to attend the signing ceremonies for the agreement between the United States, Mexico, and the International Atomic Energy Agency to carry out a technical and economic study of a nuclear sea water desalting plant to produce fresh water and electricity for arid regions in parts of Mexico and the United States.

The agreement was signed on behalf of Mexico by Hugo B. Margain, Mexican Ambassador to the United States. The text of the agreement is printed in United States Treaties and Other International Agreements (16 UST 1252).

For the President's remarks on announcing the 5-year, $200 million program of research and development to lower the cost of desalting water, see Item 417.

See also Items 325, 494, 547.

559 Remarks at the President's Salute to Congress.
October 7, 1965
[Text of remarks as delivered on October 7]

THANK YOU so very much.

I have a midnight deadline. I am back in school again and they are going to call a curfew on me.[1]

But I do want to tell you how thrilled I was this evening to have this wonderful cast come here and catch the spirit of America and portray it as I see it and as I would like for it to be.

I regret very much that all of the Members of the Congress could not be with us because they saw their duty, and I hope they are doing it. And I believe they are.

I am so happy that some of the wives of

---

[1] The President referred to the fact that he was about to leave for Bethesda Naval Hospital where he was to undergo surgery the following morning.

the Members of the House could be here. It is a somewhat unusual experience for us to sit while the House talks. That privilege has usually been reserved for the Senate through the years. But we are so happy that the Members of the Senate could be here with us, and the wives of the Members of the House that could come.

Mrs. Johnson and I particularly want to thank the members of this great cast for the sacrifices they have made. This has been a wonderful program. I wish that all America could see it, and perhaps when we have another Congress we will salute it again. And I know of no better way to salute it than just to give a repeat performance.

Thank you, good night, and God bless you.

[Text of remarks as prepared for delivery]

I CONSULTED the leadership last Tuesday at breakfast about suitable entertainment for this evening.

Speaker McCormack, Carl Albert, and Mike Mansfield volunteered to sing, "Show Me the Way To Go Home."

I don't even know that song. I was brought up singing, "Work—For the Night Is Coming."

Finally, I called a Congressman whose advice I respect, but I got no answer. When I asked him about it tonight, he said, "Mr. President, I heard the phone ringing, but I couldn't answer it. Larry O'Brien was in my office and he wouldn't let go of my arm."

Several columnists have written recently that the Congress has been "reversing the President." Well, my answer to that is in that old song we used to sing when I was a

young man in the hills of Texas: "Just Keep on Doing What You're Doing, 'Cause I Love What You're Doing to Me."

In the beginning, one evening last January, I was your guest on Capitol Hill. In my State of the Union Message, I spoke of our common challenge to enlarge the meaning of life for every American. I spoke of our goal to elevate the quality of our civilization. I spoke on that hopeful night of the "excitement of great expectations."

There haven't been many times in our history when the President could stand before Congress, at the end of a session, and express the gratitude and the pride that I feel tonight.

There were many Congresses which weren't interested in hearing what the President had to say.

All too often, the relations between the

executive and the legislative branches have been marred by bitterness.

George Washington warned that his legislature would "form the worst government on earth" if some means were not found to stem its corruption.

A great Republican, President Theodore Roosevelt, once wished he could turn loose 16 lions on his Congress. When someone pointed out that the lions might make a mistake, he replied, "Not if they stayed there long enough."

We all remember the time Harry Truman named the 80th Congress "the second worst Congress in the history of the United States." I can bring this up without fear of hurting anyone's feelings here tonight, because I was a Member of that Congress, too.

Well, now we are going to balance the ledger. Tonight, the President of the United States is going on record as naming this session of Congress the greatest in American history. And I am well aware of what that statement means.

I know the outstanding record of the 59th Congress under Theodore Roosevelt. That record included the Pure Food and Drug Act, the Meat Inspection Act, the railroad rate bill, and the Employer's Liability Act.

You have done more.

I know the outstanding record of the 63d Congress under Woodrow Wilson. That record included the Federal Reserve Act, the Clayton Anti-Trust Act, the Federal Trade Commission bill, and the tariff bill.

You have done more.

I know the great record of the 73d Congress under Franklin Roosevelt. That record included the Emergency Relief Act, the Securities Act, the CCC Act, the Home Owners' Loan Corporation, the TVA, the Economy Act, the Agricultural Adjustment Act, NRA, and the FDIC.

You have done more.

From your committees and both your Houses has come the greatest outpouring of creative legislation in the history of this Nation.

You passed legislation to fulfill the century-old promise of emancipation. Today, where once men were afraid, they now walk proudly to the polling place.

You passed legislation to ease the burden of sickness and want for older Americans. Today, though millions must face old age, they are no longer dependent on kinfolks for their medical care.

You passed legislation that should brighten every classroom in America. Once, the children of poverty began life on the hopeless road toward despair. Today they have a new chance to hope and to achieve.

You have promised to millions of American families better housing and better homes, and a rebirth for our cities.

You passed a poverty program so that poor families can train and work.

You passed a bill that will meet head-on the Nation's top murderers—cancer, heart disease, and stroke.

You told our cities and our industries that they must stop polluting our water and poisoning our air.

You passed legislation to dam our rivers, to prevent floods, to produce power, and to provide beaches and playgrounds for our children.

You gave us the blueprints for a rapid rail system to carry our commuters of tomorrow.

You passed a farm bill that puts more income in the farmer's pocket and at the same time allows him to compete at home and abroad.

You passed an immigration bill that no longer asks a man, "Where do you come from?" but, "What can you do?"

You have given local officials the tools to

restore law and order on our streets.

You passed the excise tax reduction. In a little over 20 months, at current income levels, taxes have been cut a little over $20 billion.

And tonight you serve notice on the spoilers of our landscape that we will battle with all we have to preserve the bounty of our land and the beauty of our countryside.

I read criticism in one newspaper not long ago that there was nothing new about what you have done. I read that you have simply enacted programs that have been "kicking around since New Deal days."

But let us look at the record:

This year you passed a voting rights bill that for the first time tears down the barrier of bias that barred the way to the polling booth.

This year you passed a program of rent supplements for low-income families, a program which provides a brandnew approach to meet an ancient and long-neglected need.

This year you passed, and yesterday I signed, an act to establish heart, cancer, and stroke centers throughout the Nation. It is a new way to bring the miracles of medical research to the people.

This year you passed a law to establish the Arts and Humanities Foundation—a vital new beginning to stimulate the creative talent of our Nation.

Legislation to provide hospital services for the elderly has been before Congress for a long time. But you added a voluntary plan to furnish doctors' services. You made the Medicare Act the biggest and boldest piece of health legislation ever to become law.

Federal aid to education is also a battle-scarred veteran in Congress. But the Elementary and Secondary Education Act of 1965 contains a wealth of new and imaginative ideas to enrich our Nation's schools.

It provides more money than any aid-to-education legislation ever considered by any Congress.

It offers every community a chance to bring the new techniques of teaching to the old art of learning.

The higher education bill, now in conference, also embodies daring new programs for dealing with old, old problems.

These bills and many more had their beginnings and their end in the 89th Congress.

The long list of major measures you have passed contains one example after another of new thinking, bold thinking, imaginative thinking. This has been the fabulous 89th Congress.

All of us know that much remains to be done. But you have begun a march which will not be stopped. You are on the way to a society which produces not only goods, but greatness.

It has been said that "great achievements raise a monument which shall endure until the sun grows cold." Those words, though they were written many years ago, belong to you.

You have honored the highest hopes of a Nation—and so tonight, we honor you.

Many years ago Woodrow Wilson said of a Congress: "A little group of willful men, representing no opinion but their own, have rendered the Government of the United States helpless and contemptible."

Tonight, as we balance history's ledger, I want to say of the 89th Congress: "An inspired group of dedicated Americans, representing a sense of national purpose, have written for the United States a new chapter in greatness."

I want to say to every Member of the 89th Congress—Democrat or Republican—who wrote and supported this record: Your people will revere you and reward you, and the Nation will honor you long after you are gone.

NOTE: The President spoke at 11:14 p.m. in the Department of State Auditorium as part of an evening of entertainment honoring the Members of the 89th Congress. Since the House of Representatives remained in session throughout the evening and the Members were unable to be present for the occasion, the President did not deliver his prepared remarks but spoke only briefly before leaving for the Naval Hospital in Bethesda, Md.

In the remarks as prepared for delivery the Presi-

dent referred to, among others, Representative John W. McCormack of Massachusetts, Speaker of the House of Representatives, Representative Carl Albert of Oklahoma, majority leader of the House of Representatives, Senator Mike Mansfield of Montana, majority leader of the Senate, and Lawrence F. O'Brien, Special Assistant to the President.

The text of the remarks as prepared for delivery was released at the Naval Hospital on October 11, 1965.

560 Statement by the President Upon Signing Bill Relating to Concession Rights in National Parks. *October 9, 1965*

I HAVE today signed into law H.R. 2091 establishing policies governing concession rights in our national parks.

The bill is supported by the Department of Interior and by a strong bipartisan majority in the Congress. It is designed to stimulate the development of better facilities for the tens of millions of Americans who enjoy our national parks each year. In essence it writes into law the concessions policies that have been followed by the Interior Department in the past on a regulatory basis.

It is not enough, however, to establish such policies for one department alone. Both the Department of Agriculture and the Corps of Engineers provide recreational opportunities for millions of Americans each year. To the extent that it is practical to do so, the Government should have a common policy governing concessions on federally owned lands.

Therefore, I have asked the Director of the Bureau of the Budget to make a thorough study of policies governing concessions cur-

rently in force, and to recommend a common approach to the granting of concessions by all Federal agencies. This study will be completed and recommendations made by April 1, 1966.

In order that new concession agreements entered into by the Department of Interior under the terms of this bill may be reviewed in the light of the Bureau of the Budget study, I have asked Secretary Udall to limit the terms of those concessions to 1 year, whenever practicable. This will give the administration and the Congress an opportunity to examine the desirability of new legislation affecting all publicly owned lands.

It is important that the operation of attractive facilities be encouraged in our national parks. It is just as important that lands belonging to the whole people be managed in a way that benefits the people for whom they are held in trust.

NOTE: As enacted, the bill (H.R. 2091) is Public Law 89-249 (79 Stat. 969).

The recommendations of the Bureau of the Budget were not made public by the White House.

The statement was released at the Naval Hospital, Bethesda, Md.

561 Messages to Mary Martin and the Cast of "Hello Dolly" on Tour in Viet-Nam. *October 9, 1965*

[Released October 9, 1965. Dated October 8, 1965]

To Mary Martin and the Cast of "Hello Dolly":

Your journey has been long, but I know that it will be rewarding. I want to thank each of you personally for coming to Vietnam to bring music, magic, and laughter to our sons and husbands who are so far from home.

The footlights may be dimmed after the show but they will not be dimmed in the hearts of the servicemen who see you perform. As your song goes, "For Dolly will never go away again."

LYNDON B. JOHNSON

To Mary Martin:

You are a front-line patriot in the work you are doing. You're making your President and all of Wetherford, Texas, deeply proud of you. Lady Bird and I send you our warm affections.

LYNDON BAINES JOHNSON

[Miss Mary Martin, c/o U.S. Embassy, Saigon, Vietnam]

NOTE: On October 9 the White House also released the text of the following letter to the President from Gen. William C. Westmoreland, Commander of U.S. Forces in South Viet-Nam:

Dear Mr. President:

Mary Martin and the "Hello Dolly" show have arrived in Vietnam. Before the first curtain at Bien Hoa Airfield, I read to Mary Martin and company, in front of the 5,000 spectator troops, your warm message. Mary and the cast were inspired by your words and the troops join me with appreciation for making this show available in Vietnam to your military forces who are struggling daily to support the ideals that America stands for.

Secretary McNamara has just informed me that your operation was completely successful. His message relaying this good news was also read by me at the opening show today.

Mary, the cast and all the officers and men of the Military Assistance Command, Vietnam, join me in wishing you a rapid recovery. Our prayers are with you.

Respectfully,

W. C. WESTMORELAND
General, U.S. Army

The messages and letter were released at the Naval Hospital, Bethesda, Md.

562 Statement by the President: General Pulaski's Memorial Day. *October 11, 1965*

TODAY, we pay homage to a young Polish nobleman who gave his life that this Nation might be free.

One hundred and eighty-six years ago, Casimir Pulaski, Brigadier General of the Continental Army, died of wounds received in the Battle of Savannah.

He came to America because, as he once said, "Wherever on the globe men are fighting for liberty, it is as if it were our own affair."

And so today, as we pause to honor this brave man, we are reminded of the great bonds of friendship that have always existed between the people of the United States and the people of Poland. It is now our intention to strengthen those bonds. We will build bridges across the gulf that has divided us for too many years now. They will be bridges of increased trade, of ideas, of visitors, and of humanitarian aid. We know that these bridges will be Poland's best hope for the future—and knowing that, we pledge ourselves to their completion.

And on this anniversary of Pulaski's death, we also rededicate our Nation to the cause he so nobly advanced. The torch has long since passed to us, and we know that "wherever on the globe men are fighting for liberty, it is as if it were our own affair." We pledge ourselves to that cause, too.

NOTE: Proclamation 3665 designating October 11, 1965, as General Pulaski's Memorial Day was signed by the President on August 3, 1965 (1 Weekly Comp. Pres. Docs., p. 44; 30 F.R. 9857; 3 CFR, 1965 Supp., p. 51).

The statement was released at the Naval Hospital, Bethesda, Md.

563   Statement by the President: Columbus Day, 1965.
October 11, 1965

WE celebrate Columbus Day tomorrow. It is the day when schoolchildren across the Nation marvel at the greatness of a man who braved the unknown. It is the day when adults reflect on the beginnings of our civilization.

But we honor more than Columbus the man. We honor the qualities that made him great: qualities of daring, imagination, determination, and courage. These are qualities that all Americans hold dear. They drew the Pilgrims to these shores; they prodded the pioneers westward; they spurred Lindbergh across the Atlantic; and now they urge us to explore the heavens.

But we cannot honor Columbus without being reminded of other Italians who have contributed so much to our civilization. From Vespucci to Fermi to Toscanini, America has been enriched by the blood of Italy flowing in its veins.

As we honor the first Italian-American, we honor all the others who came after.

NOTE: Proclamation 3673 designating October 12, 1965, as Columbus Day was signed by the President on September 22, 1965 (1 Weekly Comp. Pres. Docs., p. 296; 30 F.R. 12277; 3 CFR, 1965 Supp., p. 59).

The statement was released at the Naval Hospital, Bethesda, Md.

564   Message to the Congress Transmitting Ninth Annual Report on the Trade Agreements Program.   October 13, 1965

To the Congress of the United States:

This is the ninth annual report on the Trade Agreements Program, as required by section 402(a) of the Trade Expansion Act of 1962.

In 1964, U.S. and free-world trade continued to set fresh records.

—U.S. exports reached a new high of $25.6 billion, $6.9 billion more than our imports.

—U.S. farm exports rose to $6.4 billion, an all-time peak.

—Free-world exports reached a record $152 billion.

—The major trading nations agreed to take further steps under the General Agreement on Tariffs and Trade to assist exports from developing countries.

The policy of two-way trade expansion and liberalization, initiated with the Trade Agreements Act of 1934 and continued by every Administration since that time, has brought great benefits to this country. In general, U.S. goods have enjoyed progressively easier access to foreign markets. Low-cost, high-quality U.S. exports, sold and used in every corner of the world, have provided immediate evidence of the vitality of our free enterprise system. Our processors have gained ready access to essential raw materials, and have profited from the stimulus of keener competition. Consumers have enjoyed the wide range of choice which the world market provides.

But we have only begun. We must build on past success to achieve greater well-being for America, and for all the world's peoples. In particular, we must make every effort to assure the success of the current Geneva negotiations, known as the Kennedy Round.

In this International Cooperation Year of 1965, all nations should pledge themselves to work together for the steady expansion of commerce. Continuing its steady course begun in 1934, the United States will do its part in achieving that goal.

LYNDON B. JOHNSON

The White House
October 13, 1965

NOTE: The "Ninth Annual Report of the President of the United States on the Trade Agreements Program for 1964," dated August 30, 1965 (141 pp., processed), was released with the President's message at the Naval Hospital, Bethesda, Md.

---

565   Telegram to General Eisenhower on the Occasion of His 75th Birthday.   *October 14, 1965*

YOU were expressing sentiments I greatly admire on television last night. It did my heart good to see you on your 75th birthday, so strong in spirit and body—as you are indeed in the hearts of all your countrymen. Lady Bird joins me in warmest congratulations and best wishes.

LYNDON B. JOHNSON

[The Honorable Dwight Eisenhower, Gettysburg, Pennsylvania]

NOTE: The telegram was read by Bill D. Moyers, Special Assistant to the President, at his news conference at the National Naval Medical Center in Bethesda, Md., at 11 a.m. on Thursday, October 14, 1965. It was not made public in the form of a White House press release.

---

566   Letter Commending Federal and Local Groups Participating in an Urban Renewal Project in New York City.   *October 14, 1965*

[Released October 14, 1965. Dated October 11, 1965]

Dear Commissioner Brownstein:

The rehabilitation of the first building of the 114th street project in New York is a significant achievement.

It is a forerunner of other successes throughout the Nation in our aggressive attack on poverty.

This is an attack from which we cannot turn back, for to do so would be to condemn thousands of our fellow citizens to lives of degradation and despair. We cannot tolerate poverty in good conscience or in the interest of the future growth and prosperity of our great Nation.

In this specific project it is gratifying to note the cohesiveness of our effort to reach a common goal: the Housing and Home Finance Agency, the Federal Housing Administration and the Office of Economic Opportunity for the Federal Government; the City of New York under the leadership of Mayor Robert Wagner, and the City's Rent and Rehabilitation Administration and Poverty Operations Board; the Frederick W. Richmond Foundation and Carol W. Haussamen Foundation; the members of the 114th Street Block Association and their president, Curtis McFarley, and the professionals and

craftsmen whose ability and skills made this achievement possible.

Please convey my gratitude and best wishes to them. Unity in purpose and effort holds the key to our future successes.

Sincerely,

LYNDON B. JOHNSON

[Mr. P. N. Brownstein, Commissioner, Federal Housing Administration, Washington, D.C.]

NOTE: The letter was released at the Naval Hospital, Bethesda, Md.

567 The President's Greetings to the Consumer Advisory Council. *October 15, 1965*

[As read by the Vice President]

I AM ASKING our very able Vice President to convey to you my greetings and best wishes for a most successful conference.

I had planned to meet with you myself today, but my doctors claimed a prior appointment with me. However, my stay in the hospital does not diminish my deep interest in affairs of the consumer.

I have stressed to you before the vital importance of your mission, but this is something that cannot be repeated too often. You represent the voice of the American housewife in Government. That is enough to justify your efforts. But your role is vastly greater. You are working for every citizen in our land, because every citizen is a consumer.

American consumers today are benefiting from the longest peacetime expansion in history. Since 1961:

—Personal consumption has expanded 32 percent, with all this means in the way of rising living standards;

—Wages and salaries have increased by 33 percent, or $90 billion, an amount greater than the Nation's entire food bill in 1960;

—Purchasing power has increased; the average weekly earnings of manufacturing workers rose 22 percent;

—And prices have risen comparatively little.

Consumers have also benefited recently from the greatest income tax cut in our Nation's history. In the past few months the people have begun to benefit from the excise tax reduction, putting still more purchasing power into their hands. The latest report indicates that 90 percent of excise tax reductions are being passed on to consumers.

Before we reduced excise taxes, we reached a general understanding that all the reduction would be passed along to consumers. I am directing the Council of Economic Advisers to conduct a thorough recheck immediately to see that all establishments are keeping faith and passing all excise tax reductions to the consumers.

Since the Council was established, still other significant developments benefited consumers:

—The Office of Economic Opportunity

has made 17 grants, totaling over $893,000, for the development of consumer education programs throughout the country.

—The Federal Power Commission not only stemmed the rising cost of natural gas, it retroactively reduced rates. As a result, over $650 million has been refunded and there is now an annual reduction of $130 million in natural gas costs to the American consumer. Further, the Commission's National Power Survey estimates that by 1980 as much as $11 billion per year can be saved in the cost of electricity for Americans.

—The Federal Communications Commission moved to reduce the rates of interstate telephone costs. This means estimated savings of $100 million a year for American consumers.

—The Civil Aeronautics Board reduced domestic air fares, air cargo rates, and transatlantic fares which will amount to an eventual saving of over $50 million annually for consumers.

—Legislation has been passed protecting consumers from the indiscriminate sale and use of dangerous drugs.

—The National Food Marketing Commission, established last year by the Congress at my request, has held hearings to study the widening spread between what the farmer receives and what the consumer pays for food. Its recommendations, when implemented, will undoubtedly benefit consumers. In the meantime, it is gratifying to note that food prices are stable, and that good nutritional food can be obtained at reasonable prices.

The list could go on and on—for virtually every piece of legislation affects consumers. The record is indisputable—consumers have benefited greatly.

But this is not the time to look back in self-satisfaction. It is the time to look ahead.

One of the greatest contributions this Consumer Advisory Council can make will be to identify the needs of consumers, now and in the years ahead, and to recommend programs to fill their needs.

There are several areas in which I would recommend your careful interest:

First, business-consumer relations. I believe the time has come to bury forever the myth that furthering the interest of the consumer must be at the expense of the producer. There is, I am convinced, a common interest between Americans in their capacity as producers and in their capacity as consumers. This mutuality must be emphasized.

Second, adequate consumer information. Prosperity depends just as much on the freedom of consumers to make informed choices as it does on the ingenuity of business and labor. In our modern age, when the marketplace has become more complex, more impersonal, and more national in character, consumers must be kept adequately informed.

And third, groups needing special attention. Low-income consumers and other special groups—including the elderly, teenagers, and new family units—deserve adequate solutions for their particular problems.

I will continue to support the Congress in its move towards more adequate consumer legislation. Informed consumer choice among increasingly varied and complex products requires information concerning price, quantity, and quality. Greater truth in packaging will help protect consumers. More disclosure of facts in lending will help consumers to more easily compare costs of credit, and thereby help avoid the personal tragedy of being overburdened with debt.

Through the Committee on Consumer Interests, Federal agencies will continue to call on the Consumer Advisory Council for expert and timely advice on specific issues. The Consumer Advisory Council can render valuable assistance by recommending further steps:

—to improve consumer education in the Nation's schools;

—to meet the information needs of modern-day consumers; and

—to take a fresh look at how adequately the Federal Government is equipped to serve and protect the consumer interest.

I am confident that you who are gathered here today will discharge your important and unique function with honor and distinction.

A large share of credit for the progress we have made—and will make in the future—must go to Esther Peterson.

Through her leadership and her dedication, a new day has dawned for every American consumer.

We thank her—and we thank you—for the entire Nation.

NOTE: The President's remarks were read by Vice President Hubert H. Humphrey to members of the Consumer Advisory Council at noon in his office in the Executive Office Building. In his remarks the President referred to Mrs. Esther Peterson, Assistant Secretary for Labor Standards and Chairman of the President's Committee on Consumer Interests.

The Consumer Advisory Council was established as part of the President's Committee on Consumer Interests by Executive Order 11136 of January 3, 1964 (29 F.R. 129; 3 CFR, 1964 Supp., p. 110). The Council consists of private citizens appointed by the President to advise the Government on issues of broad economic policy of immediate concern to consumers.

The text of the remarks was released at the Naval Hospital, Bethesda, Md.

568 Remarks in the Hospital at the Signing of the Clean Air Act Amendments and Solid Waste Disposal Bill. *October 20, 1965*

WHEN future historians write of this era, I believe they will note that ours was the generation that finally faced up to the accumulated problems of our American life.

To us has been given the task of checking the slow but the relentless erosion of our civilization.

To us has been given the responsibility not only of stimulating our progress, but of making that progress acceptable to our children and our grandchildren.

Today, we are taking another large and forward step in this direction.

Since the beginning of the industrial revolution, we have been systematically polluting our air.

Each year the pollution grows worse.

We have now reached the point where our factories and our automobiles, our furnaces and our municipal dumps are spewing more

than 150 million tons of pollutants annually into the air that we breathe—almost one-half million tons a day.

From our automobiles alone, enough carbon monoxide is discharged daily to adversely pollute the combined areas of Massachusetts, Connecticut, and New Jersey.

This has become a health problem that is national in scope.

The air that is the very essence of life has become a carrier for disease and for early death. Between 1930 and 1960 the number of deaths from one respiratory disease alone increased by 800 percent.

But air pollution is also a drain on our resources. In the United States alone it accounts for more than $11 billion in economic damages. This amounts to nearly $30 a year for every man, woman, and child in our Nation. And yet our expenditure on air pollution control is less than 20 cents a year per citizen.

We made a hopeful beginning toward solving this problem with the Clean Air Act of 1963.

Today, with the signing of the Clean Air Act Amendments and Solid Waste Disposal Act, we are redoubling our efforts.

This act will require all 1968 model automobiles—including the foreign models that are sold here—to meet Federal control standards for exhaust.

This bill creates a Federal research and technical assistance program to seek ways of disposing of the millions of tons of solid wastes that we generate each year.

This bill gives us the tools to halt pollution before it starts in new industries.

Rachel Carson once wrote: "In biological history, no organism has survived long if its environment became in some way unfit for it. But no organism before man has deliberately polluted its own environment." [1]

Well, to those of you here in this room—members and leaders of both parties—this morning I join you in saying that together we intend to rewrite that chapter of history.

Today we make our beginning.

NOTE: The President spoke at 9:05 a.m. in his room at the Naval Hospital, Bethesda, Md. Present for the occasion were Vice President Hubert Humphrey; Representative John W. McCormack of Massachusetts, Speaker of the House of Representatives; Secretary of Health, Education, and Welfare John W. Gardner; Senators Mike Mansfield of Montana, Pat McNamara of Michigan, Edmund S. Muskie of Maine, Hiram L. Fong of Hawaii, and J. Caleb Boggs of Delaware; and Representatives Hale Boggs of Louisiana, Oren Harris of Arkansas, William L. Springer of Illinois, and Leo W. O'Brien of New York.

As enacted, the Clean Air Act Amendments and Solid Waste Disposal Act is Public Law 89–272 (79 Stat. 992, 997).

The text of the remarks was released at the Hospital.

---

[1] Rachel Carson, "Silent Spring" (Boston: Houghton Mifflin Co., 1962).

569 Memorandum on Steps Taken To Strengthen the Food-for-Peace Program. *October 20, 1965*

Memorandum for Secretary of State, Secretary of Agriculture:

I have today issued an Executive Order transferring the duties of the Director of the Food-for-Peace Program to the Secretary of State, and providing for the appointment of a Special Assistant to the Secretary to assist him in the execution of this additional responsibility.

As you know, I have always taken a deep personal interest in the Food-for-Peace Program. I regard the Food-for-Peace Program as the primary tool in our battle against hunger and privation abroad. Its accomplishments to date have more than met the hopes of its creators and have immeasurably aided the United States by advancing the cause of peace and understanding. But the time has now come to simplify and strengthen its operation within the Executive Branch—a step which I have taken today.

The administration of the Food-for-Peace Program will be transferred to the Secretary of State to coordinate, consolidate and carry out the program more effectively as part of our entire national effort for peace and progress throughout the world.

In the last four years, under your direction and leadership and under the direction and leadership of Mr. Richard Reuter, the Director of the Program, the Departments of State and Agriculture have worked together in a true example of interagency harmony and cooperation. I know that this same spirit will prevail in the future and that with your joint support the program will flourish and become stronger than ever.

I am happy that the progress of the program will be assured by Mr. Reuter's continuing direction as the Special Assistant to the Secretary of State for the Food-for-Peace Program.

I am today directing the Secretary of State to recommend what additional steps should be taken to further strengthen the Food-for-

Peace Program as an integral part of our foreign policy program.

LYNDON B. JOHNSON

NOTE: The President referred to Executive Order 11252 "Food-for-Peace Program" (1 Weekly Comp. Pres. Docs., p. 409; 30 F.R. 13507; 3 CFR, 1965 Supp., p. 181).

The recommendations of the Secretary of State were embodied in the President's message to Congress on food for freedom, dated February 10, 1966 (2 Weekly Comp. Pres. Docs., p. 194).

The memorandum was released at the Naval Hospital, Bethesda, Md.

570 Statement by the President Upon Signing the Foreign Assistance and Related Agencies Appropriation Act. *October* 20, 1965

I HAVE today signed into law the Foreign Assistance and Related Agencies Appropriation Act for fiscal year 1966.

This act is proof of the stark fact that the majority of the people in our world are living in desperate need. It is also proof of the simple fact that Americans are not going to sit idly by while others suffer.

Since World War II the nations of the free world have invested some $135 billion in foreign aid. The United States alone has contributed $115 billion of that total. I know of no more convincing evidence of the compassion in the heart of this Nation.

But compassion is not enough. While our wealth is great, it is not unlimited. It must be used not merely to apply band-aids to superficial wounds but to remove the causes of deeper and more dangerous disorders.

That is why I do not intend for American aid to become an international dole. The Congress of the United States does not want that. The people of this country do not want that. The people who benefit from our assistance, I am sure, do not want that.

Our assistance must and will go to those nations that will most use it to bring major

and far-reaching benefits to their people.

It will go to those willing not only to talk about basic social change but who will act immediately on these reforms. As I discharge my responsibilities under this act, I will look not simply to the fact of an agreement that points toward reform but to action already taken to bring reform to fruition.

Action, not promises, will be the standard of our assistance.

Accomplishments, not apologies, are what the American people expect from their desire to help others help themselves.

The amount of money appropriated in this act is only 7 percent less than my original request. This is the smallest reduction in such a request since the beginning of the Marshall plan and reflects the unusual scrutiny given the measure by both the administration and Congress.

When I sent the request to Congress, I pledged that these funds will be used wisely and effectively and in keeping with our own national interests. That pledge I intend to fulfill.

I am, for example, instructing the administrators of this program to make certain that every dollar spent is consistent with our efforts to improve our balance of payments position. If the dollar does not remain strong, no amount of foreign aid will, in the long run, prove helpful to anyone anywhere in the world.

I am also instructing the men who administer this program to be certain these funds go to the people.

And I am asking them to assure that the money invested in this program produce long-term innovations that will hasten the day when others can stand proudly on their own feet and walk steadily toward a better future.

NOTE: As enacted, the Foreign Assistance and Related Agencies Appropriation Act, 1966, is Public Law 89–273 (79 Stat. 1002).

The statement was released at the Naval Hospital, Bethesda, Md.

571 Message Greeting the Organization of African Unity Then Meeting in Accra. *October* 21, 1965

I EXTEND to the Organization of African Unity the greetings of the Government and the people of the United States of America.

We in the United States share with you a common aspiration for the advancement of human dignity and freedom. Your organization provides one means for the peoples of Africa to realize their hopes and dreams. Your past work in the peaceful settlement of disputes has demonstrated to all the world the great benefits to be derived from cooperative action.

I wish you success in your deliberations. It is our hope that they will strengthen the bonds among you and further advance the well-being of your member countries.

NOTE: The message was read by Bill D. Moyers, Special Assistant to the President, at his news conference in his office at the White House at 4:10 p.m. on Thursday, October 21, 1965. It was not made public in the form of a White House press release.

The Assembly of Heads of State and Government of the Organization of African Unity met in Accra, Ghana, October 21–25, 1965.

572 Remarks to Fellow Patients in the Naval Hospital, Bethesda, Maryland. *October* 21, 1965

I AM SORRY you are here, but there are a good many folks that are living better and enjoying freedom because you are. And I am glad that the citizens of this country are made up of men like you.

I feel like one of the fellow casualties—I have been out of circulation for a few days and kind of sliced up a little myself, but I have gone through nothing like what you have gone through.

The thing, though, that made me able to take what I did take, and with my chin up, was the knowledge that men like you are willing to do what you did for your country. I know that as far as you are concerned, you did it because that is what your duty was and what you ought to do, and what is right. But it does make your families and your countrymen—and particularly your President—mighty proud that we produce fellows like you in this country.

As long as we have the system of government we have, and as long as we have the courage and the determination, the dedication, the love of country and flag that we have, and fellows like you, we are going to continue to produce a Nation like this. Whenever we cease to love it, and whenever we cease to be willing to die for it, and whenever we are willing to throw in the towel, why then some other society will come along and take us over.

But I know some of you must think that you got a bad break. And you have. But because of what you have done there are 3 billion people in the world that will get a better break, and their kids will live better, be happier, stronger, better educated, and eat more food, and have more freedom and more liberty.

I just can't sum up in any words of mine how proud I am of the Marines, the Navy, the Army, the Air Force, and the Coast Guard, and the fellows that never look back. And when I feel pretty blue at night, and I

issue the orders that you carry out, I do it with a heavy heart. But I never see one of your performances that I am not proud of you, and I wanted to come and tell you that before I checked out.

Good luck to you. Tell all your families—your wives, your children, your mothers, and your fathers—that the President of your country is mighty proud of you.

I want to thank all the doctors, and the nurses, and the aides in this wonderful hospital for doing the best they can to make us all comfortable. They have been certainly wonderful to me and I hope they have been to you.

NOTE: The President spoke at 1 p.m., during an informal visit to Ward 6–C of the Naval Hospital, Bethesda, Md., shortly before his return to the White House following his gall bladder surgery. The patients included Marines and naval personnel who had been wounded in Viet-Nam.

573   Statement by the President Urging the Sending of Holiday Gifts and Messages to Servicemen in Viet-Nam and Southeast Asia. *October 22, 1965*

THE COMMITMENT of U.S. personnel in Viet-Nam and Southeast Asia means that thousands of our countrymen will be spending Christmas halfway around the world in an atmosphere far removed from the warm friendliness and good cheer of a typical holiday at home. More than ever, it is important that we remember our friends and loved ones who so valiantly serve us overseas.

With the expected steep increase in the volume of this year's Christmas mail for Americans in Southeast Asia, I am informed that the Post Office Department is tripling the amount of space in the San Francisco Post Office devoted to handling this mail.

There will be an addition of nearly 200 postal workers between now and mid-December to make sure that gift packages and greetings are delivered by Christmas Eve. All packages sent with regular surface postage should be mailed by November 10. Airmail packages, letters, and cards should be sent no later than December 1.

I encourage all Americans to especially remember our servicemen in Viet-Nam and Southeast Asia during the holiday season. Although they may be separated from the warmth of the family fireside, we can assure them, through our gifts and messages, that they are here in our hearts.

574   Statement by the President Following the Signing of Bill Implementing U.S.-Canadian Agreement on Automotive Products. *October 22, 1965*

I HAVE SIGNED the Automotive Products Trade Act of 1965, H.R. 9042, with particular pleasure. This legislation opens the way to a new era of even closer economic and commercial relations with our greatest trading partner, Canada.

Last January 16, Prime Minister Lester Pearson of Canada and I signed an agreement looking toward free trade in automobiles and automotive products between our two countries.

In that agreement, Canada promised to remove entirely its duties on United States automobiles and parts for the manufacture of automobiles.

I promised to ask the Congress for authority to remove United States duties on automobiles and similar parts imported from Canada.

Canada acted at once. The Canadian Government revoked a plan for the remission of tariffs that had troubled many U.S. manufacturers and that might have led to serious economic conflict between our two countries.

Canada also immediately removed its duties of 17½ percent on automobiles and up to 25 percent on parts imported from the United States. The Congress has now provided me with the authority to remove U.S. duties on imports of Canadian automotive products covered by the agreement.

Thus, we have ended a controversy that threatened to endanger our automotive trade with Canada, a trade that last year ran over one-half billion dollars in our favor.

We have assured continuation of over 25,-000 jobs for American workers directly involved in producing the automotive goods we sell to Canada, and as many more for those who work in the steel, textile, electrical, rubber, and other supporting industries.

I am confident that as production and trade expand under the encouragement of the U.S.-Canadian agreement, both our countries will benefit. These benefits will be felt by the automobile industry, our independent parts manufacturers, the employees of the automotive industry, and by our country as a whole.

These benefits have, in fact, already begun to appear. During the first half of this year our trade both ways with Canada in automobiles, trucks, buses, and automotive parts rose nearly $120 million—over 30 percent over last year's trade for the same period. Of this amount $81 million was increased sales of parts and vehicles by the United States to Canada.

During this same period total employment in the automotive industry in the United States increased by more than 45,000 workers—and many of these new jobs resulted from our increased trade with Canada.

Meantime, employment and production in Canada's automobile industry have also increased and Canadian citizens have already begun to benefit from lowered prices on automobiles.

Most important, as I said on the occasion of signing the agreement, when it appeared that our two countries were on the verge of grave differences in our mutual trade, we chose instead the road to understanding instead of the road to conflict.

Our ties with Canada are historically close, our relations cordial, our people durable friends.

This agreement, originating in our common interest, arrived at for our common benefit, will make those ties even closer and more fruitful for the future.

NOTE: As enacted, the Automotive Products Trade Act of 1965, approved October 21, 1965, is Public Law 89–283 (79 Stat. 1016).

For the President's remarks with Prime Minister Pearson upon signing the U.S.-Canadian Trade Agreement on Automotive Products, see Item 21.

See also Item 575.

575 Statement by the President on Issuing Proclamation and Executive Order Relating to the U.S.-Canadian Agreement on Automotive Products. *October 22, 1965*

I AM ISSUING a proclamation exercising the authority given me by the act to remove United States duties on automotive products covered by our agreement with Canada. The provisions of the proclamation relating to duties will become effective after 60 days. The removal of United States duties will then be retroactive to January 18, 1965, the date Canada removed its duties on United States automotive products.

H.R. 9042 also enacts special provisions for determining eligibility for the adjustment assistance already provided by the Trade Expansion Act, if there should be instances in which firms or workers suffer dislocation as a result of the agreement. These new eligibility provisions assure that there will be prompt assistance to individual firms or workers who may be temporarily affected by

this trade agreement benefiting the Nation as a whole. To administer these new provisions, I am establishing a board consisting of the Secretary of the Treasury, the Secretary of Commerce, and the Secretary of Labor, and delegating to it the functions concerning adjustment assistance conferred upon me by the act.

NOTE: The President referred to Proclamation 3682 "Implementing Agreement Concerning Automotive Products Between the United States and Canada" (Oct. 21, 1965; 1 Weekly Comp. Pres. Docs., p. 413; 30 F.R. 13683; 3 CFR, 1965 Supp., p. 68); and to Executive Order 11254 "Establishing the Automotive Agreement Adjustment Assistance Board" (Oct. 21, 1965; 1 Weekly Comp. Pres. Docs., p. 413; 30 F.R. 13569; 3 CFR, 1965 Supp., p. 183).

For the President's statement following the signing of bill (H.R. 9042) implementing the U.S.-Canadian agreement on automotive products, see Item 574.

576 Remarks at the Signing of the Highway Beautification Act of 1965. *October 22, 1965*

Secretary Gardner, distinguished Members of the leadership of the Congress and Members of the Congress, and all other lovers of beauty:

America likes to think of itself as a strong and stalwart and expanding Nation. It identifies itself gladly with the products of

its own hands. We frequently point with pride and with confidence to the products of our great free enterprise system—management and labor.

These are and these should be a source of pride to every American. They are certainly the source of American strength.

They are truly the fountainhead of American wealth. They are actually a part of America's soul.

But there is more to America than raw industrial might. And when you go through what I have gone through the last 2 weeks you constantly think of things like that. You no longer get your computers in and try to count your riches.

There is a part of America which was here long before we arrived, and will be here, if we preserve it, long after we depart: the forests and the flowers, the open prairies and the slope of the hills, the tall mountains, the granite, the limestone, the caliche, the unmarked trails, the winding little streams—well, this is the America that no amount of science or skill can ever recreate or actually ever duplicate.

This America is the source of America's greatness. It is another part of America's soul as well.

When I was growing up, the land itself was life. And when the day seemed particularly harsh and bitter, the land was always there just as nature had left it—wild, rugged, beautiful, and changing, always changing.

And really, how do you measure the excitement and the happiness that comes to a boy from the old swimming hole in the happy days of yore, when I used to lean above it; the old sycamore, the baiting of a hook that is tossed into the stream to catch a wily fish, or looking at a graceful deer that leaps with hardly a quiver over a rock fence that was put down by some settler a hundred years or more ago?

How do you really put a value on the view of the night that is caught in a boy's eyes while he is stretched out in the thick grass watching the million stars that we never see in these crowded cities, breathing the sounds of the night and the birds and the pure, fresh air while in his ears are the crickets and the wind?

Well, in recent years I think America has sadly neglected this part of America's national heritage. We have placed a wall of civilization between us and between the beauty of our land and of our countryside. In our eagerness to expand and to improve, we have relegated nature to a weekend role, and we have banished it from our daily lives.

Well, I think that we are a poorer Nation because of it, and it is something I am not proud of. And it is something I am going to do something about. Because as long as I am your President, by choice of your people, I do not choose to preside over the destiny of this country and to hide from view what God has gladly given it.

And that is why today there is a great deal of real joy within me, and within my family, as we meet here in this historic East Room to sign the Highway Beautification Act of 1965.

Now, this bill does more than control advertising and junkyards along the billions of dollars of highways that the people have built with their money—public money, not private money. It does more than give us the tools just to landscape some of those highways.

This bill will bring the wonders of nature back into our daily lives.

This bill will enrich our spirits and restore a small measure of our national greatness.

As I rode the George Washington Memorial Parkway back to the White House only yesterday afternoon, I saw nature at its purest. And I thought of the honor roll of names—a good many of you are sitting here in the front row today—that made this possible. And as I thought of you who had helped and stood up against private greed for public good, I looked at those dogwoods that had turned red, and the maple trees that were scarlet and gold. In a pattern of brown and yellow, God's finery was at its finest. And not one single foot of it was marred by a single, unsightly, man-made construction or obstruction—no advertising signs, no old, dilapidated trucks, no junkyards. Well, doctors could prescribe no better medicine for me, and that is what I said to my surgeon as we drove along.

This bill does not represent everything that we wanted. It does not represent what we need. It does not represent what the national interest requires. But it is a first step, and there will be other steps. For though we must crawl before we walk, we are going to walk.

I remember the fierce resolve of a man that I admired greatly, a great leader of a great people, Franklin D. Roosevelt. He fought a pitched battle in 1936 with private interests whose target was private gain. And I shall long remember the words that I believe he echoed at Madison Square Garden, when he declared to the Nation that the forces of selfishness had not only met their match, but these forces had met their master.

Well, I have not asked you to come here today to tell you that I have a desire to master anyone. But until the clock strikes the last hour of the time allotted to me as President by vote of all the people of this country, I will never turn away from the duty that my office demands or the vigilance that my oath of office requires.

And this administration has no desire to punish or to penalize any private industry, or any private company, or any group, or any organization of complex associations in this Nation. But we are not going to allow them to intrude their own specialized private objective on the larger public trust.

Beauty belongs to all the people. And so

long as I am President, what has been divinely given to nature will not be taken recklessly away by man.

This Congress is to be thanked for the bill that you have given us. I wish it could have been more, but I realize, too, that there are other views to be considered in our system of checks and balances.

The grandchildren of those of you in this country that may have mocked and ridiculed us today, someday will point with pride to the public servants who are here in this room, who cast their lot with the people.

And unless I miss my guess, history will remember on its honor roll those of you whom the camera brings into focus in this room today, who stood up and were counted when that roll was called that said we are going to preserve at least a part of what God gave us.

Thank you very much.

NOTE: The President spoke at 2:16 p.m. in the East Room at the White House. In his opening words he referred to John W. Gardner, Secretary of Health, Education, and Welfare.

As enacted, the Highway Beautification Act of 1965 is Public Law 89–285 (79 Stat. 1028).

On August 13, 1965, the White House made public a report to the President from the Secretary of the Interior announcing his order restricting outdoor advertising on public lands adjacent to highways.

The report stated, "I am pleased to report that I am issuing orders extending to 1,000 feet the minimum distance any billboards or advertising displays can be placed on public lands administered by this Department's Bureau of Land Management.

"The 1,000-foot minimum still permits us to bar any such signs, regardless of the distance, and is established for those acceptable signs that are not eyesores or do not otherwise impair the natural view by the public. The present restriction is 660 feet." (1 Weekly Comp. Pres. Docs., p. 91)

On November 4, 1965, the White House announced the first allocation of Federal funds to the States under the highway beautification program. The sum of $6 million was allocated for the control of junkyards and outdoor advertising, and $60 million was allocated for landscaping and scenic enhancement.

The release stated that funds would be expended

under procedures of the cooperative Federal-State highway program. The States, which would initiate projects and supervise the work, would later be reimbursed for 75 percent of the costs of controlling outdoor advertising and junkyards and for 100 percent of the cost of landscaping work (1 Weekly Comp. Pres. Docs., p. 459).

See also Items 54, 277.

577   Statement by the President Upon Signing Proclamation Relating to Imports of Lead and Zinc.   *October 22, 1965*

I HAVE TODAY issued a proclamation terminating the limits on imports of unmanufactured lead and zinc.

This action, which becomes effective immediately with respect to ores and concentrates and in 30 days for lead and zinc metals, is the result of extensive study and discussion within the executive branch. The Tariff Commission, in a unanimous decision, found that ending the quotas was not likely to have a detrimental effect on domestic producers. Additionally, the United States companies which require unmanufactured lead and zinc in their processing and manufacturing activities have made clear their great need for additional lead and zinc—in fact, many have indicated that without immediate relief they will be forced to suspend operations.

The lifting of these import controls at this time, rather than awaiting the automatic expiration in mid-October 1967, under the provisions of the Trade Expansion Act of 1962, will prevent the loss of jobs in many sections of the Nation.

Domestic lead and zinc producers who do not object to greater imports at this time have expressed concern that future relief, if necessary, should not be inordinately delayed. Accordingly, I have urged the members of the Tariff Commission to streamline its procedures and to redouble its efforts to expedite proceedings in any case where it is indicated that delay might bar effective relief. I am confident improvements can be made.

The need for a strong and vigorous domestic lead and zinc mining industry in this country is obvious. Recently the Congress demonstrated its commitment to this goal by extending the Lead and Zinc Small Producers Stabilization Act—scheduled to expire at the end of this year—to December 31, 1969. I was pleased to sign this bill into law earlier this month thereby continuing the successful program of annual payments to qualified small lead and zinc mine operators.

NOTE: The President referred to Proclamation 3683 "Termination of Quantitative Limitations on Imports of Unmanufactured Lead and Zinc" (1 Weekly Comp. Pres. Docs., p. 416; 30 F.R. 13623; 3 CFR, 1965 Supp., p. 69).

The bill extending the Lead-Zinc Small Producers Stabilization Act of October 3, 1961, was approved by the President on October 5, 1965 (Public Law 89–238, 79 Stat. 925).

578   Statement by the President Upon Signing the National Vocational Student Loan Insurance Act.   *October 22, 1965*

ECONOMISTS tell us that improvement of education has been responsible for one-fourth to one-half of the growth in our Nation's economy over the past half century.

As our population grows, the number of young people—the job seekers—will grow faster than any group among us, and employers will demand more of them. We must be sure that there will be no gap between the number of jobs available and the ability of our people to perform those jobs.

This act will help young people enter business, trade, and technical schools—institutions which play a vital role in providing the skills our citizens must have to compete and contribute in our society.

The $1,875,000 allotted to the States for insured loan programs under this act will make possible almost $19 million in loans. We estimate that in the first year as many as 25,000 young people—receiving grants of up to $1,000—will enjoy its benefits. The amount they return to our economy with their new skills and training is far beyond counting.

—This act will enable the Commissioner of Education to assist in establishing adequate State and nonprofit loan insurance programs for students in these schools;

—It will allow the Commissioner to insure eligible lending institutions against losses on such loans;

—Finally, it will empower him to make direct loans where funds are not normally available through lending institutions.

We have already done much toward providing full educational opportunity in the Nation. The benefits of the Elementary and Secondary Education Act of 1965 have already begun to flow to the States. The Higher Education Act, which will soon be signed, will provide valuable new assistance to students in our colleges and universities.

But fewer than half of our young people go to college; the quality of life in our country—and the strength of our economy—cannot depend solely upon this minority. This act will be a source of encouragement to capable young people who need training to become useful and productive citizens.

I am happy to sign it.

I want to thank the entire 89th Congress—particularly Congressman John Dent and Senator Wayne Morse, who have given much time and labor on behalf of this measure. They have helped move this country closer to the day when no ambitious young person need appear on the unemployment rolls.

NOTE: As enacted, the National Vocational Student Loan Insurance Act (H.R. 7743) is Public Law 89–287 (79 Stat. 1037).

The Elementary and Secondary Education Act of 1965 was approved by the President on April 11, 1965 (see Item 181).

The Higher Education Act of 1965 was approved by the President on November 8, 1965 (see Item 603).

579 Statement by the President Upon Signing the Health Professions Educational Assistance Amendments. *October 22, 1965*

THE RECORD of the 89th Congress is impressive in every field—and monumental in the field of health. This is the Congress which achieved Medicare, the Heart, Cancer, and Stroke Amendments, the Community Mental Health Centers Act. This is the Congress which gave to the American people the Community Health Services Extension Act, the Health Research Facilities Amendments, and many others.

To that record, we add today the Health Professions Educational Assistance Amendments.

Two years ago Congress acknowledged our tremendous need for more doctors by passing the Health Professions Assistance Act, which provided funds for constructing medical teaching facilities; it established loans to students preparing for the health professions—and in 2 years it helped create 2,000 new openings in medical and related schools.

But the need for qualified health professionals is still acute. If we are to begin to meet our health needs, we must educate 50 percent more doctors by 1975, and we must double the annual graduation rate for dentists. By 1971 we must increase by at least 3,500 the capacity of our schools to receive first-year students.

Today at least 10 medical schools are too poorly financed to continue providing acceptable education without assistance; at least three dental schools are on probationary status, in danger of losing their accreditation. Two schools of optometry also face loss of accreditation.

Because of prohibitive costs, a student from a poor family, no matter how impressive his talents, stands a far smaller chance of becoming a doctor or dentist than the child of a wealthier family. Forty-nine percent of medical students come from families with annual incomes of $10,000 or more; almost 30 percent come from families making $15,000 or more per year.

More than four out of five students in science receive grants to assist their study, yet less than one-third of American medical students receive such aid. The needy student, looking toward the long years of financial hardship in obtaining a medical education, frequently turns to graduate study in science, simply because the opportunities for financial assistance are greater. Thus the medical professions lose the services of many who might become talented—and sorely needed—doctors and dentists.

The bill which I sign today will spur the attack on these serious shortages:

—It extends construction grants to public and nonprofit medical schools to increase student capacity.

—It extends a loan program to help thousands of needy students toward medical education.

—It authorizes a new program of basic and special improvement grants to enable schools of medicine, osteopathy, dentistry, optometry, and podiatry, many of which have borne heavy financial burdens at the expense of academic standards, to improve their teaching.

—Finally, it authorizes a new program of scholarships for students in these schools and in schools of pharmacy.

I take pride in signing this measure. It symbolizes our national investment in the health and active life of every citizen—an investment which pays rich dividends in our people's productivity and happiness.

NOTE: As enacted, the Health Professions Educational Assistance Amendments (H.R. 3141) is Public Law 89–290 (79 Stat. 1052).

The Health Professions Educational Assistance Act of 1963 was approved on September 24, 1963 (Public Law 88–129; 77 Stat. 164).

580 Statement by the President Upon Signing Bill Increasing Fees for Registration of New Securities Offerings. *October 22, 1965*

IN MY Budget Message to the Congress last January, I said that, in justice to all our taxpayers, those who enjoy special benefits should bear a fair share of the costs.

In keeping with that principle I have just signed into law an amendment to the Securities Act of 1933, increasing the fees paid for registration of new securities offerings with the Securities and Exchange Commission.

The increase is a modest one when compared to the benefits enjoyed by the thousands of investors who are protected by our securities laws. These are the same persons who, in the long run, will bear the burden of the increased fees.

The new law increases the registration fee from 10 cents per $1,000 of securities registered to 20 cents per $1,000, and increases the minimum fee from $25 to $100.

This is the first increase in registration fees since the original Securities Act became

law in 1933. It is estimated that the bill will increase by about $1.8 million the fees collected by the Commission. The effect of the new fee schedule will be to place on a self-supporting basis the Commission's function of examining registration statements.

NOTE: As enacted, the bill to amend the Securities Act of 1933 with respect to certain registration fees (H.R. 7169) is Public Law 89–289 (79 Stat. 1051).

581 Statement by the President Upon Signing Bill Providing Grants for Medical Library Services and Facilities. *October 22, 1965*

THE VOLUME of published research in the field of medicine doubles every 10 years. Such a tremendous expansion of knowledge is cumulative; it feeds upon itself—no one can predict when a key discovery will be made which will unlock a whole new chain of knowledge.

This creative process cannot go on unless the results of scientific work are available to practicing physicians and to health workers across the country. The Nation's medical libraries are a vital link between medical education, practice, and research.

Yet in past years we have given too little attention to the problems of collecting and sharing scientific knowledge.

This measure provides long-needed support for our medical libraries.

—It will furnish space and facilities for dealing with the massive body of published information.

—It will advance the processing, storage, and retrieval of material vitally needed by health professionals.

—It will help us to overcome the shortage of personnel trained in science information technology.

Its result, ultimately, will be not only an increase in the growth and spread of scientific knowledge, but a gain in the health and well-being of the American people.

NOTE: As enacted, the Medical Library Assistance Act of 1965 is Public Law 89–291 (79 Stat. 1059).

582 Statement by the President Upon Signing the Service Contract Act of 1965. *October 22, 1965*

THE Government of the United States must be a model employer. Those enrolled in the service of the Nation must be assured the same labor standards and working conditions which apply to private industry. This legislation, H.R. 10238, closes the last big gap in protecting those standards where employees of contractors are doing business with the Federal Government.

Employees working on Federal construction contracts have long been protected by the Davis-Bacon Act. Those employed by businesses with Government supply contracts have enjoyed the protection of the Walsh-Healey Act. Until today, those employees of contractors who supply various services to the Government have possessed no such protection.

The McNamara-O'Hara Act, which I am signing today, corrects that deficiency. Under this act, protection is now extended to workers engaged in laundry and drycleaning, custodial and janitorial duties, guard service, packing and crating, food service, and miscellaneous housekeeping services performed on contract for the Federal Government or the District of Columbia.

All such contracts must now contain provisions regarding minimum wages, fringe benefits, and working conditions. Their wages must be no less than the rate determined by the Secretary of Labor to be prevailing for similar employees in the locality. Also, wages must not be less than the minimum rate required under the Fair Labor Standards Act. Finally, work must not be performed under conditions which are unsanitary or hazardous or dangerous to the health safety of the working men and women.

I am particularly pleased to sign this bill. I am grateful to Senator McNamara and Congressman O'Hara for their splendid efforts to achieve its enactment because so many of the employees who will benefit are among the lowest paid workers in our society.

We take justifiable pride in our growing national economy and in the ever-higher living standards being achieved by most Americans. Yet, in the midst of prosperity, there are many who continue to exist on economic levels far below that of our general prosperity. Many of those affected by this bill are so situated.

Under the terms of the McNamara-O'Hara Act we can now act to assist all such workers when they perform work financed with Federal funds.

This measure will be enforced fairly and impartially. But I want to make it clear that it is not a license for harassment of management nor is it an open door to misuse of its aims. I would hope that emerging from these new rules will be better understanding on the part of both employees and employers.

NOTE: As enacted, the Service Contract Act of 1965 (McNamara-O'Hara Act, H.R. 10238) is Public Law 89–286 (79 Stat. 1034).

583 Statement by the President Designating Two Peaks of Mount McKinley in Honor of Sir Winston Churchill. *October 23, 1965*

IT IS FITTING that these majestic peaks be named in Sir Winston Churchill's honor. Soldier, author, statesman, he was one of the greatest leaders in the history of English-speaking peoples, and he devoted his life to the twin goals of peace and freedom. Sir Winston was an honorary American citizen—the second man in history to be so honored by the people of the United States.

NOTE: The statement was made public as part of a White House release announcing that the President had designated the north and south peaks of Mount McKinley as Churchill Peaks. The release stated that designation of the peaks of the 20,320-foot mountain in Alaska was proposed by Secretary of the Interior Stewart L. Udall and the National Park Service, custodian of Mount McKinley National Park, a 3,030-square-mile subarctic wilderness area.

584 Message to the Congress Transmitting 12th Semiannual Report of the National Aeronautics and Space Administration. *October 23, 1965*

[Released October 23, 1965. Dated October 22, 1965]

To the Congress of the United States:

This report to the Congress describes a six-month period of impressive accomplishment by the National Aeronautics and Space Administration.

In a larger sense, however, this report describes America on the move.

The story of man's advancement through the ages is the story of man's victory over the forces of nature. The health and comfort he enjoys, the leisure he possesses, and the abundance of the food he eats are all the result of his unending determination to probe the secrets of the world around him.

In 1958, it was my privilege to introduce the legislation to create the National Aeronautics and Space Administration. I stated then: "I confidently believe that the developments of the Space Age will bring the beginning of the longest and greatest boom of abundance and prosperity in the history of man."

Time is bearing out that belief.

And so I take pleasure in submitting this report to Congress. It chronicles a great and exciting period of accomplishment and foreshadows an even greater one. In commending this record, I also commend the men principally responsible for making it possible. Dr. James Webb and Dr. Hugh Dryden have guided and directed our Nation's space program for nearly five years—and they have a grateful nation in their debt.

LYNDON B. JOHNSON

The White House
October 22, 1965

NOTE: The 12th semiannual report of the National Aeronautics and Space Administration covers the period July 1–December 31, 1964 (Government Printing Office, 236 pp.).

585 Message to the Congress Transmitting 18th Annual Report of the Housing and Home Finance Agency. *October 23, 1965*

[Released October 23, 1965. Dated October 22, 1965]

To the Congress of the United States:

The Housing Act of 1954 directs that I transmit to Congress the Annual Report of the Housing and Home Finance Agency, covering activities for calendar year 1964.

This report confirms the wisdom of fifteen Congresses and five administrations going back to 1934. The great Franklin D. Roosevelt first pleaded with the Congress to approve housing measures for the good of all Americans.

Consider what has been done for America by the United States Government's housing programs:

$100 billion of FHA mortgage insurance loans has been written, covering more than 7 million homes and more than one million rental units.

700,000 public housing units have been constructed since the start of that program in 1937. Two million people are living in those units in more than 2,000 communities.

More than 600,000 college students are living in dormitories made possible by government loans.

$4.3 billion has been made available for urban renewal.

4,500 communities—mostly small towns—have received urban planning assistance.

$300 million of government credit has gone into small town water and sewer facilities.

These programs were not easily begun. Cries of "socialism" and "waste" surrounded them at their birth. False propaganda and misrepresentation were used to discredit those who were to administer them. Cynicism and self-interest preyed on fear of the new and the imaginative.

But without these programs we would never have been able to push back the frontiers of blight, disease and ugliness that thirty years ago afflicted one-third of a nation. Without them the task of building a clean and safe America would have been impossible.

Today our people accept these programs. Private enterprise and public well-being depend on them. We know now that these programs—and new approaches demanded by logic and vision—are needed to meet the challenges that confront us as hour by hour we become a more urban nation.

In 1965 I requested authority for a new means of housing low-income families. We proposed to encourage private organizations to build thousands of new apartments and houses for poor people who could not afford

safe or decent housing. We proposed to help these private builders provide housing for the elderly, the poor, and the handicapped, so that they might live with safety and dignity.

Congress accepted this proposal.

Yet when the time came to provide the funds for this program, the old voices of doubt and misunderstanding were raised once more. Allegations were made that had no basis in fact. Insinuations were raised that obscured the basic purposes of the act.

For the time being, those voices have prevailed. No program funds were granted.

The national interest demands that the matter not stop there. Thousands of American families need this housing now—today. Thousands of poor children who should grow up in a world of safety and decency and promise are being treated with indifference by an affluent nation.

Next January I shall once more ask for the initial $30 million necessary to make bricks and mortar out of a promise. I am confident that the Congress will cut through the propaganda of fear and mistrust to provide shelter for the families who need it now—today. We who have raised up hopes have a duty to bring them to tangible reality.

LYNDON B. JOHNSON

The White House
October 22, 1965

NOTE: The 18th annual report of the Housing and Home Finance Agency covers calendar year 1964 (Government Printing Office, 456 pp.).

---

586   Statement by the President Upon Signing Bill Authorizing the Southern Nevada Water Project.   *October 23, 1965*

I HAVE approved S. 32, "To authorize the Secretary of the Interior to construct, operate, and maintain the southern Nevada water

project, Nevada, and for other purposes."

The southern Nevada water supply project which would be authorized by this bill consists of a system of distribution pipelines and related facilities to furnish water to Las Vegas, several other Nevada towns, and Nellis Air Force Base. I have supported Federal authorization of this project as the appropriate means for assisting this area to meet its growing water supply problems.

However, during the course of this legislation through the Congress a rider in the form of section 6 was added to it without consultation with any executive agency.

Section 6 provides as follows: "In all water supply contracts for the use of water in Nevada under this Act or section 5 of the Boulder Canyon Project Act (45 Stat. 1057) the Secretary shall recognize the intrastate priorities of water rights to the use of water existing on the date of enactment of this Act: *Provided, however,* That nothing in this Act shall be construed as validating any right diminished or lost because of abandonment, nonuse, or lack of due diligence, nor shall anything in this Act be construed as affecting the satisfaction of present perfected rights as defined by the decree of the United States Supreme Court in Arizona against California et al. (376 U.S. 340)."

Although these provisions are couched in general terms, the scant legislative history of the bill indicates that they are intended to be applicable to one company only. While there may be some equities which would justify special consideration for this company, I am advised by the Secretary of the Interior that these provisions might well have a much broader sweep. In fact, it appears that they might affect in unforeseeable ways the water rights of a number of individuals and firms amounting to 60,000 to 70,000 additional acre feet.

In these circumstances I have asked the Secretary of the Interior to develop legislation which would amend section 6 to limit its effect to that intended by the Congress. I am confident that those members concerned with this legislation will agree that the uncertainties surrounding the broader than intended effect of section 6 make its amendment desirable.

NOTE: As enacted, the bill (S. 32), approved October 22, 1965, is Public Law 89–292 (79 Stat. 1068).

587 Statement by the President Upon Signing the Omnibus Rivers and Harbors Bill. *October 26, 1965*

I HAVE today signed S. 2300—the omnibus rivers and harbors bill.

In so doing, I want to point out clearly and strongly that I cannot abide by one provision of the bill which flies in the face of the Constitution.

S. 2300 authorizes the construction of water resource projects totaling almost $2 billion.

These projects are needed.

They will bring economic vitality to almost every region of America and thus strengthen our national economy.

They have had and will continue to have my full support—because I deeply believe in them.

However, I do not support and I do not plan to implement section 201(a) of this legislation.

To do so would make the President a partner in the abdication of a fundamental principle of our Government—the separation of powers prescribed by the United States Constitution.

Section 201(a) provides that, "No appropriation shall be made to construct, operate, or maintain any such project [certain water resource development projects] if such project has not been approved by resolutions adopted by the Committees on Public Works of the Senate and House of Representatives, respectively."

Twice this year I have vetoed bills containing similar language.

Those provisions, like this one, were repugnant to the Constitution.

I have weighed this problem very carefully.

My legal advisers tell me that insofar as our system of checks and balances is concerned, this bill would do to the executive branch what neither House of Congress would want.

It would dilute and diminish the authority and powers of the Presidency.

I believe the Senate would understand my point of view, if I tried to contend that the Senate had no right to advise and consent.

And the House would understand, I am sure, if I attempted to insist that revenue measures did not have to originate in the House.

This is not a personal matter, but I cannot stress too strongly the seriousness with which I view this particular section.

The people of this country did not elect me to this office to preside over its erosion. And I intend to turn over this office with all of its responsibilities and powers intact to the next man who sits in this chair.

So just as I would not want to infringe upon the power of the Senate or lessen the jurisdiction of the House or disregard the decisions of the Supreme Court, I do not want the legislative—through two committees—to encroach upon the responsibilities of the Presidency.

Absolute legal consistency would require that I veto what is otherwise a sound bill because of this one objectionable provision.

But, after counseling with legislative leaders, I have chosen not to veto, for these reasons:

—Unlike the bills earlier this year, section 201(a) permits, but does not require, the executive branch to use the objectionable procedure in order to carry out its responsibilities. Therefore, I believe that by refusing to use the procedure, by noting my objections to it, and by seeking its repeal in the next session of Congress, it is possible to approve the remainder of the bill without yielding to encroachment.

—A veto would have denied to the people of the various congressional districts the desirable benefits of the improvements provided by this legislation.

—And finally, I have the greatest respect for this Congress and for the tremendous accomplishments which it has realized. We have worked together for the common good of the greatest number of people. I think we have been successful.

For these reasons I have signed the bill into law.

But I repeat, again and again, that I do not intend to accept this infringement upon the office of the Presidency.

The section containing the objectionable provision is a grant of authority and does not require any action to be taken. The Senate and the House were divided as to the legal interpretation of the provision.

One point is clear: Enactment of the bill will not commit the executive branch to participate in the procedure to which I have objected. And as soon as the Congress convenes again, I will request it to repeal the provision.

In the meantime, I have instructed the Secretary of the Army to refrain from exercising the authority which section 201(a) attempts to vest in him.

NOTE: As enacted, the omnibus rivers and harbors bill (S. 2300) is Public Law 89–298 (79 Stat. 1073).

The President referred to earlier vetoes of the Northwest disaster relief bill (vetoed June 5, Congressional Record, June 7, p. 12216), and of the military authorization bill (vetoed August 21, Item 440).

The statement was released at Austin, Tex.

588 Statement by the President in Connection With the Award of a Presidential Unit Citation to the 42d Ranger Battalion, Republic of Viet-Nam. *October* 26, 1965

THE HEROIC action of the 42d Ranger Battalion of the Republic of Viet-Nam affords the world still another example of the courage and steadfast determination with which a brave people struggles to preserve its freedom.

Few nations have been subjected to such a ruthless and relentless assault on their basic liberty; none have fought more heroically in defense of that liberty than the people of South Viet-Nam.

The Republic of Viet-Nam is today on the frontier of freedom—a frontier which exists wherever force and violence attempt to subvert a nation's independence. The undaunted courage and indomitable spirit of the Vietnamese 42d Ranger Battalion, which we honor by this citation, strengthens our faith in the ultimate triumph of the cause of freedom.

PRESIDENTIAL UNIT CITATION TO THE 42d
BATTALION OF THE REPUBLIC OF VIET-
NAM ARMED FORCES

By virtue of the authority vested in me as President of the United States and as Commander-in-Chief of the Armed Forces of the United States I have today awarded

THE PRESIDENTIAL UNIT CITATION

TO THE 42d RANGER BATTALION

REPUBLIC OF VIET-NAM ARMED FORCES

FOR EXTRAORDINARY HEROISM

The 42d Ranger Battalion is cited for extraordinary heroism in connection with military operations against a hostile force in Bac Lieu Province, Vietnam on 13 May 1965. On this date the 42d Ranger Battalion was committed as part of a larger force in operation Dan Chi 135, a search and destroy operation against a suspected Viet Cong Battalion. At 1210 hours elements of the Battalion were Heli-lifted into battle and made immediate contact with the fanatic forces of the provincial battalion of Soc Trang, an elite Viet Cong unit, which occupied well-prepared defensive fortifications. With undaunted courage and steadfast determination elements of the 42d Ranger Battalion immediately closed with the enemy in a fierce assault which overran a flank of the enemy position. As the Battalion continued its attack, heavy flanking fire was received from the right. The Battalion immediately redisposed to hold in the direction of attack while taking aggressive action to eliminate the threat to the flank and rear. A courageous attempt to assault across the open field was halted by withering grazing fire. Repeated attempts by the attacking elements using fire and short rounds resulted in only slight advance against the fanatically defending insurgent forces. At 1335 hours another company of the Battalion was committed to assist in destroying the enemy. Although this unit also met with murderous fire from enemy machine guns which swept the open fields, steady pressure was maintained on the defending Viet Cong. With undaunted courage and indomitable fighting spirit, continuous fire and movement was used to steadily close on the enemy position. At 1735 hours the reserve element of the 42d Ranger Battalion was committed in a coordinated Battalion assault to destroy the enemy.

The assault by this unit was so resolute that the aggressor was routed from his emplacement and the flank was rolled up. The shock action and dogged determination of this unit destroyed the enemy's will to fight. Those enemy not killed or wounded fled the scene of battle. The gallant actions and victory of the 42d Ranger Battalion cost the lives

of 11 of its members, with 22 others wounded in action. This highly effective combat operation was an eminent success and resulted in a body count of 114 insurgents killed, and a total of 59 VC weapons captured, for a favorable ten to one kill ratio. The actions of the 42d Ranger Battalion reflect conspicuous gallantry and extraordinary heroism in keeping with the finest traditions of the military service, and reflect great credit on the Republic of Viet-Nam.

NOTE: The statement and text of the citation were released at Austin, Tex.

589 Statement by the President Following the Signing of the Federal Employees Salary Act of 1965. *October 30, 1965*

THE first session of the 89th Congress enacted much historic legislation. It created new horizons for education, for health and medical care, for conservation, for civil rights and the war on poverty.

In one of its final actions, the Congress also made an important contribution toward helping us reach those new horizons. It passed the Federal Employees Salary Act of 1965.

We have the legislation and the legacy. It remains for us to fulfill them. How well we succeed will depend, to a large degree, on the ability and dedication of the men and women who work for our Government.

As I stated in my message to the Congress requesting this legislation, I am proud of the progress we have made toward lean and fit competence in the discharge of Federal responsibilities. Much of that progress results from our efforts during the past 3 years to make sure that salaries paid to our civil servants are neither more, nor less, than those paid for equal efforts in private industry. This bill brings us close to that objective.

In every field of endeavor, the American

system strives to give the worker an honest day's pay for an honest day's work, and to give his employer a maximum return for every dollar he spends on salaries. This is the system that has made us great. It applies to Government no less than to industry.

In Government, as in industry, rapid change will continue to cause dislocations in employment. Responsible employers, throughout the Nation, have recognized their responsibilities to employees whose jobs are affected by the march of progress. Government can do no less.

The burden of change, which is for the benefit of all, should be borne by all. I am pleased that this bill enables the Government to provide severance pay to Federal employees whose jobs are eliminated.

Above all, the benefits conferred by this bill are made possible within the wage-price guideposts developed by the Council of Economic Advisers. Wages in private industry have generally remained within these guideposts through the dedicated cooperation of both management and labor. I am proud that the Federal Government is showing the same sense of responsibility in conducting its own affairs.

We are now in the 56th month of the longest uninterrupted peacetime economic expansion in the history of our country. Wages, profits, and other income continue to increase. Significantly, these gains have not been diluted by inflation. The responsible action taken by Congress in passing this legislation insures continuation of that responsible partnership of industry, labor, and Government to which we owe so much.

We now have one more reason for looking forward with renewed confidence to the continued growth of America's prosperity.

NOTE: As enacted, the Federal Employees Salary Act of 1965, approved on October 29, is Public Law 89–301 (79 Stat. 1111).

On November 13, 1965, the President signed Executive Order 11257 entitled "Delegating to the Civil Service Commission Certain Authority Relating to Severance Pay under the Federal Employees Salary Act of 1965" (1 Weekly Comp. Pres. Docs., p. 500; 30 F.R. 14353; 3 CFR, 1965 Supp., p. 187). The statement was released at Austin, Tex.

590 Statement by the President on Reviewing Reports on the National Economy. *October* 30, 1965

I HAVE just finished reviewing the reports on our national economy for the first 10 months of this year. The reports show that 1965 will be the most prosperous year in our history.

During these past 10 months we have achieved new records in almost every part of the economy. Some of those achievements are:

—Employment is at an alltime high, and nearly 10,000 new employees are being added to our payrolls every workday.

—The layoff rate for factory workers is now the lowest in more than 12 years, and production workers on manufacturing payrolls are averaging $3.49 more earnings each week than they were a year ago.

—Unemployment has dropped below 3 million for the first time in 8 years. Unemployment among teenagers is at the lowest level in 3 years, despite the record numbers in which they are now entering the labor force.

—Long-term unemployment is now below 1 percent of the labor force, the lowest in 8 years.

—Increased wages over the last 10 months have more than compensated for the slight increase in consumer prices, making it possible for the American worker to buy more with his earnings today than ever before.

—Small business failures have dropped to an 8-year low. After-tax earnings of small manufacturing companies were 41.7 percent higher in the first 6 months of 1965 than in the same period of 1964.

—Investment in new plants and equipment has risen 11 percent since the end of last year.

Between the closing months of 1964 and this past September, the personal income of Americans rose some 6½ percent. Farm income is up some 16 percent over last year, and corporate profits, after taxes, are up more than 17 percent.

This month of October marks the 56th consecutive month of economic prosperity. At no time in our history have we enjoyed such an uninterrupted period of peacetime economic expansion. And during this entire expansion our prices have remained more stable than those of any industrial country in the world.

There is every reason to believe that this prosperity is going to continue. Automobile sales, for example, have an important effect on our whole economy—and during the first 20 days of October, automobile sales were the highest of any 20-day period in history.

This remarkable record is an outstanding tribute to our American system. It shows that where management and labor and Government work together, there are no limits to what they can accomplish.

Our free enterprise system has produced the greatest abundance in history. It is the strength of that economy, no less than our

military might, which supports our defense of freedom in Viet-Nam and throughout the world.

The magnificent record of that economy during 1965 shows that we are moving steadily toward our ultimate goal: the end of want and the beginning of opportunity for all who seek it.

NOTE: On November 19, 1965, the White House made public a report by the Council of Economic Advisers on economic activity during October. The report stated that the economy continued to advance on a broad front with an increase in industrial production and retail sales and a decline in unemployment. In the third quarter of 1965, the report noted, the gross national product had risen $11½ billion (1 Weekly Comp. Pres. Docs., p. 512).

The statement was released at Austin, Tex.

---

591   Memorandum Announcing a New Drive To Improve the Government's Services to the Public.   *November 1, 1965*

Memorandum for Heads of Departments and Agencies:

The task of government is to serve the public. It has been my deep and continuing concern to assure that each American receives from his Government the fastest, most efficient and most courteous service. As our society grows more complex and our population expands we must explore every path in our quest to provide the best possible service for our individual citizens.

Some months ago I asked Chairman Macy of the Civil Service Commission to survey our existing practices and to suggest ways to improve our efforts. He has reported that progress has been made. But we must continue to forge ahead, for in a real sense we have only begun.

The time for action is now. This is particularly so in view of the new programs recently passed by Congress which reach all of our people.

I am today placing Chairman Macy in

charge of a new and concerted government drive aimed at bringing better service to our individual citizens. I am directing him to coordinate the activities of each department and agency and to report to me every 90 days on our progress to improve the quality of service and to make the government more accessible to the people it serves.

To build further on the steps we have already taken, I am requesting:

First, that you assign a top member of your staff to develop within your Department or Agency a program to improve the quality of service to the public. The name of the official you select should be promptly forwarded to Chairman Macy.

Second, that you report to Chairman Macy by December 15, 1965 the steps taken in your Department or Agency to improve the quality of service and your plans for future improvement.

Third, that your agency take full advantage of the new and special training courses developed by the Civil Service Commission to improve standards of service to open up more lines of communication to the public.

I regard this as a vital undertaking. As our programs expand and increase, it is essential that each of our citizens receive prompt, efficient and courteous service and from each of our government employees.

We must have your personal support and leadership to translate the promise of a better and more responsive government into a reality.

LYNDON B. JOHNSON

NOTE: On November 1, 1965, the White House made public a progress report to the President from John W. Macy, Jr., Chairman of the Civil Service Commission, on improving the Government's services to the public (1 Weekly Comp. Pres. Docs., p. 447). The report, announcing that in 20 departments and agencies a high level official had been assigned to lead the campaign to improve the organization's communications and contacts with the public, stated in part:

"To improve service to the public, some departments are consolidating field offices to provide 'one stop' service; others have centralized their general information service to make it easier for the public to get the help it needs. Several departments and agencies have extended their office hours in Washington and in other localities to give better service to the public.

"To help Federal agencies further improve the ability of their employees to communicate clearly and responsively and to better serve the public, the Civil Service Commission has taken a number of steps:

"—We have developed new training programs to improve the standards of the Government's communications and public contact.

"—We have developed a new test of writing ability as a part of our important Federal Service Entrance Examination.

"—As a part of our inspection program, we will look to see what agencies are doing to improve their communications and services, and we will evaluate the efforts made.

"—We are preparing a fact leaflet to go to each employee expressing your personal interest in improved communications, enlisting employee support, and outlining what they can do to help.

"—We have developed a new incentive program for excellence in communications and service to the public and have urged agencies to make awards to their employees for outstanding achievement.

"—We have asked the Chairman of each Federal Executive Board to take action to improve communications and service and to encourage interagency action along these lines.

"—We have begun an interchange of information among agencies on new ideas and methods to improve communications and service."

The memorandum was released at Austin, Tex.

592   Statement by the President Upon Signing the School Disaster Aid Act. *November 1, 1965*

THE LEGISLATION I have approved today—H.R. 9022, the School Disaster Aid Act—recognizes a national responsibility to share the burden of assisting schools in communities which are struck by major disasters.

It recognizes that we must not allow the unpredictable forces of nature to disrupt the education which our children so vitally need.

In early September I saw with my own eyes the terrible devastation that was visited upon the Mississippi Delta region by a great storm. Members of the Congress accompanied me to that ravaged area. Every community in America poured out its sympathy.

We all know only too well that there is not a region of this country which can be confident that it will not suffer from an uncontrollable and unforeseeable catastrophe.

Flooding in the Mississippi Delta, or an earthquake in Alaska—these events are an inevitable consequence of man's continual battle with nature.

We are, and we should be, concerned when any school is put out of operation by a disaster. This bill will augment the assistance now being advanced to schools in major disaster areas by the Federal Government under the Federal Disaster Act (Public Law 81–875). The Nation will lend a helping hand as local communities rebuild schools damaged by hurricane, flood, or earthquake; as they replace books and desks and essential tools of learning; as they return school operations to normal after a great catastrophe. This new authority is limited to disasters occurring within a two-year period and we will carefully examine its operation in relation to other disaster assistance programs to determine whether it should later be continued or revised.

Physically handicapped and mentally retarded children will be aided by this bill which extends the benefits of the new Elementary and Secondary Education Act of 1965 to schools for deaf, speech-impaired, visually handicapped, emotionally disturbed, and crippled children. These children require special education programs which are extremely costly. It is fitting that we should recognize this need and assist our States and local school districts to educate all their children—even these for whom education is so difficult and expensive to provide. I am particularly pleased that Congress included this provision in the bill.

This bill also includes an amendment to the impacted areas education legislation (Public Law 81–874) which will provide funds to schools attended by substantial numbers of children of the military and civilian personnel of the Federal Government on the same basis for our large cities as for our smaller communities. Both large and small school districts will now be eligible for impacted areas aid if three percent of the children in the schools are there because of the Federal Government's activities in the area.

The entire impacted areas program is currently being reviewed in the light of a recent study completed at the request of Congress, and in the light of the relationship between this program and other recently enacted Federal education legislation. This is but one aspect of this Administration's firm commitment to be responsive to the need for constructive and comprehensive changes in existing legislation and to eliminate unnecessary expenditures.

This legislation also makes certain adjustments resulting from the base closing announcement of November 19, 1964. Some school districts had made plans for school construction under the impacted areas education legislation (Public Law 81–815) and had gone forward with their plans on the basis of their expectations that they would remain eligible for aid. This bill restores their eligibility because the facilities will shortly be required for new residents in these areas.

Finally, this legislation takes a further step in improving the educational resources of the Nation by providing more funds for our State educational agencies. I want especially to congratulate Senator Mansfield and Senator Metcalf for sponsoring this provision which gives each State department of education no less than $75,000 for administering programs for disadvantaged children under the Elementary and Secondary Education Act of 1965.

I also would like to congratulate Congressman William Ford who, as a freshman member of the House of Representatives, was the original sponsor of H.R. 9022.

LYNDON B. JOHNSON

NOTE: In his statement the President referred to Senator Mike Mansfield of Montana, majority leader of the Senate, Senator Lee Metcalf of Montana, and Representative William D. Ford of Michigan.

As enacted, the School Disaster Aid Act is Public Law 89–313 (79 Stat. 1158).

For the President's remarks of April 11 upon signing the Elementary and Secondary Education Act of 1965, see Item 181.

The statement was released at Austin, Tex.

593 Message Concerning U.S. Participation in the Buenos Aires
Meeting of the Inter-American Economic and Social Council.
November 1, 1965

Dear Mr. Chairman:

I was pleased to receive your telegram of October 20. The United States will participate in the meeting of the Inter-American Economic and Social Council (IA-ECO-SOC) at Buenos Aires on March 13 if that date is concurred in by most of the member states. The United States warmly appreciates your fixing the date to coincide with the Fifth Anniversary of the Alliance for Progress as a tribute to the memory of President Kennedy.

In accordance with your excellent suggestion, the United States Representative to the IA-ECOSOC will be included in the United States Delegation to the Inter-American Conference scheduled to open in Rio de Janeiro on November 17. Mr. Jack H. Vaughn, United States Coordinator of the Alliance for Progress, will shortly be named United States Representative. He will be prepared to exchange ideas on matters raised in the CIAP letter.

I take this opportunity to express again my deep personal interest in individual and collective efforts to give greater impetus to our vital Alliance for Progress.

Sincerely,

LYNDON B. JOHNSON

[His Excellency Edgardo Seoane, Chairman, Inter-American Economic and Social Council]

NOTE: Señor Seoane's telegram of October 20, 1965, was not made public by the White House.

Establishment of an Alliance for Progress was proposed by President Kennedy on March 13, 1961 (1961 volume, this series, Item 78). The Alliance was formally established on August 17, 1961, by the Charter of Punta del Este.

The President discussed the CIAP letter at the ceremony marking the fourth anniversary of the formal establishment (Item 429 above).

The text of the cable was released at Austin, Tex.

594 Message to the White House Conference on Health.
November 2, 1965

I HAVE CALLED this Conference with one purpose in mind: to bring together the best minds and the boldest ideas to deal with the pressing health needs of this nation.

The urgency of those needs is undeniable:

—Nearly 15 million people suffer from heart disease;

—Forty-eight million people, healthy today, will become victims of cancer;

—One-fifth of our children under age seventeen are afflicted with chronic ailments.

Many citizens have been left behind in our advance toward better treatment and better health—some because of inadequate health manpower; others because of obsolete or scarce treatment facilities; and others because health services are not organized efficiently enough to provide first-rate service.

I believe that a great nation can do better.

I believe that this Conference can give new strength and energy to our national effort to recruit health professionals, extend health services and improve treatment.

If we are to launch a new era for medicine—an era even more dramatic than the last 2 decades—we must begin by setting new goals:

—To increase the life expectancy of our citizens;

—To achieve a healthier environment;

—To decrease the infant mortality rate in the United States;

—To improve our understanding and care of the mentally ill;

—To eliminate such diseases as tuberculosis, measles, whooping cough.

Ours is a great opportunity to advance ideas which will contribute not only to a healthier America, but to a better world.

We have the resources; we need only the will and the leadership.

Let us raise our sights—and unlimber our imaginations.

LYNDON B. JOHNSON

NOTE: The President's message was made public as part of a White House release announcing that 600 leaders in the health professions, education, and other fields would attend the White House Conference on Health to be held on November 3–4 at the Shoreham Hotel in Washington.

On August 30 the White House announced the formation of a group of the Nation's leading health experts to serve as an executive committee to make plans for the conference. The release stated that the committee would assist the conference chairman,

Dr. George Beadle, Nobel Prize winner and President of the University of Chicago, and the executive vice chairman, Boisfeuillet Jones, President of the Woodruff Foundation of Atlanta, Ga.

The membership of the executive committee follows: Marion Folsom, former Secretary of Health, Education, and Welfare, and Chairman, Eastman Kodak Co., Rochester, N.Y.; Dr. George James, Commissioner of Health, City of New York; Dr. Leona Baumgartner, New York, former Deputy Administrator, Agency for International Development; Dr. Lowell T. Coggeshall, trustee and former dean of the Medical School, University of Chicago; Ray Brown, director of the Graduate Degree Program in Hospital Administration, Duke University, Durham, N.C.; Dr. Montague Cobb, professor of anatomy, Howard University, Washington, D.C.; Dr. Nelson H. Cruikshank, Director of Social Security, AFL–CIO, Washington, D.C.; Dr. Michael DeBakey, professor of surgery, Baylor University, Houston, Tex.; and Dr. Dwight Wilbur, surgeon, San Francisco, Calif.

On October 28 the White House announced that 500 health leaders would participate in the conference discussions which would be led by 81 panelists (1 Weekly Comp. Pres. Docs., p. 435).

See also Item 424.

The text of the message was released at Austin, Tex.

595 Remarks at the LBJ Ranch at the Swearing In of John A. Gronouski as Ambassador to Poland. *November 3, 1965*

General Gronouski and members of his family, ladies and gentlemen:

Mrs. Johnson and I deeply regret our lack of influence on the weather, but we are happy that we could be here together. And even though we may have inconvenienced some of you, we have done the best we could under the circumstances.

We are particularly delighted that we should have here with us this morning some of our most cherished friends and some of the best executives of the Johnson administration.

I am very pleased that Mrs. Gronouski and the Gronouski children could be here,

in this living room in front of this aged fireplace, while we administer the oath of office to what I consider to be one of the best public servants and one of the best human beings that I have known.

I did not know General Gronouski when he came to Washington, but his performance as Postmaster General and his counsel to me on other matters have been what I would say is exemplary.

I asked the Postmaster General to talk to Mrs. Gronouski and his advisers and to give some thought to follow in the steps of, I guess, Justice Goldberg, to consider ways and means that we might try to find a breakthrough to peace in the world, and to convince the peoples of 120 nations that we meant what we said—that we wanted to live in the world together and have peace and goodwill among men.

I said that to him because of his peculiar and particular attributes and qualifications that I had observed, and I did so only after it had first been suggested to me by the distinguished Secretary of State.

We cannot predict today what the results of that conversation will be, or how successful the new Ambassador will be with his mission as the spokesman for this country to the country of Poland. But we do have more hopes this morning for Eastern Europe and for that area of the world, and better belief that we will be better understood than I have had at any time since I have been President.

If for any reason the Ambassador does fail—and I would not anticipate that at all—or if Mrs. Gronouski prefers to return and enjoy the beautification campaign that she and Lady Bird began some time ago, I have assured them that there are a number of more important positions that await their doing.

But as I see it now, Ambassador Goldberg is doing a very fine job at the United Nations and we need to have the type of work that he is doing carried on all over the world. And this is not only the second, but it will be only one of several more that will unfold in the months to come that will be calculated to give the world a true picture of this country.

Poland is celebrating 1,000 years as a Christian nation next year. In that time she has made contributions to Western civilization, of which she is such a distinguished part.

Behind the legendary figures of Polish champions are scores of other Poles who

have illuminated the path of freedom and learning for mankind. So, this morning, we honor them as brothers in the quest for liberty.

Our ties with Poland began two centuries ago, when Pulaski came to our shores to help us in our struggle for independence. As so often happens, the gift was returned almost at once. The Polish Constitution of 1794 drew heavily on America's charter of government, and since that day Poles and Americans have understood one another without difficulty when they spoke of man's yearning to be free.

The future of our relations is bright with hope.

So, as I told you, I have asked John Gronouski, my friend and my colleague, to report to me often, directly, on the ways by which he feels that we in America could multiply the relationships through travel, particularly through trade, through scholarship, and just through better understanding between the peoples of America and the peoples of Eastern Europe.

The new children's hospital in Cracow, built with funds that are being derived from our farm community's sales in Poland, is just one of the many opportunities that I see lie ahead.

So, it is very satisfying to me that one of the great products of our Polish-American citizens, John Gronouski, should be willing to go to Warsaw in this year of remembrance and hope.

I take great pride in reading every day some of the letters from some of the boys in their teens—18, 19, 20 year olds—who are willing to leave and go into battle and give their lives in order that you can enjoy the freedom you have this morning. And I am glad that there are other people in the Government who are willing to go where their President thinks they should go, and could go, and be helpful. John Gronouski and Mrs. Gronouski and their little ones belong in that group.

He is an economist. He is a great administrator. But above all, in my months of association with him, I have found him a decent man, a human being, a fellow with ideas, with initiative, with imagination, and I think he is ideally suited for what I am going to ask him to do.

He will be an Ambassador first of peace and goodwill, whose mission is to build new bridges not just to Poland but to the people of Eastern Europe.

So, he carries with him not only the official papers of an Ambassador, but he carries with him my great personal confidence and my deep desire for peace with those that we really feel are our oldest friends.

And we are going to do our part to try to find a way to live in the world together a little better, a little closer, and, we hope, a little more peacefully.

Thank you very much.

NOTE: The President spoke at 11:13 a.m. at the LBJ Ranch, Johnson City, Tex. In his opening words he referred to John A. Gronouski, former Postmaster General. During his remarks the President referred to Arthur J. Goldberg, U.S. Representative to the United Nations and former Associate Justice of the Supreme Court of the United States, and to Dean Rusk, Secretary of State.

596 Remarks at the Post Office, Hye, Texas, at the Swearing In of Lawrence F. O'Brien as Postmaster General. *November 3, 1965*

Ambassador Gronouski and members of his family, Larry O'Brien and members of his family, the people of Hye, members of my family, Postmaster Deike, ladies and gentlemen:

It was about 53 years ago that I mailed my first letter from this post office. And Larry O'Brien told me a few moments ago that he is going out to find that letter and deliver it.

But that is not the real reason that I asked Larry to come over here to our post office at Hye, in Blanco County, this morning and join us in this ceremony.

This little community represents to me the earliest recollections of the America that I knew when I was a little boy. It was a land of farms and ranches and people who depended on those farms and ranches for a living.

Since then, I am fearful that this way of life has slowly passed. As wages in our cities have gone up, the labor on the farms has gone down and the people have gone on the move. Slowly at first, then more swiftly, they filled the cities of America to the bursting point. And I am told now by our students of urban America that by the year 2000 more than three out of every four Americans will live in the cities of this land.

I do not advocate and, of course, I realize that we cannot return to the America that I knew when I was a boy. Our task, then, is to make our cities good places to live, expensive and demanding as we realize that task is going to be.

I have given no subject more thought in the last week I have been here than that problem. But the price of progress must not be two kinds of America—one rural and one urban, or one northern and one southern, or one Protestant and one Catholic. The spirit of this land of ours must always be one, and the Government of this land must always be the servant of all the people—all of those who fill our teeming cities and all of those who live near the land in thousands and thousands of little communities like this one.

Larry O'Brien's new job will extend to every corner of America. Larry O'Brien will be the boss of a department that has 600,000 employees. Of the 33,000 post offices, more than one-fourth of them are no larger than Hye.

And Larry's coming here today reminds all of us in America that the large and the small are equally the concern of their Government—and of us all.

I have no doubt that Larry has been fully schooled and trained and acclimated in the highways and the byways and the corridors of Boston, but what I want to be sure is that he has the feeling and the understanding and the common touch of Hye as well.

I think most people know that Larry O'Brien is slightly Irish. Well, I tell you no secret when I inform you that the Irish are no strangers to the Post Office Department. Our old friend Jim Farley is one of several Irishmen who have served this country with great distinction as Postmaster General.

President Roosevelt actually appointed Levi Deike in 1934 as the postmaster here at Hye, but Levi thought it was Jim Farley, and when we asked him awhile ago, he said, "Jim Farley named me postmaster." And Jim, in fact, I guess, did make the recommendation.

Now, several misapprehensions have stemmed from the fact that the Irish have handled the mail because they have occasionally engaged in a little bit of political activity on the fringes. And there has been some tendency to believe that they carried their political interests all the way over into the Postmaster Generalship.

Well, I want to lay that to rest—just as soon as this cattle truck passes. Mr. O'Brien

has dabbled from time to time in politics. He at least believes that there may still be a two-party system—as of this morning—but I wanted to be sure that before he signed on that he knew that we run the Post Office on a bipartisan basis.

He told me firmly that from the time he was a small boy he understood there were two great, historic parties in America—the Democratic Party, and the Boston Tea Party.

Now, I don't need to have any more exhibits that this is a bipartisan operation than to point out that Roosevelt appointed Levi Deike, and Eisenhower kept Levi Deike, and we all honor Levi Deike this morning.

He's come a long way since he and I played baseball out here in his backyard. At that time we had a team known as the "Deike boys," and I think they filled every position—didn't you?—nine positions, all by brothers. And I am glad that we can accept his hospitality and be here on his front porch at his post office this morning.

Now, I don't need to list in detail the accomplishments that will attend Larry O'Brien's name as long as he lives. But I want to point them out in the presence of his family who have come here. They were not achieved for Democrats alone, and they were not special tasks that were performed only for our great, beloved President, John Fitzgerald Kennedy, and the present President, Lyndon Johnson.

But they are the laws and they are the programs that give new hope to millions of people, and that we will be implementing and strengthening and administering and perfecting all the rest of your lifetime.

They are the breakthroughs in educating your children, in providing medical care for our senior citizens, in providing housing for all people—and with emphasis on poor people, in providing voting rights for all Americans, and providing for a sound and stable fiscal policy for this country.

They are the instruments of wise and creative governments in the 1960's.

Larry O'Brien helped achieve so much because he understands, I think, the first principle of democratic government. And what is that? Tolerance of the other man's viewpoint. He believes in every man's right to fight for what he actually believes in. And I think this is important to us.

Here in the Hill Country of Texas, as well as in the proud land of New England where Larry was raised, we put a pretty high price on strong opinions that are firmly held. We appreciate a man who insists on his views without insisting that we adopt them.

That is one of the first things that impressed me about Larry O'Brien. He could frequently disagree with you without being disagreeable, and a good many times you joined his viewpoint before he joined yours.

So, this administration took Larry O'Brien to its heart. We came to know him, and as our respect for him has grown with every passing week, our affection for him has grown with every passing bill.

And this is not Q.E.D., or not "30," Larry. You have not seen anything yet.

Now, he is moving on to a great department of this Government, a department whose work is to keep Americans in touch with each other, and to keep them in communication with the world.

So, it must be a very proud moment for that proud State—that Bay State—as I know it is for the hundreds of Larry O'Brien's friends on the Hill and the thousands of his friends in all the 50 States.

So, we welcome him into our Cabinet family.

And for you cynical newspapermen—if there be any in the group—or women, in keeping with this administration's policy of complete candor, Larry's ZIP Code at Hye, Texas is 78635.

Thank you, and goodby.

NOTE: The President spoke at 11:54 a.m. at the post office in Hye, Tex. In his opening words he referred to John A. Gronouski, the new U.S. Ambassador to Poland and former Postmaster General, Lawrence F. O'Brien, former Special Assistant to the President, and Levi Deike, postmaster at Hye, Tex.

---

597   Statement by the President Upon Signing the Food and Agriculture Act of 1965. *November 4, 1965*

THE AMERICAN farmer in the last 30 years has advanced more in agricultural abundance and farm fertility than all the farmers in all the history of recorded time.

One American farmer now feeds and clothes himself and 32 others besides—an achievement unmatched anywhere on earth.

One man on the farm today does all the work that was performed by four in 1939. If this were not so, we would need 23 million farmworkers to feed and clothe ourselves, instead of the 6.5 million we have.

Thirty years ago, the city worker toiled 85 hours each month to feed his wife and children. Today he works less than half as long, and the food his family eats is both more appetizing and more nourishing.

The miracle of American agriculture is thus an example to all the world's billions of the wisdom and the rewards of our democratic system. For more than a century, that system has encouraged development of the family farm and the free and independent farmer.

Government has assisted land distribution. It has provided agricultural research and education. It has extended credit and helped to stabilize prices, but the holding and working of the land has remained with the independent farmer in the basic American tradition.

The preservation of that tradition has been the goal of all our farm policies of the last three decades.

In 1930, rural poverty was widespread; only one farmer in two owned the land he worked upon. And because the farmer was poor, the merchants, tradesmen, bankers, and factory workers, who depended on him for a customer, also suffered.

During the 1930's the Nation faced up to the tragic waste of human and natural resources in our rural areas. Government changed its policies. New laws provided stable prices and technical assistance and credit.

As a result, today, four out of five of our farmers own all or part of the land they till. The value of that land increases year by year. The average American farm today is worth 50 percent more than it was worth only 7 years ago. The net income per farm will be nearly $1,200 higher this year than in 1960.

This progress represents the achievements of a constructive partnership between the farmer and his Government.

The Food and Agriculture Act of 1965, which I sign today, opens a new chapter in the history of that relationship and in the miraculous story of American farming.

With this legislation, we reap the wisdom acquired during more than three decades of trial and effort.

Our objectives remain what they have been for more than 30 years:

—To let the free American farmer use all his skill and initiative to produce agricultural abundance, in return for a fair reward.

—To bring every American a plentiful supply of food, at the lowest possible cost.

—To avoid accumulating costly surpluses of commodities we do not need.

Until now, despite their great achievements, all our programs have not met those goals. Despite years of great abundance, farm incomes have remained far too low, and farm surpluses have remained far too high. In addition, methods used to support farm income have interfered with price competition and a free marketplace.

The Food and Agriculture Act of 1965 is a major step toward correcting those deficiencies. It takes its place proudly with expanded aid to education, immigration reforms, medical care for the aged and other health care legislation, and voting rights for all Americans, as a milestone of the most productive and constructive legislative session in our history.

The Food and Agriculture Act of 1965 sets the course of a farm policy geared to growth.

In combining the principles of competitive pricing for farm products with direct payments to producers, Congress has forged a new link with the future.

The new act:

—assures the farmer a fair income.

—assures the American family that expenditures for food will continue to take a smaller and smaller share of family income.

—strengthens the competitive position of U.S. cotton, wheat, and feed grains in world markets and, at the same time, stabilizes those markets.

—assures the reduction and makes more possible the final elimination of surplus stocks of farm products.

By combining individual commodity programs with a long-range cropland adjustment program, the legislation will:

—help reduce the cost to the taxpayers of all our farm programs.

—begin a new era of city-country cooperation as we use surplus cropland to increase outdoor recreation and beautification.

—insure our ability to produce food and fiber in the quantities we need, when we need them.

A wise and continuing partnership between American farmers and their Government, as reflected in this legislation, will produce great benefits for the entire Nation. As a result of the programs now in progress:

—By 1970 our grain surpluses will have disappeared, and our surpluses of cotton and tobacco will be greatly reduced.

—Net farm income will average nearly $2 billion higher per year during the last half of the 1960's than in the last half of the 1950's.

—By 1970, American consumers will have $7 billion a year more to spend for other purposes because of the lower cost of food.

—By 1975, American farm exports will be more than 50 percent greater than today.

Yet, all of this can be—and should be—only a beginning. In a time of technological revolution and rapid change, which is occurring on our farms no less than in our factories and laboratories, we must constantly look to the future. New ways must be explored to keep agriculture and agricultural policy up to date, to get the full benefit of new findings and of new technology, to make sure that our bountiful land is used to the best of our ability to promote the welfare of consumers, farmers, and the entire economy.

I am, therefore, establishing today a Committee on Food and Fiber, to be chaired by the Secretary of Agriculture, and a National Advisory Commission on Food and Fiber, to be chaired by Sherwood Berg, the outstanding dean of the School of Agriculture at the University of Minnesota. I am placing on the Commission Americans of broad experience and great talent.

I am asking this Commission to make a penetrating and long-range appraisal of our agricultural and related foreign trade policies. This Commission will undertake this review in terms of the national interest, the welfare of our rural Americans, and the well-being of our farmers, the needs of our workers, and the interests of our consumers.

These men will construct the most thorough study ever conducted of the effects of our agricultural policies on the performance of our economy and on our foreign relations.

This Commission will report to me within 18 months.

But a program which places agriculture on a sound and stable basis is only half of the battle.

The task of achieving a life of quality and dignity in rural America—a life which offers opportunity for rural people equal to that enjoyed by their urban brothers—will engage our minds and hearts and our energies for a lifetime.

If our farmers can succeed in making America a place where abundance flows from one unparalleled harvest to the next, then surely we can also make rural America a place of opportunity for all who dwell there.

NOTE: As enacted, the Food and Agriculture Act of 1965, approved on November 3, is Public Law 89–321 (79 Stat. 1187).

On November 4 the President signed Executive Order 11256 "Establishing the President's Committee on Food and Fiber and the National Advisory Commission on Food and Fiber" (1 Weekly Comp. Pres. Docs., p. 457; 30 F.R. 14137; 3 CFR, 1965 Supp., p. 184).

A list of the members of the National Advisory Commission on Food and Fiber is printed in the Weekly Compilation of Presidential Documents (vol. 1, p. 458).

The statement was released at Austin, Tex.

598 Statement by the President on the Unemployment Rate
During October. *November 4, 1965*

I WAS very pleased to learn today that the unemployment rate fell to 4.3 percent in October. This is the lowest rate of unemployment since August 1957—more than 8 years ago—and is substantially below the 5.2 percent rate of October 1964. Over the past year, more than 2 million jobs have been created by our vigorously advancing economy, and unemployment has fallen by nearly one-half million.

There were welcome declines in unemployment from September to October among less privileged groups of workers. Unemployment among nonwhite workers was down from 8.2 percent in September to 7.9 percent. Unemployment among blue-collar workers was down from 5.1 percent to 4.9 percent. The long-term unemployed were down from 736,000 to 703,000. The unemployment rate for married men fell to 2.1 percent in October, the lowest rate since December 1955.

As we look back, we see the great progress made in the longest period of peacetime prosperity in our Nation's history. In early 1961, the unemployment rate was 6.7 percent and nearly 5 million workers were without jobs.

As we look forward, the need and opportunity for further improvement are obvious. Unemployment of teenagers is still far too high, although the rate of 13.1 percent in October is better than the 14.3 percent of a year earlier. The unemployment rate for nonwhite Americans is still a painful 7.9 percent, although it has improved markedly from 9.8 percent a year ago.

We tend too often to think of employment and unemployment in statistical terms alone and not in personal terms. We are inclined to forget that our task is not merely to reduce percentages but to help men and women find meaningful work and fulfill their dignity as human beings.

To be able to work but unable to find a job is one of the most demoralizing experiences a man can suffer. The loss of a job to one man may only slightly, if at all, affect a statistical chart, but to that man and his family it means heartache and sacrifice. That is why our goal remains full employment. We must assure equality of job opportunity for all and pursue diligently the private and public policies that will maintain noninflationary prosperity. Next to the pursuit of peace, I know of no challenge greater than this.

NOTE: The statement was read by Bill D. Moyers, Special Assistant to the President, at his news conference at 4:15 p.m. on Thursday, November 4, 1965, at Austin, Tex. It was not made public in the form of a White House press release.

599 Statement by the President Upon Signing Bills Authorizing
Release of Zinc and Nickel From the National Stockpiles.
November 5, 1965

THE TWO BILLS which I have just signed will enable us to reap the benefits of past prudence and apply them to our present needs.

H.R. 9047 authorizes the release of 200,-000 tons of zinc from our national stockpiles of strategic materials.

H.R. 10305 authorizes the release of 200,-000,000 pounds of nickel from those stockpiles.

These valuable metals were acquired to prevent possible shortages of strategic materials in a time of national emergency. But our inventories now contain many millions of pounds for which our military planners foresee no future military need. Yet these metals can be put to essential use today.

The time has come to start moving these excess inventories from the stockpile to the smelter. They are needed at home, and they are needed to support our effort in Viet-Nam.

The United States first began stockpiling strategic materials in 1939. We did so to meet possible national defense needs and free the United States from dependence on foreign supplies in times of national emergency. These stockpiles served us well in World War II and in Korea. They are serving us now in Viet-Nam.

Vast quantities of copper, tin, zinc, aluminum, and other metals win no battle while they lie in a storage bin. Instead, they must give us the weapons and the airplanes, the trucks and the helicopters needed on the field of combat in Viet-Nam. We must move them from the stockpile to the factory and we must move them faster.

Since I have been President, we have greatly speeded up that process. During the past fiscal year alone, more than $430 million worth of excess materials were moved from our stockpiles and put to productive use. That was more than three times the value of excess stocks disposed of in the preceding fiscal year, and six times more than the Government disposed of in fiscal year 1961.

By using the excess stocks we have, we greatly benefit both American industry and American consumers. For example, zinc from our stockpiles has been used in this year's recordbreaking production of automobiles. Recent releases of copper were essential to the continued high production of our brass and wire mills, our manufacture

of copper tubing, and will be the sole source of the large quantities of core material for our new coinage made necessary by the increasing gap between silver supply and demand.

By using the excess stocks we have, we benefit the taxpayer and the national economy. The excess stocks removed from the stockpile during the past fiscal year returned to the Treasury $50 million more than their original cost. And to the extent that metal is withdrawn from our own stocks, the need for imports from abroad is reduced, and thus our balance of payments position is improved. The excess stocks disposed of last year alone saved nearly $400 million in foreign purchases.

Experience has proved that all of this can be accomplished while:

—meeting the present and future needs of our national defense.

—maintaining an orderly market for the continued prosperity of our industries.

—reducing the cost to the taxpayer of maintaining excess, unnecessary stockpiles of strategic materials.

This has not been accomplished by the executive branch alone. It has been achieved in close partnership with the Congress and American industry. During these past 2 years, for example, in addition to daily and weekly consultations, more than 25 formal industrywide meetings have been held between industry and representatives of our Government agencies. Out of such cooperation have come the benefits I have described.

By continuing this partnership, I am confident that in the year ahead we can improve our records still further.

NOTE: As enacted, H.R. 9047, approved November 4, is Public Law 89–322 (79 Stat. 1213); H.R. 10305, approved November 5, is Public Law 89–323 (79 Stat. 1213).

On November 6, 1965, following an increase in aluminum prices, the White House made public a statement by Gardner Ackley, Chairman of the Council of Economic Advisers, announcing that the Council had concluded, following a review of the situation, that the increases by the aluminum industry "have no justification under the wage-price guidelines and therefore are inflationary."

Also made public on November 6 were statements by Secretary of the Treasury Henry H. Fowler, recommending the release of stockpiled aluminum as an essential step to defend the U.S. balance of payments, and by Secretary of Defense Robert S. McNamara, discussing proposed formulas for disposing of stockpiled aluminum.

The text of all three statements is printed in the Weekly Compilation of Presidential Documents (vol. 1, pp. 474, 475).

The President's statement was released at Austin, Tex.

600 Statement by the President Upon Signing Bill Authorizing the Sale or Loan of Warships to Friendly Powers. *November 5, 1965*

I HAVE today signed H.R. 7812 which authorizes the sale or loan of 11 warships to friendly foreign countries in Europe, South America, and Asia.

It will authorize:

(1) The sale or loan of two destroyers to Argentina and three destroyers to Brazil.

(2) The loan of two conventional submarines to Italy; one helicopter carrier to Spain; two destroyers to Turkey; and one destroyer escort to the Philippines.

This marks the first addition since 1961 to the Defense Department's ship loan program which was started in 1951. Instead of being maintained in an inactive reserve fleet, these ships will now be able to make a significant contribution to the defense of the free world when operated by friendly foreign nations. As in the past, this program continues to give selected navies the capability to fill defense gaps around the world which the United States itself cannot reasonably fill.

During the first 10 years of the program—1951 through 1961—11 public laws have enabled the United States to loan, sell, or grant 82 ships to 23 foreign countries.

In addition to the earlier programs and the new proposed sales or loans, the U.S. Navy has sponsored, under the military assistance program, two other programs of great value to friendly navies and to the defense of the free world.

Under one program 17 ships, minesweepers, patrol boats, and motor gunboats, are today being constructed under contract by foreign governments in United States shipyards. Six guided missile destroyers, three for the Royal Australian Navy and three for the Republic of Germany, have been authorized since 1962, and also are under construction.

The second program involves the Navy's training of foreign navy personnel who are or will be responsible for the operation of U.S. equipment installed on their ships. They undergo technical training at the various U.S. Navy service schools throughout the United States. Friendly foreign ships and their crews also are trained operationally, as units, in U.S. waters under the direction of U.S. Navy personnel. The value to the United States of this assistance has been demonstrated in the regularly scheduled fleet exercises involving various free world navies. These fleet exercises provide allied operational training on a realistic basis, and demonstrate the effectiveness of our military assistance program to the defense of the free world.

NOTE: As enacted, H.R. 7812 is Public Law 89–324 (79 Stat. 1214).

The statement was released at Austin, Tex.

601 Statement by the President on the Agreement Covering Movement of Cuban Refugees to the United States. *November 6, 1965*

I AM pleased with the understanding which has been reached. It is an important forward step in carrying out the declaration I made on October 3 to the Cuban people. I said that those who seek refuge here will find it. That continues to be the policy of the American people.

NOTE: The statement was read by Bill D. Moyers, Special Assistant to the President, at his news conference at 10:04 a.m. on Saturday, November 6, 1965, at Austin, Tex. It was not made public in the form of a White House press release.

On November 6 the White House announced that the Swiss Embassy in Havana, representing U.S. interests in Cuba, and the Cuban Foreign Ministry had exchanged diplomatic notes establishing procedures for the movement of Cuban refugees to the United States. The text of the notes is printed in the Weekly Compilation of Presidential Documents (vol. 1, p. 471).

For the President's declaration of October 3, made at the ceremony for the signing of the immigration bill on Liberty Island, see Item 546.

See also Item 618.

602 Statement by the President in Response to Science Advisory Committee Report on Pollution of Air, Soil, and Waters. *November 6, 1965*

I AM PLEASED at the thoroughness with which the panel has investigated pollution. This report will surely provide the basis for action on many fronts.

We have made much progress. Legislative action by the 89th Congress—the Water Quality Act of 1965, amendments to the Clean Air Act, the Highway Beautification Act—has moved us along the way to a cleaner world. Now we intend to move much more rapidly. The fact that there are more than 100 recommendations in the report is evidence that there is much to be done.

I am asking the appropriate departments and agencies to consider the recommendations and report to me on the ways in which we can move to cope with the problems cited in the report.

Ours is a nation of affluence. But the technology that has permitted our affluence spews out vast quantities of wastes and spent products that pollute our air, poison our waters, and even impair our ability to feed ourselves. At the same time, we have crowded together into dense metropolitan areas where concentration of wastes intensifies the problem. Pollution now is one of the most pervasive problems of our society. With our numbers increasing, and with our increasing urbanization and industrialization, the flow of pollutants to our air, soil, and waters is increasing. This increase is so rapid that our present efforts in managing pollution are barely enough to stay even, surely not enough to make the improvements that are needed.

As we look ahead to the increasing challenges of pollution we will need increased basic research in a variety of specific areas, including soil pollution and the effects of air pollutants on man. I intend to give high priority to increasing the numbers and quality of the scientists and engineers working on problems related to the control and management of pollution.

NOTE: The report of the Environmental Pollution Panel, President's Science Advisory Committee, dated November 1965, is entitled "Restoring the Quality of Our Environment" (Government Printing Office, 317 pp.).

The President's statement was made public as part of a White House release summarizing highlights of the report. The release stated that a panel of 14 outstanding physicians, scientists, and engineers, chaired by John W. Tukey of Princeton University and Bell Telephone Laboratories, and assisted by 11 subpanels, had spent 15 months in preparation of the report.

Significant findings of the Committee, the release noted, include the following:

Pollution is an inevitable consequence of an advanced society, but we need not suffer from the intensity and extent of pollution we now see around us. If we are to manage our pollution as we should, we must give more nearly the same attention to how we dispose of our waste materials as to how we gather and transform our raw materials. Society must take the position that no citizen, no industry, no municipality has the right to pollute.

We must rely on economic incentives to discourage pollution. Under this plan special taxes would be levied against pollutors.

Carbon dioxide is being added to the earth's atmosphere by the burning of coal, oil, and natural gas at the rate of 6 billion tons a year. By the year 2000 there will be about 25 percent more carbon dioxide in our atmosphere than at present. Exhausts and other releases from automobiles contribute a major share to the generation of smog.

Water pollution control decisions should not be based entirely on health considerations. Present water treatment practices, if vigorously applied, appear adequate to permit our use of almost all waters for domestic purposes.

Shallow waters of our coasts and estuaries are essential in the life cycles of the fish and shellfish that provide nearly 60 percent of our total seafoods. The filling in of these shallow waters must be regarded as an important kind of pollution.

The manpower, knowledge, and facilities now at hand are insufficient for the complete task of pollution abatement and management. Large numbers of well trained technicians, engineers, economists, and scientists will be needed (1 Weekly Comp. Pres. Docs., p. 476).

On November 17, 1965, the President signed Executive Order 11258 "Prevention, Control, and Abatement of Water Pollution by Federal Activities" (1 Weekly Comp. Pres. Docs., p. 506; 30 F.R. 14483; 3 CFR, 1965 Supp., p. 188).

The statement was released at Austin, Tex.

---

603 Remarks at Southwest Texas State College Upon Signing the Higher Education Act of 1965. *November 8, 1965*

Dr. McCrocklin; members of the faculty and the student body; Congressman Pickle; Mr. Kellam, the chairman of the Board of Regents; Dr. Crook; my old friend and conspirator and collaborator and former coworker and cosecretary to Dr. Evans—Tom Nichols; my former superintendent, Dr. Donaho; distinguished guests; ladies and gentlemen:

In a very few moments, I will put my signature on the Higher Education Act of 1965. The President's signature upon this legislation passed by this Congress will swing open a new door for the young people of America. For them, and for this entire land of ours, it is the most important door that will ever open—the door to education.

And this legislation is the key which unlocks it.

To thousands of young men and women, this act means the path of knowledge is open to all that have the determination to walk it.

It means a way to deeper personal fulfillment, greater personal productivity, and increased personal reward. This bill, which I will make law, is an incentive to stay in school.

It means that a high school senior anywhere in this great land of ours can apply to any college or any university in any of the 50 States and not be turned away because his family is poor.

This bill is only one of more than two dozen education measures enacted by the first session of the 89th Congress. And history will forever record that this session— the first session of the 89th Congress—did more for the wonderful cause of education in America than all the previous 176 regular sessions of Congress did, put together.

I doubt that any future Congress will ever erect a prouder monument for future generations.

Last May, 2,700,000 boys and girls graduated from all the high schools in America— 2,700,000. One million, four hundred thousand—about half of them—went on to college. But almost as many—1,300,000— dropped out and never started college.

This bill, which we will shortly make into law, will provide scholarships and loans and work opportunities to 1 million of that 1.3 million that did not get to go on to college. And when you, the first year, with the first bill, take care of 1 million of that 1.3 million through this legislation, we are hopeful that the State and the local governments, and the local employers and the local loan funds, can somehow take care of the other 300,000.

So to thousands of young people education will be available. And it is a truism that education is no longer a luxury. Education in this day and age is a necessity.

Where a family cannot afford that necessity:

—We can now make available scholarships up to $1,000 a year, awarded on the basis of need alone to an individual.

—We can award part-time jobs so one student can earn as much as $500 a year.

—We can provide loans, free of interest and free of any payment schedule until after you graduate, to worthy, deserving, capable students.

And in my judgment, this Nation can never make a wiser or a more profitable investment anywhere.

In the next school year alone, 140,000

young men and women will be enrolled in college who, but for the provisions of this bill, would have never gone past high school. We will reap the rewards of their wiser citizenship and their greater productivity for decades to come.

This bill that I am signing will help our colleges and our universities add grasp to their reach for new knowledge and enlightment.

From this act will also come a new partnership between campus and community, turning the ivory towers of learning into the allies of a better life in our cities.

It ensures that college and university libraries will no longer be the anemic stepchildren of Federal assistance.

And this act makes major new thrusts in a good many other directions:

—in assisting smaller, undernourished colleges obtain better teachers;

—in adding first-class equipment in order to have first-class classrooms;

—in establishing a new National Teacher Corps to help our local communities receive extra help in the training of our neglected children, whom our teachers have been unable to reach. When Congress convenes again in January, I intend immediately to ask again for the money to take the Teacher Corps off the drawing boards and put it in the classrooms.

I consider the Higher Education Act— with its companion, the Elementary and Secondary Education Act of 1965, which we signed back in the spring of this year—to be the keystones of the great, fabulous 89th Congress.

This Congress did more to uplift education, more to attack disease in this country and around the world, and more to conquer poverty than any other session in all American history, and what more worthy achievements could any person want to have? For it was the Congress that was more true than any other Congress to Thomas Jefferson's belief that: "The care of human life and happiness is the first and only legitimate objective of good Government."

Too many people, for too many years, argued that education and health and human welfare were not the Government's concern.

And while they spoke, our schools fell behind, our sick people went unattended, and our poor fell deeper into despair.

But now, at last, in this year of our Lord, 1965, we have quit talking and started acting. The roots of change and reform are spreading, not just throughout Washington, but throughout every community in every State of this great Nation.

On my way here this morning, I visited the Job Corps Center, and I looked into the faces of boys who all their lives had been denied opportunity because they came from large families and poor families, but who today are now receiving that opportunity.

They are learning how to be mechanics and welders and operators of heavy machinery, and they will have jobs that are some more enduring and more profitable than some of you that go out to lead in our classrooms.

One fellow told me that he had been offered—when he completed his course in underwater welding—more per day than Dr. Donaho paid me per month in 1928.

I have seen other signs of progress and new determination. I have seen it throughout the States of this Nation. I saw it this past week, I am proud to say, in our own great Lone Star State of Texas.

The people of Texas went to the polls and they approved constitutional amendments which leave no doubt that the people of this State want decent treatment for their aged.

They want decent treatment for the handicapped and the unfortunate children. They want an education system that fits the needs of the 20th century. And they expect the Federal and the State governments—both of whom are the servants of all the people—to join shoulder to shoulder and work together to get this job done.

I want to make it clear once and for all, here and now, so that all that can see can witness and all who can hear can hear, that the Federal Government—as long as I am President—intends to be a partner and not a boss in meeting our responsibilities to all the people. The Federal Government has neither the wish nor the power to dictate education.

We can point the way.

We can offer help.

We can contribute to providing the necessary and needed tools.

But the final decision, the last responsibility, the ultimate control, must, and will, always rest with the local communities.

Today, then, we embark on a new adventure in learning. And it has a very special meaning to me.

This is a proud moment in my life. I am proud to have a part in the beginning that this bill provides, because here a great deal began for me some 38 years ago on this campus.

It was here in these surroundings that I first understood the deeper meaning of the Bible's promise that: "Ye shall know the truth and the truth shall make you free."

Here the seeds were planted from which grew my firm conviction that for the individual, education is the path to achievement and fulfillment; for the Nation, it is a path to a society that is not only free but civilized; and for the world, it is the path to peace—for it is education that places reason over force.

As a student, I lived in a tiny room above Dr. Evans' garage. I lived there 3 years before the business manager knew I occupied those quarters and submitted me a bill. I shaved and I showered in a gymnasium that was down the road. I worked at a dozen different jobs, from sweeping the floors to selling real silk socks. Sometimes I wondered what the next day would bring that could exceed the hardship of the day before.

But with all of that, I was one of the lucky ones—and I knew it even then.

I left this campus to become a teacher under one of the great teachers that I have known. I want him to stand because he did much in my life. Dr. Donaho, please stand.

He came here and looked over my credentials and somehow or other offered me a job at $125 a month to teach a Mexican school at Cotulla when I was a sophomore, and it was necessary that I leave that year to teach.

I shall never forget the faces of the boys and the girls in that little Welhausen Mexican School, and I remember even yet the pain of realizing and knowing then that college was closed to practically every one of those children because they were too poor.

And I think it was then that I made up my mind that this Nation could never rest while the door to knowledge remained closed to any American.

So here, today, back on the campus of my youth, that door is swinging open far wider than it ever did before.

The rest is up to you. The rest is up to the teachers and the citizens and the educational leaders of tomorrow. I want to say this to each of you, finally. You are witnessing a historic moment. You should carry the memory and the meaning of this moment with you throughout your life.

And when you look into the faces of your students and your children and your grandchildren, tell them that you were there when it began. Tell them that a promise has been made to them. Tell them that the leadership of your country believes it is the obligation of your Nation to provide and permit and assist every child born in these borders to receive all the education that he can take.

I looked over some editorials that I wrote when I was editor of the college paper here last night. Some I wasn't too proud of. But in one I urged our people to know no North or no South, or no East or West, to strive to be no sectionalist, but only an American.

And I pointed out to the 1,357 students then enrolled here at this college what I thought vision required of each of us. Some of that vision has been supplied to this student body that has gone from 1,300 to 5,500.

So, when we leave here this morning, I want you to go back and say to your children and to your grandchildren, and those who come after you and follow you—tell them that we have made a promise to them. Tell them that the truth is here for them to seek. And tell them that we have opened the road and we have pulled the gates down and the way is open, and we expect them to travel it.

And when we meet back here again a few years from now, there will be many more than the 1,300 and the 5,500 that will be here seeking and receiving the knowledge that is an absolute necessity if we are to maintain our freedom in a highly competitive world.

All you have to do is look at the morning paper this morning to see the rockets that were paraded down the avenues in the Soviet Union yesterday or the day before, and realize that until we banish ignorance, until we drive disease from our midst, until we win the war on poverty, we cannot expect to continue to be the leaders not only of a great people but the leaders of all civilization.

Thank you very much.

NOTE: The President spoke at 12:30 p.m. in the Strahan Gymnasium at Southwest Texas State College, San Marcos, Tex. In his opening words he referred to James H. McCrocklin, President of Southwest Texas State College, J. J. Pickle, Representative from Texas, Jesse C. Kellam, Chairman of the State Board of Regents of Texas State Colleges, Dr. W. H. Crook, Regional Director of the Office of Economic Opportunity, Dr. C. E. Evans, President of South-

west Texas State College when President Johnson was a student there, Tom W. Nichols, professor of business administration at the college and formerly President Johnson's college journalism instructor, and William T. Donaho, superintendent of Cotulla, Tex., public schools when the President was a teacher there.

As enacted, the Higher Education Act of 1965 is Public Law 89–329 (79 Stat. 1219). A summary of the major provisions of the act is printed in the Weekly Compilation of Presidential Documents (vol. 1, p. 482).

For the President's remarks on signing the Elementary and Secondary Education Act of 1965, see Item 181.

604 Statement by the President Following the Signing of Bills Providing for Duty-Free Entry of Scientific Instruments. *November 8, 1965*

DURING the past few days, I have signed 14 bills which would provide duty-free entry for specific scientific instruments imported for the use of 18 universities and educational institutions located in almost every section of the country.

I have approved these bills because each entry conforms to the standards for duty-free entry of scientific instruments under the agreement on the importation of educational, scientific, and cultural materials, commonly known as the Florence Agreement, to which the Senate gave its advice and consent in 1960 and for which implementing legislation is pending before the Congress. Earlier this year, I strongly recommended the enactment of such legislation.

The growing volume of special bills like the 14 I have just approved underscores and emphasizes the present need for general legislation in this area. In the interest of economy of effort and of consistent and equal treatment for all educational and scientific institutions and in furtherance of international cooperation, I earnestly hope that the Congress will give early favorable consideration to such general legislation during the forthcoming session.

NOTE: As enacted, the 14 bills providing for duty-free entry of scientific instruments, approved October 30–November 8, are Private Laws 89–172, 89–174, 89–175, 89–177, 89–181, 89–187, 89–193, 89–195—89–199, 89–208, 89–209 (79 Stat. 1400–1415).

The statement was released at Austin, Tex.

605 Statement by the President Upon Signing the Southeast Hurricane Disaster Relief Act of 1965. *November 8, 1965*

I HAVE today signed H.R. 11539, the Southeast Hurricane Disaster Relief Act of 1965.

This legislation is a fine example of constructive cooperation by the Congress and the executive departments and agencies in providing promptly additional authority needed to aid the victims of disaster.

The act has two major purposes. First and most immediate is the provision of more adequate financial assistance to those suffering property damage or loss from Hurricane Betsy, which struck Louisiana, Mississippi, and Florida early in September.

I am advised that the property loss from Betsy will probably equal or exceed the loss in any other disaster in the past two decades. We have been doing everything we can under present Federal authority jointly with State and local authorities and the Red Cross, but under present law direct Federal aid to property owners who have suffered losses is limited to the provision of long-term loans at low interest rates. Private insurance companies are absorbing hundreds of millions of dollars in losses. But thousands of families have had their homes severely damaged or destroyed by floods or other water-caused damages against which they could not purchase insurance protection, because insurance for this type of risk was not available for them to buy.

The legislative history of this act makes it clear that both the Senate and the House of Representatives desired to give special assistance to those victims of the hurricane who suffered losses for which no insurance was obtainable. Accordingly, within certain limitations the act permits a person who receives a disaster loan from the Small Business Administration or an emergency loan from the Farmers Home Administration, because of loss or damage resulting from Hurricane Betsy, to obtain a cancellation of part of the principal, or a waiver of part of the interest, due from him under the loan agreement. One of the most important of these limitations is that this relief will be given only in the case of uninsurable loss or damage—such as that resulting from flood, high water, or wind-driven water. It cannot be extended, nor should it be, to those who did not take advantage of available insurance protection.

In accordance with the intent of the law, the loss-sharing will be governed by an equitable formula designed to provide in general the most liberal assistance to those suffering the greatest loss in relation to their resources.

And for those not eligible for disaster or emergency loans, and hence not eligible for relief under this legislation, I am confident that Red Cross assistance will continue to be available.

The second major purpose of this bill and its most significant potential contribution is to authorize the immediate initiation of a study by the Secretary of Housing and Urban Development of alternative permanent programs which could be established to help provide financial assistance in the future to those suffering property losses in floods and other natural disasters, including but not limited to disaster insurance or reinsurance.

Such a basic study is long overdue.

This act is the sixth law passed in 18 months for the specific purpose of broadening Federal aids for the victims of the unusually severe succession of disasters experienced since the spring of 1964. In every case, we have had to act on such legislative proposals on an emergency basis. In three of the six cases the legislation was limited to one specific disaster.

This administration has long supported action to undertake such a basic study, and the Senate has twice passed legislation to authorize it. I am happy to note that the Congress now has not only provided the necessary statutory authority but also has appropriated funds to get the study underway. Hopefully when it is completed it will provide the basis for developing a workable program of protection for property owners in disaster areas either by extending the insurance plan of pooling the risks or by joint Federal-State sharing along with the private

owners the cost of losses arising from uninsurable risks.

NOTE: As enacted, the Southeast Hurricane Disaster Relief Act of 1965 is Public Law 89–339 (79 Stat. 1301).

The statement was released at Austin, Tex.

606   Proclamation 3686 Designating a Day of Dedication and Prayer for Those Risking Their Lives for Peace in Viet-Nam. *November 9, 1965*

[Released November 9, 1965. Dated November 6, 1965]

By the President of the United States of America a Proclamation:

WHEREAS, in assisting the people of South Viet-Nam to resist unprovoked aggression, the United States and other nations are carrying on the honored tradition of defending a people's right to freedom; and

WHEREAS the purpose of the United States in Viet-Nam is to help to open the way for social justice in place of unprovoked aggression and peace instead of war; and

WHEREAS there can be no social justice or economic progress without security from external attack and from terror in the night; and

WHEREAS the Government of the United States remains ready without condition for the international discussions that can lead to lasting peace; and

WHEREAS it is the sense of the Congress in S. Res. 159 and H. Res. 626 that it would be fitting for the President to set aside a national day of remembrance dedicated to those Americans who are committing their

lives, blood and energies in the defense of world peace.

Now, THEREFORE, I, LYNDON B. JOHNSON, President of the United States of America, do hereby designate Sunday, November 28, 1965, as a day of dedication and prayer, honoring the men and women of South Viet-Nam, of the United States, and of all other countries, who are risking their lives to bring about a just peace in South Viet-Nam.

IN WITNESS WHEREOF, I have hereunto set my hand and caused the Seal of the United States of America to be affixed.

DONE at the City of Washington this sixth day of November in the year of our Lord nineteen hundred and sixty-five, [SEAL]   and of the Independence of the United States of America the one hundred and ninetieth.

LYNDON B. JOHNSON

By the President:
   DEAN RUSK
      Secretary of State

NOTE: The proclamation was released at Austin, Tex.

607 Telegram to General Eisenhower Wishing Him an Early Recovery. *November 9, 1965*

YOU'RE so much in our thoughts that an expression like this is hardly necessary. Millions of Americans who regard you with such high affection and respect, joined by millions of people throughout the world who share that feeling, are saying, "Get well, Mr. President."

LADY BIRD AND LYNDON B. JOHNSON

[The Honorable Dwight Eisenhower, Fort Gordon Army Hospital, Augusta, Georgia]

NOTE: The text of the telegram was read by Joseph Laitin, an assistant press secretary, at his news conference at 10:20 a.m. on Tuesday, November 9, 1965, at Austin, Tex. It was not made public in the form of a White House press release.

Mr. Laitin also announced that the President had telephoned Mrs. Eisenhower in Augusta and had instructed Secretary of Defense McNamara to make needed facilities available to members of the former President's family.

General Eisenhower entered the Fort Gordon Army Hospital on November 9 following a mild heart attack. His condition was termed satisfactory, and on November 23 he was transferred to Walter Reed Medical Center in Washington to complete his recovery.

608 Memorandum Concerning the Power Failure in the Northeastern United States. *November 9, 1965*

Memorandum for Honorable Joseph C. Swidler, Chairman, Federal Power Commission:

Today's failure is a dramatic reminder of the importance of the uninterrupted flow of power to the health, safety, and well being of our citizens and the defense of our country.

This failure should be immediately and carefully investigated in order to prevent a recurrence.

You are therefore directed to launch a thorough study of the cause of this failure. I am putting at your disposal full resources of the Federal Government and directing the Federal Bureau of Investigation, the Department of Defense and other agencies to support you in any way possible. You are to call upon the top experts in our Nation in conducting the investigation.

A report is expected at the earliest possible moment as to the causes of the failure and the steps you recommend to be taken to prevent a recurrence.

LYNDON B. JOHNSON

NOTE: The text of the memorandum was read by Bill D. Moyers, Special Assistant to the President, at his news conference at 8:30 p.m. on Tuesday, November 9, 1965, at Austin, Tex.

At 10:35 p.m. Mr. Moyers announced that Mr. Swidler had communicated to the President the following steps to implement the foregoing memorandum:

"1. A telegram has been sent to all of the major companies involved, requesting that they assemble the relevant facts as to the impact of the interruption on their systems and the steps taken to restore service.

"2. A group of electric power system operation experts from various private and public power systems throughout the country will meet tomorrow in Washington to help plan the details of the investigation.

"3. Mr. Swidler has been in communication directly with the Attorney General and the Secretary of Defense to assure continuing liaison.

"4. A Federal Power Commission staff team has been dispatched to the operating offices of the Niagara-Mohawk system so that the Commission can be fully informed on the steps taken to locate faults which precipitated the breakdown of service.

"5. Another Federal Power Commission staff team has been dispatched to the operating offices of Con-Edison in New York to cooperate and coordinate with the efforts of that company to restore service."

Mr. Moyers also announced that Mr. Swidler had informed the President that the Commission staff would work through the night on these, as well as other steps now being planned, to carry out the President's directive.

For the President's statement in response to the Federal Power Commission report on the electric power blackout in the northeastern States, see Item 640.

609 Statement by the President: American Education Week. *November 11, 1965*

THIS is a time of great need—and a time of great progress in American education. In the past year the 89th Congress enacted more than a score of major measures to underwrite excellence in America's classrooms.

But the pursuit of excellence requires more than money; it requires vigorous and enlightened leadership of our schools at the local level.

I believe in local direction of school affairs—and I have firmly committed my administration to that policy.

I hope, therefore, that citizens everywhere who want better schools will recognize their obligations—and live up to them.

We need better teachers; we need more library books and trained librarians; we need more and better courses about our Nation, its history and government; we need more knowledge about our neighbors around the world.

I urge all citizens:

—To visit your local schools, to learn their problems and their possibilities;

—To take an active part in the work of your local parent-teachers association;

—To consider the contribution you can make to better education, and to begin making that contribution today.

NOTE: On September 29, 1965, the President signed Proclamation 3674, designating the period November 7–13, 1965, as American Education Week, 1965 (1 Weekly Comp. Pres. Docs., p. 328; 30 F.R. 12623; 3 CFR, 1965 Supp., p. 60).

The statement was released at Austin, Tex.

610 Proclamation 3687: Thanksgiving Day, 1965. *November 11, 1965*

[Released November 11, 1965. Dated November 10, 1965]

By the President of the United States of America a Proclamation:

For all the blessings that have been bestowed upon our nation during the past 12 months, it is a small thing to give thanks to Almighty God.

When the pilgrims first observed Thanksgiving nearly 350 years ago, life was harsh and unrelenting. Cold and sickness had diminished their ranks. Their shelter was crude. Their future was uncertain. Yet when their harvest was abundant, they considered themselves blessed—and their hearts were filled with gratitude.

Today we have much more than an abundant harvest. Our nation is rich and strong and united in the cause of liberty and justice. Our physical comforts are unmatched anywhere in the world. Our medicine has conquered ancient diseases.

In the past year we have added greatly to that national legacy. We have guaranteed the right to vote to all our citizens. We have pledged dignity to our elderly—even in sickness. We have added new dimensions to the education of our youth. We have broadened the horizons of opportunity for our poor. And all the while, we have enjoyed the greatest prosperity in history.

But our real blessings lie not in our bounty. They lie in those steadfast principles that the early pilgrims forged for all generations to come: the belief in the essential dignity of man; the restless search for a better world for all; and the courage—as shown by our sons in Viet-Nam today—to defend the cause of freedom wherever on earth it is threatened.

These are the eternal blessings of America. They are the blessings which make us grateful even when the future is uncertain. They are the blessings which give us the strength to complete the unfinished tasks that remain before us.

For these blessings should we thank God most of all.

Now, THEREFORE, I, LYNDON B. JOHNSON, President of the United States of America, in consonance with the Joint Resolution of the

Congress approved December 26, 1941, 55 Stat. 862 (5 U.S.C. 87b), designating the fourth Thursday of November in each year as Thanksgiving Day, do hereby proclaim Thursday, November 25, 1965, as a day of national Thanksgiving.

On that day, let us gather in our homes and in our places of worship to thank God for His generosity. Let us make ourselves worthy of that generosity by pledging to Him our everlasting devotion. And let us pray to Him that the forces of violence, indifference and intolerance may soon vanish from the face of the earth so that peace and understanding and love may reign supreme.

IN WITNESS WHEREOF, I have hereunto set my hand and caused the Seal of the United States of America to be affixed.

DONE at the City of Washington this tenth day of November in the year of our Lord nineteen hundred and sixty-[SEAL]   five, and of the Independence of the United States of America the one hundred and ninetieth.

LYNDON B. JOHNSON

By the President:
  DEAN RUSK
    Secretary of State

NOTE: The proclamation was released at Austin, Tex.

---

611   Statement by the President on Approving the Appointment of Members of the Health Insurance Benefits Advisory Council. *November 11, 1965*

THE SUCCESS of this program which means so much to our older people will depend in considerable part on the help provided by the many professional groups and organizations who will contribute to its administration.

I am grateful to all those who have agreed to serve on this Council. Their contribu-

tions and the continued assistance of physicians and other members of the health professions will assure that the new health insurance program will operate for the greatest benefit of our 19 million older citizens.

NOTE: The President's statement was made public as part of a White House release announcing the appointment of a 16-member Health Insurance Benefits Advisory Council to help formulate policies for the administration of the Medicare program. The release stated that the Council would be chaired by Kermit Gordon, Vice President of the Brookings Institution and former Director of the Bureau of the Budget. The members of the Council, appointed by Secretary of Health, Education, and Welfare John

W. Gardner and drawn from the fields of medicine, health care, business, labor, insurance, and the general public, are listed in the Weekly Compilation of Presidential Documents (vol. 1, p. 490).

For the President's remarks at the signing of the Medicare bill, see Item 394.

The statement was released at Austin, Tex.

612   Memorandums on the Need for Coordinating the Practices of Federal Wage Boards. *November 16, 1965*

Memorandum for Chairman Macy, U.S. Civil Service Commission

Subject: Coordination of wage board activities

I am deeply concerned by the differences in the systems and practices used by the departments and agencies to fix the pay for Federal wage board employees and by the extent to which resulting wage rates differ for similar work within a community. These wage board pay fixing programs affect more than 617,000 Federal employees in trade, craft, and manual labor occupations. They involve payroll expenditures in excess of $4 billion annually.

From the facts available it seems clear that the pay disparities are inequitable, and result primarily from differences among the agencies in basic principles, policies, and practices under which wage board pay is fixed.

Accordingly, I have addressed the attached memorandum to the heads of the executive departments and agencies.

You will note that this memorandum assigns to you, as Chairman of the Civil Service Commission, three responsibilities: (1) leadership in coordination of the collective effort, including consultation with appropriate employee organizations; (2) keeping me informed of significant developments;

and (3) reporting to me not later than July 1, 1966, on the corrective actions adopted.

LYNDON B. JOHNSON

Attachment

Memorandum for the Heads of Executive Departments and Agencies

Subject: Coordination of wage board activities

It has come to my attention that different executive departments and agencies follow different practices, and continue to pay different wage rates for the same trades and labor jobs in the same locality. Such differences constitute inequities which I believe can and should be corrected by cooperative action.

In its report of April 15, 1965, the Special Panel on Federal Salaries recommended that steps should be taken to eliminate the pay differences and to bring about equitable coordination of wage board practices. I agree with this recommendation.

I ask you, accordingly, to join with the heads of other executive departments and agencies in the development of common job standards and wage policies and practices which will insure interagency equity in wage rates based upon statistically valid wage surveys.

The policies and practices should be based

upon the principles that (1) wages shall be fixed and adjusted from time to time as nearly as is consistent with the public interest in accordance with prevailing rates, and (2) there shall be equal pay for substantially equal work, and pay distinctions shall be maintained in keeping with work distinctions.

At appropriate stages in the development of the system, there should be consultation with representatives of employee organizations whose members are paid under the wage system.

I have asked Chairman Macy of the Civil Service Commission to take leadership in coordinating this collective action to develop a common Federal wages system, including consultation with appropriate employee organizations; to keep me currently informed of significant developments, and to report to me not later than July 1, 1966, on the actions adopted.

LYNDON B. JOHNSON

NOTE: The report of the President's Special Panel on Federal Salaries, dated April 15, 1965, is printed in House Document 170 (89th Cong., 1st. sess.), page 12.

613   Remarks at a Reception for Participants in a Planning Session for the White House Conference "To Fulfill These Rights." *November 16, 1965*

Mr. Chairman Randolph, Mr. Vice President, Mr. Attorney General, Chairman Abram, Chairman Coleman, distinguished delegates:

Last spring I spoke at Howard University about the next challenge to American democracy.

I said that it is to help the Negro fulfill the rights which, after a very long time of injustice, he is finally able to secure:

—To move beyond opportunity to achievement;

—To shatter forever not only the barriers of law and public practice, but the walls which bound the condition of man by the color of his skin.

I spoke at the twilight of a revolutionary decade.

America had awakened—after a century of uneasy slumber—to the cry for justice. Every branch of this Government had been brought into action. Ancient beliefs and customs were being transformed.

Yet millions of Negro Americans re-

mained in bondage.

They are the jobless, the unskilled, the broken families that are housed in squalor—a prey to crime and violence, their children destined to the same bleak fate.

This administration is attacking these evils through our poverty program that we began last year, through our education program that we began this year, through our Medicare and our other health programs that are now being inaugurated. In numberless ways this administration is acting and not just talking.

But there is no single easy remedy. The causes and the results of past injustices are much too complex for that.

And that is why I have asked you to come here tonight, and to stay here for the next few days. You men and women that are gathered in this beautiful East Room, where Abigail Adams once hung out her washing, have given lifetimes of thought to this American dilemma.

Some of you are scholars of the heart

who dreamed dreams of a new America. Some of you are administrators who must deal with Negro life as it is. Some of you are the captains of peaceful armies, who have led your people with great courage.

And I salute all of you. I welcome all of you to 2 days of intense labor for your country's sake.

The work that you do, and the recommendations that will be built on your work next spring, will vitally affect the future of over 200 million people.

For you will not be dealing with the abstractions of political science.

You will be dealing with human lives—and each human life lost through racial hatred, each life diminished by blind prejudice, saps the strength of this great land that we all love.

You will not be working in a vacuum. This administration, under the great leadership of this great man, Nicholas Katzenbach, has already put powerful and just laws on the statute books of this land. And I am here tonight to assure you that we have the determination and we have the resourcefulness to translate those laws into better lives for all Americans—this year and next year and for as many years as it takes to get this job finally done.

Now let us review tonight some of our accomplishments, and then let us look frankly at what remains to be done.

In the few weeks that elapsed since I originally proposed and signed into law the Voting Rights Act of 1965, this year, over 200,000 Negro citizens have been newly registered to vote. But many hundreds of thousands have not, and it is the "have nots" that we are concerned about from here on out. This is a challenge, I think, not only to your Government but it is a challenge to Negro leadership throughout this country. And I urge you, I plead with you, I beg you

to work around the clock. Tell those who have been barred from the polls that a new day has come, that at last they may have a voice in shaping the destinies of their own land. That voice will be heard from the sheriff's office to the halls of Congress—but only if it is used.

One clear concern is the jury—the cornerstone of our system of justice in this country. If its composition is a sham, its judgment is a shame. And when that happens, justice itself is a fraud, casting off the blindfold and tipping the scales one way for whites and another way for Negroes.

Your Government has already moved and joined in three lawsuits which challenge a biased system of jury selection. In three counties, including Lowndes County, the United States has taken its cause to court, on the grounds that Negroes have been deliberately excluded from jury service.

But we must do more. We will do more.

I have asked the Attorney General to prepare for me, to recommend to the Congress in January, jury legislation that is clear in its purpose and specific in its aim. That aim is to prevent injustice to Negroes at the hands of all-white juries.

We intend to make the jury box, in both State and Federal courts, the sacred domain of justice under law.

In the field of education, the common goal of white parents and Negro parents alike is the best possible education for their children, and it is a national shame that the vast majority of Negro children are schooled even worse than they are housed and fed.

Tomorrow I will ask the Commission on Civil Rights to turn its careful attention to the problems of race and education in all parts of this country. I am asking them to develop a firm foundation of facts on which local and State Governments can build a school system that is colorblind.

It has been 11 years—11 years since the Supreme Court decision in the Brown case.[1] Eleven long years ago, and still while the decision is the law of the land, tonight it is not yet a fact. And I would hope that every school board in this land would examine its conscience tonight, for if not 11 years, then how long must it take?

In our assistance programs, we are seeking to make racial justice a positive purpose rather than a distant goal. I will expect immediate results from the letter that has just been sent out by the Attorney General. This letter calls on all agencies to ferret out discrimination in all assistance programs rather than just to simply sit and wait for complaints.

The plight of the Negro American can never be solved, though, just by laws alone. Despite all of the doors that we have opened in the past 10 years—and all the doors that we intend to open in the years ahead—there will be far too many who are unable to pass through them without our help. Because millions are trapped in ghettoes and shanties, millions are discouraged and hopeless. They will be as far from sharing in the promise of America as if they really inhabited another planet.

A guarantee of a job is useless to a man who cannot even read an application.

A college scholarship is useless to a child who drops out of school in the eighth grade.

The promise of a new skill is useless to a man who doesn't believe in the future.

A new classroom is useless to a child whose stomach is so empty that he cannot study, or whose eyes cannot recognize what he sees.

So the energy, and the fire, and the dedication that have gone into the American past, struggles for justice, and it struggles for it now, and it's needed for the day-to-day work that lies ahead of each of us.

I have asked you to come here to help me because this is not a job for one man alone. We need you to make these laws work. We need your guidance in what lies ahead. But most of all, I just must emphasize, we need your leadership for the Negro community in this country.

The tide of change is running with the Negro American on this mid-November evening. Neither the ignorant violence of the Ku Klux Klan nor the despairing violence of Watts can reverse it.

For this tide is moved by decency and by love and by justice. It rises in the breasts of a people whose mission on this earth is now what it was really in our own beginning. And that mission is for each of us a very personal obligation—a mission to strengthen the brotherhood of man.

Thank you.

NOTE: The President spoke at 8:30 p.m. in the East Room at the White House before a planning session for the White House Conference "To Fulfill These Rights" to be held in Washington June 1–2, 1966. In his opening words he referred to A. Philip Randolph, President of the Brotherhood of Sleeping Car Porters and honorary chairman of the meeting, Vice President Hubert H. Humphrey, Attorney General Nicholas deB. Katzenbach, and to Morris Abram of Atlanta and New York City and William Coleman of Philadelphia, cochairmen of the meeting.

For the President's address at Howard University on June 4, see Item 301.

The Voting Rights Act of 1965 was approved by the President on August 6, 1965 (see Item 409).

The President's message to the Congress on civil rights, dated April 28, 1966, is printed in the Weekly Compilation of Presidential Documents (vol. 2, p. 581).

See also Items 548, 615.

---

[1] *Brown* v. *Board of Education of Topeka, Kans.,* was one of the cases involved in the Supreme Court decision of May 17, 1954, declaring racial segregation in the public schools unconstitutional. The text of the decision is printed in United States Supreme Court Reports, 1954 (349 U.S. 294, 99 L. Ed. 1083).

614 Remarks Upon Receiving the Parents' Magazine Award for Outstanding Service to the Cause of Education. *November 17, 1965*

Mr. Hecht, ladies and gentlemen:

I look upon this award that you have just given me as a symbol of victory. Not victory for me or my administration, and not victory even for the Congress—not even victory for educators. But the victory is for American youth and for America itself.

Today, more than ever before, our boys and girls face a life of hope, a life of meaning, and, I think, a life of achievement.

The poor among them can look to opportunity and advancement. The sick among them can look to care. The mentally disturbed among them can now look for some treatment. And all among them can look to an education that will take them as far as their abilities will permit.

And this really is the great victory of our time.

I am proud to have been able to play a part in it. That pride, along with the honor you do me today, I will carry with me to the end of my days. And I am personally very grateful to you for your thoughtfulness and for this token of your recognition.

Thank you.

NOTE: The President spoke at 1:35 p.m. in the Cabinet Room at the White House. In his opening words he referred to George Hecht, publisher of Parents' Magazine. The medal was presented by Mr. Hecht and Robert Cramer, associate publisher of the magazine. The text of Mr. Hecht's remarks upon presenting the award is printed in the Weekly Compilation of Presidential Documents (vol. 1, p. 508).

Since 1928 Parents' Magazine has presented medals to distinguished Americans for outstanding service to children and to the cause of education. This was the first time such an award was made to a President of the United States.

615 Letter Requesting a Study of Racial Isolation as a Barrier to Quality in Education. *November 17, 1965*

Dear Mr. Chairman:

The future of our Nation rests on the quality of the education its young people receive. And for our Negro children quality education is especially vital because it is the key to equality.

In the past decade this Nation has moved with increasing speed toward the elimination of discrmination and segregation in education, and in housing, employment, voting, and access to public facilities and accommodations. However, long after we have done all we can to eliminate past inequities, we will continue to pay their costs in stunted lives. Because millions of Negroes were

deprived of quality education and training in basic skills, because they were given to believe that they could aspire only to the most menial and insecure places in our society, they are seriously handicapped in taking advantage of opportunities afforded by new laws, new attitudes and an expanding economy. We can no longer tolerate such waste of human resources.

Although we have made substantial progress in ending formal segregation of schools, racial isolation in the schools persists—both in the North and the South—because of housing patterns, school districting, economic stratification and population movements. It has become apparent that such isolation presents serious barriers to quality education. The problems are more subtle and complex than those presented by segregation imposed by law. The remedies may be difficult. But as a first and vital step, the Nation needs to know the facts.

These problems of race and education fall within the responsibilities which Congress has assigned to your Commission, and I request it to gather the facts and make them available to the Nation as rapidly as possible. I know that the Commission will wish to consult with Secretary Gardner and Attorney General Katzenbach to obtain the benefit of their experience, and I am sure they will make the facilities of their Departments available to assist the Commission.

I trust that the task can be completed expeditiously and that your findings may provide a basis for action not only by the Federal Government but also by the states and local school boards which bear the direct responsibility for assuring quality education.

Sincerely,

LYNDON B. JOHNSON

[Honorable John A. Hannah, Chairman, United States Commission on Civil Rights, Washington, D.C.]

NOTE: Mr. Hannah's reply to the President, made public by the White House on November 20, follows:

Dear Mr. President:

I write in reply to your letter of November 17, requesting that the Commission on Civil Rights conduct a study of problems of segregation in education and make the facts available to the Nation as rapidly as possible. The Commission will meet on December 2 to review plans and to assess the additional resources that may be needed to carry out adequately the program you have requested. In the meantime, I wish to assure you of our complete cooperation.

From its past studies the Commission has become convinced that the problem of securing equal educational opportunity for American citizens is one which faces the entire Nation rather than any particular region. We also believe that the segregation or racial isolation of children in schools, whatever the causes, does serious harm to all children—harm that demands the urgent attention of the Nation.

We hope that our studies will make a contribution to the goal you have articulated—education of a quality that will enable each child in this Nation to develop his mind and his skills to the fullest, and that it will help to point the way to additional action on the local, state and federal levels to achieve this goal.

Respectfully yours,

JOHN A. HANNAH
Chairman

616 Toasts of the President and Princess Margaret. *November 17, 1965*

Your Royal Highness, Lord Snowdon, ladies and gentlemen:

Mark Twain once said: "I have traveled more than anyone else, and I have noticed that even the angels speak English with an accent."

Tonight I know that is true. And I am confident that millions of my fellow Americans agree with what I have said, because they have seen and they have heard Your Royal Highness these past few days throughout America.

Your coming has been very good for us. You have reminded us that we are a young nation and a gay people who respond to the smile and the warmth of a young couple. You can tell a great deal about a man simply by knowing to whom he will give his heart—and a country by knowing who can claim hers. You have claimed our heart, and we are very proud to give it to you.

But you have done more.

Your travels throughout our land—in the company of a large number of the press—

have helped our balance of payments problem.

And you have given a new lift to my "See America First" campaign.

So I am very grateful to you in many ways and for many reasons.

Your countrymen should be grateful, too. Lord Nelson once said: "England expects every man to do his duty." And I say to-night, every woman, too. And you have done your duty while in America. You have represented well the people that you serve—with dignity and grace and spirit and joy. You have in fact proved that your fellow countryman, Mr. Thackeray, was wrong when he said that it is so "hard to make an Englishman acknowledge that he is happy."

I am personally very glad that you could be here on the evening that marks the beginning of my 32d year with the most wonderful woman in all the world.

You are somewhat younger than I, Lord Snowdon, and you have been married a few years less than I. And I trust that you will not be offended if I take this occasion to offer you a little senior advice. I have learned that only two things are necessary to keep one's wife happy.

First, let her think that she is having her way.

And second, let her have it.

That philosophy has worked very well for me—and, I might add, for Lady Bird, too.

Very seriously, my marriage has been like that described by Charlotte Brontë. "Al-fred and I," she wrote, "intended to be mar-ried in this way almost from the first; we never meant to be spliced in the humdrum way." Lady Bird and I always intended to be married in this way—happily—and I wish the same for both of you.

I am told by my protocol people that this visit of yours is an "unofficial" visit. I can only wish that "official" visits, of which I am something of a veteran, would have such favorable results. Everywhere you have gone in the United States you have encount-ered an affectionate warmth of feeling and a very friendly interest on the part of the American people. This has been both a tribute to Your Royal Highness and to Lord Snowdon and, through you, it has been an expression of the affection of all the American people for Great Britain.

A bond of friendship and common pur-pose has existed between our two great na-tions for more than 150 years. In a world of change, that bond is constant. In a world of uncertainty, that bond is unfailing. In a world of strife, that bond is our security.

In the name of that bond—and in the hope and belief that it will never weaken—I would now like to propose a toast to Her Majesty the Queen.

Ladies and gentlemen, the Queen.

NOTE: The President spoke at 10:04 p.m. in the State Dining Room at the White House. In his opening words he referred to Princess Margaret of the United Kingdom and her husband, Lord Snow-don. Princess Margaret responded as follows:

"Thank you so much, Mr. President, for your very kind welcome.

"May I first of all say congratulations to you and Mrs. Johnson on your 31st wedding anniversary.

"We would just like to tell you how excited we are to be here with you in the White House tonight. We are so glad to see that you have made such a splendid recovery from your operation.

"We are having the most wonderful time in the United States. The hospitality and kindness that we have received everywhere has touched us greatly, and it will make us take home superlatively happy memories of all we have done and seen. And we only wish we could have stayed longer.

"Ladies and gentlemen, I give you the toast to the President of the United States."

617 Memorandum Approving the Release of Copper From the
      National Stockpile. *November 18, 1965*

Memorandum for Honorable Buford Elling-
ton, Director, Office of Emergency Planning

I accept your recommendation and the recommendations of the Secretaries of State,
Treasury, Defense and Commerce and the
Chairman of the Council of Economic Advisers regarding the immediate release of
200,000 tons of copper from the national
stockpile.

In accordance with the provisions of Section 5 of the Strategic and Critical Materials
Stockpiling Act, as amended (50 U.S.C.

98(d)), I herewith determine that such release and disposition is required for purposes
of the common defense.

LYNDON B. JOHNSON

NOTE: On November 18 the White House also made
public a memorandum to the President from the
Director, Office of Emergency Planning, concurring
in the recommendations of the Chairman of the
Council of Economic Advisers and the Secretaries
of State, Treasury, Defense, and Commerce that
200,000 tons of copper be released immediately
from the national stockpile for purposes of the
common defense (1 Weekly Comp. Pres. Docs.,
p. 510).

618 Letter Establishing a Task Force on the Impact of the Cuban
      Refugee Program. *November 18, 1965*

[Released November 18, 1965. Dated November 17, 1965]

Dear Mr. Secretary:

I was pleased to learn from you and Governor Ellington that your visit to Miami
accomplished its objective of assuring the
community of the continuous concern of the
Federal Government about the impact of
the Cuban Refugee program. We must
continue to place prime emphasis on swift
resettlement outside the Miami area. The
voluntary agencies, which have been of material assistance in the past, will, I am sure
also continue to be of great aid in meeting
this new challenge. At the same time, we
must make a concerted effort to help the
Miami community in a number of ways
now, making the fullest possible use of existing Federal programs to maintain and stimulate economic growth in the Miami area

and to avoid an undue additional burden on
the community as a result of the influx of
refugees.

To assure interagency coordination in
minimizing the impact on Miami, I am
asking you to form a Task Force under your
Chairmanship, to include the Departments
of State, Labor, Agriculture, Commerce,
Housing and Urban Development, the
Office of Economic Opportunity and Small
Business Administration, with the Bureau
of the Budget as an observer. You may
add such other departments and agencies as
you believe will be useful in this effort.

As a result of the refugee program
launched in 1961, more than 180,000
refugees have been aided to resettle and
integrate in Miami and elsewhere in the

United States. Less than 16,000 now require financial assistance in the Miami area. This is a good record of which Americans can be proud. I want our new program to be even better.

Please keep me informed from time to time on your progress in handling this program.

Sincerely,

LYNDON B. JOHNSON

[Honorable John W. Gardner, Secretary of Health, Education, and Welfare, Washington, D.C. 20201]
NOTE: See also Items 546, 601.

619 Statement by the President on the Death of Henry A. Wallace. *November* 18, 1965

THE DEATH of Henry A. Wallace stills an original American voice. He always spoke his mind—and always from a deep sense of social justice. His views may not always have been popular, but they were always sincere. I considered him a good man and a good public servant. His country will miss him.

NOTE: The statement was read by Bill D. Moyers, Special Assistant to the President, at his news conference at 4:15 p.m. on Thursday, November 18, 1965, in his office at the White House. It was not made public in the form of a White House press release.

Mr. Wallace served as Secretary of Agriculture 1933–1940, as Vice President of the United States 1941–1945, and as Secretary of Commerce 1945–1946. In 1948 he was a candidate for President of the United States on the Progressive Party ticket.

620 Statement by the President Upon Announcing the Recess Appointment of William Gorham as Assistant Secretary (for Program Coordination), HEW. *November* 19, 1965

THE legislative successes of the 89th Congress have placed a heavy responsibility on the executive branch of Government. Good management is now the top priority concern of my administration.

That is why I asked Secretary Gardner and other department heads to take full advantage of the latest techniques in program planning and evaluation. And that is why I am appointing, on Secretary Gardner's recommendation, William Gorham to the new position of Assistant Secretary (for Program Coordination) in the Department of Health, Education, and Welfare.

Mr. Gorham has exhibited unusual qualifications in this area. He is a graduate of the Massachusetts Institute of Technology and studied at the Graduate School of Economics at Stanford. He has served more recently as Deputy Assistant Secretary of Defense (Manpower). Secretary McNamara tells me that he has been one of his ablest assistants. I believe this appointment will further strengthen Secretary Gardner's capacity to coordinate the wide range of programs for which his Department is responsible.

621 Remarks in San Antonio at a Reception Honoring Representative Henry Gonzalez. *November 21, 1965*

Congressman Gonzalez, Senator Yarborough, Mr. Cantinflas, distinguished guests, ladies and gentlemen:

Thirty-one years ago last week I came to this beautiful city of San Antonio in an attempt—and it was a successful attempt—to find a bride. We were married here, with the help of Postmaster Dan Quill, in the Episcopal Church.

Four years ago, with the help of "Pepe," we came here to San Antonio to campaign for Henry Gonzalez for the United States Congress.

For me, that election had a very special meaning. That meaning was the love and the respect that I had developed over many years for Americans of Mexican descent.

As a young teacher in a Mexican school in Cotulla I came to know what it meant to many of your children not only to be poor, but to be poor without hope.

As a young assistant to the Congressman from this very district, I came to know your dreams and your ambitions.

As a State Director of the National Youth Administration during the great depression, I came to know your dignity and your dogged determination.

As a Congressman for 12 years, and later as a Senator for 12 years, I came to know your great loyalty.

And that is why I had such a very special interest in your election 4 years ago—and that is why I have come back here to San Antonio today. This is part of my home. You are part of my people. You have never, never deserted me throughout my long career in public life—and that has been for more than 34 years—and I hope that it can always be said that I never deserted you.

With us on that memorable day here in this same place in November 1961, was a very old and very dear friend of mine and a good friend of yours: Cantinflas. He spent the weekend with me and in my home last night, and he came here today to join us again in this reunion. All the world knows Cantinflas as one of the greatest and one of the best loved comedians of all times. But we know him best as a man whose heart always goes out to his fellow man. We know him as a man who believes in human dignity. We know him as a man who has done more to further good relations between the United States and our neighbor to the south, Mexico, than most professional statesmen have done.

But we came here today for another purpose. Henry Gonzalez is a man of the people who is devoting his life to the cause of people. I can pay him no higher tribute than that.

For to me, that is what America is all about.

America's greatness is guaranteeing to every child all the education that he or she can take.

America's greatness is bringing the miracle of modern medicine to every humble citizen of this land.

America's greatness is equality of race, respect of religion, and blindness of color.

America's greatness is food for hungry people.

America's greatness is the helping hand to the child of the slum.

America's greatness is training for the unemployed.

America's greatness is willingness to lend a helping hand to our neighbors from other lands who seek freedom here in our shores.

And in the search for that greatness, we search also for a real and lasting peace. We want to help build a world where reason will replace rockets. We want to build a world where trust will replace terror.

All these goals are possible. They are possible because we believe in them. And if we believe in them, and we unite ourselves, then we can do them.

And that is what American greatness means to me. And that is what it means to this great Congressman, Henry B. Gonzalez.

There is no man in the House of Representatives who has supported your people and your President more loyally than your Congressman, Henry B. Gonzalez.

And I can take great pride in saying the same thing: There is no man in the United States Senate that has supported the program of the people of this country or the program of the President of this country more than the senior Senator from Texas, your able Senator and my friend, Ralph Yarborough.

By sending Henry Gonzalez to the Congress to speak your voice and to vote your purpose, you have helped to share and to shape America's greatness. For a long time I have felt deeply in the debt of the good people of San Antonio and Bexar County, and I came here this afternoon to again express to you the appreciation and the gratitude that I feel for your loyalty and for your friendship and for your patriotism throughout the years.

To those of you who would feel at home if I said, *Buenas tardes, mis amigos,* I would say this, that I know that you are glad that you are American citizens, but you are also, and you can always be very proud that you have Mexican blood in your veins.

It was 2 years ago this afternoon that we came here to this friendly city with the great President of the United States, our late beloved leader, John Fitzgerald Kennedy. You met him with cordiality and with hospitality. You opened your arms to him, and you received him, not knowing that just one day removed, he would no longer be with us.

But tomorrow at noon, we will go to a little Catholic church in Fredericksburg where we will be led by the priest and by ministers of other denominations in a memorial church service, a memorial to our late beloved President John Fitzgerald Kennedy.

We would like to ask each of you that might care to, to join us in that service tomorrow, if you have the time and you feel that you could come. We would be glad to have you in the Catholic Church at Fredericksburg.

This afternoon though, before closing, I think that each of you would want to join with all of us in standing and bowing our heads in respect and in memory to our great leader, John Fitzgerald Kennedy, who was here with us in San Antonio 2 years ago today.

NOTE: The President spoke at 4 p.m. at the Las Palmas Shopping Center in San Antonio, Tex. In his opening words he referred to Representative Henry B. Gonzalez of Texas, Senator Ralph Yarborough of Texas, and Cantinflas (Mario Moreno), Mexican comedian and star of the film "Pepe."

Some 30,000 persons attended the reception which marked the fourth anniversary of the special election which sent Representative Gonzalez to Congress.

622 Telegram Greeting John Nance Garner on His 97th Birthday. *November 22, 1965*

I HAVE BEEN wishing you "Happy Birthday" for as long as I can remember. But each time it is an even happier privilege to be counted among the thousands of your friends who are thinking of you and wishing you well. I hope you enjoy this one and many more to come.

LYNDON B. JOHNSON

[Vice President John Nance Garner, Uvalde, Texas]

NOTE: The telegram was read by Bill D. Moyers, Special Assistant to the President, at his news conference at 9:10 a.m. on Monday, November 22, 1965, at Austin, Tex. It was not made public in the form of a White House press release.

623 Remarks in Fredericksburg, Texas, at a Memorial Service Marking the Second Anniversary of President Kennedy's Assassination. *November 22, 1965*

NO ONE of us who lived on that terrible November day will ever be able to forget what happened then or what we lost there.

The years will make more bearable the burden of grief we felt, but not even the passing of time will dim the memory of John F. Kennedy's life.

It is not for us to know how many great things he might have accomplished had he been spared the assassin's hand, but of this we are certain—he lived long enough, and well enough, to rekindle our spirit, to renew our faith, and to reaffirm our commitment as a people to all the great purposes for which this Nation was created.

NOTE: The President spoke at 12:15 p.m. in St. Mary's Roman Catholic Church in Fredericksburg, Tex., before a gathering of 400 persons at a memorial service for President Kennedy.

Eulogies and prayers were delivered by the Reverend Dr. John Barclay, pastor of the Central Christian Church of Austin, the Right Reverend Joseph L. Manning, representative of the Catholic Archdiocese of Austin, and Rabbi Judah Fish, representative of the Jewish community of Austin. The text of their remarks is printed in the Weekly Compilation of Presidential Documents (vol. 1, p. 525).

624 Message to the Rio Conference of the Organization of American States. *November 22, 1965*

AS I STATED on August 17, on the fourth anniversary of the Alliance for Progress, our vital alliance is perhaps the greatest adventure that this hemisphere has embarked upon since Columbus reached our shore five centuries ago. I also pledged my administration to helping all of our countries meet the goals of the alliance.

Recognizing that fulfillment of our goals will require the continuation of the joint effort beyond 1971, I wish to inform the Conference—and through you, your respective governments—that the United States will be prepared to extend mutual commitments beyond the time period foreseen in the charter of Punta del Este. In determining the scope of the United States effort, we will want to examine carefully with you at that time the requirements of the hemisphere, in the light of progress made through self-help measures and the contributions which by then some of your countries will be able to make to one another to further the common effort.

NOTE: The President's message was read to the Second Special Inter-American Conference at Rio de

Janeiro on November 22 by Secretary of State Dean Rusk, who served as the U.S. representative to the Conference.

For the President's remarks on August 17 at a ceremony commemorating the fourth anniversary of the Alliance for Progress, see Item 429.

The text of the message was released at Austin, Tex.

625   Statement by the President in Response to a Progress Report by the Council on Physical Fitness. *November 23, 1965*

THE STRUGGLES to preserve freedom and to advance human hopes and aspirations will not be won by nations whose citizens let themselves grow soft and weak. Despite the ease and convenience of modern life, the crucial tasks of our times demand as much strength and stamina as any in the past.

Physical fitness is, therefore, a matter of national concern. It should also be a matter of personal concern for every citizen. People who spend some leisure time in vigorous and enjoyable activities are far more likely to lead long, productive lives than those who confuse leisure with laziness. More and more, we are coming to recognize that physical fitness in the young is the best insurance against infirmity and enforced idleness in old age.

I am pleased to report that we are responding to this challenge. Our abundance is not producing apathy, and our leisure has not led to lethargy. Instead, there is every evidence that our citizens are employing those gifts to bring about a vast renewal of health, strength, and energy.

The Council on Physical Fitness informs me that there has been remarkable progress toward the goals of providing all Americans with inspiration and opportunity to achieve new levels of physical fitness:

—21 States have strengthened their school physical education requirements.

—44 percent of the schools have increased the amount of time devoted to vigorous games and exercise.

—The number of health and physical education specialists employed in the schools has increased 26.3 percent.

—In 36 States, local school systems have established adult fitness programs, most of them in cooperation with YMCA's and municipal recreation departments.

—Private business has stepped up spending for employee recreation programs to more than $1 billion a year.

—Companies, foundations, and professional and commercial associations have spent approximately $1 million on special fitness projects initiated or suggested by the Council.

—22 States have established Governor's Physical Fitness Councils or Commissions to assist the national effort.

The results of this progress are predictable. Tests administered to thousands of schoolchildren last year showed that today's average boy or girl is as strong and skilled as the superior youngster of only 5 years ago.

These are solid and tangible gains, and they were given new impetus in the last session of Congress. For the first time, the

Federal Government has made available to the schools funds which can be used to strengthen health and physical education programs. In many communities, plans already have been drafted to put these funds to work.

All of us can assist in this effort to maintain the vigor and vitality of our free society. Every community ought to come to grips with the problem of increasing the availability of the sports and fitness facilities in our schools—for more hours each day, for more days each year, and for more of the people who live in the neighborhoods around them.

We have made much progress. But we still pay a terrible price each year for neglect of the health and fitness of our people, young and old alike. I hope that in the year ahead all Americans—parents, teachers, and community, government, business, and military leaders—will take further action to assure all of our citizens the opportunity for healthy exercise and active recreation.

NOTE: The report of the President's Council on Physical Fitness was submitted to the President by Stan Musial, Consultant to the President on Physical Fitness. The report is entitled "4 Years for Fitness, 1961–1965, a Report to the President" (Government Printing Office, 1965, 24 pp.).

The President's Council on Physical Fitness was established by Executive Order 11074 of January 8, 1963 (28 F.R. 259; 3 CFR, 1959–1963 Comp., p. 691).

See also Item 645.

The statement was released at Austin, Tex.

---

626   The President's Thanksgiving Day Message to Members of the Armed Forces.   *November 24, 1965*

TODAY Americans of all faiths gather in their homes and places of worship to give thanks for the blessings of our great land.

Not least in their minds and their hearts will be prayers for the valiant members of our Armed Forces, at home and abroad. We ask of God that He watch over you and give you strength.

The bounty of our land has always been great. It has allowed us to grow and prosper. Our fields are rich. Our cities are vibrant. Our industry and technology have brought to each generation a better way of life. These are the blessings of America.

But there are other blessings as well—and perhaps the greatest is the blessing of freedom. This we cherish above all, for it gives meaning to all the others. And for this we must sacrifice if we wish to enjoy all the rest.

A man does not inherit freedom as he in-herits the land.

A man can plow a field, but it will not make him free.

He can harvest a crop, but it will not make him free.

He can build a mansion, but it will not make him free.

To each generation belongs the task of advancing freedom; of guarding it jealously; of nurturing it; of strengthening its institutions. To each generation belongs the task of defending it in its hour of need.

Today you are the guardians and defenders of that freedom in such an hour.

Many of you are spending this Thanksgiving away from your families. Many of you serve under fire in a lonely and dangerous land. Some of your comrades have fallen. We, the people of this Nation, want you to know that our thoughts are with you.

Today we do not march in support of your

unfinished task. We carry no placards to bolster your cause. We sign no petitions to show you our unity.

But we do much more. Today we raise our voices in a single prayer of thanks for your courage and your dedication.

And that is the most powerful voice of all.

NOTE: The President spoke at 10:20 a.m. over the Armed Forces Network at Austin, Tex.

627   Statement by the President on the Death of Queen Elisabeth of Belgium. *November 24, 1965*

OUR COUNTRY is saddened by the passing of a majestic lady. Queen Elisabeth of Belgium became to her people—and indeed to the world—a stirring symbol of dignity and courage when we most needed a demonstration of those qualities.

On behalf of the people of this country, Mrs. Johnson and I extend our deepest sympathy to King Baudouin and the people of Belgium.

NOTE: The statement was read by Bill D. Moyers, Special Assistant to the President, at his news conference at 10:20 a.m. on Wednesday, November 24, 1965, at Austin, Tex. It was not made public in the form of a White House press release.

628   Statement by the President on U.S. Participation in the Founding of the Asian Development Bank. *November 26, 1965*

A DELEGATION headed by Eugene R. Black, my adviser on economic and social development in Asia, leaves Washington tomorrow for Manila, where it will participate in the founding of the Asian Development Bank.

I regard the organization of this new institution as one of the most hopeful events of our times. The Asian Development Bank has been put together by Asians. They are contributing the greater part of its capital. They will direct its lending for development in Asia.

But, most of all, it is an important and hopeful event, because the Asian Development Bank will bring so many of Asia's diverse peoples together in a cooperative effort for peaceful development and human betterment in Asia.

The basic conflict of our times is not over economic ideas or between economic systems. We do not believe any one people stands as the sole possessor of all the truth. I am confident that in its work, as in its charter, the Asian Development Bank can make a major contribution toward creating an environment in which men and nations exercise the right to develop their own systems and their own societies without fear of interference from others.

I intend to request the approval of Congress early in the next session for a United States subscription of at least $200 million to the Bank's regular capital. This would be paid in to the amount of $100 million over 4 years.

Mr. Black, and his alternate, Under Secretary of the Treasury Joseph W. Barr, have closely followed and encouraged the organization of this great venture in collaboration for peaceful construction in Asia. The Asian Development Bank has had our enthusiastic support.

I am very glad that the United States

delegates from the executive branch of the Government will be accompanied to the Manila conference by 16 Members of the Congress and that others will join them in Manila. I take particular pleasure in the fact that many of these are new, young Members of Congress, who reflect the deep interest of the American people in this vital part of the world.

It is gratifying to note that the most industralized Asian nation, Japan, is prepared to subscribe as large a sum as our own— $200 million—to the Bank's capital. Australia and New Zealand will provide approximately $100 million of the Bank capital, while less developed Asian countries will put up $300 million out of their resources.

Apart from the $200 million pledge of the United States, six nations outside the Asian region have signified their intention to subscribe to the Bank's capital. They are Belgium, Canada, Germany, Italy, the Netherlands, and the United Kingdom.

Others are considering participation in the Asian Development Bank. Even so, I should note that the problems of Asia are of an order and a diversity requiring the widest possible participation in their solution by the economically developed nations. Consequently, it is my hope that the industrialized nations of both Western and Eastern Europe that have not yet signified their support of the Asian Development Bank will do so, and that other nations will carefully assess the adequacy of their capital subscriptions.

One such effort is the establishment of special funds to be administered by the Asian Bank, and to augment its resources. Last summer, I authorized Mr. Black to pledge $100 million to funds for southeast Asia, provided other developed countries also contributed to such special funds.

Our pledge to the Asian Development Bank will help fulfill the promise I made earlier this year of American participation in cooperative efforts for economic development in Asia. We stand ready to join in other cooperative development efforts to heal the sick and wounded, feed the hungry, and spread the blessings of education and training in that part of the world.

Creation of the Asian Development Bank will mean that the Asian region will have its own sound financial institution, closely attuned to meeting the particular development needs of the area. The Bank will be an important supplement to existing international financial agencies. Of equal importance, the Bank can initiate and lead new moves toward regional cooperation, and provide the institutional framework through which substantial volumes of financial and technical assistance resources can be administered.

NOTE: On the same day the White House made public the membership of the U.S. delegation to the founding conference of the Asian Development Bank, held at Manila on December 2–4, 1965. The release stated that organizers of the Bank, which was to be affiliated with the United Nations, expected to raise $1 billion initial capital of which approximately $900 million had been pledged, $600 million from countries in Asia and the Far East (1 Weekly Comp. Pres. Docs., p. 530).

The President's message to the Congress recommending approval of U.S. participation in the Bank is dated January 18, 1966. The President signed the Asian Development Bank Act on March 16, 1966 (Public Law 89–369; 80 Stat. 71). (See 2 Weekly Comp. Pres. Docs., pp. 56, 396, pending publication of the 1966 volume, this series.)

See also Item 637.

The statement was released at Austin, Tex.

629 Telegram to the New Amir of Kuwait on the Death of His Brother, Shaikh Abdullah al-Salim al-Sabah. *November 26, 1965*

[Released November 26, 1965. Dated November 25, 1965]

Your Highness:

It is with deep regret that I have learned of the death of Shaikh Abdullah al-Salim al-Sabah. He will be long remembered for the notable progress of his country during the more than 15 years of his leadership and for his wise guidance of Kuwait into the ranks of independent, peace-loving nations. He was highly esteemed and admired in this country.

LYNDON B. JOHNSON

NOTE: The text of the telegram to Shaikh Sabah al-Salim was read by Bill D. Moyers, Special Assistant to the President, at his news conference at 4:20 p.m. on Friday, November 26, 1965, at Austin, Tex. It was not made public in the form of a White House press release.

630 Message to the White House Conference on International Cooperation. *November 29, 1965*

I HAVE CALLED this conference for one reason: I am determined that the United States shall actively engage its best minds and boldest spirits in the quest for a new order of world cooperation.

This Nation recognizes that international cooperation is not merely a lofty ideal. It is a fact of life, a necessity of our age.

The General Assembly of the United Nations has designated this year International Cooperation Year, and by proclamation of its President and resolution of its Congress, the United States rededicated itself in 1965 to the ideal and practice of international cooperation.

Throughout its history, by word and deed, this Nation has always demonstrated its understanding of the wisdom of cooperative efforts to solve world problems. And we know that a great nation remains great because it remembers that it can always do better.

I believe this conference will show us specific ways to do better.

I have directed the agencies of our Government to participate in your deliberations—and to study your recommendations with a view to immediate action.

Together we seek

—new ways to raise the world's millions up from poverty;

—new policies to conserve and develop the world's resources;

—new methods to rid the world of destructive disease;

—new means to increase commerce between nations;

—new safeguards against the overriding danger of war;

—new avenues to world peace.

This conference is a town meeting of leaders of the Nation. Its purpose is peace and cooperation.

Let us raise our sights to the limits of this goal.

And let us free our imaginations to the tireless pursuit of this high ideal.

NOTE: The President's message was read before the conference by Vice President Hubert H. Humphrey on November 29 at 9:30 a.m. In his message the President referred to Proclamation 3620 of October 2, 1964, designating 1965 as International Cooperation Year (29 F.R. 13627; 3 CFR, 1964 Supp., p.

76); and to Senate Concurrent Resolution 36, agreed to June 22, 1965, providing for the White House Conference on International Cooperation (79 Stat. 1429).

The conference was held in Washington November 29–December 1, 1965.

The text of the message was released at Austin, Tex.

631 Letter to the Chairman, Civil Service Commission, on the Need for Quality and Excellence in Government. *November 30, 1965*

[Released November 30, 1965. Dated November 27, 1965]

Dear Mr. Chairman:

I believe firmly that our merit system is the keystone of good government. Your plan for modernizing and improving staffing in government clearly illustrates the flexibility of our system and the potential still open for affirmative changes in ongoing programs through critical review and imaginative thinking.

In the past year we have made more progress in enacting creative legislation in the interests of all the people than in any other time in the history of our Nation. All of us know that much remains to be done. We have a tremendous job ahead in the coming months and years to make sure that what Congress has passed will be carried forward efficiently, with dispatch, and with economy and good management. We have to make sure that the people get a full measure of value for every dollar authorized by the Congress.

I want real achievement. This will require tighter management, more efficient organization, better methods and equipment, and concentration of resources on high priority activities. I know that the key to success in achieving our goals is in the quality of the career men and women in the Federal service.

I am deeply concerned that we continue to take advantage of the flexibility of the merit system to update methods and procedures to attract capable people who can translate our new programs into action. I want to make sure that we have a system that will challenge each employee to work at his maximum capability and will identify those who have high potential for movement into jobs of greater responsibility in their own or other agencies.

The concern I have for quality and excellence in government is a concern that all members of the Cabinet, heads of agencies and managers at all levels share. I am, therefore, pleased that the new network of Interagency Boards will be a cooperative endeavor in which all the participating agencies share in the cost of running the system under the control and guidance of the Civil Service Commission.

In view of my continuing personal interest in improving our services and communications with the public, I am particularly pleased that each Interagency Board will have a one-stop job information center so that interested citizens will not have to go from agency to agency to learn about Federal job opportunities. This is an excellent beginning. Eventually there should be a central information office in every major metropolitan area where citizens can get information, not only about Federal job opportunities, but about all functions of the Federal Government.

This is a high priority program which has my full endorsement and I shall look to you to provide the leadership for implementation at the earliest possible date. I am sure you will enjoy the full support of heads of departments and agencies in the pursuit of our common goal for quality and excellence in the Federal service.

Sincerely,

LYNDON B. JOHNSON

[The Honorable John Macy, Chairman, Civil Service Commission, Washington, D.C.   20415]

NOTE: The text of the letter was released at Austin, Tex.

632   Telephone Remarks to the Members of the Business Council. *December 2, 1965*

Mr. Murphy and members of the Business Council:

When Bev Murphy called me last night, here at the ranch, and invited me to speak to the Business Council, I was pleased and proud to do so. I regret so much that my physical condition would not permit my attending your session in Washington.

The Business Council and I have the same objectives: strengthening and preserving America's free enterprise system. This system can be strengthened and will be preserved so long as responsible business, progressive labor, and dedicated government work together with understanding. So long as I am your President, that is my goal.

A year and a half ago I outlined a set of objectives for our Nation which, when achieved, will bring us into an era of a Great Society.

Those goals included: equal opportunity for all, education to the limit of every child's ability, employment opportunities for all who want to work, abolishing of poverty for all time to come, adequate medical care for every citizen, a decent home for every family, an end to our slums, and a restoration of our natural beauty. And the most important goal of them all—a durable and lasting peace throughout the world.

It was clear to us then—as it is clear to us now—that one of the foundation stones of the Great Society must be a vital, growing economy.

A growing economy creates, of itself, more opportunities for more citizens.

A growing economy provides added revenues for the programs that only our governments—Federal, State, and local—can carry out.

In brief, the Great Society goes hand in hand with national prosperity.

It used to be said that the basis of prosperity could be summed up in a single word: confidence.

In our time, we have learned that a second word should be added. That word is "cooperation": business cooperation, labor cooperation, and Government cooperation.

Mere confidence is not enough. Neither is mere cooperation. But working together, they can build and sustain an economy unmatched in the history of man.

That is the story of our own generation.

We have built a sense of national confidence because we have committed our Government to the well-being of every sector of our economy.

We are not a labor government.

We are not a business government.

We are not a farmer's government.

We are the Government of all America. We have made it clear that we support a fair profit, a fair wage, and a fair price.

We understand the complex workings of our society. We know that if one sector falters, the others will soon falter as well.

Out of this interdependence has come a new sense of national cooperation. In the past year alone, every segment of our economy has made major contributions toward advancing our American prosperity.

The Government enacted an excise tax reduction to further stimulate sales—and the vast majority of manufacturers and retailers passed these reductions on to the American consumer.

Representatives from both management and labor of the steel industry worked around the clock for days and nights on end to avert a strike and to agree on a new wage contract that was within the administration's noninflationary guideposts. And the average annual wage increase in all major contracts worked out this year—involving some 4 million workers—was 3.3 percent, very close to the suggested guideposts.

The Congress acted with equal restraint in passing a noninflationary pay raise for our Federal civilian workers. Your President made it clear that any pay raise beyond the guidepost boundaries would be vetoed.

The guideposts are designed to help American labor and American business achieve full employment while avoiding a wage-price spiral.

They provide reasonable standards for responsible behavior by labor and business.

Another vital example of Government-industry cooperation came in the areas of excess aluminum stockpiles. It has been a source of major concern to me that we should be maintaining a stockpile far in excess of any conceivable Government requirement—while at the same time importing aluminum from abroad to meet increased Government defense needs.

The aluminum industry and the Government agreed on a plan to eliminate our excess surplus in an orderly manner. The copper industry and the Government also worked out an agreement to release copper from the stockpile to meet rising demands in the face of interruptions to foreign supplies.

These agreements will help meet our defense requirements, eliminate costly storage that the Government is paying, help improve our balance of payments deficit, and are part of a program to add almost a billion dollars a year to our national treasury.

Also during the past year, Government, industry, and labor have been working together on an expanded manpower development and training program. This is adding a fresh flow of workers with needed skills to the labor market. It is reducing unemployment. It is creating more consumers. It is adding to our revenues.

Thus with confidence in our future, with cooperation across the board, with commonsense, unselfishness, and wisdom, business, labor, and Government have sustained the longest peacetime expansion in American history—58 months of unbroken prosperity.

Since early 1961:

—Our gross national product has risen more than 35 percent—$174 billion.

—Our consumers are spending $104 billion more a year.

—Our unemployment rate has dropped to its lowest in 8 years, and the number of unemployed is now 3 million, the lowest since 1957.

—Disposable personal income has been lifted from $1,950 to $2,400 per capita, a rise of 25 percent.

—Wages and salary income have increased 33 percent.

—And corporate profits after taxes have increased 84 percent.

In short, more workers are employed, more citizens are living better, and more businesses are earning higher profits than ever before in our history.

This prosperity is all the more meaningful because during our 58-month expansion we have been able to avoid inflation. Our American prices have remained more stable than those of any other industrial nation in all the world.

From 1961 through 1964, wholesale prices remained virtually stable, while consumer prices rose only 1.2 percent a year. This record was made possible by the stability of unit labor costs in industry, by general stability of material costs, by an abundant capacity to produce, and by responsible key price and wage decisions.

In the past 12 months wholesale prices have risen by 2.3 percent, and consumer prices by 1.8 percent. Increases in farm and food prices from March to July account for most of the faster advance in consumer prices, and for about half of the advance in wholesale prices. This situation has now fairly stabilized, and we do not expect such an outbreak next year. In the past 4 months both wholesale prices and consumer prices have been advancing at a rate of less than 1 percent a year.

We expect next year to be another record year for the American economy. We are ever alert to danger signs, of course, and when we see them, we will promptly act accordingly. But we do not anticipate any major problems that confidence and cooperation cannot solve.

Our needs are growing, but our economy is growing too. We can produce the goods and services we require without "overheating" our economy!

Looking well into next year, we see strong markets and excellent profits.

We see further expansion of business investment.

We see a higher standard of living for our citizens.

We see more than $3 billion of hospital and supplemental health insurance benefits for our elder citizens going into effect next July—on top of this year's already nearly

15 percent expansion in social security payments.

We see attainment of our goal of equilibrium in balance of payments (a quarter of a billion dollars either side of balance in our accounts).

We see a further reduction in unemployment below the present 4.2.

In short, we see continued expansion at a reasonable pace.

This is the confidence that our prosperity requires.

And the other element—the element of cooperation—will be there, too. The record of the past year says that it will.

So this morning, as we Americans visit together, your boys and our boys fight to preserve freedom and to defend justice in the rice paddies of Viet-Nam. They have put the needs of their country and their Government ahead of their personal desires and their personal hopes. We must pray not only for their safe return, but to unite behind them, as they unite among themselves. We must support them from here, as they support each other there. We must equal their sacrifice and uphold their cause with the same devotion here at home as they give so willingly out there.

No one of us—businessman, laboringman, Government employee—can ever forget that what American fighting men are doing in Viet-Nam may very well determine the shape and the form of your future—and of our Nation's future.

Here at home we have built strength and prosperity. In Viet-Nam the American soldier is exerting that strength, and using that prosperity, to construct a durable road to peace in the world.

For all that we are and all that we ever hope to be is nothing, if our passion and our purpose is not peace.

Today, all around the world, Americans are working for peace:

—In Santo Domingo the OAS and Ambassador Ellsworth Bunker have shown a patience and an understanding that have banked the hot fires of violence.

—In Rio de Janeiro, Dean Rusk and Averell Harriman have led the way to a rededication of our Alliance for Peaceful Progress.

—In Rome, Orville Freeman has taken the lead in new planning for the peaceful victory of humanity over hunger—by cooperation and by self-help.

—In Paris, Robert McNamara has led in enlarging the conception of peaceful cooperation in the common defense of the Atlantic Community.

—In New York, Ambassador Arthur Goldberg has made it plain that we are working for disarmament with all who will work with us.

—In Washington, some 1,500 American citizens have gathered for 3 days to work on ways for international cooperation and peace and they have joined in frank and helpful discussions with the members of their Government.

—And, most of all, the Americans in Viet-Nam serve peace as they work and as they fight—side by side with gallant allies from Korea and Australia and New Zealand, and side by side with the people and soldiers of South Viet-Nam, and with the active support of more than 30 other nations in the world. Our common purpose there is to end aggression and to open the path to peaceful choice. All the world can be sure that the Americans in Viet-Nam have the firm and have the solid backing of the overwhelming majority of their countrymen.

So we stand for peace and we work for peace—in our own land and in every land—in our own time and for all time. There can be peace, especially in Viet-Nam, whenever men in other capitals are ready.

I have said it before. I say it again now. This Nation is ready to talk, unconditionally, anywhere, with peace as our agenda.

Peace will come, because it just must come. It will come from courage, from constancy, and from concern. It will come because there is no other answer.

Peace is our commitment. Peace is our goal. Peace will be the only victory that we seek. And peace will come.

Thank you, and good morning.

NOTE: The President spoke by telephone from the LBJ Ranch, Johnson City, Tex., at 11:05 a.m. on Thursday, December 2, 1965. In his opening words he referred to W. B. Murphy, President of Campbell Soup Company and Chairman of the Business Council.

During his remarks the President referred to Ellsworth Bunker, U.S. Representative to the Organization of American States, Dean Rusk, Secretary of State, W. Averell Harriman, Ambassador at Large, Orville L. Freeman, Secretary of Agriculture, Robert S. McNamara, Secretary of Defense, and Arthur J. Goldberg, U.S. Representative to the United Nations.

---

633 Statement by the President Upon Signing Executive Order 11259, Incentive Pay for Hazardous Duty Involving Parachute Jumping. *December 3, 1965*

DURING his visit to South Viet-Nam several days ago, Secretary McNamara informed me that certain technical restrictions were preventing our paratroopers from earning incentive pay.

The rules were that a paratrooper had to perform one or more jumps from an airplane during any 3 consecutive months to qualify for incentive pay for that period. In many instances, however, while paratroopers were engaged in ground actions, they were thus unable to make the jumps, and, as a result, lost their eligibility for incentive pay.

This was the situation that called for prompt corrective action. I have today taken that action by approving an amendment to Executive Order 11157. Under the change, a paratrooper can now earn incentive pay if his commanding officer waives the jump requirements when a paratrooper is unable to meet them because he is engaged in operations in a hostile-fire area.

NOTE: The statement was read by Joseph Laitin, an assistant press secretary, at his news conference at 10:45 a.m. on Friday, December 3, 1965, at Austin, Tex. It was not made public in the form of a White House press release.

The President referred to Executive Order 11259 of December 3, 1965 "Amending Executive Order No. 11157 as It Relates to Incentive Pay for Hazardous Duty Involving Parachute Jumping" (1 Weekly Comp. Pres. Docs., p. 548; 30 F.R. 15057; 3 CFR, 1965 Supp., p. 192), and to Executive Order 11157 of June 22, 1964 "Prescribing Regulations Relating to Incentive Pay for Hazardous Duty, Special Pay for Sea Duty and Duty at Certain Places, Basic Allowances for Subsistence and Basic Allowances for Quarters" (29 F.R. 7973; 3 CFR, 1964 Supp., p. 139).

634   Statement by the President on the Death of Dr. Hugh L. Dryden. *December 3, 1965*

NO SOLDIER ever performed his duty with more bravery and no statesman ever charted new courses of action with more dedication than Hugh Dryden.

He was a scientist who understood nonscientists. He looked out on the unknown and was not dismayed. He never lost what Einstein called "a holy curiosity," for he was far more interested in becoming a man of value than merely a man of success.

Whenever the first American spaceman sets foot on the moon or finds a new trail to new stars, he will know that Hugh Dryden was one of those who gave him knowledge and illumination. On that day devoutly to be wished when peace comes to the world, this space adventurer will be among those honored for having helped bring it about.

He and I were side by side in the creation of the American space program 7 years ago. For me his passing is a deep personal loss and a reason for national sorrow.

NOTE: The statement was read by Joseph Laitin, an assistant press secretary, at his news conference at 10:45 a.m. on Friday, December 3, 1965, at Austin, Tex. It was not made public in the form of a White House press release.

Dr. Dryden served as Director of the National Advisory Committee for Aeronautics from 1948 to 1958 and then as Deputy Administrator of the National Aeronautics and Space Administration until his death on December 2, 1965.

635   Telegram to May Craig Upon the Announcement of Her Retirement. *December 3, 1965*

IT'S A long time from May to September, but May will always be May to me.

LYNDON B. JOHNSON

[Mrs. May Craig, 717 North Carolina Avenue, S.E., Washington, D.C.]

NOTE: The telegram was read by Joseph Laitin, an assistant press secretary, at his news conference at 4:40 p.m. on Friday, December 3, 1965, at Austin, Tex. It was not made public in the form of a White House press release.

For many years Mrs. Craig served as Washington correspondent for a group of Maine newspapers.

636   Statement by the President on the Flight of Gemini 7.
      December 4, 1965

ONCE AGAIN, two brave Americans have carried the quest for knowledge to the threshold of space. They also take with them our prayers, and our pride.

As they orbit the earth in the days and weeks ahead, Astronauts Frank Borman and James Lovell will broaden our knowledge of space.

But they will do more.

Their voyage will be a continuous reminder that the peaceful conquest of space is the only form of conquest in which modern man can proudly and profitably engage.

In this struggle, all men are allies, and the only enemy is a hostile environment.

The victory over this final enemy will belong not just to Americans but to all the world.

We are proud that these fine young Americans have brought us one step closer to that goal.

NOTE: On October 28, 1965, the White House made public a memorandum to the President from James E. Webb, Administrator of the National Aeronautics and Space Administration, announcing plans to retain the Gemini 7 launching pad for use in launching the delayed Gemini 6 project. The memorandum stated that it might be possible to rendezvous the two projects in space before the end of the 14-day Gemini 7 flight (1 Weekly Comp. Pres. Docs., p. 434).

See also Items 647, 651, 656.

The President's statement was released at Austin, Tex.

637   Statement by the President on the Signing of the Charter of the
      Asian Development Bank.   *December 4, 1965*

I WAS particularly pleased to learn that the Asian Development Bank Charter has now been signed, and I look forward to early ratification by the member countries, including the United States. My adviser for Asian development, Eugene Black, and Treasury Under Secretary Joseph Barr have informed me that they have signed the charter in Manila along with other nations—both Asian and non-Asian. The signing of the charter is a milestone in economic cooperation among the Asian countries and between them and countries outside the region. It gives great promise for the future for peaceful cooperation in a vital common effort—to help improve man's life in Asia.

NOTE: The Asian Development Bank Charter is printed in House Document 361 (89th Cong., 2d sess.).

See also Item 628.

The President's statement was released at Austin, Tex.

638   Letter to Secretary Fowler Approving the Recommendations of
      the Cabinet Committee on Balance of Payments.
      December 5, 1965

[Released December 5, 1965. Dated December 2, 1965]

Dear Mr. Secretary:

I have reviewed the report of the Cabinet Committee on the Balance of Payments and approved its recommendations for action. I would like you, Secretary Connor, and Chairman Martin to announce, explain, and

1135

put into effect the proposed changes in Government policy, and specifically the improvements in the Voluntary Program of February 10, 1965.

In explaining the changes in the Voluntary Program, I would like you, and all other responsible officials of the Government, to make it clear that:

1. The February 10 program has worked. During the first three quarters of this year, the overall deficit ran at an annual rate of $1.3 billion—less than half the deficit in 1964.

2. A large measure of the credit must go to the bankers and businessmen of America who have taken part in the program. At the White House last February, I asked them "to join hands with me in a voluntary partnership . . . to show the world that an aroused and responsible business community in America can close ranks and make a voluntary program work." They have answered that call.

3. We have done well, but we must do even better. The deficit has been much smaller since February 10 than for several years past. At its peak, in 1960, it reached $3.9 billion, three times the rate so far this year. But the present deficit is still too large. To assure that the dollar will remain as good as gold, we have to show the world that we can bring our accounts into sustainable balance, and keep them in balance.

4. To do the job, we propose not a new program, but an improved and strengthened version of the Voluntary Program that we tested in 1965. The improvements reflect the experience since February 10, and have been worked out in close consultation with Secretary Connor's senior business advisors and with the banker advisors of Chairman Martin and Governor Robertson of the Federal Reserve.

5. The Government will continue to do its part. Since 1960, Secretary McNamara has reduced the balance of payments cost of military spending abroad by about 40%—despite the increase in spending on Viet Nam. Administrator Bell has reduced the balance of payments impact of foreign assistance by 50%. I have instructed both of them, and all other senior officials of the Government, to spare no effort in reducing the dollar drain of their spending still further. But I reject the counsel of those who would have the Government do the entire job, at whatever cost to American security and leadership. It is private outflow that has grown so sharply since 1960. Some further reduction in that outflow is essential if we are to solve this problem without crippling our economy at home, or compromising our leadership abroad.

6. I know that this will involve some pain and sacrifice. But the stakes are great. What is at issue is whether we can meet our critical responsibilities abroad, and maintain the expanding prosperity of the past four years at home—the decline in unemployment, the rising profits, the improving standard of life for all our people—by relying on the voluntary cooperation of business, labor, and government. This is a test which America has met with dramatic success during the past few years. I am confident that we will continue to meet it in the future.

You and the other members of the Cabinet Committee are to be congratulated for your work in the preparation of the revised program for 1966.

Sincerely,

LYNDON B. JOHNSON

[The Honorable Henry H. Fowler, the Secretary of the Treasury, Chairman, Cabinet Committee on Balance of Payments]

NOTE: In his letter the President referred to John T. Connor, Secretary of Commerce, William McC. Martin, Jr., Chairman of the Board of Governors, Federal Reserve System, J. L. Robertson, member of the Board of Governors, Federal Reserve System, Robert S. McNamara, Secretary of Defense, and David E. Bell, Administrator of the Agency for International Development.

A summary of the Committee's recommendations, dated December 3, 1965, was made public by the White House on December 5 (1 Weekly Comp. Pres. Docs., p. 560). In the summary it was noted that the Committee recommended that:

"1. The present voluntary commerce program to reduce the outflow of business capital be reinforced by the establishment both of an overall target, similar to that of 1965, and a new target specifically applicable to direct investment calling upon corporations to limit direct investments during the 2-year period 1965–1966 to 90 percent of the amount invested during the 3-year period 1962–1964. . . .

"2. The interest equalization tax on purchases of foreign securities and acquisitions of other long-term claims of foreigners by Americans be made applicable to Abu Dhabi, Bahrain, Indonesia, Iran, Iraq, Kuwait-Saudi Arabia Neutral Zone, Libya, Qatar, and Saudi Arabia.

"3. The present ceiling for bank lending to foreigners under the Federal Reserve program be raised from 105 percent of the December 31, 1964 base, in stages of 1 percentage point per quarter, to a new ceiling of 109 percent in the final quarter of 1966. . . .

"4. The ceiling for lending by nonbank financial institutions to foreigners under the Federal Reserve program be increased, in the case of credits with maturities of 10 years or less, from 105 percent of the December 31, 1964 base in stages of 1 percentage point per quarter to a new ceiling of 109 percent in the final quarter of 1966. In the case of acquisitions by such institutions of foreign securities with maturities of more than 10 years, a ceiling of 105 percent of the September 30, 1965 amount would be set for securities of developed countries other than Canada and Japan.

"5. The basic arrangement with Canada regarding Canadian access to the United States capital market and exemption from the interest equalization tax for an unlimited amount of new Canadian security issues both be continued. . . .

"6. The current efforts by all Government agencies to reduce to a minimum the balance of payments impact of their operations be intensified. . . .

"7. Legislation to encourage foreign investment in the United States now before the Congress be enacted as soon as possible.

"8. Present efforts to encourage both foreign and domestic tourism in the United States be stepped up, and efforts by the Government to encourage and expand the activities of the private sector in this area be increased. . . .

"9. Present efforts both by Government and by private enterprise to expand U.S. export trade should be sharply stepped up."

639 Statement by the President on the Raising of the Discount Rate by the Federal Reserve Board. *December 5, 1965*

THE Federal Reserve Board is an independent agency. Its decision was an independent decision.

I regret, as do most Americans, any action that raises the cost of credit, particularly for homes, schools, hospitals, and factories.

I particularly regret that this action was taken before January when we will have before us the full facts on next year's budget, Viet-Nam costs, housing starts, State and local spending, and other elements in the economic outlook.

The decisions to be taken within the next few weeks by the administration will significantly affect the course of economic development.

My view and the view of the Secretary of the Treasury and the Council of Economic Advisers is that the decision on interest rates should be a coordinated policy decision in January, when the nature and impact of the administration's budgetary and Viet-Nam decisions are known. This view was apparently shared by three of the seven board members.

The action has already been taken. Under the circumstances, I will continue to do my best to give the American people the kind of fully-coordinated, well-integrated economic policy to which they are entitled, which has been so successful for the last 58 months, and which I hope will preserve the price stability so necessary for America's

continued prosperity.

NOTE: The President's statement was released at Austin, Tex.

640 Statement by the President in Response to Federal Power Commission Report on the Northeastern Electric Power Blackout. *December 6, 1965*

IN A brief instant on November 9, 1965, 30 million Americans were suddenly plunged into darkness. Nothing has so vividly demonstrated our increasing dependence on an uninterrupted flow of electric power as the blackout which then descended upon the great cities of the Northeastern United States.

On that same evening, less than a month ago, I directed the Federal Power Commission to conduct a thorough investigation of the causes of the failure and to recommend means for preventing a recurrence.

With the help of experts from American and Canadian power companies, the Commission has now completed the first phase of the investigation I requested. Its findings and recommendations are contained in the report issued today.

We now know just what triggered the original power failure and why, in a few brief minutes, its effects were felt throughout the Northeastern United States and parts of Canada.

We also know that steps can be taken to prevent such failures. Many of the Commission's initial recommendations are already being implemented by the power companies. This effort must be continued until we have so perfected our power systems that widespread power failures will be not only improbable but impossible.

The lights that failed on November 9, 1965, will then be remembered not as a calamity, but as the beginning of renewed efforts to further perfect what is already the world's greatest and most efficient electrical system.

NOTE: The Federal Power Commission's report is entitled "Northeast Power Failure, November 9 and 10, 1965, A Report to the President by the Federal Power Commission, December 6, 1965" (Government Printing Office, 95 pp.).

See also Item 608.

The President's statement was released at Austin, Tex.

641 The President's News Conference at the LBJ Ranch. *December 6, 1965*

[*With Joseph C. Swidler, Jr., Chairman, Federal Power Commission; Henry H. Fowler, Secretary of the Treasury; William McChesney Martin, Jr., Chairman, Board of Governors of the Federal Reserve System; and Gardner Ackley, Chairman, Council of Economic Advisers*]

OPENING STATEMENT

THE PRESIDENT. [1.] I have been meeting with members of the Quadriad. I met with them last on October 6 and, as Joe Laitin[1]

[1] Joseph Laitin, an assistant press secretary.

told you some time last week, they were going to meet with me in the next few days, and we arranged it this Monday.

I asked Mr. Swidler, instead of going into Austin to take his plane back, to await your coming to the ranch where you could have a chance to hear from him on his report[2] and ask him any questions you might desire, and also to hear from the Secretary of the Treasury, the Chairman of the Council of Economic Advisers, Mr. Martin of the Federal Reserve Board, and any of the other members, about the subjects of our discussions this morning, and the views we have concerning the state of the Nation and the economy in the days ahead.

I am going to ask Mr. Swidler first to talk to you. He has just completed a study—at least some inquiries into the most recent blackout over in East Texas, the most recent power failure, and I will ask him to take any questions about his report, make any statements he may care to, and then the other members of the party will be available to you. Mr. Swidler?

RECENT POWER FAILURES

MR. SWIDLER. Thank you, Mr. President. I had the opportunity this morning to present the Federal Power Commission report to the President, to discuss it with him, and to answer the President's questions.

As I think you know, on the evening of November 9[3] the President asked the Commission to make this investigation and we have been at it ever since. We were interested not only in what triggered this massive blackout, the largest that this country has ever had, but also in the sequence of events: to look at the question of whether the cas-

cading of the failure was preventable and also to look at the question of whether the restoration of service was in a sequence that perhaps could have been improved.

The report, of which you all have copies, goes into each of these questions, and, on the basis of the study that we made, we have made a number of recommendations which I hope that the power industry and the equipment industries will look into.

We are continuing our studies and investigations. This is not a matter of a day. It is a matter of making this electric power system in this country, which is already probably the best in the world, even better, so that the risks of outages can be minimized to the absolute minimum that is made possible by the use of the best American technology.

QUESTIONS

Q. Is there any discussion in the final chapter on possible Federal legislation?

MR. SWIDLER. I told the President that we would expect to make some recommendations along that line at a later date. We have not made any specific recommendation as yet.

Q. Could you tell us what sort of things you are considering?

MR. SWIDLER. No, I am afraid I can't at this date.

Q. Mr. Swidler, you did mention specifically the question of Federal jurisdiction over service reliability. Is this right?

MR. SWIDLER. Yes, sir.

Q. Is that pretty firm in your mind as a recommendation?

MR. SWIDLER. I don't think I want to anticipate the results of the Commission's discussions of this matter. This is very high on our list of priorities and I am hoping that we can make a recommendation to the President very soon.

---

[2] See Item 640.
[3] See Item 608.

Q. Do you have any report yet on the East Texas blackout?

MR. SWIDLER. The East Texas or West Texas?

Q. West Texas—El Paso and Mexico.

MR. SWIDLER. El Paso. We have a report from our staff, and Mr. Brown [4] and I—Mr. Brown is our Chief Engineer and is with me here today—have explained this situation to the President, and we also have had a preliminary report on the East Texas blackout which occurred this morning.[5]

Q. Do you think that if all of the recommendations were carried out and all the legislation enacted, that you could say there would never be another blackout on the scale we had in the last one?

MR. SWIDLER. Well, "never" is an awfully strong word. I think I can say that I don't know any reason why there should be one. It seems to me that if all these recommendations are carried out, and if the companies build the additional interconnections and strengthen their internal systems in the way that we recommend, that this should preclude the risk of widespread blackouts.

Q. Would you expect to have any legislative recommendations ready for the next session of Congress?

MR. SWIDLER. I just don't want to anticipate our discussions on legislation. I might say, of course, that in one way or another we will make them as early as we can, and the President has instructed us to make our recommendations to him as soon as we possibly can.

Q. Can you tell us how severe the East Texas blackout was?

MR. SWIDLER. The East Texas blackout was not severe. The outage lasted 25 or 30 minutes, and all of the lines are now back in service. The generating plant that was out briefly is now back in service. This was not an outage of the same proportions.

Q. What cities?

MR. SWIDLER. Beaumont, Sabine——

MR. BROWN. The Navasota section, north of Dayton, was out for awhile.

MR. SWIDLER. The Navasota section, north of Dayton, Mr. Brown tells me.

Q. Do you see anything strange with these blackouts—they've never occurred in our history apparently on a national scale—all occurring within a month as they did?

MR. SWIDLER. Well, these two more recent blackouts are not unprecedented by any means. Blackouts of short duration have occurred. And, of course, to the extent that power failures are due to calamities—to tornadoes or floods—that kind you can always expect. But what we ought to be able to prevent is the cascading of failures into areas that are not directly affected by equipment loss.[6]

Q. Mr. Swidler, I have heard it said by some of the private power people that if the country had established the grid system nationwide it would have been a major catastrophe. Is that true? Could this have happened if we had the grid system nationwide; and what would have been the result?

MR. SWIDLER. I am not sure what a grid system nationwide is. This is nothing that we have ever recommended, and that is just

[4] F. Stewart Brown, Chief Engineer and Chief of the Bureau of Power, Federal Power Commission.

[5] The reports by the Federal Power Commission to the Senate Committee on Commerce are entitled "El Paso Power Failure, December 2, 1965," dated April 11, 1966 (31 pp., processed), and "Gulf States Utilities Company Power Failure, December 6, 1965," dated April 28, 1966 (23 pp., processed).

[6] On December 8, 1965, the White House made public a report to the President from Mr. Swidler on the power failure which affected communication equipment at Port Hardy, Vancouver Island, B. C. (1 Weekly Comp. Pres. Docs., p. 568).

too vague a term for me to be able to answer. I think that stronger interconnections would certainly have helped, assuming that before the interconnections between regions were made that the regional systems were themselves strengthened. This is a matter not only of building from one part of the country to the other. It is a matter of strengthening each company and each regional pool along the way.

Q. Mr. Swidler, each one of these recommendations seems to call on the private companies to make changes in their own systems. I'm wondering what happens if they don't. Who is responsible here for ensuring that the right changes are made?

MR. SWIDLER. There is no authority now to ensure that these recommendations will be followed. We expect a very high degree of cooperation.

MR. MOYERS. The Chief Engineer who is here is Mr. F. Stewart Brown of the Federal Power Commission.

THE PRESIDENT. I commended Mr. Swidler and Mr. Brown for the dispatch and the comprehensiveness of their report, and I want to thank them again for their prompt action this morning in connection with the Beaumont-Navasota matter.

DISCUSSION WITH MEMBERS OF THE QUADRIAD

[2.] THE PRESIDENT. We spent an hour or more before lunch exchanging viewpoints with the members of the Quadriad. It ranged all the way from the action taken last Friday by the Federal Reserve [7] to the anticipated investment figures for the next few months, and the revenue figures for the year ahead, the budget figures.

We will meet tomorrow—a preliminary meeting that will lead to our first budget discussion—and that meeting tomorrow will be with Secretary Rusk and Mr. McNamara, and Mr. Bundy and Mr. Komer,[8] and others from the national defense area, in connection with the national defense needs for the next year.

We discussed the housing situation, the machine tool situation, the price situation, and aluminum and copper stockpiles. We reviewed all the economic factors that are important in our economy. We had a free flow of information and a rather thorough exchange, and we will continue with those discussions after we have completed with Mr. Swidler and with you this afternoon.

I want to ask Secretary Fowler to make a brief statement to you covering any high points that he may care to observe, and I will also ask any of the other members who are present to state their views and they will be glad to have you ask any questions you choose to ask.

SECRETARY FOWLER

SECRETARY FOWLER. Ladies and gentlemen. There is very little to add to what the President said about our meeting this morning.

For your background information, we have these meetings about once a month to give the President a coordinated and updated look at the economic outlook for the period ahead, and of course our focus varies on the outlook for the calendar year 1966.

I undertook to review with the President

---

[7] See Item 639.

[8] Dean Rusk, Secretary of State, Robert S. McNamara, Secretary of Defense, McGeorge Bundy, Special Assistant to the President, and Robert Komer, Special Assistant to the President for Peaceful Reconstruction in Viet-Nam.

the results of some conferences that Treasury has had with various outside informed persons.

We had a full day's meeting with a group of very outstanding academic economists back on November the 23d. We had a meeting last week for a full day with about 12 or 14 of the leading business executives—Treasury Department Business Council consultants.[9]

The Chairman of the Board of Economic Advisers, Mr. Ackley, updated the last reports we had given the President on the outlook in October, and a staff report we had made in November.

Chairman Martin gave an account and a detailed explanation of the reasons for the Board action—Federal Reserve Board action—last Friday.

There was a general exchange of views on the meaning and significance of some of the new economic indicators. Particular attention was given in our exchange to an assessment of some forthcoming figures on plant and equipment expenditure forecasts for 1966 that I think will be released in the next day or two by the Department of Commerce and the SEC.

We reviewed some of the fiscal alternatives or options that are related to the budgetary decisions the President will have to make in the next few weeks.

In general, I think you can just sum it up by saying we tried to give the President the background information that he might find useful in making up his 1967 budget, and the related legislative program, particularly as it involves fiscal questions.

THE PRESIDENT. There will be some half-dozen departments and agencies here at the ranch in the next few days. We will meet with them either Friday or Saturday, here or

in Washington. I think it will be here. Bill will keep you informed as they are scheduled.

Any questions? Secretary Fowler will be glad to take them.

QUESTIONS

Q. Mr. Secretary, what is your prediction of the economic outlook?

SECRETARY FOWLER. The economy is burgeoning. The growth—and economic growth is particularly included—and prognostications of gross national product figures indicate that we will have a better year in terms of absolute growth than 1965, if the forecasts hold up.

I think the general pattern over the last few months has been that both private and public economists have tended to upgrade their forecasts from early autumn into the recent weeks, and, in general terms, we expect a rather big year for 1966.

Q. Do you think the new Federal Reserve Board action will have any kind of a brake on this burgeoning economy?

SECRETARY FOWLER. I think it is much too early for me to have any opinion on that. You may wish to ask Chairman Martin his views.

MR. MOYERS. Thank you, Mr. Secretary.

MR. ACKLEY

THE PRESIDENT. Next is Mr. Ackley. Gardner, do you want to review some of the area you went over this morning?

MR. ACKLEY. Mr. President, I think you and Secretary Fowler have covered it pretty well. I tried to review for the President the recent progress of the gross national product and the factors which affect the outlook for the year ahead.

As Secretary Fowler has said, the out-

---

[9] See Item 632.

look is extremely strong; a healthy progress of the kind we have had seems to be in the cards for the year ahead.

MR. MARTIN

THE PRESIDENT. Mr. Martin?

MR. MARTIN. I was glad to have an opportunity to review with the President the statement which the Federal Reserve Board issued yesterday with respect to the action which the Board took on Friday.

I think that it was a welcome opportunity for me to explain to the President that I had nothing to add to that statement and I made no predictions with respect to the effect of that action.

I told the President that I thought he had made a very fair statement yesterday, very fair indeed. And certainly apart from that statement, in which he in no way placed me in the role of defying the President or the Johnson administration, I want to make it clear I don't think the press ought to cast me in that role.

I am very grateful to be a part of this Quadriad setup and I can assure you that the Federal Reserve System wants to work as closely as it can with the President and with his administration.

QUESTIONS

Q. Mr. Martin, I wonder if you and the President are any closer in accord on the rise of the interest rate as a result of your meeting this morning?

MR. MARTIN. I made no predictions and the President didn't ask me to make any predictions.

Q. What is your opinion of the economic outlook for the coming year, Mr. Martin?

MR. MARTIN. I am optimistic about it.

Q. How do you view the present inflation?

MR. MARTIN. I think it is a very real one but it is one that I believe we will have the resources to contain.

Q. Was that the primary reason for raising the discount rate?

MR. MARTIN. I don't want to add to what I said in the statement, as I already indicated. I think you can see that it was directed toward the domestic economy and I don't want to add to that statement.

Q. You're not concerned, sir, about the timing in advance of this disclosure of budget figures?

MR. MARTIN. This is a matter of judgment and you can have positions in either way, but the Board by a split majority, as you know, after careful consideration decided that it should go ahead.

Q. Was there any key factor, sir, in your decision? Viet-Nam, for instance?

MR. MARTIN. No, other than the problems that the money market is resolving.

Q. Mr. Martin, what do you expect, if things go as you hope they will—what will be the effect of your increase in the discount rate?

MR. MARTIN. It will improve the flow of funds, make possible sustainable advance. It is directed toward helping, not hindering in any way, the advance.

Q. Will it not then slow down the flow of funds in any way?

MR. MARTIN. It depends on what the demand for funds are, and I am not going to make any prediction on that.

Q. Mr. Martin, would you say that you are in any way in basic disagreement with the President on the economic policy?

MR. MARTIN. I think the President and the Federal Reserve System have exactly the same objectives, and I know I speak for the entire System when I say that we are doing everything in our power to promote the President's program. We sometimes have differences in our particular field with respect to what is the most effective way to promote that program. This is only in the Federal Reserve's specific field and is not in any way intended to defy the administration.

The President's Closing Remarks and Questions

THE PRESIDENT. Thank you for coming out. If you have any questions of me I'll be glad to attempt to answer them.

Q. Mr. President, are these gentlemen staying over for your meetings tomorrow or have they concluded?

THE PRESIDENT. No, they will return when our discussions are finished today.

Q. Mr. President, do you feel that you and Mr. Martin are any closer together in your views on this discount increase now?

THE PRESIDENT. I think both of our positions have been clearly and fairly and accurately stated, and as Mr. Martin so well said, it is a matter of judgment as to whether you would act Friday, or next Friday, or next month, or whether you would act at all or not.

We all recognize the Federal Reserve is a board of experts in money and marketing, and I make no pretense of being a monetary expert. But even the experts have a division of opinion, 4 to 3, and we do have divisions all the time within the Government. One Cabinet officer may see one matter from one viewpoint and another from another. But there is one thing you can be sure: I believe the public is served by competent and dedicated men in the Federal Reserve and in the Treasury and the financial agencies, fiscal agencies of the Government. And we are going to continue to exchange views and express differences and try to reach agreements and promulgate policies

and do what we think is best for the country. This meeting has been very helpful, very fruitful. They always are.

I am not here to discuss post mortems. I am here to talk about how we can make this country better in the next year. Your job is to provoke a fight. Mine is to prevent one.

Q. Mr. President, do you see the action by the Federal Reserve Board as posing any serious threat to the current economy?

THE PRESIDENT. I expressed my views yesterday on the action of the Federal Reserve Board and I don't think I'll add to it.

[3.] Q. Mr. President, do you have any plans for the future, this month, on where you will meet President Ayub and Prime Minister Wilson? [10]

THE PRESIDENT. Yes, we are working on those plans now, and as we have told you over and over and over again, we will explain them to you in detail just as soon as a decision has been reached between the governments concerned.

[4.] Q. Mr. President, did anything that Mr. Martin said this morning change your mind about the statement you issued late yesterday?

THE PRESIDENT. No, no. He did not address himself to changing my mind, nor did I address myself to changing his.

[5.] Q. Mr. President, do you have any plans for changing the oil imports program regulations?

THE PRESIDENT. That is a matter that Secretary Udall [11] has under consideration and when he makes his recommendations they will be acted upon.

[6.] Q. Mr. President, do you feel there

---

[10] President Mohammed Ayub Khan of Pakistan and Prime Minister Harold Wilson of the United Kingdom (see Items 648–650).

[11] Stewart L. Udall, Secretary of the Interior.

is a need for stronger legislation to ensure service on interconnected power systems?

THE PRESIDENT. That will depend, I think, on the recommendations that the people who are studying it will make, and as the Chairman told you, they have not completed their study. They have not made any recommendations as yet. We will have to examine them when they do and act on them.

[7.] Q. Mr. President, is there any possibility of your going to the AFL–CIO convention this week?

THE PRESIDENT. No. I explained to them at the time they invited me that I did not think I would have a very heavy speaking schedule between now and the first of the year.

[8.] Q. Mr. President, would you entertain a question on Viet-Nam?

THE PRESIDENT. Yes.

Q. There have been some reports that the total amount of Americans——

THE PRESIDENT. What reports? Now let me get this clear, these reports and rumors. I have got to identify them before I can comment on them intelligently.

Q. Do I have to say it's one of my colleagues?

THE PRESIDENT. I want to just be sure it's reliable.

Q. Mr. Mohr,[12] of the New York Times, as you know, reported recently from Viet-Nam that there were discussions there of increasing the American commitment up to the capability of the Korean war perhaps. Is there a possibility of that?

THE PRESIDENT. I wouldn't want to make any predictions or prognostications or question Mr. Mohr's judgment. I think I'll go back to my July statement and say that we are very anxious to have peace in that area

in the world, and as soon as folks there are willing to leave their neighbors alone, why, we can have peace. But until we do have peace we are going to continue to help the people of South Viet-Nam resist aggression and we are going to supply whatever men may be needed in that effort.

Now, from day to day those numbers will change and we no doubt, between now and the first of the year, will have to make plans for what changes will take place. But so far as I am aware, those plans have not been made yet, and those decisions have not been made.

Maybe Mr. Mohr has some information I don't have. It takes time to get in. And sometimes our reports don't come as fast as you newspaper people.

Q. Will that be taken up tomorrow, Mr. President, at this meeting you are going to have with Secretary McNamara?

THE PRESIDENT. I would doubt that Mr. Mohr is on the agenda. We will discuss the defense needs rather fully.

[9.] Q. Mr. President, can you give us your expert political opinion of what happened to General de Gaulle?[13]

THE PRESIDENT. No.

[10.] Q. Mr. President, we had a report the other day from your doctors on how you're feeling. I wonder if you could give us a personal measure of your physical condition and your outlook for the next few weeks?

THE PRESIDENT. Well, I feel as well as I expect to feel. I don't feel as good as I did before the operation,[14] but I have no reason to feel that I won't be up to my normal operating strength the first of the year.

I think each day I get a little stronger and I have about reached my objective so far as

---

[12] Charles Mohr, New York Times correspondent in Viet-Nam.

[13] President Charles de Gaulle of France.
[14] See Item 549.

weight and exercise and everything is concerned. I think things are going well.

Reporter: Thank you very much, Mr. President.

NOTE: President Johnson's fifty-second news conference was held at the LBJ Ranch, Johnson City, Tex., at 2:10 p.m. on Monday, December 6, 1965.

642 Statement by the President on the Members of the Advisory Committee on Older Americans. *December 9, 1965*

THE NEW Committee represents a wide range of knowledge about the Nation's older people—their needs, their hopes, their abilities. The extensive and varied experiences of the members selected by Secretary Gardner will be invaluable in the pioneering work that lies ahead to make life better for our older citizens.

NOTE: The President's statement was made public as part of a White House release announcing the appointment by Secretary of Health, Education, and Welfare John W. Gardner of the Advisory Committee on Older Americans, established by the Older Americans Act of 1965 (Public Law 89–73; 79 Stat. 218). The release stated that the Committee would advise Secretary Gardner on national policies and programs to improve the status and well-being of older people.

William D. Bechill, Commissioner on Aging, Department of Health, Education, and Welfare, was appointed Chairman of the Committee. The names of the public members follow: William C. Fitch, Executive Director, American Association of Retired Persons and National Retired Teachers Association, Washington, D.C.; Rubin M. Hanan, Alabama League of Aging Citizens, Inc., Montgomery, Ala.;

Garson Meyer, President, National Council on the Aging, Rochester, N.Y.; Mrs. A. M. G. Russell, Chairman, Citizens Advisory Committee on Aging, Atherton, Calif.; Mrs. Margaret Schweinhaut, Chairman, Maryland Coordinating Commission on Problems of the Aging, Baltimore, Md.; James F. McMichael, Executive Director, State Commission on Aging, Madison, Wis.; Dr. Edward T. Ximenes, general practitioner, San Antonio, Tex.; Dr. I. P. Davis, dentist and community leader, Miami, Fla.; Dr. Harold Sheppard, staff social scientist, W. E. Upjohn Institute for Employment Research, Washington, D.C.; Zalmen Lichtenstein, Executive Director, Golden Ring Council of Senior Citizens, New York, N.Y.; Dr. Arnold M. Rose, Professor of Sociology, University of Minnesota, St. Paul, Minn.; Jay Roney, Director, Project on Aging, American Public Welfare Association, former Director, Bureau of Family Services, Social Security Administration, Chicago, Ill.; Dr. Wilma Donahue, Chairman, Division of Gerontology, Institute for Human Adjustment, University of Michigan, Ann Arbor, Mich.; Charles E. Odell, Director, Older and Retired Workers Department, United Auto Workers, Detroit, Mich.; and James C. O'Brien, Executive Director, United Steelworkers Committee on Older and Retired Workers, United Steelworkers, Washington, D.C.

643 Telephone Remarks Upon Accepting an Award From the Salvation Army Association of New York. *December 9, 1965*

Mr. Buckner and my good friend, Fred Kappel, ladies and gentlemen:

I feel a very special gratitude in receiving this honor today—because I think I know something of the men and women who extend it. Your standard of service is high, your record of accomplishment proud and long.

For a century now, the Salvation Army has offered food to the hungry and shelter to the homeless—in clinics and children's homes, through disaster relief, in prison and welfare work, and a thousand other endeavors. In that century you have proved time and again the power of a handshake, a meal, and a song.

But you have not stopped there. You have demonstrated also the power of a great idea. The voice of the Salvation Army has reminded men that physical well-being is just not enough; that spiritual rebirth is the most pressing need of our time and of every time; that the world cannot be changed unless men change.

That voice has been clear and courageous—and it has been heard.

Even when other armies have disbanded, I hope that this one will still be on the firing line: an army whose foes are hunger and hopelessness; an army whose happy battle cry is a call to "brighten the corner where you are."

With a pledge to heed that good advice, and with genuinely warm appreciation, I proudly accept your award.

NOTE: The President spoke at 1 p.m. by telephone from the LBJ Ranch, Johnson City, Tex., to a meeting of the Salvation Army Association at the New York Hilton Hotel. In his opening words he referred to Walker G. Buckner, Chairman of the Salvation Army Advisory Board, and Frederick R. Kappel, Chairman of the Board, American Telephone and Telegraph Company, and member of the Salvation Army Advisory Board.

644   Telephone Remarks to the Delegates to the AFL–CIO Convention. *December 9, 1965*

President Meany, delegates to the convention, my friends in the AFL–CIO:

I had planned to say that I would be following your deliberations with interest, but it occurred to me that there has been enough interest for one week already.

As you meet in San Francisco this week, you will be looking back over 2 years since your last convention. They have been the years, too, of my responsibilities as your President.

These years started from tragedy. Nothing will ever erase that terrible day from our memory.

But working together as a united people, we have moved down the road to increased progress for all Americans.

Our economy is surging. December marks the 58th consecutive month of economic prosperity. That is the longest period of uninterrupted expansion in America's peacetime history:

—Three and one-half million more people are at work.

—Unemployment, down by a million, is at its lowest ebb in 8 years.

—Business profits, after taxes, have increased by $11 billion.

—Total personal income for all Americans has increased by $69 billion.

—The average take-home pay of a factory worker with three dependents has risen to a record high of $98 a week.

—The number of people on payrolls in November of this year increased almost 2½ million—4 percent—over November 1964. That includes a phenomenal 800,000 increase in manufacturing alone.

That is our record of prosperity. I believe that we can maintain it. The increased knowledge, skills, and spirit of cooperation among management, labor, and Government justify full confidence in our ability to open even wider the doors of opportunity to all of our fellow Americans.

No challenge cries out for greater cooperation than the need to preserve the stability of prices and costs. Here the battle to keep our economy growing in a healthy way must be constantly waged.

You in labor have a very special stake. No one suffers more—or suffers sooner—

1147

than the workingman when rising prices erode the amount of goods and services that he can buy with each paycheck.

We must—and I believe we can—avoid the kind of price-wage spiral in which labor blames business for rising prices and steps up its wage claims to counter them, while business blames labor's wage demands for rising costs which require prices to go up.

From 1955 to 1960, this 5-year period, the income that a factory worker with three dependents had to spend in 1 week rose 15 percent. But the prices that he had to pay also rose—and they cut his 5-year gain to 4 percent.

From 1960 to October of this year, 1965, his spendable income rose 22 percent. And because the rise in prices was much more moderate, his real gain was a hefty 14 percent.

I believe that you want to do your part. In the last 2 years the labor cost per unit of output has remained relatively stable. By acting responsibly you have secured wage gains that mean real gains in purchasing power.

Future progress will depend on future responsibility. I am confident that we will continue on the dynamic but balanced pace that has led us this far in 58 months.

But economic progress is only one measure of the distance that we have traveled these past 2 years. Statistics can describe past trends, can analyze present developments, and can predict future possibilities.

But they cannot tell us about the soul of man.

The quality of our life must become as much a national issue as the quantity of our goods. Human progress is much more than a summary of our economic transactions.

It is a matter of how well we live.

It is not just a question of "How much do we make?" or "How much do we spend?"

It also asks: "What is the purpose of it all?"

We have pledged every American child the right to all the education that he can take. Will he use it to enlarge the meaning of his life and the good of us all?

We have pledged every American the right to full protection under law—the right to full citizenship—the right to exercise that citizenship at the polls. Will we welcome him now for what he is—an equal citizen, blessed with the same promise, afflicted with the same frailty, as all of his fellow humans? Will we now turn to the great work of reconciliation—forgiving past wrongs, healing old wounds, forging a new fellowship of Americans?

We have pledged our elderly the right to the best treatment that medical science can provide. We have pledged every American family the right to a decent home. And we have pledged our poor the right to opportunity.

But the right to something is not to realize it. A beginning has been made, but what will the outcome be?

Will the men of medicine, casting aside old superstitions and groundless fears of a nonexistent adversary, help to fulfill the bright promise of Medicare for 19 million Americans?

Will those to whom the Constitution gives the power of the purse provide the money for a new way of using an old principle— private enterprise—to solve our housing needs?

Will the poor find not only freedom from charity but the liberty of spirit and purpose no power can ever really again shackle?

These are not questions that legislation can answer. This Congress passed more legislation than any other Congress this century; 85 percent of our 1964 platform was translated into law.

And more is to come. Some business, already on the agenda, must be cleaned up soon after Congress returns.

I recommended to the Congress last year, and will urge on it further, basic improvements in the unemployment insurance program and in our minimum wage law. With your help, we will pass them both.

I recommended to the Congress last year, and we will urge on it further this year, the repeal of section 14(b) of the Taft-Hartley Act. With your help, we will pass it.

But legislation deals with the means and not the ends of our existence. And it is the ends and the moral purposes to which we give ourselves as a people that we are really concerned with at this season. No amount of economic progress can bury the inescapable fact that it is not how much we have but why we have it, and for what we use it, that determine the kind of society we live in and the kind of people we become.

WHY WE ARE IN VIET-NAM

Every day someone asks: "Why are we in Viet-Nam?"

And every day I want to answer: Not for economic reasons; we are spending our treasure, not reproducing it, out there.

And not for reasons of selfish pride; the lives of our sons are too great a price for national vanity.

Not for reasons of empire; our own sense of others' rights and the harsh judgments of history on the conquerors do not speak well of either the morality or the logic of imperial ambitions.

We are there because for all of our shortcomings, for all of our failings as a Nation and a people, we remain fixed on the pursuit of freedom as a deep and moral obligation that will not let us go.

I know it does not always seem that way. Political uncertainties often obscure our underlying purpose. Our own failures as men—politicians and generals, diplomats and reporters—cause us to question the wisdom of our course.

And nothing, perhaps, appears so contradictory to the cause that we serve as the use of force to advance it. Not even the absence of alternatives to the use of force to meet aggression lessens our distaste for it.

Only when petition and persuasion failed was the shot fired that was heard around the world. Not until appeals to commonsense brought forth the cannon's roar at Fort Sumter did Lincoln, with heavy heart, reply in kind. And not until reason perished in the aggressor's path did we turn—first in 1916 and again in 1941—to force as the ally of freedom.

I know it is said by a few: "But Viet-Nam is different. Our stake there hardly justifies one boy's life."

Well, Viet-Nam is different. The aggressor has chosen a different terrain, a different people, and a different kind of war to satisfy his appetite. But his goal is the same—someone else's freedom.

To defend that freedom—to permit its roots to deepen and grow without fear of external suppression—is our purpose in South Viet-Nam. Unchecked aggression against free and helpless people would be a very grave threat to our own freedom here in America and would be an offense to our own conscience.

In the past few days I have reviewed with my top counselors the situation in Viet-Nam. We are carefully studying how we can best continue to turn back that aggression. We are all determined to do all that is necessary.

At the same time, we are equally determined that every prospect for peace be exhausted before other hard steps are taken.

Only this week we reviewed our efforts for peace in some detail. Our efforts to communicate our desire to talk about peace were met with silence from some and met with shrill propaganda from others. On the crucial questions of readiness to meet without conditions, the response in Hanoi—and still more in Peking—remains completely negative.

Let us hope, however, that even at this hour reason might prevail in the minds of other men who hold the key to peace.

All over the world, in every capital where we are represented, America's Ambassadors are waiting for some word that those men, too, want peace and are willing to talk about it. I have given the Secretary of State special instructions to make sure that no one is uncertain about our purpose.

Our devotion to freedom is unyielding. So, too, is our hope for peace. Those who insist on testing either will find us earnest in both.

Thank you.

NOTE: The President spoke at 4:30 p.m. by telephone from the LBJ Ranch, Johnson City, Tex., to the AFL–CIO convention in San Francisco. In his opening words he referred to George Meany, President of the AFL–CIO.

645 Statement by the President Upon Announcing the Creation of the Physical Fitness Awards Program. *December 11, 1965*

IT IS essential that our young people develop their physical capabilities as well as their mental skills. Sports and other forms of active play promote good health and help provide our country with sturdy young citizens equal to the challenges of the future.

NOTE: The President's statement was made public as part of a White House release announcing the creation of a Presidential physical fitness awards program to give recognition to children between the ages of 10 and 17 who achieve a superior level of physical fitness.

The release stated that the President's Council on Physical Fitness, designated to administer the program, had estimated that approximately 1 million of the 27.7 million students in grades 5 through 12 could qualify for the award. Certificates bearing the President's signature and embroidered award emblems will be presented, the release noted, to students who score well on all seven items of the physical achievement test of the American Association for Health, Physical Education and Recreation, a department of the National Education Association.

See also Item 625.

The statement was released at Austin, Tex.

646 Statement by the President Upon Announcing the Recipients of the National Medal of Science Awards. *December 11, 1965*

THIS MEDAL serves as a symbol of the Nation's desire to recognize outstanding achievement, to set an example for our youth, and to depict to the world the depth and variety of American accomplishment in science and engineering.

This richness and diversity are well illustrated by the men being honored. Yet, these 11 awards represent only a sampling of this country's great scientific leadership.

For example, Hugh Dryden's recent death ended nearly 50 years of singleminded devotion and effort by one of the most distinguished civil servants this country has ever known. Beloved by all his associates and respected throughout the world, Dr. Dryden more than any other man let us into the age of jet aircraft and space exploration.

The careers of the other medalists are equally inspiring. All of them have contributed greatly to our knowledge of the world and the universe in which we live. They have made key discoveries ranging from the virus theory of cancer to neutrinos, superconductivity, and the transistor. Their work encompasses genetics and algebraic geometry, the principles of supersonic flight and the design of such remarkable aircraft as the U–2 and the A–11. They have extended our life span through greater understanding of the causes of disease and through devising accurate methods of understanding the composition of our bodies. They have enriched our understanding of the history of our planet and of the frontier of the mind. They have advanced our economic welfare and our national security.

Many of these men are great teachers. A few have had to defend their discoveries in the face of determined opposition. All represent the best in science.

I hope that through these awards more Americans will come to recognize and to appreciate the wealth of talent in our midst and the extraordinary progress which these gifted people inspire.

NOTE: The President's statement was made public as part of a White House release announcing the names of the 1965 recipients of the National Medal of Science. The release stated that the medal, established by Congress in 1959, was awarded to outstanding scientists on the basis of recommendations received from the President's Committee on the National Medal of Science under the chairmanship of Dr. H. E. Carter of the University of Illinois.

The names of the 1965 recipients follow: Dr. John Bardeen, Professor of Physics and Electrical Engineering, University of Illinois; Dr. Peter J. W. Debye, Professor Emeritus, Department of Chemistry, Cornell University; Dr. Hugh L. Dryden, former Deputy Administrator of the National Aeronautics and Space Administration, and first posthumous recipient of the National Medal of Science; Dr. Clarence L. Johnson, Vice President for Advanced Development Projects, Lockheed Aircraft Corporation; Dr. Warren K. Lewis, Professor Emeritus of Chemical Engineering, Massachusetts Institute of Technology; Dr. F. Peyton Rous, associated with the Rockefeller Institute; Dr. William W. Rubey, Professor of Geology and Geophysics, University of California at Los Angeles; Dr. George G. Simpson, Agassiz Professor of Vertebrate Paleontology, Harvard University; Dr. Donald D. Van Slyke, research chemist, Brookhaven National Laboratory; Dr. Oscar Zariski, Professor of Mathematics, Harvard University; and Dr. Leon M. Lederman, Professor of Physics, Columbia University.

Biographies of the recipients are printed in the Weekly Compilation of Presidential Documents (vol. 1, p. 586).

The statement was released at Austin, Tex.

---

647   Statement by the President on the Delayed Takeoff of Gemini 6. *December* 12, 1965

WE ARE all disappointed that Gemini 6 did not go off as expected. But our disappointment is exceeded by our pride in Astronauts Walter Schirra and Thomas Stafford and the flight directors of NASA. With the world watching, they acted with remarkable courage in the face of danger and potential disaster.

Their eager desire and determination to try again proves once more that men are the real heroes—and the essential factor—in space exploration.

NOTE: See also Items 636, 651, 656.

The statement was released at Austin, Tex.

648 Remarks of Welcome to President Ayub Khan of Pakistan on the South Lawn at the White House. *December 14, 1965*

Mr. President:

I am happy, on behalf of the people of the United States, to welcome you once more to our shores.

We Americans have admired Pakistan's rapid progress as a nation, and we have had particular respect for you as the leader who has been chiefly responsible for this great progress over the past 7 years.

It is also a very great satisfaction for me, personally, to have you here with us at this time. I have not forgotten the hospitality which my wife and I received during our visit to Pakistan 4 years ago. It seemed to me then, as it does now, that Pakistan and the United States have very much in common. For one thing, each of our countries began as what most people called "an impractical experiment." No one expected us to survive. Yet here we are.

I remember, most gratefully, how much at home I was made to feel on my visit to your country. I also recall my feelings when you addressed the legislature of my home State back in 1961. Mr. President, I don't know whether you felt equally at home on that occasion, but I remember thinking at the time that you could have had a very great future in American politics.

So we do have, I think, much in common. We have also had our differences. Yet I hope that the bonds which unite us are far stronger than any temporary disagreements.

Both of our nations are dedicated to government by, and for, the people.

Both you and we, each in our own way, are trying—trying so hard to provide a fuller life for all of our people. We, in America, admire Pakistan's efforts to this end, and we have sought to work with them.

We also agree, I know, that the ultimate success of all of our efforts really depends upon the restoration of peace and stability, not only in Asia, but throughout the entire world.

I am quite confident that, working together with the millions of others who share these ideals, we will ultimately reach our goal. I am confident, too, that the discussions which we are about to have will bring us—and the world—one step closer to that common objective.

Mr. President, we are delighted to have you here this morning. We hope you will enjoy your stay in our country, and we certainly want you to know that we warmly welcome you as our friend.

NOTE: The President spoke at 11:12 a.m. on the South Lawn at the White House, where President Mohammed Ayub Khan was given a formal welcome with full military honors. President Ayub Khan responded as follows:

Mr. President:

I am deeply touched by the warm welcome you have given me and my party, and also for the gracious words you used for the progress that Pakistan has made during the last few years.

May I say that we got our independence after 150 years of British rule 18 years ago, and when I became responsible for running the country, my main concern was to do such things which would improve the living standards of the people and give them hope for a better future.

Now for a country like yours, which started much earlier, perhaps such things are simpler, also simpler perhaps because of your vast resources. But for us, we had to establish the intrastructure of all descriptions to be able to embark on the road to progress.

And I am very happy to be able to tell you that we made considerable progress. And I also would like to take this opportunity of thanking your Government and you, sir, and your people, for the very generous assistance you gave us in these endeavors.

I am very happy to be here again in Washington. It reminds me, first of all, of my last visit when the President, as Vice President, under no obligation on him to waste his time on me, he very kindly, and his lady, took me to the ranch, and the amount of affection and the amount of hospitality they showed, I can never forget in my life and I keep on repeating it to my people in Pakistan. I come here again; I am looking forward to meeting you, sir, and discussing with you our mutual problems, and also to have the opportunity of meeting several other good friends of Pakistan here in Washington and in the United States.

There are several places in the world which are troubled, which are under stress; so is our part of the world. Unfortunately there has been a war, a short war, but a sharp war and bloody war. The peace there hangs on a very thin thread of cease-fire.

I know you are far away, but you, as the greatest country today, have an obligation to the rest of the world, and I have no doubt, sir, that your Government, under your dynamic and powerful leadership, will lend its full support toward the resolution of the problems which are besetting us.

We can't afford wars. We can't afford tensions. Our task is difficult. Our task is to do something for humanity. Our task is to search for peace. And we, in Pakistan, certainly make every endeavor to be able to make our contribution towards peace on honorable and reasonable terms.

Sir, again I thank you once again for a warm welcome, and I am happy to see after your very serious operation you are looking so well and you are regaining your health, and I do hope that you will completely recover soon because the responsibility you hold—not only on behalf of your own people but on behalf of the largest part of the world—is so great that your health is of tremendous importance to us all.

Thank you, sir.

See also Items 649, 650.

649   Toasts of the President and the President of Pakistan. *December* 14, 1965

Mr. President, distinguished guests, ladies and gentlemen:

There is no need to say how very pleased we are, Mr. President, to welcome you to this house this evening. The President of Pakistan comes on a new visit, but he is a very old friend. This is his third journey here as head of a young State already grown to world importance.

Mrs. Johnson and I want to thank you, Mr. President, for honoring us with your distinguished Ambassador Ahmed and his charming wife, whom we enjoy very much.

We are also particularly pleased that we could renew acquaintances with your former Ambassador, your present Foreign Secretary. I observed that perhaps when he was Ambassador and I was Vice President we were doing a little better job with our relations than we are in our new positions. But it just shows you what happens to people when they get promoted!

President Ayub and I have a great deal in common, just as our peoples share many values and many dreams.

President Ayub is a rancher as I am. His home district is a country much like Johnson City, Blanco County, where I live. He also has a special bond with Mrs. Johnson, and for that matter, all lovers of beauty in this land. President Ayub is building a new capital for his country, just as we are trying to rebuild and beautify ours.

With so much to share it is not surprising that President Ayub and I found our talks today fruitful. They will continue in the evening and we hope for more extended sessions tomorrow.

We share the basic values and beliefs: man's fundamental dignity and worth, a love of liberty, a pride of excellence, pursuit of beauty and truth, a vision of a better and a fuller life for all human beings.

I have recalled a courageous and a compassionate appeal made by President Ayub in a broadcast back in 1963. He said then— and I quote: "Hatred and anger fan the fires of hell in human minds. Why not put them out? It is nobler and better for one's own happiness to live on terms of friendliness with others."

And so tonight we share the greatest hunger and the most burning thirst of all. We want so much to find peace in the world. We want so much to bring peace to Asia and peace to all the other countries that are troubled. We want peace not only in our time, but peace for all time.

We want peace. And we shall work every minute, day and night, for peace.

President Ayub visits us as the architect of his country's inspiring struggle for economic emancipation. And nowhere have we observed a better administrative effort. Today Pakistan surges forward in a very great adventure. And Dave Bell will talk to you about it for hours if you will listen to him because we are very thrilled to observe the economic advances and the other results that the leadership of President Ayub and his associates provides and inspires. We all must rededicate our very best efforts to conquering the curses of poverty, hunger, disease, illiteracy: the human and physical problems that, as President Ayub has said, and I quote him again, "cannot be resolved by the magic wand of just freedom alone."

So, Mr. President, with your permission, I am sending a very high level team of medical teachers and scientists shortly to your country of Pakistan. This team will be led by the President's Science Adviser, my own trusted counselor, Dr. Donald Hornig. Its mission will be to work with your own medical authorities in instituting a very broad improvement in medical training, and in working with all of your fine people in the attempt to improve rural health and public health among your fellow countrymen.

This will be a beginning. If our purposes are as one, we can continue and expand the dynamic partnership that we have had in the past. Together we can press the

battle against waterlogging and salinity; against devastating cyclones, cholera, heart and eye disease. Together as friends, working shoulder to shoulder, we can improve weather forecasting and improve flood warnings, and multiply housing programs such as the Korangi project that I visited in 1961 when I met my good friend the camel driver. He came to this country and he spread good will from one end of it to the other, and he is remembered most affectionately by all who met him. We can speed in many ways the transition from a subsistence economy to a life of plenty and a life of purpose for every Pakistani.

This has been a stimulating and inspiring day for me. It is always so when I am in your presence.

So tonight, here in this, the first house of our land, I would like to ask those friends of mine whom I have asked to come here from various parts of this country—from California to New York—to raise our glasses to salute the spirit and the success of the Pakistan nation, and the dedicated leadership of the great President of Pakistan, Mohammed Ayub Khan.

NOTE: The President proposed the toast at 10:15 p.m. at a dinner in the State Dining Room at the White House. During his remarks the President referred to Ghulam Ahmed, Pakistan Ambassador to the United States, Ali Bhutto, Foreign Minister of Pakistan, David E. Bell, Administrator, Agency for International Development, and Donald F. Hornig, Special Assistant to the President for Science and Technology.

President Ayub Khan responded as follows:

Mr. President, Mrs. Johnson, Your Excellencies, ladies and gentlemen:

I am deeply touched by the warm reception given to me and my party and by your great hospitality tonight. You are a generous man. I am only talking to a friend now. May I have the liberty of doing so with a great heart.

I am so very happy that this great country has a man like you, sir, at its head, and that is how it should be. It is only people with large hearts, broad understanding, forgiveness, and so on, that can tackle the sort of responsibilities that devolve on you. Not only responsibilities on behalf of your country, but, in fact, on behalf of the world even, because you are the head of the mightiest country in the world.

As far as Pakistan is concerned—the people in Pakistan are concerned—there has been very friendly and warm relations between our people.

Lately—and I would be less than honest if I did not admit it, since I was largely responsible for this friendship and understanding between our two countries—it hurts me to say that our relations have, to a certain extent, been soiled, and I think that has happened because of a lack of understanding of each other's difficulties and problems.

You have certain obligations and certain problems which you are facing, of which we are aware. We have certain difficulties in the location and the situation in which we live.

You have been very generous and kind to invite me to come to your country to see you and talk to you in heart-to-heart fashion. And I have with all sincerity and honesty put to you our problems, and you have been good enough to tell me your problems.

I think that in countries like yours and mine, situated so far away, with different sorts of obligations, locations, and so on and so forth, friendships can be maintained—and they must be maintained. And the way to maintain them is to bear friendship with friendship and understand each other's difficulties, and don't do anything which is against the interests of a friendly country.

I have no doubt in my mind if that principle is observed—we certainly will observe it, sir— there is no reason why our friendship should not continue.

Your country and your people have in many ways been assisting us, and I am the first one to admit it. Not only do I do so in my heart, but I do so in front of my people. And it has been a very stimulating experience for our mutual relationship.

We regained our independence after a long time. In a period when the world has shrunk, peoples' expectations have risen. They want the good things of life quickly. Demands on government, therefore, have increased enormously. After all, it takes time with the best will in the world and the best effort in the world to produce results.

The people are not prepared to wait. They are impatient. Therefore, there is great pressure, tremendous pressure, in our country to produce results to the satisfaction of the people. We have been, in our humble way, trying to improve the conditions of our people, and remove sufferings and wants, and so on.

I think we made a considerable success in that. One lesson I learned from that was that the people really try to improve their lot once they are given the right direction and the opportunity.

Lately, unfortunately, we have been bedeviled with a major conflict. My own hope and prayer is that we shall be able to overcome. My endeavor always has been to live in peace with our neighbors, especially with our big neighbor, India. They have tremendous problems and we have tremendous problems.

We need peace. We need peace not only for the sake of peace but also for the sake of doing a very noble task of improving the lot of our people.

In that connection, I am very grateful to you, sir, for sending this mission out. I am sure that it will be appreciated, and I am sure that they will get the fullest cooperation from our people and they will benefit by their experience.

The last time I was here President Kennedy and I had long discussions. I mentioned to him about this problem of waterlogging and salinity in West Pakistan. Those of you who are familiar know the circumstances there. Our agriculture is totally artificial in West Pakistan. It is dependent on artificial irrigation. I think—I don't know whether I am right in saying—but it is probably the biggest, shall we say, artificially irrigated area in the world in one block—some 32 million acres of land.

And through this process of irrigation the water table has gone out, the salts have come up, and we were facing tremendous problems. And he was good enough to send a team of scientists out, and they have done, in conjunction with our people, a tremendous job. I am sure if your set of people come they will have a second look at these things. We made a start in this project and we made a great success.

So, I am very grateful to you for this offer. Our effort really is to do the very best we can for our people.

We also find that our population is growing at a rate which is not acceptable, and which can create serious problems. That is another thing that we are putting our major efforts on.

Similarly with our agriculture, and so on, results have been very heartening. And so any advice and assistance of that nature will be most welcome, in keeping with the wishes and the desires and endeavors of the people.

I am glad to see that after your major operation— apparently it has been a very serious one—you are looking so well and regaining your health. I hope you will regain your full vigor.

May I say that the talk we had together has been very exhilarating for me. You have been patient enough to listen to me and I do hope that you will be convinced of my sincerity. I may be wrong in my approach but you can be assured of my sincerity of approach.

I have no doubt that if we understand each other's difficulties there is no reason why our friendship can't last forever.

So, I thank you for all the understanding you have given me and us all, and this warm welcome and great hospitality, and also given me the opportunity of meeting you again. It has done my soul a lot of good.

So, in return for that, may I ask you ladies and gentlemen to join me in drinking to the health and happiness of the President of the United States of America and to the well-being and happiness of the people of the United States of America.

Mr. President, sir.

See also Items 648, 650.

650 Joint Statement Following Discussions With the President of Pakistan. *December* 15, 1965

PRESIDENT JOHNSON and President Ayub have had frank, wide-ranging, and productive talks for the past 2 days. President Ayub's visit has given the two Presidents the opportunity to renew their warm personal acquaintance and to recall with pleasure their respective visits to Pakistan and the United States in 1961.

The two Presidents discussed at length recent events in south Asia, including the tragic conflict between India and Pakistan. In this context, they reaffirmed their Governments' support for the U.N. Security Council resolution of September 20, 1965, in all its parts, as well as the resolutions adopted on September 27 and November 5, 1965.

President Johnson reaffirmed that the United States regards as vital to world peace the preservation of the independence and integrity of Pakistan and expressed the continuing interest of the United States in Pakistan's economic and social development. President Ayub reaffirmed the importance that Pakistan attaches to a close and cooperative relationship with the United States and expressed the continuing desire of his Government to contribute to this objective.

The two Presidents agreed on the need for a peaceful resolution of all outstanding differences between India and Pakistan, so that the energies and resources of the peoples of the subcontinent would not be wastefully diverted from their efforts to meet their vitally important social and economic problems.

Within the context of a review of worldwide developments, the two Presidents discussed in depth the problem of achieving peace and stability in southeast Asia. They expressed the hope that the conflicts in that area would be peacefully resolved. They agreed that their diplomatic representatives would remain in close touch on these wider and critical Asian problems.

NOTE: See also Items 648, 649.

651 Telegram to the Administrator, NASA, Following the Meeting in Space of Gemini 6 and Gemini 7. *December* 15, 1965

I WANT to congratulate the astronauts and the thousands of scientists, technicians, and administrators for the success of today's rendezvous. You have all moved us one step higher on the stairway to the moon. By conducting this adventure for all the world to see, you have reaffirmed our faith in a free and open society. We invite those throughout the world who have shared our suspense and suffered with us during our temporary failures to share with us this triumph, for it belongs not just to the United States but to all mankind. Our efforts in space will take us not only to the moon but, by increasing our knowledge of technology and the world around us, to a better life for all.

"Without adventure," Alfred North Whitehead said, "civilization is in full decay." Today's accomplishment is a new declaration of the vigor of our society and the hope all men can hold for the future.

LYNDON B. JOHNSON

[Mr. James Webb, Administrator, National Aeronautics and Space Administration, Washington, D.C.]

NOTE: See also Items 636, 647, 656.

652 Statement by the President on the Death of Dr. William Randolph Lovelace II. *December 16, 1965*

A DAY of great achievement in space was marred by news of the death of Dr. William R. Lovelace II. His life was too short, although his legacy to space medicine will endure and will be a resource of assurance to future astronauts whose names and deeds are yet unknown.

NOTE: The statement was read by Bill D. Moyers, Special Assistant to the President, at his news conference at 4:50 p.m. on Thursday, December 16, 1965, in his office at the White House. It was not made public in the form of a White House press release.

Dr. Lovelace was killed in a plane crash near Aspen, Colo., on Sunday, December 12, 1965. The wreckage of the plane was discovered on Wednesday, December 15, the day of the rendezvous of Gemini 6 and Gemini 7. Dr. Lovelace had served as Director of Space Medicine for Manned Space Flight in NASA since April 20, 1964.

653 Remarks at the Lighting of the Nation's Christmas Tree. *December 17, 1965*

Mr. Prime Minister, Mr. Vice President, my fellow countrymen:

Once again it is Christmas.

Once again that time has come when the heart of man opens to the holiness of life.

Once again we tell the ancient story of a baby, born into poverty and persecution, whose destiny it was to lift the iron burden of despair from his fellow men.

In the 20 centuries that have transpired since the sacred moment of His birth, mankind has never been wholly free of the scourge of war and the ravages of disease, illiteracy, and hunger. Yet the star of Bethlehem burns in our hearts on this December evening with a warmth that is not diminished by the years or discouraged by our failures.

It reminds us that our first and most compelling task is peace.

As in other Christmas seasons in the past, our celebration this year is tempered by the absence of brave men from their homes and from their loved ones.

We would not have it so. We have not sought the combat in which they are engaged. We have hungered for not one foot of another's territory, nor for the life of a single adversary. Our sons patrol the hills of Viet-Nam at this hour because we have learned that though men cry "Peace, peace," there is no peace to be gained ever by yielding to aggression.

That lesson has been learned by a hundred generations. The guarantors of peace on earth have been those prepared to make sacrifices in its behalf.

On this platform with me this evening is the very distinguished and very great Prime Minister of Great Britain. He speaks for a people who have made such sacrifices in behalf of peace. On the battlefield and at the conference table, his countrymen have fought and have labored to create a just peace among the nations.

The distinguished Prime Minister, Harold Wilson, and I have spoken of this task this afternoon. We have spoken not only of the security of mankind, but of the countless opportunities for cooperation that are the true works of peace.

He has told me that his Government will renew the quest for peace as cochairman of the Geneva Conference. I have told him that any new way he can find to peace will have a ready response from the United States.

We know too that peace is not merely the absence of war. It is that climate in which man may be liberated from the hopelessness that imprisons his spirit.

In this strong and prosperous land, there are many that are still trapped in that prison where hope seems but a dream. We shall never rest until that dream becomes a reality.

But hope cannot be our province alone. For we shall never know peace in a world where a minority prospers and the vast majority is condemned to starvation and ignorance. This evening, inspired once more by Him who brought comfort and courage to the oppressed, we offer our hand to those who seek a new life for their people.

Above all things, we dedicate ourselves to the search for a just settlement of disputes between nations. We declare once more our desire to discuss an honorable peace in Viet-Nam. We know that nothing is to be gained by a further delay in talking. Our poet Emerson once said that "the god of victory is one-handed—but peace gives victory to both sides."

So in the name of a people who seek peace for their brothers on this earth—"that we may be the children of our Father which is in heaven; for He maketh His sun to rise on the evil and on the good, and sendeth rain on the just and on the unjust"—I turn on the lights of this tree, and pray that the Spirit that we revere this evening may illuminate the heart of every man on earth.

NOTE: The President spoke at 5:19 p.m. just before lighting the National Community Christmas Tree at the 12th annual Pageant of Peace ceremonies on the Ellipse near the White House. In his opening words he referred to Prime Minister Harold Wilson of the United Kingdom and Vice President Hubert H. Humphrey.

---

654   The President's Christmas Message to the Men and Women in the Armed Forces. *December 18, 1965*

THIS is a season of hope and rejoicing as we celebrate the birth of the Prince of Peace. It is a time for renewing ties of brotherhood with all men of good will, everywhere on earth.

Our thoughts are especially with the men and women in uniform. We ask that you may enjoy a full measure of this season's happiness. Far from your homes and loved ones, you make it possible for all the rest of us to enjoy more fully the meaning of Christmas. For your sacrifice we are forever indebted.

We grieve for those who have made the supreme sacrifice, for those who bear wounds for freedom's sake, and for their families.

We rededicate ourselves in this season of good will to the ultimate promise of peace made 2,000 years ago. To fulfill that hope remains our urgent quest.

---

655   Messages to the President-Elect and to the President of the Republic of the Philippines. *December 18, 1965*

Dear President-Elect:

I extend to you warmest congratulations on your election to the Presidency of the Republic of the Philippines. I send the good wishes of the American people for your success in leading the Philippine people in continued progress. Our two nations are bound by friendship and alliance, and you may be assured of our enduring support and good will.

It is with genuine pleasure that I look forward to continued close partnership between our peoples, and cooperation between my administration and yours. We have much work to do both in our own countries and together to further the hopes of our peoples for dignity, well-being and peace.

Sincerely,

LYNDON B. JOHNSON

[His Excellency Ferdinand Marcos, President-elect of the Republic of the Philippines]

Dear Mr. President:

As you prepare to relinquish the duties and responsibilities of your high office, I send you my warm good wishes. I know that you must take great satisfaction in having served your country with such distinction in its highest office. The friendship of our two nations has grown even closer under your leadership.

Mrs. Johnson and I recall with great pleasure the State Visit which you and Mrs. Macapagal made to our country and send you now our sincere affirmation of friendship and good will.

Sincerely,

LYNDON B. JOHNSON

[His Excellency Diosdado Macapagal, President of the Republic of the Philippines]

---

656   Letters to the Gemini 6 and Gemini 7 Astronauts After the Successful Completion of Their Mission. *December 18, 1965*

Dear Captain Schirra:

Once again you have journeyed to the outer limits of the earth's environment. Once again you have captured the imagination of the entire world. And once again you have returned safely to the applause and admiration of your fellow countrymen. For them

I can offer you the highest praise a President can bestow: You have made us all very proud.

Your remarkable rendezvous with Gemini 7 was unparalleled. Certainly we will go on to other accomplishments, but we will never forget that suspenseful moment, last

Wednesday, when you and your colleagues met in space and together circled the globe in history.

Sincerely,

LYNDON B. JOHNSON

[Capt. Walter Schirra, USN, Manned Space Center, Houston, Texas]

Dear Major Stafford:

No words of mine can add luster to the splendid triumph in which you have just shared. I do want to say, on behalf of the people of the United States, that all of us are immensely proud of your adventure and its success. You have our lasting thanks, and our hope that the years ahead will bring continued success in our reach for the stars.

I have just sent to the Secretary of the Air Force a memorandum authorizing your promotion to the rank of Lieutenant Colonel in the United States Air Force. In a small way this symbolizes our gratitude for your courage.

Sincerely,

LYNDON B. JOHNSON

[Major Thomas P. Stafford, USAF, Manned Space Center, Houston, Texas]

Dear Commander Lovell:

The flight you have just completed will be remembered for all time as one of man's great achievements in making his environment. I want history also to record the deep gratitude for your skill and courage, which all Americans feel, and which, as President, I express on their behalf.

You may be interested in knowing that I have approved your promotion to the rank

of Captain in the United States Navy. The promotion will be submitted to Congress for confirmation the moment it reconvenes.

Sincerely,

LYNDON B. JOHNSON

[Cdr. James A. Lovell, Jr., USN, Manned Space Center, Houston, Texas]

Dear Colonel Borman:

I know I speak for the entire nation when I tell you how proud we are of your tremendous accomplishment. We watched your lift-off anxiously. We followed you with pride, orbit by orbit, as space records fell to Gemini 7 and her gallant crew. We cheered your rendezvous with Gemini 6. And now we congratulate you on your safe return after fourteen days in space.

I know the satisfaction which you must personally feel from your vital part in this historic mission. But perhaps I can add to that satisfaction just a little by telling you that I have just approved your promotion to full Colonel.

You have earned that promotion, just as you have earned the gratitude and admiration of every American citizen.

Sincerely,

LYNDON B. JOHNSON

[Lt. Col. Frank Borman, USAF, Manned Space Center, Houston, Texas]

NOTE: On December 16, 1965, the Gemini 6 spacecraft, manned by Captain Schirra and Major Stafford, returned to earth after nearly 26 hours in space. The Gemini 7 spacecraft, manned by Commander Lovell and Lieutenant Colonel Borman, came down in the Atlantic Ocean on December 18 after 14 days in space. It had served as the target for Gemini 6 in man's first space rendezvous.

See also Items 636, 647, 651.

657   Statement by the President on the Treaty of Basic Relations
      Between Japan and Korea. *December 18, 1965*

AS A FRIEND of Japan and the Republic of Korea, we welcome their exchange of instruments of ratification of the Treaty of Basic Relations and its associated agreements. We believe that this final step in the establishment of normal relations between these two neighbors will bring important and lasting benefit to both peoples, and will strengthen the community of free nations.

NOTE: The statement was read by Bill D. Moyers, Special Assistant to the President, at his news conference at 12:15 p.m. on Saturday, December 18, 1965, in his office at the White House. It was not made public in the form of a White House press release.

Mr. Moyers stated that the treaty was signed in Tokyo on June 22, 1965, and by the Korean Government on August 13, and was ratified by the Japanese Government on December 11. The instruments of ratification were exchanged in Seoul, Korea, on December 18, 1965.

658   Statement by the President Upon Signing Order Providing for the
      Manner of Election of the Chief Executive, Ryukyu Islands.
      December 20, 1965

I HAVE today signed an amendment to Executive Order 10713, as previously amended, which provides for the administration of Okinawa and other Ryukyu Islands. The new amendment specifies that the Ryukyuan Chief Executive, heretofore appointed by the U.S. High Commissioner, shall henceforth be elected by the legislative body of the Government of the Ryukyu Islands, as the popularly chosen representatives of the Ryukyuan people.

This amendment is another forward step in the continuing policy of the United States to afford the Ryukyuan people as great a voice in managing their own affairs as is compatible with the essential role of the Ryukyus in maintaining the security of Japan and the Far East.

I am happy to announce this change at this time, so as to insure that the Ryukyuan Chief Executive for the next term can be elected directly by the representatives of the Ryukyuan people.

NOTE: The President referred to Executive Order 11263 "Further Amending Executive Order No. 10713, Providing for Administration of the Ryukyu Islands" (1 Weekly Comp. Pres. Docs., p. 608; 30 F.R. 15777; 3 CFR, 1965 Supp., p. 195); and to Executive Order 10713 "Providing for Administration of the Ryukyu Islands," dated June 5, 1957 (3 CFR, 1954–1958 Comp., p. 368).

659   Toasts of the President and Chancellor Ludwig Erhard of
      Germany. *December 20, 1965*

Mr. Chancellor, distinguished members of your party, ladies and gentlemen:

The great German writer, Goethe, once said that the formula for a happy life was each day to read a beautiful poem, listen to beautiful music, look at a beautiful painting, and, if possible, say some reasonable thing.

Today, Mr. Chancellor, we may have lacked the beauty of poem, painting, and music. But we did, I believe, say reasonable things to each other.

We are privileged tonight to have in our

country and in the first house of our land one of the world's most reasonable and versatile leaders.

He is a man of many talents: educator, author, amateur musician, economist, politician, and statesman.

As a politician, he can look with great satisfaction to the vote of confidence that the people of West Germany gave him in last September's national election.

As a statesman, he can look with great pride to nearly 20 years of dedicated and effective service to the Federal Republic. The miracle of Germany's economic recovery following World War II stands as a towering monument to his service.

So, Chancellor Erhard, we welcome you this evening, not only as a politician and as an economist, but as a statesman. But really, most of all, we welcome you as a friend. You are aware, I am sure, of the high regard and the deep affection in which I personally hold you. That regard and that affection are reflected throughout America.

And there is no truth to the rumor that your reputation as an economist prompted us to invite you here to visit us at budget time.

In other areas, however, we will not be so reticent in seeking your advice.

We live in a world of change. In that world, nations have much to gain from an open exchange of information—and we have much to lose by ignoring the potential contribution of other peoples.

We have already begun a mutual adventure in space.

Only last summer, our two Governments worked out an agreement whereby we will launch a German-built satellite to probe the inner radiation belts.

Now, we would like to discuss with you— and with others—an even more ambitious plan to permit us to do together what we cannot do so well alone. Examples would be two projects which stand high on the space agenda. Both are very demanding and both are quite complex. One would be a probe to the Sun, and another a probe to Jupiter. To cooperate on such a major endeavor would contribute vastly to our mutual knowledge and to our mutual skills.

So, I propose, early in the year, to send a commission—headed by our able Administrator of NASA, James Webb—to consult with you and other governments of Europe wishing to participate in a joint exploration of space.

In all our efforts we seek to learn as well as to contribute.

And we are now watching with great interest the pioneer work that you in Germany are doing to make your cities more livable. We are especially interested in your antipollution programs, which are said to be among the most effective in all the world. So, I propose sending a working group, headed by our distinguished Secretary of the Interior, Mr. Udall, to West Germany next month to visit with your own Minister of Science and Education and to view some of your accomplishments firsthand.

I am told that some of your air pollution experts feel that the only thing that now stands between them and final success is the daily quota of their Chancellor's cigars.

Mr. Chancellor, in welcoming you to our shores this Christmas season, we are aware that we have much to be thankful for: a stable political system and healthy economies in both our countries; a North Atlantic Alliance that has met every challenge of the past; and an effective relationship that binds our countries together within the framework of an Atlantic partnership. We applaud the role of Germany in these great affairs.

And for our part, the United States is especially grateful for the support which your

Government has given to the common cause in Viet-Nam, and which you may give in the days ahead.

The great effort which my country is making tonight in Viet-Nam is in fulfillment of the clear commitment of the American people, the American Congress, and three American Presidents. The people of South Viet-Nam need our support, and they are getting it. The credible commitment of the United States is the foundation stone of the house of freedom all around the world. If it is not good in Viet-Nam, Mr. Chancellor, who can trust it in the heart of Europe? But America's word, I can assure you, is good in Viet-Nam, just as it is good in Berlin.

Our object in Viet-Nam is not war but peace. There will be peace in Viet-Nam the very moment that others are ready to stop their attacks. We will push on every door for peace. We will go anywhere to talk. We set no conditions. We neglect no hopeful step. But, as all of you know, it takes two to talk and it takes two, as well, to stop the fighting.

Meanwhile, we are going to keep this country moving in the spirit of the Great Society and the Formed Society. Though we are defending freedom abroad we must continue to enlarge freedom at home and around the world.

In Europe much remains to be done. The reunification of Germany in peace and freedom is a major goal. We share your hopes for a continued development of a united Europe. The strength of the Atlantic partnership will require the best efforts of both sides of the Atlantic. A just solution to the crisis in Viet-Nam just must be found, and the entire fabric of world peace must be strengthened. As we agreed today, there is work to be done by your country and by ours.

There are no easy answers to any of these questions. They will require a new spirit of trust and cooperation among all the nations of the world. That spirit, Chancellor Erhard, is embodied in the friendship of our two great nations.

And so, ladies and gentlemen, in honor of a country whose people and whose future are represented here tonight by my old and dear friend, Chancellor Ludwig Erhard, I now ask you to join me by raising your glasses to the President of the Federal Republic of Germany.

NOTE: The President proposed the toast at 10:05 p.m. in the State Dining Room at the White House. Chancellor Erhard responded as follows:

Mr. President, Mrs. Johnson, ladies and gentlemen:
It is certainly a very great honor for me to be your guest tonight, Mr. President, at such a festive occasion, and I would like to thank you for this reception on behalf of all my fellow countrymen who are here tonight. And we had a very valuable, very enjoyable day today. I consider it always to be a very great distinction to be here and I am fully aware of what the friendship with you, Mr. President, means to me personally, to my country, and to all my fellow countrymen.

Looking back on the past, on the time during which I had to accept and bear political responsibility—and that covers a period of nearly 20 years—on thinking back of the moment when we were completely broken down, facing the collapse of our country, and there the Americans were first in their generosity to extend to us a helping hand. And this, Mr. President, ladies and gentlemen, is a deed we will never forget.

When we then had to start building up and reconstructing the economy of our country, and I had to take over responsibility for that job, I was looking around for a model. Where was the country adhering to the same ideals, to the same principles, living by these principles and ideals, which we now needed, which I felt we had to live by after the tragedy through which we had gone? And here again the generosity and the cooperation, the help of the United States and the Americans proved itself so immensely helpful. And it was quite obvious that this should become the basis of real friendship.

In those years, we have won friends, and I say, with the feeling of pride and with the feeling of satisfaction, that the friendship that exists between you and me, and our personal relations, is the coronation; it is the crowning of this friendship between our two countries.

You do not know, Mr. President, how much that means to me, and I am not speaking from vanity. I speak sincerely and honestly. And because this is so, because of this friendship, we know how much we still have to do together, our two countries— how much is still to be done.

We have discussed a number of problems today. You have mentioned some of them. We cannot live in a peaceful world unless we stand together, formally and resolutely. We are living in a world economically, socially, politically, where great demands are made on all of us, but particularly on the United States of America, and particularly on you, Mr. President. And all these principles and ideals by which you and the Americans are living are indivisible. No country, however great it may be, is any longer an end in itself. No country, however great it may be, is self-sufficient today. It is necessary today to rely on one's neighbor, to rely on one's friends. And that is one more reason why we have to get more closely together in order to make this world more peaceful.

I think this is a particularly appropriate idea in this Christmas season, which should inspire us with glad and happy hope.

Today and tomorrow we will have another opportunity to continue our talks, and I hope we will be able to bring our talks to fruitful conclusion, to fruitful results.

You, Mr. President, mentioned one particular project which is very close to my heart, and that is: How can the industrialized society of a highly developed country be given a new shape, a new form?

It is perhaps no accident that at the same time when you, Mr. President, developed your concept of the Great Society, I put forth another concept, that of the Formed Society.

It may be difficult here tonight to explain in detail what we have in mind with these two new concepts. But I think what we have in common, both of us, is the feeling that all the "isms" of the 19th century, be it capitalism, be it socialism, are no longer enough to solve the problems of today. These won't do any more. But what we require is something new.

These two concepts are perhaps not fully identical, but there is this common desire to create something new, which would not lead people astray but would make people live together with their neighbors, with their friends, would establish sound relationships between the people and their environments. And I would particularly welcome close cooperation between our two countries in this particular field, in developing these new concepts.

You also included, Mr. President, in the enumeration of subjects we discussed, cooperation in the field of space research. Of course, we, the Ger-

mans, would not like to get too close to the sun because we wouldn't like to burn our wings, but I think such ambitious plans would serve us well because it has been my experience that when you try to achieve only little things, you are very often bound to fail, but if you have a great objective, which will fascinate the imagination of the people, then you will very often succeed, because it arouses the enthusiasm, the support, and the imagination of the people.

Mr. President, we are also in agreement that we need integration, economic cooperation, a sound economy, sound currency, as a basis for our policies. This has become evident again and again in our talks, in our meetings. And this may perhaps constitute the real, the inherent value of the friendship of the alliance to which we both belong.

You also mentioned Viet-Nam, Mr. President. We know that the United States of America is making great sacrifices in Viet-Nam in order to defend the security of the people there. But that is also our security, and if you appreciated our contribution we are making to that effect, I must confess, quite frankly, I feel ashamed, because what we can contribute is very modest compared with what you do.

Mr. President, I am very proud of our friendship, and in going back to Germany, I'll tell the German people that the United States of America is a reliable ally.

You may be convinced that we, on the other hand, will also be ready not to betray this confidence and this trust. The measures and criteria may be different, but the spirit is identical: we must stand together; we must unite.

What would our future have been, what would our faith have been had not the United States and the Americans, in their generosity giving us hope after our collapse, had they not shown the way to us?

It is perhaps not only incidental that for the second time we have met in this Christmas season. Two years ago we had the pleasure of being your guest after Christmas at the ranch in Texas. Today, we are meeting here under the Christmas tree, so to speak, the shine of the candles. Christmas tree and candles—a symbol of peace, symbol of charity. In all we do, we should be inspired by these auspicious ideals.

If we have to undertake efforts in the military fields, some people may incline to believe that this would be an end in itself and that we wanted to disturb the peace. But this is not true. The fact that we are getting together in this Christmastime, that we are aware of the Christian ideals, is evidence to the contrary. Because we want to serve peace, we want to maintain peace, so that the old message, the tidings may come true—peace on earth and good will to men.

In this spirit, Mr. President, I wish you and Mrs. Johnson Merry Christmas and a Happy New Year.

Let me thank you once again for this wonderful reception, for this wonderful evening you have prepared for us here.

To your health, sir.

Chancellor Erhard had arrived at Andrews Air Force Base at 4 p.m. on Sunday, December 19, where he was greeted by Vice President Humphrey and other officials.

See also Item 660.

660   Joint Statement Following Discussions With Chancellor Erhard. *December 21, 1965*

PRESIDENT JOHNSON and Chancellor Erhard have completed 2 days of intensive, cordial, and candid conversations in Washington. They were accompanied by Secretaries Rusk, Fowler, and McNamara; Ministers Schroeder and von Hassel and other advisers. They discussed all major matters of joint concern to the United States and the Federal Republic of Germany and of general import for the free world.

The future of the Atlantic Alliance was a central topic in the conversation. The President and the Chancellor agreed that close political and military cooperation among the nations of NATO was necessary. They affirmed the determination of both Governments to maintain and to strengthen the alliance and its political and military institutions.

The President and the Chancellor gave close attention to the nuclear problems confronting the alliance. They agreed that the Federal Republic of Germany and other interested partners in the alliance should have an appropriate part in nuclear defense.

In this connection the Chancellor emphasized that the Federal Republic of Germany neither intended nor desired to acquire national control over nuclear weapons, that it had in 1954 given an undertaking to its allies not to produce such weapons in Germany, and that, finally, it is the only State in the world to have subjected itself to international supervision of such an obligation.

The President and the Chancellor noted with satisfaction that the Defense Ministers of a number of NATO countries have started discussions on the possibility of improving present nuclear arrangements within the alliance.

The President, after noting that the deterrent power of the alliance had proved completely effective and was being constantly modernized, stated the views of the United States that arrangements could be worked out to assure members of the alliance not having nuclear weapons an appropriate share in nuclear defense. The President and the Chancellor agreed that discussion of such arrangements be continued between the two countries and with other interested allies.

The President and the Chancellor were in agreement in upholding the principle of nonproliferation of nuclear weapons into the national control of states. They were of the view that alliance nuclear arrangements would not constitute proliferation of nuclear weapons and in fact should contribute to the goal of preventing the spread of nuclear weapons. They stressed the importance of continuing efforts to reduce the threat of war and bring about effective arms control.

The President and the Chancellor voiced mutual satisfaction at the arrangements worked out, and already successfully underway, between the United States Space Agency and the Germany Ministry of Scientific Research for a joint project to launch a German-built satellite to probe the inner radiation belt. The President suggested several other possible cooperative projects, including a probe to the Sun and a probe to Jupiter. He also indicated his intention to send a commission to Europe early in 1966 to consult with the German Government and other European governments which wish to join in the cooperative exploration of space.

The President and the Chancellor had an intensive exchange of views on the question of Germany's reunification. They reaffirm their strong determination to pursue all opportunities for attaining as soon as possible the common objective of the peaceful reunification of Germany on the basis of self-determination. The President and the Chancellor reject malicious allegations designed to cast doubt on the peaceful intentions of the Federal Republic of Germany. The exchange of views between the two Governments on the German problem and related questions will be continued.

The President and the Chancellor emphasized that pressures on Berlin would continue, as in the past, to be met with firmness and determination. They underlined that a lasting solution of the problems of Berlin can only be found in a peaceful solution of the German problem on the basis of self-determination.

The President and the Chancellor reaffirmed the view that a lasting relaxation of tension in Europe and in West-East relationships will require progress toward the peaceful reunification of Germany in freedom. Both leaders restated their intention to continue to seek improvement in relations with the nations of Eastern Europe. The Chancellor reaffirmed Germany's fundamental commitment to European unity and his confidence in the ability of the effective institutions already created to contribute to its achievement. The President assured the Chancellor that the United States remained convinced that a united Europe is important to the achievement of an effective Atlantic partnership.

The President and the Chancellor agreed that the successful conclusion of the Kennedy Round trade negotiations is of major importance to the progress of the free world, for developed and developing countries alike. They also agreed that, to attain their full promise, these historic negotiations must move forward as rapidly as possible with the active participation of the EEC.

Recent developments in other parts of the world, particularly in the Far East, were also examined. The President described the situation in Viet-Nam and the efforts of the Governments of South Viet-Nam and the United States, together with their allies, to bring about a peaceful and just settlement. He expressed his appreciation for the support of the Federal Republic of Germany in the struggle to deter Communist aggression against South Viet-Nam. The Chancellor stated the determination of his Government to continue to assist in this effort for the cause of freedom.

The President and the Chancellor reviewed the aid programs of their Governments and emphasized the great importance of effective aid to developing countries. In this connection, they noted that over 90 percent of all external resources flowing to these countries is provided by the free world. They agreed that there was need for increased effort on the part of developed countries to provide funds to assure that adequate levels of aid are maintained. At the same time, they emphasized the need for greater self-help by the developing countries. The

President was pleased to hear the Chancellor's description of the progress of the German Development Aid Service (German Peace Corps).

The President and the Chancellor welcomed the establishment of the Asian Development Bank, to which their Governments would make substantial contributions. They reemphasized the value of economic and social development in southeast Asia as a way of promoting peace in that region.

They also discussed the arrangements between the two Governments whereby United States military expenditures in Germany entering the balance of payments are offset by the Federal Republic through its purchase of United States military equipment and services. It was agreed that these arrangements were of great value to both Governments and should be fully executed and continued.

The President and the Chancellor discussed social developments in the United States and in Germany. They expressed the view that their concepts of the Great Society and the *Formierte Gesellschaft* have much in common and that a joint discussion of experiences should take place as soon as possible.

The President and the Chancellor agreed that the tradition and practice of effective consultation between their Governments—reflecting the friendship and trust which has grown up between the people of the United States and Germany—would lead to even closer and more fruitful relations in the future between the United States, the Federal Republic of Germany, and their partners.

NOTE: See also Item 659.

661 Memorandum to the Secretary of State on Export Sales of Surplus Agricultural Commodities to the United Arab Republic. *December 29, 1965*

Memorandum for the Secretary of State
Subject: Determination that Sale of Surplus Agricultural Commodities to the United Arab Republic is Essential to the National Interest

In accordance with your recommendation of 17 November, I hereby determine pursuant to Section 107 of the Agricultural Trade Development and Assistance Act of 1954, as amended, that it is essential to the national interest of the United States to finance export sales of surplus agricultural commodities to the United Arab Republic under title I of that Act.

LYNDON B. JOHNSON

NOTE: The memorandum was read by Joseph Laitin, an assistant press secretary, at his news conference at 4:20 p.m. on Wednesday, December 29, 1965, at Austin, Tex. It was not made public in the form of a White House press release.

662 Telegram to Senator Saltonstall Following His Announcement That He Would Not Seek Reelection. *December 31, 1965*

[Released December 31, 1965. Dated December 30, 1965]

I KNOW you are doing what you feel you must do from your personal standpoint, but I am compelled to say that you will be missed in the councils of Washington where your high purpose and great personal integrity have counted so much in the years you were here. I have been privileged to know you well and to serve with you in the Senate. Your friendship is one of the treasures I shall always value most devotedly.

LYNDON B. JOHNSON

[The Honorable Leverett Saltonstall, Smith Street, Dover, Massachusetts]

NOTE: The telegram was read by Joseph Laitin, an assistant press secretary, at his news conference at 10:25 a.m. on Friday, December 31, 1965, at Austin, Tex. It was not made public in the form of a White House press release.

663   Statement by the President on the Price Increase by the Bethlehem Steel Company.   *December 31, 1965*

THE Chairman of the Council of Economic Advisers has informed me that the Bethlehem Steel Company's response to his statement earlier today contains no information on the price increase that was not in its original press release and no justification for the action. This is a critical hour in our history and it is highly important for responsible representatives of this one steel company to meet with the President's Council of Economic Advisers right away. This is certainly no time for unwarranted price increases which can lead to inflation. It is the time to consider the larger national interest, to weigh the impact of unnecessary price action against the sacrifices of our men in VietNam, and to act accordingly.

NOTE: The statement was released at Austin, Tex.

*Appendix A—*White House Releases

NOTE: Includes releases covering matters with which the President was closely concerned, except announcements of personnel appointments and lists of public and private laws.

Releases relating to Proclamations and Executive orders have not been included. These documents are separately listed in Appendix B.

For list of Press Conferences, see subject index under "News conferences."

In many instances the White House issued advance releases of addresses or remarks which differ from the text as delivered. These have been noted in brackets, thus: [2 releases].

January

1 Message to the Finnish people on the centennial of the birth of Jean Sibelius

4 Annual message to the Congress on the State of the Union [2 releases]

6 White House announcement of the President's birthday gift to Carl Sandburg

6 Letter to Alice Roosevelt Longworth on the 46th anniversary of the death of Theodore Roosevelt

7 Remarks to a group of business leaders upon their return from a visit to Moscow [2 releases]

7 Special message to the Congress: "Advancing the Nation's Health"

7 Statement by the President on his message on the Nation's health

11 Remarks to the National Committee for International Development

12 Remarks of welcome at the White House to Prime Minister Sato of Japan

12 Special message to the Congress: "Toward Full Educational Opportunity"

12 Statement by the President on his message on education

12 Recorded remarks on the message on education [2 releases]

12 Remarks to the members of the U.S. Industrial Payroll Savings Committee [2 releases]

12 The President's toast at a dinner in honor of Prime Minister Sato

13 Special message to the Congress on immigration

January

13 Letter on the need for further savings in the procurement of office equipment for Federal agencies

13 Joint statement following meetings with the Prime Minister of Japan

13 Statement by the President on announcing photographic program "The President's Choice"

13 White House announcement of invitation to a group of artists and writers to be the President's guests at the inaugural ceremonies

14 Remarks upon presenting the Enrico Fermi Award to Admiral Rickover

14 Special message to the Congress on foreign aid

14 Letter to the President of the Senate and to the Speaker of the House on highways in the Nation's Capital

15 Letter to the President of the Senate and to the Speaker of the House on continuing the Agency for Arms Control and Disarmament

16 Remarks with Prime Minister Pearson upon signing U.S.-Canadian Trade Agreement on Automotive Products

16 Statement by the President reviewing the economic gains of 1964

16 Letter accepting resignation of Dr. Janet Travell as White House Physician

16 Letter accepting resignation of Meyer Feldman as Special Counsel to the President

16 Letter accepting resignation of Kenneth O'Donnell as Special Assistant to the President

16 Letter accepting resignation of David F. Powers as Special Assistant in the White House office

Appendix A

February

25 The President's questions at a briefing on Mariner 4 at the National Aeronautics and Space Administration

25 Remarks following a briefing at the National Aeronautics and Space Administration

26 Remarks to a group of Italian artists

26 Letter to the President of the Senate and to the Speaker of the House on the Peace Corps

28 Remarks recorded for the opening of the Red Cross campaign.

28 Letters in response to a report on equal opportunity in Federal farm programs

28 Statement by the President on the Neighborhood Youth Corps

March

1 Message to the Chancellor of Austria on the death of President Schaerf

1 Remarks to the winners of the Science Talent Search

1 Remarks before the National Conference on Educational Legislation

2 Special message to the Congress on the Nation's cities

2 White House announcement of supplemental appropriations request

2 Remarks at the Federal Woman's Award ceremony

2 Letter to the President of the Senate and to the Speaker of the House transmitting the national oceanographic program

2 Letter to the President of the Senate and to the Speaker of the House on Government use of automatic data processing equipment

3 Remarks at the unveiling of a portrait of Abraham Ribicoff

3 Remarks at the Smithsonian Institution's Museum of History and Technology

3 White House release on civilian employment in the executive branch

4 Statement by the President on the observance of International Cooperation Year

March

4 Letter to the President of the Senate and to the Speaker of the House on high-speed interurban ground transportation

4 Remarks at the swearing in of Buford Ellington as Director, Office of Emergency Planning

4 Statement by the President on his annual manpower report

5 Annual message to the Congress: The Manpower Report of the President

6 Excerpt from a letter thanking Nicholas G. Morgan, Sr., for a plate originally part of the Lincoln dinner service

8 Special message to the Congress on law enforcement and the administration of justice

8 White House announcement of forthcoming visit by the President of Upper Volta

8 White House statement on the war on poverty

9 Remarks upon signing the Appalachia bill

9 Statement by the President on the situation in Selma, Ala.

10 Statement by the President on the proposed National Foundation on the Arts and Humanities

12 White House announcement of plans for a White House Conference on Natural Beauty

15 White House announcement of supplemental appropriations request for Inter-American Development Bank

15 White House announcement of further supplemental appropriations request and amendments to 1966 budget

15 White House announcement of supplemental appropriations request for the District of Columbia

15 White House announcement of supplemental appropriations request for Appalachia

15 Special message to the Congress: The American Promise [2 releases]

15 Special message to the Congress on the right to vote

16 White House announcement of supplemental appropriations request

March

29 White House announcement concerning anti-poverty programs in the Nation's poorest counties

29 Remarks of welcome at the White House to President Yameogo of Upper Volta [2 releases]

29 Toasts of the President and President Yameogo of Upper Volta

29 Letter to the President of the Senate and to the Speaker of the House on the saline water conversion program

30 Joint statement following meetings with the President of Upper Volta

30 Statement by the President on the bombing of the U.S. Embassy in Saigon

30 White House announcement of amendment to 1966 budget

31 Letter accepting resignation of Douglas Dillon as Secretary of the Treasury

31 Letter to the President of the Senate and to the Speaker of the House on the auomotive products agreement with Canada

31 Letter to the President of the Senate and to the Speaker of the House on the proposed Public Works and Economic Development Act

31 Special message to the Congress on the food for peace program

31 Remarks to district directors of the Internal Revenue Service

April

1 Letter from Birmingham officials following the disarming of dynamite bombs

1 Letter to Senator Byrd following House reductions in the District of Columbia budget

1 Letter to the President of the Senate and to the Speaker of the House on the need for a new chancery in Saigon

1 Letters to the Secretaries of Labor and Commerce on the unemployment record for March

1 Statement by the President on the unemployment record for March

1 Remarks at a ceremony in observance of Cancer Control Month

April

1 Remarks at the swearing in of Henry H. Fowler as Secretary of the Treasury

1 Statement by the President following Senate subcommittee approval of the education bill

1 White House announcement of amendment to budget for the Bureau of Reclamation

1 White House announcement of request for progress report on the natural beauty program

1 Letter accepting resignation of Everett Hutchinson from the Interstate Commerce Commission

2 Remarks at the dedication of the Carl Vinson Hearing Room in the Rayburn House Office Building

2 Remarks at the retirement ceremony of Gen. John K. Gerhart, USAF [2 releases]

2 Remarks at a ceremony in honor of Stephen Addiss and William E. Crofut II [2 releases]

2 Letter to Representative Moss stating administration policy as to claims of "executive privilege"

3 Letters relating to the disarming of bombs in Birmingham by members of an Army unit

3 Remarks with Prime Minister Pearson to the press at Camp David

3 Statement by the President upon appointing a committee to review the closing of veterans hospitals

5 Statement by the President on savings by American families during 1964

5 Further statement by the President on unemployment during March

5 White House announcement of order permitting Federal Reserve inspection of returns under Interest Equalization Tax Act

5 White House announcement concerning first meeting of the National Council on the Arts

5 Statement by the President upon appointing new members of the Science Advisory Committee

5 White House announcement of members of Special Presidential Committee on U.S. Trade Relations with Eastern European Countries and the U.S.S.R.

Appendix A

Appendix A

May

1 Statement by the President on the OAS mission to the Dominican Republic

1 Statement by the President on the new speed records set by the United States Air Force

1 Statement by the President in response to a progress report by the Antarctic Policy Group

2 Radio and television report to the American people on the situation in the Dominican Republic

3 Summary of reports by State highway departments on the roadside beautification program

3 White House announcement of results of survey on roadside clutter

3 White House announcement of U.S. delegation to 18th World Health Assembly

3 Remarks at a ceremony honoring physical fitness winners

3 Remarks to the 10th National Legislative Conference, Building and Construction Trades Department, AFL–CIO

3 Statement by the President on approving a program to find summer jobs for young people

3 White House announcement of plans to expedite tax refunds for Armed Forces personnel serving in Viet-Nam

3 Statement by the President announcing grants to four universities under the Science Development Program

3 Statement by the President on making public a report of the Council of Economic Advisers on steel prices

4 Letter from General Eisenhower in support of the President's conduct of foreign relations

4 Remarks to committee members on the need for additional appropriations for military purposes in Viet-Nam and the Dominican Republic

4 Remarks of Representatives Rivers and Mahon at the conclusion of the President's remarks to committee members

4 Remarks upon presenting Distinguished Service Medal to Adm. Harold Page Smith

4 Citation accompanying Distinguished Service Medal awarded to Adm. Harold Page Smith

May

4 Special message to the Congress requesting additional appropriations for military needs in Viet-Nam

4 Remarks at a dinner meeting of the Texas Electric Cooperatives, Inc.

5 Remarks upon presenting a social security check to the 20-millionth beneficiary

6 Remarks at the presentation of lifesaver medals to 13 members of school safety patrols

6 Letter to Mary McGrory reappointing her to the Distinguished Civilian Service Awards Board

6 Letters on the need for a unified and flexible foreign affairs personnel system

7 Report to the President by the Special Committee on U.S. Trade Relations with East European Countries and the Soviet Union

7 Remarks upon signing resolution making appropriations for military requirements in Viet-Nam [2 releases]

7 Remarks broadcast on the 20th anniversary of V–E Day [2 releases]

7 White House announcement concerning forthcoming White House Conference on Natural Beauty

8 Remarks by telephone for the dedication of the Sam Rayburn Dam in Texas [2 releases]

8 Remarks in the Capitol at the presentation of the Veritas Medal to the Speaker of the House of Representatives

8 Greetings telephoned to President Truman on the occasion of his 81st birthday

8 Statement by the President on the work performed in disaster areas by members of the Neighborhood Youth Corps

8 Statement by the President on the need for a review of policy-making positions in the executive branch

9 Statement by the President upon issuing order prescribing standards of ethical conduct for Government officers and employees

10 White House announcement of Labor Department report on the job outlook for 1965 college graduates

May

10 White House announcements concerning the Equal Opportunity Commission

11 White House announcement concerning the Advisory Commission on Intergovernmental Relations

11 Remarks upon signing proclamation adding Ellis Island to the Liberty Island National Monument

11 White House release on the Ellis Island proclamation

11 Remarks to the National Association of Home Builders

12 Special message to the Congress on increasing Federal military and civilian pay rates

12 Statement by the President on the Appalachian region highway construction program

13 Address to members of the Association of American Editorial Cartoonists: The Challenge of Human Need in Viet-Nam [2 releases]

13 Special message to the Congress transmitting Reorganization Plan 2 of 1965: Environmental Science Services Administration

13 Remarks to the National Review Board for the East-West Center

13 Statement to the President on the Department of Agriculture's "War on Waste"

13 Cabinet report from the Secretary of the Treasury: The Balance of Payments Program and the Congress

13 Cabinet report from the Chairman, Civil Service Commission: Improving Communications and Contacts with the Public

14 Memorandum on the budget preview and program planning for fiscal year 1967

14 Cabinet report from the Secretary of Health, Education, and Welfare: Progress Report, Implementation of Title VI of the Civil Rights Act

14 Cabinet report from the Secretary of Commerce: Increased Efficiency in Patent Office Operations

14 Cabinet report from the Administrator of General Services: Architectural Standards for Federal Buildings

May

14 White House announcement of request for additional funds for crime control in the District of Columbia

14 Remarks to members of the American Association of School Administrators

15 Remarks upon announcing plans to reduce excise taxes [2 releases]

15 Statement by the President on the minting of silver dollars

15 Further statement by the President on the OAS mission to the Dominican Republic

16 Report by Council of Economic Advisers: The Longest Expansion in Peacetime History

17 Remarks of welcome at the White House to the President of Korea [2 releases]

17 Special message to the Congress recommending reduction of excise taxes and increases in user charges

17 White House announcement of budget amendment for the Coast Guard

17 Toasts of the President and President Chung Hee Park of Korea

18 Joint statement following discussions with the President of Korea

18 Special message to the Congress on labor

18 White House announcement concerning the Head Start program

18 Remarks on Project Head Start [2 releases]

18 Remarks to the winners of the Hearst Foundation journalism awards

18 Statement by the President on making public a memorandum on the appropriation for military needs in Viet-Nam

18 Statements by the President on announcing U.S. support for an international program to eradicate smallpox

18 Announcement of selection of panelists to participate in the White House Conference on Natural Beauty

19 Remarks at the presentation of the National Civil Service League's Career Service awards

May

19 Letter in response to report on the second national conference of Federal Executive Board Chairman

20 Remarks following a meeting with members of the Antarctic Policy Group

20 Letter in response to report on U.S. Trade Relations with East European Countries and the Soviet Union

20 Memorandum on "June Buying" by Federal departments and agencies

21 Announcement of joint meteorological research activities, U.S.-Argentina

21 Statement by the President on announcing the Youth Opportunity Campaign

23 Announcement of forthcoming presentation of Small Businessman of the Year award

23 Memorandum on announcing the names of recipients of the President's Award for Distinguished Federal Civilian Service

24 Remarks at the presentation of the Small Businessman of the Year award

24 Message to the Congress transmitting sixth annual report on weather modification

24 Statement by the President upon signing bill to carry out U.S. obligations under the International Coffee Agreement

24 Letter to Adlai Stevenson approving appointments to the Board of Trustees, Eleanor Roosevelt Memorial Foundation

24 Statement by the President on cost reduction by the Government during the first three months of 1965

25 Letter to the President of the Senate and to the Speaker of the House on the Federal Water Resources Research Program

25 Statement by the President upon signing bill authorizing a new Embassy in Saigon

25 Remarks to the delegates to the White House Conference on Natural Beauty [2 releases]

26 Statement by the President following passage by the Senate of the voting rights bill

26 Letter to the President of the Senate and to the Speaker of the House transmitting bills to improve highway beauty

May

26 Remarks at a military reception on the White House lawn

27 Special message to the Congress transmitting Reorganization Plan 3 of 1965: Locomotive Inspection

27 Special message to the Congress transmitting Reorganization Plan 4 of 1965: Abolition of Certain Committees, Councils, and Boards

27 Special message to the Congress transmitting Reorganizattion Plan 5 of 1965: National Science Foundation

27 Announcement of budget amendment for disaster relief

27 Remarks at the signing of the bill extending the Arms Control and Disarmament Act

28 Remarks at the unveiling of the President's portrait in the Texas State Capitol [2 releases]

28 Commencement address at Baylor University [2 releases]

30 Letter accepting resignation of Dr. Stafford L. Warren as Special Assistant to the President for Mental Retardation

30 Anouncements concerning the selection of the Presidential Scholars of 1965 [2 releases]

30 Statement by the President on announcing the winners of the 1965 Presidential Safety Awards

31 Statement by the President on Defense Department actions in support of the war on poverty

June

1 Announcement of reductions in overseas civilian employment

1 Announcement of reduction in Federal civilian employment

1 Remarks at the commencement exercises of the National Cathedral School [2 releases]

1 Remarks at a swearing-in ceremony for several Government officials

1 Statement by the President announcing the calling of a White House Conference on Education

1 Statement by the President and letter on the agreement on the importation of educational, scientific, and cultural materials

1179

June

1 Statement by the President on the 20th anniversary commemorative session of the U.N. General Assembly

1 Statement by the President on the distribution of food and medical supplies in the Dominican Republic

1 Statement by the President upon ordering the withdrawal of Marines from the Dominican Republic

1 Statement by the President on the need for additional foreign aid funds for southeast Asia

1 Special message to the Congress on the need for additional foreign aid funds for southeast Asia

1 Announcement of forthcoming White House Conference on Education

2 Letter accepting resignation of Kermit Gordon as Director, Bureau of the Budget

2 Announcement concerning presentation of President's Award for Distinguished Federal Civilian Service

2 Remarks at the presentation of the President's Award for Distinguished Federal Civilian Service

3 Special message to the Congress proposing changes in the coinage system

3 Remarks on the Youth Opportunity Campaign [2 releases]

3 Remarks in Chicago at the Cook County Democratic Party dinner [2 releases]

4 Joint statement following discussions with Chancellor Erhard

4 Commencement address at Howard University: "To Fulfill These Rights" [2 releases]

6 Commencement address at Catholic University [2 releases]

7 Announcement of "The President's Choice" photograph for May

7 Announcement of budget amendments for the Corps of Engineers and the Bureau of Reclamation

7 Announcement of budget amendment for construction of a new chancery in Saigon

June

7 The President's toast at a luncheon in honor of Sir Robert Menzies, Prime Minister of Australia

7 Telephone conversation between the President and Astronauts James McDivitt and Edward White

8 Remarks at the signing of the bill providing for a National Technical Institute for the Deaf

8 Remarks to the Presidential Scholars

8 Announcement of a special Neighborhood Youth Corps summer program in New York City as part of the Youth Opportunity Campaign

9 Remarks to the members of the Iowa Trade Mission

9 Remarks to winners of a contest sponsored by the National Rural Electric Cooperative Association

10 Message to the Congress transmitting annual report of the Office of Alien Property

11 Remarks in Houston at the NASA Manned Spacecraft Center

12 Statement by the President following a review of agency compliance with his memorandum on "June buying"

12 Statement by the President on extending the automated merchant vessel report system to the Pacific coast

12 Statement by the President on rate reductions by the rural electric cooperatives

12 Announcement of appointment of members of the Consumer Advisory Council

13 White House announcement following a review of income tax returns by the Internal Revenue Service

13 White House announcement of the signing of a military procurement bill

14 Remarks at the White House Festival of the Arts [2 releases]

15 Remarks to a delegation from the American Institute of Architects and the Pan American Congress of Architects

15 Remarks at the graduation ceremony of the school for Capitol page boys

June

17 Remarks at the signing of the Pacific Northwest Disaster Relief Act

17 Remarks at the presentation of NASA Exceptional Service awards following the flight of Gemini 4 [2 releases]

17 Statement by the President on cease-fire violations in the Dominican Republic

17 Statement by the President following House approval of bill establishing a Department of Urban Affairs

17 Statement by the President announcing reduction in number of areas of "substantial unemployment"

17 Statement by the President announcing a reduction in the anticipated budget deficit

17 Statement by the President on the Government's part in reducing the balance of payments deficit

17 Statement by the President following passage of the excise tax bill

17 Statement by the President on announcing resignation of Secretary of the Army Stephen Ailes

17 Statement by the President on announcing resignation of Under Secretary of the Navy Kenneth E. BeLieu

17 Remarks at a ceremony in the State Department Auditorium in honor of the Gemini 4 astronauts

17 Memorandum from the Chairman, Atomic Energy Commission

17 Announcement concerning the level of civilian employment in the executive branch

18 Council of Economic Advisers' report covering the growth pattern in May

18 Cabinet report from the Secretary of Health, Education, and Welfare: Reorganization of the Office of Education

18 Cabinet report from the Administrator, Housing and Home Finance Agency: FHA Mortgage and Loan Insurance

18 Remarks to White House correspondents following a meeting of the Cabinet

June

18 The President's statement to the Cabinet following passage of the excise tax reductions

18 Remarks at a ceremony marking the progress of the Neighborhood Youth Corps

19 The President's statement to the Cabinet on Project Head Start

19 Announcement of plans for an extended summer recreation program in the District of Columbia

20 Announcement of a pilot school lunch program in Bogotá, Colombia

20 Cabinet report from the Administrator, NASA, on the Gemini 3 and Gemini 4 accomplishments

20 The President's statement to the Cabinet on approving new guidelines for employee health service programs

20 Statement by the President on announcing an international meeting on water desalting

21 Summary of Secretary Rusk's report to the Cabinet on strengthening the Foreign Service Institute

21 Report to the Cabinet from the Chairman, AEC, on exchanges with the Soviet Union on peaceful uses of atomic energy

21 Remarks at the signing of the excise tax reduction bill [2 releases]

21 Statement by the President on the death of Bernard Baruch

22 Letter accepting resignation of Donald M. Wilson as Deputy Director, USIA

22 Announcement of budget amendments for the Department of Agriculture

22 Announcement of budget amendments for the Interoceanic Canal Commission

23 Announcement of supplemental appropriations request for the Department of Labor

23 Letter to the Secretary, Smithsonian Institution, on the transfer to the Institution of the original Corcoran Gallery of Art

23 Letter accepting resignation of Stephen Ailes as Secretary of the Army

June

23 Letter accepting resignation of Kenneth E. BeLieu as Under Secretary of the Navy

24 Announcement of supplemental appropriations request for new National Technical Institute for the Deaf and new Administration on Aging

24 Remarks at the Democratic Congressional Dinner in the Washington Hilton Hotel [2 releases]

24 Remarks at the Democratic Congressional Dinner in the D.C. Armory [2 releases]

25 Address in San Francisco at the 20th Anniversary Commemorative Session of the United Nations [2 releases]

27 Memorandum directing full use by Federal agencies of the ZIP Code system

28 Remarks at a ceremony marking the first commercial communication satellite service

28 Remarks at the White House Fellows ceremony

28 Announcement concerning the White House Fellows ceremony

28 Letter accepting resignation of Dr. Eugene G. Fubini as Assistant Secretary of Defense

29 Remarks to the YMCA Youth Governors Conference

30 Remarks at the presentation of the Young American Medals

30 Statement by the President following passage of the housing bill by the House of Representatives

30 Statement by the President upon signing bill limiting duty-free imports by tourists

30 Announcement concerning order consolidating previous delegations of authority to the Bureau of the Budget

30 Letter accepting resignation of Najeeb E. Halaby as Administrator, Federal Aviation Agency

July

1 Remarks at the swearing in of General McKee as Administrator, Federal Aviation Agency

1 Announcement of resignation of Thomas K. Finletter as Ambassador and U.S. Representative to NATO

July

2 Letter accepting resignation of John M. Kelly as Assistant Secretary of the Interior

2 Remarks before the National Education Association [2 releases]

3 Remarks at the swearing in of Homer Thornberry as Judge, U.S. Court of Appeals, Fifth Circuit

3 Statement by the President on ordering further withdrawal of U.S. forces from the Dominican Republic

3 Announcement of establishment of an Advisory Committee on International Monetary Arrangements

4 Announcement of appointment of additional members to the Citizens' Advisory Council on the Status of Women

4 Statement by the President on announcing U.S. participation in the International Agency for Research on Cancer

4 Announcement of opening of White House summer seminar for students

4 Statement by the President on announcing a mission to consider U.S. cooperation in establishing a Korean Institute for Industrial Technology and Applied Science

5 Letter accepting resignation of John C. Bullitt as U.S. Executive Director, International Bank for Reconstruction and Development

5 Announcement of resignation of Charles J. Hitch as Assistant Secretary of Defense (Comptroller)

7 Letter accepting resignation of Dr. Leona Baumgartner as Assistant Administrator, Agency for International Development

7 Remarks at the swearing in of LeRoy Collins as Under Secretary of Commerce

8 Remarks upon signing World Law Day proclamation

8 Announcement concerning agenda of forthcoming White House Conference on Education

9 Statement by the President following passage of the Medicare bill by the Senate

July

10 Statement by the President following passage of the voting rights bill by the House of Representatives

10 Reports to the President on the first year's progress under the Civil Rights Act

10 Announcement following Eugene Black's report to the President on his trip to southeast Asia

10 Announcement of resignation of Maj. Gen. C. V. Clifton as Military Aide to the President

10 Letter accepting resignation of Maj. Gen. C. V. Clifton as Military Aide to the President

10 Announcement of resignation of Eugene M. Zuckert as Secretary of the Air Force

10 Letter accepting resignation of Carl T. Rowan as Director, United States Information Agency

11 Letter to the President of the Senate and to the Speaker of the House transmitting a report on the development of the Passamaquoddy-St. John River Basin

11 Letter accepting resignation of Eugene M. Zuckert as Secretary of the Air Force

11 Letter accepting resignation of James A. Reed as Assistant Secretary of the Treasury

12 Memorandum following release of the Labor Department's employment figures for June

12 White House statement on the report on U.S.-Canadian relations prepared jointly by Ambassadors Livingston Merchant and A. D. P. Heeney

12 Report to the President on the operations of the Small Business Administration

13 Letter accepting resignation of Archibald Cox as Solicitor General

14 Remarks at the signing of the Older Americans Act [2 releases]

14 Statement by the President on hearing of the death of Adlai Stevenson

14 Remarks at a luncheon for members of the Joint U.S.-Japan Committee on Trade and Economic Affairs

14 Remarks intended for delivery at a luncheon for members of the Japanese Cabinet

July

14 Statement by the President on the death of Adlai Stevenson [2 releases]

14 Remarks to the National Rural Electric Cooperative Association

14 Statement by the President on requesting the Water Resources Council to take steps to meet the northeastern drought

14 Exchange of messages with the Secretary General of the United Nations

14 Announcement of appropriations request for the Corps of Engineers flood emergency program

14 Memorandum on cost reduction by Federal agencies

15 Remarks at the signing of the drug abuse control amendments bill

15 Remarks to members of Federal agency task forces on cost reduction

15 Letter to Mrs. Francis A. Cherry on the death of her husband

16 Letter accepting resignation of Marjorie M. Lawson as Associate Judge, D.C. Juvenile Court

16 Statement by the President following a meeting on the Dominican situation

16 Statement by the President following a meeting with the Advisory Committee on International Monetary Arrangements

16 Remarks on crime control at the signing of the District of Columbia appropriations bill

16 Announcement of appointment of members of the President's Commission on Crime in the District of Columbia

17 Letter concerning the issuance of a commemorative stamp marking the 700th anniversary of the birth of Dante Alighieri

17 Letter to the President of the Senate and to the Speaker of the House on the proposed teaching professions bill

17 Remarks on the proposed teaching professions bill [2 releases]

20 Remarks upon announcing the nomination of Arthur J. Goldberg as U.S. Representative to the United Nations [2 releases]

July

20 Remarks at the swearing in of Rear Adm. John Harllee and James V. Day as Chairman and Vice Chairman, Federal Maritime Commission

20 Remarks to the American Field Service students on the eve of their departure from the United States

20 Report by the Secretary of Agriculture on aid to drought stricken areas

20 Letter to the Postmaster General requesting the issuance of an Adlai Stevenson commemorative stamp

21 Report by the Secretary of Agriculture on economic opportunity programs in rural areas

21 Remarks to the delegates to the White House Conference on Education [2 releases]

22 Remarks at the signing of the Water Resources Planning Act

22 Remarks to the British Ambassador at the Magna Carta anniversary ceremony

22 Message to the Congress transmitting annual report of the Commodity Credit Corporation

22 Remarks to the members of the World Press Institute

23 Memorandum in response to a report on the new Executive Seminar Center

23 Announcement concerning the membership of the President's Commission on the Patent System

23 Remarks at the signing of the Coinage Act

23 Letter accepting resignation of Dr. Roy J. Heffernan as Chairman, National Committee on Selection of Doctors, Dentists, and Allied Specialists

24 Letter from the Postmaster General concerning plans for an Adlai E. Stevenson commemorative stamp

24 Announcement of report on women employed in the postal service

24 Effect of excise tax reduction on consumer prices; first report by the Council of Economic Advisers

24 Letter to the members of the President's Commission on Crime in the District of Columbia

July

25 Report by the Secretary of Health, Education, and Welfare on preparations for administering the Medicare program

26 Announcement of establishment of the President's Commission on Law Enforcement and Administration of Justice

26 Statement by the President on establishing the President's Commission on Law Enforcement and Administration of Justice

26 Announcement of report from the Secretary of the Treasury on savings under management improvement program

26 Remarks at the swearing in of Arthur J. Goldberg as U.S. Representative to the United Nations

26 Announcement of report from the Secretary of the Interior on industrial development on Indian reservations

26 Statement by the President upon announcing a White House Conference on Equal Employment Opportunities

27 Remarks on announcing the nominations of Anthony J. Celebrezze as Judge, U.S. Court of Appeals, Sixth Circuit, and of John W. Gardner as Secretary of Health, Education, and Welfare

27 Message of greetings to the Geneva Disarmament Conference Committee

28 Remarks at the Department of Defense cost reduction awards ceremony

28 Statement by the President: the Nation's Goals in Viet-Nam

28 Letter accepting resignation of Anthony J. Celebrezze as Secretary of Health, Education, and Welfare

28 Letter to the Secretary General of the United Nations expressing confidence in Ambassador Goldberg and emphasizing U.S. willingness to negotiate on Viet-Nam

29 Remarks upon viewing new Mariner 4 pictures from Mars

29 Remarks on the status of women in America

29 Letter accepting resignation of Judge Russell E. Train from the Tax Court of the United States

29 Announcement of annual report of Board of Visitors, U.S. Naval Academy

Appendix A

10 Telegram to General Eisenhower on the 91st anniversary of the birth of Herbert Hoover

10 Remarks at the signing of the Housing and Urban Development Act

10 Statement by the President in response to reports on the Federal-State program of vocational rehabilitation

10 Letter accepting resignation of Dr. Luther L. Terry as Surgeon General, U.S. Public Health Service

10 Announcement of Presidential directive facilitating entry into the United States of Mexican nationals

11 Report on the career status of returned Peace Corps volunteers

11 Remarks at the signing of the Saline Water Conversion Act

11 Remarks at a meeting of the Water Emergency Conference

11 Remarks to the members of the See the U.S.A. Committee

12 Remarks at the signing of the bill establishing the Herbert Hoover National Historic Site

12 Remarks at the swearing in of Henry Cabot Lodge as Ambassador to South Viet-Nam

12 Report by the Secretary of the Air Force on the Titan II missile silo disaster at Searcy, Ark.

13 Announcement of appropriations request for the Northeastern drought emergency

13 Excerpt of letter to the members of the President's Commission on Law Enforcement and the Administration of Justice

13 Message to the President of Korea on learning of plans to dispatch Korean troops to South Viet-Nam

13 Statement by the President on announcing plans for the White House Conference on Health

13 Announcement by the Secretary of the Interior of order restricting billboards or advertising displays on public lands adjacent to highways

13 Report by the Acting Secretary of Health, Education, and Welfare on job-training for public assistance recipients

13 Memorandum from the Attorney General reporting on activities of the Civil Division, Department of Justice

14 Report by the Chairman, Civil Service Commission, on voter registration in Alabama, Louisiana, and Mississippi

14 Announcement of allocation of work-study grants to college students from low-income families

15 Statement by the President commemorating the 30th anniversary of the signing of the Social Security Act

15 Statement by the President following the restoration of order in Los Angeles

15 Statement by the President on the ratification by Korea of the Basic Relations Treaty with Japan

16 Announcement of a grant to Hadassah University Hospital in Israel

16 Statement by the President on the need for industry-wide procedures to settle manning disputes on automated ships

17 Remarks at a ceremony commemorating the fourth anniversary of the Alliance for Progress [2 releases]

17 Statement by the President on the draft treaty to prevent the spread of nuclear weapons

17 Exchange of messages with the President of Chile concerning U.S. assistance in the Chilean flood disaster

18 Exchange of messages with Prime Minister Pearson on the 25th anniversary of the Canada-U.S. Permanent Joint Board on Defense

18 Remarks at the swearing in of Dr. John W. Gardner as Secretary of Health, Education, and Welfare

18 Remarks at a conference on the water crisis in the Northeastern States

18 Text of Elements of Agreement on Federal, State, and municipal action in the water crisis

18 Report by the Secretary of Agriculture on rental housing for senior citizens in rural areas

18 Second report by Council of Economic Advisers on excise tax reduction and consumer prices

Appendix A

1187

August

29 Statement by the President on the Gemini 5 achievement

29 Statement by the President announcing the end of the shipping strike

29 Statement by the President following a review of foreign affairs with the Secretary of State

29 Advance text of remarks upon announcing the appointment of John A. Gronouski as Ambassador to Poland

29 Advance text of remarks upon announcing the appointment of Lawrence F. O'Brien as Postmaster General

30 Letter to Secretary General U Thant at the Second United Nations World Population Conference in Belgrade

30 Announcement of Dr. Howard Rusk's mission to Viet-Nam

30 Report by the Secretary of Commerce on future motor vehicle needs

30 Statement by the President on the role of the National Export Expansion Council

30 Announcement concerning the White House Conference on Health

30 Televised statement by the President announcing postponement of a shutdown in the steel industry [2 releases]

31 Remarks on announcing plans to extend Project Head Start [2 releases]

31 Announcement of apportionment of funds for highways in or near national forests

31 Announcement concerning retroactive social security benefits

31 Remarks at the swearing in of Leonard Marks as Director, United States Information Agency [2 releases]

31 Statement by the President following a meeting with Dr. Howard Rusk on health and welfare needs in South Viet-Nam

31 Announcement of policy for the promotion and decoration of astronauts

31 Announcement of free mail privileges for members of the Armed Forces in Viet-Nam

August

31 Announcement of cost-of-living increase in Armed Forces retirement pay

31 Statement by the President reviewing progress in the desegregation of schools

September

1 Announcement of seminar to study health problems of coal miners

1 Announcement of forthcoming International Congress on Air Technology

1 Remarks at the signing of a bill establishing the Delaware Water Gap National Recreation Area

1 Statement by the President on the agreement to form a new government in the Dominican Republic

1 Statement by the President on the contributions made by the Organization of American States to the Dominican agreement [2 releases]

1 Telegram to Dr. Albert Schweitzer

1 Statement by the President on the signing of the Labor, HEW, and related agencies appropriations bill

1 Statement by the President on the appointment of Gen. Maxwell D. Taylor as Special Consultant to the President

2 Remarks at the signing of a bill authorizing the Auburn-Folsom Project, California [2 releases]

2 Remarks at the swearing in of Charles R. Simpson as Judge, Tax Court of the United States

2 Announcement of report to the President on U.S. volunteers for duty in Viet-Nam

2 Announcement of report to the President on job-training opportunities under the Vocational Rehabilitation Act

2 Announcement of allocation of funds to establish a Center for Urban Education in New York City

2 Announcement of progress report by the special Presidential task force for Los Angeles

2 Statement by the President following passage by the Senate of the higher education bill

Appendix A

Appendix A

September

13 Statement by the President to the Cabinet on cost reduction programs by civilian agencies

13 Examples of cost reduction actions by civilian agencies

13 Report to the President following Secretary Fowler's exchange of views with European leaders on international monetary matters

14 Remarks at the signing of the State Technical Services Act [2 releases]

14 Statement by the President to the Cabinet and memorandum on strengthening academic capability for science [2 releases]

15 Letter accepting resignation of Richard N. Goodwin as Special Assistant to the President

15 Letter accepting resignation of Horace Busby, Jr., as Special Assistant to the President

15 Remarks at a meeting with the Congressional Fellows

16 Remarks to the delegates to the Conference on World Peace Through Law [2 releases]

16 Message to the Shah of Iran on the 25th anniversary of his reign

16 Statement by the President upon signing the Military Construction Authorization Act

16 Remarks at the Smithson Bicentennial Celebration [2 releases]

17 Announcement concerning the Peace Corps National Advisory Council

17 Announcement of estimated personal income for August

18 Letter accepting resignation of Hobart Taylor, Jr., as Associate Counsel to the President and as Executive Vice Chairman, President's Committee on Equal Employment Opportunity

20 Message to Chancellor Erhard on his victory in the German elections

21 Remarks at the signing of a bill establishing the Assateague Island Seashore National Park

21 Memorandum for the President reporting on the progress of the job development program

September

21 Memorandum for the President on the relationship of education to employment

21 Statement by the President on Federal grants for academic research

21 Message to the ninth general conference of the International Atomic Energy Agency

22 Statement by the President on the cease-fire agreements by India and Pakistan

22 Memorandum to Federal agencies on voluntary blood donations

22 Statement by the President following the signing of law enforcement assistance bills

22 Third report to the President on excise tax reduction and consumer prices

23 Remarks after signing bill providing funds for programs under the Elementary and Secondary Education Act [2 releases]

23 Announcement of allocation of funds under the Elementary and Secondary Education Act

23 Statement by the President upon signing bill extending the incentive awards program to members of the Armed Forces

23 Remarks to members of the board of directors of the International Association of Lions Clubs [2 releases]

24 Memorandum from the Vice President recommending reassignment of civil rights functions

24 Memorandum on reassignment of civil rights functions

24 Remarks on announcing intention to nominate Dr. William H. Stewart as Surgeon General, Public Health Service

24 Statement by the President on the progress of treaty negotiations with Panama [2 releases]

28 Statement by the President following the signing of the United Nations Participation Act Amendments

29 Remarks at the signing of the arts and humanities bill [2 releases]

29 Special message to the Senate transmitting income tax protocol, U.S.-Germany

September

29 Announcement of report to the President on diseases of children and young people

30 Remarks at the signing of the High-Speed Ground Transportation Act [2 releases]

30 Message to the Congress transmitting eighth annual report on U.S. participation in the International Atomic Energy Agency

30 Letter to the President of the Senate and the Speaker of the House on the Pennsylvania Avenue National Historic Site

30 Remarks upon accepting the Charles B. Stillman award for outstanding service to education

30 Statement by the President in response to report on the Federal incentive awards program

October

1 Remarks at the annual meeting of the World Bank and the International Monetary Fund [2 releases]

1 Announcement concerning the assignments of the first group of White House Fellows

1 Statement by the President upon signing bill relating to war orphans' educational assistance allowance

2 Remarks at the signing of the Water Quality Act of 1965

2 Letter authorizing the Secretary of Health, Education, and Welfare to undertake a joint United States-Japan medical research program

2 Announcement of joint United States-Japan medical research program

2 Statement by the President making public a joint report on natural beauty in America

3 Remarks at the signing of the immigration bill, Liberty Island, N.Y. [2 releases]

4 Announcement of agreement with Mexico for a joint saline water feasibility study

4 Statement by the President welcoming the delegates to the First International Symposium on Water Desalination

5 Statement by the President concerning the White House Conference "To Fulfill These Rights"

October

5 Statement by the President announcing that he would undergo surgery

5 Statement of procedures for use in the event of Presidential inability

6 Remarks at the signing of the Heart Disease, Cancer, and Stroke Amendments of 1965 [2 releases]

6 Message to the Congress transmitting annual report on the international educational and cultural exchange program

6 Message to the Congress transmitting second annual report on special international exhibitions

6 Remarks to officials and chambers of commerce representatives of the Appalachian region of Tennessee

7 Remarks at the signing of the water and sanitation systems in rural areas bill [2 releases]

7 Remarks at the signing of proclamation "White Cane Safety Day, 1965" [2 releases]

7 Remarks upon signing proclamation "National Day of Prayer, 1965" [2 releases]

7 Remarks to the delegates to the First International Symposium on Water Desalination [2 releases]

7 Announcement of plans for the Salute to Congress

7 Remarks at the President's Salute to Congress

8 Announcement of request for supplemental appropriations

9 Statement by the President upon signing bill relating to concession rights in national parks

9 Messages to Mary Martin and the cast of "Hello Dolly" on tour in Viet-Nam

11 Prepared text of remarks for the President's Salute to Congress

11 Statement by the President: General Pulaski's Memorial Day

11 Statement by the President: Columbus Day, 1965

13 Message to the Congress transmitting ninth annual report on the trade agreements program

Appendix A

November

1 Statement by the President upon signing the School Disaster Aid Act

1 Message concerning U.S. participation in the Buenos Aires meeting of the Inter-American Economic and Social Council

2 Message to the White House Conference on Health

3 Remarks at the LBJ Ranch at the swearing in of John A. Gronouski as Ambassador to Poland

3 Remarks at the post office, Hye, Tex., at the swearing in of Lawrence F. O'Brien as Postmaster General

4 Statement by the President upon signing the Food and Agriculture Act of 1965

4 Announcement of first allocation of funds to States under the highway beautification program

4 Statement by the President on the unemployment rate during October

5 Statement by the President upon signing bills authorizing release of zinc and nickel from the national stockpiles

5 Statement by the President upon signing bill authorizing the sale or loan of warships to friendly powers

5 Telegram from New York Mayor-elect John V. Lindsay

6 Statement by the President on the agreement covering movement of Cuban refugees to the United States

6 Announcement and text of notes establishing procedures for the movement of Cuban refugees to the U.S.

6 Statement by the Chairman, Council of Economic Advisers, on the increases in aluminum prices

6 Statement by the Secretary of the Treasury on the need for releasing stockpiled aluminum

6 Statement by the Secretary of Defense on proposed formulas for disposing of stockpiled aluminum

6 Statement by the President in response to Science Advisory Committee report on pollution of air, soil, and waters

November

8 Remarks at Southwest Texas State College upon signing the Higher Education Act of 1965 [2 releases]

8 Summary of major provisions of Higher Education Act of 1965

8 Statement by the President following the signing of bills providing for duty-free entry of scientific instruments

8 Statement by the President upon signing the Southeast Hurricane Disaster Relief Act of 1965

9 Telegram to General Eisenhower wishing him an early recovery

9 Memorandum concerning the power failure in the Northeastern United States

11 Statement by the President: American Education Week

11 Statement by the President on approving the appointment of members of the Health Insurance Benefits Advisory Council

13 Announcement of new program for the economic development of qualified distressed areas

16 Memorandums on the need for coordinating the practices of Federal wage boards

16 Remarks at a reception for participants in a planning session for the White House Conference "To Fulfill These Rights" [2 releases]

17 Remarks upon receiving the Parents' Magazine award for outstanding service to the cause of education

17 Letter requesting a study of racial isolation as a barrier to quality in education

17 Toasts of the President and Princess Margaret [2 releases]

18 Memorandum approving the release of copper from the national stockpile

18 Letter establishing a task force on the impact of the Cuban refugee program

18 Statement by the President on the death of Henry A. Wallace

19 Council of Economic Advisers' report on economic activity during October

Appendix A

December

9 Telephone remarks upon accepting an award from the Salvation Army Association of New York

9 Telephone remarks to the delegates to the AFL–CIO convention

11 Statement by the President upon announcing the creation of the Physical Fitness Awards program

11 Statement by the President upon announcing the recipients of the National Medal of Science awards

12 Statement by the President on the delayed take-off of Gemini 6

14 Remarks of welcome to President Ayub Khan of Pakistan on the South Lawn at the White House [2 releases]

14 Toasts of the President and the President of Pakistan [2 releases]

15 Joint statement following discussions with the President of Pakistan

15 Telegram to the Administrator, NASA, following the meeting in space of Gemini 6 and Gemini 7

16 Statement by the President on the death of Dr. William Randolph Lovelace II

17 Remarks at the lighting of the Nation's Christmas tree [2 releases]

18 The President's Christmas message to the men and women in the Armed Forces

18 Messages to the President-elect and to the President of the Republic of the Philippines

December

18 Letters to the Gemini 6 and Gemini 7 astronauts after the successful completion of their mission

18 Statement by the President on the Treaty of Basic Relations between Japan and Korea

20 Statement by the President upon signing order providing for the manner of election of the Chief Executive, Ryukyu Islands

20 Toasts of the President and Chancellor Ludwig Erhard of Germany [2 releases]

21 Joint statement following discussions with Chancellor Erhard

29 Memorandum to the Secretary of State on export sales of surplus agricultural commodities to the United Arab Republic

30 Announcement of International Boundary and Water Commission recommendations relating to the salinity problem of the lower Rio Grande

30 Interim report to the President on the first 100 projects established to improve the schooling of children of low-income families

31 Telegram to Senator Saltonstall following his announcement that he would not seek reelection

31 Joint statement announcing a new Air Transport Agreement, U.S.-Canada

31 Report of Board of Visitors to the U.S. Air Force Academy

31 Statement by the President on the price increase by the Bethlehem Steel Co.

Appendix B—Presidential Documents Published in the Federal Register

PROCLAMATIONS

Appendix B

Appendix B

EXECUTIVE ORDERS

Appendix B

Appendix B

Appendix B

PRESIDENTIAL DOCUMENTS OTHER THAN PROCLAMATIONS AND EXECUTIVE ORDERS

Appendix C—Presidential Reports to the 89th Congress, First Session

Subject	Published	Sent to the Congress	Date of White House release
U.S. Civil Service Commission	H. Doc. 13	Jan. 6	. . . .
Peace Corps	H. Doc. 42	Jan. 6	. . . .
Weather Modification:			
5th Annual	H. Doc. 43	Jan. 6	. . . .
6th Annual	H. Doc. 188	May 24	May 24
National Aeronautics and Space Administration:			
11th Semiannual	H. Doc. 63	Jan. 26	. . . .
12th Semiannual		Oct. 22	Oct. 23
U.S. Aeronautics and Space Activities, 1964	H. Doc. 65	Jan. 27	. . . .
Housing and Home Finance Agency:			
17th Annual	H. Doc. 64	Jan. 27	. . . .
18th Annual		Oct. 22	Oct. 23
Economic Report	H. Doc. 28	Jan. 28	Jan. 28
U.S. Arms Control and Disarmament Agency	H. Doc. 66	Feb. 1	. . . .
Alaska Omnibus Act		Feb. 1	. . . .
International Educational and Cultural Exchange Program:			
Fiscal year 1963		Feb. 1	Feb. 1
Fiscal year 1964		Oct. 6	Oct. 6
National Wilderness Preservation System	H. Doc. 79	Feb. 8	Feb. 8
Rail Rapid Transit for the Nation's Capital		Feb. 10	Feb. 10
National Science Foundation	H. Doc. 89	Feb. 15 (H)	Feb. 15
		Feb. 17 (S)	
U.S. Participation in the International Atomic Energy Agency:			
7th Annual	H. Doc. 88	Feb. 15 (H)	. . . .
		Feb. 17 (S)	
8th Annual	H. Doc. 297	Sept. 30	Sept. 30
Communications Satellite Act of 1962	H. Doc. 87	Feb. 15 (H)	Feb. 15
		Feb. 17 (S)	

Appendix C

Subject	Published	Sent to the Congress	Date of White House release
Manpower Report of the President and a Report on Manpower Requirements, Resources Utilization, and Training by the U.S. Department of Labor		Mar. 5	Mar. 5
Government Employees Training Act		Mar. 10	. . . .
Surgeon General of the Public Health Service	H. Doc. 118	Mar. 16	. . . .
P. L. 480 (83d Congress)	H. Doc. 130	Mar. 31	. . . .
Office of Minerals Exploration:			
13th Semiannual		Apr. 5	. . . .
14th Semiannual		Sept. 14	. . . .
Federal Disaster Relief Program	H. Doc. 153	Apr. 26	Apr. 26
U.S. Foreign Assistance Program	H. Doc. 95	May 3	. . . .
National Capital Housing Authority		May 12	. . . .
Railroad Retirement Board		May 12	. . . .
Federal Statutory Salary Systems, Joint Annual Report of the Director of the Bureau of the Budget and the Chairman of the Civil Service Commission	H. Doc. 174	May 17	. . . .
Office of Alien Property		June 10	June 10
Saint Lawrence Seaway Development Corporation.	H. Doc. 218	June 23	. . . .
Commodity Credit Corporation		July 22	July 22
Atlantic-Pacific Interoceanic Canal Study Commission	H. Doc. 253	Aug. 3	Aug. 3
Corregidor-Bataan Memorial Commission	H. Doc. 299	Oct. 5	. . . .
Special International Exhibitions		Oct. 6	Oct. 6
Trade Agreements Program	H. Doc. 305	Oct. 13	Oct. 13

Appendix D—Rules Governing This Publication

[Reprinted from the Federal Register, vol. 30, p. 15133, dated December 7, 1965]

TITLE 1—GENERAL PROVISIONS

Chapter I—Administrative Committee of the Federal Register

PART 32—PRESIDENTIAL PAPERS

SUBPART A—ANNUAL VOLUMES

PUBLICATION AND FORMAT

Sec.
32.1 Publication required.
32.2 Coverage of prior years.
32.3 Format, indexes, ancillaries.

SCOPE

32.10 Basic criteria.
32.11 Sources.

OFFICIAL DISTRIBUTION

32.15 The Congress.
32.16 The Supreme Court.
32.17 Executive agencies.
32.18 Governmental requisitions.
32.19 Extra copies.

PUBLIC SALE

32.22 Sale of annual volumes.

AUTHORITY: The provisions of this Part 32 issued under sec. 6, 49 Stat. 501, as amended; 44 U.S.C. 306. Sec. 6, E.O. 10530, 19 F.R. 2709; 3 CFR 1954–58 Comp.

SUBPART A—ANNUAL VOLUMES

PUBLICATION AND FORMAT

§ 32.1 *Publication required.* There shall be published forthwith at the end of each calendar year, a special edition of the FEDERAL REGISTER designated "Public Papers of the Presidents of the United States." Ordinarily each volume shall cover one calendar year and shall be identified further by the name of the President and the period covered.

NOTE: This program started with the year 1957.

§ 32.2 *Coverage of prior years.* After conferring with the National Historical Publications Com-

mission with respect to the need therefor, the Administrative Committee may from time to time authorize the publication of similar volumes covering specified calendar years prior to 1957.

NOTE: The Committee has approved the publication of volumes starting with the year 1945.

§ 32.3 *Format, indexes, ancillaries.* Each annual volume, divided into books whenever appropriate, shall be separately published in the binding and style deemed by the Administrative Committee to be suitable to the dignity of the office of President of the United States. Each volume shall be appropriately indexed and shall contain appropriate ancillary information respecting significant Presidential documents not published in full text.

SCOPE

§ 32.10 *Basic criteria.* The basic text of the volumes shall consist of oral utterances by the President or of writings subscribed by him.

§ 32.11 *Sources.* (a) The basic text of the volumes shall be selected from: (1) Communications to the Congress, (2) public addresses, (3) transcripts of press conferences, (4) public letters, (5) messages to heads of state, (6) statements released on miscellaneous subjects, and (7) formal executive documents promulgated in accordance with law.

(b) In general, ancillary text, notes, and tables shall be derived from official sources.

OFFICIAL DISTRIBUTION

§ 32.15 *The Congress.* Each Member of the Congress, during his term of office, shall be entitled to one copy of each annual volume published during such term. Authorization for furnishing such copies shall be submitted in writing to the Director and signed by the authorizing Member.

§ 32.16 *The Supreme Court.* The Supreme

Court of the United States shall be entitled to 12 copies of the annual volumes.

§ 32.17 *Executive agencies.* The head of each department and the head of each independent agency in the executive branch of the Government shall be entitled to one copy of each annual volume upon application therefor in writing to the Director.

§ 32.18 *Governmental requisitions.* Legislative, judicial, and executive agencies of the Federal Government may obtain, at cost, copies of the annual volumes for official use upon the timely submission to the Government Printing Office of a printing and binding requisition (Standard Form 1).

§ 32.19 *Extra copies.* All requests for extra copies of the annual volumes must be addressed to the Superintendent of Documents, Government Printing Office, Washington, D.C. 20402. Extra copies must be paid for by the agency or official requesting them.

PUBLIC SALE

§ 32.22 *Sale of annual volumes.* The annual volumes shall be placed on sale to the public by the Superintendent of Documents, Government Printing Office, Washington, D.C. 20402, at prices determined by him under the general direction of the Administrative Committee.

[F.R. Doc. 65-13119; Filed, Dec. 6, 1965; 8:48 a.m.]

INDEX

[Main references are to items except as otherwise indicated]

[Main references are to items except as otherwise indicated]

[Main references are to items except as otherwise indicated]

[Main references are to items except as otherwise indicated]

Index

[Main references are to items except as otherwise indicated]

Index

Index

Index

[Main references are to items except as otherwise indicated]

Index

Index

Index

[Main references are to items except as otherwise indicated]

Index

Index

Index

[Main references are to items except as otherwise indicated]

Index

Index

Index

Index

[Main references are to items except as otherwise indicated]

Index

Index

Index

Index

[Main references are to items except as otherwise indicated]

Index

[Main references are to items except as otherwise indicated]

Index

Index

Index

55–947—66—index——3

Index

Index

[Main references are to items except as otherwise indicated]

Index

Index

Index

Index

Index

[Main references are to items except as otherwise indicated]

Index

Index

[Main references are to items except as otherwise indicated]

Index

Index

Index

Index

Messages to heads of state and government
African Unity, Organization of, 571
Austria, Chancellor Klaus, 87
Canada, Prime Minister Pearson, 432
Chile, President Frei Montalva, 431
Germany, Chancellor Erhard, 520
Iran, Shah Mohammad Reza Pahlavi, 517
Korea, President Park, 423
Kuwait, Shaikh Sabah Al-Salim Al-Sabah, 629
Philippines, President Macapagal, 655
Soviet Union, Chairman, Presidium of the Supreme Soviet, Anastas I, Mikoyan, 116
Metals, stockpiles, 599, 617, 632
Metcalf, Sen. Lee, 592
Mexico, 325
Ambassador Hugo B. Margain, 558 n.
Chamizal Zone agreement with U.S., 487
López Mateos, Adolfo, 119
President Gustavo Diaz Ordaz, 179, 558
U.S. relations with, 558
Water desalination agreements with U.S., 119, 558
Mexico, International Boundary and Water Commission, United States and, 119
Meyer, Albert Cardinal, 180
Meyer, André, 365 n.
Meyer, Eugene and Agnes E., Foundation, 70
Meyer, Garson, 642 n.
Miami, Fla., 618
Michelangelo, 200
Michigan
Area redevelopment programs, 132
Disaster relief, 239
Michigan State University, 223
Middle East and Near East, 117 [6], 378
United Nations operations, 169
Yemen cease-fire agreement, 463 [6]
See also specific countries
Migrant workers, 5, 100, 406
Miki, Takeo, 15, 355 n.
Mikoyan, Anastas I., 116
Milburn, Gen. C. L., Jr., 229
Military assistance and defense support, 26, 60, 319 [17], 476, 495, 600
Asia, 26, 106 [4], 130, 176 [3], 179
Dominican Republic, 217, 227

Military assistance and defense support—
Continued
Europe, 235
Israel, 117 [6]
Korea, 254, 257
Laos, 26
Less developed countries and new nations, 18, 176 [3]
Viet-Nam, 2, 51, 106 [4], 117 [2, 8], 130, 145, 152, 172, 194, 206, 208 [2, 14, 16, 20], 227, 229, 234, 246, 254, 257, 261, 316, 388 [1, 2, 5, 11, 14], 476, 588
See also Foreign assistance
Military Command System, National, 26
Military Construction Authorization Act, approval, 518
Military construction authorization bill, 440, 448 [22]
Military installations, U.S., 261 n., 277
Closing of, 26, 222, 440, 518
Panama Canal Zone area, 532
Review and study of, 360
Ryukyu and Bonin Islands, 15
Surplus, use by Job Corps, 288 n.
Military pay raise bill, 439
Military personnel, 395 [2], 396
Dependents overseas, 51
Education, 26
Housing, 26
Overseas, 60
Pay, 26, 32 (p. 96), 244, 439, 633
Reception for, 280
Retirement, 49
See also Armed Forces, U.S.
Military rejectees, training and rehabilitation, 5, 9, 26, 100, 156 [2]
Military research, 26, 32 (p. 90)
Military strength, U.S., 2, 20, 26, 32 (p. 90), 37, 185, 347 [9], 353 [6], 387, 388 [1], 396
Draft requirements to maintain, 388 [1], 395 [2]
Miller, Repr. George P., 134
Miller, Herbert J., Jr., 366
Miller, J. Irwin, 266
Miller, Sen. Jack, 420
Miller, Neal E., 56 n.
Milliken, Frank R., 11

Index

Index

[Main references are to items except as otherwise indicated]

Index

Index

Index

Index

[Main references are to items except as otherwise indicated]

Index

Index

Index

[Main references are to items except as otherwise indicated]

Schreiber, Walter R., 353 [4]
Schröder, Gerhard, 660
Schultze, Charles L. (Director, Bureau of
the Budget), 249, 290, 297, 319 [6, 8],
324, 332, 347 [8], 362, 404, 418, 447,
506, 512, 560
Schurmeier, Harris M., 134
Schwartz, Carl H., Jr., 263 n.
Schweinhaut, Mrs. Margaret, 642 n.
Schweitzer, Dr. Albert, 474
Schweitzer, Pierre-Paul, 541
Schwinger, Julian, 56 n.
Science
    Education, 2, 32 (p. 95), 88, 225, 271, 514,
        522
    Exchange programs, 292, 519
    Research, 9, 32 (p. 95), 56, 71, 88, 92, 115,
        166, 170, 196, 220, 225, 247, 257, 265,
        271, 319 [5], 514, 522, 523, 558
    U.S.-Korean cooperation, 257, 344, 407
    Waste products, 54
Science, Korean Institute for Industrial
    Technology and Applied, 257, 344, 407
Science, National Medal of, 56, 646
Science, President's Committee on the Na-
    tional Medal of, 646 n.
Science Adviser to the President. See
    Science and Technology, Office of,
    Director
Science Advisory Committee, President's,
    166, 602
Science Board, National, 283
Science Foundation, National, 9, 32 (p. 95),
    71, 220 n., 225, 271, 283, 514
Science Talent Search, remarks to winners
    of, 88
Science and Technology, Federal Council
    for, 92, 271, 275, 514
Science and Technology, Office of, Direc-
    tor (Donald F. Hornig), 4, 12 n., 54,
    56 n., 88, 92 n., 257, 344 n., 375, 404,
    407, 417, 418, 446, 514, 547 n., 649
Scientific, and Cultural Materials, Agree-
    ment on the Importation of Educational,
    292, 604
Scientific Cooperation, United States-Japan
    Committee on, 15
Scientific instruments, approval of bills for
    duty-free entry of, 604
Scientists
    American, comments on, 56

Scientists—Continued
    Exchange programs, 319 [5], 519
    Training, 514
Scranton, Gov. William W., 417, 418, 434,
    471
Seaborg, Glenn T. (Chairman, Atomic En-
    ergy Commission), 17, 88, 196, 319 [1,
    5], 417, 418, 523
Seamans, Robert C., Jr., 120, 121, 134, 310,
    462, 463 [2, 13]
Seashores, national, 222, 521
SEATO. See Southeast Asia Treaty
    Organization
Second Supplemental Appropriation Act,
    1965, 215
Securities
    Corporate, 60
    Foreign, 60, 638 n.
    Government, 60
    Registration fees, 580
Securities Act of 1933, amendments, 580
Securities and Exchange Commission, 164,
    580, 641 [2]
Security, national. See National security
Security Council. See United Nations Se-
    curity Council
Security Industrial Association, National,
    211
Security Medal, National, 209 n.
See the U.S.A. Committee, 418, 419
"See the U.S.A." program, 60, 419
Seitz, Frederick, 56 n.
Selective Service System, 100
    Draft increase, 388 [1], 395 [2]
    Rejectees. See Military rejectees, train-
        ing and rehabilitation
"Self Renewal; the Individual and the In-
    novative Society," John W. Gardner,
    385 n.
Selma, Ala., 201, 409
    Civil rights demonstrations in, 106 [1,
        7], 107
    Civil rights march to Montgomery, 104,
        114, 117 [1, 5, 10], 126 n., 135
    Voting registration, 46 [3, 13]
Senate youth program participants, remarks
    to, 48
Senior citizens. See Older persons
Senior Citizens Month, 72
Seoane, Edgardo, 593
Separation of church and state, 302

A–66

Index

Index

[Main references are to items except as otherwise indicated]

[Main references are to items except as otherwise indicated]

Statements by the President—Continued
  Southeast Asia—Continued
    U.S. assistance to, 176 [1], 295 [3]
  Steel dispute, agreements, 208 [3], 466,
    483
  Steel prices, 62, 226, 663
  Stevenson, Adlai E., death of, 356
  Surgery, plan to undergo, 549
  Unemployment statistics, 156 [1], 165,
    319 [7], 598
  United Arab Republic, U.S. relations with,
    46 [2]
  United Nations
    Meetings with U.S. Representative,
      395 [3]
    Twentieth anniversary, 295 [2]
  U.S. Embassy in Saigon, bombing of, 145
  Veterans hospitals, committee to review
    closing of, 163
  Viet-Nam, 130, 194
    Appropriations for military require-
      ments in, 261
    Health and welfare needs in, 469
    Negotiations proposal, 208 [2]
    U.S. dependents, withdrawal from, 51
    U.S. policy in, 117 [2], 388 [1, 2]
    Visit of Secretary McNamara and Am-
      bassador Lodge, 353 [1]
  Vocational rehabilitation, Federal-State
    program, 416
  Voting Rights Act of 1965, compliance,
    448 [9]
  Voting rights bill, 201
    House action on, 349
    Senate passage, 278
  Wage-price stability in 1965, 208 [4]
  Wallace, Henry A., death of, 619
  Water Desalination, International Sym-
    posium on, 325, 494, 547
  Water Resources Council, Ad Hoc, 358
  White House conferences
    Education, 291
    Equal employment opportunity, 384
    Health, 424
    "To Fulfill These Rights," 548
  White House staff, 22 [1]
  Yemen agreement, 463 [6]
  YF–12A aircraft, world speed record, 219
  Youth Opportunity Campaign, 268
  See also Legislation, remarks or statements
    upon approval

Staten Island, N.Y., 467
States
  Appalachian area. *See* Appalachian area
  Charters for private organizations, 508
  Depressed areas. *See* Depressed areas
  Eastern Kentucky, 195
  Educational agencies, 9
  Federal aid. *See* Federal aid to States
  Governors, 98, 119, 388 [14]
    Appalachian area, 103
    Northeastern area, 434
  Land development, Federal aid, 90
  Middle Atlantic, 358
  Midwestern, floods and tornadoes in, 187,
    188, 189, 190, 191, 193, 215, 239, 477
  National Guard, 26
  New England, resources development,
    350, 358
  Northeastern
    Power failure, 608, 640, 641 [1]
    Water problems, 358, 375, 417, 418, 434,
      477
  Northwest-Southwest power transmission
    intertie, 186
  Pacific Northwest, floods in, 317, 477
  Southern
    School desegregation, 470
    Voting registration, 448 [9]
  Voting discrimination, 104, 107, 108
  See also Federal-State-local governmental
    responsibilities; *specific States*
Steel
  Prices, 22 [2], 35 (p. 111), 46 [14], 62,
    226, 448 [11], 663
  Production, 208 [21], 226
Steel industry, 62, 448 [11, 15], 459
  Employment, 226
  Labor dispute, 448 [11, 15], 454 [1, 3],
    463 [10, 12, 14], 466, 478
    Agreements, 208 [3, 21], 483, 632
  Profits, 226
Steelworkers of America, United, 208 [3,
    21], 226, 454 [1], 466, 483
Stellar, Raymond, 288 n.
Stennis, Sen. John, 353 [13]
Stephens, Col. Robert L., 219
Stevens, Roger L., 177 n.
Stevenson, Adlai E., 176 [1, 3], 210
  Commemorative stamps, 373, 504
  Death of, 355, 356, 359, 370, 371, 373, 376,
    383

[Main references are to items except as otherwise indicated]

Index

Index

Index

[Main references are to items except as otherwise indicated]

Index

[Main references are to items except as otherwise indicated]

Index